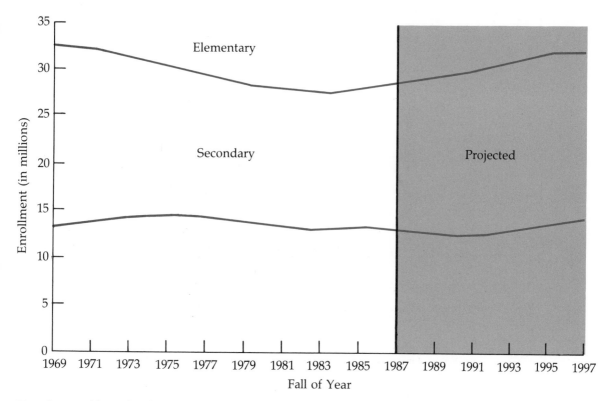

IMPORTANT: *State law requires the loyalty affidavit to be signed and notarized on each application and requires the applicant to keep one copy.*

LOYALTY AFFIDAVIT

T3-BEC-776

I solemnly swear (or affirm) that I will support the Constitution of the United States of America, the Constitution of the State, and the laws of the United States and the state, and will, by precept and example, promote respect for the flag and the institutions of the United States and of the state, reverence for law and order, and undivided allegiance to the government of the United States of America.

Signed _____
(Applicant)

Subscribed and sworn to before me, a Notary Public, this _____ day of _____ 19 ___

My commission expires _____. Notary Public _____

NOT VALID WITHOUT STAMP OR SEAL OF NOTARY PUBLIC

Sample loyalty oath

Trends in public school enrollment: Fall 1969–1997

Introduction to the Foundations of Education

SECOND EDITION

Introduction to the *Foundations* of *Education*

Robert F. Hessong
Thomas H. Weeks
Butler University

Macmillan Publishing Company
New York
Collier Macmillan Canada
Toronto

Editor: Robert Miller
Production Supervisor: Charlotte Hyland
Production Manager: Rick Fischer
Text and Cover Designer: Sheree Goodman
Cover Illustrator: Tim Foley
Illustrations: Vantage Art, Inc.

This book was set in Trump by Ruttle, Shaw & Wetherill, Inc. and was printed and bound by R. R. Donnelley & Sons Co. The cover was printed by New England Book Components.

Macmillan Publishing Company
866 Third Avenue, New York, New York 10022

Collier Macmillan Canada, Inc.
1200 Eglinton Avenue East, Suite 200
Don Mills, Ontario M3C 3N1

Library of Congress Cataloging-in-Publication Data

Hessong, Robert F.
    Introduction to the foundations of education / Robert F. Hessong, Thomas H. Weeks.—2nd ed.
        p.   cm.
    Rev. ed. of: Introduction to education. c1987.
    Includes bibliographical references.
    ISBN 0-02-354395-7
    1. Education—United States—History. 2. Educational sociology—
—United States. 3. Education—Philosophy. 4. Education and state—
—United States. 5. School management and organization—United
States. 6. Teaching—Vocational guidance—United States.
I. Weeks, Thomas H. (Thomas Harold), 1938–   . II. Hessong, Robert
F. Introduction to education. III. Title.
LA205.H47   1991
370′.973—dc20   90-35530
                    CIP

Printing: 1 2 3 4 5 6 7   Year: 1 2 3 4 5 6 7

Photo Credits. Essay 1: Allen Zak. Essay 2: Paul Conklin; Paul Conklin; Macmillan/St. Joseph's Montessori School, Columbus, Ohio; Larry Hamill; Stuart Spates; Macmillan/St. Joseph's Montessori School, Columbus, Ohio; Macmillan/ Gail Meese; Larry Hamill; Richard Hutchings/Info Edit.

To our wives, Dotty and Kathy,
whose patience and understanding made
the completion of this work possible

Preface

The second edition of this book is designed to present foundations of education material to the beginning student in teacher education, the graduate student in education, and to the layperson interested in schools. Potential and current school-board members will find this book helpful in gaining perspective on the primary issues that affect schools and education today.

At Butler University, we recommend that our students obtain the textbook for their first course in foundations, currently known as "Concepts of Education," taken during their sophomore year, and keep the book for a course called "Exit Foundations," taken during their senior year. The book will serve as a main text, handbook, and reference throughout this important learning and developmental period.

Organization

The chapters are ordered in such a way that instruction and learning begins logically with Chapter 1 and moves sequentially through the text. The first two chapters orient teacher candidates to teaching as a career. The major and traditional units of foundations are placed in this section of the book; the next seven chapters cover social, historical, and philosophical foundations. The study of the curriculum from past, present, and future perspectives is the next content area. The final sections cover school law, educational control, governance, finance, and teacher organizations.

The organization of material moves from the general to the specific. However, as the units and chapters can stand on their own, individual instructors can easily change the sequencing of topics. Instructors benefit when material can be ordered conveniently to fit their own special interest areas, their teaching styles, and the learning styles of their students.

Theoretical Base

The first two chapters cover the orientation of the teacher candidate to teaching. Chaper 1 discusses major topics in the orientation of a new teacher, and Chapter 2 surveys current trends and reforms in the teaching profession.

Chapter 3, in the sociology unit, identifies most of the important social issues that have a direct impact on the schools. Chapter 4 follows with a discussion of the issues that have a more indirect impact on education. It is the authors' wish that students will thus have some practical solutions they can apply in their work as teachers. Graduate students in foundations should be able to relate well to this unit, gaining new insight and relating their own experiences and ideas to the issues.

The history unit presents a sequential history of education built around significant headings and divided among three chapters; we feel that the logical headings highlight the accomplishments in each area. Chapter 5 explores the ancient foundations of education and European ideas, because it is important for students to know that American educational history did not begin with the colonial settlements but rather has much older roots. Chapter 6 presents more traditional material about the three colonial areas and their educational contributions, which have been identified by many authors. Chapters 6 and 7 provide the reader with an understanding of the contributions of the federal, private, and public areas to the growth of education in America and of the logical relationships among them.

The philosophy unit, Chapters 8 and 9, is designed to help the student understand the traditional philosophies (as they apply to education), the educational philosophies, and their applications to current practices in education. The curriculum chapter, Chapter 10, is based on 12 significant questions that should give the student a broad understanding of curricular background. In Chapter 11, recent curricular reforms, the Effective Schools Movement, and technology in education are surveyed. From Chapter 12, students will be able to gain an understanding of the many ways in which the law is applied to schools and to teachers, including the topics of teacher certification, teacher contracts, control of students, teacher liability, and religion in the public schools. In Chapter 13 through 16, the governance, control, and financing of education are discussed in detail. The state, local, and federal aspects of each topic are also explored. These same chapters could be used as a separate course. Chapter 17 reviews the background of educational organizations and outlines the collective bargaining process.

New to This Edition

Numerous changes have been made to this edition of *Introduction to the Foundations of Education*. New chapters entitled "Trends in the Teaching Profession" and "Waves of Reform, Effective Schools, and Technology in Education" have been added. The "Trends" chapter surveys recent reform movements in teacher education, whereas the "Waves of Reform" chapter looks at reforms, effective schools, and technology from the viewpoint of the curriculum process in elementary and secondary education.

In addition to these entirely new chapters, many other chapters have been extensively revised and reorganized. The orientation unit has been moved from the last unit in the textbook to the first unit on the assumption that the orientation of teacher candidates to the profession should precede the other foundations presented. This orientation unit has also been expanded from one chapter to two chapters to cover this area more thoroughly. The sociology unit has been extensively revised to bring the societal impact issues and the responses to each issue into closer proximity. The curriculum unit has been revised by augmenting the section on values education, by rearranging the topics in the final section to make them more cohesive, and by adding a new chapter on reforms and technology in the curriculum process. The unit on school law has been condensed from two chapters into one, emphasizing the application of school law to the classroom teacher. The finance unit has been condensed, and any repetitive material has been eliminated. The final chapter on educational organizations has been updated and extensively revised to bring prospective teachers the most current information on professional organizations.

Learning Aids

This edition adds significant new learning aids that students and instructors will find helpful. Among the new pedagogical features:

- *Cue words* have been added in the margins to almost every paragraph in the textbook to aid the reader in identifying the major topic or concept in each paragraph.
- *Glossary terms* have been italicized within the text, listed at the end of each chapter, and defined in a new glossary in the back of the textbook.
- An *annotated bibliography* has been added at the end of each chapter for students who want to read further on each topic.
- Two four-page *color photo essays*, one on multicultural education and the other on ways to best improve education, have been added to this edition.

The second edition also retains the key pedagogical features of the first edition. Two of the most useful learning/reading aids are the introduction and summary of each chapter. Each unit of subject matter is followed by a list of *questions;* these questions can serve as a review, as a stimulus before reading, or as a point of departure for class discussion. The *activities* at the end of each unit serve as hands-on or involvement projects; activities include interviews, debates, simulations, and research topics. A list of *references* is placed near the end of the book to facilitate the search for more information on a topic. A useful *appendix* is placed in the back of the book. It contains key educational dates, the *NEA Code of Ethics,* the *AFT Bill of Rights,* and a list of professional organizations. Finally, the illustrations, photographs, figures, charts, and tables have been updated. The bibliography has been augmented and updated also.

Supplements to the Second Edition

Additional aids to learning are located in the *Instructor's Manual*, which includes suggestions for organizing the course with either a traditional or a progressive approach and additional activities and questions for student use. The *Instructor's Manual* also provides test questions for each unit. These test questions are available in computerized form on a *Computer Test Bank* for use on IBM or IBM compatible equipment.

Acknowledgments

We gratefully acknowledge the assistance of many dedicated people in the writing of this book. First, we wish to express our appreciation to Butler University for the generous support and encouragement given to this lengthy project through the Butler Academic Grants Committee for funding and to the Butler Leaves Committee, which provided the time for reflecting on, researching, and writing this textbook. In particular, we want to express our appreciation to Joseph F. Lamberti, Dean of the College of Education, and to Louis Chenette, Dean of Faculty, without whose encouragement and support this project would have been impossible. We are indebted to Dr. Joseph M. Nygaard, Professor of Education Emeritus at Butler, for the preparation of the chapter on the legal foundations of education. We appreciate the assistance of Larry DeWester, Janet Hudson, Ann Riemer, and Ann Arvidson, whose work as our graduate assistants propelled the book toward completion. We extend thanks specifically to Larry for his analysis of data on market trends and for his work on revising the initial chapters, and to Janet Hudson and Ann Arvidson for revising the manuscript, proofreading, obtaining the necessary permissions, rewriting material, compiling photographs, drawing charts and illustrations, writing test questions for the *Instructor's Manual*, and generally assisting with the majority of the manuscript. Their work was truly invaluable to us and to the project as a whole, and we are indebted to them for more than a year of diligent work. We are also grateful to Gina Lawrence, Brenda Davis, and Ginger B. Williams for typing the manuscript with ease and speed, and to Brenda also for coming to our aid numerous times with secretarial help on short notice. We are indebted to the Butler undergraduate and graduate students of educational foundations who have field-tested the material in this text and have offered helpful suggestions over the past several years.

For their assistance in providing photographs for this book we are indebted to the Indianapolis Public Schools; the Metropolitan School Districts of Washington and Lawrence Townships in Marion County, Indiana; the Indiana State Teachers Association; the Indiana Federation of Teachers; the Indiana State Department of Education; the Library of Congress; the Archdiocese of Indianapolis; the Arthur Andersen Company; the Children's Museum of Indianapolis; the National Education Association; Robert Keeshan Associates; the Pentathlone Institute; Project Charlie; The Comprehensive Health Education Foundation; and photographers Dan Axler, William Locker, D. L. Harless, Robert Schafer, and Gradie Franklin. We also want to thank all of the parents and young people who graciously consented to our using their photographs in this book. In addition, we wish to acknowledge the professional help given by librarians at the Library of Congress, the Indiana State Library, the library of the Indiana Department of Education, the Karl Kalp Library of the Indianapolis Public Schools, Indiana University Library, and the Irwin Library at Butler University. We are also indebted to the Indiana Farm Bureau for information on school finance and to Dr. Paul Krohne for the material on the early history of education in Indiana.

We gratefully acknowledge the encouragement and assistance of the following people from Macmillan: Lloyd Chilton, without whose help this project would not come to fruition; Charlotte Hyland, production supervisor; Robert Miller, education editor; Peter Knapp, assistant education editor; and Sheree Goodman, designer. We are also grateful for the counsel of Dr. John Best, Professor of Education Emeritus at Butler University, whose book *Research in Education* served as an inspiration for this project. We wish to express our appreciation for the extremely helpful comments of the professionals who were chosen by Macmillan to critique the text:

Frank R. Asbury, University of Georgia
Shelby Crowe, Wright State University
Donald R. Ferris, Purdue University
J. Donald Hawk, Georgia Southern College
Tony L. Williams, Marshall University

Finally, thanks are due to our wives, Kathy and Dotty, our families, who encouraged us in this long project, and to Dotty for her aid in revising and editing several early chapters of the manuscript. Without their forbearance and support, the writing of this text would have been impossible.

R.F.H.
T.H.W.

Brief Contents

IX

Educational Organizations *515*

Contents

V

The School Curriculum 285

VI
_____

Legal Elements of Education   *375*

VII

Control and Governance of Education   *419*

VIII

Financing Education   *469*

IX

Educational Organizations 515

Introduction to the
Foundations of Education

(Photo by Grady Franklin.)

I

Orientation to Teaching

CHAPTER 1

On Becoming a Teacher

Introduction to the Orientation Unit

After reading this unit, it is hoped that you will be better able to state why you want to become a teacher. The characteristics of the ideal teacher are discussed here, not to make you as a prospective teacher feel inadequate, but as a standard for comparison. Knowing where the potential problems lie ahead of time may allow you as a teacher to recognize what is happening to you and to take corrective action. Teaching is a discipline, and beginners should know why it is so and should treat what they are learning about teaching with great respect. Stress and stress management are discussed so that you may become aware of and prepare to cope with the different situations. No one can anticipate all of the new experiences that you will have in your first year of teaching, but some concerns are discussed to assist you in the transition from student to teacher. Incentives for teachers are being implemented in various places to stimulate and motivate the professional teacher and some examples are presented. Finally, a new concept called teacher empowerment, which gives the teacher a sense of dignity and stimulates creativity, is explored.

Why Become a Teacher?

LOVE KIDS

Many motives are involved in choosing a career in teaching. The one we have all heard many times is that a teacher must love "kids." Liking children is definitely a major reason that people choose teaching, especially in elementary education. Research (Lasley, 1980) indicates, however, that simply liking children is not enough.

ART VS. SCIENCE

Teaching is really a combination of an art and a science. Teaching as an art is reflected in the first grade teachers who, despite unorthodox methods and unusual techniques, consistently enable all their students to read. Teaching as a science is exemplified when a teacher uses known principles of learning (Lasley, 1980). Someone who likes children but can neither identify basic instructional principles nor weave those principles together to form coherent lessons will have difficulty in achieving learning goals. Liking children is a definite asset, but teachers must also possess more specific skills.

SUBJECT MO-TIVE

On entering teaching, many students comment that they like a specific subject, such as science, history, mathematics, or music. It is very common for secondary students to want to teach a subject because they have done well in that subject in both high school and college. Love of a subject is a good reason to want to teach, but it has to be joined with other desires, such as a love of kids. The authors have noted several education majors who have relied too heavily on their subject-matter interest and not enough on other motivations for teaching; thus, student teaching did not turn out to be a pleasant experience for them.

The desire to serve others is a good reason to enter teaching because

The purpose of this chapter is to address several topics of particular interest to students in teacher-training programs. These topics merit consideration by anyone who wishes to become a teacher.

SERVICE
MOTIVE

teaching is a service occupation. Helping a student to learn is not very much different, from a service point of view, from nursing a patient back to good health, putting out fires, policing a city, or making laws to protect others. Some people are filled with an almost missionary zeal in teaching a child how to read, helping a child learn a trade, or assisting a child in finding a career. Being of service to others has traditionally been the primary reason most teachers teach. Many priests and nuns dedicate their entire lives to education and to teaching. The Jesuit Order has a worldwide reputation for its high standards of education. Many young men and women

COACHING IS
TEACHING

enter teaching because they like to coach. Coaching is teaching with a greater emphasis on development of psychomotor skills. Most coaches like kids; therefore, there is a compatible combination for their success.

OTHER MO-
TIVES

Other reasons for teaching are not verbalized as much but may be as important to many people. These would include ego satisfaction, teaching as a status position, lifestyle, the unique vacation schedule of teachers, the powerful position that the teacher has to influence others, and a love of learning. Whatever your reasons for teaching, you will need a magic combination of the aforementioned motivational factors to be highly successful as a teacher.

What Are the Characteristics of the Ideal Teacher?

A BASIS FOR
COMPARISON

In using the term *ideal*, the authors mean "as close to perfection" as one can come. Becoming an ideal teacher is a process that good students of education and practicing teachers should strive for during their careers. Theoretically, no teacher can ever reach the ideal, that is, reach a level of perfection where he or she need no longer exert effort toward improvement; thus, growth would stop. Personal and academic growth in one's chosen career are essential to staying fresh and interesting as a teacher; therefore, there must always be something better to reach for. Use the following list of characteristics of the ideal teacher as an ultimate goal toward which to strive.

Being Knowledgeable

To be knowledgeable one must possess knowledge or understanding. When teachers begin to practice what they have learned in the college classroom, they are expected to be knowledgeable. Being knowledgeable also carries

CONFIDENCE
WITHOUT
ARROGANCE

with it a feeling of self-confidence without arrogance. The main reason for going to college is to gain knowledge and understanding in one's chosen field. Just as you expect your professors to be knowledgeable about their subjects, your students expect you to know the content of the subjects you teach. No teacher knows the answers to all of the questions pupils ask, but you should be able to steer them to the appropriate references for further

A teacher must be knowledgeable, yet must always be willing to learn and to expand in knowledge and outlook.

(Photo used by permission of the Indianapolis Public Schools.)

information. Also, truly exceptional teachers are scholars who constantly read and upgrade themselves in their subjects.

Being Humorous

Being humorous is the faculty of perceiving, appreciating, or expressing what is amusing or comical. This part of teaching must be done in good taste or it will become a negative rather than a positive feature. On the positive side, teachers must be able to laugh at themselves when things go wrong in the classroom. One young science teacher hurriedly moved a mobile laboratory into a classroom to demonstrate some experiments. The drain in the portable laboratory led to a small bucket. As the students and the teacher became involved in the experiments and more water was used, the bucket filled up and began emptying on the floor. None of the students said anything until the pool of water had reached the rear of the classroom. When the teacher finally discovered the problem, there was a big gasp, followed closely by laughter. Her eighth grade science class enjoyed the joke they had played on the teacher, and they appreciated the ability of the teacher to laugh at herself.

ON THE LIGHTER SIDE

Another teacher enjoyed making jokes about the cute girl in the front row. In the beginning, the jokes were funny to the rest of the class, but later in the school year, his jokes became stale. Eventually, the rest of the class felt that this girl was receiving special treatment. The teacher was unaware that the rapport he had had with his class had slipped; therefore, he was unable to correct the problem.

In the first example, the teacher was able to turn a negative situation into a positive one with an appropriate humorous response. In the second example, the teacher used bad judgment in his use of humor and lost the rapport with his class. The appropriate use of humor is a personal matter, and it demands the use of good common sense. As you work on your sense of classroom humor, think about the teachers you most admired and how they used humor. Also, examine the humor you have used in the past and contemplate how it could be adapted for future use in the classroom. Be cautious, but be humorous.

CAUTIOUS BUT HUMOR-OUS

Being Flexible

MODIFY AND ADAPT

To be flexible, one must be able to adapt. Teachers need to be flexible because some days the best lesson plan does not work. How often are teachers heard to say, "I couldn't do anything with my classes today"? Being flexible is being able to talk about problems that have arisen in the classroom and eventually to get back to the lesson. For example, suppose the miniseries *Roots* was shown on television the previous night, and the children have questions about the series involving serious racial and ethical considerations. Even though you are ready to go on with the lesson for the day, you need to take some time to deal with this important matter.

After the *Roots* situation has been resolved, you may notice that you have gained greater attention from your class, who can now focus more intensely on the lesson. In not recognizing important learning opportunities as they occur in the classroom, on the playground, on television, or elsewhere, the teacher misses learning moments that may not naturally arise again. Flexibility in teaching is a definite asset.

Being Upbeat

POSITIVE AT-TITUDE

Upbeat is a term borrowed from the field of music that has come to mean a positive spirit and demeanor. An upbeat person genuinely likes kids and enjoys the task of teaching. Teaching is not simply a job for thse people; it is a source of great pleasure, and they show it in their facial expressions and in their positive attitude around the school. Upbeat people always have time to talk to a colleague or do something extra for the school or the staff. One key to being upbeat is having a good self-concept.

Being Honest

INTEGRITY

Honesty or integrity is a very important trait, particularly for a teacher. Teachers with integrity tell their class what to expect and then deliver on those promises. We have all had teachers who promised things to us but never followed through. For example, when a teacher gives an exam, it is understood that the results of that exam should be back within a reasonable period so that the student will benefit from the feedback. The student ought to be able to trust what the teacher says and does.

Being Clear and Concise

Clarity and conciseness relate to both oral and written expression in the classroom. One of the main goals of education is to help students become clear and concise communicators; therefore, we must be good models of

CLEAR COM- this learning goal. Feedback from our classes will indicate how well we are
MUNICATION getting our points across. The questions asked by students, the examination
answers received, and certain nonverbal cues should give teachers an adequate understanding of how well they are communicating with their students. The process of communication can be aided by such audiovisual devices as overhead projectors, chalkboards, film projectors, duplicated papers, textbooks, posters, and artifacts.

Being Open

RELATING TO Willingness to share a part of yourself is being open. Teachers who share
STUDENTS events in their own lives to illustrate a point or share their feelings about
a given situation often help learners to relate to situations in more meaningful ways. Young people continuously experience new emotions as they grow up, and it is helpful to them to know that teachers have experienced these same emotions. As you share yourself, you will develop a greater rapport with your students.

Being Patient

PERSEVER- Patience is often expressed as perseverence or diligence. Few people have
ANCE enough patience, and teachers need an especially large amount. Learners
come to you in every state of being, for example slow, gifted, dyslexic, and emotionally disturbed. Their parents and the general public expect you to produce outstanding results. Researchers and practitioners have developed hundreds of teaching-learning techniques to use with the diverse groups of students you will face. You may be frustrated by large classes and by your lack of ability to reach all students. Patience is required as you carefully decide what teaching-learning technique is best for each learner in your class. Also, with patience, you will learn to appreciate the gradual progress over time rather than dramatic results immediately.

Being a Role Model

POSITIVE IN- Every teacher should be an excellent role model. Young children and young
FLUENCES adults need and seek role models on which to pattern their lives. Unfortunately, however, many children are attracted to less desirable role models seen on television or in movies or to other children in the neighborhood. Although some of the models in the media may be good, many are quite negative. Children who do not have loving parents, grandparents, uncles, and aunts and positive teacher models are operating at a disadvantage as they make critical decisions about who they are going to be. Being a good role model to all the children you teach is one of the greatest contributions you can make to society.

Being Able to Relate Theory to Practice

Often it is very difficult to relate the theories advocated in college classes to actual practice in the schools. Throughout this text, in the Activities section at the end of each unit, there are suggestions for individual and

FIELD EXPERI-
ENCES

group activities to enhance your interest and motivation in teaching. Most states and teachers' education colleges try to provide field experiences while you are in training to tie in with the theories presented in the college classroom. For example, many states stipulate that laboratory or field experiences shall be initiated as soon as possible and continued throughout the student's program of preparation.

SIMULATION
AND ROLE
PLAYING

Simulation games and role-playing exercises can be very important in teacher training. Cruickshank and Broadbent (1968) found the actual teaching problems to be less numerous for students receiving simulation training. They also found simulation experiences to be at least as effective as an equal amount of student teaching. The more you become involved with actual classroom situations and ask questions of experienced teachers, administrators, school board members, teachers' organization personnel, parents, and students, the sooner you will experience the reality of teaching. Do not be like those college students who later look back on their student life and are sorry that they did not take advantage of every learning opportunity. Many opportunities will be provided to help you relate theory to practice.

Being Self-Confident

LEADERSHIP
EXPERIENCES

We have all met individuals who seem to know themselves very well. Chances are these people feel self-confident. The best way to gain self-confidence is to test yourself and to become comfortable in as many teaching experiences as possible. Students who have taught church school classes, have been counselors in summer camps, have been senior scouts, or have participated in other youth-related activities generally feel more confident about teaching.

POSITIVE
FEEDBACK

Positive feedback for work well done goes a long way in enhancing one's self-confidence. Successful athletes exude confidence, as do successful students of education. As we gain self-confidence from others' positive comments on our work, we need to remember to give positive feedback to our students. If we are models of self-confidence, not egomaniacs, our students will want to model themselves after us.

Being Diversified in Your Preparation

IMPORTANCE
OF A MINOR

Most successful schoolteachers do not have a single concentration. They major in certain areas such as elementary education or history at the secondary level, but if they are wise, they also choose a minor. A minor certification, such as special-education endorsements in elementary education or a subject area in secondary education, gives prospective teachers a better opportunity for employment as well as more latitude on the job. In the 1990s, there will continue to be a demand for science and math teachers. With the rise in the status of women's athletics, the ability to coach will benefit women who enter the employment arena.

INTERESTS
AND HOBBIES

Being diversified also means having outside interests or hobbies, for example, music, chess, bridge, minor sports, and travel. Potential employers are attracted to applicants with outside interests, because such teachers will be able to sponsor extracurricular activities and to be a more interesting staff member. Today, the curriculum comprises a multitude of offerings and administrators are often hard-pressed to fill the empty slots.

Being Well Groomed and Having Good Personal Hygiene

FORMALITY?

An expensive designer wardrobe is not a necessity in the teaching field. It is important, however, to be clean and neat and to wear clothing that is acceptable in the school building in which you teach. Some school staffs prefer casual clothing; others favor more formal attire. Teachers' clothing is nearly always different from and more formal than student clothing. This contrast is good because it sets the teacher apart as an adult model for the students.

COMMON
SENSE

Personal hygiene may be a problem. Unpleasant odors or an unkempt appearance can be a distraction to students. The ideal teacher needs to be a model who is looked up to, and so must maintain her or his body in a hygienic manner. Excellent body hygiene pays off for the teacher in both better health and a better rapport with students.

Being Unique

BEING
UNIQUE

As in all such characterizations, there is danger in identifying the ideal teacher. There will always exist that unique person who may not meet all the criteria but possesses other qualities that cause her or him to excel at teaching. We must be open to such people because they often act as change agents in our schools. As we strive toward the ideal, we may become more conservative and less likely to take chances. The latter problem may be avoided be reevaluating our ideal teacher list.

The Discipline of Teaching

EDUCATION
VS. MEDICINE

The authors believe that becoming a good teacher is as much a learning experience as becoming proficient in one's chosen subject or subjects. Neither of these learning endeavors begins in college, and neither ends in college; for the professional, teaching is a continuous process of growth. A physician may say that he or she has learned all that is necessary about physiology. A teacher may say that he or she knows all that is necessary about child psychology and the elementary subjects. And, indeed, there are physicians and teachers who have stopped learning and growing after completing their formal schooling. But this is a gross mistake. Whatever one does to be a professional, she or he must learn the subject matter and the means of practicing the profession. We want our physicians to understand us as people and to know how to heal our physical wounds, and we want

PAY AND
PROFES-
SIONAL STA-
TUS

our teachers to understand our growth levels and to be able to focus learning where we, as students, can maximize our intellectual potential.

Is it easier to become a teacher or a physician? I hope your answer was that neither profession is easier than the other if one wants to achieve the degree of excellence that we hope all future teachers will strive to attain. The pay and the professional status that physicians enjoy may mistakenly lead one to believe that being a teacher is easier, but there is no difference with respect to excellence in performance. Both are disciplines, in which certain facts and skills must be learned. A physician must be a careful and precise diagnostician, an informed prescriber of medicine, and often a skilled surgeon; teachers must test and analyze a student's abilities, must devise a teaching style or a learning method that will meet a certain child's needs, and must be able to use various techniques to meet individual children's learning patterns.

THE IMPOR-
TANCE OF
FOUNDA-
TIONS

The traditional foundations-of-education subjects presented in this text (history, sociology, and philosophy) are all very important in understanding how to become a fully disciplined teacher. Other subjects mentioned in this text and other teachers' education subjects are important as well. To emphasize the point that studying and learning the foundations of education are a real art of studying about pedagogy as a discipline, we present two illustrations.

Illustration 1

EXAMPLES
AND REAC-
TIONS

- *Situation:* A student has failed biology exams repeatedly.
- *Reactor A* is a teacher who thinks of teaching mainly in the narrow sense of teaching a subject.
- *Reactor A* says that the only answer for some students is to fail the class; thus, it is unevitable that some students will fail. Academic standards must be upheld in this school.
- *Reactor B* is a teacher who has become well informed about the whole child and her or his needs. This teacher studies his or her teaching technique as much as the subject matter area and is a scholar in the foundations area of education.
- *Reactor B* says that it would be a good idea to look into the family background of the child, his or her academic potential, the classes he or she is placed in, whether he or she is taking the class for the first or second time, and whether good rapport with the child has been established through meaningful dialogue. Further examination of the child's background may show a need for additional testing, a family conference, and the establishment of a definite plan to facilitate the child's study habits. The child is not written off by *Reactor B.*

Illustration 2

- *Situation:* Every year teachers are bombarded with some new idea, such as the back-to-basics movement.
- *Reactor A* tends to see these media trends as fads and feels that if one waits long enough, they will go away. There probably will be no noticeable teaching adjustment in this teacher's class, although the curriculum that he or she teaches may be affected eventually by outside forces.

One-on-one teaching is one of the best ways to determine a child's strengths, weaknesses, and interests.

[Photo used by permission of the Metropolitan School District of Lawrence Township.]

- *Reactor B* accepts new ways of doing things as another challenge. Although he or she may wish that some new fads had not appeared, he or she accepts these adjustments as part of teaching. *Reactor B* knows that historically, education has gone through both liberal and conservative trends and that neither is a bad omen. He or she feels that any new idea offers a chance to look at and evaluate one's approach to teaching and education. Big publicity items, like the back-to-basics movement, will lead to more money for education, changes in text-books, special conferences, and reforms in teachers' education.

Students in teacher education classes who understand the foundations sequence and the purpose behind it will become better teachers. Such students will become teachers who not only read about how to improve their subject, but who also keep informed about current trends in education

HOW VS.
WHAT?

as they read such journals as *Phi Delta Kappan* and *Educational Leadership.* These teachers know that how they present subject matter to young people is as important as what they present.

Items That Cause Teachers Stress

CHALLENGES

Teaching is a challenging career, and some of these challenges and problems produce **stress.** In one study, 400 kindergarten through twelfth grade teachers in a midwestern community were asked to rank eleven stressful conditions in teaching. Table 1–1 summarizes the results of this study.

Disruptive Students

STUDY THE
SYMPTOMS

Disruptive students seem to emerge close to or at the top of about everyone's list. All public school teachers and administrators are confronted with the problems of a disturbed society and must deal daily with the symptoms of the sociological problems in their communities. As discussed in Chapters

TABLE 1–1
Rank Order and Male/Female Rankings of Items That Cause Stress

OVERALL RANKING	MALE RANKING	FEMALE RANKING
1. Disruptive students	Disruptive students	Lack of time
2. Lack of time	Student apathy	Disruptive students
3. Student apathy	Financial pressure	Nonteaching duties
4. Nonteaching duties	Lack of support from parents/community	Student apathy
5. Financial pressure	Lack of positive feedback from administrators	Lack of support from parents/community
6. Lack of support from parents/community	Lack of time	Financial pressure
7. Dealing with multiability students	Nonteaching duties	Dealing with multiability students
8. Lack of positive feedback from administrators	Dealing with multiability students	Lack of positive feedback from administrators
9. Lack of input into curricular/administrative decisions	Lack of input into curricular/administrative decisions	Lack of input into curricular/administrative decisions
10. Lack of recognition for teaching excellence	Lack of recognition for teaching excellence	Lack of recognition for teaching excellence
11. Lack of colleague support	Lack of colleague support	Lack of colleague support

SOURCE: Dedrick, C. V., Hawkes, R. R., & Smith, J. K. (1981). Teacher stress: A descriptive study of the concerns. *National Association of Secondary School Principals Bulletin, 65,* 32.

3 and 4, symptoms are manifested in drug and alcohol problems, teacher assaults, vandalism to the school, verbal abuse of teachers and administrators, pregnancies, dropouts, decline in test scores, increased student apathy, and many more. The schools alone cannot hope to solve the deep-seated causes of these problems, yet the schools are often the scapegoat for society's problems. Educators can only hope that religious institutions, government agencies, community organizations, and the home will unite with them in an effort to solve the real problems. In the meantime, preservice

DEVIANT BE-
HAVIOR

teachers need to study deviant behavior and to learn a multitude of ways to minimize its effect on them and on the students they teach.

Lack of Time

TIME MAN-
AGMENT

Lack of time also rated very high on all three lists in the midwestern study. As a teacher, you will be asked to do many things that take up your time, for example, lunchroom duty, playground duty, study hall supervision, ticket taking, bus-loading supervision, and so on, none of which are actual teaching responsibilities. Because of strained education budgets, you may have to deal with large classes, which require more time for paper grading and class preparation. Lack of time correlates strongly with the dislike of nonteaching tasks.

Student Apathy

RELEVANT?

Student apathy also rates high as a stressful part of teaching. There are probably many factors that cause student apathy in our schools today. Slow or learning-disabled students sometimes give up trying to participate in school after experiencing frustration and failure. Many young people see the subject matter taught in school as irrelevant to their lives. Students may be turned off by schools and learning because of the influence of television. Many students watch television more hours per week than they go to school, and the shows they observe are far more exciting than an orderly, disciplined classroom. The threat of nuclear war, often discussed on television, also has an effect on our children. Some actually feel that there is no sense in getting an education because they will be killed by the bomb anyway. Apathy may also arise in certain subcultures of students who are out of the mainstream as a result of heavy use of alcohol and drugs. Whatever the reason for apathy, teachers have to expend far more energy to motivate and teach apathetic students.

Nonteaching Duties

DISTRAC-
TIONS

Nonteaching duties are probably the least publicized and the most misunderstood problem of teachers. Most of the American public visualizes teachers in the act of teaching and not as curriculum planners, paper graders, ballgame ticket takers, hall duty monitors, lunchroom overseers, activity sponsors, playground supervisors, and so on. Nearly all teachers are on task not only during the school day, but also after school hours, in the evenings, on weekends, and in the summers. These nonteaching expectations, when added to the problems of disruptive students and excessive class size, can and often do place additional stress on dedicated teachers.

Financial Pressure

The current financial pressures on families and on individuals are tremendous. Teachers are intelligent individuals who are leaders in our communities, and they may be dissatisfied when they compare themselves with other professionals in the community who reap giant financial rewards for their services.

Lack of Support from Parents and Community

WORKING EF-
FECTIVELY
WITH PAR-
ENTS

Lack of support from parents and the community also rated high as a source of stress in the midwestern study. Again, as a teacher, you must learn to cope with this problem and know that its causes are deeply rooted in society. Most elementary school teachers receive a reasonable amount of support from parents, but at the secondary level, parent support drops off considerably. On parent nights, many junior high or middle schools and high schools are fortunate to greet one fourth of their parents. The following guidelines offer some positive first steps toward working more effectively with parents (Bordeaux, 1982).

1. Make home visits so that the parent(s) can remain on familiar territory. (Though teachers may be ill at ease in settings out of their control, benefits accrue in development of trust and better understanding of children.)

2. Write letters of welcome to children and parents, including brief information about your aspirations for the children, and invite the support of parent and child.

3. Organize several group planning meetings for parents at different times to accommodate work schedules, with follow-up telephone calls or personal contact to reaffirm that parents are needed to help plan for their children.

4. Organize a corner, table, or bulletin board for parents, making available announcements, schedules, brochures, and books appropriate to parent interests.

5. Design a one-page memo to parents for regular distribution, including class highlights, films viewed, projects initiated or completed, trips planned, etc.

6. Develop an open-door policy for parents to visit the classroom whenever they can, teaching children to greet, introduce, and see to the comfort of parents visiting the classroom during instruction.

7. Survey parents for topics or problems they would like to discuss or have considered.

8. Contact parents with words of caring when circumstances warrant.

9. Develop lists of seasonal activities and places to visit with children on weekends and holidays.

10. Write letters of appreciation or arrange for other recognition of parents who participate in the instructional program or commit time to special projects.

11. Help children plan an afternoon, evening, or weekend reception for parents so they may meet one another and get acquainted.

12. Help children get acquainted through classroom activities that highlight strengths of each child. (p. 276)

Although the list may seem to be best suited to elementary teachers, many of these guidelines are as well suited to secondary teachers. Common sense and the literature tell us that home visits can be very productive in **HOME VISITS** eliminating most of the problems that students are having in school. The most important single ingredient of a home visit is establishing a common understanding between you and the parents on how to work with that child in a more constructive and consistent manner. Getting on the same wavelength with parents is absolutely essential to making real progress with a problem learner and is nearly as essential with other students.

When going to students' homes, each teacher will want to gather different information, but most will want answers to the following questions (Bordeaux, 1982):

1. Do you think your child likes school?

2. What activities interest your child at school?

THE VISIT!   3. What does your child enjoy doing at home? (This is needed so that teachers and parents can get together and withhold activities from either home or school, when children misbehave.)

4. What is your child's favorite subject at school? (This is necessary so that teachers can check with each other to find out if the child's behavior is consistent in every class; and if not, why not?)

5. Do you have any concerns about your child with which the school can help? (p. 276)

In your preservice training you may wish to go on a few home visits to gain some practical experience in this challenging area.

COMMUNITY The members of the community must also be a part of the educational **INVOLVE-** establishment; they are the ones who, acting through legislators, fund our **MENT** schools. As a new teacher, you will be too busy to be concerned unduly with community understanding, but there are some ways you can help. Teachers should assist citizens by:

1. Showing courtesy and genuine pleasure toward all visitors

2. Actively participating in parent–teacher organizations and other community affairs

3. Seeking, through invitation, use of the community's human resources both in curriculum planning and in instruction

4. Emphasizing the unique value of citizen contributions ("The School's Role in Community Life," 1982, p. 125)

Getting to know your community better, especially if you are a newcomer, is an exciting part of living. Many people in your community can enhance your curriculum with valuable expert knowledge on many subjects, and they will be flattered to be asked to speak to your classes.

Dealing with Multiability Students

VARIATIONS
AND ABILITY

Teachers are confronted with the problem of individual differences in students. Even in very homogeneous classes, individuals may vary considerably in ability. Meeting these individual needs is not easy even for the most experienced teachers. It is often frustrating to teach a concept to your class and have only about half the students grasp the meaning the first time. Even after the third time, a few will need some individual tutoring. The nongraded type of school mentioned in Chapter 10 is an administrative setup intended to meet this need.

Lack of Input into Curricular/Administrative Decisions

NEED FOR
EMPOWER-
MENT

Teachers generally enjoy being a part of the curricular decision-making process, but too often, their curricular ideas are not sought. Administrators pressured to facilitate things, make decisions about curriculum or important school policy with little or no input from classroom teachers. Teachers, then, who must abide by these decisions, are angered as they must implement these same policies. Many teachers are stressed by the frustration

Being able to deal with students of widely ranging abilities is a problem faced by all teachers.

(Photo used by permission of the Indianapolis Public Schools.)

that results from their having little or no input into decisions that affect them.

Lack of Positive Feedback and Support

COLLEGIAL SUPPORT

Positive feedback and support depend on your administrators, your colleagues, and the students you teach. Lack of positive feedback from school administrators is an additional cause of stress for teachers. It appears that many administrators are so concerned with the daily tasks involved in running a school that they overlook the internal human-relations aspect of their jobs. Teachers may seldom get positive comments when things go wrong. Feedback, especially positive feedback, from administrators means a great deal to the teacher. In fairness to administrators, they themselves seldom get positive feedback from the public they are trying to serve; they actually receive more negative feedback from the public than do teachers.

FORCES LIMITING COLLEGIALITY

It is always great to receive support from those you work with on the job, but often we get too busy to be concerned about others as we go about our daily concerns. Frequently, in teaching, we let envy or jealousy creep in as a deterrent to real dialogue with our fellow teachers. Colleague support among the members of a department or a school group is very rehabilitative. It results in much greater productivity, and the students are the greatest beneficiaries. In addition, teachers want to be and deserve to be recognized for teaching excellence, but often it goes unnoticed. In the military, there are awards for about every type of excellence imaginable, but teachers must rely on their students to praise them. Students may remember to thank their teachers, but teachers need more immediate recognition for excellence.

MANAGING STRESS

Stress is a part of everyone's life to a certain extent; but of representative occupations especially at risk, education ranks at or near the top (Matthews, 1989). The big question for all of you who are about to embark on a teaching career is: How can I manage stress so that it will least harmfully and most positively affect me and the students I instruct? A well-thought-out stress management model is recommended for your use (Matthews, 1989, p. 1). The Matthews formula is $A + B + C + D = R$. A stands for *awareness* of the physiology of stress; B stands for *benefits* of a healthy body; C stands for the various *components* of various stress management techniques; D focuses on the *dependency* of practice of the skills throughout the curriculum; and R stands for the sum of the four factors of the equation, or *relaxation*. Whether you are now in preservice training or are currently employed as a teacher, the Matthews formula can be of help.

AUTONOMIC

With respect to the A factor, one needs to study how the autonomic nervous system functions. At this early stage procedural matters should include the use of biofeedback devices. Such devices demonstrate vividly and conclusively the mind–body relationship. For example, changes in peripheral temperature indicate changes in physiological factors, such as blood flow, which are indicative of the degree of stress.

BENEFITS   Concerning the *B* factor, the student needs to realize the benefit that accrues as a result of having a healthy body. A holistically healthy person is one who is mentally healthy, having all of the implicit intellectual, physical, emotional, and social functions. Some stress is normal; in fact, optimal stress may produce exhilaration, high motivation, mental alertness, high energy, improved memory and recall, sharp perception, and calmness under pressure. It is important that you as a student realize the benefits that come from effective stress management.

COMPO-   The *C* factor is concerned with such components as time management,
NENTS   cognitive restructuring, relaxation training, progressive relaxation, quieting reflex, autogenics, and biofeedback; but it does not overlook dieting, budgeting of rest, and the allowance for optimum individual exercise procedures as parts of stress management. One must as much as possible eliminate any dependence upon medication. The following components of the *C* factor are accompanied by a brief explanation of how each might be implemented.

TIME MANAGEMENT

IMPORTANCE 1. *Time Analysis.* Explore how you spend your time in the present. For
OF TIME   approximately two weeks, record what you do every half hour.
MANAGE-   2. *Goal Setting.* Set both long-range and short-range goals that are both
MENT   measurable and realistic.
            3. *Prioritization.* Arrange the goals in three columns: goals that are essential (must do), those that you desire but are not essential (should do), and those that are good but can be delayed (can do). The first set of goals is the set you strive to achieve. The second and third sets of goals remain dormant until the first list is completed.
            4. *Delegation.* You may at times elect to hire secretarial help or other technical services. Delegating work at home with household chores helps because all family members share in the operation of the home.
            5. *Action*—At this step, you plan strategy to accomplish goals and perform the tasks outlined in the strategy.

COGNITIVE RESTRUCTURING

The process of restructuring involves (1) examining the interaction between events and beliefs that lead to perceptions and emotional reactions, (2) recognizing when the reactions are unwarranted or negative, and (3) alter-
APPEARANCE ing the way one thinks about the situation in order to alter the emotional
VS. REALITY reaction. For example, we all try to read the minds of others and attribute thoughts and feelings to other people without evidence. We need to realize that failure to give the expected reaction does not mean the person disapproves of what you said. So then we can alter how we think about a given situation in order to change our emotional response.

RELAXATION TRAINING

RELAXATION
RESPONSES When stress causes an alarm reaction, eliciting the relaxation response can counter the physical changes of alarm and maintain a calm, relaxed state. Some examples of these relaxation responses follow:

1. *Progressive Relaxation.* Here one focuses on a single muscle, muscle group, or area of the body and alternately tenses and relaxes the muscle(s). This is one of the simplest relaxation techniques, but it is somewhat limited in variety.

2. *Quieting Reflex.* This six-second "quieting reflex" technique has proved highly successful for persons with demanding schedules. It permits a person to function with an alert mind while in a calm body. When you become aware of something frightening and annoying in the environment, like tension or anxiety, follow these steps in order:

   - Smile inwardly with both eyes and mouth.
   - Take an easy deep breath.
   - While exhaling, let the jaw, tongue, and shoulders go limp; the person should then feel a wave of heaviness and warmth flowing through the body from the head to the toes.
   - Resume normal activity.

AUTOGENICS

SELF-GENER-
ATING RE-
SPONSES The word *autogenics* means self-generating and is a high-level cognitive technique for triggering the physiological relaxation response.

One of the common techniques used in autogenic programs capitalizes on the ability of the body to follow the commands of the conscious centers of the brain. Typical phrases a person can use during the exercises are I am relaxed, I am calm, I am quiet, My right leg is heavy, My right arm is heavy and warm, My left arm is heavy and warm, and I am quiet and at peace. If a person can imagine warmth or the feeling of a heavy sensation in the limbs, the body has the tendency to reproduce that state.

BIOFEEDBACK

LISTENING
TO THE
BODY If you listen to the body, it tells you about its functioning. For example, peripheral measurements of skin temperature can indicate blood flow changes to a particular region of the body.

DEPENDENCY
ON PRACTICE The *D* factor, or dependency on practice, of the stress management model is most important. This factor deals with the application of the skills learned to everyday living. Matthews (1989) sees this model of stress management as being used throughout your preservice years and all through the curriculum. Ideally, by the time you have graduated and become a teacher it is as much a part of you as lesson planning. You can use these techniques to calm yourself before taking tests and/or during student teaching.

RELAXATION The *R* factor, or result, is relaxation. If you are successful in implementing the program of stress management, you will become a free and functioning individual in major control of your life. Stress management is not included in this chapter to alarm you; it is mentioned so that you can learn to cope with the stresses and pressures of the occupation and thus become a more successful teacher. Not only will stress management help you be a better teacher, it will help you become a better person too.

The First Year

CHALLENGES Getting through the first year of teaching is a tremendous challenge. Any occupation presents more difficulties in the first year than in the years following, but teaching has so many facets that it is especially demanding. Many of the challenges are of a practical nature, such as learning to get along with colleagues, learning whom to trust and whom not to trust, getting to know your supervisors, learning the school's accepted disciplinary procedures, and following school policy. Also, the first-year teacher is challenged by the academic responsibility of providing a workable lesson plan for each day.

Many articles have been written about how to induct a new teacher into a school and into a system. Myers (1981) wrote that beginning teachers generally identify the six items as being most significant in helping them to adjust to teaching:

ADJUST-
MENTS

1. Achieving status with peers and co-workers
2. Gaining the attention and concern of the principal
3. Having ample opportunity to know and understand the local situation with emphasis on general school policies, school facilities, and school routines
4. Opportunities to make unique and personal contributions to the school
5. Opportunities to grow and progress personally and professionally
6. Opportunities to associate socially with peers (pp. 71–72)

Myers commented on all the items in this list from the principal's point of view, and he discussed many excellent suggestions for the principal and the new teacher. One of the most meaningful comments by Myers (1981) is one made in connection with opportunities to make personal contributions to the school. If

NO ONE WAY

> beginning teachers are convinced that they are at liberty to be themselves, to implement their own techniques, to exercise their own personalities, what a tremendous boost to morale! Most beginning teachers have come to recognize that teaching is so much more a personal affair that there can be no one way of teaching. Rather, each teacher must be permitted to discover his optimum efficiency in a climate that not only permits but encourages experimentation and self-expression. It would be argued that this attitude on the part of the principal is by far the most significant contribution he can make to the development of the beginning teacher. (pp. 73–74)

This statement will be very meaningful to use as you begin to teach. For some of you, that first year may seem far away, but it is closer than you

POWERFUL
RESPONSIBIL-
ITY

think. Although the comment by Myers is directed to the principal, it is an ideal that you can help to facilitate for yourself. The latitude you have as a teacher, within your own classroom, to be yourself and to direct your own unique style of learning is a powerful responsibility.

Working with Other Adults, Parents, Administrators, and Aides

To better prepare yourselves for the first full year of teaching, there are some things you can do for yourself or that your college can help you

LACK OF
PREPARA-
TION

accomplish. Research indicates that beginning teachers are not well prepared to work with other adults, parents, administrators, and aides (Hitz and Roper, 1986, p. 66). These working relationships can be practiced and critiqued during preservice training.

PEER PROB-
LEM SOLVING

Learning to work with other adults can be facilitated by informal problem-solving sessions with peers. During student teaching, student teachers can participate in support groups with other teachers where they can share classroom experiences and help generate potential solutions. Students can jointly plan lessons and observe one another and thus promote colleague relationships.

PARENT–
TEACHER
CONFER-
ENCES

As a **preservice teacher** you can gain experience in conducting parent–teacher conferences as an observer in a field setting, in simulations in college classes, and in conducting some actual conferences yourself during student teaching. As you work in a field setting with other students, one of you can serve as an aide to the other at alternate times. If, during student teaching, your **cooperating teacher** uses an aide, then you have an excellent opportunity to gain direct experience working with an aide. Administrators and aides can be invited to college classrooms to talk about their jobs. These are only some of the ways one can better prepare for the first year and for the years that follow as well as bridge the gap between preservice and inservice training and experiences.

Finding a Buddy

As you know, your first year of teaching is so important in gaining the confidence you need to become a professional teacher. If your first year does not go well, you may not remain in teaching. Experienced leaders know what it takes to get the type of assistance you need to achieve success in the classroom. During your first year some of you will be in internship

MENTORS

programs and will be assigned a **mentor teacher.** A mentor is normally trained to give you instructional assistance and to make classroom observations. Some mentors fulfill all of your needs, but in case you are not assigned a mentor, a support teacher or a buddy can help to make your first year more constructive. If your principal does not appoint a buddy for you, ask him or her to do so. According to Hamlin and Hering (1983, p. 126), "a buddy could be any willing, successful teacher with good listening skills and compassion." According to Hamlin and Hering (1988), buddies can do the following things for you:

- Aid you in making learning assessments by testing or other means
- Help you make parent communications and arrange parent conferences
- Setting up your grade book
- Adapting materials to match the individual needs of students
- Constructing lists of classroom rules
- Writing field trip permission slips
- Calling parents when discipline problems occur
- Help in organizing the class period
- Develop realistic expectations of appropriate student behavior
- Help decipher building and district policy, both written and unwritten (p. 177)

This is by no means a complete list, but it gives you some feel for how useful a buddy can be during your first year.

Beginning Teacher Internship Programs

One of the reforms in teacher education that appears to be very promising is the beginning teacher **internship program.** Internships operate differently from state to state, but basically they are in place to help the teacher adapt to the teaching environment. Not only does the beginning teacher benefit

Buddy teachers can help beginning teachers arrange parent-teacher conferences.

ASSISTANCE
AND SUP-
PORT

by receiving assistance and support, but the schools are also able to assess and encourage those teaching practices that improve their program the most.

INDIANA BEGINNING TEACHER INTERNSHIP PROGRAM

MIDWEST
PROGRAM

Indiana began a program for interns during the 1988–1989 school year. The beginning teacher is hired by a school district and paid the regular beginning teacher's salary. Once the intern is hired by the school district, he or she is assigned a mentor teacher for the entire internship year. The mentors are recognized in their school corporations as effective and outstanding teaching professionals. By law the mentors must have at least five years of teaching experience and ideally teach the same/similar grade level and same/similar subject in the same building as the beginning teacher. Not only are the mentors recognized as outstanding teaching professionals, they are also paid an annual stipend of $600 by the state.

The intern is·evaluated by the building principal before May 1 of the school year. She or he uses an internship checklist developed by the state department of education. If the intern does not successfully pass the internship program, she or he can repeat for a second year in the same district or another school district. The school district in which the internship was completed is not obligated to reemploy the intern. Also, beginning teachers may select a university advisor to provide assistance and support during the year. It is too early to assess the ultimate value of the Indiana program, but it appears to be a move that will result in better teacher performance.

FLORIDA BEGINNING TEACHER PROGRAM

SOUTHERN
PROGRAM

The state of Florida is providing support services for their beginning teachers during the first year. This program was begun in 1982; and in 1986–1987, a total of 8,047 teachers successfully completed the program. Beginning teachers receive full pay for a beginner in that district, and they are assigned a support staff consisting of a building administrator, a peer teacher, and another professional educator. The support staff conducts at least five observations of the beginning teacher. In Florida the experienced teacher must teach at the same level and in the same subject area as the beginning teacher. Successful completion of the state-approved Beginning Teacher Program is required to obtain a teaching certificate.

The Florida program specifies thirty-five essential generic competencies with special emphasis upon the following:

1. The ability to comprehend and interpret a message after listening
2. The ability to orally communicate information on a given subject in a coherent, logical manner
3. The ability to comprehend patterns of physical, social, and academic development in students, including exceptional students, in the regular classroom, and to counsel the same students concerning their needs in these areas

4. The ability to recognize and be aware of the instructional needs of exceptional students (Florida Department of Education, Rule 6A-5.61, p. 306)

Among other things, Florida wants to emphasize listening and communication skills. They want their teachers to be very sensitive to student needs and interests. A professional development plan must be designed to assist each individual to improve and to demonstrate performance on the minimum essential competencies specified in the rule.

BROWARD
COUNTY

In Broward County, Florida, the district specifies the following:

A Professional Development Plan is written for each beginning teacher in the year-long and Alternate Certification Program. The plan is developed by the support team with the knowledge and participation of the beginning teacher. It includes specific objectives, learning experiences which should lead to satisfactory demonstration of those objectives, and target dates of completion. A set of resource materials has been provided to each media center to assist the support team. The plan includes three formative conferences which are based upon at least one observation by a support team member. Upon completion of the Professional Development Plan and the demonstration of the minimum essential competencies, the portfolio is signed by the principal and beginning teacher. It is sent to the district office to be checked. After the portfolio is signed off by the coordinator of the Beginning Teacher Program, an official statement of completion is sent to the Department of Education in Tallahassee. The beginning teacher is then able to apply for a regular Florida teaching certificate. (Sedinger, 1988, p. 3)

Broward County is only one of the county plans in Florida. The Broward plan is very specific; it leaves little doubt of what is expected of the beginning teacher. The state will benefit by having better trained teachers and the teacher will feel comfortably supported.

FIRST-YEAR TEACHER SUPPORT/INDUCTION PROGRAM IN CALIFORNIA

WESTERN
PROGRAM

When asked what kind of help they needed, new teachers in the Encinitas Union School District in California answered knowledge, administrative support, and peer support. After being sensitized to new teacher needs, the district devised the following plan:

1. Give new teachers an overview of policies/procedures
2. Ask administrators and supervisors to meet with new teachers to discuss short- and long-term needs
3. Observe new teachers in class
4. Encourage both sides to initiate meetings

New teachers are assigned mentor teachers to help with class management, discipline, and other items. It is a confidential relationship and nonsupervisory in nature. Also, inservices are held for parent/teacher conferencing, student testing, and grading.

TREND TO-
WARD ASSIS-
TANCE

As you can see, the trend is toward either an internship program or other

First-year teacher internship programs help first-year teachers learn about their profession.

(Photo used by permission of the Metropolitan School District of Washington Township.)

types of assistance for beginning teachers. Whatever the program, it is designed to help a beginning teacher adapt to the teaching role. School corporations want to hold on to their teachers and thus reduce the high dropout rate in the teaching profession. The authors feel that these moves constitute a positive step toward helping the teacher become a better trained professional. States and school districts will need to be sensitive to the needs of some older individuals entering the profession after having been in another line of employment. Not all programs fit all individuals entering the profession for the first time; thus, some degree of flexibility is in order.

Teacher Incentives

There has been a lot of talk in recent years about offering teachers the kinds of **incentives** needed to do an outstanding teaching performance. According to Mitchell and Peters (1988),

INTRINSIC
VS. EXTRIN-
SIC BENE-
FITS?

Effective incentive systems should reflect the principles that intrinsic rewards are more powerful than extrinsic ones and that encouraging collegiality is preferable to rewarding individual teachers. (p. 74)

In particular what is needed to motivate teachers are intrinsic benefits like exciting work, commodious working conditions, interesting co-workers, or the joy of competently performing important tasks, not extrinsic benefits like promotions and wages (Mitchell and Peters, 1988, p. 75). The extrinsic rewards are important, but research has demonstrated that teachers are most sensitive to intrinsic rewards directly linked to their relationships with students and co-workers. One of the authors of this book recalls the joy he experienced as a result of working closely with one of his students on a science fair project but he does not remember as well the salary increases that came along at various times.

As you enter the teaching profession, consider carefully the school district you select to work for as a teacher. The good school districts have built in intrinsic rewards that help you feel good as a professional. None of these are more satisfying than having the opportunity to work cooperatively with fellow teachers or participate fully in the implementation of adopted school programs (Mitchell and Peters, 1988, p. 77).

TREATED
LIKE CHIL-
DREN

Mary Hartwood Futrell, recent past president of the National Education Association, has often said "that teachers are treated like very tall children instead of professionals" (Futrell, 1988, p. A-10). If teachers can be given more opportunities for intrinsic rewards, Futrell and others are more likely to describe the treatment given teachers as professional.

In recent years there has been much talk and discussion about installing a merit pay system for teachers. Others have said that public school teachers would benefit from a career ladder system similar to the university model. Reform is needed in this area because, traditionally, teachers' salary schedules have offered few incentives to teachers to improve themselves or the program of the school where they are employed. Once you are hired into a system, the salary schedule yields yearly increases automatically; therefore, all one needs to do is come to work and teach. Outstanding teachers are

SELF-MOTI-
VATION

nearly always self-motivated and do extra things routinely; but they, along with all the other teachers, deserve some rewards beyond the regular pay schedule. Both merit pay and career ladder pay have their advantages and disadvantages, but creative minds are at work thinking up still other incentive pay systems of rewarding teachers.

AN EXAMPLE
INCENTIVE
SYSTEM

One incentive system for rewarding teachers has been proposed in Jefferson County, Kentucky (JCK) (Schlechty and Ingwerson, 1987). This plan rewards the quality of results and the quantity of effort. JCK used the airline frequent-flyer incentive system as a model for their proposal. Teachers accumulate bonus points. For every 1,000 accumulated bonus points, they receive one award unit. JCK teachers put together what they call an action plan for accumulating bonus points. The plan is then reviewed by a panel of teachers and administrators to assign bonus points ranging from 0 to

12,000. After the project is completed, a panel of evaluators review it to see how the action plan was carried out. Bonus points are awarded based on the extent to which the previously agreed upon task was carried out. Consequently, if the task is accomplished, the individual or group receives all the bonus points originally assigned. Bonus points beyond 1,000 points can be converted into teacher supplies, equipment, and even cash awards. Also, built into this incentive system is the nudge to cooperate with colleagues and work on action plans together to earn collective bonus points. These bonus points can then be used to buy items needed for a department or a class. Whole schools can work on an action plan to earn points for the unit. According to the designer of the JCK program,

> The implementation of the program should help faculties begin to see that recognizing and honoring the stellar performance of an individual also helps that person's colleagues. For example, teachers who earn the top number of bonus points will not only receive personal awards, but their efforts will also increase the average number of bonus points earned by the faculties of which they are members. (Schlechty and Ingwerson, 1987, p. 590)

The JCK program is only one proposal for offering incentives to teachers in which exceptional teaching performance is rewarded. The authors estimate that during the 1990s, most school systems will experiment with ideas to establish incentives to do excellent work. Incentive systems for the public schools constitute one of the most discussed topics in the current reform movement in education. The more intrinsic the reward systems are, the more long-lasting and successful they will be.

Teacher Empowerment

FEELING OF
ISOLATION

Of all of the educational reform movements currently afloat, none is more important than teacher **empowerment.** Most teachers feel isolated and unable to influence school reform themselves. These feelings can cause stress and have a negative influence on how one teaches.

Leanna Landsman, editor-in-chief and publisher of the *The Instructor,* is concerned about the need for greater teacher empowerment and offers ten resolutions that teachers can make to empower themselves.

1. Do Not Give up Your Birthright

PRIMARY JOB

If you wake up and find that you are nothing but a traffic cop in a dysfunctional classroom, do something about the problem. As a teacher your primary job is to teach, not to discipline. Make a plan for solving the problem; involve the principal if necessary or change things on your own in your own classroom.

> In every action, think about what a teacher *ought* to do. Take the lead professionally. Don't be flattered when the curriculum director asks you to help select new textbooks. Assume it's your birthright and your professional responsibility to help choose the materials you use to teach. (Landsman, 1988, p. 373)

2. Remove the Words "They Won't Let Us" from Your Vocabulary

"WE CAN"
APPROACH

So often we humans pass the blame off on someone else—the principal, the superintendent, or the school board. Maybe there is no time for the first grade teacher to meet and talk about common problems. Do not blame it on the principal; decide on a special time such as breakfast one day a week.

> Nothing hurts teachers more than the downtrodden postures they sometimes assume, and they've paid the price for "being done to" for a long time. Sometimes the "they" is really "we." (Landsman, 1988, p. 373)

3. Market Your Profession

SELLING
TEACHING

We need to sell teaching as a profession to the community. Let local service clubs know that you are willing to speak and perhaps appear on a local talk show with a few of your students. Also, do not forget to cultivate your local reporters.

> Decide once a month to tell the world what a teacher does and what teaching is all about. Call it publicity, call it PR, call it survival. Let people outside of education know what you do and why it is important that they understand it. (Landsman, 1988, p. 373)

4. Do Not Let Your School Try to Be All Things to All People

INVOLVE-
MENT IN SO-
LUTIONS

This textbook addresses itself to social issues that impact upon schools, but teachers and schools cannot solve these problems alone. As a teacher you need to be involved in the solution of social problems; but it takes many entities to solve such complex issues as child abuse. Certainly, churches, hospitals, social agencies, universities, and service clubs have a role to play.

> Although public education cannot back away from problems created by the urge to provide for the needs of all children, we must also keep the school's primary academic purpose before the public. (Landsman, 1988, p. 373)

5. It Takes Only a Few Waves to Make a Sea of Change

YOU CAN
INITIATE A
CHANGE

You may have a schoolwide problem such as an ineffective principal. Do not just sit around and complain in the faculty lounge. Perhaps you can use your best professional skills and political expertise to get this person transferred. This scenario has occurred before and often the principal ends up in a job or a position that is better suited to his or her expertise, enabling the faculty of the school to carry out their agenda in a more constructive manner.

> If you have a big school problem, don't wait for an act of God to solve it. (Landsman, 1988, p. 373)

6. Build Your Professional Base from the Bottom up

BOTTOM UP
APPROACH

Whatever happens to you the first year depends a lot on your own initiative. It is easy to become isolated and lonely in a school. Some teachers have a desire to save the world all in one school year by stepping out without a network of colleagues and with ties to the administration, thus building barriers of resistance among fellow teachers and administrators.

> Establish your own brain trust. Network. Find colleagues whom you respect and whose advice you can count on. No one needs to deputize you to get yourself business cards with your school address, phone number, and the title "teacher." (If enough parents call, perhaps schools will finally provide one of the things that teachers really need: telephones in individual classrooms.) (Landsman, 1988, p. 374)

7. Shape Up Your School's Recruitment, Selection, and Induction System

This is probably one resolution that can wait until after your first year, but it is still a worthwhile idea.

WAYS TO IM-
PROVE THE
PROFESSION

> Does your school hire teachers who share the same goals for students and the same beliefs about teaching? If not, all the curriculum alignment in the world won't make for smooth transitions between grades. (Landsman, 1988, p. 374)

Landsman believes that teachers should be a part of the process for hiring new faculty members. This is one way of making sure that new teachers are in sync with the direction in which the school is headed.

8. Acknowledge That There Are and Will Continue to Be Certain Tensions in the Area of Curriculum

ONGOING
DEBATES

All teachers have certain ideas concerning what ought to be covered in the curriculum. There is ongoing debate over First Amendment issues such as religion in the public schools. Should school prayer be used? Can we teach about how religion has been an important part of our history?

> The curriculum crisis is really a national identity crisis. What should an American student study? And who should decide? Teachers should not be defensive about these matters. It's a national debate, and you should be an informed and guiding participant in it. (Landsman, 1988, p. 374)

9. Enlist Your Local, State, and National Unions on the Professional Team

ASSISTANCE
FROM PRO-
FESSIONAL
ORGANIZA-
TIONS

Often, teachers become involved in minor, indeed picky, issues and lose sight of the big picture—what being a professional teacher is all about. Landsman says it is important for all teachers to sing the same professional tune at local, state, and national levels.

10. Provide for Your Own Renewal

THREAT OF
BURNOUT

If teachers do not take time for themselves once in a while, they will burn out.

> Teaching is exhausting work, even when it is exhilarating. Know when you need a mental health day. Know when you need to take a sabbatical. Know when you need to change jobs—for a day or for a year. Your continued empowerment depends on it. (Landsman, 1988, p. 374)

The authors feel that you cannot wait for others to empower you; you must be instrumental in making those changes yourself. If you do help to bring about some of the ten resolutions suggested by Landsman, you will have taken a giant step toward improving your own professional life. Much can be said for an affirmative stance; little can be said for the "poor me" negative stance. Not only will an affirmative position help your professional life, but it will also help your personal life!

Summary

In this chapter, you have been presented with several reasons for choosing teaching/education as a career. Being a teacher involves more than enjoying a subject or liking children, although these are important. Some characteristics of the ideal teacher were discussed to help you focus on what a teacher is capable of doing. Other chapters will relate to important considerations about becoming a teacher, and it is hoped that you will take every opportunity during the remainder of your training to relate theory to the practice of teaching in the classroom.

You have learned that teaching is both a discipline and a profession, as is the practice of medicine or, for that matter, any of the other learned professions. We hope that we have given you some constructive ideas to assist you in your first year of teaching.

It would be unwise for us to be dishonest about some of the causes of teacher stress—and, in some cases, teacher burnout—but these can be found in other occupations as well. We think that you should know from the beginning what to expect from the occupation you are about to enter, so that you can better prepare yourself to handle some of the difficulties you will encounter. It is, indeed, a worthy occupation to serve our fellow human beings and to help, as others have said, make the world a better place in which to live.

Several hints to make your first-year experience more successful have been presented. There are many people and agencies out there ready and willing to help just for the asking. School districts and state school systems want you to be successful, and most of them are providing an organized effort to fulfill this need.

Finally, the term *teacher empowerment* was introduced. Ten suggestions were offered as to how you can become empowered to do more for yourself and your school. An empowered teacher is one who will make some waves and become a valuable leader in the school or school system.

Glossary Terms

Stress, 13   Internship Program, 23
Preservice Teacher, 22   Incentives, 26
Cooperating Teacher, 22   Empowerment, 28
Mentor Teacher, 22

Questions

1. Teachers, like everyone else, experience pressures as they practice their occupation. Discuss some of the pressures alluded to in the chapter and how they might be overcome.

2. Teaching is both an art and a science. Why are both of these aspects important to being a successful teacher?

3. Discuss why the motivation to be an elementary school teacher differs from the motivation to be a secondary school teacher. Why should these motivating reasons be similar rather than so far apart?

4. Why are the theories presented in the college classroom often remote from actual practical application? How can you as a student, with the instructor's assistance, overcome this disadvantage?

5. Who was the most influential role model in your life? Discuss the importance of this favorite role model with other students in the class.

6. Think of some teachers you know who are models of self-confidence. Why are these teachers self-confident?

7. Of the list of stress-producing items in Table 1–1, which would you currently choose as potentially most stress producing? Discuss your choice with other members of the class.

8. Myers alludes to the teacher's being at liberty to be himself or herself. How can you best prepare yourself for this challenge?

9. Discuss the problems of the first-year teacher as you perceive them and identify ways in which internship programs and buddy systems can help alleviate these problems.

10. Why do you think teacher empowerment is such a strong emotional issue in teacher education?

Annotated Bibliography

1. Dedrick, C. V., Hawkes, R. R., & Smith, J. K. (Dec. 1981). Teacher Stress: A descriptive study of the concerns. *National Association of Secondary School Principals Bulletin, 65,* 32.

   Stress, as the authors point out, is not new. This article analyzes stressful conditions as perceived by teachers, not by administrators or counselors. A very useful article.

2. Hamlin, K., & Hering, K. (Sept. 1988). Help for the first-year teacher: Mentor, buddy or both? *National Association of Secondary School Principals Bulletin,* pp. 125–127.

   A mentor is compared with a buddy teacher. This reading tells new teachers what some of their needs are as they begin their career. The article contains many useful tips for the beginning teacher.

3. Landsman, L. (Jan. 1988). 10 resolutions for teachers. *Phi Delta Kappan, 69,* 373–374.

   A large part of this article is included in the textbook. It is hoped that these ten resolutions might free teachers to effect real school reform. The article tells teachers how they can make a difference.

4. Mitchell, D., & Peters, M. (Nov. 1988). A stronger profession through appropriate teacher incentives. *Educational Leadership, 46,* 74–78.

   In this high-quality article much emphasis is placed upon intrinsic rewards rather than extrinsic rewards. The authors maintain that encouragement of collegiality is preferable to rewards for individual teachers.

5. Myers, P. E. The principal and the beginning teacher. (Apr. 1981). *National Association of Secondary School Principals Bulletin, 65* (444), 70–75.

   This article is directed to administrators, but the author, a former principal, has some useful suggestions for the beginning teacher. He emphasizes how important it is that the beginner feel and be a part of the group or school staff.

OBJECTIVES

After reading Chapter 2, the student will be able to:

- Compare and contrast the reform initiatives proposed by NCATE, the Holmes Group, and the Carnegie Foundation
- Identify the criticisms of these reform initiatives
- Be aware of the advantages and disadvantages of alternative routes to teacher certification
- Identify lessons that teacher education can learn from the business community
- Recognize the importance of minority participation in teacher education
- Describe the advantages of two well-known professional development programs in education
- Quote the approximate salaries and fringe benefits paid to teachers
- Project, for the near future, the supply-and-demand probabilities for positions within the teaching profession

Trends in the Teaching Profession

Introduction

TRENDS IN THE PROFESSION

This chapter describes some of the trends in the teaching profession. Currently, the profession is taking a close look at itself in light of some severe criticisms launched at it in the 1980s and continuing into the 1990s. The reform movement in teacher education is viewed from the initiatives taken by three organizations that have made some bold moves and created some waves in education. See the "Visions of Reform Matrix" in Table 2-1 for specific reform proposals.

A trend in alternative teacher certification is considered detrimental and wrong for the children, who deserve to have fully certified personnel as their teachers. Another trend is to look to business and industry for ideas to improve the profession—Disney may have some answers! A dangerous trend is the increased testing of teachers which may inhibit many needed minority students from joining the profession. Two professional growth

TABLE 2–1

Visions of Reform Matrix

	NCATE Redesign	Holmes Group	Carnegie Forum
Recruit minority teachers	X	X	X
Require basic skills and liberal arts background	X	X	X
Ensure subject-matter competence	X	X	X
Develop clinical experiences and demonstration schools	X	X	X
Promote internships and residencies	X	X	X
Support teacher induction	X	X	X
Encourage multiple evaluations	X	X	X
Implement a systematic knowledge base	X	X	X
Develop a coherent professional curriculum	X	X	X
Provide additional resources for teacher preparation	X	X	X
Encourage experimentation and innovation	X		
Develop school technology	X		X
Increase teacher responsibilities and authority		X	X
Require bachelor's degree prior to professional study		X	X
Extend formal preparation and certification period		X	X
Admit novices contingent upon testing		X	X
Differentiate career opportunities		X	X
Improve teacher salaries and working conditions		X	X
Relate student performance and teacher incentives			X
Create a national board			X
Eliminate undergraduate education majors		X	X

programs that are enhancing the expertise of members of the profession are presented. Finally, the latest trends in financial rewards and in supply and demand of teachers are given.

NCATE Reforms

The accrediting agency that oversees the business of teacher education is the **National Council for Accreditation of Teacher Education (NCATE).** The mission of NCATE is twofold: (1) to require a level of quality in professional education that fosters competent practice of graduates, and (2) to encourage institutions to meet rigorous academic standards of excellence in professional education. It is important to note that NCATE is recognized by the U.S. Department of Education as the only authorized accrediting agency in the field of school personnel preparation.

FIVE CATE-
GORIES

NCATE's standards address five categories having a bearing on teacher education. With respect to the first category, *knowledge base for professional education*, NCATE sees to it that all professional education programs are based on established educational research and essential knowledge of sound professional practice. In the second category, *relationship to the world of practice*, the emphasis is on relating theory to practice in clinical and field settings. The third category addresses the *students*; specifically, the unit or school's admission procedures must encourage the recruitment of a culturally diverse student population with potential for professional success in the schools. The fourth category addresses the *faculty*: these are faculty members that teach one or more courses in professional education, and they should be committed to the continuing improvement of the teaching profession. The fifth category is *governance and resources*; the governance system clearly identifies and defines the unit submitted for accreditation, clearly specifies the governance system under which the unit is enabled to fulfill its mission, and demonstrates that in practice the system operates as described.

A board-of-examiners team visits a campus after certain preconditions have been met. The team talks to all important people involved in teacher education on a campus and makes their recommendations regarding approval of the institution. The college or institution is advised within a few weeks of its status. The Unit Accreditation Board can give full or partial approval of the program. If an institution receives partial approval, certain stipulations are spelled out that must be met prior to full approval.

CONTINUITY
TO TEACHER
EDUCATION

The standards for NCATE approval are specific enough to give some continuity to teacher education; yet they are general enough to allow each college or unit to individualize its program. Among all the things it accomplishes for teacher education, NCATE is constantly evaluating older standards and developing new standards. NCATE tries to stay on top of the changes taking place in teacher education.

The Holmes Group

Several groups are proposing many new initiatives directed at teacher education and aimed at general reform. One of the most powerful of these groups is the **Holmes Group,** which comprised ninety-six universities in 1988. Most of these universities are large research-oriented schools with many graduates. The Holmes Group includes the University of California at Berkeley, Ohio State University, and Teachers College at Columbia University.

FIFTH-YEAR PROGRAM

What is startling about this group is that it wants to eliminate undergraduate education and establish the master's degree as the initial teaching certificate. Some critics say that this would result in a needless delay and would cause teachers' education to be more expensive, with no guarantee that teachers would receive compensation at the conclusion of their education to cover the increased costs. Lanier and Featherstone (1988, p. 21) of the Holmes Group maintain that majoring in the arts and sciences is demanding and they make no apologies for making big demands on tomorrow's teachers. There is no doubt that the Holmes Group is at the forefront as far as teacher education reform is concerned and will be the one to watch in the future.

PROFESSIONAL DEVELOPMENT SCHOOLS

The Holmes Group is pushing the idea of forming partnerships with the school systems to create "professional development schools," which would function as teaching hospitals. At these schools a team could be composed of two classroom teachers, a professor from the university, a first- or second-year teacher's aide, an intern (a fifth-year student in the program), and two residents (sixth- and seventh-year students from the university). The team would be responsible for teaching between 75 and 100 students. All of these team members working together would give more adult time to the students, would provide experienced teachers with new chances for professional growth, would improve preservice education and induction, and would enable the district to draw on a well-prepared pool of applicants to fill a large number of teacher vacancies (Lanier and Featherstone, 1988, p. 19).

A TRUE PROFESSION

Creating a true profession of teaching is not something that universities can do alone; it will require coalitions and alliances with people in the schools. Thus, creating bridges across customary boundaries is part and parcel of the Holmes effort. Underneath that effort is a vision of active learning that is at odds with passive sitting and listening that reigns in too many schools and colleges. (Lanier and Featherstone, 1988, p. 20)

At the time of this writing, the Holmes Group has been in place two years. The Group is moving ahead on its initial agenda, which includes the following:

- Restoring the intellectual soundness of teacher's professional education
- Recognizing differences in knowledge, skill, and commitment among teachers [The group supports three career levels.]

HOLMES'
AGENDA

- Elevating standards for entry into teacher preparation programs and the nation's classrooms
- Establishing cooperative relationships between schools and universities
- Enhancing teacher and student learning through improved working conditions (Holmes Group, 1986, pp. 66–73)

SMALL VS.
LARGE
SCHOOLS

As these Holmes Group universities march ahead on their agenda, many smaller teacher education colleges and universities are reassessing their own programs. Most smaller schools are concerned mainly with complying with NCATE standards, but they will take a look at what the large research-oriented universities are doing too. Many smaller schools pride themselves, and justly so, on their undergraduate efforts in teacher education.

The Carnegie Forum

Another group that has immense public respect whenever it comes to reform is the Carnegie Foundation. In 1985, the Foundation established the **Carnegie Forum** on Education and the Economy with the goal of defining a ten-year agenda to explore the link between economic growth and education of the people who will make that growth possible (Carnegie Forum 1986, Preface). The Forum established a Task Force on Teaching as a Profession in recognition of the central role teachers play in the quality of education. This Task Force consisted of top-rated business and educational leaders, who made their recommendations in six categories in the spring of 1986 (Carnegie Forum, 1986, Recommendations).

TASK FORCE
ON TEACH-
ING

First, they called for an improved professional environment for teaching. They wish to give teachers greater autonomy in setting goals for their schools and to make them accountable for achieving agreed-upon standards of performance. They wish to foster collegial styles of decision making and teaching in schools in which "lead teachers" play a central role. These lead teachers should hold advanced teacher's certificates from a new **National Board for Professional Teaching Standards** (see next paragraph). Additionally, teachers should be provided the support staff they need to be more effective and productive; and school districts should consider a variety of approaches to school leadership. The authors of this textbook propose that the principals of the schools be chosen from among the lead teachers. From candidates suggested by the superintendent, the teachers in a particular school would select one to lead them for the next four years. Under this presidential model, the lead teacher would be eligible for two four-year terms. It is further suggested by the authors that lead teachers and principals never completely leave the classroom, teaching at least one class per day.

LEAD TEACH-
ERS

Second, the Task Force wished to employ new standards for excellence in teaching by establishing a **National Board for Professional Teaching Standards.** The board would grant teacher's certificates that attest to a high level of competence. The board would also grant advanced teacher's certificates that indicate outstanding teaching competence and demonstrate ability for school leadership. Opposition to this bold move would come

STANDARDS
BOARD

from state certification agencies who think they are doing very well at present and do not wish to see this power taken from the state. The Task Force plan is not intended to take state licensing authority away from the states, but to strengthen certification through the National Board.

GRADUATE LEVEL ENTERPRISE

Third, the Task Force wishes to restructure teacher education by abolishing the undergraduate degree in education and making professional teacher education a graduate-level enterprise. This concept of graduate-level entry into teacher education is similar to that of the Holmes Group. The Task Force would like to see college faculties and disciplinary societies undertake a thorough reexamination of undergraduate programs in the arts and sciences to ensure their appropriateness for the preparation of professional teachers. In addition to offering financial aid to minority students for this graduate training, the Task Force asks for financial aid to qualified applicants interested in specific fields experiencing severe shortages, such as physics.

RECRUITING MINORITIES

Fourth, the Task Force is very interested in recruiting and maintaining minority students in the profession. They suggest assisting the predominantly black institutions of higher education in preparing students for graduate professional education in teaching. They would like to see the federal government establish fellowships for minority students who enroll in professional teacher education programs at the graduate level. These fellowships would then be repaid as the recipients commit themselves to a fixed period of teaching service.

INCENTIVES

Fifth, the Task Force wishes to establish incentives for teacher performance and productivity. They believe that states and school boards, working closely with teachers, should establish incentive systems that link teachers' compensation to schoolwide student performance. Their argument is that if teachers are hard working and successful, they should be rewarded for their accomplishments.

BASIS FOR INCREASED SALARIES

Sixth and finally, the Task Force wants teachers' salaries increased to levels adequate to attract and retain the best qualified teachers. They want salaries to be based upon the following attributes:

1. *Job Function*—Level of responsibility
2. *Competence*—As determined by level of Board certification
3. *Seniority*—Experience in the classroom
4. *Productivity*—Contribution to improve student performance

The Task Force admits that the teacher's contribution to student performance is the hardest attribute to assess. They suggest that teachers be actively involved in the design of performance-based compensation systems.

Critics of the School Reform Movement

Orlich (1989) is critical of the suggestions of both the Holmes Group and the Carnegie Forum Task Force. Among his criticisms of the Holmes Group's proposals, the following are highlighted:

CRITICISMS
OF HOLMES

- The proposed six-year teacher preparation program would cost new teachers about $35,000 in lost salaries and about $15,000 in extra tuition.
- The field-oriented master of teaching degree would be built on courses better suited to undergraduates.
- The Holmes Group report exhibits naive amateurism. It provides wonderful cliches but no practical ideas. (p. 514)

As to the Carnegie Forum Task Force's suggestions, the following criticisms are presented:

CRITICISMS
OF CARNEGIE

- There are 50 states and 50 different school systems and contractual agreements exist between several thousand school districts and their teacher bargaining units.
- A six- or seven-year program of higher education leading to a teaching certificate would reduce, not encourage, the entry of students into the profession.
- The master of teaching degree would be an anti-intellectual degree. [He feels that this degree would be more hands-on and would lack the academic rigor expected normally in a master's degree program.]
- How can one jump into graduate study with no prerequisite undergraduate work in the field?
- States would have to raise taxes by 100% to 200% just to pay the suggested teacher salaries. (p. 514)

With respect to both groups' suggestions, Orlich (1989, p. 514) voices the concern that the end result would be to reduce the number of minority teachers.

LACK OF SPE-
CIFICS

Orlich is critical of most school reforms for their seeming lack of specifics and concrete results. The Holmes and the Carnegie efforts toward teacher education reform are to be commended, but the power structures that are in place will inhibit the realization of their suggestions. It appears that the cooperation between federal, state, and local entities of government and agencies will need to be smoother than it has been in the past to achieve the much needed school reform.

In 1988 the Carnegie Foundation for the Advancement of Teaching surveyed more than 13,500 teachers to find out how they feel about the school reforms now in progress. Ernest L. Boyer, author of this report, stated

TEACHERS'
VIEWS OF RE-
FORMS

that in the past five years, this nation has been engaged in the most sustained drive for school renewal in its history. Governors have placed education at the top of their agendas. Corporate leaders have, for the first time, argued vigorously on behalf of public schools. And federal involvement in the education debate has become increasingly intense. (Boyer, 1988, p. 1)

The results of this survey were not very supportive of the reform movement in education. Nearly 70% of the respondents said that the reform movement deserved a C or lower grade.

C GRADE?

After all the studies, reports, and conferences on how to reform our nation's schools, it is still the teacher in the classroom who provides an

Ernest L. Boyer is one of the leaders in the school reform movement.

(Photo used by permission of the Carnegie Foundation.)

Reform Movement

If you were to give a grade to the
education reform movement, what would it be?

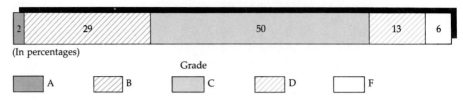

(In percentages)

Grade

A   B   C   D   F

Teacher Morale

How, from your experience, has the
morale of teachers changed since 1983?

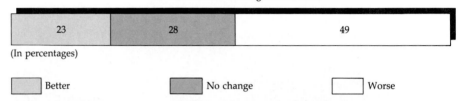

(In percentages)

Better   No change   Worse

SOURCE: Boyer. E. L. (1988). *Report card on School Reform.* The Carnagie Foundation for the Advancement of Teaching, p. 16.

accurate assessment of what has really happened. A measure of how successful the reform movement has been is teacher morale. In this same study nearly 80% of those teachers surveyed said their morale was no better.

The momentum of the drive to reform has not been lost, but one wonders when it will be felt in the classroom.

Alternative Teacher Certification

TEACHERS VS. DOCTORS
Many states permit **noncertified teachers** to be hired where there are shortages of teachers, and some permit noncertified teachers to be hired even if there is no shortage. What would happen if hospitals hired noncertified doctors? Perhaps some ex-medics out of the service could be hired at low salaries—why not? We all know what would happen; few, if any people would go to that hospital, and the American Medical Association (AMA) would be very disturbed. Also, the laws would not permit this practice, yet the same lawmakers would allow noncertified teachers to be hired by the districts. This obviously is not a fair practice, but some people believe that simply going through college makes one an expert on education.

PROFESSIONAL CONTROL?
Most, if not all, **alternative certification** programs must meet standards. What legislatures have done in some cases is to take away the university's role in teacher training and give it to the school corporations. Again, if this would have been attempted in the medical profession, the AMA would have stopped it immediately. Teachers are well organized, but they are not

together as a profession. Otherwise this type of incursion into certification would not have happened.

Universities have had their faults and they have made some mistakes in the training of teachers.

DISILLUSION-
MENT?

One reason for the growth of alternative certification is disillusionment with traditional teacher preparation programs. Complaints about these programs emphasize their inability to attract the best and brightest students as well as fundamental problems with their structure. (McKibbin, 1988, p. 32)

LACK OF
UNIVERSITY
CONTROL

All of the alternative programs surveyed by McKibbin (1988, p. 34) required that candidates have a baccalaureate degree, pass certification tests, and participate in a training program and in a field practicum. This does not sound like a very bad curriculum, but in many cases it takes away the university's control of teacher education.

INFERIOR RE-
QUIRE-
MENTS?

According to Watts (1986, p. 25) the requirements for alternative certification are inferior to those for **standard preparation** programs in at least one of four areas. First, applicants may be permitted to teach in subject fields in which they have less academic preparation than is required for standard programs. Second, alternative routes may require less college preparation in academic foundations. Third, they may be required to have little or no pedagogical preparation. Fourth, regulations for alternative preparation programs may not require participants to pass competency exams and achieve performance standards that are mandatory for teacher trainees in standard preparation programs. It is true that some of this could be worked out and improved over time, but is it necessary to improve teacher education?

PARTNER-
SHIPS

Schools of education and the local school corporations are forming more and better partnership relationships. As these partnerships grow stronger and teacher education improves, the authors of this textbook think we will see less interest in alternative certification programs. Somehow, professional teachers' organizations and teacher colleges must not allow state legislatures and state departments of education to dictate what happens in the training of teachers. Legislatures do control education, but they should also listen to what is best in the long run for children in their states.

Mirrors of Excellence

IDEAS FROM
BUSINESS

Reformers in teacher education have also taken a close look at what industry has done and is doing to educate their employees. The Association of Teacher Education (ATE) sponsored a book, ***Mirrors of Excellence*** (1986), to show how industries train their employees and how implications for the education of teachers can be drawn from these examples.

INSTILLING
PROFESSION-
ALISM

One exemplary company is Arthur Andersen and Company, one of the world's largest accounting and auditing firms. The firm has identified several shared values that they feel are integral to their success: professionalism, quality, integrity, and client service. When a new employee enters the firm, these values are instilled from the beginning. Even though their employees have had extensive education by the time they arrive, they immediately go to school to learn the Arthur Andersen way of doing business.

CULTURAL
VARIABLES

As educators we assume that our clients or our students are shaped by the society from which they come, but we also know that cultural and climatic/support variables are related to school achievement and student attitudes toward schooling (Byrd, Shrock, and Cummings, 1986, p. 14). Outside cultural forces can be changed by manipulation to support and aid student learning. For example, parents can be contacted, tutors can be hired, and extra attention can be given to certain students.

IMPLICA-
TIONS FOR
TEACHER
TRAINING

As we look at industry or business, in this case Arthur Andersen, there are some very clear implications for the training of teachers. Teachers can be instilled with the values of an outstanding profession. Some of these values are strong leadership in instruction, commitment of staff to the mission of a school, clear enunciation of expectations for students, formative feedback and remediation of key concepts and skills, a belief that all students can learn, communication of expectations to parents, parental involvement, and a recognition that school is a meaningful and important part of a child's life (Byrd et al., 1986, p. 14). This is a mirror of excellence that can be learned from Arthur Andersen and Company.

REEDUCA-
TION OF EM-
PLOYEES

Arthur Andersen and Company invests approximately 9%, or about 100 million dollars, each year to educate or reeducate their 26,000 employees (Byrd et al., 1986, p. 11). They have a 125-acre campus near Chicago that accommodates 900 participants at one time. Along with this fine facility, they have a support staff in the Professional Education Division that includes technicians, writers, graphic artists, instructional designers, evaluators, educational researchers, and instructors. It is safe to say that this type of facility is not available to public and private school educators in the United States. The authors of this textbook feel that if schoolteachers were cared for in the manner that Arthur Andersen employees are, the United States would be number one in all aspects of educational achievement.

WALT DISNEY

Another mirror of excellence is the Disney Corporation. One of the things Disney does is to treat each employee as a cast member who has a specific role in the show. This is so much more dignified than being treated as a peon, as is done in some companies and in some school systems. We as teachers are members of a large cast of characters involved in the education of children for the greatest show on earth—life itself! Both education and Disney rely heavily on motivation to achieve a common end product, that of enjoyment and learning (Funk, Sharpe, and Usher, 1986, p. 29). Disney

EVERY PER-
SON A VIP

treats every guest as a VIP. Good teachers look at the children they teach as VIPs, too; but there are too many teachers who have forgotten why they are there. Anyone who has visited Disney World or Disneyland feels the comfort of being wanted in this magical world. I wonder what it would do to the learning atmosphere if the children in our schools had this same comfort level. We all need to remember that the children are the reason for our existence.

The training center for Arthur Andersen and Company.

SETTING A
GOOD
MODEL

One of the reasons visitors like the Disney parks so much is that the grounds are always kept clean and neat and the employees are well groomed and in costumes. Our schools and our teachers are not generally as neat and well groomed. The model that we set for students is not always the best.

THE
BROADER
THE BASE . . .

At Disney they hold the philosophy that the broader the base, the higher the peak. In other words, they consider the hourly jobs the most important because these are the employees who meet the people. Therefore, it is very important that these employees reflect the philosophy and the direction of the Disney organization so that they in turn can help the company reach greater heights. In education, children often do not know their mission as students and learners in the organization. It is our responsibility as teachers to continue to enunciate and instruct them in their role so that they can be proud and motivated to be a part of the school organization. It is also

. . . THE
HIGHER THE
PEAK

the job of school administrators to keep the teachers informed about the philosophy and direction of the school. Again, the broader the base, the higher the peak!

There are many incentives to move up in the Disney organization. In

INCENTIVES

fact, when a job within the company opens up, priority is given to a competent Disney employee over an outside applicant. Few such incentives are available in teaching. A career ladder incentive would be beneficial in helping to provide teachers with more opportunities.

ENOUGH RE-
WARDS?

Some people would say that teachers really do not need incentives to teach young people. It is true that a smile on a student's face when he or she answers correctly or understands a concept for the first time is a nice reward. To be realistic, however, teachers need other rewards just as people in industry do. Such rewards may be a new type of job or a promotion to a higher rank. Disney does offer another mirror of excellence for educators to look at for direction.

Minority Participation in Teacher Education

LIMITING MI-
NORITIES

It is extremely important to have equal representation among all **ethnic groups** in the teaching profession! Currently there is a great need for minorities in teacher education. At the same time, however, tests are being pushed to ensure quality teachers; and sometimes blacks and other minorities are not able to pass these tests. Years of prejudice, discrimination, and poverty have hurt blacks in relation to mastery of test content. Because they have been kept out of the mainstream of society, blacks find it very difficult to score well on mainstream-type tests. Gregory R. Anrig (1986), president of the Educational Testing Service, says

> that by the year 2000, if there is not significant change in the current status of teacher preparation, the percentage of minorities in the teaching force in the U.S. could be cut almost in half, from the current level of approximately 12%. (p. 449)

A partial answer appears to be assistance for blacks recruited into the teaching profession to be successful teacher-education students.

RETENTION
OF MINORI-
TIES

In addition to the above-mentioned difficulties with testing, many young black people want to enter other professions. According to Daisy F. Reed (1986), "the most critical problem in education today is the precipitous decline in the number of talented young black people who are entering the teaching profession." (p. 31) The black colleges have trained large numbers of black teachers in the past, but as career opportunities for black students have increased, fewer black students are entering the teaching profession. Black colleges are not the only institutions experiencing this difficulty; all higher educational institutions are experiencing this problem.

BLACK
TEACHERS AS
ROLE MOD-
ELS

Black teachers are needed as role models for black students. Part of their role is to pass on black cultural heritage and to instill a sense of black pride; it is the black teacher who will feel a sense of obligation to teach in an inner-city school when others will not. Also, black teachers are needed in the suburban schools to help promote racial understanding and discourage many misconceptions and prejudices (Reed, 1986, p. 33).

The need to train teachers to help Hispanic students will be even greater by the year 2000.

(Photo by Grady Franklin.)

HISPANIC
GROWTH

The Hispanic population is growing in size, especially in California. It is estimated that by the year 2000, minority students in California will make up 52% of the total school-aged (K–12) children compared with 42% in 1980 (Nieto, 1986, p. 2). The largest number of these will be Hispanic. Hispanics are decreasing in number at the state universities and in the teaching ranks. Hispanics also drop out of school at higher rates than do other groups.

HISPANICS AS
ROLE MOD-
ELS

The Hispanic minority group within our population has enormous needs that must be met in our educational institutions in the next few years and beyond. Similar to blacks, Hispanics need role models among the teacher population. It is important for teachers to be able to communicate to students in Spanish as well as English. When a good bilingual program is in place in the schools, a student's self-esteem is enhanced.

OTHER MI-
NORITY
GROUPS

Other minority groups, including Native Americans and immigrants from Southeast Asia, need our assistance as well. We need teachers sensitive to the cultural needs of these people. In its report, the Commission on Minority Participation in Education and American Life proposed:

> That in 20 years, a similar examination will reveal that America's minority population has attained a quality of life as high as that of the white majority. No less a goal is acceptable. For if we fail, all Americans—not just minorities—will be the victims. But if we succeed, all Americans will reap the benefits. (Rhodes, 1988, p. 1)

REVERSAL OF
THE TREND?

The authors think that part of this progress and success must come from the recruitment of minority teachers into the profession. The trend is toward fewer minority teachers, but this must be and can be reversed by our teacher colleges! It is so true that if the Commission's goal is not achieved, then all of America fails to some degree.

Professional Growth Programs

Madeline Hunter's Proposals

Madeline Hunter is a professor at the University of California, Los Angeles; she has influenced how teachers teach about as much as any person now living. The Hunter model increases the probability of learning by (1) identifying professional decisions teachers must make, (2) supplying research-based cause-and-effect relationships to support those decisions, and (3) encouraging the teachers to use data emerging from students and classroom situations to augment or correct those decisions (Hunter, 1985, p. 57). Her **Clinical Theory of Instruction** is based upon the premise that the teacher is a decision maker. It follows then that she helps the teacher, the decision maker, to make better decisions based upon sound theory.

CLINICAL
THEORY OF
INSTRUC-
TION

> My purpose is to tell teachers what to consider before deciding what to do and, as a result, to base their decisions on sound theory rather than on folklore and fantasy. (Hunter, as quoted by Brandt, 1985, p. 63)

Madeline Hunter's techniques emphasize the local classroom teacher as an important decision maker.

(Photo used by permission of the Indiana Department of Education.)

TEACHERS AS DECISION MAKERS

Hunter claims that her model identifies decisions all teachers must make regardless of content, age, or ethnicity of the learner, style of teacher, or mode of teaching. Her model is based upon propositional knowledge or generalizations validated by psychological research, which identify behaviors affecting learning. The following material states in a practical way how the Hunter model can be used by teachers to improve their performance:

DISTRIBUTING PRACTICE

> Take these two Hunter principles for instance: (1) massing practice increases speed of learning, and (2) distributing practice increases retention of what has been learned. These are two generalizations that guide teachers' decisions about practice. The teacher should first be able to translate them into procedures so that massed practice remains meaningful and interesting, and then make decisions about scheduling distributed practice for maximum learning efficiency. (Hunter, 1985, p. 58)

FROM INTUITIVE TO PURPOSEFUL

Practicing teachers do many things because they seem to work. These acts may be positive; but if they are told that on the basis of the Hunter model, their practice is sound and based on proven research, they can move from intuitive to purposeful behavior. Purposeful behavior results when one knows what he or she is doing and why.

THREE STAGES

Teachers learn to use the Hunter model in three stages. They learn the propositions first. For example, one proposition is that the beginning and end of any sequence are the most powerful times for learning. Second, the students must learn the procedure, or how to carry out the proposition. This is done through simulation of an actual teaching situation. Finally, the teacher or student tries it out with students in the classroom; this is where conditional decision-making takes place. As you teach, you will make decisions as to how a given proposition fits your personal teaching style.

TESA (Teacher Expectations and Student Achievement)

SENSITIZING TEACHERS

A program sponsored by Phi Delta Kappa and known as **TESA (Teacher Expectations and Student Achievement)** is available to school corporations across the country. What it does for teachers is to put them in touch with all of their students. It sensitizes a teacher to the unique needs of the children or young adults in his or her classroom. Low-achieving students in ordinary classrooms seldom are called on; in TESA classrooms teachers try to involve all students.

FIFTEEN INTERACTIONS

The TESA program originated in the Los Angeles County Schools as an ESEA Title III grant in 1970. The project was originally titled Equal Opportunity in the Classroom (EOC). The researchers identified fifteen separate interactions that were supportive and motivating to students. It was later proved that in the classroom, these interactions were more frequent with high achievers than with low achievers. The researchers conducted workshops to assist teachers in interacting with *all* of their students in an equitable manner; the results were quite favorable.

GAINS BY
LOW ACHIEV-
ERS

At the conclusion of the three-year study, approximately 2,000 identified low achievers in experimental classes showed statistically significant academic gains over their counterparts in the control classes. Not only were academic gains noted; also, there was a significant reduction in absenteeism and a significant reduction in discipline referrals. (Kerman, 1979, p. 717)

RESPONSE
OPPORTUNI-
TIES

One interaction model is known as response opportunities. A response is any specific opportunity provided by the teacher for a pupil to respond to a question, recite, read aloud, express an opinion, give a report, do a problem on the chalkboard, demonstrate something, confirm a response given by another student, and so on. Teachers characteristically seldom call on low-achieving students because they do not want to embarrass them or because they want the class to hear the correct or most thoughtful response. To help teachers respond to all students equally, classroom observers are taught how to code a teacher's interactions with various types of students. Examples of both positive and negative responses follow:

PLUS

Positive Codes
- *Primary Grade Level*—"Jimmy, please spell 'cat'."
- *Intermediate Grade Level*—"Sarah, what is the product of 10 times $325.95?"
- *Secondary Grade Level*—"Todd, what are the advantages of using solar energy instead of fossil fuels?"

NEGATIVE

Negative Codes
- *Primary Grade Level*—Teacher calls on Terry twice while ignoring a target student (a low achiever) whose hand is up.
- *Intermediate Grade Level*—"Louise, I told you not to shout out answers when it is not your turn! Don't you ever listen!?"
- *Secondary Grade Level*—"Shut up, Henry! You're always talking out of turn." (Kerman and Martin, 1980, pp. D-2 and D-3)

Other interaction models are feedback and personal regard.

PAIRED PAR-
TICIPATION

The TESA program is clearly outlined and is generally presented to teachers in a workshop. Teachers are then divided into pairs to observe and code each other's classes. Participants learn both by participating and by coding. The purpose of this program is not evaluation; it is to help teachers become more effective. The following statements indicate some views of the concept:

TESTIMONI-
ALS

I was amazed at some of my perceived "lower" students. . . . TESA made one conscious and aware of each student as an individual without the stigma of preconceived expectations. (Seventh/Eighth Grade Core Teacher)

TESA has been a very rewarding experience. My only regret is that all teachers don't use these methods which would enable all students to have an equal opportunity to learn. (Third Grade Teacher)

TESA can be summed up in one word—rewarding. The strategies and skills taught in the program would be of value to any educator. I heartily encourage

The TESA program strives to make classroom teachers aware of the special needs of individual students.

(Photo used by permission of the Indiana State Teachers Association.)

every educator to participate. (High School English Teacher) (Kerman and Martin, 1980, p. A-3)

TESA, like other special exercises, does not fulfill all needs in the classroom, but it is of real assistance with student interactions.

The Financial Rewards for Teachers

Salaries

FINANCIAL
PRESSURE

Financial pressure rates high on lists of concerns of teachers. As a preservice teacher, you deserve to know more about the financial standing of teachers. Although the information given here is not the worst news, it is not what teachers think their financial situation ought to be.

GEOGRAPHIC
VARIATIONS

Teachers' beginning salaries vary slightly by geographic region in the United States. Table 2–2 indicates that the mideast region has the highest average beginning salaries; the lowest average beginning salaries are found in the Rocky Mountain region. The mean average beginning salary for all regions is $19,510. Table 2–2 also includes minimum salaries offered for other professional positions in education. Teachers usually must have several years of classroom experience, as well as additional credits, to be eligible for promotion to principal or superintendent. Many districts also mandate that the superintendent have a doctorate.

TABLE 2-2 ██

Mean Minimum Scheduled Salaries for Personnel in Selected Professional Positions in Reporting School Systems, by Geographic Region, 1988–1989

POSITION	GEOGRAPHIC REGION[a]								
	New England	Mideast	Southeast	Great Lakes	Plains	Southwest	Rocky Mountains	Far West	Total All Regions
Superintendents (contract salary)	$66,200	$73,826	$69,999	$67,125	$67,256	$77,092	$64,573	$78,352	$71,190
Elementary school principals	41,096	42,353	34,598	40,255	38,171	35,783	35,658	44,152	39,299
Senior high school principals	46,614	47,973	39,496	47,855	44,814	42,432	40,682	50,642	45,397
Classroom teachers	19,454	20,831	18,897	18,994	18,354	19,018	17,901	21,219	19,510
Counselors	20,170	21,384	20,303	19,801	19,061	21,621	18,760	24,850	20,923
Librarians	19,951	20,965	19,296	19,376	18,607	19,688	18,220	21,522	19,824
School nurses	16,329	19,497	15,642	18,157	16,732	18,727	16,625	21,582	18,511

[a] States included in geographic regions: New England—CT, ME, MA, NH, RI, VT; Mideast—DE, DC, MD, NJ, NY, PA; Southeast—AL, AR, FL, GA, KY, LA, MS, NC, SC, TN, VA, WV; Great Lakes—IL, IN, MI, OH, WI; Plains—IA, KS, MN, MO, NE, ND, SD; Southwest—AZ, NM, OK, TX; Rocky Mountains—CO, ID, MT, UT, WY; Far West—AK, CA, HI, NV, OR, WA.

Source: Educational Research Service, Inc., Scheduled Salaries for Professional Personnel in Public Schools, 1988–1989. Part 1 of National Survey of Salaries and Wages in Public Schools. Arlington, VA: ERS, p. 14.

COMPARI-
SONS WITH
CPI

The Educational Research Service (ERS) has graphically compared the **composite indicator of changes in average salaries and wages paid by public school systems (CIC)** with the **consumer price index (CPI)** from 1980 through 1989. In observing Figure 2–1 note that educational salaries were falling behind increases in the CPI by almost 5 percentage points in the school year 1979–1980, by 2.6 percentage points for 1980–1981, and by 1.2 percentage points for 1981–1982. In 1982–1983, the average change in public school salaries was 0.5 of a percentage point higher than the CPI, to the delight of public school teachers and other school personnel. The following school years saw a rise of 1.7 percentage points in 1983–1984, 3.5 percentage points in 1984–1985, 3.0 percentage points in 1985–1986, 3.1 percentage points in 1986–1987, 1.8 percentage points in 1987–1988, and only 0.7 percentage point in 1988–1989.

KEEPING UP
WITH INFLA-
TION?

Previous to 1983, the CPI ran ahead of teacher salary increases. Teachers were receiving more pay, but were falling further behind because of inflation. So, since 1983 teachers have bettered their economic position with regard to inflation, but as we write, classroom teachers' salaries are about even with the CPI.

The goal of education organizations or unions is not only to keep up with inflation, but to decrease the differential between teachers' salaries and salaries of other professionals.

COMPARISON
TO BUSINESS
AND INDUS-
TRY

In Table 2–3 a comparison is made between the average starting salaries of teachers and those of business and industrial groups. Teachers' beginning salaries are lower than those of other professionals because of their nine-

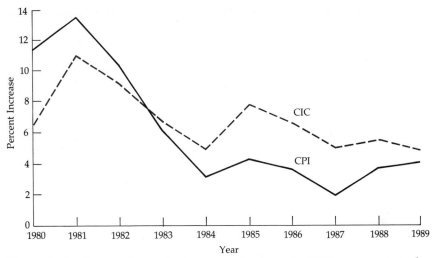

Figure 2–1 Comparison of percentage increase in ERS composite indicator of changes (CIC) with increases in the consumer price index (CPI), 1980 through 1989. CIC data are for the school year ending in the year shown; CPI data are the averages of monthly changes for the calendar year in which the corresponding school year begins.

SOURCE: *Measuring changes in salaries and wages in public schools: 1989 edition.* Educational Research Service, Arlington, VA

to ten-month working schedule, compared with the twelve-month working schedule common to most professions. The stress and tension that teachers experience during the school year from grading student homework, interacting with a large number of children, contacting parents and sponsoring extracurricular duties add many hours to the work day and the work week. Some would say that teachers deserve the same or nearly the same wages as other professionals despite their "shorter" working schedules. Many teachers claim that their working schedule is the barrier to receiving a salary equal to those of other groups. As this may be true, the year-round school concept may be the solution to attracting higher salaries from school boards.

Part-Time Employment

Many teachers find part-time employment to help sustain them. Moonlighting is not new for teachers, but it is now more commonly accepted as a way of life. Men, in particular, have traditionally painted houses, played in bands, taught driver's education, sold insurance, and followed other similar lines of employment during the summer break or during the school year. TREND TO-WARD MOONLIGHT-ING At present, both men and women teachers work at a variety of jobs part-time; waiting on tables at a restaurant seems to be very common. Although the trend is toward moonlighting, and the economic situation seems to demand extra work, it is best for a teacher to concentrate on only one

TABLE 2–3 ████████████████████████████████████

Average Starting Salaries of Teachers and Other Professionals in 1987

FIELD OF EMPLOYMENT	AVERAGE STARTING SALARY, 1987
Beginning public school teachers with bachelor's degree	$17,500
Graduates with bachelor's degree	
Engineering	28,932
Accounting	22,512
Sales—Marketing	21,232
Business administration	21,972
Liberal arts	20,508
Chemistry	27,048
Mathematics—statistics	25,548
Economics—finance	21,984
Computer science	26,280

Source: Statistical Abstract of the United States 1988, 108th ed. U.S. Department of Commerce, Bureau of the Census, p. 137.

occupation. As pointed out earlier, teaching as an occupation demands large amounts of physical, mental, and emotional energy. On the plus side, some teachers say that the side jobs provide a good diversion from teaching. Still others feel that the part-time jobs keep them in touch with the "real world," and enhance their performance in the classroom.

Year-round Schooling

Moonlighting and all the benefits and disadvantages that go with it could disappear if our schools change to a year-round schedule. Additional compensation in the form of higher salaries would naturally accompany the extended school year. In addition to attracting more bright students into teaching, the year-round schedule would offer great continuity for all of our students. The long summer vacation disrupts the continuous learning pattern needed by the slower student (Ballinger, Kirschenbaum, and Poimbeauf, 1987, p. 9). Those who have been in teaching a while know that a method or condition that enhances the education of a slower learner is generally applicable to other students as well.

LONG VACA-
TIONS?

There are many year-round plans. One, the 45–15 single-track plan,

VARIOUS
FORMS

divides the year into four nine-week terms, separated by four three-week vacations or intersessions. Students and teachers attend school for nine weeks (45 days), then they take a three-week vacation (15 days). This sequence of sessions and vacations repeats four times each year, thus providing the usual 36 weeks or 180 days of school. Four additional weeks each year are allocated to winter holidays, spring vacation, and national, state, or local holidays. (Ballinger et al., 1987, p. 16)

An extended contract would then be available for teaching additional sessions or days. There is little doubt that teachers would gain economically with the year-round schedule.

More information on year-round education can be found in Phi Delta Kappa Fastback No. 259, *The Year-Round School: Where Learning Never Stops*, by Ballinger et al. (1987).

Fringe Benefits for Teachers

Fringe benefits for teachers are extensive and vary by geographic region and by school district. In most school districts, fringe benefits are determined through the collective bargaining process.

VARIATIONS

Teachers receive many and varied fringe benefits in addition to their contracted salary. Although your interest in fringe benefits may not be great at this stage in your preparation for teaching, we have included a comprehensive list of items that you should consider when seeking a job. Most school corporations provide all or some of the fringe benefits found in Table 2–4, which give the teacher an underlying sense of security. Table 2–4 lists the major fringe benefits offered to teachers in eight geographic regions in the United States. The survey questionnaire used to obtain the data in Table 2–4 was sent to 1,808 school systems enrolling 300 or more pupils.

SICK LEAVE

Sick leave is offered almost universally across the country, and it is designed to protect the teacher against loss of compensation because of illness. Most school systems provide ten to fifteen days of sick leave per year, which can accumulate to an unlimited number of days. The majority of systems reporting allowed no sick leave credit toward retirement benefits; however, a growing number of systems are allowing full or partial credit for unused sick leave days toward retirement. Sick leave days normally cannot be transferred from one district to another.

PERSONAL LEAVE

Personal and emergency leave days generally fall between three and six days per year and are to be used for personal business, civic affairs, and severe illness or accident to a member of the immediate family of the teacher. Most commonly three days are granted by school systems. A few school systems agree to an "unlimited/as needed" phraseology. More than half the systems do not allow unused emergency or personal leave days to be charged to sick leave, but over 38% of the school systems charge all or some unused days to sick leave.

SABBATICAL

Sabbatical leaves, paid or unpaid, are provided in 70% of the school systems for the purpose of advanced study. In a typical school system, one must teach seven years before becoming eligible for a sabbatical leave. A few systems allow a sabbatical leave after one year of employment. Monetary compensation for sabbatical leaves varies from no salary to full salary. Seventy-two percent of the school systems pay a certain percentage of the teacher's salary during her or his leave.

HEALTH INSURANCE

Group health insurance is provided by most school corporations. Both single coverage and family coverage are provided. Most health insurance plans are very generous and include hospitalization, medical/surgical, and

TABLE 2–4

Summary of Selected Fringe Benefits for Teachers in Reporting School Systems, by Geographic Region, 1987–1988

PROVISION	GEOGRAPHIC REGION[a]								
	New England	Mideast	Southeast	Great Lakes	Plains	Southwest	Rocky Mountains	Far West	Total, All Regions
Number responding	59	167	162	196	102	86	46	126	944
Percent providing vacation leave	1.7	1.2	21.6	1.5	4.9	3.5	.0	1.6	5.4
Percent Providing Sick Leave	100.0	99.4	99.4	97.4	99.0	100.0	97.8	100.0	99.0
Specified number of days per year[b]	100.0	99.4	100.0	99.0	96.0	98.8	100.0	100.0	99.1
Provided as needed[b]	—[c]	0.6	—	1.0	4.0	1.2	—	—	0.9
Sick leave counts toward retirement service	16.9	27.1	47.2	27.7	16.8	20.9	20.0	74.6	34.4
Percent providing Personal/emergency leave charged in whole or part to sick leave[b]	100.0	98.2	97.5	94.4	96.1	95.3	93.5	95.2	96.3
	8.5	11.6	45.6	22.2	46.9	56.1	23.3	86.7	37.7
Percent providing sabbatical leave	93.2	80.2	48.1	71.4	73.5	57.0	80.4	75.4	70.2
Mean number of leave days									
Vacation leave									
Days credited per year	20	16	13	11	8	13	—	9	12
Maximum accumulation	—	—	29	25	15	90	—	7	28
Sick leave									
Days credited per year	15	12	11	13	12	10	11	11	12
Maximum accumulation	175	180	121	172	129	113	97	168	150
Personal/emergency leave, days allowed per year	4	3	4	3	3	3	3	6	4
Percent providing insurance group hospitalization	96.6	99.4	94.4	97.4	96.1	95.3	97.8	99.2	97.1
Single coverage[b]	94.7	97.0	81.7	95.8	84.7	69.5	80.0	78.4	86.9
Fully paid[b]	94.7	96.4	70.6	95.3	81.6	61.0	80.0	76.0	83.4
Family coverage[b]	94.7	97.0	74.5	94.2	77.6	63.4	77.8	77.6	83.9
Fully paid[b]	31.6	64.5	4.6	44.0	22.4	2.4	31.1	50.4	34.6
Medical/surgical	94.9	98.2	91.4	96.9	95.1	94.2	97.8	98.4	95.9
Single coverage[b]	92.9	97.0	81.8	95.8	84.5	69.1	80.0	78.2	86.7
Fully paid[b]	92.9	96.3	70.9	95.3	81.4	60.5	80.0	75.8	83.3
Family coverage[b]	92.9	97.0	74.3	94.2	77.3	64.2	77.8	77.4	83.8
Fully paid[b]	28.6	64.6	4.7	44.2	22.7	2.5	31.1	50.0	34.6
Major medical	93.2	98.8	93.2	98.0	94.1	94.2	100.0	98.4	96.4
Single coverage[b]	92.7	97.0	80.8	96.4	84.4	69.1	78.3	78.2	86.6
Fully paid[b]	92.7	96.4	68.9	95.3	81.3	60.5	78.3	75.8	82.9
Family coverage[b]	92.7	97.0	72.8	94.8	77.1	64.2	76.1	77.4	83.5
Fully paid[b]	29.1	64.2	4.6	44.8	21.9	2.5	28.3	50.0	34.4
Percent providing insurance									
Dental	52.5	95.2	53.1	85.7	76.5	65.1	76.1	97.6	78.0
Single coverage[b]	93.5	94.3	74.4	96.4	84.6	67.9	77.1	82.1	86.5
Fully paid[b]	93.5	92.5	61.6	94.0	82.1	53.6	74.3	81.3	82.5
Family coverage[b]	80.6	86.2	64.0	94.6	69.2	62.5	68.6	77.2	79.3
Fully paid[b]	32.3	52.2	9.3	50.6	16.7	1.8	22.9	55.3	37.5
Vision care	13.6	37.1	19.8	37.8	17.6	23.3	28.3	82.5	35.1
Single coverage[b]	75.0	90.3	65.6	97.3	77.8	70.0	61.5	82.7	83.7
Fully paid[b]	75.0	85.5	50.0	97.3	77.8	60.0	53.8	80.8	79.8
Family coverage[b]	75.0	79.0	65.6	97.3	61.1	60.0	46.2	66.3	74.3
Fully paid[b]	12.5	43.5	21.9	64.9	5.6	5.0	15.4	44.2	40.2

PROVISION	GEOGRAPHIC REGION[a]								
	New England	Mideast	Southeast	Great Lakes	Plains	Southwest	Rocky Mountains	Far West	Total, All Regions
Prescription drugs	64.4	64.7	64.2	72.4	66.7	82.6	84.8	92.1	72.7
Single coverage[b]	89.5	94.4	81.7	94.4	85.3	67.6	79.5	78.4	85.0
Fully paid[b]	89.5	92.6	65.4	93.7	83.8	54.9	79.5	76.7	80.3
Family coverage[b]	89.5	92.6	77.9	94.4	79.4	66.2	76.9	75.9	82.8
Fully paid[b]	21.1	63.0	3.8	52.8	19.1	4.2	28.2	50.0	35.0
Mean percent of insurance premium paid if less than full									
Hospitalization									
Single coverage	70.3	85.8	75.0	87.3	71.8	63.6	66.5	76.0	77.7
Family coverage	71.2	80.5	55.2	79.9	65.4	51.4	52.2	81.9	71.8
Medical/surgical									
Single coverage	69.9	86.0	74.7	87.5	71.8	63.6	66.5	76.0	77.7
Family coverage	70.9	80.6	55.7	79.3	65.4	51.4	52.2	81.9	71.7
Major medical									
Single coverage	71.3	85.0	74.6	87.4	72.0	63.6	71.0	76.0	77.9
Family coverage	72.2	79.9	55.7	78.3	65.2	51.4	56.1	81.9	71.5
Dental									
Single coverage	76.6	79.5	72.0	81.2	73.4	65.8	66.5	85.0	77.3
Family coverage	74.8	71.6	50.5	80.2	61.7	62.0	61.0	87.9	72.8
Vision care									
Single coverage	80.0	69.6	99.0	85.8	70.0	62.5	75.0	83.3	78.1
Family coverage	80.0	70.5	49.5	84.9	77.0	65.0	—	86.0	77.3
Prescription drugs									
Single coverage	71.6	80.9	78.3	84.3	74.4	65.5	78.3	86.3	77.4
Family coverage	71.6	77.4	56.1	75.7	69.6	51.4	68.0	86.8	70.4
Percent providing income Protection Insurance	10.2	20.4	30.2	49.0	54.9	45.3	54.3	19.0	34.9
Mean salary coverage	64%	59%	63%	69%	66%	65%	65%	66%	66%
	8.5	13.2	27.2	43.4	51.0	29.1	47.8	15.1	29.0
Mean monthly benefit/ limit	$5,000	$1,426	$2,021	$2,626	$2,901	$2,117	$3,133	$2,499	$2,420
	1.7	10.8	17.9	25.5	24.5	24.4	30.4	9.5	18.0
Percent providing group life Insurance	72.9	62.3	61.1	88.3	88.2	75.6	78.3	69.0	73.8
Mean policy amount	$21,688	$55,107	$20,974	$28,332	$24,978	$17,509	$38,721	$23,256	$28,787
Fully paid[b]	46.5	73.1	68.7	74.6	76.7	66.2	77.8	71.3	71.0
Mean percent of premium paid if less than full	66%	67%	44%	63%	54%	67%	63%	52%	61%
	32.2	6.0	6.8	12.8	3.9	1.2	4.3	2.4	7.9
Percent providing professional liability insurance	79.7	69.5	72.8	78.1	75.5	68.6	78.3	53.2	71.3
Percent with retirement plans									
State retirement system	98.3	98.2	98.1	97.4	96.1	97.7	97.8	100.0	98.0
Local retirement system	1.7	2.4	4.9	4.6	6.9	2.3	2.2	—	3.4
Social security coverage	18.6	88.6	76.5	48.5	61.8	45.3	58.7	21.4	56.6
Tax-sheltered annuity	66.1	79.6	83.3	71.4	77.5	74.4	78.3	66.7	75.2
Early retirement option	39.0	40.7	29.0	60.7	64.7	31.4	80.4	58.7	48.8
Percent providing severance pay	44.1	53.3	29.0	59.2	41.2	29.1	45.7	8.7	39.9
Percent with tuition reimbursement provisions	69.5	68.3	30.9	34.7	17.6	15.1	21.7	11.1	34.7
Percent reporting collective negotiations agreement	98.3	97.0	24.1	94.9	80.4	32.6	65.2	95.2	74.7
Percent paying all or part of teacher organization membership dues	—	1.2	1.2	—	—	2.3	2.2	—	0.7

[a] States included in geographic regions: New England—CT, ME, MA, NH, RI, VT; Mideast—DE, DC, MD, NJ, NY, PA; Southeast—AL, AR, FL, GA, KY, LA, MS, NC, SC, TN, VA, WV; Great Lakes—IL, IN, MI, OH, WI; Plains—IA, KS, MN, MO, NE, ND, SD; Southwest—AZ, NM, OK, TX; Rocky Mountains—CO, ID, MT, UT, WY; Far West—AK, CA, HI, NV, O, WA.
[b] Percentages in detail lines based on number of school systems providing coverage.
[c] —,Data not available.

Source: Education Research Service, Inc. (1988). *Fringe Benefits for Teachers in Public Schools, 1987–1988*, pp. 52–54.

major medical coverage. Many of these comprehensive plans are fully or nearly fully paid for by the school corporation for the individual, and partially for the family plan. Dental coverage is increasing in importance as part of the teacher's health-care package. Many systems have provisions for orthodontic work. Vision care is provided by only 35% of the school corporations reporting, but prescription drugs are provided by 73%.

LIFE INSUR-
ANCE

Income protection and group life insurance are also offered by many school corporations. Thirty-five percent of the corporations provide income protection insurance for their teachers. The average salary percentage covered is 66%, and the mean monthly benefit (limit) is $2,420. Sixty-nine percent of the corporations reporting provide group life insurance with a face value averaging about $28,787.

LIABILITY IN-
SURANCE

Other fringe benefits include professional liability insurance, provided by 71% of the school corporations; retirement plans, generally state-supported, but supplemented by local school corportions; severance pay; and tuition reimbursement provisions.

Teacher Supply and Demand

CYCLE

The authors have experienced the **supply-and-demand** cycle during their careers in education. There was a huge demand for math and science teachers after the launch of *Sputnik* in the late 1950s and early 1960s. Figure 2–2 indicates that math and science teachers are still in demand and there are acute vacancies in physics and chemistry. Social studies teachers continue to be the least in demand.

Obviously, the number of students enrolled in schools affects the demand for teachers. Figure 2–3 depicts the trends in public school enrollments with projections to 1997. Total public elementary and secondary enrollment declined steadily throughout most of the 1970s and into the early 1980s. The "baby boomers," born between 1946 and 1964, tended to delay marriage and childbearing; thus their offspring did not begin to produce a rise in public school enrollment until about 1985. It is projected that elementary school enrollment will rise through 1996 and then level off. Secondary school enrollment will rise steadily during the 1990s.

A large number of teachers leave the profession each year, many because of age. Added to this problem, many good female and minority prospects are not attracted to teaching as a career because of the attractiveness of other careers that formerly were not available to them. Also, there are those who demand that we improve the quality of the teaching force and reduce class size, which would increase the demand for teachers.

PREDICTED
SHORTAGES

The annual average supply of new teachers projected for the five-year period 1989 to 1993 is about 137,000 (Pipho, 1988, p. 32). The greatest shortages will be in the areas of special education, general elementary education, bilingual education, biological and physical sciences, and math-

TEACHER
TURNOVER

ematics.

The National Center for Education Statistics (NCES) projects a constant

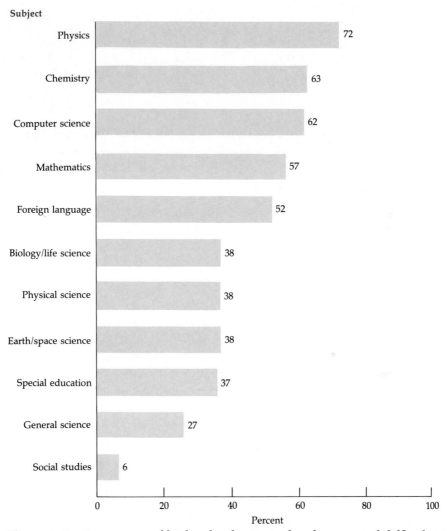

Figure 2–2   Percentage of high school principals who reported difficulty in hiring fully qualified applicants for teaching vacancies, by subject: School year ending 1986.

SOURCE: National Science Foundation, National Survey of Science and Mathematics Education, 1985–1986.

6% turnover of teachers each year, based on a rise in student enrollment and a slight reduction in student–teacher ratios. Some surprise factors could push the demand for teachers either up or down:

CHANGE
FACTORS

- The changes in federal tax law under charitable giving could influence donations for private or religious institutions resulting in fewer private schools and more students enrolling in the public schools.

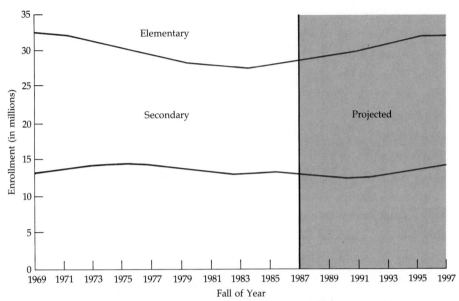

Figure 2–3   Trends in public school enrollment: Fall 1969–1997.

SOURCE: National Center for Education Statistics, *Projections of Education Statistics to 1997–1998.*

- State or federal governments could adopt a modified or full voucher plan resulting in the loss of state money and students to the private sector.
- A change in the overall economy could influence the amount of money for education. A downturn in the economy could reduce or reverse the drive for smaller class sizes as part of the reform movement, but an economic surplus in states could speed up the process or lower class sizes even more.
- The complex personal variables that determine when a teacher decides to drop out of the profession or take early retirement could be influenced by many factors. (Pipho, 1988, p. 33)

The NCES reports that in 1983, only 14% of the total of 146,000 new teacher candidates became teachers. To solve this problem state policy leaders have called for alternative certification procedures to increase the pool of available teachers. Teacher educators and other citizens are very concerned about attracting people into the profession via the alternative route because of the lowering of standards. Most teacher educators feel that these shortages could be avoided by improving the status of the profession and working conditions. It is unfortunate that this problem occurs, but the fact is teachers and teacher educators do not have the power alone to change the system because the state legislatures are the real force in education. Legislators can increase salaries and working conditions for teachers by allocating more needed monies to the local school districts.

AVOIDING
SHORTAGES

GATHERING
DATA

To be fair, the legislators need precise statistics at least four to six years in advance. These data could be gathered if there was an interest in doing so. Education is a statewide function, and some states plan and care for their schools better than others.

POSSIBLE SO-
LUTIONS

Some possible solutions to the teacher shortage include the following:

1. *Technology.* Through the use of instructional television, rural areas of the country can be reached by some of our finest teachers. Satellite technology, video tape recorders, and two-way communication lines can be utilized to better reach all parts of the country. All students will soon have top quality instruction available to them.

2. *Foreign Teachers.* Some school districts have already started to meet teacher shortages by hiring foreign teachers. Currently there is an oversupply of well-trained teachers in Canada and Western Europe and they speak fluent English. This pool of teachers may never be large, but it could give us all some new ideas to think about.

3. *Certification Changes.* As we have already mentioned, alternative certification programs are being tried and some wish to phase out the bachelor of arts degree as a starting point for teacher training.

4. *Public Opinion.* Changing public opinion of teaching from the negative image it now has to a more positive image will be difficult, but it can happen! These changes must occur in order to give teaching a deserved status and attract some of our nation's brightest and best into the profession. (Pipho, 1988, pp. 35–37)

Summary

This chapter highlighted reform initiatives taken by three prominent groups that have attempted to influence educational reform. These three organizations are NCATE, the Holmes Group, and the Carnegie Foundation. Both the Holmes Group and the Carnegie Foundation would like to see the professional education degree given at the graduate level, thus eliminating undergraduate teacher education programs. NCATE is a national organization that accredits teacher education programs and, in the process, influences what goes on in education in many ways. Also, a controversial National Board for Professional Teaching Standards is recommnended by Carnegie, but the state departments of education will very likely want to retain control, as mentioned by one of the critics of school reform.

Alternative teacher certification programs were mentioned, and some of the weaknesses of this solution were explained. One of the models for possible school reform lies in business and industry. Both Arthur Andersen and Company and Disney were cited as examples of companies that train their employees well and use positive motivation to maintain high morale. The need to bring minorities into the profession and the difficulty involved in attracting minority students in whose way lie so many obstacles were discussed.

A number of professional growth programs are available. Madeline Hunter's techniques and the TESA devices were brought to the reader's attention.

Both of the authors have been impressed with the results of these two efforts.

Salaries, fringe benefits, and teacher supply and demand were discussed to give you a rough idea of what to expect. Economic rewards for teaching may suddenly escalate, although that has not been the trend in recent years. As far as teacher supply and demand is concerned, keep in tune with local, state, and national trends. This area of teachers' welfare is very important, but consider the entire picture before deciding on a career in teaching.

Glossary Terms

National Council for Accreditation of Teacher Education (NCATE), 36

Holmes Group, 37

Carnegie Forum, 38

National Board for Professional Teaching Standards, 38

Noncertified Teacher, 42

Alternative Certification, 42

Standard Preparation, 43

Mirrors of Excellence, 43

Ethnic Groups, 46

Clinical Theory of Instruction, 48

TESA (Teacher Expectations and Student Achievement), 49

Composite Indicators of Changes in Average Salaries and Wages Paid by Public School Systems (CIC), 52

Consumer Price Index (CPI), 52

Fringe Benefits, 55

Supply and Demand, 58

Questions

1. How can one justify becoming a teacher, considering the current monetary problems? What are greater reasons, other than monetary considerations, for entering the teaching profession?

2. List the key components of the three reform movements mentioned in this chapter. Compare and contrast the advantages and disadvantages of each.

3. What aspects of Arthur Andersen and Company and the Disney Corporation could realistically be adapted for use in education?

4. What innovative solutions to the problem of minority participation in teacher education are in use in colleges and universities in your area? Can you think of some additional solutions to this problem?

5. Discuss the effects of year-round schooling on salaries and part-time employment of teachers.

6. What do you perceive as the advantages and disadvantages of year-round schooling?

7. With respect to your teaching specialty, how will the current forces of supply and demand affect your career in education?

8. What is your reaction to a five-year program in teacher education?

9. View a Madeline Hunter videotape and write a critique of one of her teaching skills.

   10. Interview a teacher who has been involved in the TESA program and obtain her or his reactions as to the effectiveness of this program.

Activities for Unit I

1. Teaching is a service occupation. List as many reasons as you can why teaching is service oriented. Similarly, list the service aspects of another occupation in the private sector. Compare the two occupations, and make three generalizations about your findings.

2. List ten characteristics of the ideal teacher. Be prepared to present to the rest of the class your rationale for choosing these characteristics.

3. When you observe classes, identify as many types of deviant behavior as possible. Write down what you think are the best remedies for these deviant behaviors and discuss them with other members of your class.

4. Interview a teacher about the benefits of being a teacher. How does he or she feel teachers have been treated monetarily in relation to the private sector, and what does he or she think is more important than money? Discuss your interview with the rest of the class.

5. Interview some experienced teachers about the pressures of disappointments they have had in teaching. Ask them how they handled these problems.

6. Arrange with a teacher in the public schools to help plan a home visit, and accompany the teacher on the home visit. If the home visit cannot be arranged, simulate a visit before the class.

7. Invite outstanding teachers to your class for a panel discussion. Have them share some of their accomplishments as teachers, and then open the discussion up for questions and answers.

8. Invite an official of the state department of education to discuss or explain the first-year teacher internship in your state.

9. Interview master teachers about the incentives that have motivated them during their professional teaching careers.

10. Read a recent article on teacher empowerment in a professional journal and report to your class on the progress of this movement.

Annotated Bibliography

1. Ballinger, C. E. (1987). *The year-round school: Where learning never stops.* Bloomington, IN: Phi Delta Kappa Educational Foundation.

   The *Year-round School* fastback describes in detail many plans or options that school systems can adopt. Some successful programs of year-round education are highlighted.

2. *Carnegie Forum on Education and the Economy.* (May 1986). *A nation prepared: Teachers for the 21st century.* New York: Task Force on Teaching as a Profession.

The *Carnegie Forum on Education and the Economy* is a program of the Carnegie Foundation of New York which was established in 1985. The report of the Forum is a document of valuable importance as the United States re-evaluates its educational policies in the 1980s and 1990s.

3. *Holmes Group Forum*. The Holmes Group, 501 Erickson Hall, East Lansing, MI 48824-1034.

   The *Holmes Group Forum* is published for the purpose of keeping interested members and nonmembers informed of its progress. The *Forum* is published in fall, winter, and spring to stimulate exchanges of ideas and opinions with the Holmes Group.

4. Houston, W. R. (Ed.) (1986). *Mirrors of excellence—Reflections for teacher education from training programs in ten corporations and agencies*. Reston, VA: Association of Teacher Educators.

   This sixty-seven-page book contains many valuable models and lessons from industry besides what has been noted in this chapter for the Arthur Andersen and Company and Disney.

5. Kerman, S., & Martin, M. (1980). *Teacher expectations and student achievement*. Bloomington, IN.: Phi Delta Kappa Educational Foundation.

   A teacher handbook is available from Phi Delta Kappa that details the entire *TESA* program. Among other important information, the handbook explains the concept of positive and negative coding of teachers in practice.

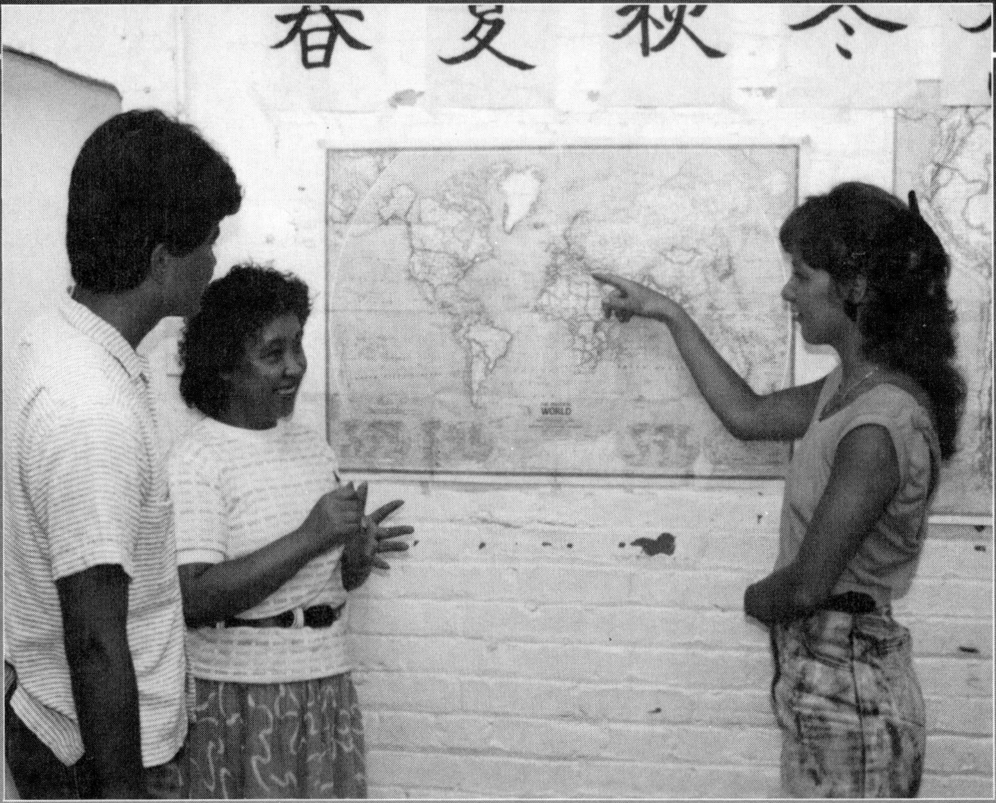
春夏秋冬
WORLD

II

Sociology and Education

Social Problems and the School's Responses: Direct-Impact Issues

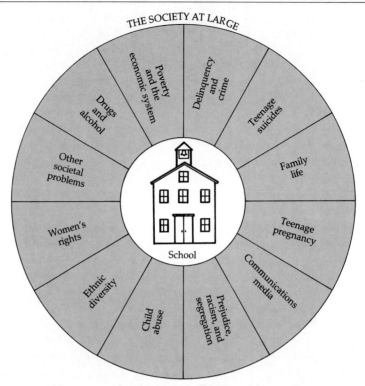

THE SOCIETY AT LARGE

Poverty and the economic system

Delinquency and crime

Teenage suicides

Drugs and alcohol

Family life

Other societal problems

School

Teenage pregnancy

Women's rights

Communications media

Ethnic diversity

Child abuse

Prejudice, racism, and segregation

Many societal problems affect our schools.

Introduction

There are at least two ways of looking at the sociology of education that are helpful in gaining a perspective on past, present, and future events in education: functional theory and conflict theory. Both theories have historical roots worth noting. Emile Durkheim (1858–1917) was a sociologist who devoted much of his time to relating sociology to education. He believed that different parts of society related to each other in a functional orderly manner, for example, schools should support the home and industry. Therefore, it was the job of the school to teach values to prepare one for the workplace; and the home should support this task. Representing the other side was Max Weber (1864–1920), who exposed the conflict theory. Conflictists believe that there are always groups in society that are in conflict with each other. Concerning the school situation, there are the power structure, which wishes to maintain the school and the culture in its present position, and the poorer classes, who wish to see their status in society improve.

From the 1960s through the early 1990s, we have witnessed the struggle

DURKHEIM

WEBER

POWER
STRUGGLE

CONFLICT
THEORY

FUNCTIONAL
THEORY

of blacks, women, hispanics, American Indians, and other disenfranchised groups to better their lot in society. Also, during the 1980s we saw the government, through a national study, *A Nation at Risk*, try to empower our educational institutions to become more functional by teaching the so-called fundamentals in a more thorough manner. The first example is explained best by the conflict theory, and the second, by the functional theory. These two forces are at work all of the time and represent a continuum (see Table 3–1) that can help us better understand sociological trends in education.

RADICAL VS.
MODERATE
APPROACHES

In this unit several current social issues affecting our schools at the present time are dealt with in some detail. The most radical functionalists would say that these are not the schools' business and that it is up to the families to send their children to school ready to learn. Many functional thinkers claim that substance abuse programs and sex education programs are necessary to a functional society. The most radical conflictists maintain that teachers need to be very sensitive to social differences and social problems, in general, to develop a meaningful rapport with their classes. Many conflicts thinkers place the self-concept of the child at the top of the list and would be willing to sacrifice some academics to more closely achieve equal educational opportunity.

SYMPTOMS
VS. ROOT
CAUSES

Another important theme the authors have in mind as they present the sociological foundations of education is that with many of these sociological issues that impact upon the educational system, only the symptoms are treated; the real problem is never solved. For example, recognition of the potential danger signs of a suicidal youth is treatment of a symptom, when teachers should be seeking the reasons for the suicide attempt. A student teacher seeking a real solution to teen suicide might look at family problems, the school testing program, peer relationships, and many other root causes. It is important to be knowledgeable of both the symptoms and the root causes of social problems so that lasting solutions can be found.

The issues in this unit are divided between those that have a direct impact upon our youth (Chapter 3) and those that have an indirect impact

TABLE 3–1 ■■■■■■■■■■■■■■■■■■■■■■■■■■■■■■

Sociological Change Continuum

FUNCTIONAL VIEW Toward Fewer Changes	CONFLICT VIEW Toward More Changes
More traditional and conservative	More liberal and more on the cutting edge
Pro *Nation at Risk*	Pro multicultural education
Pro testing	Pro alternative education
Pro college prep curriculum	Pro women's rights

AIDS, along with alcohol and drug abuse, presents additional challenges for educators into the 1990s.

(Photo used by permission of the Indianapolis Children's Museum.)

upon our youth (Chapter 4). The direct issues are generally more visible and obvious; the indirect issues are less obvious and not as easy to identify. Indirect issues, however, can be just as profound in their impact upon the schools. Each social issue is dealt with in terms of its impact upon the schools, and then examples of how some schools respond to the various issues such as AIDS are given.

Impact of Drug and Alcohol Abuse

Drugs

TOP SOCIAL
ISSUE

The 1988 Gallup Poll of the Public's Attitudes Toward the Public Schools published by the Phi Delta Kappa Educational Foundation lists the use of drugs as the biggest problem in the public schools. During the 1988 presidential campaign both candidates cited drug abuse as a top priority.

DAMAGE TO
BODY

More evidence is accumulating daily to indicate that damage is done to the body by the continued use of drugs such as marijuana. Although this problem was once confined primarily to the ghettos of large American cities, today it can be found in any neighborhood. Sometimes, the more money children have to spend, the more likely they are to be involved in drugs.

ELEVEN
TYPES

The U.S. Department of Health and Human Services listed the prevalence and recency of use of eleven types of drugs by the high school class of 1986. Figure 3–1 lists marijuana as the third most-used drug by young people and adults, after alcohol and cigarettes. Note that these statistics are percentages, and the total number of youths involved in drugs is enormous.

THE REAL
CAUSE?

The question is why do people want to alter their minds with drugs in the first place. If we could answer this question fully, we would be well underway to finding a solution to the problem rather than continuing to treat the symptoms. People have many reasons for using drugs, and society needs to seriously consider all the underlying causes of drug use. Treatment programs often overlook the real causes of drug misuse. Treatment must often involve more than just the user if there are to be real results; many treatment centers around the country address this concern by involving other family members.

A CON-
CERNED SO-
CIETY?

Is society, as a whole, concerned about the problem? There are both signs that society does care and signs that it does not care enough. We try to arrest drug pushers and to discourage the use of harmful drugs. At present, the federal government—and the U.S. Coast Guard, in particular—is arresting illegal importers of marijuana and other drugs; however, most importers are not caught. Because enormous profits are to be made on drugs, even established businesspeople and government leaders sometimes find it difficult to resist the profits. Rock stars are admired by teenagers, but some are known users of drugs who are allowed to perform in arenas where the use of drugs is public. Respected businesspeople, who control the keys to these arenas, tacitly accept the use of drugs in this way, and often these

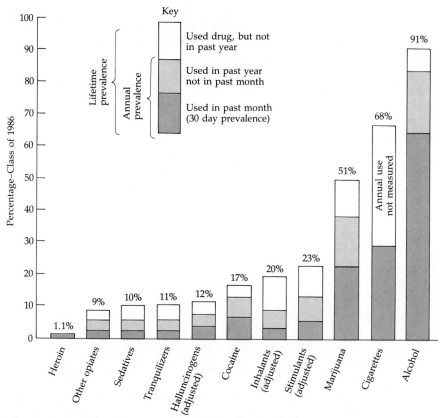

Figure 3–1   Prevalence and recency of use of eleven types of drugs, class of 1986. The bracket near the top of the bar indicates the lower and upper limits of the 95% confidence interval.

SOURCE: U.S. Department of Health and Human Services (1987). *National trends in drug use and related factors among American high school students and young adults, 1975–1986.* National Institute on Drug Abuse, Rockville, MD.

same people wonder what is happening to our young people in the schools. Does society really care?

Alcohol

LOSS TO SO-
CIETY

Alcoholism is a growing health problem in the United States, claiming more victims than any disease with the exceptions of cancer and heart disease (Coorsch, 1982). Note in Figure 3–1 that 91% of the class of 1986 have used alcohol. The problem is causing our country so many difficulties that it is hard to estimate the magnitude of the loss both in dollars and in human agony. Some estimate the financial loss resulting from alcoholism and alcohol abuse to be nearly $50 billion a year. Employers lose as a result of employees' lack of productivity on the job, poor morale, high medical costs, absenteeism, and replacement costs. Workers with alcoholism are at least 25% less productive than their co-workers (Coorsch, 1982). A family suffers whenever a member deteriorates because of alcoholism, particularly if that person is the main source of income. The victim of alcoholism is one who faces great adversity. Other than the money factor, distorted attitudes and values affect families because of alcoholism. These problems can cause psychological problems in the children and affect their school performance.

MAGNITUDE OF THE PROBLEM

The magnitude of the alcohol problem is not so surprising when we consider that Americans drink 180 million barrels of beer a year, that is, forty-two gallons for each person in the United States aged fourteen or older, and that statistic does not include wine or hard liquor (Strong, 1983). Drinking is a part of the lifestyle of many people in the United States. Problems related to the use of alcohol impact heavily on education.

Responses to Drug and Alcohol Abuse

TENTATIVE STAGE OF ADOLES-CENCE

Fortunately, we have had the benefit of numerous studies on the process of adolescent growth and development. Now that we know what a tentative stage adolescence is in one's life, why do we not treat it with more care? One principal writes that

> adolescents regard their new size, new sensations, and new capacities with a good deal of positive anticipation, but these same developments are also occasions for unexpected awkwardness, worry, and loss of personal control. Both the drama and the awkwardness of adolescence are developmentally necessary. (Hawley, 1987, p. 4)

Teens, to escape the dilemmas they face in adolescence, often use drugs to gain **peer acceptance.** A simple answer seems to be to give these adolescents some viable and positive alternatives for their life adjustments. As we know, there are no simple answers to complex problems, but some of the materials and suggestions that follow may be useful.

TALKING ABOUT THE PROBLEM

Alcohol may be the cause of as many as 50% of all fatal accidents. Kevin Tunnell was arrested and convicted of manslaughter for the death of an eighteen-year-old girl while driving under the influence of alcohol. Kevin had been drinking with his friends, who had warned him not to drive home; they had even tried to take his car keys. The unique thing about Kevin's case is that he was sentenced to spend the next year reliving that New Year's Eve before groups of high school students in Virginia. The judge wanted him to lecture to peers and their parents on the evils of drunk driving several hours each week for a year. At first, many people thought that his sentence was too light, but he felt that it was harder to relive the incident each time he told the story than to have been in jail. Generally, he concluded his talks with "I wouldn't want anybody here to go through what I've had to go through. If it just helps one person, though, it will make me feel better" (Moore, 1982, p. 10).

Dr. George Valliant, a noted researcher on alcoholism, believes that we

MAKING IN-
TELLIGENT
DRINKING
DECISIONS

should teach children how to make intelligent drinking decisions (cited by O'Reilly, 1983). He himself is a social drinker, and he serves wine on special occasions to his two teenage children. In this case, the model he sets for his children is that moderate drinking is permissible; it makes sense that teaching them about his lifestyle is a good idea because children tend to follow adults whom they love and respect. Some children are not so fortunate as to have parents who drink moderately, and the example these youngsters see is excessive drinking. Other children come from homes where alcohol has never been a part of the family's lifestyle. No doubt Dr. Valliant's idea is a good one for some families, but a number of approaches will have to be used in the home and in the schools to educate most children.

Another teenage death, that of Cari Lightner, age thirteen, occurred in California. Cari was struck by a drunk driver who had already been convicted twice for drunk driving. Cari's mother wanted to do something to get drunk drivers off the road. Ms. Lightner and several other mothers who had lost relatives in automobile accidents caused by drunk drivers formed

MADD

MADD (Mothers Against Drunk Drivers) to campaign for tougher laws against drunk driving (Gorman, 1982). A related group, **SADD (Students Against Drunk Driving),** is active in the schools.

SADD

In 1988 the National Association of Secondary School Principals published an article that the authors feel is very helpful to those seeking answers to the drug prevention dilemma. The article begins, "Research

ABILITY TO
LEARN AND
REMEMBER?

indicates that drug use diminishes students' ability to learn and remember, increases their likelihood of skipping school or dropping out, contributes to suicides, accidents, teen pregnancies, and sudden deaths" (Dogoloff, 1988, p. 1). This statement does describe the problem, but educators hear these things all the time and most of them have become bored rather than shocked into taking action. This action-oriented article written for principals spells out what schools can do. A "model" drug policy per se is almost impossible to describe because differences in schools' educational philosophy, source of financial support, and composition of student body, as well as state and local laws and community outlook, influence the way a school formulates, communicates, and implements any new policy. Nevertheless,

EIGHT PRIN-
CIPLES

some basic principles about drug use and its prevention, as well as some techniques for addressing student drug use, are useful for educators to consider when developing a drug policy, regardless of how a school is organized. Eight of these principles are listed here:

LEGAL AND
ETHICAL OB-
LIGATION

- *Principle I.* All students have a right to attend school in an environment conducive to learning. Since alcohol and other drug use is illegal, contagious, and interferes with both effective learning and the healthy development of young people, the school has a fundamental legal and ethical obligation to prevent drug abuse and to maintain a drug-free educational environment.

DRUG EDU-
CATION

- *Principle II.* Given the extensive abuse and the formal and informal promotion of alcohol, tobacco, and other drug use in our society, the school has an obligation to provide drug education units integrated with the standard curriculum at all grade levels. These units are necessary to prepare students to decide against drug and alcohol use.

BASED UPON VALID INFOR- MATION

- *Principle III.* Drug education must be based on accurate and scientifically valid information concerning the health and developmental hazards of all abused drugs, including such socially sanctioned substances as alcohol and tobacco.

CLEAR AND UNAMBIGU- OUS

- *Principle IV.* Drug policy guidelines must be clear and unambiguous. They should be communicated formally to students, staff members, and parents, every year, in writing, as part of the code of conduct.

LEGALLY SOUND AND CONSISTENT

- *Principle V.* Policy guidelines must be legally sound and consistent with the right of all students to be educated in a drug-free environment conducive to learning.

- *Principle VI.* Policy guidelines must be applied uniformly.

APPLIED UNI- FORMLY

- *Principle VII.* Whenever possible, support for the policy should be obtained from parents, teachers, other community institutions, and the students themselves.

GAINING SUPPORT

DEGREE OF TOLERA- TION?

- *Principle VIII.* Although parents have the ultimate, primary responsibility for their children's drug use, individual differences in parental standards regarding their children's alcohol and drug using behavior in non–school-related settings cannot be permitted to compromise the environment. Schools cannot respond to the least common denominator. Even if parents tolerate their child's illegal drug and alcohol use, the school cannot do so, either legally or ethically. (Dogoloff, 1988, p. 2)

FIVE SUC- CESSFUL PROGRAMS

This article concludes by listing five successful drug education programs that are appropriate for our schools. It is assumed that these five programs are successful because they implement the eight basic principles listed above to some degree. We list all five programs because we felt that they are in tune with the concept of reaching solutions rather than just treating the symptoms of the drug problem.

Drug Education Programs

Here's Looking at You, 2000 Comprehensive Health Education Foundation, 20852 Pacific Highway South, Seattle, Washington 98198; (206) 824–2907

This is a complete drug education curriculum that begins in kindergarten and continues through high school, according to the program's promotion brochure.

TEACHER'S GUIDES

The heart of the program is the teacher's guides, with more than 150 lesson plans. Each grade level kit contains a guide with complete step-by-step instructions and detailed learning objectives. These lessons are augmented by dozens of reference sheets, worksheets, and handouts to help minimize preparation time. Overall, the K–12 curriculum includes more than 30 videotapes, more than 60 posters, and dozens of books, cards, hand puppets, reference materials, costumes, charts, scripts, and other materials.

FOCUS ON THREE AREAS

The curriculum focuses on three areas: providing information, developing social skills, and promoting bonds with institutions and prosocial groups. In early grades, friendly animal characters link lessons and activities. Lessons for later grades provide information about drug effects and teach critical social skills.

RISK FAC-
TORS EM-
PHASIZED

The curriculum emphasizes risk factors such as family history of alcoholism, family management problems, early antisocial behavior, favorable attitudes toward drug use, and friends who use drugs.

The program addresses known risk factors, focuses on gateway drugs, and contains clear "no drug use" messages. It engages students in a variety of learning activities, presents information appropriate for the grade level, and teaches social skills to the point of mastery, so students can use them immediately.

The following are three regionally representative schools that have participated in the *Here's Looking at You, 2000* program:

Bellevue School System
Bellevue, WA 98009
(206) 455–6024
Contact: Bob Collins

Alaska Council on Alcoholism
Anchorage, AK
(907) 394–6602
Contact: Carolyn Peter

New Hanover County Public Schools
J. P. Hoggard High School
Wilmington, NC 28403
(919) 791–0230

*Skills for Adolescence—**The Quest Program,*** Quest National Center, 6655 Sharon Woods Boulevard, Columbus, Ohio 43229; (800) 446–2700

GEARED FOR
MIDDLE
SCHOOL

Developed in cooperation with the Lion's Club, this is a program geared specifically for middle school–aged children, grades 6–8. It is designed to be taught as a semester-long course in a class that meets everyday, but it also could be implemented in a church, scout troop, or some organization other than a school. Though one of the goals of the curriculum is drug-free youth, drug education is not the only focus.

OPPORTU-
NITY FOR IN-
VOLVEMENT

An unusual aspect of the course is the opportunity for the pupils to become involved in a community or school service project. The rationale is that through service to others, young people can develop self-confidence and maturity. They can also practice leadership and other skills. Once they are involved constructively in helping others, young people are less likely to feel alienated and to act out by using drugs or exhibiting other negative behaviors.

IMPLEMEN-
TATION

A curriculum for implementing the service project is included in the program. Seven other units also are provided. The first three, "Entering the Teen Years: The Challenge Ahead," "Building Self-Confidence Through Better Communication," and "Learning About Emotion: Developing Competence in Self-Assessment and Self-Discipline," concentrate on helping the pupils get to know themselves better, to communicate more effectively, to accept responsibility, and to understand and manage their emotions. Units Four and Five, "Friends" Improving Peer Relationships" and "Strengthening Family Relationships," are self-explanatory.

CRITICAL THINKING SKILLS

Unit Six, "Developing Critical Thinking Skills for Decision Making," is the drug education segment. The first five lessons in this unit emphasize clarifying values, making decisions, and thinking critically about the consequences of making choices.

FACTS AND REALITIES

The next 11 lessons explore the facts and realities about alcohol, marijuana, tobacco, and other drugs. They include word games and activities that help reinforce the negative consequences of use. Also, there is a lesson on how to say "no." In this lesson, students identify circumstances that might lead to use and develop a plan of refusal.

HOW TO SET GOALS

Unit Seven, "Setting Goals for Healthy Living," includes lessons that teach how to set goals, to take charge of life, to accept responsibility, and to accept successes and failure.

SKILLS FOR LIVING

The curriculum focuses on skills for living. Though there is a drug education unit, the real thrust is to help youngsters to understand themselves, to communicate, to make decisions, and to learn other social skills not taught in an ordinary classroom.

The following are three regionally representative schools that have participated in *Skills for Adolescence—The Quest Program:*

Chinquapin Middle School
900 Woodbourne Avenue
Baltimore, MD 21212
(301) 396–6424
Contact: Craig Spilman, Principal

Campbell Junior High School
295 West Cherry Lane
Campbell, CA 95008
(408) 378–4955
Contact: Edward McCauley, Principal

Hillsboro Middle School
Grand & Jefferson
Hillsboro, KN 67063
(316) 947–3297
Contact: Marilyn Jost, Principal

Project SMART, Institute for Prevention Research, USC, c/o Project SMART, 35 North Lake Avenue, Pasadena, California 91101, (818) 405–0472

SAYING "NO"

Project SMART is geared toward seventh graders and addresses alcohol use only. The program's main thrust is what the authors call ***resistance training***, which is practicing saying "no" to the forces pressuring a young person to drink.

ROLE PLAYING

The *Project SMART* approach relies heavily on role playing and group work; very little of it is didactic or information centered. Scattered through the sessions are occasional "lecturettes," but this is definitely a process-oriented rather than a content-oriented program.

SKILL LEAD-
ERS

An integral feature of the program is the use of "skill leaders," students who are chosen by the other students for their leadership qualities. These skill leaders are used to help demonstrate some of the techniques being taught before the other students begin to practice. They also serve as *role models,* the rationale being if they are cooperative and willing to try the activities, the other students may be more likely to participate.

AS A GROUP
FACILITATOR

The teacher acts more as a *group facilitator* than an instructor. The teacher's duties are to help the students learn to give helpful and specific feedback to their students, to give feedback, and to praise and reinforce positive student behavior. Some facts and information about alcohol are included in the teacher's guide so if the teacher is asked specific questions, he or she can answer readily and accurately.

TEN SES-
SIONS

There are 10 sessions in *Project SMART,* each with a central theme such as identifying the consequences of alcohol use and nonuse, resisting peer pressure to use alcohol, or identifying media influences to use. Some sessions include constructive activities such as making up a skit promoting the nonuse of alcohol or videotaping each student as he or she assertively resists alcohol offers.

METHOD
BEST FOR
THEM

The program does not suggest any right or wrong techniques of refusal; the students find what method is best for them. Their peers and teachers tell them if they sound convincing and effective. Students who say they would not want to refuse an offer of alcohol are encouraged to practice resistance training on something they would want to refuse.

RECOGNIZ-
ING THE IN-
FLUENCES

The focus on this program is recognizing the influences that encourage alcohol use and learning and practicing effective ways of saying "no." Some information is given, but the main focus of the program is on learning how to refuse, not why to refuse.

Project Charlie, 5701 Normandale Road, Edina, Minnesota 55424, (612) 925–9706

ELEMENTARY
AGES

Project Charlie (Chemical Abuse Resolution Lies in Education) consists of a primary segment for grades K, 1, 2, and 3 and an intermediate segment for grades 4, 5, and 6. Each segment contains units on self-awareness, relationships, and decision making; the intermediate segment also contains a unit entitled "Chemical Use in Society."

SELF-ESTEEM

The idea underlying this program is that drug problems can be prevented by raising children's self-esteem—if they feel good about themselves, they will not use drugs.

The self-awareness units try to convey the point that "you are someone special." Students document ways they are unique, respond to "risk cards" with statements like "I would be happier if . . . ," learn to identify feelings, give "warm fuzzies" (compliments) to each other, and engage in many other activities designed to promote self-knowledge and self-acceptance.

RELATION-
SHIPS?

The relationship units focus on family relationships as well as friendships. Ways of getting positive attention from family and friends are explained. Accepting differences in each other is encouraged and stereotyping of sex roles and minorities is discouraged. The power of peer pressure is examined, as are ways of functioning in a group (leader, follower, observer, etc.).

Project CHARLIE tells every child: "YOU ARE SOMEONE SPECIAL"

(Photo used by permission of Project Charlie.)

DECISION
MAKING

The decision-making units focus on what a decision is and how values influence our decisions. They also include exercises in which students "role-play" making a decision, though not a decision that is drug related.

CHEMICAL
USE?

The chemical use unit includes drug education information, explores reasons people use drugs, and discusses responsible (medicinal) and irresponsible (getting high) use.

PROCESS ORI-
ENTED

The focus is on raising young people's self-esteem through activities and exercises designed to make them feel lovable, capable, and accepted. It is process oriented; most exercises are processed by having the students sit in a circle and share their feelings about the effect of the activity. Almost all the lessons are experimental rather than didactic.

The following are three regionally representative schools that have participated in *Project Charlie*.

Bolles School
7400 San Jose Boulevard
Jacksonville, FL 33217-3499
(904) 733–9292
Contact: Fred Scott

Kingston City School
61 Crown Street
Kingston, NY 12401
(914) 339–3000
Contact: Theresa Pabon

Grand Junction Schools
Grand Junction, CO 81501
(303) 242–2588
Contact: Oneta Smith

Building Drug-Free Schools, American Council for Drug Education, 204 Monroe Street, Rockville, Maryland 20850, (301) 294–0600

DISTINCTIVE

This drug education program is distinctive on a number of counts. First, it is comprehensive. The program is targeted for both public and private schools, and the instructional activities span grades K–12. The program's thrust is that school policymakers combine the student's learning activities with school policies that aim to create a drug-free school.

DRUG-FREE
SCHOOLS

Another distinctive feature of this program is that it calls for drug-free schools. This goal is not as obvious as it may sound. Drug-free students and drug-free schools are not the fundamental aims of most drug education programs; "responsible use" of drugs, effective decision making, and increased self-esteem are more typically the stated aims of alternative programs.

DRUG-FREE
BODY AND
MIND

Building Drug-Free Schools begins with the assumption that a drug-free body and mind are essential conditions for learning and for healthy maturation.

TO STAND
ALONE

A third feature of the program is that it is designed to stand alone, without other costly drug education resources. Teaching guides, drug-related information, and references are all included in one compact binder.

The program has four components:

SAMPLE POLI-
CIES

A guide to school drug policies includes guidelines and numerous sample policies from all types of schools and communities. Policy issues addressed include enforcement procedures for school drug rules, suspension, expulsion, confidentiality, referral for help, etc.

EXTENSIVE
DRUG INFOR-
MATION

A model curriculum, K–12, includes extensive drug information and background material for teachers. The learning activities are designed to match the developmental capabilities of learners at each grade level. Each exercise is clearly outlined, although improvisation is encouraged also. Learning exercises are not limited to a specific department, i.e., health, physical education, science, but rather appear in all instructional areas, as drug education is a shared school goal.

A VARIETY
OF SUGGES-
TIONS

A guide to building community consensus includes a variety of suggestions and successful models for forming parent organizations, parent–school partnerships, and community resolve to work for a drug-free youth. Names and addresses of resource organizations are also provided.

A 28-minute film documents the need for drug-free schools, drawing on the experience of specific schools that have successfully addressed student drug use.

SYSTEMWIDE
FOCUS

The program's focus is systemwide, not merely schoolwide. The conviction that ties together administrative efforts, classroom exercises, parent organizations, and community consensus building is that young people should be, and can be, drug free. The curricular emphasis is on building an informed conviction among students of all ages that their healthy nervous systems are too valuable to injure with illegal chemicals.

HEALTHY
AND SAFE
DECISIONS

In the early grades, students are asked to practice making healthy and safe decisions about drugs and other threats to health. As they proceed into the middle school and high school grades, the exercises provide an increasingly thorough grounding in where drugs come from, how they affect human functioning, and how their use affects society generally.

COMPREHEN-
SIVE AND
FIRM

Building Drug-Free Schools is both a comprehensive and firm program; it aims to eliminate, not to accommodate, student drug use. Although clear in its aims, it is very sophisticated. For while its language is clear, many of its concepts, particularly those relating to child development, are challenging.

Classroom exercises must be read closely and carefully. Implementation of the instructional program may require workshop and planning time, but it should not require additional, costly materials.

STRENGTHS
OF THE PRO-
GRAM

The program's strengths are its clarity of purpose and its systemwide, comprehensive nature. (Dogoloff, 1988, pp. 2–6)

After-School Discussions

LISTENING
TO KIDS

Another important principle to consider is that of listening to kids when they really want to talk. Teachers, counselors, and administrators are normally more than willing to talk to students, but their time is often very limited. Schools can make special time for students, for example, a time for group discussion after school. Some principals at Decatur Central High School in Indianapolis, Indiana, designed a program for helping students with problems. These assistant principals believed that school-related problems are tied to student personal problems. These problems might be drug related, but they could have other root causes as well. Although the agendas for these groups were flexible, the principals identified ten topics, including decision making, interpersonal communication, stress management, personal responsibility and accountability, crisis management, peer relationships, organizational management, self-examination, self-concept, and planning for success (Bourke and Furniss, 1987, p. 241). To get their group discussions off to a good start they would ask the students to tell about their most prized possession and why they cherished it. The topic for the meeting would then be introduced with the intention of getting the students involved as participants as they would role-play classroom and real-life situations. These student participants were given written assignments such as speaking to a teacher they disliked or developing a foolproof plan for getting to school on time. The entire after-school program was goal directed with very excellent follow-up activities. In line with the authors' idea for solving the problem, Bourke and Furniss said, "We believe that all students could benefit from a program such as this, which seeks to treat the causes, not merely the symptoms, of their problems" (Bourke and Furniss, 1987, p. 242).

ROLE PLAY-
ING

After listing and describing the five drug prevention programs for our schools, we feel that even though these programs offer some hope, they will not ultimately lead to a solution until the American people drastically alter their lifestyles. On the basis of our public school experience, personal family experience, and indirect but valuable experience at the university level, working with adolescent children for nearly thirty years, we believe that the only solution that will work must involve a realignment of our national commitment from materialism and wealth to a commitment to our own children. We feel that it would be a better society if we moved from less day-care to more parent care involving both fathers and mothers, from less emphasis on high-technology jobs to greater emphasis on jobs in general so that children can visualize greater hope for an occupation once they complete their schooling, and from special interest dominance to a greater commitment to equal educational opportunity. The latter comment relates to the fact that often we as a society emphasize what is best for "me" rather than what is best for "us."

ALTERING
LIFESTYLES

A COMMIT-
MENT TO
CHILDREN

Now that we have made a statement and given some suggestions, what is your concept of a solution to the drug problem? There is hope for a bright future because you are among the leaders who will guide our young people toward a positive new horizon.

Impact of Delinquency and Crime

ARREST
RATE!

No matter how you measure crime in the United States the results do not look good for such an advanced nation. There were 12.7 million arrests in 1987 for all criminal infractions except traffic violations. To put this in better perspective, in 1987, in cities of 250,000 or more people, the arrest rate was 7,808 per 100,000 inhabitants; in suburban county areas, the rate was 3,949; and per 100,000 in rural areas, the rate was 3,423 (Uniform Crime Report, 1987, p. 163). With respect to age, 5% of all persons arrested nationally in 1987 were under the age of 15, and 16% were under 18. Most (82%) of those arrested in 1987 were males. Fourteen percent of the males were arrested for driving under the influence. All of the preceding statistics were taken from The Federal Bureau of Investigation (Uniform Crime Reports, 1987, p. 163).

Responses to Delinquency and Crime

GENERAL RE-
SPONSES

Students get into trouble for many and varied reasons, but the schools are making some rather general responses to this problem. Schools can do a great deal by offering a fine academic program, hiring teachers that make the curriculum exciting, and promoting a sensitive and caring faculty with a good guidance program. Schools and communities are addressing the problem of troubled youth in various ways. Dropout prevention programs have sprung up all across the country. Two specific examples follow.

Preventing Dropouts

PEER MEN-
TORS

In Washington, DC, a peer mentor program is busy helping to keep youth in school. About 12.5% of all sixteen- to nineteen-year-old youths living in the District of Columbia have not completed nor are currently enrolled in high school (Lee, Bryant, Noonan, and Plionis, 1987, p. 16). Recognizing this important need in the community, a joint effort between the public and private sector was designed to help keep these youths in school. Basically, older youths are selected to be role models for younger endangered or at-risk children. The organizers of the project recognized the importance of peer influence during adolescence, and this has become the most important aspect. The objective then is to motivate youths to stay in school through role modeling, advice giving, and reinforcement of positive behaviors. Some of the peer mentors were undergraduates enrolled at Catholic University and their duties included counseling, tutoring, monitoring school progress, making appropriate referrals, recommending specific changes, and exposing youths to a variety of social or cultural activities in and around the University and the District. Youths were introduced to the

THE JOB
WORLD

job world by the time they reached sixteen by the Marriott Corporation. The youths can, and do, work their way up in the Marriott restaurant hotel system. This employment feature of the program is used as an incentive to complete high school. Although the project is too new to evaluate objectively, the youths were observed to enjoy the attention given by their peer mentors and to improve their study habits and attitudes toward school. A fine beginning!

Another idea that seems to be helping is the Miami Boys Club Delinquency Prevention Program (George and Mooney, 1986, p. 76). This program

TUTORING

addresses hard-core male delinquents and focuses on counseling and tutorial instruction in basic mathematics, reading, and writing competence. The chief fund raiser for the projects believes this 3Rs approach is the right way to help these kids. The students to be tutored are between eight and fourteen years old and have had at least three court appearances.

A RIGID
SCHEDULE

Once the kids are enrolled they must adhere to a rigid schedule. Their school attendance is monitored daily; if they are not at school they are picked up and transported to school. At the end of a school day the student is met by his or her counselor and transported to the local Boys Club for a session of academic instruction, counseling, and recreation. At the Boys Club they begin with a snack, which is followed by two hours of tutoring; each tutor sees only two boys. After tutoring, the boys engage in team and individual games, and receive counseling before being driven home after 8:00 P.M. Later in the evening, counselors make spot checks to make sure the boys are home.

The program is very successful and much less expensive then other boarding establishments. At $4,200 per year the cost is only one third that of a state training school (George and Mooney, 1986, p. 78). The following statement sums up why the authors believe this is a solution-type program:

COMMIT-
MENT FROM
THE PRIVATE
SECTOR

> The Juvenile Foundation's innovative and successful approach to rehabilitation through education and counseling, in an era of shrinking funds for social programs and disenchantment with established institutions, is a striking example of how strong commitment from the private sector can fill some of this void and salvage the lives of youths who otherwise might have little chance to succeed. (George and Mooney, 1986, p. 78)

Preventing Juvenile Crime

Sociologists and criminologists are examining the crime cycle of the juvenile offender to find the critical point at which to intervene and remove the youth form the cycle. Society wants an answer to the crime problem; and, logically, the earlier we can identify a potential juvenile offender, the better are our chances of helping him or her to lead a life free of crime. At the highest levels of government, including the U.S. Senate, work is underway to address this major issue. David P. Farrington of the Institute of Criminology, Cambridge University, England, testified before the Senate Subcommittee on Juvenile Justice in October 1981. According to Dr. Farrington, these are some of the requirements for delinquency prevention:

EARLY IDEN-
TITY!

1. Emphasis should be placed on early environment and upbringing. The earlier the intervention, the better.

ESPECIALLY
AT RISK

2. Educationally retarded children from large, poor, and criminal families are especially at risk of committing criminal and delinquent acts. Scarce welfare resources should be concentrated on this high-risk group.

FIRST CON-
VICTIONS

3. All the evidence indicates that first convictions are followed by a worsening of delinquent behavior. (Subcommittee on Juvenile Justice, 1981, pp. 50–54)

A community leader takes time to talk about his occupation.

(Photo used by permission of the Indianapolis Public Schools.)

RESEARCH
STUDY

Also testifying before the Senate Subcommittee on Juvenile Justice was Gerald R. Patterson, a research scientist at the Oregon Social Learning Center. Patterson's group studied 200 families of antisocial children and then 200 normal families for a fifteen-year period. The parents of the antisocial children were taught how to monitor their children, and they were paid $10 per week to do the monitoring. Parents were taught to find out where their children were when they did not come home, who they were with, what they were doing, and when they were coming back. All of these children were practicing predelinquent behavior (described as stealing at least twice a month). Most of these parents did not know very much about what their children were doing; and even when they saw the child perform an antisocial act, such as assaulting another family member, they did not

PARENTS
TAUGHT
HOW TO
PUNISH

punish the child. The parents were also taught how to administer sane punishment, which means a confrontation with the child that results in a work detail, the withdrawal of a privilege, or a time-out period for smaller children. The result of the experiment was that the stealing stopped for the six months during which the monitoring and sane punishment were carried out. The experiment ended when the children were six, seven, and eight years old. By the time they had reached the age of fourteen the parents had removed all controls, and 57% of these children had become chronic juvenile offenders (Subcommittee on Juvenile Justice, 1981, pp. 55–59). The experiment gives us some hope that early intervention may work, but more research is needed to detect whether a longer term of supervised parent monitoring and sane punishment would yield a higher success rate.

According to John Monahan, professor of law, psychology, and legal medicine at the University of Virginia School of Law, who also testified before the Subcommittee on Juvenile Justice, three clusters of factors relate to future violent behavior:

THREE CLUS-
TERS OF FAC-
TORS

A. Parent factors
  1. Parents themselves criminals
  2. Lack of supervision of child
  3. Conflict between parents
  4. Harsh physical discipline
B. Child factors
  1. Gender
  2. Race
  3. IQ
  4. Temperament
  5. Age of onset of delinquency
C. School factors
  1. Interpersonal difficulties
  2. Academic difficulties (Subcommittee on Juvenile Justice, 1981, p. 9)

COMPLEX SO-
LUTION

As teachers, we would be more concerned with the final cluster, but as we look at all three clusters, we can detect how complex the solution to the whole problem would be. Working with the parents, the child, and the school at the earliest possible time appears to be the best plan. The school problems a child may be having are tied to several other factors over which teachers have no control, but the results of this complex problem have a negative impact on the public schools. How many hours per semester do teachers have to stop teaching to deal with a predelinquent or delinquent student, and thus spend a large portion of their time desciplining and counseling young people while academic learning is set aside?

SOCIAL IN-
EQUALITY

Blau and Blau (1983), who examined the influence of social inequality on the violent crime rate, came to some interesting conclusions and inferences. The Blaus collected data from 125 of the largest American metropolitan areas, and they concluded that socioeconomic inequality engenders alienation, despair, and pent-up aggression, which find expression in frequent conflicts, including a high incidence of criminal violence. It is important that teachers understand these facts because in the daily operation of schools, there arise so many opportunities to verbalize or demonstrate

ECONOMIC
INEQUALITY

principles of human equality. Blau and Blau (1983) also found that economic inequality itself may be an alienating experience that engenders conflict and violent crimes in a democracy; but when overall inequality and its

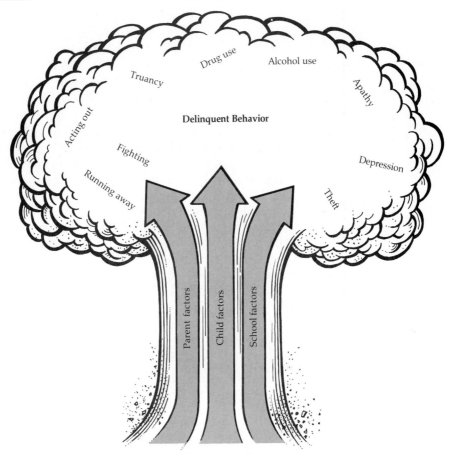

Possible causes and results of delinquent behavior.

mediating influences are controlled, racial inequality still exerts an independent influence on criminal violence. Obviously, all inequality has a negative effect, but racial inequality has a far worse negative effect.

The answer to the problems of crime and delinquence can be found through research and a greater public commitment. When we decided, as a country, to land on the moon before 1970, we achieved that goal; likewise, we can set a goal to eradicate juvenile crime by the year 2000 and accomplish that, too. Any country like the United States, with a nearly $5 trillion GNP (Economic Report of the President, 1989), can afford monetarily to solve this problem.

Impact of Racial Prejudice, Racism, and Segregation

The topics of prejudice, racism, and segregation are not pleasant ones. Some might claim that these problems do not exist in their hometowns or that the country took care of these problems back in the turbulent 1960s and

1970s. It is true that we, as a country, have made progress in solving them, but as they all still exist, they do have adverse effects on education.

Prejudice and Racism

PREJUDICE DEFINED

The Random House College Dictionary (1980, revised edition) defines *prejudice* as "an unfavorable opinion or feeling formed beforehand without knowledge, thought or reason" (p. 1046). One example, of prejudice concerns a black professional worker in a northern city in 1983. This man told of having to change his bike path frequently on his way to work because he was stopped by the police and asked all types of questions about his bike license when he passed from one area of the city to another.

RACISM DEFINED

Racism is even stronger than prejudice; it is the doctrine that "inherent differences among the various human races determine cultural or individual achievement, usually involving the idea that one's own race is superior" (p. 1088). Racism may take the form of an action or an institutional structure that subordinates a person or a group because of race. Racism was a legal part of the southern lifestyle in the United States before the *Brown v. Board of Education of Topeka* (347 U.S. 483) U.S. Supreme Court case of 1954 and the Civil Rights Acts of the 1960s changed laws and their interpretation. Blacks were to use separate drinking fountains and restrooms, sit in the rear of buses, and attend separate schools. Racism remains a part of the lifestyle of many U.S. citizens, both northern and southern, although it is no longer legally sanctioned.

Institutional Racism

The denial of equal opportunities to all races in the various institutions in our society affects schools both directly and indirectly. Institutional racism

THREE TYPES OF RACISM

> that has obstructed and in some cases continues to impede realization of status equality is of three types: (1) Prerequisites or preconditions that cannot be justified on grounds of necessity and that disproportionately bar minorities; these prerequisites are frequently economic or have economic antecedents. (2) Freezing, which occurs when standards are rigorously imposed on all applicants, regardless of race, but only after most whites have qualified during a period of less stringent requirements. (3) Mapping—the drawing of district lines in a way that dilutes minority political strength and produces racial isolation in the public schools. (Bullock and Rogers, 1975, p. 54)

MINORITIES HURT THE MOST

An example of the first type of institutional racism (prerequisites or preconditions) is housing. Because minority Americans are found in disproportionate numbers among our nation's poor, minorities are hurt most when there is a housing configuration based on economic considerations. Consequently, suburban areas are mostly white, whereas urban areas contain three times as many blacks as whites. Blacks often share overcrowded housing because of their low income. The government has tried to help solve the housing problem either by building low-income housing or making available older housing units at reduced rents. Low-income housing is only a partial interim solution for the poor, particularly blacks and other minority groups; the real solution is equal opportunity in the job market. Schools feel the pressure from blighted neighborhoods and communities that suffer from inadequate opportunities.

JOB DISCRIM-
INATION

An example of the second type of institutional racism (freezing) is found in employment. Criteria for employment may be equally applied to all racial groups now, but whites were able to obtain jobs when there were less stringent requirements. As a consequence, minorities find themselves discriminated against, but not overtly, in applying for certain jobs because of institutional requirements.

REALIGN-
MENT

Mapping is a type of institutional racism that directly affects the schools and education. Since the *Brown* decision in 1954, school districts have been realigned because of their *de jure* (deliberate) placement or *de facto* (not deliberate, but as a result of circumstances) placement of students. The goal, of course, has been to distribute minority groups equally within a district or across districts to achieve the best balance possible among all groups. In the South, this has meant abolishing exclusively white and exclusively black public schools. Busing for racial reasons is continuing across the United States at the present time.

Segregation

RESTRICTING
THE ACTIONS
OF ONE OR
MORE
GROUPS

No doubt segregation of one form or another has been in effect from the beginning of human history, but in the United States, it is more pronounced between white and black people. Basically, racial segregation means restricting the actions of one or more groups on the basis of racial or ethnic membership. Because of civil rights legislation in the United States in the 1960s and 1970s, legal segregation came to an end. Segregation in the South had been legal since the *Plessy v. Ferguson* (163 U.S. 537) case was decided by the Supreme Court in 1896. In this case, the Court ruled that it was legal to segregate white people from black people on railroad cars as long as equal facilities were provided. Eventually the practice spread to schools, waiting rooms, buses, and drinking fountains. Northerners practiced segregation in different ways, and the effect was that black people were denied equal access to jobs, housing, schools, and private clubs.

ROSA PARKS

December 1, 1955, marked a day in our nation's history when old segregational tactics began to change. It was on this day that Rosa Parks boarded a bus in Montgomery, Alabama, and sat in a seat normally reserved for white people. Because she refused to move from her seat, she was arrested and convicted of breaking the law. This one act signaled the start of the civil rights movement just as *Sputnik* signaled the beginning of space exploration twelve years later. Rosa Parks, in the words of Martin Luther King, Jr., was

MARTIN LU-
THER KING,
JR.

> anchored to that seat by the accumulated indignities of days gone by and the boundless aspirations of generations of unborn. She was the victim of both the

forces of history and the forces of destiny. She had been tracked down by the Zeitgeist—the spirit of the time. (Lindsey and Lindsey, 1974, p. 60)

VIOLENT
ACTS

Among the violent acts that occurred in the 1960s were the bombing of a Sunday-school room in a black Baptist church in Alabama, killing four little girls, and the slaying of three civil rights workers in Mississippi. The three civil rights workers, James Chaney, Andrew Goodman, and Michael Schwerner, were in Mississippi to encourage blacks to register to vote and to take advantage of their civil rights. Minorities have had a long struggle to gain their rights guaranteed by the U.S. Constitution.

APARTHEID

The United States has not had a monopoly on segregation in the world. As one illustration, South Africa today has one of the most racist school systems in the world. Under apartheid in South Africa, different racial groups are educated separately for entirely separate career goals; for example, most blacks are trained for blue-collar work and most whites for professional positions. It would be very difficult to estimate the losses in the United States alone in dollars to our gross national product because of prejudice and racism, but it is, no doubt, in the billions.

INHERENTLY
UNEQUAL

After the *Brown* case in 1954, separation by race in American schools was declared inherently unequal. This one court case has changed the way Americans relate to one another more than any one act since before the turn of the century. The Supreme Court mandated the desegregation of American public schools, whether segregation was purposeful *(de jure)* or the result of neighborhood placement *(de facto)*. Desegregation did not move rapidly after *Brown;* but inch by inch, court decision after court decision, progress has been made. As lawsuits have been brought against various school districts across the country and court decisions have been made, various solutions have been proposed; most of these solutions have involved busing or changes in school-district boundaries.

EASIER COM-
MUNICATION

Many white parents have been angered by the court orders and have moved their families to the suburbs. Other white families have remained in their old districts and participated in the great experiment. Frequently, white children have met black children, made new friends, and become learning and social partners. As integration has proceeded, it has become easier for all groups in our society to meet and communicate better. Greater opportunities for minority groups have opened up, and a good many members of minorities have climbed and are climbing the ladder of economic success. Many suburban housing developments are no longer all white, and a number of school districts have integrated themselves naturally.

STILL WORK
TO BE DONE

Today, legal segregation is part of the past. The attitude in the nation is much better than it was in 1955, when Rosa Parks made her initial protest; however, some workers in skilled trades are opposed to accepting black workers in their ranks. In many places, fair housing laws have not been passed; blacks are still harassed when they move into neighborhoods or communities where they are not wanted; and minority businesses still must fight for their existence. Much work still remains before Martin Luther King's dream for America is fulfilled.

Response to Desegregation

DENIAL

CURRICULUM ADJUST-MENTS MADE

HUMAN RE-LATIONS GROUPS

LEARNING FROM STU-DENTS

INTERRACIAL ACCEPTANCE

When the desegregation orders were handed down by the various federal and district courts, school systems and communities knew that they must do something to prepare for the changes that were to come. Although white and black families had lived near each other and worked together for years, they had not been familiar with each other's cultural differences. Denial of equal educational opportunity to blacks in segregated schools had resulted in their having many learning deficiencies; but more important, their learning expectations were very low. Now it was imperative for schools to gear their programs to meet these new teaching challenges. Schools had training sessions for their teachers and staff, community desegregation groups got together, and some important curriculum adjustments were made.

Human relations groups were set up to deal with teacher–pupil relationships within the schools. One ninth grade student, who was a member of one of these committees, made the following statement (Bash, 1973):

> Why is it that people put blacks and whites in some kind of separate categories?
> The students have fears and prejudices only because they were taught this. Even adults have this feeling and try to hide it instead of listening to the student's side of it. Why not let the teachers learn from their students sometimes? If teachers can learn from their students whom they are trying to teach, they will find they have a much better communication with people, black and white.
> Let the child take the job for a while, listen to your students, each one, and your subject will be taught and learned. Talk to your class, you will find that more students in your class will let their feelings out about the subject or whatever is being talked about.
> Relate to people now!!! Don't wait. They will relate right along with you. (p. 16)

Not only did this young man have a good idea for bettering race relations, but he also hit on the good teaching technique, listening to your students. Many immediately useful suggestions, as well as long-lasting suggestions, on how to improve race relations have come from the human relations groups that were set up. Actually, by the time you have entered teaching, the work of the human relations committee may be on the back shelf, but one could benefit greatly by talking with former leaders and reading documents written by committee members.

Some research has been done on interracial acceptance in desegregated schools. The findings by Bennett (1979) in one large midwestern school district indicate that where there is a climate of acceptance, teachers do not distinguish between the learning potential of their black and white

Integration means that students of different races learn to work together.

[Photo used by permission of the Indianapolis Public Schools.]

students. These teachers also tend to be strong and directing, fair, warm, spontaneous, and involved in the teaching profession. Bennett also found that although there was much student initiation in "acceptance" classrooms, the teacher still controlled the classroom interaction.

QUALITY ED-
UCATION IS
POSSIBLE

In the face of all the turmoil and change surrounding the process of desegregation, quality education is possible. Desegregation practices can have a positive effect on students, teachers, and administrators through changes in curricula, instructional practices, and attitudinal adjustments. Hawley (1983) suggested several strategies that are helpful in the desegregation process:

HELPFUL
STRATEGIES

1. Desegregate as early as possible before racial prejudices are ingrained.
2. Employ instructional strategies that retain heterogeneous classes and work groups. These strategies deemphasize competition and encourage student interaction. Rigid forms of ability grouping should be avoided and possible misuse of special programs should be monitored closely.
3. Develop interracial extracurricular activities which provide contact in cooperative, nonthreatening situations.
4. Develop a rigorous but fair disciplinary program that can be enforced in consistent, firm, and equitable ways.

TEST OF OUR
NATIONAL
COMMIT-
MENT

5. Involve parents directly in the education of their children. (pp. 335–336)

These are only a few ideas that have assisted in the desegregation process. If you find yourself in a school with some desegregation problems, the literature is full of helpful suggestions. Hawley (1983) wrote that desegregation is more than a challenge to the capacity of schools to provide high-quality education; it is a test of our national commitment to social mobility and to racial equality.

Busing and School Integration

Busing has been one solution to the integration problem used in our public schools. Busing has given many opportunities to both minority and white majority children to mix socially, athletically, and intellectually in the schools. Busing was implemented after extensive court litigation, some of which was bitter, and after the expenditure of millions of dollars for school buses and bus transportation. In 1978–1979, Los Angeles spent $375 per pupil on the mandatory busing program alone. In spite of all the busing efforts and all the other types of programs that have been devised to integrate our schools, the National Task Force on Desegregation says that racial bias is still pervasive and that government policies and practices that result in school segregation still exist (Summers, 1979).

RACIAL BIAS
IS STILL PER-
VASIVE

A Midwest research study of seven Marion county school districts by Indiana University in Indianapolis offers some insights into the progress of school integration. The study is a longitudinal type of study and the results constitute only one step of a three-stage design. The research team developed a Student Needs Assessment Survey to measure students' perceptions in desegregating school districts in the area of school climate (that is, interracial attitudes, attitudes toward school and learning, staff/student interaction, student/student interaction, incentives and structure, parent involvement, proximity, and self concept/self-esteem).

MIDWEST
STUDY

The population used in the study included black and white transported and nontransported students in Grades 3, 5, 7, 9, and 11 in the Indianapolis public schools. Students were divided into four groups for purposes of the study.

FOUR
GROUPS

- *Black Resident*—black student who attends the assigned school within his or her own district.
- *Black Nonresident*—black student who is transported for the purpose of desegregation
- *White Resident*—white student who attends the assigned school within her or his district
- *White Nonresident*—white student who is transported for the purpose of desegregation

Selected Findings

MORE TO
RACE

1. Differences in interracial attitudes do not appear to be a function of desegregation. The difference was related more to race than to residence status.

POSITIVE AT-
TITUDE

2. Overall, the students perceived a positive attitude toward school and learning.

3. Seemingly, desegregation contributes to a perceived stress in children's and adolescents' peer group relationships.

4. Overall, the students perceived a positive school self-concept.

Recommendations

1. That school districts continue to take affirmative actions to ensure that staff and students see the schools as egalitarian

2. That school districts initiate or continue programs to help students transported for purposes of desegregation (and their families) feel part of the school family

3. That increased attention be given to multicultural experiences in the schools; also, that teachers should be educated in methods of multicultural education

4. That schools continue efforts at recruiting qualified black faculty and staff

5. That schools take active steps to eliminate activities and barriers which effectively foster resegregation

6. That teachers must be educated to the character of prejudice (Harris, Heid, Ingersoll, and Pugh, 1985, pp. 321–331)

The findings and conclusions of this study indicate more of a positive support for busing than the opposite. The fact that children transported for purposes of desegregation are more likely to see themselves as "outsiders" is a negative factor that the research group has some suggestions for improving. Almost all six recommendations relate to helping bused students feel less isolated and more a part of the entire school program.

A study published by Harvard University Graduate School of Education and authored by Charles V. Willie offers some new ideas on school desegregation and busing. First, Willie maintains that from all levels of government, including the executive branch, we have heard that "busing has not worked." The truth is that school desegregation has worked and Willie offers the following facts to support his claim:

1. Back in 1940 before the *Brown* decision, the median school year completed by whites was 53 percent higher than that of blacks. But by 1979, 25 years after *Brown*, the median school year completed by the majority was only 3 percent above that of the minority.

2. Back in 1940 before the *Brown* decision, of all blacks 25 years of age and over only 7 or 8 percent had graduated from high school. By 1979, 25 years after *Brown*, a majority of black adults over 25 years were high school graduates.

3. Back in 1940 before the *Brown* decision, less than 2 percent of blacks over 25 years had graduated from college. But by 1979, 25 years after *Brown*, 10 to 11 percent of all black adults had earned college degrees.

4. In summary, the median school year completed by blacks increased from 5.7 years in 1940 to 12.1 years in 1979. This represents a 110 percent increase in less than a half century. (Willie, 1984, p. 16)

Multicultural education helps to bridge the gaps between different racial and ethnic groups.

(Photo used by permission of the Metropolitan School District of Washington Township.)

Second, Willie believes that school desegregation has benefited whites as well as blacks and other minorities:

WHITES ARE DOING BETTER

In 1940, for example, before *Brown* only one third of the white adults over 25 years graduated from high school. In 1979, 25 years after *Brown*, the proportion of white high school graduates had doubled and represented almost two thirds of those over 25 years. (Willie, 1984, p. 6)

WHITES A MINORITY

Third, Willie states that desegregation and busing have been successful because they have made it possible for whites to be a minority, to not be in charge. Whites often worry that their children will not learn in schools where there is a black majority, but there is growing evidence that they may learn things they could not learn as a majority.

DESEGREGATION WORKS!

From these two studies there is solid evidence that busing and school integration are working. Professional educators need to speak out in favor of this evidence and become greater advocates of desegregation to overcome the negative effects voiced by politicians and others in the community.

Magnet Schools and School Integration

One method of desegregation that has worked to some degree in several school systems throughout the country is the magnet school. It was believed that if certain schools were made especially attractive to children and parents, students throughout the school district would attend, thus facilitating the integration process. Magnet schools can be set up at all levels in the educational process and can include specializations that are limited only by the imagination.

SCHOOLS MADE ATTRACTIVE

The magnet school plan in Houston has been one of the nation's most successful. In Houston's Independent School District, there are sixty-one magnet schools. In one magnet school for the performing and visual arts, the school's marquee notes student performances in dance, drama, media arts, music, and the visual arts. Academic instruction is correlated with history, theory, and technique in each art area. The future artists of Houston and the United States are blooming here (McIntire, Hughes, and Say, 1982). Houston also has a program called Vanguard for the academically gifted, which begins in kindergarten and ends in high school. A definite measure of the success of Houston's magnet program is that these schools attract nonminority students back into the city. The greatest advantage of the magnet schools is that they are voluntary.

SIXTY-ONE MAGNET PROGRAMS

Schools that focus on the fine arts are good examples of magnet schools.

(Photo used by permission of the Indianapolis Public Schools.)

INNOVA-
TIONS
SPREAD
In Tucson, the magnet concept has helped to successfully integrate the schools. Some magnet schools have implemented such innovations as bilingualism. As Tucson has a large bilingual population, this type of magnet school is very popular (Grant, 1983). Successful innovations have spread to other magnet schools.

EDUCATION
BY CHOICE
In Boston, as many as one third of the school population attends magnet schools, which are racially balanced. Fantini (1982) wrote that although many magnet schools have committed themselves to basic academic skills, they also identify and cultivate talent and introduce the concept of education by choice, as does the alternative school program.

LINK TO ED-
UCATIONAL
NEEDS
One of the keys to their success is that magnet schools are more closely linked to the educational needs and interests of the students than are the traditional schools. Magnet schools often have waiting lists, and children attending them have shown improved test scores. We are living in a complex society where many options must be tried to answer our population's diverse educational needs.

Impact of Child Abuse

CAUSES OF
ABUSE
The number of child abuse cases reported in the United States is rising each year. In 1978, the American Humane Association reported 607,000 cases of child abuse; by 1981, the count had risen to 846,000, and by 1985, to 1,299,000. Child abuse strikes all socioeconomic levels and all racial groups, and for every case reported, four go unreported. The exact causes of child abuse are not known, but several theories have been proposed. The most disturbing finding about child abusers is that they themselves grew up being abused and that their children will very likely become abusers also. The cyclical pattern of child abuse must be broken, and teachers can be of much assistance in the identification of victims.

CHILD ABUSE
DEFINED
In 1974, Congress passed the Child Abuse Prevention and Treatment Act (P.L. 93-247), which defines child abuse and neglect as "the physical or mental injury, sexual abuse, negligent treatment, or maltreatment of child under the age of eighteen by a person who is responsible for the child's welfare under circumstances which indicate the child's health or welfare is harmed or threatened thereby" (U.S. Department of Health, Education, and Welfare [USDHEW], 1976). There are thus four basic types of child abuse: physical abuse, neglect, emotional abuse, and sexual abuse.

PHYSICAL
ABUSE
A child is physically abused when any physical injury is inflicted on him or her by other than accidental means. Typical injuries are unusual bruises, welts, burns, fractures, and bite marks.

NEGLECT
ABUSE
Abuse in the form of neglect is failure to provide a child with the basic necessities of life, such as food, clothing, shelter, medical care, and education. Typically, neglected children appear dirty, tired, and lethargic; they come to school with no breakfast; they are alone for long periods; they may need glasses, dental care, or other medical attention.

EMOTIONAL
ABUSE
The emotionally abused child has parents with excessive, aggressive, or

unreasonable behavior that places demands on the child to perform above her or his capabilities. Typically, the emotionally abused child's parent blames or belittles the child, is cold and rejecting, withholds love, or treats the children in the family unequally.

SEXUAL
ABUSE

The sexually abused child is exploited for an adult's own sexual gratification; sexual abuse takes the form of rape, incest, fondling of genitals, or exhibitionism. Typically, children who have been sexually abused appear withdrawn or engage in fantasies or babylike behavior, have poor relations with other children, are unwilling to participate in physical activities, and may state that they have been assaulted by a parent or caretaker.

REPORTING
ABUSE

Most people have a stereotypical image of parents as always caring and overly patient; therefore, they find it hard to believe that parents may act otherwise. As a result, most cases of child abuse remain unreported. A greater percentage of child abuse cases are reported among the poor and nonwhite population, mainly because public agencies, such as welfare agencies, hospitals, and outpatient clinics, have greater access to these groups.

MULTIDI-
MENSIONAL
PROBLEM

No one knows the exact breakdown of the percentage of child abusers by socioeconomic level, but poverty, drugs and alcohol, poor housing, unemployment, and racial discrimination produce stress, which aggravates any problem. Gil (1969) sees child abuse as a multidimensional problem, but he is a leading exponent of the theory that environmental stress is a major cause.

CHARACTER
DISORDER

No matter what environmental problems contribute to it, child abuse is a form of character disorder in some adults who need to be treated. Organizations such as Parents Anonymous and family support centers, as well as a government agency called Child Protective Services, have been set up to help both abusers and victims, providing they can be identified.

COVERUP

Violent crimes like murder are nearly always reported and recorded, but child abuse is often covered up and unreported. Victims of child abuse exist in larger numbers than most of us realize, and inside they are crying out for assistance. The cover article in *Time* magazine of September 5, 1983, attests to the importance of recognizing child abuse in our society so that we can begin to solve the problem for larger numbers of offenders and victims.

Figure 3–2   Child abuse is a multidimensional problem.

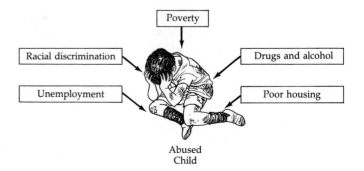

MORE CASES REPORTED — The number of cases of child abuse reported is rising rapidly, indicating greater public awareness of the problem. There is better detection of child abuse in schools, hospitals, and social agencies. Some studies (Magnuson, 1983) indicate that as many as 90% of inmates in prision claim to have been abused as children. There is no doubt that helping children and adult abusers overcome their emotional and/or psychological problems would have some effect on reducing the prison population. One cannot estimate the number of child abuse victims who cause problems for business and industry, as well as for themselves. How much more productive these citizens might be if they could be relieved of the legacy of their childhood trauma.

AN EXTREME CASE — An article in *Time* magazine (Magnuson, 1983) contained a case study of a girl named Mary, which illustrates a very extreme case of child abuse. It serves to point out the cyclical effect of child abuse from one generation to another:

ABOUT MARY — Her name is Mary. She is 34 years old and lives in a suburb of New York City. With her neatly tailored beige suit, pink designer blouse, and necklace of seed pearls, she has the well-scrubbed preppie look of someone who has had a safe, comfortable life. When she begins to speak, the words seem strange, as if they belong to some other person.

What I remember most about my mother was that she was always beating me. She'd beat me with her high-heeled shoes, with my father's belt, with a potato masher. When I was eight, she black-and-blued my legs so badly, I told her I'd go tell the police. She said, "Go, they'll just put you into the the darkest prision." So I stayed. When my breasts started growing at 13, she beat me across the chest until I fainted. Then she'd hug me and ask forgiveness. When I turned 16, a day didn't pass without my mother calling me a whore, and saying that I'd end up in Potter's Field, dead, forgotten, and damned for all eternity. Most kids have nightmares about being taken away from their parents. I would sit on our front stoop, crooning softly of going far, far away to find another mother.

FIND AN-OTHER MOTHER — What she did to my young brother was worse. When he was two years old, she tried to hang him from the shower curtain and drown him in the toilet. He still has tic-tac-toe marks across his chest from being held down across a red-hot heating grate. From the time he was born, my mother groomed my brother to kill my father. When Daddy came home, she made us tell him how much we hated him. I went to bed and prayed he didn't believe me. It was after I'd been married two years that my mother and brother bludgeoned my father to death in the cellar with his own pool cue. They stuffed his body in the car trunk and drove him to the middle of town and left him there.

TAUGHT TO HATE

CYCLICAL PATTERN — I started abusing my boy because his birth was an accident and he was a screamer. When he was four months old, I hit him so hard my engagement ring carved a deep bloody furrow across his soft face. His screams shattered my heart. I sank to the floor with self-loathing. Then I held him tightly in my arms, so tight he turned blue. I told him he had to do his share. Why didn't he help out? Why didn't he stop screaming. Deep down, I knew he couldn't understand. But I also thought he was doing it on purpose. He'd start crying and I'd hit him again, and I felt so helpless when this happened.

When he was ten, I got so angry with him, I panicked. I was rushing to kill him. But I managed to tell him to go to his room and lock himself in and not to open the door no matter what I said. He fled. He was really afraid. I could hear him breathing like a frightened rabbit behind the door. I was fulfilling my predictions. I was no good and I'd never be any good. I went to Mass every Sunday, and every Sunday I'd say, "I'll confess." I couldn't. I'd go into the confession box and choke on the words. When you abuse your child, it seems like you're watching someone else do it. There is guilt, horror, pain. Society need not hate us. We hate ourselves. No one hates an abusing parent more than the abusing parent.

WE HATE
OURSELVES

Most abused children, of course, do not murder their fathers. A parent who tries to kill or succeeds in killing a child is also relatively rare. Unfortunately, Mary's account of the physical and emotional humiliation inflicted on her by an out-of-control parent and the recycling of the same kind of abuse when she became a mother is all too typical. What is hopeful, although unusual, about Mary's story is that she realized she needed help, found a group, Parents Anonymous, that knew how to help her, and made peace with her son. In high school now, he is a straight-A student and a starter on the baseball team. Mary says, "He is always telling me that when he is very rich, he'll build a beautiful house and put me and his father on the second floor with a sauna bath, a fireplace and a jacuzzi. Now we are a warm, happy family." (Magnuson, 1983, p. 20)

PARENTS
ANONYMOUS

As you can see, it is possible for people to heal and live a normal life, thus breaking the abuse cycle.

Response to Child Abuse

Schools and teachers are in an excellent position to help the victim of child abuse and, indirectly, the abusers.

THREE STEPS

Three steps are involved in protecting an abused child: (1) identification, (2) investigation, and (3) intervention. It is at the identification step that educators have the best opportunity to help. In some states, teachers and administrators are mandated to report all suspected cases of child abuse and neglect; therefore, legal action could possibly be taken against them for not reporting such violations. The important thing to remember is that by reporting suspected cases, one is not meddling in someone else's private problem but instead is helping to protect the life of a child: "Because we in America respect the privacy of the home, we have adopted a 'don't get involved' attitude that has sent many a child to an early grave" (Overton, 1979, p. 7). Suspected abuse cases are to be reported to the nearest office of the Department of Public Welfare, Child Protective Services Division, or the nearest police agency. Your job, as a teacher, is only to report, not to conduct a unilateral investigation.

WHERE TO
REPORT
CASES

As a teacher responsible for identifying a child abuse victim, suspect abuse if a child

WHEN TO
SUSPECT
ABUSE

- Is habitually away from school and constantly late
- Arrives at school very early and leaves very late because he does not want to go home

- Is compliant, shy, withdrawn, passive, and uncommunicative
- Is nervous, hyperactive, aggressive, disruptive, or destructive
- Has an unexplained injury—a patch of hair missing, a burn, a limp, or bruises
- Has an inordinate number of "explained" injuries such as bruises on his arms and legs over a period of time
- Exhibits an injury that is not adequately explained
- Complains about numerous beatings
- Complains about the mother's boyfriend "doing things" when the mother is not at home
- Goes to the bathroom with difficulty
- Is inadequately dressed for inclement weather with, for example, only a sweater in winter for outer wear
- Wears a long-sleeved blouse or shirt during the summer months to cover bruises on the arms
- Has clothing that is soiled, tattered, or too small
- Is dirty and smells or has bad teeth, hair falling out, or lice
- Is thin, emaciated, and constantly tired, showing evidence of malnutrition and dehydration
- Is unusually fearful of other children and adults
- Has been given inappropriate food, drink, or drugs (Fraser, 1977, pp. 14–16)

Educators should also suspect child abuse if the parents

PARENT IN-
DICATORS

- Show little concern for their child's problems
- Do not respond to the teacher's inquiries and are never present for the teacher's visits or for parents' nights
- Take an unusual amount of time to seek health care for the child
- Do not adequately explain an injury
- Continue to complain about irrelevant problems unrelated to the injury
- Suggest that the cause of an injury can be attributed to a third party
- Are reluctant to share information about the child
- Respond inappropriately to the seriousness of the problem
- Cannot be found
- Are using alcohol or drugs
- Have no friends, neighbors, or relatives to turn to in crises
- Have unrealistic expectations for the child
- Are very strict disciplinarians
- Were themselves abused, neglected, or deprived as children
- Have taken the child to different doctors, clinics, or hospitals for past injuries
- Show signs of loss of control or fear of losing control
- Are unusually antagonistic and hostile when talking about the child's health problems (Fraser, 1977, pp. 14–16)

These problems and others will help you identify victims and, hopefully, start the recovery process so that these children can become productive citizens and much better students.

HUGGING
KIDS?

There is also growing concern that many of our excellent teachers will refrain from touching and showing affectionate behavior toward children because they fear being accused of child abuse. This fear arises from some allegations of sexual abuse in schools and daycare centers. A recent teacher of the year said that he had, as a goal, being able to hug all the members of his classes. Team teaching and leaving classroom doors open are ways to prevent accusations, but we hope that our teachers will not need to cease their affectionate behavior toward children.

> Schools should teach students to say "no" to unwelcome physical contact. At Riverside, we taught even the youngest children to say "I don't like that" when someone grabs, hits, or otherwise touches them in a way they don't want. (Goodhue, 1988, p. 48)

Child abuse is a very bad problem in our society, but overreaction to abuse and false accusations can be just as damaging. We as teachers need to identify and report abused children, and we must use proper discretion as we are affectionate with the children we teach.

Impact of Adolescent Suicides

The following quotation from a Phi Delta Kappa task force on adolescent suicides places the problem in the proper perspective.

DRAMATIC
INCREASE IN
SUICIDES

> Over the past 35 years there has been a steady and dramatic increase in the number of youth suicides. During this period the increase in suicides among young males has been 300%; among females, 230%. In the decade of 1970 to 1980, the suicide rate among young males between the ages of 15 and 25 increased 50%. Suicide is now the second leading cause of death among high school students, exceeded only by motor vehicle fatalities. (Garfinkel and others, 1988, p. 2)

POSSIBLE
CAUSES

Emile Durkheim, an authority on suicide, believed that the rising suicide rate was a reflection of the state of the society. Durkheim (1897) viewed the rising suicide rate in the civilized world as a function of the failure of state, church, and family to act as the forces of social integration they had been before the Industrial Revolution. If the Industrial Revolution caused such trouble, what do we have to look forward to from the high-technology revolution? On the positive side, high technology may free us to explore and deal with the causes of suicide, but it could also put a lot more stress on people and thus cause more suicides.

THE DRUG
LINK

Alcohol and drug abuse among teenagers appear to be related to teen suicides. According to Greuling and DeBlassie (1980), "based on statistics in several large cities, it is not unreasonable to assume that at least 50% of the teenagers who committed suicide were involved in moderate to heavy drinking and abusive use of dangerous drugs prior to their death" (p. 589). These authors were not suggesting, however, that drinking and drug abuse

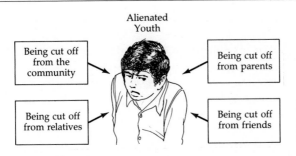

Figure 3–3 Factors contributing to the alienation of our youth.

are the causes of suicides. The key here is to find out what led to the alcohol and drug abuse.

ISOLATION

In most of the literature, alienation of youth is noted as a factor contributing to teen suicides. Being cut off from parents, friends, and relatives causes loneliness and depression. Many studies have indicated that isolated youngsters, particularly boys, are most likely to commit suicide (Greuling and DeBlassie, 1980).

LACK OF COMMITMENT TO CHILDREN

No matter what experts think the specific causes of suicide may be, many feel that individuals in society have withdrawn their commitment to children and substituted "self" as the most important priority. Spencer (1979) wrote that adults were once willing to suffer genuine material hardships to have and raise children, but now the greatest priority appears to be a country house, a larger air conditioner, a microwave oven, or a better retirement. Blame for the increase in teen suicides cannot be attributed to any one factor when all of society is somewhat the cause.

Responses to Potential Suicide Victims

HOW TO TREAT POTENTIAL VICTIMS

As a teacher, you may never have a student who commits suicide, but learning how to treat potential victims is not a waste of your time. Learning the methods of treatment used to help students with potential suicide problems will affect how you treat all members of your classes.

SCHOOL EVALUATION AND INTERVENTION TECHNIQUES

School officials, particularly guidance counselors, need to know how to evaluate potential victims. The schools must help teachers and staff understand the factors associated with childhood suicidal behavior. In addition, schools should develop effective intervention services within the school and between schools and community mental health facilities. It is also important for you as a teacher to know your own attitudes and skills in responding to a potentially suicidal child (Pfeffer, 1981).

As a teacher, you should keep in mind some general characteristics of potential suicide victims. The majority of adolescents who have attempted suicide have shown evidence of some of the following changes (McKenry, Tishler, and Christman, 1980):

SOME IMPORTANT CUES

1. A drastic change in the student's personal appearance, generally from good to bad

2. Inability to concentrate and exhibition of problems in judgment and memory

3. A dramatic shift in quality of school work

4. Changes in daily behavior and living patterns, such as extreme fatigue, boredom, stammering, and/or decreased appetite

5. Changes in social behavior such as falling asleep in class or becoming a discipline problem in class

6. Open signs of mental illness, such as delusions and hallucinations

7. A sense of overwhelming guilt and shame

8. Loss of friends (p. 43)

LOOK AT A
COMPOSITE
OF THESE
CHANGES

Some of these changes occur from time to time in many students, but a composite of these behavioral changes may fit into the overall pattern of a potential suicide victim. In addition, dramatic changes in the family or school situation can precipitate a teen suicide. Two examples are a marriage breakup or a family member's death. Certainly, boy–girl relationships are very important, and a breakup in a relationship could create a crisis. Also, "studies of adolescents who have attempted suicide indicate that school adjustment is often one of the major precipitating factors" (McKenry et al., 1980, p. 44).

Early Childhood Intervention

EARLY AC-
TION IS BEST

Some experts feel that the early childhood teachers can do a lot toward suicide prevention by identifying the child with dysfunctional coping behaviors (Seibel and Murray, 1988, p. 50). Children are known to act out because of internal frustrations or extreme turmoil within the mind. These acts may include setting fires, talking back to teachers, fighting with peers, skipping classes, or being truant. It follows then that we as educators can take action early in a child's education to break these patterns of destruction. Elementary teachers often do not have the support they need from guidance counselors; but often principals, social workers, and school nurses can assist. If we can stop these maladaptive behaviors, which are symptoms of the real problems, then we can help find lasting solutions.

Teacher and Guidance Counselor Intervention

TRUSTING
RELATION-
SHIPS

After you have identified students who may be potential suicide victims, talk to them about what you have observed about their behavior and ask them how they see themselves. Chances are that if you have developed trusting relationships with your students, they will be willing to talk to you about their problems. Because your time is limited, find out from the students if they would like to talk to a guidance counselor. After you have a student's permission to talk to a counselor on his or her behalf, do so cautiously at first, until you are sure that the student will get the care needed. Many good school guidance departments insist on a psychological evaluation of the student, and counselors are in touch with other community agencies capable of giving the proper assistance. Some schools have an organized plan for crisis intervention that can help you as a teacher at the time of crisis.

Peer Counseling

COUNSELING OTHER STUDENTS

Peer counseling can help prevent teen suicides as well as a number of related problems. All through junior and senior high school, students are trying to identify who they are in this complicated world. The value that schools and society put on academic achievement often causes them to overlook the development of the personality and self-concept. It is fairly easy for children to develop intellectually and socially when they come from families that are free of trauma, but many of today's young people are exposed to alcoholism, child abuse, divorce, poverty, drugs, and a number of other negative influences. Some schools and communities are trying to help students through peer counseling programs. In peer counseling, selected students counsel other students.

EASIER TO DISCUSS PROBLEMS

ACCEPTANCE OF FEELINGS

In a high school in Jericho, New York, the suicide of a promising senior provided the impetus for starting a peer counseling program. Peers began to lead rap sessions on such adolescent problems as personal freedom, dating, family difficulties, and interpersonal relationships. Counselors at Jericho found that students could discuss problems more freely with their peers. Peer leaders, students in senior high school, were selected from groups that had been led by adults. They were trained and assigned to small groups of ten to twelve junior high school students. After five years of peer counseling activities, a survey showed that 80% of the participants found the experience enjoyable and valuable enough to continue and 65% said that they were more aware and accepting of their own and other people's feelings. Only 26% of the participants said that they liked themselves better, but 54% of the parents felt that the peer counseling program had caused their youngsters to feel more positive about themselves. Ninety percent of the student counselors felt an enhanced self-concept as a result of their participation (Hamberg, 1980). Jericho has refined its peer counseling procedure over the years, and it represents an exemplary effort to meet student needs.

A POSITIVE PEER COUNSELING PROGRAM

At Laredo Middle School in Colorado a successful program of peer counseling has been developed at the middle school level. The school community backs the program, which is a real key to its success. The students are well trained and carefully selected to perform a number of counseling tasks. Peer counselors meet once a day in a regularly scheduled class. Their assignments include counseling at least one student regularly in a one-to-one relationship; working as aides in a preschool housed in the same building; tutoring peers; working as aides in a learning disabilities program; hosting visitors who come to the school; and introducing new students to their school, teachers, and classes. School officials conclude that the Laredo program of peer counseling works because it is educational and because it makes the school a place where students, teachers, and parents like to spend their time (Grady, 1980).

These two examples of the use of peer counselors at both the senior high and middle school levels show how students can become more involved through training and through development of leadership responsibility. Such a program requires careful planning on the part of staff, at least one capable adult leader, community support, and, most of all, administrative support and encouragement. These programs are bound to increase school spirit and support for other aspects of the academic program.

SUPPORT IS
NEEDED

Summary

In this chapter an attempt has been made to discuss those social issues that have direct impact on society. Because of the profound impact of drug and alcohol abuse on our society, this issue was given prime attention. Several exemplary drug education programs for use in the schools were described. Drugs and alcohol contribute greatly to juvenile crime and delinquency, but there are other causes as well. Factors related to parents, children, school, and community contribute to future violent behavior.

Next, some of the sources of racism in our society and racial segregation were described. As teachers and school corporations can do much to stop or block these problems in our schools, possible remedies were delineated.

Because child abuse can often be detected by teachers, the law in many states requires teachers to report instances of suspected child abuse. Details on how to recognize child abuse were included in this chapter. The tragedy of adolescent suicides as presented in this chapter can be avoided in most cases; all responsible adults, especially teachers, need to be aware of the danger signals that can be detected in a student's lifestyle.

Glossary Terms

Peer Acceptance, 75

MADD (Mothers Against Drunk Driving), 76

SADD (Students Against Drunk Driving), 76

Here's Looking at You, 2000, 77

The Quest Program, 78

Project SMART, 79

Resistance Training, 79

Role Models, 80

Group Facilitator, 80

Project Charlie, 80

Building Drug-Free Schools, 82

Questions

1. Would a conflict theory or a functional theory supporter be more likely to solve the nation's drug problem by adding to the school curriculum and increasing classroom time? Why?

2. Did Kevin Tunnell receive enough punishment by having to relive his experiences before groups of high school students? Do you support or oppose this unique solution?

3. With respect to the eight principles of drug use and prevention, which principles do you agree with and which ones do you have concerns about? Why?

4. Rate the five drug education programs described in this chapter as to how well they implement the eight basic principles.

5. A program for prevention of school dropouts in Washington, DC, was described. What are some of the merits of this program? What additional items would you suggest?

6. Some experts have suggested a fourth factor in addition to the parent, child, and school factors mentioned by Monahan—the community factor. What community factors might relate to future violent behavior? What are some possible solutions?

7. Whether it be race relations or any other tense or controversial subject, it is good to listen to your students. How can you best facilitate this in the classroom?

8. Is the magnet school or busing a better solution to school integration? Why?

9. Provide some examples in which environmental stress appeared to be the major cause of child abuse.

10. In line with Durkheim, what could the state, the church, and the family do (that they are not now doing) to influence the suicide rate and improve society?

Annotated Bibliography

1. Ballantine, J. H. (1983). *The sociology of education.* Englewood Cliffs, NJ: Prentice-Hall.

   Chapter 1 of this text desribes the contributions of Durkheim and Weber, as well as the functionalist and conflict theories.

2. Besharov, D. J. (1987). Policy guidelines for decision making in child abuse and neglect. *Children Today, 16,* F-N.

   This article reports on policy guidelines for improved reporting and investigative decision making regarding child abuse.

3. Dogoloff, T. (1988). Drug prevention programs—Strong policies, strong actions. *Curriculum Report of the National Association of Secondary School Principals, 17,* 1–6.

   This article includes eight principles schools can use to combat the drug and alcohol problem. Five successful drug education programs are described.

4. Garfinkel, B., et al. (1988). *Responding to adolescent suicide,* pp. 1–29. Bloomington, IN: Phi Delta Kappa Task Force on Adolescent Suicide, Phi Delta Kappa Education Foundation.

   This publication is from the task force on adolescent suicide established in 1987 by Phi Delta Kappa. Educators can play an important role when suicide occurs; thus, the school's response is crucial.

5. Hawley, W. D. (1983). Achieving quality integrated education—with or without federal help. *Phi Delta Kappan, 64,* 335–336.

    Dr. Hawley has written extensively on desegregation. This article is part of a larger paper entitled, "Effective Educational Strategies for Desegregated Schools." Practical commonsense suggestions are offered that are still important considerations for achieving quality integrated education.

6. Pfeifer, Jerilyn K. (1986). *Teenage suicide: What can the schools do?* Fastback No. 234. Bloomington, IN: Phi Delta Kappa Educational Foundation.

    Adolescent suicide is approaching an epidemic stage and this fastback examines possible factors leading to the decision to commit suicide. It shows how parents and teachers can help.

7. Subcommittee on Juvenile Justice of the Committee on the Constitution, U.S. Senate (Oct. 22, 1981). *Oversight hearing to fashion programs to remove the juvenile from a crime cycle,* Serial No. j-97-70.

    A copy of this document would be useful to those who wish to delve more deeply into problems of the juvenile crime offender. The object of this hearing and study was to find ways to remove the potential juvenile offender from the crime cycle.

OBJECTIVES

After reading Chapter 4, the student will:

- Be aware of some of the changing family needs and their impact upon the schools

- Be able to describe the impact of poverty upon our society and our schools

- Be able to list some measures the teacher can use to counter the negative impact of the media upon children

- Be able to record some ways a teacher can be fair in the treatment of both sexes in classes.

- Be cognizant of the culturally and ethnically diverse society in which we live and what implications this has for the teacher

Social Problems and the School's Responses: Indirect-Impact Issues

Introduction

In Chapter 4, issues with more of an indirect impact upon the schools, but nevertheless substantial influence, are discussed. Family life in the United States is difficult to describe, but as we know, many of our families are dysfunctional. Also, the economic situation in the United States is not always fair to all citizens, and this problem is examined.

The media are probably more influential than most of us are aware of, and some important suggestions on how to cope with their influence are offered. Women in our culture have not been treated fairly and we as educators must be more aware of this inequity and do what we can to eliminate the problem.

Multicultural awareness is also an important indirect issue that warrants substantial consideration on the part of all teachers. Some specific suggestions are made on how teachers can improve their teaching by including other cultures in the curriculum.

Impact of Family Life in America

FAMILY LIFE NOT AS GOOD

Family life in America is far different than it was when the authors of this textbook were young, when intact families composed of Mom and Dad and two children were more the norm. Throughout the history of the human race there have always been **dysfunctional families,** but in the last few years statistics tell us that things at home are not as good as they once were in the United States.

Arthur J. Norton, who is the Assistant Chief, Population Division, U.S. Bureau of the Census, gives us the following insights on trends in American family life:

TRENDS IN FAMILY LIFE

- In the last decade the labor force participation rate for women with very young children (under three years old) has increased from one third to one half.

- Parents are moving away from using care in the child's home and care in another private home to group care arrangements like day-care centers and nursery schools.

- In the past decade the age for the first marriage has risen from 23.1 to 25.7 and this has meant a drop in family size. Women are currently bearing children at a rate of slightly under two per woman.

- The divorce rate, currently about one of every two marriages, may drop in the future. Still the United States has the highest reported divorce rate in the world.

- About 43 percent of all one-parent families in 1986 were maintained by a divorced parent.

- Nine of every 10 single-parent families in the United States are mother–child(ren) families. This has not changed in 30 years. These families suffer more deprivation than other families.

- Sixteen percent of all married couple families today involve step situations.

- One of every five of the seven million single-parent families is maintained by a never-married woman. (Norton, 1987, pp. 6–9)

All of the situations presented by Norton describe changes taking place in our family structure. Not all of these are negative forces, but most, if not all, present challenges to society in general and to parents in particular. As educators, we are most interested in children and how they fare in the schools.

Because of how the family structure is changing in the United States, one might wonder what type of family organization or pattern is really the INTACT FAM- best. Not surprisingly, Nunn and Parish (1982) found that children who ILIES fared the best in their personal, family, and school adjustment came from

Figure 4–1   Eight trends in American family life.

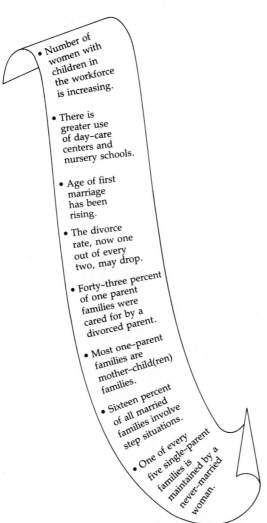

- Number of women with children in the workforce is increasing.

- There is greater use of day–care centers and nursery schools.

- Age of first marriage has been rising.

- The divorce rate, now one out of every two, may drop.

- Forty-three percent of one parent families were cared for by a divorced parent.

- Most one–parent families are mother–child(ren) families.

- Sixteen percent of all married families involve step situations.

- One of every five single-parent families is maintained by a never-married woman.

intact families; the next best were children from families in which the fathers had died; and the least well adjusted were children from homes broken by divorce. All options were not measured by the Nunn and Parish study, but the results were based heavily on the child's self-concept, anxiety level, and adjustment to home and school.

In this section, we are obviously more concerned about families with children, as they are the ones that the schools must work with in the educational process. The family with children has a tremendous influence on educational practice through the attitudes and values the family instills in its children toward education, teachers, and life in general.

When one of the authors asked one of his college classes to describe a dysfunctional family they know, one student related the following:

A DYSFUNC-
TIONAL FAM-
ILY

In my life's experience a dysfunctional family I know well became troubled early. After only two years the marriage ended in divorce, and the mother was pregnant with her second child. She moved back to her mother's home and was severely criticized by her own three sisters. Her ex-husband frequently came by to see her and his daughter and infant son, but he was usually extremely intoxicated and became violent during his visits. For about six years or so, both grandparents helped raise the children, then their grandfather died.

The mother was very bitter about her life's situation, but kept a full-time job to which she commuted over an hour a day. She also kept late hours on the weekends with gentlemen friends which her children were aware of at the time.

After fifteen years, the grandmother died, and the mother took her two teenagers and moved to a trailer park. Through these years both of the children struggled in school, and the son was now thought to be "slow."

A few more years passed, and the daughter dropped out of college only a few hours short of a bachelor's degree. Her self-esteem and self-confidence were so low she could not deal with the expectations and pressures of college.

The mother finally remarried about four years after her daughter dropped out of college. The mother refused to believe that the daughter had any problems that are remotely as severe as her own have been.

To date both children have had very little emotional support in their lives. Both are barely supporting themselves, but they live together in a rent-free house owned by their mother. Their father died about a year ago from a liver disease. The daughter has not taken his death very well. The son seems uncaring and bitter.

Neither of the children have very good interpersonal skills and neither of them dates. Both children have compulsive tendencies: the girl for food and the boy for alcohol. (R. J. McAtee)

As you can tell from this description of a classic dysfunctional family, the cause of the dysfunction was probably the father's alcoholism. Attending school was difficult for both of these students because of this huge family distraction. These children became a burden to their family, to themselves, and to society because of their lack of productivity. The ques-

INTERVEN-
TION?

tion remains: How much should society and the schools intervene in students' personal lives to improve their futures? Of course, first the students must be willing to accept some help.

OURSELVES
COMPARED
TO THE
THIRD
WORLD

Poor and disadvantaged families living in crowded urban areas of our country may need much assistance from the public schools. The government must find ways to help the poor, economically and educationally, or eventually this country may face some of the same problems faced by other countries that have no organized system to help the disadvantaged citizens improve their lot in society. The poor in India and other Third World countries travel the streets begging for money, living wherever they can. Our growing numbers of homeless people in the United States have some advantages over Third World people in that there is an organized system to take care of them, but often they are out of touch with the system. If the children of economically and socially disadvantaged citizens are to move up the socioeconomic ladder, they must get vocational assistance along with basic assistance for food, housing, and medical care; and these children must be given the opportunity to secure a good education. People who have the good life in America want the best for their own children; yet, when asked to pay more taxes for the poor and oppressed, they often do not see these people as being their problem. Where are we in America in reaching the goal of dignity for all people?

Teenage Pregnancy

ONE MILLION
PER YEAR!

Another problem with huge educational implications is the increasing number of teenage pregnancies, which is related to two phenomena: the first is a dramatic shift in the age of menarche in young girls from a mean age of 14.2 in 1900 to a mean age of 11.8 today; the second is the steady increase in the number of sexually active young people (Bell, Casto, and Daniels, 1983). Some experts say that the number of teenage pregnancies may now be around one million per year.

ALIENATION

Because most of these births occur to women in the lower socioeconomic strata, where there is a lack of proper nutrition or medical care, these children start life in a handicapped position. The mothers themselves are still adolescents and have not completed their own education. More often than not, because unmarried teen mothers find themselves alienated from the mainstream of society, they do not get all the help they need, and they often receive very little or no help from their families.

PRENATAL
CARE ESSEN-
TIAL

Prenatal care is essential during the first trimester of a pregnancy. Some estimates indicate that only 20% of girls under the age of 15 receive any prenatal care. Low-birth-weight babies are generally the result of poor or no prenatal care, and low birth weight contributes to the higher infant morality rates among teens. Poverty influences this whole process; thus, the lack of care in low-income areas influences the number of teen pregnancies, low birth weight, and infant mortality.

The infant mortality rate is much lower in the United States, Europe, and the Soviet Union than in other regions of the world, but this does not diminish the fact that every child lost is a tragic statistic. See Figure 4–2 for a comparison of infant mortality rates in different regions of the world.

Some estimates indicate that only 20% of the girls under the age of fifteen receive any prenatal care.

(Photo used by permission of the Indianapolis Children's Museum.)

A UTAH
MODEL
     Utah has initiated an intervention program to help a few young mothers that could serve as a model for other states. This program helps both the mothers and the children, taking advantage of materials from Parent Effectiveness Training and Head Start. So far, the results from the program indicate that its graduates have had significantly higher employment rates, less dependence on **AFDC (Aid to Families with Dependent Children)** and fewer referrals for child abuse (Bell et al., 1983, p. 172). As the trend toward increased teen pregnancies continues, programs of this type will be needed to improve opportunities for the next generation of children.

Response to Changing Family Needs

Dysfunctional families have many needs. The authors have chosen to highlight several innovations and/or educational plans and demonstrate how they can help solve dysfunctional families' problems.

Parenting

Formal schooling in America today includes much training that in earlier times might not have been considered in the curriculum; some of these new courses have been added as a result of changing family life. Schools commonly offer courses in sex education, drug and alcohol abuse, food and nutrition, and other similar areas. The newest course may be parenting, whose purpose is to help young people be better parents. Schools in Tacoma,

NEWEST
COURSE

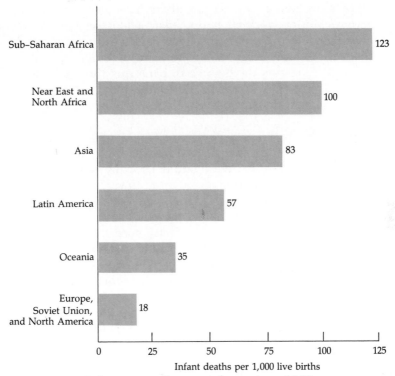

Figure 4–2   Infant mortality rates by region: 1985.

(SOURCE: U.S. Department of Commerce, Bureau of the Census.)

Washington, are in their fifth year of a parenting program that has resulted in better communication between adults and teenagers about child rearing. The Tacoma program has a three-part structure: traditional academic instruction in child development, small group discussions with parents from the community, and firsthand experience in a nursery located at the high school (Brown, 1980). Many sex education courses include units on parenting; therefore, it is evident that schools, as they reflect society's needs in their curriculum, are not overlooking the parenting aspect of family life. However, only a small percentage of high school students take these elective parenting courses.

ONE-PARENT   One-parent families are growing in America. In 1980, 18% of the nation's
FAMILIES   schoolchildren were living with one parent (Brown, 1980). In a study of one-parent families, Brown found that they accounted for 100% of the expulsions, 42% of the dropouts, 39% of the discipline problems, and only 9% of high academic achievement when compared with two-parent families and no-parent families (foster families and relatives). One-parent families and no-parent families represented only 25% of the total group, and so they were disproportionately represented in the negative statistics. Some concrete suggestions made at the conclusion of the study were that schools

make provisions for single parents to have access to school personnel and activities after working hours, that school services be revised to better accommodate the unique needs of children from one-parent families, and that schools' adult education programs assume a major role in providing

SCHOOLS A
PLACE FOR
HELP

effective programs in the area of parenting (Brown, 1980). Whether composed of one or two parents living together or separately, many families need help, and the schools are a logical place for families to get this help.

Head Start

One government program, **Head Start,** which has much meaning to poor families, is still intact, but a strong effort by advocates is required to keep

EARLY STIM-
ULATION

it alive. Early stimulation of the mind toward learning is just as important for poor children as it is for mainstream Americans. Unfortunately, 80% of the American children eligible for Head Start will never see a Head Start center (Edelman, 1983). If the nation's poor children were better fed, better cared for, and better educated, we could save money. Edelman (1983) of the

ANTIWEL-
FARE AND
ANTIDEPEN-
DENCY

Children's Defense Fund wrote, "Child care is an antiwelfare and antidependency measure, because it will help reduce federal spending on income transfers more than any other program" (p. 26). The Bush Administration recommended a substantial increase in the Head Start budget in 1989, and Congress was considering increased funding for child care.

Egalitarian Marriage

SHARE
EQUALLY

The **egalitarian marriage,** in which all roles in the family are shared equally by the husband and the wife, is a reality for a few, and may increase in future years. Changing patterns in the family, for example, when the wife works outside the home as much as the husband, are common today for more than half of the married women in the United States (Smith and Reid, 1982). By egalitarian marriage, we refer not to the wife who has a part-time job or a job that supplements the husband's income, but to one who is an equal partner in the breadwinning role. Sharing of duties around the home tends to be along the lines of traditional roles for men and women, but it is predicted that this pattern will change. Studies have indicated that fathers have shown just as much competence in taking care of newborn infants as mothers. Implications for schools include the development of courses in family life that teach examples for living in family patterns other than the traditional nuclear family.

The Whole Child Initiative

One idea appears to be more of a solution-type program to help children. **The Whole Child Initiative (WCI)** brings people and resources together to benefit children and youth. These people include parents, teachers, and community members who have a vision of excellence and a place for realizing the vision. The Minnesota Department of Education formed a partnership with the First Bank System of Minneapolis and the Center for Youth Development and Research at the University of Minnesota to orga-

OTHERS CAN
HELP

nize, provide resources, and evaluate programs. Specific centers in Minnesota created programs to make people responsible, within limits, for shaping the conditions under which they live, work, learn, play, and otherwise spend their time (Freidmann, 1987). One of the outcomes resulted in matching children who were willing to work with community people, especially senior citizens, who needed work done. The program, called "Lean on Me," emphasized building positive relationships among youths and developing peer support networks. By the year 2000, it is hoped that several hundred communities will be involved in the WCI.

The Latchkey Child

As you probably know, **latchkey children** let themselves out and in with their own keys. When they return home from school, no adult is present to supervise them. This is not only a lonely time for the child, but generally a nonproductive time as well. As more and more families work, after-school programs are becoming a national need. In a 1984 survey conducted by *Woman's Day* and the Wellesley College Center for Research on Women, 63% of the respondents said that public schools should provide after-school child care (Seligson, 1986, p. 638). Schools are natural places for this activity, as children are often dropped off before 8:00 AM and they have no place to go after school.

> Schools that begin to offer child care for school-age children recognize the value of being "open" systems, of modifying and expanding their institutional boundaries to incorporate new services for their clientele. The overriding reason that schools become involved in the provision of child care is that it is in the best interests of both the school and the community. (Seligson, 1986, p. 638)

SCHOOL-
BASED PRO-
GRAMS

Many school-based programs are sponsored by the local YMCA, day care centers, or some social service agency. School-based child care seems to be an answer to the needs of the latchkey child. According to Seligson (1986), "after-school child care poses a number of problems for schools, but the benefits can be significant" (Seligson, 1986, p. 637). Changes in family life in America are real, and this is another way schools are responding to this impact.

Childbearing as "Symptom of Alienation"

In the following excerpt, Leon Dash, a reporter for the Washington Post, suggests that the young mothers he interviewed became pregnant as a response to their isolation from mainstream society:

> In the end, I discovered that not a single one had become pregnant out of ignorance or by accident.
> Some of the people I interviewed were couples. Some were single parents. Some were people living on welfare stipends. Some were working people living on what little they had earned each day. One was an adolescent mother who had been abandoned by her family. What they all shared was poverty and a long legacy of racial oppression.

LEGACY OF
RACIAL
OPPRESSION

POVERTY IS
THE DOMI-
NANT FAC-
TOR

I had believed, even before we moved in, that the patterns of alienation acted out in Washington Highlands every day parallel the behavior patterns of innumerable other poor Americans. Their poverty is the dominant factor of their lives. Their poverty produces predictable responses and predictable choices.

LAYERS OF
ALIENATION

I also knew that among black Americans I would find another dimension of antagonism. Our American experience has added layers of alienation, starting three and a half centuries ago with slavery, followed by a demure system of ethnic oppression, then de facto discrimination, and rejection at every level of the larger, white society.

SOCIAL
CLASS IS A
FACTOR

I do not believe that any black American, even one born into comfortable levels of economic well-being or privilege, has completely escaped the feeling of alienation. Blacks of different income groups and of varying economic mobility handle the alienation differently, more because one's class often governs one's behavior and outlook, but all blacks can readily agree on the source of the alienation.

REJECTION
OF A VALUE
SYSTEM

In Washington Highlands, one of the many black-adolescent symptoms of alienation from mainstream America is having a child, a rejection of the larger society's value system regarding what is rational and irrational behavior. The patterns of child-bearing were laid down long before the children of Washington Highlands were born. The patterns are viewed by many of them as rational responses to human needs, requirements that cannot be met by other means.*

Schools and Teen Pregnancies

BIRTH CON-
TROL INFOR-
MATION

Schools have addressed the teen pregnancy problem by disseminating birth control information, installing school-based clinics, and providing some flexibility for pregnant and young mothers to go to school. Birth control information may be given to young people in health classes and in sex education programs. Ideally, all of our children need ongoing sex education as they mature and become acquainted with what is happening to their bodies. Sex education classes of any kind have not been added to the school curriculum with the greatest of ease. In fact, it has been a battle against traditional forces.

NOT JUST
FOR SENIORS

One instructor known to the authors has a well-established class that includes marriage, parenting, and sex information for seniors. The course is one of the most popular programs in this suburban school, but the disadvantage is that only seniors can take this elective course.

INVOLVE-
MENT OF
PARENTS

There is no doubt in the mind of most educators that information on sexuality needs to be a part of the school's curriculum. Also, an integral part of such a sex information program is the involvement of parents so that they can support the school in this important task.

With all the talk about sex information for children, however, there is still another factor that needs to be addressed. Children living in poverty may not care about sex information or birth control as much as their own identity. Leon Dash (1989, p. 22) had assumed that teen pregnancies were

---

* Excerpted from *When Children Want Children: The Urban Crisis of Teenage Childbearing* by Leon Dash. Copyright © 1989 by Leon Dash. Reprinted by permission of William Morrow and Company Inc. Page 22.

due to ignorance about birth control methods, adolescent reproductive capabilities, and the cynical manipulation by boys, but he learned he was wrong on all counts. "In time," he writes, "it became clear that for many girls in the poverty-stricken community of Washington Highlands, a baby is a tangible achievement in an otherwise dreary and empty future" (Dash, 1989, p. 22).

Dash also found that in his direct experience the desire for more welfare was not a motivating factor because the girls were aware that the welfare checks would not cover their expenses (p. 22). One must draw the conclusion that poverty and racial prejudice are the significant contributing factors to teen pregnancies in the black ghetto. Schools can help some through education and counseling, but poverty and prejudice from the larger society must abate before the ultimate solution can be achieved.

PARENTS AS AN INTE-GRAL PART

As we move into the 1990s and beyond, educators should still be guided by one single purpose: to do what is best for the students who come to them. Parents are an integral part of the educational process and ought to be treated as such. If either the teachers or the parents fail in the coeducator's role, society will ultimately lose. Public criticism of schools is most often directed toward teachers and administrators, but parents have failed in their educational role at least equally. Educators often blame poor family situations for the students they receive, and parents blame the schools for the poor education their children receive, when both should be working together for the good of the children.

Impact of the Economic System and the Poverty Cycle

The system of capitalism and free enterprise brings with it both pluses and minuses. On the plus side, capitalism allows Americans to invest money in an endless variety of enterprises to meet the needs of society. If the entrepreneurs have been careful in their investments, they make a profit,

DEVELOPING CYCLE

and they may decide to expand their businesses. As long as the economy is in a developing cycle, the gross national product (GNP) will increase, and most citizens will be employed. On the minus side, there will be down

DOWN CYCLE

cycles in the economy when a certain percentage of the population will not be able to work. People in lower socioeconomic strata find it difficult to make a living during a developing cycle and find life grim in down cycles.

LAND OF OP-PORTUNITY

America is a land of opportunity where one can rise in social and economic status; the system also allows one to fail in all aspects. Many Americans feel good about their country because in the United States there are not as many serious economic problems and because there are fewer poor people than in most countries of the world. Some well-meaning people say that the poor will always be with us; having said this, they feel released from caring about the poor in our country. The material goods or rewards that one can attain in America are tremendous, and these, too, tend to insulate us from dealing with the poor and the social problems that are part of poverty. Because they have become widespread, crime and drug problems have tended to excite the average citizen more than in the past. Keeshan (1983), known popularly as Captain Kangaroo, placed our society's problems in perspective:

20% OF OUR CHILDREN IN POVERTY

> Forty percent of our preschoolers are not immunized against polio. How quickly we forget. Incredible. Twenty percent of our childrn live in poverty. Many of our children go to bed hungry, many more go to bed ill-nourished. Many go to bed in detention centers and jails. Incredible. Why do we allow this to happen in the wealthiest, most technologically advanced nation in the world? Incredible. (p. 55)

Most of us save money, perhaps give a little to charity, and fight to keep all the money we can from going into unnecessary taxes. Some change agents in our society are constantly searching for new and better ways to serve the poor. A few people design programs that would lead to solutions, but many, mostly through ignorance, are content to treat the symptoms of poverty. This treatment of the symptoms does make a few people feel better, but no solution is ever reached.

SYMPTOMS OF POVERTY

A SENSE OF DIGNITY

Our welfare system, with its food stamps and unemployment payments, does not appear to give people a sense of dignity; instead, it may lead to idleness and purposeless behavior. The welfare system operates on the premise that feeding a hungry stomach will solve the poverty problem, but it may only treat the symptoms. Parents who operate under this welfare system influence children who attend our schools. The solution-type thinkers would say that whatever the cost to our economy, we must do something to give all people a sense of dignity in our economic system. It appears that a solution must be found that involves putting more people in the work-force—ultimately, all people who want to work. Including most Americans in the regular work force would possibly do more to solve educational problems than would most proposed and current in-service educational solutions.

WEALTH IN THE HANDS OF A FEW?

The authors are not suggesting that if the United States abandoned capitalism and substituted socialism in its place, society would be any better. We in the United States must maintain our free enterprise system, but we also need to put limits on the system so that more of the wealth does not end up in fewer hands.

EDUCA-TIONAL IM-PLICATIONS

Teachers need to be aware of the economics of our society so that they can better understand its educational implications. Teachers are public servants who are trying their best to help students become productive citizens, but teachers are also citizens who have a stake in ensuring the continued existence of our country. Informed citizens and teachers may need to recognize that neither a completely free enterprise system nor a nonproductive welfare system will work. Perhaps all concerned citizens will need to work together to modify the system before it is too late. Some have said that neither the idle rich nor the idle poor are good for our public schools or for America's future.

Responses to the Impact of Our Economic System

UNIQUE
CHANGES

Schools are responding to the impact of our economic system in various ways. Some school systems change very little; they hold on to a very traditional curriculum that serves the interests of the children best who are high achievers and on the college track. Some unique changes are taking place, however, largely in response to our economic system, and these are described in the following pages.

The Alternative School Movement: A Response to Dropping Out

A SEARCH
FOR ALTER-
NATIVES

Among the specific school changes taking place today is the **alternative school movement.** This movement was begun to try to meet the needs of more of our student population. One of the target groups receiving aid through an alternative school are children from low-income families who drop out of school. In earlier days, it was easy for young people who dropped out of schools to be absorbed into the workforce, either on the farms or in the factories. As the industrial age became increasingly complex, and society became more troubled, students without a high school diploma found it increasingly difficult to find work. In the 1960s, the existence of so many dropouts from the public schools and the increased demands of business and industry caused school systems to search for alternatives.

HARLEM
PREP

PARKWAY
PROGRAM

Many innovations were tried within traditional schools in the 1960s and the early 1970s, and after evaluation, the general conclusion was that none made a significant difference (Raywid, 1981). Then, in 1974, David Tyack wrote an interpretive history of American education that led many to question whether there is one best way to conduct school, that is, a single best set of aims for all, an ideal curriculum, and one best way to organize and administer schools and to prepare teachers. Tyack encouraged the promotion of alternative schools. Harlem Prep came into being in 1967, and Philadelphia's Parkway Program started in 1968. These two alternative schools popularized the movement. Money from the Ford, Carnegie, and Rockefeller Foundations supported the experimental programs. Today, more than 10,000 alternative schools can be found in 80% of the nation's larger school districts.

HUMANIZE
SCHOOLS

Alternative schools originally set out to humanize education, to make schools more relevant, and thus to reduce the school dropout rate. Now, in the 1990s, alternative schools or programs are looked on as a way to effect reform in education and perhaps to humanize the entire system; thus, the alternative schools of the 1980s and 1990s are far different from those that inspired the movement in the 1960s.

ERA OF VARI-
ETY

Many movements or innovations in education last only a short time, but the alternative school movement appears to be long-lasting. Educational movements of the past seem to have had an either/or outlook; however, the 1980s and 1990s are an era of variety, and alternative schools fit this variety. How long the alternative school movement will remain with us is

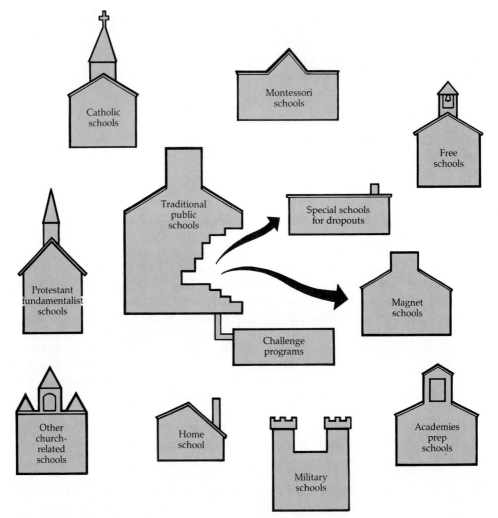

Alternative education.

not as important as the problems it may help to solve in the meantime and the legacy it will leave after its demise. Currently, evaluations show that alternative education is an extraordinarily effective solution to the problems of school vandalism and violence, high truancy, and high dropout rate (Raywid, 1981). The following quotation from Kammann (1972) is an analogy that illustrates how school systems have been doing business, and one can infer how the use of alternative schools may put selecting a school on the same basis as selecting the family doctor:

ARBITRARY
SCHOOL AS-
SIGNMENTS

Imagine a town where every family is assigned arbitrarily to one local doctor by a ruling of the board of health. Imagine that the board of health assigns families only on the basis of the shortest distance from the home to the doctor's office. Imagine, finally, that when a family complains that the assigned doctor is not helping one of its ailing members, the board of health replies: "Sorry, no exceptions to doctor assignments."

If this sounds like a totalitarian nightmare, it also is a description of the way school boards assign children to schools and teachers. (p. 37)

Example of an Alternative School

EDUCATING
SCHOOL
DROPOUTS

In Denver, the Metropolitan Youth Education Center was created to educate school dropouts. To be eligible students must be between the ages of sixteen and twenty-five, and they must have dropped out of school at least six months previously. The center's basic goal is to get students back into the mainstream of education. The curriculum focuses on basic skills, the academic requirements for a high school diploma, and the preparation necessary to pass the **General Educational Development (GED) test.** The center issues no diplomas; instead, records of credits earned are sent to the schools that the students last attended, which issue the diplomas, avoiding the permanent stigma of dropping out. Although most of the students who attend the center are much like students at regular high schools as far as intelligence and family backgrounds are concerned, they do have a higher-than-average incidence of personal problems (Jacques, 1982).

Helping the Bottom Half

A study by the William T. Grant Foundation calls attention to the approximately 20 million Americans between the ages of sixteen and twenty-four who are not likely to go on to college (Halperin and others, 1988, p. 409). Some of these millions are making it by working more than one job, living with parents, delaying marriage and family, and at the same time searching for extra training that can advance their careers. These young people are as

LARGE BUT
RATHER SI-
LENT

visible as those that are involved in crime or are considered "troubled and irresponsible" by the media and other people.

The Grant Foundation study has several suggestions for schools to improve services to the bottom half (Figure 4–3). Schools can help students bridge the gap between school and work in the following ways:

SUGGES-
TIONS

1. Being more flexible about allowing people over 18 to return to high school
2. Using monitored work experience which exposes students to adult supervisors and models in the workplace, and relating their academic learning to the world of work
3. Encouraging community and neighborhood service
4. Offering hands-on experience through vocational education
5. Making students aware of career information through counseling
6. Utilizing school volunteers for tutoring and realizing that they will also serve as friends and mentors to expand students' career horizons (Halperin, 1988, p. 412)

COMMIT-
MENT TO
ALL GROUPS

All of these suggestions are good ones, but we educators must ensure that these programs and others are offered, that quality is controlled, and

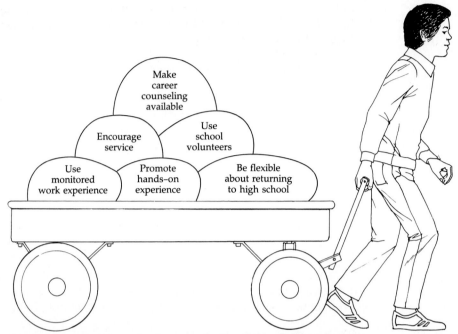

Figure 4–3   Helping the bottom half of the children between ages sixteen and twenty-four.

that funding is adequate. Our true and steadfast commitment to the non–collegebound student is as important as our commitment to college-bound students.

The Urban School Response

Urban schools are largely inhabited by poor black and Hispanic students and are generally filled with doom and gloom. Most of the teachers and students have low expectations about what is supposed to happen in these places called schools:

FILLED WITH
DOOM AND
GLOOM

> In one urban high school, where the dimly lit corridors and the shabbiness of the building belied its relative newness, there was no cheerleading squad, the band was shrinking from a shortage of members, and the student newspaper had stopped publishing for lack of money. "There is virtually no enthusiasm among the students," said one young woman, an honors student who had found that being chosen editor of the school newspaper was an empty honor. "The kids need incentives to keep them from being down on themselves." (Maeroff, 1988, p. 635)

A NATIONAL
DISGRACE

Schools like this one, and there are many of them, are a national disgrace. If we as a nation really want to help the poor and the underprivileged, we must improve these schools as soon as possible!

MARVA COL-
LINS

The story of Marva Collins from the inner city of Chicago is truly an urban school success story. She has obtained outstanding results in her school because of her gifted teaching ability. She is positive, determined, and caring all at the same time. The children have no choice but to learn and enlarge upon their own expectations. Marva has said many things that deserve to be quoted, and here is one:

ANY CHILD
CAN LEARN

> Adults should take a positive approach with children. The most important thing we can do as parents and teachers is build a child's self-confidence. Any child can learn if he or she has not already been taught too thoroughly that learning is impossible. Children need reassurance and encouragement. They have to be told that it is all right to make mistakes because mistakes are part of learning. I tell my students: "If you knew everything there is to know, then you wouldn't have to be in school." (Tarcher, 1982, p. 42)

If Marva can do such a wonderful job in Chicago, there is hope that others will follow.

Marva Collins' School is an example of an urban success story in education.

(Photo used by permission of the Indianapolis Children's Museum.)

SMALLER
GROUPS

Some of the very best thinkers of our time say that we must deal with smaller groups in urban schools and personalize our teaching much more. We must offer a much more supportive environment for these students to bolster their confidence (Sizer, as cited by Maeroff, 1988, p. 638). Theodore Sizer says that urban high schools must embrace the philosophy that "less is more." The scope of the curriculum should be reduced and focused on a more limited body of material that can be taught in depth—adapted to individual needs along the way—so that it is better understood and serves as a possible base for widening interest (p. 638).

A MUST IN-
VESTMENT

All of this "smaller" talk is educationally sound, but it will take much more money and very enlightened leadership to make it happen. It is an investment that we as a country must make if we are to become a truly gentler nation.

A SAFETY
NET

Schools have responded to our economy that inevitably treats some people better than others by creating alternative schools for dropouts, by addressing the needs of the non–college bound, and by demonstrating success in the urban schools with magnet schools and other programs such as the one developed by Marva Collins. It is evident that a safety net is in place, but it has some holes. Improving our schools and instituting some job training or vocational programs are both ultimately solution-type responses, but if they remain minimal and poorly funded, they will treat only the symptoms of our economic problems.

U.S. Government Programs

JOB TRAIN-
ING PART-
NERSHIP

Historically, since the New Deal programs of the Franklin Roosevelt administration in the 1930s, the federal government has helped the poor and disadvantaged by providing jobs and/or job training for those in need. Currently, the **Job Training Partnership Act of 1982 (JTPA)**, among other things, provides a system of block grants to states to support local training and employment programs for the economically disadvantaged. Close to 94% of those receiving help are considered economically disadvantaged.

THE JOB
CORPS

Another government program, the **Job Corps**, has 107 residential centers in 43 states that provide basic education, vocational training, counseling, and health care to help disadvantaged young men and women prepare for jobs and responsible citizenship (U.S. Department of Labor, p. 103). Since 1965 when the program began, more than 800,000 young people between the ages of sixteen and twenty-one have been helped. The basic education provided includes reading, mathematics, social studies, and preparation for the GED high school equivalency examination. Besides the academic and the vocational training, they also receive instruction in general living skills, such as hygiene and grooming, getting along in the world of work, and constructive use of leisure time (p. 103).

POTENTIAL IS
GOOD

Despite their flaws, these two government-sponsored programs are in place, and many of our nation's young people have been given the opportunity to attain economic self-sufficiency. If individuals work hard and take the training seriously, the program can become a real **"safety net"**, saving them from an otherwise deprived and dependent life. The savings in dollars is no doubt in the billions; thus, it is very important that we maintain these "safety nets."

The schools are responding in many ways to our economic system. Good school systems, teachers, and administrators are changing constantly to

SOME NEEDS
ARE NOT
MET

meet needs that arise from our economic system. Still, the budgets of school corporations are not flexible enough to suit the needs of all people, and the needs of the poor are often not met at all.

Impact of the Communications Media

Mass media is the term commonly used to refer to communication by television, radio, newspaper, magazines, and the film industry. No doubt, television has the greatest influence of all the mass media. Television is

A BABYSIT-
TER?

often used as a babysitter by parents who do not care to be bothered with their children. Captain Kangaroo (Keeshan, 1983) was often told that he was the parent's best friend, the very best babysitter. Because much of television programming is aimed toward adult audiences, most of the programs that children watch are adult oriented. The fact is that children do watch a lot of TV, and the influence of TV programming on their lives is tremendous (Figure 4–4). The authors do not suggest that the government

PARENTAL
ROLE

completely regulate the television industry; our wish is that parents become more aware of what their role should be and that television production become more responsive to the child audience.

The **National Institute of Mental Health (NIMH)** produced a report in 1971 for the U.S. Surgeon General entitled *Television and Growing Up:*

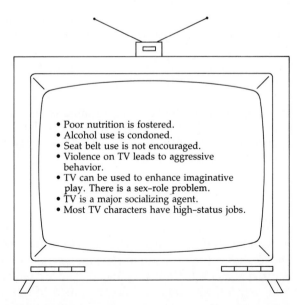

• Poor nutrition is fostered.
• Alcohol use is condoned.
• Seat belt use is not encouraged.
• Violence on TV leads to aggressive behavior.
• TV can be used to enhance imaginative play. There is a sex-role problem.
• TV is a major socializing agent.
• Most TV characters have high-status jobs.

Figure 4–4 What is TV doing for/against our children?

TELEVISION
AND BEHAV-
IOR

The Impact of Television Violence. Ten years later, the NIMH published an undated report, *Television and Behavior: Ten Years of Scientific Progress and Implications for the Eighties.* Some findings in this latest report are highlighted here:

1. Much of television's content seems to foster poor nutrition, especially in commercials for sweets and snack foods. The fact is that children who watch a lot of television have poorer nutritional habits than children who do not watch as much.

2. Alcohol consumption is common on TV, and it is condoned as a regular social practice.

3. When people drive cars on television, they do not wear seat belts. Correlational studies suggest that people's attitudes are influenced by these portrayals.

4. After ten more years, the consensus among most of the research community is that violence on television does lead to aggressive behavior by children and teenagers who watch the programs. Not all children become aggressive, of course, but the correlations between violence and aggression are positive.

5. Television can be used to enhance children's imaginative play if an adult watches with the child and interprets what is happening.

HIGHLIGHTS
OF STUDY

6. Women on television are generally stereotyped more as passive and feminine and men as strong and masculine.

7. About 10 percent of the television characters are **black,** but few are **Hispanics, Native Americans,** or **Asian Americans**.

8. Television characters usually have higher status jobs than average people in real life. Few characters are blue-collar workers.

9. In general, researchers seem to agree that television has become a major socializing agent of American children.

10. People who are heavy viewers of television are more apt to think the world is violent than are light viewers. They also trust other people less and believe that the world is a "mean and scary" place.

11. Television, according to some observers, reinforces the status quo and contributes to a homogenization of society and a promotion of middle-class values.

12. Television broadcasters of religious services bring religion to those who cannot get out, but they also may reduce attendance at churches and, thus, opportunities for social interactions. (U.S. Department of Health and Human Services, 1982, pp. 5–8)

SUBTLE CON-
TROL

Television has a tremendous impact on American society. It subtly controls much of our thinking and actions. The NIMH report conservatively estimated that during an average day's viewing, a child would see 10 episodes involving drinking, adding up to about 3000 episodes per year. The effect of this type of repeated modeling on young children is very powerful. No wonder we have a drinking problem among our teenagers! Also, if most characters are portrayed as middle class or above, no wonder many children and adults who are not middle class are disillusioned in life as a result of

Multicultural Education

Students now benefit from bilingual education programs in many of our schools.

Children are made more secure in the learning process when their native cultures and languages are not forgotten.

The goal of most successful bilingual programs is to move students into the mainstream language as soon as possible, while at the same time enriching them in their native language and culture.

One of the long-term benefits of bilingual and multicultural programs is the assimilation of adults and their families into the everyday world of their new culture.

Continued appreciation of heritage, culture, and language is another long-term goal of bilingual–multicultural education.

The ultimate goal in the United States is to have children of all races and cultures cognizant of their own background and culture, yet also become contributing citizens of their new culture.

the influence of the media. Some racial groups are almost entirely left out, and this omission does not represent the **pluralism** that is truly America.

DEREGULA-
TION

Deregulation of the broadcasting industry began soon after the Reagan administration took office. Deregulation has changed the way toy manufacturers and the television industry do business. According to Paige and Levin, "TV programming since deregulation has resulted from the industry's drive to increase sales and profits—not from a desire to promote what is best for children" (Carlsson-Paige and Levin, 1989, p. 32). These same authors say that a child's natural play is being disrupted by single-purpose toys that lock kids into repeating a narrow range of actions (p. 32). These comments are not the result of a scientific study, but simply the words of two educators who plead for some regulation to protect our children.

Advertisers as well as television executives share the problems that society faces in relation to TV. According to one prominent cereal company president (Mason, 1979),

MAKING SO-
CIAL SENSE

this attitude on the part of broadcasters and advertisers is plainly and simply irresponsible—because it does not make social sense. U.S. broadcasters have operating control of one of the most economically and socially important assets—the U.S. broadcast spectrum—in the world today. The TV medium is clearly the most pervasive influence in our society. This is particularly true in the case of children, who, by the time they reach college age, will have spent more time in front of a TV set than they will have spent in school, church, or in conversation with their parents. (p. 14)

The inference from this statement is that if nonnutritious breakfast foods are being advertised, then the cereal industry is as much to blame as anyone. Auto manufacturers are irresponsible when they supply free or discounted automobiles for use on TV shows and allow them to be used improperly, without seat belts.

SMOKING?

The print media can also be accused of diminished social responsibility in advertising, particularly as it applies to cigarettes. Despite the heavy evidence of the link between cigarette smoking and cancer, advertisements picture healthy, good-looking people smoking while at work or during leisure activities. Is it any wonder that our young people want to smoke to imitate the adult models pictured in these expensive advertisements? Again, the advertisers as well as the media share the responsibility.

POSITIVE IN-
FLUENCE

In some countries in Asia, the media is used to promote positive changes to effect better health standards. For example, in a few Asian countries, the media plays an important role in promoting breastfeeding and in educating women away from infant formula (Banerjee, 1983). (In the undeveloped countries of the world, there have been problems with contamination of bottled milk for infants.) So here we see the media being used to effect a positive change for a country. Most of these countries have a state-controlled press, whereas in the United States we have a free press. The hope is that our free media will become more responsible and will turn many of these negative effects into positive ones. In fairness to the American media, they do act responsibly in many situations.

Responses to the Media

IMPROVE AT-
TITUDES
ABOUT
DRINKING

A recent study on Youth and Alcohol in Television Stories offered some suggestions on how best to use the medium to improve attitudes about drinking:

1. Honesty plays well on television as it does in real life. Where an adult faces a difficult situation involving youth and admits his or her lack of godlike qualities, the message comes across with clarity and force, often winning over the young person who would otherwise remain unconvinced.

2. While humor is often a way of relieving tension in a difficult situation, it must be used with care. Alcohol and youth is a serious, perhaps deadly, subject. If humor is subordinated to the message, it can be effective. But if the humor obscures or trivializes the subject, it is counterproductive.

3. Peers have great power to deliver an intervention message. They are eminently believable to youthful viewers. The formula that seems to work best is: one youth learns the lesson and then shares it, at considerable risk to the friendship bonds with a buddy. The problem of the adult talking down to a youth is obviated.

4. Advertisers have learned a valuable lesson: their message is better received when pitched by a believable person. Creators of TV programs can follow this example. A coach, an athletic star, a hero or heroine of any sort or a respected peer—all have validity with youth.

5. Programs which dramatize the message seem most convincing. "Don't tell them, show them." Dramatize the strained relationships and the painful consequences. No preaching is needed. Viewers are left to draw their own conclusions.

6. Since there are many myths surrounding alcohol and youth, a clear statement of the facts, without fear or exaggeration, is essential. Young people are quick to spot a small variance from the truth, and as a result, discard the whole message.

7. Young people tend to equate drinking with adulthood. Television has the means to point up this fallacy, and to dramatize the results. A more appropriate test for adulthood is realizing that they have a responsibility to act prudently when alcohol is involved.

8. In real life, a wrong approach to drinkers can lead to serious consequences for young people. Viewers, however, can watch a program and learn what to avoid from negative examples. A lesson is learned without risk in real life. (Defoe and Breed, 1988, pp. 546–548)

COMMON
SENSE

These suggestions all seem to make a lot of common sense, and common sense is what is needed to solve the problem of substance abuse. All of the suggestions fit in well with what we know about adolescent psychology as well; for example, we know about the power of peer influence and how young people look up to certain heroes. Also, as teens watch an enormous amount of TV per week, we should focus on this medium and use it in a positive way.

The negative impact of the media on the children we teach is profound.

THE USE OF
NEGATIVES

Teachers and schools can, however, turn some of these negative influences into stimulating intellectual topics for the benefit of their students. For example, nutrition-poor foods advertised on TV can be used as a topic of discussion in many classes. Some creative teachers have been known to form nutrition committees composed of administrators, teachers, parents, and children to look into the eating habits of students and the nutritional compositions of the school lunches. The poor use of safety belts in TV movies can be a stimulus for a discussion on the advantages of buckling up for safety. Students might also get involved in a study of the use of safety belts and the use of nutritious foods through a problem-solving approach. Many negatives can form the curricular content for positive class activities.

HOW TO
HELP YOUR
CHILD

Parents need to be shown how to help their children learn by watching TV. Some thought-probing TV shows might be watched by both parents and children, with the parents reinforcing certain key concepts. To aid parents, teachers might send home special papers on important points for discussion brought up in a TV program. The socializing that parents and children do as they learn together by watching and discussing a TV show could be both educationally and personally beneficial.

FACING THE
MEDIA HEAD-
ON

Another way to respond to the impact of the media is to face it head-on. What this implies is that we as educators must know what is presented on TV and in other media as well. Our students have seen or heard things before they come to us, and we are in competition with television in particular. For example, when we try to teach cooperative learning and sharing we are up against TV programs that have taught that power and influence are the way to win and be successful. Knowing how this concept has been taught to our students is an important first step in recognizing the dilemma they face. "If we are to do our job, we will have to be aware of what TV teaches and of what its 'students,' our students as well, have learned from it" (Condry, 1987, p. 24).

THE VALUE
OF DOCU-
MENTARIES

The broadcast media have tremendous resources and produce some very valuable documentaries. Using this material as a resource can bring classroom discussions to bear on information and ideas unavailable in traditional school materials. Assignments for older students can include viewing a program for discussion in class the following day. A drama such as *Roots* or *The Color Purple* can be of immense help to social studies teachers. Television can be a positive educational tool if only we learn to use it properly.

Impact of the Women's Rights Movement

Many established societal norms in the United States were in the process of social revolution from the mid-1960s until the early 1970s. Among these were women's rights and place in society. The attempted passage of the **Equal Rights Amendment (ERA)**, the National Organization for Women (NOW), Bella Abzug, Gloria Steinem, and other events, organizations, and leaders emerged from that turbulent era in American politics. Although the initial thrust behind the women's movement may have dissipated, the message continues to be evident in our daily lives. We might ask ourselves two questions: What is at the bottom of the women's movement now and in the past? Why should women be disturbed about the role they play in American society? These questions will not be answered entirely in this textbook, but the authors hope to arouse their readers' curiosity about this important impact on the schools.

EVIDENT IN
OUR DAILY
LIVES

IMPORTANCE
OF WOMEN'S
RIGHTS

The importance of women's rights and their place in history has been documented in a congressional resolution:

> Whereas American women of every race, class, and ethnic background helped found the Nation in countless recorded and unrecorded ways as servants, slaves, nurses, nuns, homemakers, industrial workers, teachers, reformers, soldiers, and pioneers; and

The women's rights movement has opened doors to new areas of endeavor.

(Photo courtesy of the Indiana State Department of Education.)

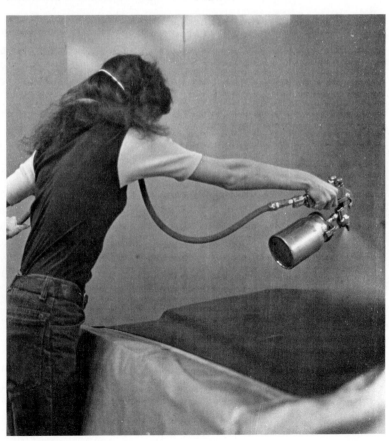

Whereas American women have played and continue to play a critical economic, cultural and social role in every sphere of our Nation's life by constituting a significant portion of the labor force working in and outside of the home; and

Whereas American women have played a unique role throughout our history by providing the majority of the Nation's volunteer labor force and have been particularly important in the establishment of early charitable, philanthropic, and cultural institutions in the country; and

Whereas American women of every race, class, and ethnic background served as early leaders in the forefront of every major progressive social change movement, not only to secure their own right of suffrage and equal opportunity, but also in the abolitionist movement, the emancipation movement, the industrial labor union movement, and the modern civil rights movement; and

Whereas despite these contributions, the role of American women in history has been consistently overlooked and undervalued in the body of American history:

Now, therefore, be it resolved by the Senate and the House of Representatives of the United States of America in Congress assembled, that the month of March is designated as "Women's History Month," and the President is requested to issue a proclamation calling upon the people of the United States to observe such month with appropriate ceremonies and activities. (National Women's History Project, 1989, p. 2)

For more information, contact the National Women's History Project, P.O. Box 3716 Santa Rosa, CA 95402, (707) 526–5974.

CONGRESSIO-
NAL EN-
DORSEMENT

The fact that Congress has endorsed the movement, by writing this resolution supporting an increased effort to show how women have been an integral part of American history, is an encouraging sign that the movement is still very much alive.

THE ORIGIN

When did the unfairness in the treatment of women begin? Some feminists (Dixon, 1978) have argued that the ability women have to give birth is the limiting factor in women's work activities. They say that when the communal kin group was broken up and individual families became isolated units, the female of the species was relegated to doing domestic work for her husband, which subjugated her into virtual slavery.

LEADING
ROLES IN
THE COM-
MUNAL KIN
GROUPS

Women in the tribal societies are known to have had leading political and economic responsibilities despite their childbearing role; therefore, the argument that women are limited as to the work they can do does not hold up. The other argument concerning the breakup of communal kin groups is a more logical reason for the historical unfair treatment of women when you consider the communal decisions and group problem solving that must have taken place; no doubt, women were not left out of communal decisions and group problem solving while the kin groups were intact.

A SHIFT TO
DEPENDENCE

As capitalism and the Industrial Revolution became a part of Europe and America, families increasingly became consumers rather than producers. Before the Industrial Revolution, families lived in communal kin groups and constituted a production unit as well as a consumer unit. Families in the industrial period became a dependent unit, as the husband sold himself as a laborer while the wife worked in the home. The important decisions in life were made away from the family; thus, there was a shift away from the family as the central unit of social organization. Because of the reduction in the importance of the family unit, the wageless nature of female domestic labor, and women's dependence on their husband's wages, women found themselves in a position of low power both economically and politically (Dixon, 1978). This scenario may not be entirely correct, but it offers some explanation of the beginnings of the unfair treatment of women in an industrialized society.

A NEW SCE-
NARIO FOR
WOMEN

Today, the woman's role is changing, and for some, it has already changed; most activists would say there is still a long way to go. Alice Rossi (1971) wrote a proposal for changing the status of women from birth throughout life. At the conclusion of her essay, Rossi described the hypothetical case of a woman who is reared and lives out her life under the changed social conditions proposed in her essay. The Rossi proposal for change seems to offer a commonsense solution to the powerless and unrewarding dilemmas that women face because of their established role in the family in an industrialized society.

The Rossi Proposal

A HYPO-
THETICAL
CASE

I shall describe a hypothetical case of a woman who is reared and lives out her life under the changed social conditions proposed in this essay. She will be reared, as her brother will be reared, with a combination of loving warmth, firm discipline, household responsibility, and encouragement of independence and self-reliance. She will not be pampered and indulged, subtly taught to achieve her ends through coquetry and tears, as so many girls are taught today. She will view domestic skills as useful tools to acquire, some of which, like fine cooking or needlework, having their own intrinsic pleasures, but most of which are necessary repetitive work best gotten done as quickly and efficiently as possible. She will be able to handle minor mechanical breakdowns in the home as well as her brother can, and he will be able to tend a child, press, sew, and cook with the same easy skills and comfortable feeling his sister has.

NOT BE PAM-
PERED AND
INDULGED

During their school years, both sister and brother will increasingly assume responsibility for their own decisions, freely experiment with numerous possible fields of study, gradually narrowing to a choice that best suits their interests and abilities rather than what is considered appropriate or prestigeful work for men and women. They will be encouraged by parents and teachers alike to think ahead to a whole life span, viewing marriage and parenthood as one strand among many which will constitute their lives. The girl will not feel the pressure to belittle her accomplishments, lower her aspirations, learn to be a receptive listener in her relations with boys, but will be as true to her growing sense of self as her brother and male friends are. She will not marry before her adolescence and schooling are completed, but will be willing and able to view college years as a "moratorium" from deeply intense cross-sex commitments, a period of life during which her identify can be "at large and open and various." Her intellectual aggressiveness as well as her brother's tender sentiments will be welcomed and accepted as human characteristics, without the self-questioning doubt of latent homosexuality that troubles many college-age men and

TO THINK
AHEAD

women in our era when these qualities are sex-linked. She will not cling to her parents, nor they to her, but will establish an increasingly larger sphere of her own independent world in which she moves and works, loves and thinks, as a maturing young person. She will learn to take pleasure in her own body and to view sex as a good and wonderful experience, but not as an exclusive basis for an ultimate commitment to another person, and not as a test of her competence as a female or her partner's competence as a male. Because she will have a many-faceted conception of her self and its worth, she will be free to merge and lose herself in the sex act with a lover or a husband.

MARRIAGE
AN EN-
LARGEMENT
OF HER LIFE
EXPERIENCES

Marriage for our hypothetical woman will not mark a withdrawal from the life and work pattern that she has established, just as there will be no sharp discontinuity between her early childhood and youthful adult years. Marriage will be an enlargement of her life experience, the addition of a new dimension to an already established pattern, rather than an abrupt withdrawal to the home and a turning in upon the marital relationship. Marriage will be a "looking outward in the same direction" for both the woman and her husband. She will marry and bear children only if she deeply desires a mate and children, and will not be judged a failure as a person if she decides against either. She will have few children if she does have them, and will view her pregnancies, childbirth, and early months of motherhood as one among many equally important highlights in her life, experienced intensely and with joy but not as the exclusive basis for a sense of self-fulfillment and purpose in life. With planning and foresight, her early years of childbearing and rearing can fit a longrange view of all sides of herself. If her children are not to suffer from **"paternal deprivation,"** her husband will also anticipate that the assumption of parenthood will involve a weeding out of nonessential activities either in work, civic, or social participation. Both the woman and the man will feel that unless a man can make room in his life for parenthood, he should not become a father. The woman will make sure, even if she remains at home during her child's infancy, that he has ample experience of being with and cared for by other adults besides herself, so that her return to a full-time position in her field will not constitute a drastic change in the life of the child, but a gradual pattern of increasing supplementation by others than the mother. The children will have a less intense involvement with their mother, and she with them, and they will all be the better for it. When they are grown and establish adult lives of their own, our woman will face no retirement twenty years before her husband, for her own independent activities will continue and expand. She will be neither an embittered wife, an interfering mother-in-law, nor an idle parasite, but together with her husband she will be able to live to an independent, purposeful, and satisfying third act in life. (Rossi, 1971, pp. 162–164)

TOWARD IN-
DEPENDENCE

WHOLE SOCI-
ETY ADJUSTS

The Rossi proposal is one of many ideas for revamping the role and the lifestyle of American women. In the Rossi scenario men will need to change their roles as well. If Rossi's proposal plays out in real life, our whole society will be adjusting to these changing patterns over a long period. The authors know of some families that practice something like Rossi has in mind, but still many other American families are not much different than they were in the 1950s. While these adjustments are taking place, children will be neglected and marriages will dissolve, but after some years of change all families could be better off.

SCHOOL'S
ROLE

Schools and teachers can assist the whole realignment process by recognizing what is happening and teaching children about these new family roles. It is not likely that family life will ever return to what it was like in the 1950s and earlier when most women served exclusively as housewives and mothers. Now we turn to some responses that schools should make to the women's movement or, more accurately, the family revolution.

Response to the Women's Movement

OVERCOM-
ING OLD
STEREOTYPI-
CAL VIEWS

In your role as a teacher, you will influence children not only in a positive way; you will have many opportunities to influence them in a negative way as well. Negative results occur when teachers continue to reinforce old **sex role stereotypes.** It is difficult for teachers to overcome the media image, which seems to reflect commonly held stereotypical views. The media often picture women in the roles of housewives or sex objects. Men are pictured more often in decision-making roles as bankers or business executives.

SEXIST MATE-
RIAL

The sexist printed resources used by teachers are another difficulty that is hard to overcome. Gough (1976) made a study of basal readers published for the third grade in 1972 and 1973 and found that males outnumbered females both in content and in illustrations. The great heroes in history are generally depicted as males, and some textbooks even go so far as to intimate that girls lack competence in math: "Jane couldn't figure out how to do . . . , so John helped her" (p. 19).

GOVERN-
MENT AC-
TION!

As in all forms of unfair treatment, society loses. The people with top ability, whether they be girls or boys of whatever race, need to be encouraged to rise to their potential in any career opportunity. In 1972, the federal government took some action to end discrimination against females; Congress enacted **Title IX,** which says, "No person in the United States shall, on the basis of sex, be excluded from participation in, be denied the benefits of, or be subjected to discrimination under any education program or activity receiving financial assistance." As a result of the Title IX legislation, girls have received much better treatment in the athletic programs of our nation's public schools. In some states, where the boy's basketball tournament was the high school event of the year, there is now a state girl's basketball tournament, and girls as well as boys participate in an annual all-star game. Equality of treatment in athletics appears to be ahead of the academic programs in schools.

SEX ROLE EX-
PECTATIONS

No solid evidence (Gough, 1976) indicates that men and women are born with psychological differences that cause them to behave in different ways. It follows, then, that cultural influences have the greatest impact on determining sex roles. Research (Gough, 1976) seems to indicate that sex role expectations are repressive for members of both sexes, inhibiting both boys and girls from achieving their full psychological and intellectual capabilities. Careers for women in our society are limited primarily by the sex roles imposed on them by society: "Choices for women in our society are limited

Women in administrative roles in education serve as role models for students.

(Photo by Axler.)

today only by interests, talents, motivations, and attitudes, and the school can play a part in influencing each of these" (Gough, 1976, p. 37). Schools and teachers can play an important part in helping to change traditional sex roles, thus freeing children of both sexes to become what they really want to be.

On so many issues, schools wait until there is public awareness or a public outcry before anything is really accomplished because schools tend SCHOOLS ON to reflect society's needs. **Feminists** and others like them think that schools THE "CUT- should be more on the "cutting edge" than on the "trailing edge." The TING EDGE"? authors wonder if progress in human rights or equality in educational opportunity would advance more rapidly if teachers would take a more active role.

Foxley (1979) offers some concrete suggestions to help teachers eliminate sexism in our schools. In the area of self-awareness, Foxley suggested the following activity:

> Much of the literature dealing with sex role stereotyping in the schools tends to focus on the problems rather than directions for constructive change. Yet, there is a great deal teachers can do to help free the student's environment of sexist elements. The purpose of this article is to highlight actions teachers can take in three areas: (1) self-awareness, (2) classroom practices and behaviors, and (3) out-of-classroom efforts. (Foxley, 1979, p. 316)

Self-Awareness

To help others overcome the detrimental effects of sex role stereotyping and become fully aware, functioning, and human persons, we as teachers must first be able to recognize our own biases and work to change them, for our own benefit as well as that of our students. There are many ways to begin this self-assessment regarding sex bias. The following activity is one way.

OVERCOM-
ING OUR
OWN BIASES

Listed below are sex role stereotypic characteristics that have generally been attributed to men/women and girls/boys. Read through the lists carefully.

Characteristics Generally Attributed to Men/Boys	*Characteristics Generally Attributed to Women/Girls*
1. Aggressive	1. Passive
2. Independent	2. Dependent
3. Dominant	3. Talkative
4. Good at math and science	4. Emotional
5. Mechanical ability	5. Considerate
6. Good at sports	6. Easily influenced
7. Competitive	7. Excitable in crises
8. Skilled in business	8. Tactful
9. Worldly	9. Gentle
10. Adventurous	10. Helpful to others
11. Outspoken	11. Home oriented
12. Interested in sex	12. Sensitive
13. Decisive	13. Religious
14. Demonstrates leadership	14. Neat in habits
15. Intellectual	15. Indecisive
16. Self-confident	16. Supportive
17. Ambitious	17. Submissive
18. Autonomous	18. Devoted to others
19. Strong	19. Conforming
20. Unemotional	20. Concerned about appearance

- Do you agree with the categorizing of these characteristics for men and women in general?
- Do you see yourself as having more of the stereotypic traits of your sex than those of the opposite sex?
- Do you view your spouse and/or other members of your family (parents, siblings, children, other relatives) as having the characteristics generally attributed to their sex rather than those of the opposite sex?
- Do you view your friends and colleagues as having the sex role stereotypic characteristics?
- Do you view your students as having the sex role stereotypic characteristics? (Foxley, 1979, p. 316)

After taking this simple test, readers should feel more in tune with themselves and how they perceive this problem. Earlier, we talked about the intelligent young lady belittling her accomplishments and lowering her aspirations or goals. The reason girls often act this way is that they want to conform to the usual expectations that teachers, and particularly their peers, have of them. We may be losing a fine physician or an outstanding research scientist by not recognizing the problems that these young women ENCOURAGE have to overcome. By being aware that a young woman can have, and NONSEXIST indeed often has, many of the characteristics generally attributed to young BEHAVIOR men, we as teachers can encourage nonsexist education in our schools.

Impact of Our Culturally and Ethnically Diverse Society

RACIAL DI-
VERSITY
We Americans live in a society composed of many diverse ethnic groups. Some estimate of the degree of racial diversity in America can be obtained from a look at the listings in the U.S. Census. Racial groups listed do not include those of various Spanish origins, such as Mexicans, Puerto Ricans, and Cubans, which were included in the Census under other headings. In 1987, there were approximately 238 million people living in the United States. Table 4-1 lists the racial groups and their population in millions. White ethnic groups, such as Polish-, Italian-, and Irish-Americans, add to the diversity in the population.

American Indians are the only ethnic group native to America; therefore, all other group members came to this country as immigrants. Immigrants could have chosen to blend in with other Americans when they arrived, and some of them did; but others felt more comfortable remaining in their **ethnic enclaves.** Most people would agree that a certain amount of "melt-

TABLE 4-1
Racial Groups Found in America

RACE	TOTAL PERSONS (in millions)
Total	238.79
White	202.45
Black	28.93
Hispanic	18.79
American Indian	1.48
Chinese	0.81
Filipino	0.78
Japanese	0.72
Asian Indian	0.39
Korean	0.36
Pacific Islander	0.26
Vietnamese	0.25

SOURCE: U.S. Department of the Census. (1987). Statistical Abstract of the United States. Washington, D.C.: U.S. Government Printing Office, p. 35.

"MELTING POT" CONCEPT

ing" is necessary for the survival of our society, that is, for our national security, for the maintenence of our republic, and for the promotion of our economic system. Historically, many Americans have been forced to melt into the system either more than they wanted to or more than was necessary for the common good. Still other groups have had to come up from slavery or have suffered the indignity of being placed on a reservation, as have blacks and American Indians have had to do. Also, many Japanese-Americans were placed in **internment camps** during World War II.

BUILDING TOWARD

Since World War II, more Americans have come to see their ethnic background as a source of identity in a complex world. In addition, educators and intellectuals think it important to know more about other cultures and ethnic groups. During World Wars I and II, we did not trust German-Americans and Japanese-Americans, but time has brought a change. As we build more trust in each other, our ethnically and **culturally pluralistic society** seems to be an asset instead of a liability.

Response to Cultural and Ethnic Issues

In this section, the school's response to cultural and **ethnic diversity,** is illustrated by **multiethnic education,** and **bilingualism.**

Multiethnic Education

MORE ACCEPTING OF DIVERSITY

One of the main proposals for reforming education that emerged from the social unrest of the 1960s and the early 1970s was multiethnic education, the type of curriculum that acquaints students with the many ethnic groups in our society so that they will become more familiar with and accepting of the diversity of the population in the United States. Advocates of multiethnic education feel that it should be an integral part of every social studies course from kindergarten through high school, so that our schools will reflect the reality of our society in the curriculum. Most American schools' curricula today represent the views of the dominant cultural group.

PROBLEMS WITH THE CURRICULUM

In conscience, at least, we believe in democracy and equality of opportunity for all Americans, but in practice, our schools and our curricula are not equal in their treatment of our diverse cultures. Several events in our nation's history have led to the present curricula. Puritan New England set the tone for education by being strongly in favor of education from the very beginning. Most of the trained teachers and early textbooks emerged from the New England area. Later, McGuffey's Readers influenced many more generations of schoolchildren, especially throughout the Midwest. Both the early school literature in New England and later the McGuffey's Readers espoused the dominant cultural group viewpoint of America, without the intentional exclusion of other groups.

ASSIMILATION CONCERNS

When immigrants started arriving in large numbers, the dominant cultural influence on the school curriculum was not so innocent. The policy of assimilating new immigrants into American society became known as the **"melting pot" concept.** New immigrants were forced to comply with certain national laws and to melt into American society. "Anglo-Saxon ideals were taught in the schools in order to bring these new people into the American race," according to Elwood P. Cubberley, a noted educational historian at the turn of the century (cited by Banks, 1977, p. 11). Despite the efforts of our government and our schools to combine all ethnic groups into one new **megaethnic group,** influenced mostly by the dominant culture's philosophy, many ethnic groups settled into their own enclaves, where they could continue their unique cultural practices. Other cultural groups wished to become assimilated; not all newcomers were unwilling participants.

CIVIL
RIGHTS?

Some Americans immigrated not by choice, but by force; they were brought from Africa and forced into slave labor. Their descendants constitute our large ethnic group of black Americans. Lincoln's Emancipation Proclamation legally liberated them from slavery, but the *Plessey v. Ferguson* (163 U.S. 537) ruling by the U.S. Supreme Court in 1896 legitimized their unequal position until the *Brown v. Board of Education of Topeka* (347 U.S. 483) decision in 1954. The *Brown* case set in motion numerous civil rights actions, both peaceful and violent, throughout the country, which eventually resulted in various forms of civil rights legislation, such as the *1964 Civil Rights Law* and the *1965 Elementary and Secondary Education Act* with all of its titles. During the upheaval, every established American institution was questioned, including our educational system.

PLURALISM
PROMOTED

Leaders in the multiethnic education movement realize that as a nation, we are more pluralistic than monolithic, and that our cultural differences ought to be promoted and celebrated rather than diluted and lost. The first real evidence of a multiethnic impact on the curriculum was the outcry for black history, which at first was offered as a separate course to satisfy the demands of black students and civil rights organizations. Sometimes, history teachers inserted black history as an additional topic to be covered in their courses, but the course of study largely reflected the dominant culture.

CURRICULUM
CHANGES

As there were increasing signs of alienation among certain minority ethnic groups, particularly blacks, other steps were taken to change the curriculum and the school staff. For example, more minority teachers were hired; textbooks were written that reflected the contributions of most ethnic groups to our society; illustrations in textbooks were changed to show minorities fulfilling major roles; and in general, a much greater sensitivity was shown to ethnic and cultural diversity.

NEED FOR
MULTIETH-
NIC EDUCA-
TION

In addition to other obvious reasons for instituting multiethnic education, the busing of schoolchildren to achieve racial balance in our schools has resulted in an even greater need for multiethnic education. School districts are eager, for the most part, to meet the needs of all children in their schools, and most districts want their curriculum to be interesting and challenging to all their students. James A. Banks, an outstanding leader

Children enjoy learning about different cultures and different languages.

[Photo used by permission of the Indiana Department of Education.]

DIAGRAM
FOR CURRIC-
ULUM RE-
FORM

in multiethnic education, has suggested two exciting models for curriculum reform that offer the most inclusive and most commonsense approach to multiethnic education.

According to Banks' diagram of innovative strategies for ethnic studies (see Figure 4–5), teachers in Model A talk only about mainstream perspectives of our history and culture. In Model B, the teachers use **additives,** such as American Indian, but retain **mainstream emphasis.** Banks suggested that teachers using Model A skip Model B and go to Model C, where the mainstream perspectives appear among several others and are in no way superior or inferior to the other perspectives. He called Model C the **multiethnic model.** Finally, in Model D, social or historical events are viewed in terms of other nations, and this type of curricular organization helps students to better understand the lands and cultures from which the various groups have come (Banks, 1987, p. 22).

What the future holds for multiethnic education and other related federally sponsored programs is difficult to estimate, but the need for such reforms has been well documented. There remain horror stories of how our

ROLE FOR
THE
SCHOOLS

Native Americans are treated on and off their reservations, and Hispanics and blacks still have to fight for the rights due all Americans. All minority ethnic groups must strive, to some degree, for acceptance, and there is no doubt that sound, well-thought-out, school-system–wide multiethnic curricular programs would be very helpful.

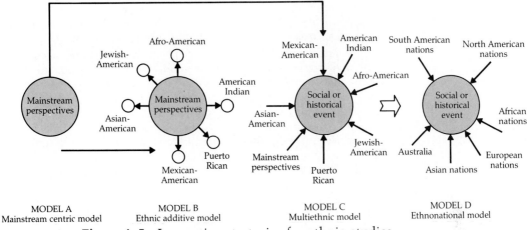

MODEL A
Mainstream centric model

MODEL B
Ethnic additive model

MODEL C
Multiethnic model

MODEL D
Ethnonational model

Figure 4–5   Innovative strategies for ethnic studies.

(SOURCE: Adapted, by permission, from Banks, J. A. (1987). *Teaching strategies for ethnic studies,* 4th ed. Allyn and Bacon, Newton, MA, p. 22.)

BANKS'
TYPOLOGY

All Americans, indeed all planet earth dwellers, fall somewhere on a continuum of acceptance of those who are different from themselves. The degree of acceptance ranges from none at all to total acceptance of other groups. The authors believe that the Banks typology, or study, of ethnic acceptance offers the reader a road map that helps individuals to understand where they "come from" and where they might "go" in becoming more accepting of diversity. Figure 4–6 on page 147 illustrates Banks's (1987) emerging stages of ethnicity:

> We often assume that ethnic groups are monolithic and have rather homogeneous needs and characteristics. Rarely is sufficient attention given to the enormous differences within ethnic groups. We also tend to see ethnic groups as static and unchanging. However, ethnic groups within modernized democratic societies are highly diverse, complex, and changing entities. I have developed a **typology** that attempts to describe some of the differences existing between individual members of ethnic groups. The typology assumes that individual members of an ethnic group are at different stages of ethnic development and that these stages can be identified and described.

AN IDEAL
CONSTRUCT

> The typology is a preliminary ideal type construct in the Weberian sense and constitutes a set of hypotheses based on the existing and emerging theory and research, and on my observations and study of ethnic behavior. The typology is presented here since it can be used as a departure point for classroom discussions of ethnicity. However, its tentative and hypothetical nature should be emphasized in class discussions.

ETHNIC SELF-
REJECTION

Stage 1:   Ethnic Psychological Captivity. During this stage, the individual has internalized negative ideologies and beliefs about his or her ethnic group that are institutionalized within the society. Consequently, the Stage 1 person exemplifies ethnic self-rejection and low self-esteem. The individual is ashamed of his or her ethnic group and identity during this stage and may respond in a number of ways, including avoiding situations that lead to contact with other ethnic groups or striving aggressively to become highly culturally assimilated.

Stage 2:   *Ethnic Encapsulation.* Stage 2 is characterized by **ethnic encapsulation** and ethnic exclusiveness, including voluntary separatism. The individual participates primarily within his or her own ethnic community and believes that his or her ethnic group is superior to that of others. Many Stage 2 individuals, such as many Anglo-Saxon Protestants, have internalized the dominant societal myths about the superiority of their ethnic or racial group and the innate inferiority of other ethnic groups and races. Many individuals who are socialized within all-white suburban communities and who live highly **ethnocentric** and encapsulated lives may be described as Stage 2 individuals. Alice Miel describes these kinds of individuals in *The Short-changed Children of Suburbia.*

SUPERIORITY
FEELING

Stage 3:   *Ethnic Identity Clarification.* At this stage, the individual is able to clarify personal attitudes and ethnic identity, reduce intrapsychic conflict, and develop positive attitudes toward his or her ethnic group. The individual learns to accept self, thus developing the characteristics needed to accept and respond more positively to outside ethnic groups. Self-acceptance is a requisite to accepting and responding positively to others.

DEVELOPING
POSITIVE AT-
TITUDES

Stage 4:   *Biethnicity.* Individuals within this stage have a healthy sense of ethnic identity and the psychological characteristics and skills needed to participate in their own ethnic culture. The individual also has a strong desire to function effectively in two ethnic cultures. We may describe such an individual as biethnic.

CAN FUNC-
TION IN TWO
ETHNIC CUL-
TURES

Stage 5:   *Multiethnicity.* Stage 5 describes the idealized goal for citizenship identity within an ethnically pluralistic nation. The individual at this stage is able to function, at least at minimal levels, within several ethnic sociocultural environments and to understand, appreciate, and share the values, symbols, and institutions of several ethnic cultures. Such multiethnic perspectives and feelings, I hypothesize, help the individual to live a more enriched and fulfilling life and to formulate more creative and novel solutions to personal and public problems.

CAN FUNC-
TION IN SEV-
ERAL CUL-
TURES

Stage 6:   *Globalism and Global Competency.* Individuals within Stage 6 have clarified, reflective, and positive ethnic, national, and global identifications and the knowledge, skills, attitudes, and abilities needed to function in ethnic cultures within their own nation as well as in cultures within other nations. These individuals have the ideal delicate balance of ethnic, national, and global identifications, commitments, literacy, and behaviors. They have internalized the universalistic ethical values and principles of humankind and have the skills, competencies, and commitments needed to act on these values. (Banks, 1987, pp. 64–65)

UNIVERSALIS-
TIC

The important thing to remember when reading about these stages is that they are just stages and no person needs to remain fixed in a stage. Movement either horizontally or vertically is taking place in all of our lives

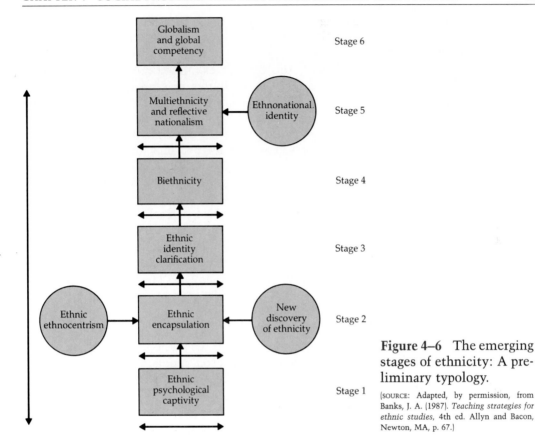

Figure 4–6   The emerging stages of ethnicity: A preliminary typology.

(SOURCE: Adapted, by permission, from Banks, J. A. (1987). *Teaching strategies for ethnic studies*, 4th ed. Allyn and Bacon, Newton, MA, p. 67.)

SETTING
GOALS

most of the time. The ultimate goal for most of us would be Stage 6, but Stage 5 or Stage 4 is a more realistic goal for most Americans. To avoid nuclear holocaust, however, the more urgent goal in the 1990s for all people should be Stage 6.

TOWARD
FAIRNESS
AND DIG-
NITY

It is important for all teachers and educators to recognize that they do live in a pluralistic nation. The spirit of the 1960s and the early 1970s caused all of us in the United States to realize that failure to treat every ethnic group with fairness and dignity can result in violence. For many reasons, children often come to school with attitudes that place them at either Stage 1 or Stage 2 in Banks' typology. Teachers can and do have a role to play in helping children, through multicultural and multiethnic education, advance in the typology.

Teaching About Race and Prejudice

A TEACHING
TECHNIQUE

An innovative teacher wanted to teach her six-year-olds about racial prejudice. To find out where her students stood at this early stage in their lives, she showed them a series of pictures and asked them some questions. For example, she showed them a card with two identical girls, one seated in a wheelchair and the other seated in a regular chair. She then asked, "Who was the better student?" The majority chose the girl sitting in the regular chair.

As the lesson progressed, the teacher examined and challenged their views. The students examined the attributes of a good student, and all agreed that good listening skills, good communication skills, and the ability to follow directions were necessary. When the teacher asked them if the wheelchair prevented the girl from possessing these attributes, the students realized that their choice was based on **learned bias** and snap judgments (Davis, 1988, p. 28).

This exercise was carried out by a very creative and resourceful teacher who wanted to expose her students to some stereotypes before talking about Martin Luther King's birthday. She reasoned correctly that her students would say no to the question, "Is it fair to judge someone by the color of his or her skin?" (Davis, 1988, p. 28). She wanted them to think more deeply and realize their own stereotypes before talking about the larger issue of prejudice. She may well have motivated most of her class to advance in the typology of ethnicity suggested by Banks.

MOVING UP
BANKS' TY-
POLOGY

Bilingualism

Related to multiethnic education is bilingual education. Bilingual education was developed to help Hispanic students better understand standard English curricula and thereby improve their chances to compete for economic and social advantages in the mainstream of society. As we go about our busy lives, progressing through school and attaining economic success, we often overlook the feelings of others, especially those less fortunate than we are. Hispanic children often come to school and face teachers and other children who do not understand their language or their culture. Without assistance, Hispanic children may not be able to master their language and a new one (English) at the same time; hence, they drop out early.

HISPANIC
CONCERN

Bilingualism and **biculturalism** are ways to reach out to these disadvantaged students and give them a better chance (Valverde, 1978):

REACHING
OUT

> Language is learned in the intimacy of one's family and around those we care about and cherish. It is in these comfortable surroundings that we express our most intimate feelings and emotions. Educators must accept and nurture, both verbally and nonverbally, the language children bring with them from the home. In doing this, not only do we indicate that the child's language is worthwhile, but also that the child is a worthy individual. As children sense this worth, educators can help them develop and reinforce a sense of efficacy. (p. 9)

In bilingual–bicultural programs, the child's native language is used as a mediator between the child's culture and that of the school and the society at large. As teachers better understand their students, they build important bonds of trust with the students, which results in a greater readiness to learn the second language (Valverde, 1978).

An often-heard complaint is that bilingualism and biculturalism are bad

Hispanic students receiving bilingual education in the public schools.

(Photo by Grady Franklin.)

for the child who is trying to learn a second language, but the contrary is true. We have learned that bilingualism and biculturalism are not detrimental to cognitive development, and that cognitive skills are transferable across cultures and languages (Ovando, 1983).

A POLITICAL PROBLEM

Another problem with bilingualism—and it is a political problem—concerns the enactment of Title VII of the Elementary and Secondary Education Act in 1968. The intent of Congress with this bilingual legislation was to get students to learn standard English as soon as possible and to drop their home-language instruction. As a result, the schools were no longer encouraging the pluralistic development of our society. The 1968 legislation was not intended to maintain the rich linguistic resources that these children represented (Ovando, 1983). One of the great debates regarding bilingual–bicultural education, therefore, is maintaining the child's home language versus keeping bilingual instruction as short as possible.

CULTURAL LOYALTY

The public is very concerned that the new immigrant groups may have divided linguistic and cultural loyalties. Many people new to our society find that they can move into the mainstream without giving up their first language and their cultural traditions. The political issue with respect to cultural loyalty surrounding bilingualism and biculturalism is not resolved. The question is "Should **linguistic minority** groups have the right to participate fully in American life without being completely assimilated into the mainstream culture?" (Ovando, 1983, p. 567). The issue of cultural loyalty seems to be one of trust; thus, time will tell us whether this situation will present a serious problem.

According to Ovando (1983), "It would be pedagogically unsound and sociopolitically imprudent to return to the sink-or-swim methods of the WAVE OF THE past" (p. 567). In fact, bilingual instruction could be the wave of the future FUTURE? because it can be personally satisfying to all students involved and can help students develop the interpersonal skills and attitudes essential to a healthy society. Bilingual–bicultural education could play a major role in helping us to prepare ourselves to participate in a global society.

Bilingualism was still a very controversial topic when the Bush administration took over in Washington. California has declared English the official language of the state, and according to educators like Nicholas Sanchez,

> By shielding them from the linguistic rigor of both English and the parent tongue, the dialect serves to keep the children from properly learning either language, and separates them from the mainstream of American society and from their parents as well. (Sanchez, 1987, pp. 42–43)

Sanchez (p. 43) speaks in favor of some degree of bilingualism as long as MOVE TO EN- it is committed to helping children move quickly into English-language GLISH-LAN- classrooms.
GUAGE
CLASSROOM   Sanchez quotes Sarah Hudelson, who speaks in favor of bilingualism from her direct experience as a teacher and a language educator:

> Hudelson believes that the first benefit of a strong native language literacy program is that it develops in children an understanding of what reading and writing are for, using the medium of a language that the children speak fluently and that they have used to make sense of their life experiences to this point in time. As they read and write in a language they already speak, children become aware of the scope of reading and writing in people's lives. (Hudelson, 1987, p. 830)

As children develop fluency in their native language, they gain the confidence to learn and write English as well (Hudelson, 1987, p. 837). Hudelson provided some examples from her personal experience and background that are proof of the merits of bilingual instruction. She is very much a professional and has the knowledge and the sensitivity to work with language-minority children. No doubt there are problems in the implementation of A SOUND bilingual instruction in certain areas, but the theory behind it seems to be THEORY sound.

> Early in 1987 the United States General Accounting Office asked ten experts to review the research done to that time. Almost all of them concluded that quality bilingual education is beneficial to children's English language and academic achievement. (Hudelson, 1987, p. 829)

Where the federal government and the states will be on this issue in the future is uncertain. The point of view presented here has much support, but at least as many detractors.

Summary

In this chapter selected social issues that have an indirect impact on the schools were discussed. One issue, family life in America, was discussed in some detail, and suggestions on how this critical area can be improved were offered. Poverty in the United States and the problems that accompany poverty were examined in terms of the ramifications of our economic system.

There is mounting evidence that what children see and hear in the media affects their lifestyle and moral character. Many of these implications were described here. Because in many instances women in our society have not been treated fairly, women's issues were discussed, and some specific suggestions were made for positive improvement.

The fact that we live in a culturally and ethnically diverse society can present problems; but, as suggested in this chapter, this diversity can be turned into a positive experience for all of us. These then are some of the issues that have an indirect impact on our society and profound influence on our young people.

Glossary Terms

Dysfunctional Families, 112
AFDC (Aid to Families with Dependent Children), 116
Head Start, 118
The Whole Child Initiative (WCI), 118
Egalitarian Marriage, 118
Latchkey Children, 119
Alternative School Movement, 123
General Educational Development Test (GED), 125
Urban Schools, 126
Job Training Partnership Act of 1982 (JTPA), 128
Job Corps, 128
"Safety Net," 128
Mass Media, 129
National Institute of Mental Health (NIMH), 129
Blacks, 130
Hispanics, 130
Native Americans, 130
Asian Americans, 130

Pluralism, 131
Equal Rights Amendment (ERA), 133
Paternal Deprivation, 137
Sex Role Stereotype, 138
Title IX, 138
Feminists, 139
Ethnic Enclaves, 141
Internment Camps, 142
Culturally Pluralistic Society, 142
Ethnic Diversity, 141
Multiethnic Education, 142
Bilingualism, 142
Melting Pot Concept, 143
Megaethnic Groups, 144
Additives, 144
Mainstream Emphasis, 144
Multiethnic Model, 144
Typology, 145
Ethnic Encapsulation, 146
Ethnocentric, 146
Learned Bias, 148
Biculturalism, 148
Linguistic Minority, 149

Questions

1. Describe in your own words what you perceive to be a dysfunctional family. What are three things society can do to help these families?

2. Is it realistic to propose that we have egalitarian marriages? What is the key to making such marriages work? How could these marriages help our schools?

3. Why would after-school programs be of great assistance to latchkey children?

4. What are some solutions to the massive teen pregnancy problem we have in the United States?

5. What are some of the educational implications for children who live in poverty and what can educators do to help?

6. What can you as a teacher do to counter the tremendous impact of the media on formation of children's values?

7. Discuss how you as a teacher can incorporate into your classes a fair approach to young women and men and eliminate sexism, taking into consideration the Rossi proposal.

8. Why is Banks' Model D approach considered an ideal? Suggest how some social and historical events could be viewed in this context.

9. What are some advantages and disadvantages of bilingual programs? Would a good bilingual program help in achieving Stage 5 or 6 of the Banks' typology?

Activities for Unit II

1. Choose any social issue that impacts on the schools, define the problem, gather data about the problem, and draw conclusions about how the problem could be solved.

2. Identify a school using Title I funds, visit the school, and report to the class on the status of the program.

3. Interview a social worker and/or a probation officer about his or her perceptions of how the criminal justice system works.

4. Read and report to your class on Phi Delta Kappa Fastback No. 46, *Violence in Schools: Causes and Remedies.*

5. Read and report to your class on Phi Delta Kappa Fastback No. 26, *The Teacher and the Drug Scene.*

6. Examine some selected school textbooks on your subject or at your grade level for sex bias in text and illustrations.

7. Invite a local authority on child abuse to talk to your class and/or visit a local family support center.

8. Look up the national statistics on teenage suicides and compare those figures with the rates in your own community.

9. Observe a videotape of the first episode of *Eyes on the Prize* and discuss the factors that may have led to this violence.

10. Research and write about a dysfunctional family. What were some of the critical dilemmas faced by this family?

11. You are on a committee formed to design a parent education curriculum. What subject matter would you include?

12. Visit a Head Start program in your community. How would you evaluate this program?

13. Considering Banks' typology, what are some steps you would take to move your classes to Stages 5 and 6?

Annotated Bibliography

1. Banks, J. A. (1987). *Teaching strategies for ethnic studies*, 4th ed. Newton, MA: Allyn and Bacon.

    This book is an excellent source for information on multicultural education. The fourth edition has been updated to reflect current and emerging theory, research, and scholarship in the fields of ethnic studies and multicultural education.

2. Condry, J. (1987). T.V. as educator. *Action in Teacher Education*, 9, No. 2, Summer, 15–26.

    In this excellent article, Condry concludes that TV affects all who watch it—our actions, our attitudes, our beliefs, and our values. Those of us in education are in competition with television.

3. Gough, P. (1976). *Sexism: New issue in American education*, Fastback No. 81. Bloomington, IN: Phi Delta Kappa Educational Foundation.

    Sexism may not be as new an issue in the 1990s as it was in the late 1970s and 1980s, but it still exists in the schools. This fastback calls attention to those things we as educators need to be aware of as we teach.

4. Seligson, M. (1986). Child care for the school-age child. *Phi Delta Kappan*, 67, 637–640.

    This article examines the need to have some type of after-school program available to latchkey children.

5. Tarcher, J. (1982). *Return to excellence and quality in our classrooms Marva Collins way*. New York: St Martin's Press.

    This is the story of Marva Collins, who teaches in a private school in the inner city of Chicago. An inspiring story!

III

The History of Education

CHAPTER 5

OBJECTIVES

After reading Chapter 5, the student will be able to:

- View from a historical perspective the roots of American education

- Recognize why the emergence of the written language about 6000 years ago made a more formal type of schooling and education possible

- Identify noteworthy accomplishments of the Greeks and the Romans

- List specific periods and individual leaders who made significant contributions

- State why certain historical advances in education were important to American accomplishments in education

Origins of Educational Thought

Introduction

The main goal of this chapter is to discuss the influence that developments in other countries have had on American education. Two events seem so obvious and so essential to us today that they hardly need to be mentioned: the development of written language and the invention of the printing press. These two events were 5,000 years apart, yet without them education would not have progressed as it has in America.

The Development of Written Language

About 5,000 to 6,000 years ago, nomadic tribes began to grow their food rather than to hunt for it. The agricultural revolution led to the rise of cities as the new and expanded food sources led to an increase in population. Surplus food was traded with other newly emerging towns and cities, and INSTILLING THE CULTURAL HERITAGE writing was invented to keep commercial records. The new society that grew out of the agricultural revolution developed new institutions, one of the most important of which was education. There was a need not only to teach reading and writing, but also to instill the cultural heritage in the young members of the society. The Sumerians developed the first written language 5,000 to 6,000 years ago. Perhaps 6,000 characters were used in the Sumerian language, a few of which are shown in the accompanying illustration.

MAKING SOCIETY RESPONSIBLE FOR EDUCATION The impact of the development of the written language on the growth of education is obvious. But we seldom recognize that it was some 6,000 years ago that the responsibility for education began to move from the family to society. In the 1980s, more instruction outside the home is being demanded; many advocate earlier nursery school experience.

LANGUAGE CONTINUES TO EVOLVE Nomadic tribes came together in early times to achieve a better social order and higher agricultural production; today, people organize for many of the same reasons. As these diverse groups come together, our language continues to evolve, and more importantly, understanding languages other than our own has become a necessity to transact world commerce, to establish cultural ties, and to achieve greater human understanding and world peace. Our world is exciting because we can communicate, but the world situation can be frustrating when we cannot find adequate avenues

Early Sumerian pictographs.

(SOURCE: Kramer, S. N. (1963). *The Sumerians*. University of Chicago Press, Chicago, p. 102.)

Plow   Boat   Chisel   Ax   Saw

of communication. To the degree that we as educators can facilitate human understanding, we can aid in the peace-making process.

LANGUAGES
MAKE SOCI-
ETY MORE
PREDICTABLE

The introduction of written languages helped to make society more sophisticated, orderly, and predictable. The first teachers, who were probably also scribes, emerged about the same time that written languages were invented at the beginning of the Sumerian and Egyptian civilizations.

The Printing Press (Fifteenth Century)

GUTENBERG

Johannes Gutenberg, a German, is given most of the credit for inventing a press using movable metallic type in the mid-1400s. Gutenberg and others improved the printing press and refined the paper-making and ink-making processes. The implications of the development of the printing press were enormous; had it not been for this mechanical invention, the dissemination of the writings of scholars during the Renaissance, the Reformation, and since would not have been possible. The current computer suggests a close parallel to the original printing press in that both were revolutionary in their time periods.

Contributions of the Greeks

ADVANCED
THINKING

The ancient Greeks, during the Golden Age of Athens, made great advances in art, literature, and philosophy. Philosophers such as Socrates (470–399 BC), Plato (427–347 BC), and Aristotle (384–322 BC) were responsible for the advanced thinking that has affected education to the present time. They possessed wisdom far beyond what humans had previously experienced.

Socrates

DIALECTICAL
METHOD

Socrates used a logical method of argumentation known as the *dialectical method*, more often called the **Socratic method** because of Socrates' finely tuned ability to use the process. Socrates wanted people to think logically; therefore, he used the dialectical method, or logical discussion, to induce them to think. His goal was a more ethical and moral society. An example of the Socratic method follows (Meyer, 1975):

> "Do you believe," Socrates would ask an unsuspecting victim, "that Zeus leads a stainless life?"
>
> "Of course I do," comes the swift retort.
>
> "And do you believe," Socrates leads on, "that Zeus had intercourse with certain mortal women?"
>
> The man can but affirm, for long ago his elders had told him tales of the god's amorous adventures with mundane females, and the resultant increase in the Hellenic population.
>
> "Is it your belief then," Socrates drives on, "that Zeus is an adulterer?"
>
> The hard-pressed respondent begins to fidget, for he knows full well that

Socrates advanced Greek wisdom by using his dialectical method to cause people to think logically. This skill is important for all teachers.

(Photo courtesy of the Library of Congress.)

Zeus is a married god, and so, whether he likes it or not, he emits a doleful affirmation.

The implications are obvious. If Zeus committed adultery, then his life is not without stain, and his divinity must be suspect. But remark how different the business would have been had Socrates accosted the stranger with the blunt query, "Do you believe that Zeus is a god?" The very question breeds alarm and, maybe, even a call for the police. (p. 8)

Socrates' method of questioning emphasized that mental discipline is necessary for acquiring knowledge, and has had an everlasting effect on education. The questioning approach used by Socrates was the forerunner of the inquiry approach used in education today, in social studies and in the sciences.

Plato

Plato was a student of Socrates. He came from the upper class, whereas Socrates came from the middle class. Plato's aristocratic ideal included division of the state into three classes. He wrote that the masses were fit for doing the work of the state; the courageous and physically developed were fit to fight and protect; and the intellectually gifted were fit to be the kings or rulers.

CONDITION-
ING

Plato believed in using the conditioning process to shape the child's mind. Today, Plato and B. F. Skinner would have much in common as advocates of the manipulation of pleasure and pain to educate the child.

Plato believed that shaping young men (women were not educated at the time) was the best way to find the roles for them to fill in adult society. All instruction was based on what was best for the society. He attached great importance to the physical aspect of education, but games and sports were to be used for practical purposes, not for pleasure and entertainment as they are today. The practical philosophy of Plato is also found in the type of music he recommended for the young. Musically, pupils should be allowed to hear the two modes that expressed manliness and temperance, but never for pleasure or entertainment. The educational methods and curriculum ideas of Plato were well summarized by Butts (1955): "Plato doubtless did a great service in showing that a system of education is integral with the welfare of the state, but he also doubtless did a great disservice to democracy by idealizing an antidemocratic kind of state (p. 31).

CULTIVAT-
ING ONE'S
INTELLECT

Philosophically, Plato believed in the existence of a body of absolute, unchanging, spiritual ideas, which could be absorbed only by some men through contemplation. He believed that only as a man concentrated on the external truth could he cultivate his intellect. Such subjects as mathematics and philosophy were the best subjects to help students achieve intellectual discipline. The effect on Western education of Plato's idealist philosophy has been profound.

Aristotle

STRESSED IN-
TELLECTUAL
DISCIPLINE

Many feel that Aristotle was the wisest of all Greeks. He had an inquiring mind that probed into every facet open to intellectual examination. He was a student of Plato, but he believed in empiricism as the road to knowledge, whereas Plato believed in the concrete embodiment of ideas. Both Plato and Aristotle stressed intellectual discipline as the mode of accumulating knowledge.

SCIENTIFIC
THINKING

Perhaps more than anything, we owe a debt of gratitude to Aristotle for his introduction of scientific thinking. He was the first person to organize logic into a technical system of thought (Meyer, 1975). After Aristotle, most teachers taught logic as formal **mental discipline.** He gave us the tools to find rational explanations for complex matters.

Solon and Pericles

POLITICAL
DEMOCRACY

Solon (ca. 630–ca. 560 B.C.), another Greek, was considered the first great lawgiver in Athens. As a leader, Solon improved the lives of the lower classes by changing such practices as imprisonment and slavery for debt. Under Solon, the lower classes were admitted to citizenship and were given a place in the assembly, and the power of the aristocrats was weakened. As the common people in Athens gained economic opportunity, political democracy in Athens throve (Butts, 1955).

GOLDEN AGE

Pericles led the Athenian Greeks between 460 and 430 B.C. during the so-called Golden Age when democracy was at its height. Education also evolved and was most vital and rewarding during this period (Butts, 1955). In the beginning of our republic, Thomas Jefferson stressed broad educational opportunities; he must have learned this lesson from the Greeks. But just as the Greeks became very democratic for their times, they also lost some of their momentum through excessive individualism.

Contributions of the Romans

The Roman Empire spread throughout the known world, where it eventually extended a common religion and a common language with the aid of a common political bond. During the Hellenistic period from the third century B.C. to the first century B.C., Greek culture and influence spread throughout the area conquered by Alexander the Great. Along with their conquests, the Romans acquired a system of schools with a large Greek influence by the end of the third century B.C. The elementary school in

LUDUS

Rome was known as the **ludus,** and in it, children aged seven to twelve were taught how to read, write, and count. The secondary schools were

GRAMMAR SCHOOLS

entirely Greek in character. They were called **grammar schools,** and the teacher was known as a **grammaticus.** Between the ages of twelve and sixteen, boys were taught Greek grammar and literature; thus, the first secondary schools in Rome were foreign language schools. During the first century B.C., Latin grammar schools developed as well. Emperor Vespasian

HIGHER EDU-CATION

(A.D. 9–79) took the first steps toward establishing higher education in Rome by setting up library facilities with endowed chairs of rhetoric in Greek and Latin.

Quintilian

By far the most outstanding educator in Roman times was Quintilian (A.D. 35–95). He believed that the purpose of education was to uphold and protect

IMPROVE SO-CIETY

society. He also believed that education could improve society. Quintilian was chosen as rhetor from Spain, a part of the Roman Empire, and he eventually rose to the rank of senator in Rome. His high rank was due to his intellect, to his teaching, and, no doubt, to the admiration of the emperor Vespasian. Some of Quintilian's ideas on education are worthy of our consideration today.

BEING A GOOD MODEL FOR YOUR STU-DENTS

Quintilian maintained that it was important that a teacher be a good model for students and that study of a foreign language was helpful in learning the native language. Quintilian was also an advocate of group schooling rather than private tutoring, for he felt that there was great value in socialization and comradeship.

These educational ideas of Quintilian are taken from his famous book *Institutes of Oratory,* which is primarily about what an orator needed in

INSTITUTES
OF ORATORY

the way of education and training to be successful in Roman society. During the Renaissance, the *Institutes* were rediscovered and became the educational bible for generations of **Humanist** educators (Butts, 1955). Quintilian also advocated a list of great books to be read for a liberal education.

Meyer (1975) summarized best the contributions of this great educator when he outlined some of Quintilian's lasting contributions:

RIGHTS AND
DIGNITY AS
A HUMAN
BEING

> the importance of the home in the child's early education; the necessity of understanding the peculiar nature of the individual child, and, by corollary, the recognition of his rights and dignity as a human being, even though he is not yet fully formed; the value of play and joy as spurs to learning; the desirability of learning not from books alone, but from experience as well; and so on. The memory of the planter of these and other seeds of progression may have faded, but his pedagogy in the main has been kept alive. (p. 52)

SPREADING
GREEK IDEAS

The importance of the Roman period in world educational history is that the Romans not only preserved some of the important ideas of the Greeks but spread these ideas throughout the known world. The contributions of Quintilian are noteworthy because they were no doubt read by Jean-Jacques Rousseau, Johann Heinrich Pestalozzi, and other subsequent educational reformers. The strong authority of Roman rule did not, however, contribute positively to the development of democratic forms of education.

The Middle Ages (480–1350)

The church, the monastery, the manor, and the guilds were all important institutions of the Middle Ages. The pope exercised control over the kings; thus, it was important for all people to please the church in Rome.

CHARLE-
MAGNE

The Emperor Charlemagne (742–814) was a strong political leader of the era; he was able to establish a central government over most of western Europe. Charlemagne became Roman emperor in 800, when he was crowned by the pope. Under Charlemagne's rule, improvements were made in economics and agriculture, and reforms in religious and educational matters were achieved. Charlemagne invited one of the greatest scholars

ALCUIN

and teachers of his age, Alcuin of York, to be his educational adviser. The palace school that Alcuin established was attended by young members of the court and by Charlemagne himself, although he never personally learned to read and write. Along with Alcuin, other scholars were invited to teach the clergy and other officials of the government. A serious attempt was made to improve learning among the privileged classes.

The Middle Ages lasted another six centuries after Charlemagne's death. Feudal emperors ruled their individual domains through their vassals, and the lack of a united empire under a strong king contributed to the continuation of the feudal system.

During this period the monasteries worked to keep religious spirit alive and to preserve and copy ancient manuscripts. As a result, ancient documents were available to the many lay people who became interested in them in the Renaissance. The world owes a great deal to the patience, wisdom, and scholarship of these medieval monks.

LIFE AFTER
DEATH

During the Middle Ages, there was so much stress within the church and society that life after death took on prime importance rather than life on earth. The development of the individual, through education, for life in the society in which he or she lived was mostly absent in the Middle Ages. It is an important lesson of the Middle Ages that we keep the act of learning and development of the individual alive, as well as maintain a keen sensitivity to anyone's possible disenfranchisement from an educational opportunity.

The Renaissance (Fourteenth to Seventeenth Centuries)

LIFE IN THE
PRESENT

The Greeks, at their peak of power and influence, had altered the perspective of human thought, focusing on life in the present and viewing nature from a scientific rather than a mystical viewpoint. In the Middle Ages, the pendulum swung back to a more mystical focus on the hereafter. But a new revolution of thought began during the fourteenth century. The rediscovery of classical civilization, the increase in trade and commerce, the revitalization of science and technology, and the rise of a new aristocracy whose wealth came from trade and banking rather than land and whose base of power lay in the cities signaled the beginning of the Renaissance. Life again centered on earthly existence rather than the hereafter. The newly emerging Italian Renaissance witnessed the appearance of a new political, social, and economic order that would sweep across Europe, ending forever the old **feudal system.** Florence, Italy, under the stimulation of the very wealthy Medici family, was a major center of the newly emerging Renaissance culture.

NEW ARIS-
TOCRACY

When the Renaissance began, the church was dominant, but this was to change as the kings built strong national states. Further weakening of the church occurred after the Protestant Reformation began in 1517. The breakdown of the church contributed to the dissolution of the feudal system that held so many people in virtual slavery. Many serfs found new opportunities in the lively new cites that were springing up, where increased commercial trade resulted in an increase in the growth and vitality of city life. Art and architecture, with brighter colors and inspiring designs, also helped to give a lift to city life.

BRIGHTER
COLORS

The Greeks had focused on humans and what they could do with art, literature, science, education, and other facets of life just as the Humanist writers of the Renaissance focused on humans rather than the church. Bonds that held people to the church were broken in favor of more secular approaches to life. The Humanists of this period were people who found new interest in human nature, thus freeing them from the restricting demands of the church, the guilds, the manors, and the monasteries. Scholars could now think more independently and with fewer restrictions.

Erasmus was an independent thinker, the foremost humanist of the Renaissance.

(Photo courtesy of the Library of Congress.)

ERASMUS   Desiderius Erasmus (1466–1536) of the Netherlands, one of the greatest
                   scholars of the period, is considered the foremost Humanist of the Renais-
                   sance. Like most scholars of that era, he believed that human nature was
                   perfectable if only it was allowed to develop through an understanding of
                   ancient classics. Among his accomplishments was the first critical version
                   of the New Testament, which marked the beginning of modern higher
PRAISE OF   biblical scholarship. His *Praise of Folly*, written in little more than a week,
FOLLY   gave him an international reputation. In this book, Erasmus wrote lines
                   that were considered humorous and innocent at the time but that, in fact,
                   were critical of the church and of what he perceived as corruption within

the church. The book contributed to the spiritual rebellion that is now known as the Reformation. Erasmus also wrote the *Colloquies*, which were schoolbooks for children, which contained many suggestions on how children could lead an upright Christian life. As did the *Praise of Folly*, the COLLOQUIES *Colloquies* criticized the established church, but Erasmus did not join the leaders of the Reformation by using his powerful pen to help their cause.

INDIVIDUAL THOUGHT The Renaissance gave the world back the freedom of individual thought that had been lost before Europe settled into the Middle Ages. Institutions such as the church, the arts, music, the sciences, and education would never be the same. The spirit of the Renaissance needs to be preserved by modern-day educators as they stimulate young learners to discover the wonders of the world.

The Reformation (Sixteenth Century)

The Reformation grew out of a seed planted in the Renaissance. For years before the Reformation, there had been rumblings of discontent within the MARTIN LU-THER established church. One of the leaders was a priest named Martin Luther (1483–1546), a very popular professor of religion at the University of Wittenberg. The pope, through intermediaries, authorized the selling of indulgences (spiritual pardons). One of the conditions for gaining an indulgence was to give a money donation for the building of Saint Peter's Church at Rome. Luther was very upset and, in 1517, he nailed ninety-five "theses" (problems with the church) to the church door at Wittenberg. This act PROTES-TANTS officially signaled the beginning of the Protestant Reformation, which has never ended. Although Luther, at first, wanted to reform the church from within, many Reformation forces rejected the church altogether. Protestants, searching for their own interpretation of Christianity, formed numerous denominations: the Lutherans, the Presbyterians, the Anglicans, the Baptists, the Quakers, and many others.

Education benefited greatly from the Reformation. Luther insisted that solely through our faith in God could we be saved; therefore, it was imperative that we learn to read and interpret the Bible for ourselves. Luther suggested that every prince should provide primary schools for both boys and girls, and he translated the Bible into peasant German so that they could understand. Later, in 1528, Luther wrote his famous catechism, which became the child's basic book for religious instruction. Unfortunately, Luther was not able to educate all of his followers quickly because most education still took place in the home, and many parents were illiterate.

SEEDS FOR DEMOCRACY Perhaps the true importance of the Reformation was that it sowed the seeds for the democratic type of education that emerged in the late eighteenth and nineteenth centuries (Butts, 1955). The reformers, including both Luther and John Calvin (1509–1564), gave lip service to universal education for all, but they ended up supporting the more classical type of secondary education for the upper classes. Democratic education emerged

Martin Luther marked the beginning of the Protestant Reformation when he nailed his ninety-five theses to the door of the church of Wittenberg.

(Photo courtesy of the Library of Congress.)

several centuries later in America about 1840, where equal opportunity was afforded to all except a few minority groups.

READ THE BI-
BLE

No matter what trials and tribulations Luther and his fellow reformers had with education, the precedent had been set that being able to read the Bible or a catechism was the pathway to salvation. The Puritans and other religious groups arriving in America established schools for their children so that they could read the Bible.

As a reaction to the Protestant Reformation, the Catholics began to use education to counter the growth of Protestantism. Ignatius of Loyola (1491–

LOYOLA AND
THE JESUITS

1556) started the Society of Jesus, more commonly known as the Jesuits. The Jesuits' weapon against the spread of Protestantism was superior education. They established schools to train teachers all over the world, and as a result, they became a successful **Counter-reformation** agency.

STIMULUS TO
PUBLIC EDU-
CATION

The Reformation has been and continues to be a stimulus to mass or public education. Currently, in America, education is regarded as a major pathway to social mobility and economic security, but the Puritans and other religious groups originally intended only that their children learn to read and write in order to read and interpret the Bible. In some religious groups, schooling is still first and foremost in promoting their faith. In recent years, private, church-based Protestant schools have been established across the country to provide religious training similar to that given by the long-established Catholic and Lutheran schools. The results of the Protestant Reformation are still very much a part of what is happening in education today.

The Development of Science and Reason

THE SCIEN-
TIFIC SPIRIT

The study of science was condemned by Martin Luther as "that silly little fool, that Devil's bride, Dame Reason, God's worst enemy" (cited in Butts, 1955, p. 217). People were burned at the stake for advocating scientific explanations of natural and supernatural phenomena. Both Catholics and Protestants advocated a strict and narrow curriculum, consisting mainly of God's Holy Word. Reformers such as Luther could not control all people's minds, however; thus, Luther had opened the door to the questioning of traditional ways of thinking. The **scientific spirit** was one of the most long-lasting nonconventional phenomena to emerge from this period.

Sir Francis Bacon

THE SCIEN-
TIFIC
METHOD

Because of his writings and his influential political position as lord chancellor in England, Sir Francis Bacon (1561–1626) was able to popularize the scientific method. He determined that through the scientific investigation of known facts, one could make some generalizations that would fit many situations. In *Novum Organum* (1620/1901), Bacon set down his theories: the following example is an important part of the inductive process that he is famous for enunciating:

> CVI.   In forming our axioms from induction, we must examine and try whether the axiom we derive be only fitted and calculated for the particular instances from which it is deduced, or whether it be more extensive and general. If it be the latter, we must observe, as it were, in pointing out new particulars, so that we may neither stop at actual discoveries, nor with a careless grasp catch at shadows and abstract forms, instead of substances of a determinant nature: and as soon as we act thus, well authorized hope may with reason be said to beam upon us. (pp. 83–84)

In this instance, Bacon was warning his readers not to be taken in by the first set of observations, but to test the axiom to see if it fits a particular instance or can be generalized further:

KNOWLEDGE
ARISES OUT
OF EXPERI-
ENCE

Today Bacon would be criticized for recording masses of useless data just because he observed them and for a neglect of the supreme importance of mathematics in modern science. Nevertheless, his insistence that knowledge arises out of experience rather than through traditional authority and his perception of the use of a controlled method of investigation were of supreme importance. (Butts, 1955, p. 219)

Bacon was not the first person to use these procedures as a method of investigation, but because of his important political position, he was able to popularize the method and make it respectable.

The result of Bacon's contribution to education and to science today is the growth of scientific inquiry as a discipline. As a result, the causes of some of our worst diseases, as well as answers to some of the most preplexing problems in the universe, have been discovered or are under study. As a teacher and a promoter of a point of view, one never knows what long-range effect he or she may have on others—evidence the writings of Bacon.

The Origin of Secular Education

COMENIUS

Students often ask when religious teachings and God as the center of the curriculum faded from our schools. The concept that children should be prepared for life in general and not just for entering the heavenly gates entered our thinking soon after the Reformation. John Amos Comenius (1592–1670) was a Moravian bishop who believed that children were not born human but became humanized by being educated in society. Eventually, Horace Mann (1796–1859) borrowed some of these secular ideas as he designed and modeled for us in America our common school system; however, both Comenius and Mann were very devout Christians.

THE VISIBLE
WORLD

Comenius was considered the most distinguished educational reformer of his time. His most famous textbook, *Visible World*, was published in 1658. It was among the first illustrated schoolbooks ever written. Comoenius felt that the best way to learn about the world was to observe it firsthand, and the next best way was through pictures. He felt it was the purpose of education to prepare children for happiness on earth as in heaven, thus breaking with the tradition of the Middle Ages of preparing one for life after death. Comenius also felt that learning was within the reach of every child, rich or poor, male or female.

Secular education originated in this early period because of the logic of educating the child for all of life rather than just for the church. The candle of religious fervor within the schools did not burn low until more recent times. The curriculum and schools gradually became less religious; however, the *New England Primer*, used as a text in colonial Massachusetts, is a reminder that the Puritans were one religious group that did not ride the

John Amos Comenius believed in education for life and learning through experience.

(Photo courtesy of the Library of Congress.)

Comenius bandwagon. It was difficult to shed the effects of the medieval period of pious religious teachings, but most of the public high schools in America today are virtually devoid of direct religious influence.

HOW TO TEACH CHILDREN AT HOME

Comenius wrote a special handbook, *The School of Infancy*, to instruct mothers how to teach their children at home. He urged mothers to teach their children values as soon as they were able to understand. Comenius also described a vernacular school for teaching the basics, which included much material of a moral/ethical nature. He also suggested a Latin school and a school of higher learning. Some of his schoolbooks continue to be used 100 years after his death.

LEARNING BY
PRACTICE

Comenius firmly believed in learning by practice. Like Jean-Jacques Rousseau, he believed that sense experiences stimulated a student's intellect. Comenius commented on what we in educational circles now call *hands-on experience:*

> Artisans do not detain their apprentices with theories, but set them to do practical work at an early stage; thus they learn to forge by forging, to carve by carving, to paint by painting, and to dance by dancing. In schools, therefore, let the students learn to write by writing, to talk by talking, to sing by singing, and to reason by reasoning. In this way schools will become workshops humming with work, and the students whose efforts prove successful will experience the truth of the proverb: "Our work makes us." (Cited in Piaget, 1957, p. 88)

The Effect of the Age of Reason and Enlightenment

By the eighteenth century, people in Europe were weary of the authoritarian regimes that had appeared during and after the Reformation. Arbitrary rule by kings in the various countries, as exemplified by the reign of Louis XIV of France, continued to keep the common people from participating in government. All monarchs (some were women) were **elitists** who maintained their power by supporting loyal armies and a privileged nobility. As a result of the disenchantment that the people, particularly the emerging middle class, felt with the noble classes, the **Enlightenment** was born.

ORIGIN OF
THE EN-
LIGHTEN-
MENT

Reformers during the Enlightenment period protested the domination of the nobility, who thought their inherited rights put them above the law. Leaders of the Enlightenment emphasized the natural rights of all human beings, which were supported by the new scientific conceptions of the world. Hereditary rights eventually gave way to more democratic forms of government.

EMPHASIS ON
NATURAL
RIGHTS

JOHN LOCKE

One reformer, John Locke (1632–1704), was among the intellectual giants of the period. Locke was born into the aristocratic class in England, but as a philosopher, he produced some very democratic ideas for government. He supported the social contract theory of government whereby citizens delegate authority to the government, in turn for which the government agrees to protect the natural rights of all citizens. Locke's social contract theory greatly affected the framers of the American Constitution. As our government is basically democratic, his influence has indirectly affected our need in America to sustain a good educational system to produce citizens who are intelligent voters.

SOCIAL CON-
TRACT THE-
ORY

EDUCATION
THROUGH
THE SENSES

In his eductional theory, Locke emphasized education through the senses rather than from memory. He attacked narrow classical training and favored curricular items like arithmetic, writing, science, carpentry, gardening, and sports. He popularized the concept of education as achievement of "a sound mind in a sound body." He was not the first nor the last of the great thinkers to emphasize the senses as the road to knowledge.

ROUSSEAU

Jean-Jacques Rousseau (1712–1778), a writer and philosopher, was a child of the Enlightenment. Rousseau held the view, characteristic of the Enlight-

DO EXACTLY
OPPOSITE
enment, that the best way to do things in the future was the opposite of how they had been done in the past; this view reflected a contempt for authority. In the schools of Rousseau's day, the child was thought of as evil and sinful; the teacher's job was to drive the evil from the child. Rousseau espoused the opposite philosophy—that the child is born with inherent impulses that are right.

HUMAN NA-
TURE IS PER-
FECTABLE
Teachers and others inspired by Rousseau began to look at children in a different, more positive way. From this emerged the principle that human nature is perfectable and can be constantly improved. Key words in Rousseau's writings were *naturalism, freedom, growth, interests,* and *activity,* which would be incorporated into John Dewey's progressive educational philosophy at the turn of this century. Rousseau argued that education should be designed to follow the natural stages of development of the child. For example, in the infancy stage, Rousseau suggested free play and activity:
ADAPT TO
THE CHILD
"In general, Rousseau did a great service in directing attention to the desirability of studying the child so that education can be adapted to the child's characteristic needs" (Butts, 1955, p. 291).

ÉMILE
Rousseau wrote about what he felt was the ideal teaching-learning situation in his book *Émile* (1762). This very famous book describes in detail how the boy Émile is to be brought up and nurtured into manhood. According to Boyd (1963), the book indicates many parallels to Rousseau's own life as a child. Even though Rousseau was not an educator and his philosophy, as noted in *Émile,* was never put into practice, he influenced the works of many other educational reformers.

PESTALOZZI
One of the great educators was Johann Heinrich Pestalozzi (1746–1827), who was an avid admirer of Rousseau's ideas on the natural development of the child. Unlike Rousseau, Pestalozzi was a practicing educator who tried out his ideas. Some of his experiments with education failed, for a number of reasons, but eventually, he was successful and gained many followers all over the world, including the United States.

DEVELOP
FROM
WITHIN
Pestalozzi believed that religion and moral instruction were very important but that they should be developed from within the individual and not imposed on him or her from without. He emphasized individual development, maintaining that every faculty of the body and mind should be harmoniously and uniformly developed. Society, he felt, could be improved if individuals were helped to develop their own powers, abilities, and feelings of self-respect and security. He was a champion of the poor and down-trodden and an advocate of discipline through cooperation and sympathy, not physical punishment. He was opposed to mere repetition as a means of learning, the method used in his day to learn the rules of grammar. He
EXPERIENCE
believed that experience had to precede or accompany learning, emphasized practical activities, and developed **"object-teaching lessons"** related to the step-by-step study of objects in the child's environment. The principles and ideas of Pestalozzi were used by other reformers to shape the schools in Germany and in America.

Johann Heinrich Pestalozzi was a Swiss educator who believed that all children should be educated to develop their individual talents through experience.

(Photo courtesy of the Library of Congress.)

In a portion of a letter to a James Greaves, Pestalozzi wrote:

We must bear in mind that the ultimate end of education is not perfection in the accomplishments of the school, but fitness for life; not the acquirement of habits of blind obedience and of prescribed diligence, but a preparation for independent action. We must bear in mind that whatever class of society a pupil may belong to, whatever calling he may be intended for, there are certain faculties in human nature common to all, which constitute the stock of the fundamental energies of man. We have no right to withhold from any one the opportunities of developing all his faculties. It may be judicious to treat some of them with marked attention, and to give up the idea of bringing others to high perfection. The diversity of talent and inclination, of plans and pursuits, is a sufficient proof for the necessity of such a distinction. But I repeat that we have no right to shut out the child from the development of those faculties also which we may not for the present conceive to be essential for his future calling or station in life. (cited in Anderson, 1931, p. 166)

This letter points to the need for general education, which Horace Mann and others called for in this country in the 1840s. Mann was strongly influenced by the German educational system, which was influenced greatly by Pestalozzi.

The origin of the kindergarten goes back to Pestalozzi and one of his star

The early kindergarten was less regimented than schooling for older children.
(Photo courtesy of the Library of Congress.)

FROEBEL AND
KINDER-
GARTEN

students Friedrich Wilhelm Froebel (1782–1852). Froebel very much admired Pestalozzi, for whom he taught in Switzerland, but Froebel returned to his native Germany to make his unique contribution to educational history. Froebel believed that educational reform must start in the nursery school, and he dedicated himself to this task.

Froebel made his kindergarten a land of song, story, and play. The kindergarten was designed to be child's world, not an adult world into which the teacher forced the child. Emphasis would be placed on socialization or helping the child learn to function freely and agreeably with his mates (females were not permitted to attend kindergarten). Among Froebel's curricular offerings were what he called "gifts" which were cubes, spheres, cylinders, and circles. All the "gifts" had symbolic meanings. Froebel's "occupations" were items that could be transformed when they were put to use, for example, sand, clay, cardboard, and paper. The story was also made part of the kindergarten, and it stimulated interest in all areas.

FIRST AMERI-
CAN KINDER-
GARTEN

Froebel's invention came to America as early as 1855 in Watertown, Wisconsin. Here Mrs. Carl Schurz, a former pupil of Froebel, opened the first kindergarten in America. Elizabeth Peabody of Boston opened the first English-speaking kindergarten in 1860, and the first public tax-supported kindergarten was opened in St. Louis in 1873. Most public school systems in America today provide kindergartens, but it took more than 100 years for this innovation to become standard educational practice. In the current curriculum of the kindergarten, one can still see the influence of Rousseau's naturalism and Pestalozzi's practicality.

IDEALS OF
THE EN-
LIGHTEN-
MENT

Even though practice lags behind theory, sometimes by hundreds of years, the Enlightenment brought us hope for democracy and the theory of the natural development of the child. Common people began to be recognized as persons who were important and worthy of being educated. The United States has demonstrated the ideals of the Enlightenment probably better than any other nation, but much work remains before it can be said that there is truly equal educational opportunity in American schools.

Summary

The ideas and events described in this chapter may seem ancient to most of us, but even 6,000 years is only a fraction of a tick of the clock in the history of the human race. All of the people and events portrayed in this chapter were very influential in the development of education in the United States. The early symbols that made up the first written language were a start toward the development of modern language. The Greeks used languages to communicate and make great advancements in society, and the Romans spread their culture throughout the known world. The Renaissance was a reawakening of individual freedom and spirit. The printing press was and continues to be a catalyst in cultural development. The Reformation caused people to think about their individual salvation and thus about the need for common schooling. Science and the beginning of secular education promoted the concept that human beings could benefit from learning about life here on earth as well as life in the hereafter. And the Enlightenment brought us our government, our democratic way of life, a new way of looking at humankind, and the kindergarten.

Glossary Terms

Socratic Method, 159
Mental Discipline, 161
Ludus, 162
Grammar Schools, 162
Grammaticus, 162
Humanist, 163
Feudal System, 164

Counter-Reformation, 168
Scientific Spirit, 169
Secular Education, 169
Elitists, 171
Enlightenment, 171
Object-Teaching Lessons, 172

Questions

1. What are some factors contributing to the transfer of responsibility for education from the family to society?

2. Why are Greeks admired for their education contributions? What were some of the prime factors leading to these contributions?

3. What does it mean when a political leader, such as the Roman Emperor Vespasian, takes a real interest in education? Are there some parallels to this leadership role at the local, state, and national levels of American government at the present time?

4. Quintilian had some ideas about education that are as relevant today as they were in Roman times. What are some of his ideas?

5. What were some of the problems of the Middle Ages that tended to slow down inquiry and the advancement of knowledge? Could these problems occur again? Why or why not?

6. Why was Erasmus an important figure in history? What did he do during the Renaissance that made his name synonymous with the period?

7. What immediate and long-lasting changes came about as a result of the Reformation?

Annotated Bibliography

1. Butts, R. F., & Cremin, L. A. (1953). *A history of education in American culture.* New York: Holt.

   This book, according to the authors, should help educators to review our history to recognize the constructive ideas/methods that can be used in the future and the destructive ideas/methods that need to be changed. It is filled with many interesting facts about education.

2. Kramer, S. N. (1963). *The Sumerians: Their history, culture, and character.* Chicago: University of Chicago Press.

This volume covers the political history of the Sumerian people and the nature of their social and economic institutions. It describes how the Sumerians and their language were discovered and brought to our attention.

3. Froebel, F. (1887). *The education of men.* (translated from the German by W. N. Hailmann). New York: D. Appleton.

    Considered Froebel's greatest work, this book helps us to understand Froebel's philosophy and the principles upon which he based the kindergarten system.

4. Erasmus, D. (1942). *The praise of folly.* New York: Published for the Classics Club by W. J. Black.

    Erasmus, a humanist, took only about one week to write this book, which promotes the humanists' program for educational, religious, and theological reform. This witty work was bitterly attacked as expected.

5. Jelinik, V. (1953). *The analytical didactic of Comenius.* Chicago: University of Chicago Press.

    The reader is introduced to some of the practical ideas of Comenius. His special methods for instilling knowledge are interesting and useful.

Colonial and Federal Developments in Education

OBJECTIVES

After reading Chapter 6 the student will be able to:

- Describe the three basic areas of colonial development in America

- Understand how the three areas of colonial development have influenced American education in different directions

- Identify some of the early practices in education

- Recognize the depth of federal involvement in education from 1785 to the present

- Appreciate the role that the federal government has played in stimulating education

Introduction

This chapter focuses on the growth of schooling in the American colonies and the expansion of the federal government's role in education since the adoption of the U.S. Constitution in 1789.

The colonial period was marked by significant differences in the development of educational resources in the northern, middle, and southern geographic regions. Each area made lasting contributions to the nation's educational growth.

As America made the transition from an aggregate of colonies to a republic, the federal government took a very inactive role in education because of the Tenth Amendment to the Constitution. Over the years, however, the federal government has had tremendous influence on the growth and climate of education. U.S. Supreme Court decisions as in the *Dartmouth College* case and *Brown v. Board of Education of Topeka* have affected all school systems. Acts of Congress such as the Morrill Act of 1862, the Civil Rights Act of 1964, and the Elementary and Secondary Education Act of 1965 have furthered education for many citizens. The executive branch has also been active, most recently with the study *A Nation at Risk* (National Commission on Excellence in Education, 1983). The federal government has probably done more to influence the direction of education, but has spent less money than either states or local communities.

Colonial Developments in Education

Introduction

THE SCOPE OF PUBLIC EDUCATION

MORALITY FOR RELIGION

MORE THAN FORMAL EDUCATION

During the colonial period in America, from 1607 to 1784, educational practices reflected Old World traditions. Commager (1976) outlined three areas in which the colonies were different from the Old World. First was the enlargement of the scope of public education. Most of the expansion was in the New England area, but it occurred in other areas as well. The second difference was the substitution of **morality** for religion in the schools. Generalized religion was present in the schools rather than one particular religion. Third, schools provided more than a just formal education for students. This section highlights developments in three distinct geographic areas in colonial America, and some early educational practices are noted. (See the Appendix for Dates of Key Educational Events in America.)

The Northern Colonial Development

The first settlers in the northern colonies were the Pilgrims, who were of English descent, but who, because of religious persecution, left England to go to Holland. The Pilgrims were of the Puritan faith, and most found life

THE JOINT
STOCK COM-
PANY

in Holland agreeable at first; however, some eventually returned to their homeland and, together with others from England, formed a joint stock company. The formation of the joint stock company made it easier for groups to get together and pool their resources: English farms were being turned into sheep enclosures, and farmhands were being put out of work;

The 1908 schoolroom was ruled by the schoolmaster and was populated with scholars of all ages, studying and reciting their lessons.

[Photo courtesy of the Library of Congress.]

and vital natural resources, such as timber, were being depleted, so that it was increasingly urgent to find new resources. Many laborers were being put out of work, and because help from the government was not available as it is today, the economic motivation to emigrate was as intense as the religious motivation. Thus, it was a joint stock company of English and Dutch Pilgrims that left England for America on the Mayflower in 1620.

GRAMMAR
SCHOOL

HARVARD

Once in America, the Puritans at first left education up to the church and individual households, but in 1635, they established the first **grammar school.** Only one year later, in 1636, Harvard College was established to train the clergy. The colony needed the clergy, but only half of the first few years' graduates went into the ministry; thus began Harvard's role of training other professional groups.

LAW OF 1642

OLD DE-
LUDER SA-
TAN ACT

LAW OF 1647

ALL CHIL-
DREN

Because by 1642 concern had been raised in the communities that the youth were not learning to read, the Commonwealth of Massachusetts decided to enact a law regarding education. The law of 1642 was the first law in America to establish the principle of compulsory education, but it did not specify any schools, nor did it require attendance. The Old Deluder Satan Act of 1647 was a tougher law: it called for every town with 50 or more households to offer reading and writing so that the children could avoid hellfire and damnation by reading the Scriptures. Also, the law of 1647 instructed towns with 100 or more households to provide Latin grammar schools to enable the young to prepare themselves for college. Thus, we see that the colony had enlarged the scope of education to include all children, whereas people in the Old World, especially England, had been concerned only with the education of certain elite groups.

The fact that education was specified by law did not mean that there was instant compliance. Nevertheless, there was a real interest in the communities in providing basic education. Apparently, the Massachusetts colonists complied better with the mandate for grammar schools than they did for basic schooling, for all twelve towns of over 100 inhabitants established grammar schools. In these early days, as in more recent times, farmers needed their boys at home to help with the work; therefore, they did not encourage schooling as much for their sons as the city dwellers did.

UNITY

There was more unity in New England than in other colonial areas. The unity among people in the North was probably due to their common religious ties, their town meetings, and their close proximity to one another. Although they did not always agree on issues, there was better communication within their settlements, and the result was that they were quicker to support education than either the middle or the southern colonies.

The Middle Colonial Development

VERY PARO-
CHIAL

The colony of New Amsterdam was established in 1621 by the Dutch. From the start, this colonial establishment was very parochial. The Dutch did their own teaching, as did the Anglicans, the Catholics, the Quakers, and others. Because of this lack of unity, a university (Princeton) was not established until 1746, or 110 years after New England's Harvard.

TOLERATION
OF OTHERS

Pennsylvania, another middle colony, was established in 1681 by William Penn (1644–1718). Penn's influence and the Quaker belief in **toleration** of other religious groups led many other groups, such as Anglicans, Lutherans, Presbyterians, Dunkers, Mennonites, and Moravians, to move into the colony (the population was 12,000 by 1689). All of these groups made immense contributions to the society, but the different religious sects generally stayed to themselves, worshiping and educating their children in their own churches and schools. Thus, they also were very parochial in their educational activities.

WILLIAM
PENN

William Penn expressed his concept of education:

> We press their memory too soon, and puzzle, strain and load them with words and rules; to know grammar and rhetoric, and a strange tongue or two, that it is ten to one may never be useful to them; leaving their natural genius to mechanical and physical, or natural knowledge uncultivated and neglected; which would be of exceeding use and pleasure to them through the whole course of life. (cited in Cremin, 1970, p. 305)

PRACTICAL
EDUCATION

HUMAN
EQUALITY

Penn was concerned that all children should be educated, but he also felt that a college curriculum was unnecessary because of the impracticality of the courses.

The Quakers also brought with them the concept of human equality. The Quakers believed in working with and educating blacks and Indians. Penn himself tended to be rather **paternalistic** toward blacks and Indians, but later Quaker leaders came out very strongly against the evils of slavery. Quakers in the mid-1800s helped slaves escape through the underground railroad, and they were active in the abolition movement before the Civil War.

BENJAMIN
FRANKLIN

SELF-EDUCA-
TION

*POOR RICH-
ARD'S ALMA-
NAC*

Benjamin Franklin (1706–1790), though he was born in Boston, the son of a candlemaker, spent most of his adult life in Philadelphia. A common theme that Franklin espoused most of his life was the need for self-education. Franklin himself was the perfect model of self-education, having had no more than two years of formal education. He wrote and distributed *Poor Richard's Almanac*, which was filled with proverbs that encouraged industry and frugality as a means of obtaining wealth. Typical of these proverbs is (Cremin, 1970) "It being more difficult for a man in want to act always honestly, as it is hard for an empty sack to stand upright" (p. 374). The *Almanac* was widely disseminated and read by the average American, who understood the commonsense proverbs.

JUNTO CLUB

Franklin's desire for practical education led to the establishment of the Junto Club in Philadelphia. The Junto was a club for mutual self-improvement and was put together by Franklin and his friends for that purpose. Franklin was influenced by John Locke, who had established a similar club for self-improvement in England. The club served Franklin for forty years as an intellectual sounding board for his creative ideas.

Franklin was very interested in practical education, as was Penn. He reflected in his famous autobiography the pride he had felt in establishing

PHILADEL-
PHIA ACAD-
EMY
the Philadelphia **Academy** in 1751, which later became the University of Pennsylvania. Franklin wanted his students to acquire a good education in the English language; thus, Latin and Greek were not high on his list. The curriculum included natural history and gardening, the history of commerce, principles of mechanics, physical exercise, experiments with scientific apparatus, and field trips to farms for natural observations. The academy became the second type of secondary school established in America, the first being the Latin grammar school, and the third being the high school. (The first high school was established in Boston in 1821.)

The Southern Colonial Development

JAMESTOWN,
1607
In the southern colonial area, Jamestown, Virginia, was established in 1607. This colony's basic motivation for settlement was economic. The settlers' interest in the land and in what it could do for them led eventually to the use of slaves as a source of cheap labor.

PRIVATE TU-
TORS

OLD FIELD
SCHOOL

SLAVERY
The plantation system was not conducive to universal education because of the sparseness of population over a large geographical area. The planters installed private tutors in their homes to teach their sons, whom they later sent to Harvard, Princeton, Yale, William and Mary, or England for a university education. Poorer whites received very little education, but occasionally planters would get together and build a one-room school on an abandoned tobacco field—sometimes called an **old field school**. Generally, instruction was meager, and the teachers were ill-prepared.

The institution of slavery, set up to provide cheap labor, had a profound psychological effect on all who lived in the South, both white and black. To generalize, the whites developed a superior attitude, and as a result, the slaves suffered terrible indignities. Life in the South, and public education in particular, would lag behind the other areas of the country far beyond the colonial years.

One example of the degree to which this superiority–inferiority attitude existed is a whipping given a slave owned by Colonel Lloyd, the same man who owned Frederick Douglass (1817–1895). The beating in question was witnessed by Frederick Douglass (cited in Preston, 1980):

> One of the most heart-saddening and humiliating scenes I ever witnessed was the whipping of Old Barney, by Col. Lloyd himself. Here were two men, both advanced in years; there were the silvery locks of Col. L., and there was the bald and toil-worn brow of Old Barney; master and slave: superior and inferior here, but equals at the bar of God; and in the common course of events, they must both soon meet in another world. . . . "Uncover your head!" said the imperious master; he was obeyed. "Take off your jacket, you old rascal!" and off came Barney's jacket. "Down on your knees!" Down knelt the old man, his shoulders bare, his bald head glistening in the sun, and his aged knees on the cold, damp ground. In this humble and debasing attitude, the master—that master to whom he had given the best years and the best strength of his life—came forward, and laid on thirty lashes, with his horse whip. The old man bore it patiently, to the last, answering each blow with a slight shrug of the shoulders,

Private family tutoring was the main method of education for sons of southern plantation owners in the colonial South.

(Photo courtesy of the Library of Congress.)

and a groan. I cannot think that Col. Lloyd succeeded in marring the flesh of Old Barney very seriously, for the whip was a light, riding whip; but the spectacle of an aged man—a husband and a father—humbly kneeling before a worm of the dust, surprised and shocked me at the time; and since I have grown old enough to think on the wickedness of slavery, few facts have been of more value to me than this; to which I was a witness. It reveals slavery in its true color, and in its maturity of repulsive hatefulness. (pp. 69–70)

THOMAS JEF-
FERSON

GENERAL
DIFFUSION
OF KNOWL-
EDGE

Slavery was a negative force in the South with respect to the development of education, but there were positive factors in the South as well, such as Thomas Jefferson (1743–1826) and his creative mind. Jefferson's contributions to the young republic were many, but he should be most remembered as a strong advocate of public education. Jefferson wrote a bill in 1779 for the Virginia legislature, the Bill for the More General Diffusion of Knowledge. Under the guidelines of the bill, Virginia was to be divided into parts, called *hundreds*, and each hundred was to provide elementary schools where reading, writing, arithmetic, and history were to be taught gratis to all free inhabitants. (The economic system in the South at this time hinged on the institution of slavery, and slaves were to be kept ignorant. Thus, slaves were left out of Jefferson's educational plan.) The bill went on to propose that Virginia build twenty grammar schools throughout the commonwealth to teach more promising students such subjects as Latin, Greek, and English grammar, and advanced arithmetic. The brightest scholars of the lower school whose parents could not pay tuition were to be granted scholarships to the grammar school. Finally, Jefferson's bill provided to ten scholarship students of the grammar schools free tuition, board, and clothing for three years of study at William and Mary College (Cremin, 1970).

The immediate results of the Bill for the More General Diffusion of Knowledge for Virginia were disappointing, for the legislature failed to pass it until seventeen years after it was proposed. Then, they left it up to the courts in each county to decide whether they needed to implement the law, and none of the countries wanted it. The inspiring words and the educational ideals written into the bill were not lost, however, as they eventually helped to bring free education to New England, the Midwest, the Far West, and eventually to Jefferson's own South (Brodinsky, 1976). The bill that Jefferson authored reflected the thinking of Locke and Rousseau, whose writings Jefferson was very fond of reading.

Jefferson's educational interest expanded to the University of Virginia, where he designed the buildings, organized the curriculum, and assembled a faculty. The university opened in 1825, a year before his death; the University of Virginia was truly "Mr. Jefferson's University" (Meyer, 1967, p. 128).

In an effort to expand education, the Society for the Propagation of the Gospel in Foreign Parts (SPGFP) was established in 1701 to educate slaves and Indians. This Anglican educational group felt that if they could be taught to read and write, slaves and Indians would have a chance at salvation. Naturally, SPGFP had trouble in the South because the society's principles were antagonistic to those of the southern establishments; slaves, by law, were not to be taught, and Indians resisted SPGFP teachings. SPGFP was to have better luck in the middle and northern colonies.

Although public schooling was long in arriving in the South, southerners founded a secular college in 1693 in the town of Williamsburg, known as William and Mary College. Among other things, William and Mary was the first college to establish modern languages and modern history as part of the curriculum. The first chair of law, occupied by the famous George

Wythe, who instructed Thomas Jefferson, was established as William and Mary. Here also was founded in 1776 the famous honor society known as Phi Beta Kappa.

The achievements in education in the southern colonies were mixed. William and Mary College and the University of Virginia were landmarks in higher educational achievement. And the educational ideals of Thomas

Jefferson were inspirational. Yet, forever overshadowed by the economic needs of the plantation system, the South lagged far behind the North in the development of public education.

Some Early Practices During the Colonial Period

Several practices during the colonial period are interesting from a historical point of view. Most of these practices originated in Europe, and some lingered on many years after the colonial period (Johnson, 1963):

The Hornbook

The hornbook was not a book in the usual sense of the word, but it was usually a piece of printed paper about three by four inches fastened on a thin piece of board. The name "hornbook" came from the fact that it was a custom in those days to cover the written material on the hornbook with the translucent covering from a cow's horn. Covering of the letters was important to save them from being smudged by little fingers. At one end of the board was a handle with a hole in it so a string could be attached; therefore, the youngster would be able to hang it around his neck. Generally, the alphabet was printed on the hornbook in both capitals and in small letters; and then in orderly array the vowels, then double lines of ab, eb, ibs, and the benediction, "In the name of the Father, and the Son, and of the Holy Ghost. Amen." The remaining space was devoted to the Lord's Prayer, unless, as was sometimes the case, this was supplemented at the bottom by Roman numerals. (p. 28, emphasis added)

FROM A
COW'S HORN

First Schoolhouses

The first school buildings were described by Johnson as having been built of logs exclusively. This type of log building was common even fifty years after the Revolution. Often the floors were bare and very dusty—especially when some young scholars would deliberately kick up some dust to amuse themselves and their schoolmates. Sticks were inserted around the walls on the inside of the cabin, and boards were nailed to them for desks. There was a fireplace at one end, and some windows were cut where greased paper was inserted to break the wind and cold and to let in some light. These early colonial schools had no blackboards and no maps. Some schools had globes, but there were no slates and pencils until much later. (p. 38)

FLOORS WERE
BARE AND
VERY DUSTY

Writing Practices

Most young scholars of this era learned the skill of penmanship very well. They generally wrote in **"copybooks"** which were hand-made and ruled by the students. Writing was done with quill pens and ink, and early schoolmasters needed to be experts on how to sharpen quill pens. Some schools made their own ink, while others used ink powder which was put to use by dissolving it in water. The most important thing for a schoolmaster to teach was penmanship; spelling mattered little. (p. 40, emphasis added)

COPYBOOKS

PENMANSHIP

The New England Primer

Like the hornbook, the ***Primer*** was brought over from England. It was first published in Boston about 1690 and was used as late as 1806. The *Primer*

VERY SMALL
BOOK

Paper was expensive and books scarce in colonial America, so young scholars studied their basic lessons from the hornbook.

(Photo by Axler.)

was a very small book, three by four inches in length and breadth and ninety pages thick.

Every *Primer* had a page devoted to the alphabet, followed by two pages of curious word fragments called "easy syllables for children," like *ba, be, bi, bo,* and *bu;* then three pages of words from one to six syllables long. MORAL VERSES The rest of the book was filled with religious and moral verses and prose, including the picture alphabet with a two- or three-line jingle after each letter. For the letter *A* there was

> In Adam's fall
> We sinned all.

For the letter *C* there was

> Christ crucified
> For sinners died.

For the letter *Y* there was

> While youth do cheer
> Death may be near.

BORN IN ORIGINAL SIN The Puritans who used this book felt that their children were born in original sin and that much help was needed if it was to be driven from them.

Another part of the *Primer,* labeled Lessons for Youth, laid down some extremely strict rules for children to follow. The following three verses illustrate how harsh the book was on the young scholars:

- Foolishness is bound up in the Heart of a Child, but the Rod of correction shall drive it from him.
- Liars shall have their Part in the Lake which burns with Fire and Brimstone.
- Upon the Wicked God shall rain a Horrible Tempest.

OUT OF FEAR Modern-day teacher-educators would not agree with this philosophy of education because they believe, as did Rousseau, that children are born innately good.

The Dame School

Another Old World practice carried to this continent was the **dame school.** The school dame was a woman who lived in the neighborhood and taught reading. She received a modest fee for her efforts. As she also performed her normal housekeeping chores, she may well have been America's first ENGLISH home economics teacher. Dame schools were an English institution and were described by the English poet George Crabbe in these words (Johnson, 1963):

> A deaf, poor, patient widow sits
> And awes some thirty infants as she knits;
> Infants of humble, busy wives who pay
> some trifling price for freedom through the day.

> At this good matron's hut the children meet,
> Who thus becomes the mother of the street.
> Her room is small, they cannot widely stray,
> With band of yarn she keeps offenders in,
> And to her gown the sturdiest rogue can pin. (p. 25)

Summary of Colonial Education

The colonial period was a difficult era in all three geographical regions, but important seeds were planted that later bloomed into educational developments. Among the most important colonial advances were the establishment of compulsory education in New England in 1642; the establishment of a practical rather than a classical secondary school curriculum at Franklin's academy in 1751; and the enunciation by Jefferson of the educational theory of a more democratic educational system in 1779. It was also during this period that some of our nation's greatest universities were established—Harvard in 1636, William and Mary in 1693, and Princeton in 1746.

Federal Developments in Education

Even before ratification of the U.S. Constitution, the federal government became involved in education with the Ordinances of 1785 and 1787. Although the Tenth Amendment to the Constitution placed the primary responsibility for education with the states, the federal government has over the years stimulated education by giving money back to the states for priority items considered crucial to the nation. The federal government has also influenced educational process through the U.S. Supreme Court and its interpretation of the Constitution. Beginning with the ordinances of 1785 and 1787 and continuing through the study of *A Nation at Risk* in 1983, the highlights of federal action are presented.

Ordinances of 1785 and 1787

As the western areas of the country were being developed, the Congress passed the Land Ordinances of 1785 and 1787. Under these ordinances, every township was to contain thirty-six sections, each with 640 acres; the

SIXTEENTH
SECTION

sixteenth section of each township was to be sold, and the money used to support education. This aid to public schools was a very important precedent very much supported by Thomas Jefferson.

IMPORTANT
PRECEDENT

In 1787, another land ordinance was passed, the Northwest Ordinance, which set aside not only the sixteenth section for schools but also two whole townships for a university. These two townships were to be taken from the entire 1,500,000 acres under the Northwest Ordinance. In addition to the provision for land to be sold and used for public education, Article III states:

FOREVER BE
ENCOUR-
AGED

> Religion, morality, and knowledge being necessary to good government and the happiness of mankind, schools and the means of education shall forever be encouraged. (Butts, 1978, p. 17)

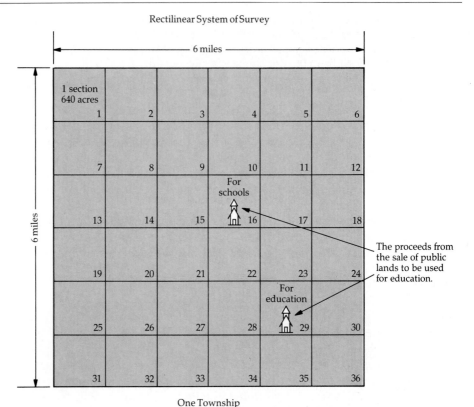

Rectilinear System of Survey

One Township
The ordinances of 1785 and 1787, the beginning of federal aid to education.

Even though there was a lack of compliance with these ordinances because of greedy land speculators, they truly stimulated public education. These ordinances are examples of federal action for the general welfare of all citizens.

Adoption of the U.S. Constitution in 1789

THE TENTH
AMENDMENT

The matter of education was scarcely mentioned at the Constitutional Convention; thus, the U.S. Constitution itself does not cover education anywhere within its contents. The precedent that public education was a responsibility of the state had not been set by any country. Most of the framers of the Constitution felt that education was mainly a private matter, generally under religious control. The **Tenth Amendment** says that powers not delegated to the federal government by the Constitution, nor prohibited by it to the states, are reserved to the states, or to the people (Hicks, 1957). Therefore, education became the responsibility of the states.

It was unfortunate that at this time in our history, the states were not ready to establish an educational system. Most states were occupied with political and economic problems during the early years of the republic, and the development of education in most states did not start until the second quarter of the nineteenth century.

Morrill Land Grant for Colleges (1862)

The Morrill Act of 1862 was one of the most notable congressional decisions in support of public higher education and the general welfare. Since at least 1838, there had been interest in agricultural instruction, and some states had established agricultural schools. Senator Justin S. Morrill of Vermont took up the cause to establish college where both agricultural and industrial education were to be taught. Senator Morrill reasoned that public lands GIANT LAND could be sold, and the proceeds used to build colleges in each of the states. SALE In 1862 President Lincoln signed into law the Morrill Land Grant Act, which eventually endowed at least one land grant college in each of the fifty states, the District of Columbia, Puerto Rico, Guam, and the Virgin Islands. The mandate to establish the colleges included the provision of agricultural and mechanical arts (engineering), as well as military science and tactics. Each state would receive the proceeds from the sale of 30,000 acres of public land for each senator and representative it had in Congress. So far, proceeds from the sale of about 11.4 million acres of our public lands have been used to finance these public colleges.

One might ask, "Has this noble experiment helped the United States achieve what it intended?" More than half the nation's scientists have been prepared in land grant schools, many Noble Prize winners have earned OUTSTAND- degrees at land grant institutions, and such discoveries as hybrid corn, ING SCIEN- streptomycin, television, and talking pictures have emerged from these TIFIC AND colleges (Meyer, 1967, p. 212). The first person to walk on the moon and ACADEMIC many of our nation's astronauts graduated from these public institutions RESULTS of learning. According to Eby (1952), "The establishment and continued support of the land grant colleges proved to be the most far-reaching educational measure ever taken by the federal government" (p. 648). The Morrill Act not only established public institutions of higher education but also spurred healthy competition between the public and private sector in higher education. Because of the lower tuition costs of these institutions, millions of Americans have been extended an opportunity for a higher education.

Plessy v. Ferguson (1896)

The Morrill Act served to increase educational opportunity, but in 1896 the Supreme Court made a decision that would severely restrict the educational and personal opportunities of millions of Americans for years to come. In the *Plessy v. Ferguson* case, (163 U.S. 537), the Court upheld the right of the railroads to segregate passengers according to their race. By so doing, SEGREGA- the Court also endorsed segregation by race in the schools and affirmed the TION BY "separate-but-equal" doctrine. As a result of the *Plessy v. Ferguson* case, RACE schools in northern as well as southern states remained legally segregated until the *Brown v. Board of Education of Topeka* case of 1954.

SEPARATE
BUT UN-
EQUAL

The "separate-but-equal" doctrine proved in practice to be "separate but unequal." With inferior schools came inferior jobs and fewer opportunities for economic success for blacks. The personal indignities experienced by minorities as a result of legalized segregation were reprehensible. The civil rights guaranteed by the U.S. Constitution to all citizens were dealt a severe blow by the *Plessy v. Ferguson* decision.

Smith–Lever Act (1914)

IMPROVE-
MENTS IN
AGRICUL-
TURE AND
HOME ECO-
NOMICS

By the early 1900s, the federal government had become concerned about the quality of country life in the United States, and President Theodore Roosevelt appointed a Country Life Commission to study the problem. As a result of the commission's report, the Smith–Lever Act was passed in 1914. The Smith–Lever Cooperative Agricultural Extension Act provided national aid to people desiring information on agricultural and home economics. People not attending college were to receive instruction and practical demonstrations in agriculture and home economics. This extension work is now done through the agricultural colleges in each state under the direction of the U.S. Department of Agriculture. The educational work, under the Smith–Lever Act, has been accomplished by the publication of informational pamphlets and papers. This act has resulted in the improvement of country life through the educational process. The dissemination of vital information to farmers and their families has made their lives easier and more productive.

Smith–Hughes Act (1917)

VOCATIONAL
EDUCATION

In 1917, Congress passed the Smith–Hughes Act to provide vocational education in schools below the college level. This act called for cooperation between the federal and state governments; the states had to match federal dollars to comply. Vocational education includes courses in agriculture, home economics, trades, industry, and commerce. The Smith–Hughes Act was the first of many related acts that were to follow. Many rural communities owe a great deal to the work and dedication of the vocational agriculture teachers whose salaries were partly provided for by the act.

The Smith–Hughes Act and the Smith–Lever Act have greatly benefited rural and urban Americans. Today, less than 10% of our population is engaged in the production and distribution of food. American farmers are so efficient as a result of our great agricultural colleges, extension agents, and vocational agricultural education that most Americans are free to pursue other goals. Industries and businesses are also dependent on the trade and commercial skills developed by students in vocational programs in the schools.

GI Bill of Rights (1944, 1952, and 1966)

The generosity of the federal government continued after World War II, when Congress rewarded returning soldiers with free education by passage

HELP FOR
FORMER SER-
VICEMEN
AND
-WOMEN

of the GI Bill of Rights of 1944. In 1946, enrollment in colleges was 45% higher than it had been in 1944, and in 1947, over a million former servicemen and -women were attending colleges across the nation (Good and Terrer, 1973). The former GIs not only had their college tuition paid; they also received subsistence pay and money for books and supplies.

More former GIs received benefits below the college level than at the college level, at various vocational schools, through on-the-job training, and on farms. Both programs, college level and below college level, were administered by the Veterans Administration.

AN EXCEL-
LENT IN-
VESTMENT

Since the initial Act in 1944, the GI Bill of Rights has been extended to include veterans of Korea (in 1952) and Vietnam (in 1966). A total of 16 million persons have participated at a total cost in excess of $34 billion. Many feel that the GI Bill is one of the best investments the country has ever made (Brodinsky, 1976):

> In the early days of the GI Bill veterans returned to the college classroom eager for learning; often impatient with dull professional techniques and institutional rules, the returning veterans helped change and invigorate higher education. (p. 73)

The GI Bill has democratized education, enabling those from poorer economic backgrounds to climb the socioeconomic ladder.

Background to the Brown *Decision*

FREDERICK
DOUGLASS

Before the Civil War, Frederick Douglass (1817–1895) knew that to achieve civil rights, blacks could not be accommodationists. Instead they would need to protest. Frederick Douglass declared:

POWER

> Those who profess to favor freedom but deprecate agitation want the crops without plowing up the ground. . . . Power concedes nothing without demand. It never did and it never will. (Farmer, 1975, p. 18)

We doubt that he had in mind agitation as gross as the Civil War, but some form of agitation seemed necessary to emancipate the slaves.

BOOKER T.
WASHING-
TON
ACCOMMO-
DATIONIST

The *Brown* case (1954) would not arise until early black leaders were heard. Although Booker T. Washington (1856–1915) established Tuskegee Institute (included on page 210 in Chapter 7), he was a classic accommodationist. He spoke politely to whites and even was welcome in the White House; however, the status of blacks remained the same as far as voting rights were concerned. The power and prestige of Washington and his delicate touch with the white power structure may have set back black civil rights a number of years.

W. E. B. DU-
BOIS

Later, W. E. B. DuBois (1868–1963) helped found the National Association for the Advancement of Colored People (NAACP). DuBois worked for complete equality for blacks, and published his views in the *Crisis*, the official publication of the NAACP. Later it was the work of the NAACP that

W. E. B. DuBois was an early black activist and one of the founders of the NAACP.

(Photo courtesy of the Library of Congress.)

brought the *Brown* case before the Supreme Court. For much of his adult life DuBois fought the accommodationist tactics of Booker T. Washington, and he ignited a few fires for a change in policy.

CHARLES HOUSTON

THURGOOD MARSHALL

MARTIN LUTHER KING, JR.

The torch for change was also carried by Charles Houston (1895–1950). Houston, while at Howard University, improved the law school and helped train outstanding black lawyers to fight for civil rights. He worked in the NAACP, with Thurgood Marshall, one of his students, to attack segregation in the forms that had been permitted under the *Plessy v. Ferguson* in 1896. He realized that a lawsuit such as the *Brown* case, which was not supported by the public, would not be successsful. Houston said, "The truth is there are millions of white people who have no real knowledge of the Negro's problems and who never give the Negro a serious thought (Williams, 1988, p. 15). It was not until much later after *Brown* that people like Martin Luther King, Jr. made speeches and organized marches and sit-ins to call attention to the plight of black people living under segregation. Even though Houston died early, his courage and wisdom had a profound effect on the outcome of the *Brown* case.

Brown v. Board of Education of Topeka *(1954)*

The question of the legality of segregation on the basis of race, particularly segregation in education, once again came before the Supreme Court in 1954, sixty years after the *Plessy v. Ferguson* affirmation of "separate but equal." Because of the importance of this case, it is necessary to understand its background.

ROOTS OF A BIG CHANGE

By chance, a young housewife from Merriam, Kansas, drove her maid home through a neighborhood where a dilapidated school building was located. Esther Brown, a white housewife, became outraged when the school board in that city refused to make any improvements at the dilapidated black school until a new, modern white school could pay its building debt, forty years hence. She made speeches in Merriam and throughout the state, decrying the school's lack of a gymnasium, a cafeteria, and an auditorium. She also mentioned the smelly earthen privy, which served both sexes; the lack of plumbing or adequate heating and lighting; and the generally run-down condition of the school. Eventually, she recruited campaign workers and collected money for legal fees (Teeter, 1983).

THE LEGAL CASE

The legal case in Kansas was put together by an association formed by Esther Brown. Oliver Brown (no relation to Esther), a Topeka welder and part-time minister, sued the Board of Education, asking that his daughter be admitted to the town's all-white elementary school. The case was tried first in the U.S. District Court, and then, along with four similar cases, in the U.S. Supreme Court using Oliver Brown's name. Thurgood Marshall and a team of civil rights lawyers argued the case for Brown, and John W. Davis, one of the most able lawyers of his time, argued for continued school

Thurgood Marshall and Chief Justice Early Warren made civil rights history in the case of *Brown v. the Board of Education of Topeka* in 1954.

(Photos courtesy of the Library of Congress.)

EARL WAR-
REN

segregation. Chief Justice Earl Warren stated the majority opinion that segregated schools were inherently unequal, and that dual educational systems were to be abandoned. This case ended the rule of the "separate-but-equal" doctrine. It took a while for people to act on the new ruling, and more action was necessary on the part of the Supreme Court and the Congress, but eventually schools were integrated.

Civil Rights Act (1964)

TITLE IV

TITLE VI
A GENUINE
THREAT

Related to the *Brown* decision, Congress passed the Civil Rights Act of 1964, placing all three branches of the federal government behind black equality in education. The Supreme Court had acted in 1954, and both President Kennedy and President Johnson were squarely behind the movement. Title IV of the Act enabled the U.S. Justice Department to initiate lawsuits on behalf of individuals to force compliance with the desegregation law. Title VI allowed the federal government to withhold funds from states and school districts that were not integrating their schools. As more federal funds became available, the withholding of funds became a genuine threat.

 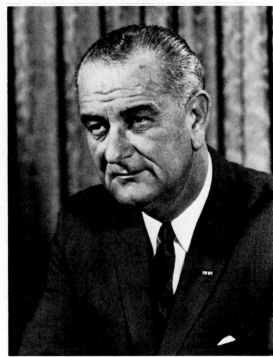

Presidents John F. Kennedy and Lyndon B. Johnson were strong supporters of civil rights and federal aid to education.

(Photos courtesy of the Library of Congress.)

The Civil Rights Act of 1964 has proved to be a needed measure to ensure compliance with the intent of the *Brown* case in 1954.

Elementary and Secondary Education Act (ESEA) of 1965

To help poor and minority children, Congress in 1965 took a giant step toward giving financial aid to the nation's public schools. When he signed the Elementary and Secondary Education Act of 1965, President Johnson believed it would have a tremendous impact on the future of the United States (Brodinsky, 1976). The act has extended the role of the federal government in elementary and secondary education. The passage of the bill hinged on the nation's interest in providing aid and assistance to poor people and minority groups. Political rhetoric at the time of the passage of the bill and the influence of civil rights groups were two factors not to be ignored.

MORE ASSIS-
TANCE TO
POOR AND
MINORITY
GROUPS

TITLE I

The act is divided into nine titles, each one specific to a certain need. For example, Title I, the main part of the ESEA, pertains to the education of poor children in metropolitan areas, in Appalachia, and in states with low literacy rates. The policy for Title I of ESEA is as follows:

Part I Elementary and Secondary Programs
Elementary and Secondary Education Act of 1965

Title I Financial Assistance to Meet Special
Educational Needs of Children

Declaration of Policy

Sec. 101. In recognition of the special educational needs of children of low-income families and the impact that concentrations of low-income families have on the ability of local educational agencies to support adequate educational programs, the Congress hereby declares it to be the policy of the United States to provide financial assistance (as set forth in the following parts of this title) to local educational agencies serving areas with concentrations of children from low-income families to expand and improve their educational programs by various means (including preschool programs) which contribute particularly to meeting the special educational needs of educationally deprived children. Further, in recognition of the special educational needs of children of certain migrant parents, of Indian children and of handicapped, neglected, and delinquent children, the Congress hereby declares it to be the policy of the United States to provide financial assistance (as set forth in the following parts of this title) to help meet the special educational needs of such children. (p. 1)

A Nation at Risk *(1983)*

Most of the events discussed so far concerning the federal government have been the result of actions taken by the congressional and judicial branches. The President and the executive branch of the government demonstrate leadership in various ways. The Reagan administration, through his then

T. H. BELL

Secretary of Education, T. H. Bell, created the National Commission on Excellence in Education in 1981. The commission was directed to examine the quality of education in the United States. The federal government took this action in part because of the decline in college entrance exam scores and complaints by business and military leaders that they were having to

TOO MANY
REMEDIAL
PROGRAMS

spend millions of dollars on remedial education, such as reading, writing, spelling, and computation.

The commission was composed of eighteen people representing all levels of education and some outside the field of education. They listened to and talked to administrators, teachers, students, parents, business leaders, and public officials, and read papers written by experts on a variety of educational issues. At last, they arrived at certain findings, and from these, they wrote their recommendations. Most college libraries have a copy of the commission's complete report. It contains many useful recommendations for education.

The following findings and recommendations are from the commission's report, *A Nation at Risk* (National Commission on Excellence in Education, 1983):

A Finding in Regard to Content

CAFETERIA-
STYLE CUR-
RICULUM

Secondary school curricula have been homogenized, diluted, and diffused to the point that they no longer have a central purpose. In effect, we have a cafeteria-style curriculum in which appetizers and desserts can easily be mistaken for the main courses. Students have migrated from vocational and college preparatory programs to "general track" courses in large numbers. The proportion of students taking a general program of study has increased from 12 percent in 1964 to 42 percent in 1979. (p. 18)

NEW CON-
TENT

A Recommendation in Regard to Content

We recommend that State and local high school graduation requirements be strengthened and that, at a minimum, all students seeking a diploma be required to lay the foundations in the Five New Basics by taking the following curriculum during their 4 years of high school: (a) 4 years of English; (b) 3 years of mathematics; (c) 3 years of science; (d) 3 years of social studies; and (e) one-half year of computer science. For the college-bound, 2 years of foreign language in high school are highly recommended in addition to those taken earlier. (p. 24)

A Finding in Regard to Time

POOR USE OF
TIME

Evidence presented to the Commission demonstrates three disturbing facts about the use that American schools and students make of time: (1) compared to other nations, American students spend much less time on school work; (2) time spent in the classroom and on homework is often used ineffectively; and (3) schools are not doing enough to help students develop either the study skills required to use time well or the willingness to spend more time on school work. (p. 21)

SOME REAL
CHANGES
RECOM-
MENDED

Three Recommendations in Regard to Time

1. Students in high school should be assigned far more homework than is now the case.
2. Instruction in effective study and work skills, which are essential if school and independent time is to be used efficiently, should be introduced in the early grades and continued throughout the student's schooling.
3. School districts and state legislatures should strongly consider 7-hour school days, as well as a 200- to 220-day school year. (p. 29)

Summary

The preceding pages have illustrated how all three branches of the federal establishment have been involved in education. At the very beginning of our republic, in the Land Ordinances of 1785 and 1787, the federal government supported education even though according to the Constitution's Tenth Amendment, the responsibility for education belonged to the states. The Morrill Land Grant Act of 1862 was a tremendous boon to state universities and to science. The Smith–Lever Act of 1914 and the Smith–Hughes Act of 1917 helped to improve rural life in the United States and to enhance the state agricultural colleges that trained vocational agriculture teachers and regulated the dissemination of information to rural people.

The GI Bill of Rights is an example of the federal government's involvement in helping those who have served our nation.

In the *Brown* case, the Supreme Court declared that all races must be treated equally, and the Civil Rights Act of 1964 placed the necessary power in the hands of the federal government to make changes in the schools. President Johnson's ESEA of 1965 set the precedent of sending huge amounts of federal aid to the schools to equalize educational opportunity. *A Nation at Risk* (National Commission on Excellence in Education, 1983) was designed to influence the directions that education was to take in the United States.

In the 1980s the Reagan administration showed interest in returning some of the responsibility for education to the states. The U.S. Department of Education had assumed a great deal of responsibility for education during the 1960s and 1970s, mainly to help minority citizens by overseeing and implementing various federal educational grants and entitlements. Now the federal government, assuming that the civil rights of most of our minority citizens were protected, wanted this responsibility returned to the states. Whether the states will truly be responsible for educating all of their citizens remains to be determined. Aside from the desire to make the states responsible, there is the current mandate to reduce federal expenditures. In the case of the ESEA of 1965, the federal government did come very close to giving general aid to the schools, but this aid has remained basically categorical, being earmarked only for particular programs. The federal government, then, has performed a vital role as a stimulator of educational innovations and as a safety net for the poor and the disadvantaged. It will be interesting to see if state governments mature to the point where they will be capable of handling most of the administrative and financial burden of education.

Glossary Terms

Morality, 179   Hornbook, 186
Grammar School, 181   Copybooks, 186
Toleration, 182   Primer, 186
Paternalistic, 182   Dame School, 188
Academy, 183   Tenth Amendment, 190
Old Field School, 183

Questions

1. Psychologically speaking, what was wrong with the teaching approach used in the *New England Primer*?
2. Describe five current educational practices that can be traced back to the Puritans and other groups of early settlers.

3. Why was the northern colonial region more inclined toward learning and education for all of its citizens than the other two colonial areas?

4. Specifically, what were the contributions of William Penn and Benjamin Franklin to educational development in Pennsylvania?

5. What effects did the plantation system and the institution of slavery have on educational progress in the southern colonies?

6. Some of the ideals of Jefferson and Franklin were ahead of the realities of their times. What factors produced this gap? Today, does progress within our educational institutions lag as a result of a similar gap between real and ideal?

7. Historically, what has been the nature of the relationship between the federal government and education in America? Do you feel that this role is changing?

8. Describe the legal milestones in the civil rights movement in America as they relate to education. How did each help or hinder the progress toward equal educational opportunity for all citizens?

9. What has been the significance of the Elementary and Secondary Education Act (ESEA) of 1965 to educational opportunities in the United States?

Annotated Bibliography

1. Butts, F. R. (1955). *A cultural history of Western education.* New York: McGraw-Hill.

   This general text on the history of education, even though old, is an excellent source of information on nearly all aspects of our educational history.

2. Commager, H. S. (1976). *The people and their schools,* Fastback No. 79. Bloomington, IN: Phi Delta Kappa Educational Foundation.

   Dr. Commager is a noted historian and he wrote this fastback as a part of a bicentennial series published by Phi Delta Kappa. This book highlights what the public schools have tried to do for the United States and he urges us to return to the ideals of public education.

3. Johnson, C. (1963). *Old-time schools and school books.* New York: Dover.

   First published in 1904 by Macmillan, this book is one of the best and most interesting references on the topic. Even though the book has no index, the table of contents and the list of illustrations are very helpful in locating information.

4. LaMorte, M. (1982). *School law cases and concepts.* Englewood Cliffs, NJ: Prentice Hall.

   Chapter 5 of this book, "School Desegregation," contains informative details on the *Plessy v. Ferguson* and *Brown v. Board of Education of Topeka* cases.

5. Meyer, A. E. (1967). *An educational history of the American people,* 2nd ed. New York: McGraw-Hill.

   In this general text on the history of education, the author shares his view that a discernible relationship exists between education and society.

Private and Public Schooling in America

Introduction

Private education and public education have developed side by side since very early times in America. The resulting competition between these two groups has generally been good for the country. In this chapter, we outline some of the historical educational events that have taken place in both the private and the public sectors. Many early endeavors in education were private only because the financial arrangements were made without local, state, or federal government assistance; however, admission to these educational establishments was frequently open to all and often free for poor children. Public schools have brought education to the masses, a task few other countries have been able to accomplish.

Private Schooling in America

The private sector has given the American educational scene several exemplary models from kindergarten to higher education. Notable educational events occurred in the early days of our republic at the private level, and they continue today. Some of the educational models that have emerged from the private sector are now examined.

Sunday Schools

The **Sunday school movement** was begun in England in 1780 by Robert Raikes. These schools were established during the Industrial Revolution, when children were employed in the factories from sunrise to sunset six SCHOOL ON days a week. The idea was to offer basic educational opportunities to A CHILD'S children on their day off, Sunday. The idea spread to America, where Sunday DAY OFF school societies were formed. At first, the goal was to teach the children the basic 3Rs in a secular manner, but then the churches took over and made the principal aim of this movement religious instruction.

Apparently, people felt sorry for these poor children who were deprived of their ABCs, and in fact, many children benefited from this philanthropic endeavor. The philanthropists benefited also, by not being taxed for education; thus, the fact that something was being done for the poor children delayed the passage of the public tax for education. The delay of the tax at this point in history led Meyer (1967) to say, "Philanthropy was a favorite stratagem of a puissant, self-interested minority in their effort to stay the EMPHASIS ON establishment of the tax-supported school" (p. 143). Nevertheless, the Sun-THE NEED day school movement did impress on the people the need for public edu-FOR PUBLIC cation. The attitude of some taxpayers today toward paying for public EDUCATION education indicates that problems concerning this issue have changed very little over the years.

Monitorial Schools

Another English innovation was the **monitorial school.** Started in England by Andrew Bell in 1797, it was brought to America by Joseph Lancaster in 1818. The monitorial school system was organized around selected students

MONITORS   known as *monitors*, who were chosen for their academic abilities. One paid
school teacher was hired to teach a monitorial school having as many as
three to five hundred students. The best scholars were then selected by the
teacher, and these scholars, or monitors, became responsible for about ten
other students. Directions and/or instructions were given to the monitors
by the teacher, and they, in turn, delivered the lesson to their ten students.
The school was run in a military manner; often orders were barked out in
a dictatorial fashion. Corporal punishment was abandoned in favor of the
dunce's cap, leg shackles, a wood log hung around the neck, or suspension
from the ceiling in a basket. The schools were set up to be efficient and
cheap, but they were also impersonal: numbers were used in place of names.
Some books were reprinted on wall charts for use in group instruction to
save money on materials. The curriculum generally consisted of the catechism, reading, writing, spelling, and arithmetic.

The contributions of the monitorial system were several. Mostly, it was
cheap (as low as $1.06 per term), and thus, education became financially
INNOVATIVE   available for the first time to nearly everyone. Lancaster's efficient ways
were innovative, but also restrictive. As a substitute for pen and paper, he
used sand trays for writing lessons. These trays are used today by teachers
who work with dyslexic children. Selden (1975) wrote that "Lancaster above
all, offered schooling to the poor at a time when they were otherwise denied
POPULARIZED   it, and in doing so planted the seed of the concept of education as a fun-
SCHOOLING   damental right" (p. 27). Many teachers today use a type of monitor system
when they ask some of their better students to help explain a previously
taught concept to individuals or small groups within the class.

Infant Schools

NURSERY   From England, another response to the Industrial Revolution was the **infant
CARE   school**, which cared for the children of poor families who worked in the
factories. Robert Owen, a Scottish manufacturer and socialist, was behind
this movement. Besides being an advocate of reducing the hours a child
could labor, Owen was able to establish infant schools, including one for
his own factory workers. These schools taught some religion and some of
the 3Rs, but the schools concentrated on play, singing, dancing, and nursery
care. The infant school served three-, four-, and five-year-olds. By the 1820s,
infant school societies had been formed in the major cities in the United
States.

Robert Owen went on to establish a socialist society in New Harmony,
Indiana, and to assemble a learned group of scientists and intellectuals at
that location. The infant school idea and related happenings promoted the
belief that society's schools had a responsibility to very young children as
well as to older children. Commitment to the education of the younger
infant-school-age group, however, is still not part of our tax-supported sys-
CONTRIBU-   tem in most areas. Butts (1955) stated that "from England came the Sunday
TIONS FROM   schools, the monitorial schools, and the infant schools, all of which helped
ENGLAND   to provide a transition from private to public school systems" (p. 491).

These three exemplary private school experiments show how private endeavors in education often do aid the development of public education.

The Dartmouth College Case (1819)

PRIVATE VS. PUBLIC?

Legally, there was confusion in higher education about who controlled the colleges until the *Dartmouth College* decision of the U.S. Supreme Court in 1818. The question was whether Dartmouth College should remain private or be controlled by the state of New Hampshire. In 1816, the state legislature passed a law converting Dartmouth into a state university. This drastic change of events in the history of the college occurred when the liberal state legislature became upset at the firing of their liberal friend, John Wheelback, who had been president of Dartmouth for sixteen years. The legislature even installed a new liberal board of trustees. The old, more conservative board went to work to gain back its power to operate the college.

The old board first took its case to the New Hampshire Supreme Court, but the plea was denied. The old board then appealed its case to the U.S. Supreme Court after having hired an able lawyer by the name of Daniel Webster. In 1819, Chief Justice John Marshall wrote the decision that reversed the lower court's ruling. Justice Marshall said, in effect, that the original charter for the college came from the king of England and had the force of a contract that the state could not impair. According to Butts (1955),

> the decision had far-reaching economic and political ramifications, but it meant specifically for colleges that the philanthropic endowments of private colleges would be safe from encroachment by the states. This encouraged private donors to give money to the private colleges and stimulated the states to establish their own universities under state control. (p. 466)

DUAL SYSTEM ENCOURAGED

As a result of the *Dartmouth College* case, the United States has a strong dual system of colleges, both private and public. Twenty state universities were established before the Civil War, but private universities had been the major influence until that time.

The Academy Movement (1800–1850)

FRANKLIN'S ACADEMY

Another precedent-setting educational institution was the academy. The academy movement in the United States began with Benjamin Franklin's Philadelphia Academy in 1751 and spread rapidly during the first half of the next century. One thing that greatly facilitated the academy movement was the *Dartmouth College* case in 1819 (Kraushaar, 1976). Academies were secondary schools that offered a variety of programs, including college preparatory education and programs that terminated at the end of a student's time at the academy. In general, the academies provided a broad, practical

PRACTICAL CURRICULUM

curriculum in tune with the great social, political, and cultural changes that were part of the growing young nation. The academy was the dominant secondary school until after the Civil War. Most of the academies were privately endowed, and with the rise of the public tax–supported high schools, only the best endowed of the academies survived (Cubberley, 1934). The Phillips Academy at Andover, Massachusetts, is probably the most famous survivor.

A BOOST TO SECONDARY EDUCATION

The academies boosted the importance of secondary education, and they offered a variety of educational opportunities. There was an emphasis on English literature and grammar, the traditional Latin and Greek, plus newer subjects on the American scene like algebra, astronomy, botany, chemistry, U.S. history, surveying, and debating. The academies bridged the gap between the more elite Latin grammar schools that had come before them and the more democratic high schools that were to follow.

Education for Women

Pioneer efforts in the area of higher education for women were made about 150 years ago. The attitude of most people at this time was that a woman's place was in the home, caring for children and other family needs. Because women's minds had not been tested, there was a feeling that women were intellectually inferior to men. Three women made notable contributions to the education of women in the early nineteenth century.

EMMA WILLARD (1787–1870)

Emma Willard received as much education as she was allowed, and began her teaching career at the age of seventeen in Middlebury, Vermont. In her husband's medical library, she was able to continue her education on her own, and when her husband ran into financial difficulty, she responded by opening up a school for girls in her home. The curriculum began with socially acceptable types of subjects, such as music, drawing, and penmanship, and gradually expanded to include foreign languages, mathematics, philosophy, history, and literature. She called her school the Middlebury Female Academy, and it was a big success. Emma pressed for state financial suport of female academies in both Connecticut and New York, but she was denied support in both places.

SOCIALLY ACCEPTABLE SUBJECTS

TROY FE-MALE SEMI-NARY, 1821

Eventually, the people of Troy, New York, invited her to start a school. She opened what became known as the Troy Female Seminary in 1821, when she was only thirty-four years old, and for the next fifty years at Troy, she dedicated herself to improving the education of women. The success of the Troy Female Seminary and Willard's efforts is reflected in the formation of Vassar, Elmira, Mary Sharp, and other women's colleges. By 1837, Willard was able to obtain some state support for Troy, and with the opening of Iowa State and Utah universities to women, her influence had become far reaching. Moorefield (1972) summed up Willard's influence:

FAR-REACH-ING INFLU-ENCE

No college anywhere—not just in the United States but throughout the world—accepted women students in 1787. By the time she died in 1870, women were not only attending American high schools but many of the brightest and most determined among them were earning college degrees and launching professional careers. (pp. 30–31)

CATHERINE BEECHER (1800–1878)

HARTFORD
SEMINARY

Catherine Beecher was part of a famous family. Her sister, Harriet Beecher Stowe, was a gifted writer, and her brother was Henry Ward Beecher, a well known pulpit orator. In 1828, she opened the Hartford Seminary, a school for girls in Hartford, Connecticut. Catherine Beecher also started a school in Cincinnati, Ohio, called the Western Female Institute for Women.

TRAINED
TEACHERS

PROMOTED
LIBERAL EDU-
CATION FOR
WOMEN

During the early 1800s, women were flocking into teaching as the only career field open to them. Beginning about 1830, Beecher dedicated herself to the recruitment and training of teachers willing to go to the western states to train the uneducated masses. She went on trips to New England to find young women who were willing to make the long trip to the West, and she worked with committees that were willing to support her cause. Her work helped to alert the public to the need for common schools and trained teachers. This pioneer woman educator organized the Woman's Education Association in 1852. Among other things, the association promoted providing liberal education for women and making women into successful wives, mothers, and housekeepers.

MARY LYON (1797–1844)

MOUNT
HOLYOKE

TAUGHT MIS-
SIONARIES

Mary Lyon dedicated her entire adult life to education, and the last twelve years to the founding and the administration of Mount Holyoke College for women in South Hadley, Massachusetts. The college opened its doors in 1837 to serve women of limited means. A small tuition was to be supplemented by two hours of domestic work daily. Lyon thought of education as a means of performing social and religious services. Her students were encouraged to become missionaries, particularly in foreign missions.

ACCEPTANCE
OF WOMEN

All three of these women did some of the initial work necessary to prove that higher education for women was worthwhile. In those days, it was necessary to mix higher education with housekeeping and other socially acceptable career areas to launch the concept of women in college. The past 150 years have seen a growing acceptance of women in colleges and universities, but the last twenty years have seen a tremendous growth of the acceptance of women into the major professions.

The Development of the Kindergarten

FIRST A PRI-
VATE INSTI-
TUTION

Kindergartens are not universally supported by the public tax dollar even to this day, but the private endeavors in this important area have been tremendous. It could be, as in the case of the Sunday school, that the very success of private efforts has delayed public support. Froebel's kindergarten came to the United States as a private institution in 1855. (Froebel's kindergarten and the American adaptions of it were discussed in detail in Chapter 5.) The kindergarten curriculum has always focused on the child, so the kindergarten movement, when it came to the United States, laid the foundation for the "child-centered" elementary school (Butts, 1955, p. 404).

Mary Lyon, who founded Mount Holyoke College for women, was one of America's great female educators.

(Photo courtesy of the Library of Congress.)

Hampton Institute (1868)

GENERAL
ARMSTRONG

After the Civil War, one of the northern generals, Samuel Chapman Armstrong, founded the Hampton Institute in 1868. General Armstrong believed that the best education for blacks was a practical type of education that would get them jobs in the post–Civil War days. According to Butts (1978), "General Armstrong argued from a humanitarian but paternalistic attitude

PRACTICAL,
BUT NOT SO-
CIALLY AC-
TIVE EDUCA-
TION

of white superiority that the racial differences as well as the economic disabilities of Negroes required a special kind of education" (p. 212). Specifically, the types of skills taught at Hampton were woodworking, metalmaking, cooking, and serving. Students at Hampton were also taught such academic subjects as English, arithmetic, geography, and history at the secondary level. The significance of Hampton was that it was here that

Booker T. Washington was an outstanding educator and spokesperson for black rights and education in the late 1800s.

(Photo courtesy of the Library of Congress.)

TUSKEGEE,
1880

EMPHASIS ON
INDUSTRIAL
EDUCATION

Booker T. Washington attended school and learned from his mentor, General Armstrong, how to set up his own Tuskegee Institute in 1880.

Booker T. Washington developed his Tuskegee model after the Hampton Institute with a very strong emphasis on industrial education. He believed that blacks would be served best by a practical or vocational education rather than a liberal arts education. Other white and black leaders of the period believed that a good liberal arts education would best serve to bring

The education of blacks to improve their economic standing was the main thrust at Tuskegee Institute, founded by Booker T. Washington.

[Photo courtesy of the Library of Congress.]

blacks out of slavery into modern society. The most prominent black leader opposed to Washington's views was W. E. B. DuBois.

Hampton Institute was a start for black education, but the direction it took, according to many modern scholars, appears to have been wrong in that blacks were given one type of educational opportunity (industrial, leading to blue-collar jobs), whereas whites were given another (liberal arts training, leading to the professions). Some would say that the direction that Armstrong and Washington took was the only one available at the time and, pragmatically, the only sensible way to move considering the social status of blacks in the South during this period. By 1900, fourteen hundred Tuskegee graduates had found jobs in thirty different industries, and the Hampton Institute model of industrial education spread to many more schools in the South besides Tuskegee.

LED TO BLUE-COLLAR JOBS ONLY

The Dewey Laboratory School and the Progressive Education Movement

THE LABORA-TORY SCHOOL, 1896

Another significant event in private education was the establishment in 1896 of the laboratory school at the University of Chicago by John Dewey (1859–1952). The entire University of Chicago had been financed privately by John D. Rockefeller, and it was here that some of the most significant experiments in education were to be carried out under the guidance and direction of John Dewey. Although Dewey gave credit to Francis Parker (1837–1902) for being the father of **progressive education**, effective publicity for the movement originated from the laboratory school in Chicago. Some of the experiments in different parts of the country were labeled as progressive, but later were to be condemned by Dewey as being unsound educationally. The Dewey philosophy is explained in detail in Chapters 8 and 9.

FRANCIS PARKER

NOTEWOR-THY IDEA

The progressive movement in educational history is noteworthy because most educators up to this time had thought there was only one way to teach: the traditional method. Francis Parker had implemented some progressive ideas in the public schools in Massachusetts, but Dewey's ideas were revolutionary. The concept of the child and how she or he learned would now become more important than forcing subject matter to be memorized. This reform did not take place at once, but as the years unfolded, we have seen increasing acceptance of these ideas.

Experimental Private Schools of the 1960s and 1970s

HARLEM PREP

During the 1960s and the 1970s, many experimental private schools were founded. No doubt, many of these schools were stimulated by the progressive school movement of an earlier era. The Harlem Preparatory School was one of several private street academies whose purpose was to rescue bright young black people from failure. Schools like Harlem Prep specialized in instilling self-confidence in the students and in getting them to understand that through a college education, they could lift themselves up the socioeconomic ladder.

MONTESSORI
AND SUM-
MERHILL
SCHOOLS

Other private schools were established on the Montessori or Summerhill model. The Montessori schools stress respect for the child and place emphasis on his or her interests. The Summerhill model places emphasis on freedom of the child to decide on his or her own learning. These two models were often more enthusiastically supported than thought out, but many of these schools show signs of stability today (Kraushaar, 1976). Private alternatives to public schools keep the spirit of competition alive, and private school ideas are being adopted by the public schools; for example, several public systems now have Montessori-type schools.

DIVERSITY

The diversity within private schools today is nearly as great as it is in the public schools. The church schools include not only Catholic and Lutheran schools, but schools of almost every other Protestant denomination as well. Hebrew schools were small in number before 1940; 90% of the present 500 or so were formed after this date (Kraushaar, 1976). There are Black Muslim schools in some of our largest cities. Some other private or nonsectarian schools prefer to carry the label *independent* rather than *private* because of the elitist connotation of the label *private*.

Public Schooling in America

There were compulsory school laws in New England as early as 1642, but these schools were not public as we understand that term today. The mandate that Massachusetts placed on its citizens to send their children to school was a helpful precedent for the future of public schools, but schools were not free. The concept of free public schools eventually won out, but it was a long, hard struggle, one of this nation's finest and most noteworthy achievements. Some of the important milestones in the development of the free public school are discussed here.

WHERE DO
WE GO FROM
HERE?

The struggle continues today as we try to maintain the public schools amid cries that they are failing to educate our children and are in a state of disarray. Are public schools worth all our efforts, or should we now change our stance to a greater emphasis on private schools through vouchers or tuition tax credits? What about poor people's education and equal educational opportunity? Where do we go from here? We hope to provide some of the answers in the following pages.

Jefferson's Model (1779)

THE "SEED"!

We described in Chapter 6 how Thomas Jefferson provided a plan for public education. His plan for Virginia served to stimulate others interested in education, such as De Witt Clinton of New York, even though Virginia did not adopt Jefferson's ideas.

De Witt Clinton

The New York Free School Society was organized in 1805 under the leadership of De Witt Clinton (1769–1828), then mayor of New York City and later governor of the state. The society was organized for the purpose of educating the poor children in the City of New York. The society was able to secure funds from the city council and the state legislature, to build schools, to train teachers, and, most of all, to get the people interested in free public education. (Other free societies were formed during this same period. One in Washington, DC, had Thomas Jefferson as a board member and a financial contributor.) De Witt Clinton was a great believer in the monitorial system of education (see the discussion earlier in this chapter), which prospered in New York with his enthusiastic approval. Eventually in 1853, the society turned over its system of schools to the city to be used as its regular public schools.

In his two terms as governor of New York, Clinton was a dedicated crusader for educational improvements throughout the state. Through his efforts, popular interest in education was intensified (Eby, 1952). Many governors today face a similar struggle in trying to reform public education in their states.

Jackson's Presidency (1829–1837)

In 1829 Andrew Jackson (1767–1845) became president of the United States, the first president to be elected by the people in general, excluding, of course, slaves and women. Advocates of popular elections had fought numerous battles to achieve their goal, known as *white manhood suffrage.*

The country was not fulfilling the spirit and the intent of the doctrines of the American and the French revolutions (Hicks, 1957). The march toward democracy was well on its way with white manhood suffrage; still there would be a long wait for universal suffrage.

Before Jackson, all presidents had been elected by the elite of the eastern states. With Jackson, the frontier states saw one of their own elected to the presidency: "The Jackson inauguration symbolized for many the triumph of the common man" (Hicks, 1957, p. 367). Now men who made their living by plowing the land, mending shoes, or working in a factory could vote along with the wealthier men. Once access to the ballot box was assured, interest in public education began to spread. White manhood suffrage was a significant step for America.

The Cousin Report (1831)

In the late 1820s, Prussia was among the strongest countries in Europe. Encompassing much of present-day Germany and Poland and parts of Russia, Prussia had a strong educational system that was to influence educational reform in many countries. Victor Cousin, a Frenchman, was instrumental in writing a report on the value of Prussian education. The Cousin Report resulted in a French school reform law, but more important for the

Andrew Jackson was the son of poor farmers; his rise to the presidency
symbolized the opportunities available in America.

(Photo courtesy of the Library of Congress.)

United States, it was translated and printed here and read by many educated
people:

THE PRUS-
SIAN SYSTEM
What the Frenchmen liked about the Prussian System of Education was its
national authority over education; its centralized secular control; its trained
and expert teachers; its up-to-date methods; its planning, financing, and supervising; and finally its bold and outspoken employment of the school as an
instrument for national ends. (Meyer, 1967, p. 178)

Through his writings, Cousin stimulated school reform on two continents.

The Stowe Report (1837)

Near the conclusion of the Jackson presidency, in 1836, Calvin Stowe, an Ohio theologian, was sent to Prussia to bring back an American report on the schools. He liked what he saw in Prussia, particularly the thoroughness of instruction, teacher education, and the Pestalozzian methods. The Ohio Legislature must have been somewhat excited because they ordered 10,000 copies of the report printed, but Ohio took very little action. The Stowe Report did find its way into notable journals of education, and it was reprinted and circulated to other states, including Massachusetts.

PESTALOZ-
ZIAN METH-
ODS

Horace Mann

Like several others who had gone before him, Horace Mann (1796–1859) visited and reported on the Prussian schools in 1843. Unlike most previous visitors, he included in his report both praise and criticism of the Prussians. While he was in Europe, he also visited England, Belgium, Holland, and France. He rated Prussia first and England last because England lacked a national system of education in which all of the people could participate. When he returned, Mann said, "There are many things abroad which we at home should do well to imitate" (Cubberley, 1934, p. 362).

BOTH PRAISE
AND CRITI-
CISM OF
PRUSSIA

Horace Mann was a dedicated public servant. Before becoming a leading educator in Massachusetts, he was president of the State Senate and was headed for the governorship. As a legislator, he led humanitarian crusades for such noble causes as psychiatric treatment of the insane, abolition of imprisonment for debtors, better prison conditions, and temperance laws. When Mann had an opportunity to organize the newly formed state school board in Massachusetts, he resigned from the legislature to become the first secretary of the Massachusetts school board. The remainder of his life was dedicated to improving public education. He spent his last years as president of Antioch College in Ohio.

DEDICATED
PUBLIC SER-
VANT

Because he was the first secretary of the Massachusetts Board of Education, Mann had great freedom in defining his position. He created a tremendous model for all school systems in the United States to follow. One of his first tasks was to inspect the schools and to assess their state. He criticized education in Massachusetts as having shanty school buildings without the slightest sanitary facilities, stupid and incompetent teachers, dilapidated equipment, and supervision that was in full collapse (Meyer, 1967). Some of today's reformers have been heard to say some equally inelegant things about current school practices.

CREATED A
MODEL
SCHOOL SYS-
TEM

On Mann's return from Europe, he instituted many needed reforms. New schools were built at a cost of $2 million—a large sum in those days for a state. Teachers' salaries were raised 62% for men and 54% for women, and three new teacher training institutions or normal schools were built, the first of their kind in America. Mann improved the quality of teaching in the state by making personal addresses, authoring twelve annual reports to the legislature, writing in the *Common School Journal*, and continually visiting the schools while in office (Monroe, 1940).

TEACHER ED-
UCATION IM-
PROVED

Schools grew in the early 1800s from isolated cabins with a few pupils to larger buildings serving many more children.

(Photo courtesy of the Library of Congress.)

NOT AN ELI-
TIST

Leaders like Horace Mann come along very infrequently. Reforming the schools as he did in Massachusetts was one of the most democratizing moves ever made in American history. Establishment of good common or public schools was a bold and courageous move because, at the time, many people felt that society should be composed of different classes of citizens. Mann, however, was not an elitist and had not forgotten his own ordinary roots. This was the beginning of our public school system, where every child would be offered an opportunity for a formal education. Keppel and Messerli (1975), during our bicentennial celebration, wrote in reference to Mann, "Our national pantheon is peopled by few visionaries and many men

A DREAMER
AND A DOER

and women of action; but it is the rare occupant who has been both a dreamer and a doer" (pp. 18–21). Some have even honored Mann by referring to him as the "father of our common schools."

Other Public School Reformers

FIRST U.S.
COMMIS-
SIONER

Another very important school reformer of the period was Henry Barnard (1811–1900). Barnard, who did in Connecticut what Mann had done in Massachusetts, eventually became the first U.S. Commissioner of Education in 1867. Barnard founded the American Association for the Advancement of Education, whose publication was *The American Journal of Edu-*

SPREADING
THE GOOD
WORD

OTHER RE-
FORMERS

cation. As editor of the journal, Barnard publicized the merits or public education and gave details on ways to accomplish the task. The journal supported every educational reform of consequence that occurred before the 1880s (Meyer, 1967). In addition to Connecticut and Massachusetts, other states picked up on the trend sweeping the country, and reformers emerged in many areas, notably, Robert J. Breckenridge of Kentucky, Calvin Stowe of Ohio, Caleb Mills of Indiana, and Jonathan Swett of California.

Catalysts in the Public School Movement

1¢ NEWSPA-
PERS

THE LYCEUM

THE LABOR
MOVEMENT

INTERNAL
IMPROVE-
MENTS

GREAT
SPEAKERS

MCGUFFEY
READERS

A discussion of the public school crusade, spearheaded by Mann and others, would not be complete without mention of other important forces or events that acted as catalysts in the process. The previously mentioned **Jacksonian democracy**, monitorial system, and use of educational or **pedagogical journals** were all instrumental in aiding public schools. Newspapers, then costing a mere cent, were cheap enough so that nearly everyone could afford them, and the urge to read them sparked an interest in schooling. Josiah Holbrook's American **Lyceum** was begun in 1826 for the purpose of stimulating citizens with lectures on varied topics, and the lecturers always sang the praises of the common schools. From the start, the labor movement favored free public education, and members demanded that the states accept full responsibility for providing schools at public expense. During this period, internal improvements, consisting of the building of canals, railroads, and turnpikes, helped to spread the news from one part of the nation to another. Speakers of note, such as Ralph Waldo Emerson, talked of unrestrained individualism that would allow one to rise to endless heights, inferring that the best way to rise was through schooling.

The first McGuffey Readers were published in 1836, and they continued to be used until 1920. The Readers were truly American, not like the books previously used, which related more to Europe. The standards of social life set up in the Readers pleased a majority of the Americans, particularly those on the frontier. Many of the stories were pleasant, and few were designed to frighten children about going to hell as earlier texts had done. The stories used by McGuffey included many of top literary merit. These improved textbooks and others helped to popularize the public schools.

IMMIGRA-
TION

Immigration, mostly from European countries, was a large factor in the increasing use of the public schools. Those who now referred to themselves as "native Americans" feared that conflicts and disputes might result from having so many immigrants in the work force building canals and railroads. Some feared the political influence of the foreigners, but eventually, the wise and broad-minded realized that assimilation of these immigrants, through education, into the democracy, rather than exclusion, would be the best policy (Monroe, 1940). One significant result was that the native population saw education as an effective means of making democracy work; therefore, the great immigrations into this country aided the development of education.

Ralph Waldo Emerson expounded in his philosophy of humanism the value of learning both from schooling and from life, as well as the importance of independent thinking.

(Photo courtesy of the Library of Congress.)

Pauper Schools and Public Taxation

OVERCOM-
ING A BAR-
RIER
The ideal of having public schools was one thing, but paying for them through taxes was another issue entirely. Unfortunately, the precedent set abroad was not helpful. In England, school reformers thought of public schools only as charity schools. This concept predominated in the thinking of most people in the colonies during the eighteenth century, and it was a difficult idea to erase. This barrier had to be overcome to establish the free

and open democratic school system that was to follow. Benevolent societies and individuals did perform a service by aiding the pauper schools, but their act carried with it the stigma of elitism.

Gradually, the view that the teacher might be paid by the people in general, or through public taxation, was accepted (Monroe, 1940). The 1809 law in Pennsylvania that provided free education to the poor made few friends, as the poor had to declare themselves as lowly paupers to qualify, and property owners objected to paying the tax (Meyer, 1967). Pennsylvania later became a model for doing away with the **pauper school** custom when it enacted the Free School Act in 1834. The trend that emerged was the use of local and county taxes for schools, with some additional help from the state.

FREE SCHOOL
ACT

RATE BILL
PROBLEM

In most states, the rate bill or tuition tax was charged to every child whose parent was able to pay. The rate bill system of collecting money for schools grew out of the Old Deluder Satan Act of 1647 in Massachusetts. This system of collecting tuition kept many children from obtaining an education, either because they could not afford the rate or because they were too proud to ask for charity. Many states allowed a certain number of free attendance days; after this period, the parents had to pay the rate. This practice encouraged some parents to hold their children out of school. The rate bill forced some poor parents to send only one child at a time (Monroe, 1940). Massachusetts ended their system of rate collection in 1827 and Delaware did so in 1829, but other states did not end the practice until much later, some even after the Civil War.

STILL
CHARGING
FEES

Even though the rate bill or tuition practice has ended, some public schools are not completely free today. One large public school system in a major midwestern city charges fees for books. Other systems are known to charge fees for certain extras, often placing those who are unable to pay for those extras in an embarrassing position. The maintenance of "free" public schools is still a live issue.

Compulsory School Attendance Laws and Child Labor Laws

One of the most important changes to affect the growth of the public school system was the passage of compulsory school attendance laws. The first of these laws was drafted in Massachusetts in 1852, but it was 1918 before compulsory attendance legislation had been passed in all states. The first decree in Massachusetts was for a period of only twelve weeks. Enforcement of most of these laws was weak because the states did not have the necessary administrative machinery (Katz, 1976).

ENFORCE-
MENT WAS
WEAK

TRUANT OF-
FICERS

Compulsory schooling regulations changed greatly between 1900 and 1930. The previously simple statutes requiring school attendance for a fixed number of days each year became a complex network of legal rules. Added to the school attendance rules were rules for hiring truant officers and defining their duties, establishing truant schools, delegating jurisdictional power, and dealing with child labor laws. The child labor laws, the first of

SCHOOL AT-
TENDANCE
AS A PRE-
REQUISITE
FOR EMPLOY-
MENT which was passed in Rhode Island in 1840, often required school attendance as a prerequisite for the employment of children or disallowed employment altogether for some youth during their schooling. After passage of the child labor laws, 90.6% of the children legally designated as too young to work were attending school (Katz, 1976). Average daily attendance helped to improve compliance with compulsory attendance laws. Some children were sent to reform schools after being convicted of truancy.

CRUCIAL
LAWS

The child labor laws and the compulsory attendance laws were crucial in furthering the development of the public schools. Today, the benefits to the growth of their children both socially and mentally motivate most parents to support their children's education, but the compulsory attendance edict is still needed for the benefit of all society, and many states are currently considering extending the age of compulsory education to eighteen.

The Kalamazoo Case (1874)

It took the action of the supreme court in the state of Michigan in 1874 in *Charles E. Stuart and others v. School District No. 1 of the Village of Kalamazoo and others* to finally decide that public high school was a legitimate part of the public school system. Some prominent citizens of the city of Kalamazoo, Michigan, objected to paying taxes to support the local public high school. Charles E. Stuart, a former U.S. Senator, was one of the citizens who objected to the tax-supported secondary school. He felt that an elementary school education was enough for the taxpayers to provide, for he, after all, had made it all the way to the Senate with only an elementary school diploma.

TAX OR
FREE?

Judge Thomas M. Cooley, an associate justice of the Michigan Supreme Court, argued that a liberal education, including instruction in the classics, was an important practical advantage to be supplied to all, not just to those whose accumulated wealth enabled them to pay for it (Selden, 1975). In addition, Judge Cooley cited, among other legislation, the Northwest Ordinance of 1787, which states that "schools and the means of education shall forever be encouraged." The effect of the *Kalamazoo* case was far-reaching. After 1874, in states across the nation, courts turned to the *Kalamazoo* decision as a precedent when faced with challenges to the public high schools. In the fifteen years following Judge Cooley's decision, the number of high schools in Michigan rose from 107 to 278, and there was a similar expansion in other states (Selden, 1975).

LIBERAL EDU-
CATION FOR
ALL

AN IMPOR-
TANT PRECE-
DENT

SLOW TO
GAIN WIDE
ACCEPTANCE

Considering the general acceptance of the public high school as a part of our American educational system, it is difficult for us to realize how hard a fight was necessary to win approval for its existence: "Even at the beginning of the twentieth century public high schools enrolled only 11% of all youth eligible to attend" (Brodinsky, 1976, p. 23). As we well know the debate continues on the content of the high school curriculum, but the right for it to exist was settled in the *Kalamazoo* decision.

The Committee of Ten (1892)

The proper curriculum for the high school was clarified and defined by the Committee of Ten in 1892. This committee was formed by the National Education Association for the purpose of improving the relationship of the secondary schools to the colleges. The committee was chaired by the legendary president of Harvard University, Charles Eliot. The rest of the membership was composed of male college presidents, professors, and teachers, mainly experts on the college preparatory curriculum. The members felt unanimously that high schools should offer academic subjects and that high school students should be subjected to academic rigor.

The Committee of Ten selected nine subcommittees, each composed of ten members, and assigned each a field of study then taught in the high schools. These subcommittees had to decide where in the high school program to place each subject, how long each subject should be studied, and by what methods each subject should be taught. According to Eby (1952),

> This was the first time in American education a group of 100 educators had undertaken to formulate a unified system of instruction for children and youth from six to 18 years of age. The report was one of the most important educational documents ever issued in the United States. (p. 592)

As a result of the work of the Committee of Ten, the curriculum of public secondary schools became more standardized than it had been in the older academies. Despite the committee's goal of treating everyone the same, whether they were college bound or not, the suggested curriculum was dominated by college preparatory courses. The committee did not study pupil abilities, social needs, interests, or capacities for learning (Cubberley, 1934). The domination of colleges over the secondary school program is still very much in evidence, and battles remain to be fought to improve programs and attitudes toward programs for the non–college-bound student.

Public Education and the Role of Religion

By the turn of the century, public education for all was well on its way to becoming a reality in America. You will find modern developments in public education explored throughout this text, from the social issues discussed in Chapters 3 and 4 to the foundations and issues of school law, governance and control, finance, and curriculum to be presented later.

One additional topic should be explored as a twentieth century concern, seen in the light of history. The issue of religion in the public schools has been and continues to be a matter for heated debate in America. To further your understanding of this controversy, the following paragraphs present some historical and legal facts.

In western and central Europe during the Middle Ages, only one established Christian denomination, the Roman Catholic Church, set the moral values and standards of behavior. The new social, political, and economic

IMPROVE
SECONDARY
EDUCATION

COLLEGE
PREP CUR-
RICULUM

A MORE
STANDARD
CURRICULUM

HEATED DE-
BATE

relationships that marked the Renaissance helped to lead to the Reformation and a split in the church, and many new Christian denominations emerged. The dilemma that we face today in our public schools was partly and indirectly caused by the division of the Christian church during the Reformation and the concept of separation of church and state, which originated during the Enlightenment.

SEPARATION
OF CHURCH
AND STATE

Diversity of religious thought did not alone cause the movement away from religion as the basis for education. Educators like Comenius believed in educating the child for all of life, not just for entry into heaven. Thinkers like Comenius and Luther—and later, in the Enlightenment period, Rousseau—set in motion a chain of events that led to the teaching of only secular subjects in public schools today.

MOVE TO
USE ONLY A
SECULAR
CURRICULUM

The movement toward secular education in America is where it is today for a number of reasons. The **First Amendment** of the U.S. Constitution was adopted to give everyone an opportunity to practice the religion of her or his choice, free from the restraints of the government. This noble idea, set down by the Founding Fathers, was meant to protect citizens from feared encroachments by federal, state, or local governments on personal religious beliefs. In addition, Horace Mann and other school reformers in the 1840s obtained their model for public school reform from Prussia. The Prussian system of schools was completely under secular control.

FIRST
AMENDMENT
INFLUENCE

During colonial times—and in some areas for a great many years after—the public schools were located in homogeneous communities with only one or two religious denominations. Practice of religion in the schools was logical and generally without controversy. But most communities grew and diversified in the makeup of their citizenry. In our present-day pluralistic society, the practice of any one particular religion in a school causes great controversy, and it was declared illegal by the U.S. Supreme Court in *Abington v. Schempp* and *Murray v. Curlett* in 1963.

PLURALISTIC
CHANGE

Today, in our country, many groups and individuals claim that the values of our young people are not what they should be, and that elimination of religious training from the schools has led to a lack of moral and values training for our children. Solutions for this problem vary from those who suggest a values clarification approach to those who propose that churches work with the schools to improve the children's value base. Some organizations, such as the National Council on Religion and Public Education (NCRPE), point out that the Supreme Court ruled in 1963 only against reading from the Bible and the use of the Lord's Prayer in the public schools. The court specifically said that study of the Bible or religion as a part of the secular school curriculum was consistent with the intent of the First Amendment. Thus, the NCRPE suggests that schools use the Bible as literature and for stories on values, that comparative world religions become a part of social studies, and that the study of the arts include religious subjects.

STUDY OF
RELIGION

The issues of religion in the public schools and the move toward secularism are still to be resolved, and involve not only the many Christian denominations but also the Jewish community, many non-Christian sects,

KNOW
WHERE YOU
STAND

and even atheist groups. As the controversy continues, it is important for teachers to know where they stand personally on this issue and what the current laws and rules of their school district are in relation to the religion issue.

Summary

This chapter provided some examples of the contributions of private education in the United States. Many of these examples paved the way for changes that were later picked up by the public schools. Many private schools operating today offer alternatives that may one day be adopted by the public schools. As long as there is a proper balance between the two systems, each of them actually helps the other. Kraushaar (1976) stated it best when he wrote:

> The new goal is to recognize the spheres and validity of public and private schools and that the dual system adds alternatives, richness, and diversity to the opportunities open to the young, while it strives to bring the two spheres into harmonious working relationship. (p. 52)

Public educational development winds its way historically from New England's quasi-public schools to the more free and open public schools we have today. These early schools were quasi-public schools because they charged a rate or a tuition even though they were open to most of the people. The great public school movement headed by Horace Mann consolidated public opinion in favor of free public education, and after the *Kalamazoo* case, we were assured of free public high schools as well as elementary schools. Many important people helped to shape the events that have built the public school system into the vast network it is today.

Glossary Terms

Sunday School Movement, 203
Monitorial School, 203
Infant Schools, 204
Progressive Education, 211
Jacksonian Democracy, 217

Pedagogical Journals, 217
Lyceum, 217
Pauper School, 219
First Amendment to the U.S. Constitution, 222

Questions

1. Were there any early practices in education that you would like teachers to use today?
2. How have educational practices begun in the private sector affected the public schools?
3. Compare the influence of the *Dartmouth College* case and the *Kalamazoo* case on the use of public money for education.

4. Compare the emphasis of the academy movement with that of the previous grammar school movement and the subsequent high school movement.

5. Describe the impact on minority education, particularly higher education, of the work of Emma Willard, Catherine Beecher, Mary Lyon, and Booker T. Washington.

6. How have the progressive education movement and the experimental private schools of the 1960s and 1970s affected the public schools?

7. How did European school systems, particularly the Prussian system, influence American education in the early 1800s?

8. What was the significance of each of the following for the growth of public education in America?
    a. Pauper schools
    b. Child labor laws and compulsory attendance laws
    c. Public taxation for education

9. Describe the controversy over religion in the public schools.

Activities for Unit III

1. Write a paper on the contributions of Friedrich Wilhelm Froebel. Compare the curriculum of a present-day kindergarten with that of Froebel's kindergarten in Germany.

2. Construct a model of an early educational device such as a hornbook, a copybook, or a quill pen.

3. Try to simulate in class the Socratic method of teaching. What aspects of the Socratic method would work today in teaching?

4. As a class, rediscover the exuberance of the Renaissance by designing new learning activities for children that will truly "light their fire." These activities could be put to use in some school during your pre–student-teaching experience.

5. Choose an educator such as Sir Francis Bacon, John Amos Comenius, John Locke, Jean-Jacques Rousseau, Johann Heinrich Pestalozzi, or Friedrich Wilhelm Froebel and report to the class on how he made a significant impact on learning and education.

6. Role-play what it may have been like in an early one-room school. One student will be the master and the rest of the class will be divided into eight grades. The members of each grade will devise a "curriculum" for themselves.

7. Invite a retired teacher to talk about the methods he or she used in teaching. Have the teacher bring to the class any historical textbooks she or he might have.

8. Locate an old McGuffey Reader and compare the values taught by it with the values taught in a modern textbook for the same grade level.

9. Create a drama illustrating the common school movement in education. Include media events, foreign influence, and men such as Horace Mann and Henry Barnard. Create minor supporting roles for interest.

10. Interview a local school official concerning the use of Elementary and Secondary Education Act (ESEA) funds. Attempt to find out the amount of funds received locally and the purposes for which the funds are used.

Annotated Bibliography

1. Cabberly, E. P. (1920). *The history of education*. New York: Houghton Mifflin.

   This comprehensive study of the history of education to 1920 contains a section on the academy on pages 696–699.

2. Goodsell, W. (1931). *Pioneers of women's education in the United States*. New York: McGraw-Hill.

   This account of the historical development of American education by certain outstanding women, including Emma Willard, Catherine Beecher, and Mary Lyon, provides details on their actual suggestions on improving the education of women.

3. Morgan, J. E. (1936). *Horace Mann: His ideas and ideals*. Washington, DC: National Home Library Foundation.

   The aim of this book was to introduce both the life and writings of Horace Mann. Reading about the philosophy of Horace Mann will give the reader insight into why he was a great believer in the common or public school.

4. Washington, B. T. (Ed.) (1905). *Tuskegee and its people: Their ideals and achievements*. New York: Appleton.

   The book contains information on what graduates did with their lives after Tuskegee. It contains many photographs of the buildings, people, and grounds.

(Photo courtesy of the Library of Congress.)

The Philosophy of Education

OBJECTIVES

After reading Chapter 8, the student will be able to:

- Speculate about the reasons for studying philosophy

- Define and give examples of the philosophical questions posed in the four major branches of philosophy

- Compare and contrast the educational beliefs and principles of the five pure philosophies

- Identify the contributions of major philosophers in each of the pure philosophies

- Decide which philosophy or philosophies incorporate the student's philosophical position

Traditional Philosophies

Introduction

As a student of the education process, you have learned that a teacher is required to make decisions about what should be taught, what methods should be used in the instruction, what learning activities should be included in each lesson, whether learning should be by group activity or individual project, and what techniques should be applied to evaluate this learning. Thus, education involves the investigation of a multitude of problems and questions, and the possible answers to all of these questions are based on the teacher's beliefs about people, about the world, about how students learn, about how students think, and about values. Every decision the teacher makes, from how the classroom should be arranged to how the learning should be evaluated, involves the teacher's philosophy of life and of education. Discipline and classroom control practices are especially dependent on the teacher's belief system and philosophy of education. Teaching without a philosophy of education would be analogous to building a house on sand instead of on a firm foundation, or to taking a trip without a road map.

Definition of the Term Philosophy

LOVE OF WIS-
DOM

What is a "**philosophy**"? The word comes from two Greek words meaning "love of wisdom." In practical terms, philosophy is the belief system that a person develops concerning existence, reality in the world, truth and knowledge, logic or thought processes, and aesthetics and ethical values. A philosophy answers such questions as What is real? How do we gain a knowledge of what is true? What is our view of the world? Are humans basically good or evil? How do we learn? What are the principles of correct thinking? What ethical values should guide us in our actions? Of what does beauty consist? Philosophy, then, is a person's fundamental belief system, on which he or she bases the answers to life's (and education's) most perplexing questions.

Why Study Philosophy?

QUESTIONS
ON DISCI-
PLINE

As mentioned in the introduction to this chapter, many of the pressing problems in education today are related to and can be answered by one's personal philosophy of education. Many of these questions are related to the three crucial areas of discipline, methods, and evaluation. What classroom control techniques should be used with students at a specific age and maturity level? Are humiliation and sarcasm ever appropriate as discipline methods? Should subject matter be used as punishment ("Johnny, do twenty more addition problems because you talked without raising your hand")? How effective are logical consequences and assertive discipline techniques in controlling the aggressive behavior of students? Are detention and isolation techniques harmonious with the teacher's general philosophy of education? Should corporal punishment be used as a last resort? The answers to many of these questions concerning classroom control depend on one's view of the student as basically good or evil and on one's ideas about how correct behavior is best learned and internalized.

QUESTIONS ON METHODS

What questions arise in the area of teaching and learning methods? Should instruction concentrate on group work or individualized learning experiences? Do you favor individualized learning contracts? Is peer tutoring an effective method for a particular age or learning level? Are calculators and computers an aid to learning math, or do they make students too dependent on machines? How do you feel about programmed instruction and teaching with television? Are current television programs an aid or a hindrance to classroom learning? How should commercial television programs be used to supplement classroom learning? What percentage of instruction should be by practical hands-on experience (philosophers have very definite opinions on this question)? Is your aim as a teacher to cover all the known subject matter in a survey fashion, or should students study fewer topics in greater depth by "postholing"? Should subjects such as history be chronological or topical in arrangement? Should the study of biology be organized by the classification system (phyla) or by the practical use of each plant or animal (niche approach)? What is "basic" for pupils to learn at a specific level in elementary school? Are physical education, music, and art basic to the learning process in elementary schools?

QUESTIONS ON EVALUATION

How should students be evaluated? Should academic test scores be the only method of evaluation? To what extent should academic ability, attitude, and effort be considered? Should evaluation be subjective, objective, or a combination of both? Would you recommend "extra credit" projects for slower students, for better students, or for all students? Would you use essay or objective exams in your subject area or grade level? What is the importance of success or failure to the self-concept of the student? Should students be passed from grade to grade with their peers whether or not they have mastered the subject matter? Is competency-based education an answer to this problem?

OTHER QUESTIONS

Numerous other examples could be given, but let these illustrations prove the point that all questions in education are basically philosophical questions.

Even the physical arrangement of classrooms should be based on a philosophy of education. Is the teacher's desk in the front, at the side, or at the rear of the classroom? Should students' seats be in rows, in a circle, or in a U-shaped arrangement? Should three or more classes be grouped together in open-concept "pods" or separated into single classrooms?

Philosophy is truly the most practical of subjects because every question is in essence a philosophical question. This chapter will help you to formulate a philosophy and to rely on it to answer these and other questions in everyday educational practice.

AGE-OLD PROBLEMS

Rosen (1968) stated that there are very few new problems in education. Therefore, we educators need to study philosophy to clarify the age-old problems, such as how to educate students for citizenship (studied by Plato and by education students today).

> One of the most immediate values in the study of a variety of philosophies of education is that it allows one to see a number of different and alternative solutions to a single problem. Each of the solutions is part of a broader framework of educational thought which in turn is part of a philosophical system. Thus, each solution is a part of a consistent view point. . . . Each point of view provides us with a different measuring stick for current educational practices. (Rosen, 1968, p. 8)

SEARCH FOR MEANING

Rosen sees philosophy as a person's attempt to give meaning to life and to search for answers to the basic problems in existence and education (p. 3). Thus, the authors of this text believe that students of education should engage in acting as well as thinking. Students are seeking in this chapter the personal beliefs and values that will serve as a foundation in their search for answers to present and future educational problems. A student's philosophy will enable him or her to make and to justify consistent choices in a future educational career.

The Language of Philosophy

Before the major pure and educational philosophies can be studied, the education student must become familiar with the special terminology of philosophy. At first you may feel as if you are studying a foreign language, but as you use the terms, they will become clear. Do not be fearful of them, and use the simple equivalent question given for each term to help you.

Metaphysics

REALITY

The first of the four major divisions of philosophy is **metaphysics**. Metaphysics concerns the universe and humankind. The main question posed in metaphysics is What is real? With respect to the world, metaphysics is concerned with the causes of events in the universe, including the theories of creation and evolution. Metaphysics also involves questions concerning the nature of humans. Is the basic human nature physical or spiritual? What is the relation, if any, between mind and body? Are we free or determined? In other words, does a person make free choices, or do events and conditions, such as mental ability, poverty, and financial resources, force one into basic decisions? Other aspects of metaphysics encompass questions about a person's existence, about the nature and existence of God, about whether there is purpose in events of the universe, and about whether ultimate reality is singular or plural: Is reality one substance (mind or body), two substances (mind and body), or more than two substances?

METAPHYSICAL QUESTIONS

The questions in metaphysics are extremely relevant to teachers and students of education, especially those questions about humanity and the universe. Theories about how the universe came to be and about what causes events in the universe are crucial to the sciences, especially biology.

The questions about humankind in metaphysics are important at all grade levels and in all subjects. To what extent can students influence and control their own lives (freedom versus determinism)? Are humans "little animals" to be treated only as physical beings, are they only a composite of the ideas they hold, or are they a combination of both? The answers to these questions influence a teacher's behavior in disciplining students, in emphasizing physical conditioning of the body versus development of the mind, and in deciding how much emphasis to place on student's learning decision-making skills.

Epistemology

TRUTH

The second major division in philosophy is **epistemology**. Epistemology deals with What is true? and How do we know? Epistemology includes the limits of knowledge, the kind or types of knowledge, and the ways of acquiring knowledge. In connection with the limits of knowledge, an agnostic believes that it is impossible to acquire knowledge of ultimate reality, whereas a skeptic questions whether it is possible to acquire such knowledge. The two major types of knowledge are knowledge based on observation and experience and self-evident knowledge that does not require proof. However, the major contents of epistemology for the teacher are the five ways of knowing. The first way of knowing is by revelation from God, such as the Ten Commandments. The second is by authority: one relies on an expert for knowledge. The third way of knowing involves reasoning ability within the mind of the individual, and the fourth is knowledge gained through sense perception by the individual (the scientific method). The fifth way of knowing is by intuition: after study of the topic, one skips the ordinary steps in the discovery process when he or she gains insight (has a brainstorm in the middle of the night, for example).

REASONING
PROCESS

How we know, or epistemology, is of paramount importance to teachers because their beliefs about learning influence their classroom methods. Should teachers train students in the scientific method, deductive reasoning, or both? Should students study logic and fallacies of the reasoning process? Under what conditions can one believe an authority figure (an athlete or a movie star) on television? Is the "grand leap" of intuition a legitimate source of knowledge? Is intuition involved in major scientific discoveries (such as pasteurization)? Teachers' knowledge of how students learn influences how they teach.

Logic

DEDUCTION
AND INDUC-
TION

Logic, or how one thinks, is the third major division of philosophy. It is closely related to epistemology and includes two major subdivisions: deductive logic and inductive logic. When one starts with a general principle and "deduces" specific facts or behaviors, one is using deductive logic. When one begins with a multitude of specifics and eventually formulates a general rule from them, one is using inductive logic. Although the scientific method encompasses both deduction and induction, it places great emphasis on the inductive method. As will be explained later, idealists tend to emphasize deduction, whereas realists and pragmatists rely on induction and the scientific method, using the systematic observation of experience. John Dewey's *How We Think* (1933) deals with this question of the scientific method. Immanuel Kant, an idealist, is associated with deduction, whereas Francis Bacon, a critical naturalist, emphasizes induction.

Axiology

The fourth major division of philosophy is also of crucial importance to teachers and schools. **Axiology** includes the questions What is morally right? and What is beautiful? It covers ethics and moral values, topics that many people think schools should emphasize. Good citizenship, honesty, and correct human relations are all learned in schools. They are not always taught directly but are learned as a by-product of other learning. Often, students learn ethics from what the teacher "is" as well as from what the teacher "says." Cheating on exams and other types of academic dishonesty have become major problems in some schools. Watergate and other instances of government corruption have placed much pressure on the schools to increase instruction in ethics and moral values. One major question to be examined is whether the end (goal) justifies any means (methods) of achieving it. To those involved in the Watergate scandal, reelection of a particular president of the United States seemed more important than the methods used to accomplish this goal, and basic violations of ethical principles and basic civil rights resulted.

ETHICS AND MORAL VALUES

In summary, problems in philosophy can be divided into questions of being (existence), knowledge, logic, and values. Such questions as Who am I? Why am I here? What is real? What is good? What is beautiful? and How can students learn? are crucial to education and to teachers. The reader is now introduced to the various positions of the pure philosophies. In Chapter 9, the related educational philosophies are described to see how each philosophy answers these relevant questions.

Pure Philosophies

The four major "pure" philosophies are naturalism, idealism, realism, and pragmatism. In addition, existentialism is included here in the pure philosophies, and its major tenets are discussed in this chapter. These pure philosophies are related to the educational philosophies of perennialism, essentialism, progressivism, and reconstructionism, which are discussed in Chapter 9.

As will be seen, naturalism and realism share a belief in the external physical world as being the real world, but they differ in that naturalism has little theory of knowing whereas realism has an epistemology based on the scientific method. Realism emphasizes the correspondence theory of truth (that something is true if it corresponds to the external world as it appears to our senses). For idealists, on the other hand, reality is an idea in our heads, not in the external physical world. Idealists emphasize the consistency (or coherence) theory of truth, which states that an idea is true if it forms part of a "system" of ideas. Idealists place much emphasis on deductive reasoning and much less on the senses and the scientific method. Pragmatism (also called *experimentalism* or *instrumentalism*) places its emphasis on changes as the only reality to be counted on. For pragmatists, everything is relative and situational, including ethics. Existentialism is oriented toward the individual and is concerned with two basic issues, individual freedom and death. Freedom of choice is crucial for the existentialists. Each of these pure philosophies is now examined in more detail.

Naturalism

Naturalism is the oldest of the major pure philosophies, dating back to ancient times. Naturalism is also the simplest of the major pure philosophies, with its belief that the physical world as it appears to one's senses is true reality. Naturalism shares this belief in the external physical universe with realism, but differs in that naturalism does not emphasize questions concerning knowledge or epistemology. Instead, naturalism places its emphasis on metaphysics (what is real). Naturalism is best conceived of as opposing "supernaturalism" because true naturalists believe that there is nothing beyond the physical world that a person sees. For the pure naturalist, there is no god outside of nature. The closest approach they have to a god is pantheism, where the totality of nature approximates "god." As Butler (1968) put it, "Naturalism is a distinct philosophy by virtue of its insistence that reality and nature are identical, and that beyond nature there is no reality" (p. 73). Naturalists believe that the human being is a child of nature, not of society. They emphasize living in harmony with nature and using the scientific (inductive) method of logic. Society, they believe, results from individuals' binding themselves together in a social contract to avoid anarchy. Naturalists believe that science yields items of knowledge that constitute a dependable source of scientific information.

Thomas Hobbes and Herbert Spencer both contributed much to the development of naturalism. Hobbes (1588–1679) believed that humans are in continual competition with others (a war of everyone against everyone). When one says, "It's a cruel and competitive world out there," she or he is espousing Hobbes' philosophy. According to Hobbes, schools should emphasize competition, not cooperation. He would emphasize high academic standards, science fairs, spelling bees, and other forms of competition, especially letter grades. Hobbes believed that "justice is exacted of men by a terror of punishment which is greater than the benefit they [students] would gain from a breach of the law" (Butler, 1968, p. 60). Thus, Hobbes's major classroom discipline technique would be the fear of punishment.

Spencer (1820–1903) was a scientist who participated in the development of the theory of evolution. He believed that the child is a little animal who must be educated according to the natural rhythms of growth and development. Scientific knowledge, he believed, was of the most worth, and the

PHYSICAL WORLD

HOBBES

SPENCER

long infancy of humans makes education a necessity. Spencer wrote specifically about education in *Education: Intellectual, Moral, and Physical* (1861). He called his theory the synthetic philosophy, involving the principles of evolution and dissolution, and he was very objective in collecting and organizing facts by the scientific method. He was an energist and an agnostic, believing that ultimate reality is a force and that it is unknowable. Spencer formulated eight principles of the education process (Butler, 1968):

1. Education must conform to the natural processes of growth and mental development.
2. Education should be pleasurable . . . [with an emphasis on readiness and interests].
3. Education should engage the spontaneous self-activity of that child. . . . The child educates himself in a great measure [the use of native self-activity].
4. Acquisition of knowledge is an important part of education.
5. Education is for the body as well as the mind. . . . Mind and body must both be cared for and the whole being of the pupil unfolded as a unit.
6. Education practices the art of delay . . . [in harmony with the rhythms of nature and maturation].
7. Methods of instruction should be inductive.
8. Punishment should be constituted by natural consequences of wrong deeds; should be certain, but tempered with sympathy. Punishment should fit the crime, be consistently administered, and avoid anger. (pp. 92–94)

ROUSSEAU   Jean-Jacques Rousseau (1712–1778) was probably the greatest modern naturalist, from the educator's standpoint. Rousseau believed that the individual is innately good but is corrupted by society. He condemned society and preferred the simple life close to nature. He wrote *Émile* (1762), a book describing the education of the son of a wealthy person through private tutoring, and *The Social Contract* (1762), a work on politics. Rousseau opposed the contemporary emphasis on habit formation and behavioral conditioning. He believed that the impetus for growth and maturation of mind and body comes from within and that a teacher should cultivate students much as a gardener tends a plant, providing the proper environment and nourishment, while preventing harmful influences from the outside world. Rousseau believed in a practical education through action rather than talking. He believed that students should not be exposed to society until they had learned how to handle this experience. Thus, he wanted to teach the student moral principles before introducing her or him to society. Rousseau believed that a person should place emphasis on studying his or her relationship to the environment. In Rousseau's words,

> The real object of our student is man and his environment. To my mind those of us who can best endure the good and evil of life are best educated; hence it follows that true education consists less in precept than in practice. We begin to learn when we begin to live; our education begins with ourselves, our first teacher is our nurse. (cited in Gruber, 1973, pp. 108–109)

Jean-Jacques Rousseau's philosophy of naturalism influenced the educational and political thought of his time.

(Photo courtesy of the Library of Congress.)

GOODNESS OF MAN

Rousseau's belief in the goodness of man and in the evil of society is evident in this statement (Gruber, 1973):

SOCIETY IS EVIL

> God makes all things good; man meddles with them and they become evil. He forces one soil to yield the products of another, one tree to bear another's fruit. He confuses and confounds time, place, and natural conditions. He mutilates his dog, his horse, and his slave. He destroys and defaces all things; he loves all that is deformed and monstrous; he will have nothing as nature made it, not even man himself, who must learn his paces like a saddle horse, and be shaped to his master's taste like the trees in his garden. (pp. 107–108)

WOMEN'S ROLES

Rousseau further stated, "Plants are fashioned by cultivation, man by education" (Gruber, 1973, p. 108). He obviously put great emphasis on education, but it must be noted that his opinions on women's role in society are dated because he devoted only one chapter at the end of *Émile* to women's role: he stated that women should be educated to be helpmates for the Émiles rather than for careers of their own. In spite of such weaknesses, Rousseau was very influential in the philosophy of naturalism and was the philosophical father of Johann Friedrich Herbart, Johann Heinrich Pestalozzi, and Friedrich Froebel, as will be seen later in this chapter.

CURRENT EX-
AMPLES OF
NATURALISM

The "back-to-nature" trend in the last few years in the United States is an example of naturalism. Backpacking, camping, and survival training reflect this trend, as does the "natural look" in cosmetics and dress. We all seem to yearn for a return to the simple life in the rhythms of nature. Anything that is artificial and unnatural seems to repel us. "Earth tones" have been popular in interior decoration, and even suburbs have arisen from a need to "get back to nature" and away from pollution. In fact, the entire environmentalist movement parallels the ideas of naturalism. This movement ranges from the protection of wilderness lands to the heating of homes with wood and solar energy rather than fossil fuels. As can be readily seen, naturalism has been the "in" philosophy in recent years.

STRENGTHS
AND WEAK-
NESSES OF
NATURALISM

Naturalism has both strengths and weaknesses as a philosophy. According to Butler (1968), the simplicity of naturalism is both a strength and a weakness. The call back to nature is a simplifying influence on the hectic pace of modern life. Naturalism is too simple, however, in that it does not have an adequate theory of knowledge (epistemology); thus, it is not a comprehensive philosophy. It ignores the fact that nature is not all rhythm and harmony because there are tornados, earthquakes, and floods. For naturalists, there is no supernatural, and the pupil remains a "little animal" with slight emphasis on mental development. Thus, physical conditioning of the human body becomes very important for the naturalists.

Idealism

IDEA-ISM

Idealism is the second pure philosophy. Idealism is important both in its own right and because pragmatism and realism were developed as counterthrusts to idealism. Idealists believe in the reality of the spirit, the mind, the soul, and ideas. As Rosen (1968) pointed out, "Idealism is a philosophical position which adheres to the view that nothing exists except as it is an idea in the mind of man, the mind of God, or in a super- or supranatural realm" (p. 12). Thus, idealism could be more accurately called *idea-ism* without the *l*. Although idealists do believe in ideals, as shown by their belief in God and the supernatural, their main emphasis is on ideas and the human mind. As contrasted with naturalism, which includes a belief in the physical world and a lack of belief in supernaturalism, idealism is the complete opposite. For idealists, the idea of a physical thing, such as a building, in the human mind is what is real, not the physical structure itself. Also, most idealists have a firm belief in God, whereas most naturalists do not believe in any supernatural power higher than nature itself. George Berkeley (1685–1753), the consummate idealist, had trouble with the following question: Does a falling tree make a sound in the forest if

Philosophies and Roles in Education

Naturalism	
Student	Teacher
Little animal to be kept attuned to nature	A. Protector from evils of world B. Transmitter of knowledge so child can cope C. Competitive mentor and strict disciplinarian (Views differ.)

Idealism	
Student	Teacher
A mind to be nurtured and protected	Model for students Emphasizes lecture and discussion of ideas
Parent	Transmitter of cultural heritage
Protector from evils of the environment	

Realism	
Student	Teacher
"Tabula rasa" Blank page Passive organism	Forms correct habits in students ("conditioner") Connects new information to old

Pragmatism	
Student	Teacher
An active problem solver moving toward the goal of an independent learner	Guide and resource person

Existentialism	
Student	Teacher
Active questioner searching for self, responsible for own learning	Helps students to make their own choices and to become their own person

there is no human there to hear it? For Berkeley, "to be was to be perceived," and he solved the problem by maintaining that God (the mind of God) was always there to perceive the sound of the tree falling.

Idealists believe in the power of reasoning (in the mind), particularly deductive reasoning, and they deemphasize the scientific method and sense perception, which they hold suspect. They believe that we look inside our own minds for the truth. They search for universal or absolute truths that will remain constant through the centuries. Rosen (1968) summarized this idealist view when he wrote that the senses deceive us and make us believe that the purely transitory world is the real world, and therefore, we must suppress the senses as much as possible. Idealists often define education as helping humans to conform to the will of God. Idealist educational beliefs include an emphasis on the study of great leaders as examples for us to imitate. For idealists, the teacher is the ideal model or example for the student. Teachers pass on the cultural heritage and the unchanging content of education, such as study of the great figures of the past, the humanities, and a rigorous academic curriculum. Idealists emphasize the methods of lecture, discussion, and imitation; and finally, they believe in the importance of the doctrine of ideas.

DEDUCTIVE
REASONING

Plato, Immanuel Kant, and Georg Wilhelm Friedrich Hegel were three very important idealists. Plato was intent on separating the permanent from the temporary, shadows from real objects, and the perceptions of our senses from realities. What one's senses perceive are illusions compared with the real world of ideas in the mind. This idea is perhaps best seen in Plato's allegory of the cave (cited in Rosen, 1968):

PLATO

> There is a cave in which men are chained facing a wall. On a ledge behind those who are chained, another group of men walk carrying things. Behind the men on the ledge is a fire which casts their shadows on the wall for the chained men to see. . . . Plato's analogy indicates that the world we know, the world of our senses, is like the shadows. It is unreal but we believe it to be the true reality because of habit and because it is the only reality with which we are familiar. The Real World, the World of Ideas, is of a different order, just as the men on the ledge are of a different order than their shadows. (p. 13)

ALLEGORY
OF THE CAVE

Kant and Hegel carried Plato's ideas further. Kant (1724–1804) emphasized the universal moral law, which he believed human beings naturally tend to fulfill. Kant's universal moral law, or categorical imperative, states that we should behave according to principles that we would want to be universal laws for everyone; for example, "Don't cheat on your income tax unless you expect everyone to do so." Also, persons must act correctly because it is right morally, not because other people will praise or condemn them for these actions. Hegel (1770–1831) believed that an individual fact or idea has no value until it fits into a system with other facts and ideas. This idea is sometimes called the **coherence theory of truth** because the facts or ideas have to stick to each other to become meaningful. Hegel also believed that most thought patterns begin with an idea (a thesis), then progress by contrasting this idea with its opposite (antithesis), and finally find the real truth in a combination of the thesis and the antithesis (the synthesis). Hegel would look at the idea that only the subject matter is important in schools (thesis), examine the opposite idea that only the child is important (anthesis), and conclude these ideas are equally important in learning (synthesis).

KANT

HEGEL

Hegel's educational theories grew directly out of his absolute idealism. He considered education to be a life process, a mental discipline that makes man religious, moral, cultured, and rational. Education should be compulsory through the state and for the state because only through education is the Will of God transmitted. (Gruber, 1973, p. 133)

CRITICISMS
OF IDEALISM

Many criticisms of idealism can be identified. It seems to ignore the physical aspects of human nature. It fails to place importance on information available through the senses. Idealists place an overemphasis on perfection and unattainable goals, and they tend to emphasize the humanities to the detriment of the sciences. Some philosophers would also criticize its goal of preserving the past and of transmitting our cultural heritage to future generations. In spite of these possible deficiencies, idealism has had a great influence on American education. Hiring officials tend to seek teachers whose personal qualities can be used as examples for students, and Hegel's system of thesis, antithesis, and synthesis is widely evident in American education. Kant's universal moral laws have also influenced values education in schools in the United States. In fact, an entire nineteenth century movement of idealists in the United States, called *transcendentalism*, has influenced our values and literature. Transcendentalism received its name from the belief that reality is to be found "beyond" the physical environment and the physical nature of a person.

Idealism is also important, as has been mentioned before, because it led its opponents to develop the philosophies of realism and pragmatism.

Realism

Realism is the third of the pure philosophies. One way to understand realism is to compare it with idealism and naturalism:

Where an idealist would say that a tree in the middle of the desert exists only if it is in some mind, or if there is knowledge of it, the realist would hold that whether or not anyone or anything is thinking about the tree, it nonetheless exists. The realist has revolted against the doctrine that things that are in the experiential universe are dependent upon a knower for their existence. (Rosen, 1968, p. 28)

REALISM RE-
LATED TO
NATURALISM

Concerning the relationship of realism to naturalism, realism is in many ways similar to naturalism, but naturalism has a better developed theory of knowledge (how we learn). Both realists and naturalists believe that the real world is the physical world as it appears to our senses, not the world of ideas in our minds. Both emphasize the senses and the scientific method.

PHYSICAL
WORLD AS
REAL WORLD

What are the philosophical beliefs of the realists? To the realists, the physical world as it appears to our senses is the real world. The realists also believe that the universe is governed by an orderly system of natural laws. Thus, they emphasize the natural sciences and a dependable fund of scientific knowledge. They place much faith in inductive logic and the scientific method, differing from the idealists, who place emphasis on deductive logic and reasoning instead of the scientific method of inquiry. A

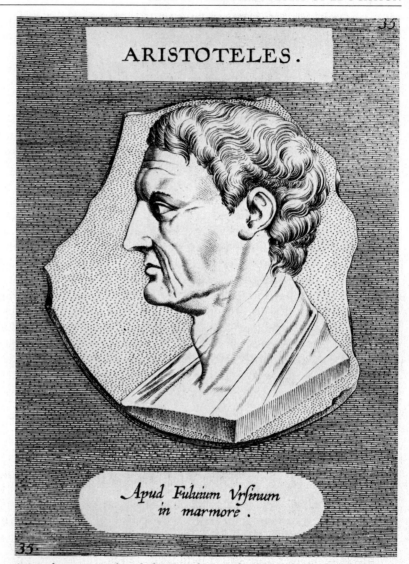

Aristotle was a realist, believing that unchanging physical realities should be studied through inductive logic and scientific investigation.

(Photo courtesy of the Library of Congress.)

further way in which realists differ from idealists is in their belief in a mechanistic universe, a universe governed by natural laws and cause-and-effect relationships, not necessarily by a supreme being. Realists do, however, agree with idealists in their belief in absolutes. Realists reinforce the idealists' belief that the purpose of education is to conserve and transmit the cultural heritage to future generations. Humans are, however, more passive spectators than active participants in the events of the universe. In the realist view, humans are analogous more to a radio wave receiver than **ARISTOTLE** to a transmitter. Whereas the idealist Plato was interested in ideas and **VS. PLATO** universal truths, Aristotle, the realist, was concerned about specific facts discovered by the scientific method. Aristotle believed in unchanging, objective, external realities. As Butler (1968) put it, "This confidence in abiding, objective, and external realities which, like the pyramids, stand unaffected by the passing processions, whether of time or inquisitive minds, is the prime confidence of realism" (p. 76). The educational beliefs of the realists are that neither teachers nor students are free; they are subject to natural laws and are spectators in the universe. The subject matter of schools, according to the realists, is the physical universe, and the scientific method and inductive logic should be used to discover and master facts. In fact, "the whole concept of teaching machines is compatible with the [realists'] picture of reality as a mechanistic universe in which man is simply one of the cogs in the machine" (Rosen, 1968, p. 41).

Realists can be divided into two groups: new realists and critical realists. The new realists believe that the objects of the real world are just as we **NEW REAL-** perceive them. They believe in the correspondence theory of truth, which **ISTS AND** says that a thing is true if it "corresponds" to the real world. In contrast, **CRITICAL** critical realists have a representational view that, as in Plato's allegory of **REALISTS** the cave, one never sees the real objects but only their shadows or "representations" of reality.

> Critical Realists felt that man could not know the world directly but only through certain vehicles or essences. Thus, objects are not presented directly to consciousness but are represented. We do not have direct knowledge of any object except as it is carried to us by our senses. It was felt by the Critical Realists that this position was the only way to explain errors of perception. (Rosen, 1968, pp. 33–34)

Thus, new realists believe that one sees the world directly, whereas critical realists believe that one sees it indirectly.

John Locke, John Amos Comenius, and William James are proponents of **LOCKE** the realist tradition. Locke (1632–1704) believed in the "blank tablet" view of the mind, that there are no innate ideas in the mind. Locke stated that the mind of a person is blank at birth and that the person's sensory experiences make impressions on this blank tablet. Comenius' view of the **COMENIUS** human mind was that it resembles a spherical mirror (of the ball type used in dance halls of the 1920s to reflect the lights). It receives images or signals rather than originating or transmitting them. Because the mirror is composed of small pieces of glass, it also distorts the images, resulting in errors **JAMES** of perception. William James (1842–1910) is classified as both a realist and a pragmatist, as we shall see later in this chapter. His realist ideas included his emphasis on habits, which he defined as tendencies to act in certain

John Locke, a realist of the seventeenth century, believed that ideas
come to the mind only through experience with the world.

(Photo courtesy of the Library of Congress.)

ways, and his emphasis on building useful systems of association in the
pupil's mind. On the topic of habits, Gruber (1973) presented James' view
in the following words:

> James' *Talks to Teachers* [1898] is a popular simplification of his monumental
> *Principles of Psychology* prepared especially for classroom teachers with little
> or no technical knowledge. . . . James writes that pupils can easily understand
> at an early age that our lives are but a mass of habits. He agrees with Aristotle
> that habit is man's second nature and with Kant that education is for behavior
> and habit. . . . Like many modern psychologists, he advises the person to
> accumulate all the possible connections (or assumptions) that will reinforce
> the right motives and warns that deferring the establishment of a new habit
> lessens the chance that it will ever be formed. (p. 176)

PESTALOZZI   In education, the realists are represented by the works of Johann Heinrich
Pestalozzi, Friedrich Froebel, and John Friedrich Herbart. First, let us look
at the realistic ideas of Pestalozzi. Pestalozzi was influenced by Rousseau

William James, who is classified as both a realist and a pragmatist, believed that education is the formation of habits.

(Photo courtesy of the Library of Congress.)

in his belief that the teacher cultivates students like the gardener tends plants and that growth is from within. The teacher cannot make a student learn but can only protect the student from harmful outside forces and provide the proper environment for learning:

> Basing all learning on sense perception and activity, Pestalozzi developed a curriculum made up of object lessons, development of language skills, arithmetic, geography, music [especially singing], drawing and modeling, geometry, gymnastics, and manual training. He rejected, as did Rousseau, the study of history, myth, and literature because they had no direct connection with sense perception. (Gruber, 1973, p. 125)

In *How Gertrude Teaches Her Children* (1801/1894), Pestalozzi emphasized a natural education and opposed education based on memorization and the mental discipline theory of learning. Pestalozzi believed that "the child's innate capacities should be awakened by a series of experiences arranged according to his maturation and that method should follow the order of nature (Gruber, 1973, p. 125).

FROEBEL

Friedrich Froebel studied under Pestalozzi, established a school for boys, and opened the first kindergarten ("child's garden") in Germany in 1837. He then spent the rest of his life on the preparation of teachers in the area of early childhood education. Froebel's unhappy childhood probably influenced his ideas on education. His father, a minister, paid little attention to his son, and his stepmother favored her own children. According to Gruber

Friedrich Froebel, who established the first kindergarten, felt that early childhood was an important time, when children should be nurtured and given many and varied play experiences.

(Photo courtesy of the Library of Congress.)

(1973), "This early unfortunate childhood probably shaped the whole course of his life and was influential in centering his interest on early childhood education, making him sympathetic to and understanding of the problems of the very young" (p. 145). Froebel, like Rousseau, believed that the child develops from the inside out and that the child should be nurtured like a plant in a garden.

EDUCATION AS A GARDEN

> He [Froebel] likened education to a garden and believed that the school should cultivate and develop the potential in each child as a horticulturist tends each tender plant. To this end he used color, motion spheres, cubes, and other geometric forms and figures for their symbolic meaning. For example, a sphere taught the child the unity of mankind to God. (Gruber, 1973, pp. 146–147)

IMPORTANCE OF PARENTS AND VOCATIONS

Froebel recommended that an actual garden of living plants be part of every kindergarten, and he emphasized vocations as an important part of a child's learning. He recognized the importance of the parents' role in educating the child, and wrote a songbook for mother and child. However, the role of the parent was to protect the child from the evils of the environment, not to prescribe exactly what the child should learn and do. Froebel emphasized the social aspects of learning by group activity because he thought that every human act has social implications (Gruber, 1973):

> Possibly Froebel's greatest contribution to educational method was the doctrine that play was itself educational. He believed that play and free self-activity were nature's way of developing the child and that the child's activities should be prompted by the development of his own nature. (p. 147)

AMERICAN KINDERGARTEN

Froebel's kindergarten in Germany led to the first American German-speaking kindergarten, established by Mrs. Karl Schurz in Watertown, Wisconsin, in 1855, and to the first English-speaking kindergarten in Boston in 1860. Gruber (1973) concluded,

> Although he [Froebel] differed in many respects from Rousseau and his teacher Pestalozzi, he shared with them a concern for the continuous development of the individual from infancy. He aimed to rear free-thinking, independent men through developing the inner nature of the child, and believed that all learning should be oriented in the direction of the child's interests and capacities. (p. 146)

Herbart (1776–1841) was born in Germany but took a job in Switzerland as a tutor. Here he was influenced by Pestalozzi, the Swiss educator. Both Herbart and Pestalozzi emphasized the importance of sense impressions, but they had many differences, as shown in the following comparison:

> Pestalozzi was active, impulsive, and developed his psychology in actual practice; Herbart, on the other hand, was thoughtful, scholarly, systematic, and developed his theory of psychology in connection with his teaching of philosophy. While Pestalozzi was interested in the education of childhood and youth through sense perception, Herbart was interested in the intellectual develop-

Modern kindergartens provide many of the types of experience recommended by Froebel in the 1800s.

(Photo used by permission of the Indiana State Teachers Association.)

ment of the secondary school pupil and the university student. (Gruber, 1973, p. 139)

HERBART

One of Herbart's major beliefs was that the learner can be conditioned to correct behavior, and Herbart agreed with John Locke that experiences make impressions on the blank tablet of the mind. Like William James, Herbart was interested in psychology, especially the conscious and unconscious states of the mind. Herbart believed that interest can call an idea or experience from the unconscious to the conscious state.

FIVE FORMAL
STEPS

APPERCEP-
TIVE MASS

Herbart's main contributions to education are his five formal steps of methodology. The first is preparation of the student to receive new information, and the second is presentation of the new knowledge. The third step is association, in which new material is compared with knowledge already in the brain, or "apperceptive mass," as Herbart called it. The fourth step is generalization, an attempt to discover a general rule, and the fifth is application of the concept learned to new situations. Rosen (1968) summarized Herbart's ideas:

> Herbart argued that all subjects are related and that knowledge of one helps strengthen knowledge of the others. As the mind acquires new contents they are assimilated with the existing contents [in the apperceptive mass]. . . . The relationship between new ideas and old ideas occurred in what Herbart called the apperceptive mass. Within the mind, new apperceptions or presentations united with older apperceptions and struggled to rise from the unconscious level of the mind to the conscious. Obviously, any teaching must be aimed at making the greatest number of connections between new ideas and those which were already held in the apperceptive mass. (p. 32)

STRENGTHS
AND WEAK-
NESSES

This discussion of the major ideas of realism has uncovered both strengths and weaknesses in this philosophy. Its strengths include its support of habits and behavioral conditioning, its emphasis on cause-and-effect relationships, and its emphasis on psychology. Criticisms include its treatment of the mind as a passive receptor of knowledge and experiences, its emphasis on cultural heritage rather than change, and its overdependence on cause-and-effect relationships, which seems to diminish a person's ability to control his or her own life. Whatever the strengths and weaknesses of realism, realist educators such as Herbart and Pestalozzi made an enormous contribution to educational thought and methodology.

Pragmatism

AN AMERI-
CAN PHILOS-
OPHY

The fourth major pure philosophy, **pragmatism**, is the only one that originated in the United States. Pragmatism, sometimes called *experimentalism* or *instrumentalism*, was developed in opposition to the principles of idealism. Ideas alone are not sufficient for reality, said the original pragmatists; action on these ideas is necessary to determine their value. For the pragmatists, the only test of truth is what works best and what ideas can be used to solve problems satisfactorily. The pragmatists were oriented more toward the present than toward the past, which is prominent in idealism

Steps to Knowledge		
Dewey's Pragmatism (student-based)		Herbart's Realism (teacher-based)
Test all hypotheses and choose a "best" solution for this situation	5	Application of the general rule to a new situation
Consideration of possible positive and negative consequences of all hypotheses	4	Generalization—formation of a general rule
Formulation of hypotheses	3	Association of new knowledge with previous knowledge
Definition of the problem in terms all participants can accept	2	Presentation of new knowledge
Recognition of the problem by students: "felt need"	1	Preparation of students to receive new knowledge

Comparison of Dewey's and Herbart's approaches to the learning process.

TRUTH IS
RELATIVE

EXPERIENCE

and realism. They grounded their thinking in present actualities and used the scientific method to solve present problems: If the idea "works" and the problem is solved, then the truth has been revealed. Truth, then, is relative to present conditions and circumstances, not an absolute as the idealists and realists believed. For pragmatists, "experience" was the medium in which thought (ideas) and action mix. They formulated the principles of interaction and continuity of experience. Americans are a very pragmatic people who like to learn by doing, engage in practical tasks, and determine the truth in each problem situation as it comes along. The pragmatists believed that change is the only thing that is permanent and that truth, reality, and values are all relevant to circumstances. Furthermore, the pragmatists did not believe in absolutes and tended to doubt that rules can be generalized over many specific situations. For the pragmatists, society and the social aspects of culture were also very important.

What are the educational principles of current pragmatists? Pragmatists see education as the reconstruction and reorganization of human experience. Educators should provide conditions that allow students to grow. They see the student as an organism capable of solving problems. The teacher, for the pragmatist, is also a continuous learner who aids and guides

PROBLEM
SOLVING

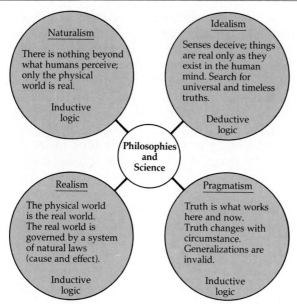

Relationships among the traditional philosophies and science.

others in the learning process without pretending to be the only source of knowledge. Teachers do not abdicate their responsibilities; they arrange conditions for learning related to students' needs and interests.

PRAGMATIST CURRICULUM   The curriculum of the pragmatists would consist of any experience contributing to growth and would be based on the needs and interests of the learner. Thus, the subject matter is centered on the problems and needs of the learner, not on universal moral laws as the idealists advocate or on the cause-and-effect relationships championed by the realists. The project method, individual problem-solving research, and class discussions are the methods of the pragmatists, who encourage students to become self-directed learners. As Rosen (1968) wrote, "Pragmatic method is rooted in the psychological needs of the students, rather than in the logical order of subject matter. Thus, method is nothing more than the helping of the students to use intelligence and the scientific method in the solution of problems that are meaningful to the child" (p. 82). As one pragmatist has asserted, "Interest is not enough. It is a necessary, but not a sufficient, condition for selecting an area of concern. It should also offer a challenge and significant educational value" (Rosen, 1968, p. 82). Thus, instead of studying biology in terms of phyla, for example, the pragmatist would help students to organize the subject in terms of significant problems of interest to the students, such as ecology, acid rain, and damage to the environment. The social consequences of our actions are of pressing importance to the pragmatists, who see every action and decision as having an effect on society at large.

FIVE STEPS OF
THE SCIEN-
TIFIC
METHOD

The pragmatic method involves the five steps of the scientific method. John Dewey himself outlined them in the booklet *How We Think*. The first step is recognition of the problem. It begins with an uneasy feeling that something is wrong, which Dewey called the "felt need." The second step is definition of the problem in terms that all participants can accept; the authors of this text see this definition stage as one of the most crucial in problem solving because a problem cannot be solved if group members are, in effect, working on different definitions of the problem. The third step is formulation of hypotheses or tentative solutions to the problem. Consideration of both the positive and the negative consequences of each possible solution is the fourth step in the process. In the final step, each possible solution is tested and the one "best solution" is chosen on the basis of the test results. It should be added at this point that pragmatists are very suspicious of broad generalizations. They believe that truth is valid only for a single set of circumstances, which are never identical from one situation to another. Pragmatists could truly say, "Never trust a generalization, including this one!"

PRAGMATIST
LEADERS

Numerous American leaders of pragmatism can be identified, such as William Heard Kilpatrick, Boyd Bode, and George Counts, but William James (already discussed under "Realism"), Charles Sanders Pierce, and John Dewey are the most influential names in this movement. Pierce, for instance, formulated the pragmatist belief that the consequences of an idea determine its meaning; however, John Dewey is discussed here as the foremost leader of the pragmatists.

JOHN DEW-
EY'S LIFE

Who was John Dewey, and what were his major philosophical ideas? John Dewey was born in 1859 in Burlington, Vermont, and lived until 1952. He came from a line of pragmatic Vermont farmers and attended local public schools. After he graduated from the University of Vermont, Dewey taught in a Vermont high school for only three years and then went back to school to earn graduate degrees. He studied idealism under George Sylvester Morris and educational psychology under G. Stanley Hall at Johns Hopkins University. Gruber (1973) summarized Dewey's professional career as follows: "He taught philosophy at the University of Michigan and Minnesota, was professor of philosophy and pedagogy at the University of Chicago from 1894–1904, and was professor of philosophy at Columbia University from 1905 until his retirement in 1931" (p. 183). After his retirement, he remained active by traveling and lecturing until his death in 1952.

Dewey rebelled against the educational ideas of his time; his thinking was a radical departure from then-current educational thought. He opposed the ideas that education is preparation for life and that facts must be stored up before thinking can occur. Dewey believed that education is life and that facts are discovered as one works on solutions to significant problems. Dewey analyzed the human thinking process and investigated the interrelationships of a great number of dualisms, such as interest and effort, mind and body, and change and permanence. In his view, every idea was conditional, a hypothesis to be tested in practice. Instead of being absolute and

DUALISMS

universal, as the idealists believed knowledge to be, Dewey emphasized that knowledge is relative and situational, requiring constant reevaluation and reconstruction of experience. Dewey called his philosophy *instrumentalism* because he saw ideas as instruments of living rather than as ends in themselves. "For Dewey, then, reality is change, the universe is process, and man is coexistent with nature" (Gruber, 1973, p. 184).

INSTRUMEN-
TALISM

DEWEY'S ED-
UCATIONAL
CONTRIBU-
TIONS

What are Dewey's major educational contributions and his legacy to American education? Dewey held a strong belief in democracy, and he believed that schools should teach democracy by using democratic principles themselves. He was also a proponent of the problem or project method of teaching and learning (Gruber, 1973):

> [W]hile the student with a proper "project" is intellectually active, he is also overtly active; he applies, he constructs, he expresses himself in new ways. He puts his knowledge to the test of operation. Naturally, he does something with what he learns. Because of this feature the separation between the practical and the liberal does not even arise. (p. 191)

As one can readily see, Dewey influenced American education in very practical directions. The following quote from Dewey (cited in Gruber, 1973) illustrates his criticisms of schooling that is unrelated to life experiences:

DEWEY'S
CRITICISMS
OF SCHOOL-
ING

> The failure [of schooling] is again due, I believe, to the segregation of subjects. A pupil can say he has "had" a subject, because the subject has been treated as if it were complete in itself, beginning and terminating within limits fixed in advance. A reorganization of the subject matter which takes into account outleadings into the wide world of nature and man, of knowledge and of social interests and uses, cannot fail save in the most callous and intellectually obdurate to awaken some permanent interest and curiosity. Theoretical subjects will become more practical, because they are more related to the scope of life; practical subjects will become more charged with theory and intelligent insight. Both will be vitally and not just formally unified (p. 425)

From this quotation it can readily be seen that Dewey was interested in the theoretical versus the practical and in interest and effort. Dewey further maintained that one problem with schools and their curricula was that cohesive and unified learning was artificially splintered into separate courses. We can understand Dewey when we hear a student say, "Why should I have to use correct spelling and grammar? My report was for science, not English."

MISINTER-
PRETATIONS
OF DEWEY

Dewey's impact on the progressive education movement in America is much debated. Dewey and the pragmatists originally provided the impetus to the progressive movement. In Dewey's view, however, his followers often misinterpreted his ideas and carried them too far. As a result, in 1938, Dewey issued a statement ending his association with the progressive education movement. In fact, he became a critic of progressive education in the United States. Gruber (1973) summarized Dewey's influence:

John Dewey's influence in American education has been considerable, not only in the mainstream of public education, but among the traditionalists and essentialists who opposed him. The impact of his writings can be traced to the fields of law and art as well as the social sciences. . . . He was not as analytic as Pierce nor as fluent a writer as James, but his often difficult style has gotten through to the minds of his countrymen and has influenced every department of American thought. (p. 189)

Dewey is often censured as responsible for the so-called progressive education of our modern schools, but Brickman (1966) made the following assessment of the responsibility for the problems that developed:

CRITICISMS
OF DEWEY

Adverse criticism of Dewey, in relation to our modern education, is due to the failure by school officials to interpret and apply adequately his principles to practical problems in the conduct of our schools. Deficiency is not in Dewey as a philosopher but in school officials as administrators of his philosophy. (p. 22)

Whether one worships Dewey or hates him, it can readily be seen that his ideas have had a great effect on American education.

Existentialism

EXISTENCE
PRECEDES ES-
SENCE

The last pure philosophy, which is examined here only briefly, is **existentialism**. For existentialists, existence (being) precedes essence (meaning). Individuals always have a choice in any situation and should make the most of the situation in which they find themselves. For instance, if you were being held as a prisoner of war by an enemy army, you could still control your thoughts and even your reaction to enemy torture. Another example in a school situation would be your attitude toward taking a subject you dislike. You can either oppose learning this subject, or you can be positive and take what is valuable to you from the lessons. If, in another instance, two children are born in the ignorance and poverty of a large-city slum, one could seek education and fight his or her way to a better life, while the other could continue as part of the welfare system. For existentialists, the future depends a great deal on one's choices and one's attitude toward the future. Existentialism emphasizes human individuality as much as pragmatism and reconstructionism place their trust in the importance of social problems. Existentialists see people as alien beings in a world foreign to their spirits, and anxiety, loneliness, and uneasiness are central to their thinking about humankind and reality.

EXISTENTIAL-
ISTS' EDUCA-
TIONAL BE-
LIEFS

Educational beliefs are not the main product of existentialist thought, but the existentialist student would have a questioning attitude and would be immersed in a continuous search for self and reasons for her or his own existence. The existentialist teacher would help students become what they themselves want to become, not what outside forces such as society, teachers, or parents want them to become. The authors of this text have seen many students pressured by parents who are trying to fulfill their own dreams and aspirations through their children. Existentialist educators deplore this interference in the child's existence and believe that the students should make these choices for themselves. In much the same manner, existentialists question the validity of educational objectives imposed on students by outside forces such as teachers or the school system. Existentialists place a great deal of emphasis on the individual and are very suspicious of any social and group activities. Thus, existentialists would welcome alternative education opportunities but would deplore behavioral objectives as another form of conditioning that usurps individual freedom of choice.

FACING
TRAGEDY
OPENLY

Existentialists believe that tragedy should be faced openly and directly and, thus, would applaud death education units as coping directly with a part of life with which all of us must deal at some time. Death for existentialists is personal. For them, life and death are two sides of the same coin. They emphasize authentic experiences in education as moments of truth dealing with the very meaning of human existence. To existentialists, the individual seems to be thrown into a world beyond his or her control. Existentialism seems to flourish in environments where ideologies have fallen apart, such as in Germany before World War II or in the age of the atomic bomb.

Existentialism can be divided into two strains, and its followers are a diverse group. The Christian or theistic existentialists are best exemplified by Søren Kierkegaard, and the atheistic existentialists are represented by Jean-Paul Sartre (1905–1980) and Albert Camus (1913–1960). Gruber (1973) summarized the origins of existentialism:

CHRISTIAN
VS. ATHEIS-
TIC

> Although existential philosophy has been traced back to Plato and St. Thomas Aquinas, it is generally agreed that the modern movement arose from the revolt of the Danish theologian Søren Kierkegaard (1813–1855) against the absolute idealism of Hegel and the authoritarianism of church and state. . . . This philosophy states that existence [being] precedes essence [meaning] and attempts to create authentic individuals who are free from the tyranny of the group. Present-day interest in existentialism grew out of the destruction and despair of the concentration camps in Germany and the occupation of France in World War II. (p. 220)

A. S. NEILL'S
SUMMERHILL

Buber (1878–1965), one of the theistic existentialists, emphasized the importance of the relationship between the teacher and the pupil. Friedman said of Buber's philosophy: "This meeting of pupil and teacher as two unique individuals is what is educative. The relation of teacher to pupil is the meeting of one who has found direction with one who is finding it" (Gruber, 1973, pp. 181–182). The English educator A. S. Neill (1883–1973) established a school, Summerhill, which further embodies existentialist principles. At Summerhill, students have much freedom. There are no rules, no requirements, no homework, no grades, no tests, and no dress codes. Neill was trying to rehabilitate students who hated authority by making the students responsible for their own learning. Neill found that many students abused the freedom at first but, after a recovery period, began to plan their own learning.

In an evaluation of existentialism as a philosophy of education, its individualism is both a strength and a weakness. Can institutions supported by the society at large be this amenable to the wishes of the individual? Can schools avoid overall objectives and group activities? Yet, the freedom of the student to become what he or she desires to become has widespread support in the general statements of goals for schools in the United States.

Summary

In this chapter the term *philosophy* as well as the major divisions of philosophy—metaphysics, epistemology, axiology, and logic—was defined. The questions examined by philosophers were noted, and reasons for studying philosophy suggested. Major tenets of the four major pure philosophies—naturalism, idealism, realism, and pragmatism—were delineated. Naturalism and realism share a belief in the external world as being the real world but differ in that naturalism has little theory of knowing while realism has an epistemology based on the scientific method. Idealism is based on reality as in a person's mind, not in the eternal physical world. Pragmatism places its emphasis on change as the only reality. The major ideas championed by John Dewey as well as his contributions to education were examined. Finally, existentialism's beliefs in the importance of personal choices, anxiety, and loneliness were shown in relation to the educational contributions of this philosophy of individualism.

Glossary Terms

Philosophy, 230

Metaphysics, 232

Epistemology, 233

Logic, 233

Axiology, 234

Naturalism, 235

Idealism, 238

Coherence Theory of Truth, 240

Realism, 241

Pragmatism, 249

Existentialism, 254

Questions

1. Define and differentiate among metaphysics, epistemology, axiology, and logic as divisions of philosophy.
2. Having read the section Why Study Philosophy? in this chapter, describe in your own words the rationale behind the study of philosophy.
3. Compare and contrast idealism with both realism and pragmatism. What is the relationship of these three philosophies?

4. What naturalistic influences do you see in today's society (for example, the environmentalist movement and the "back-to-nature" movement)?

5. Explain in your own words what Plato meant in his allegory of the cave. What was the significance of the allegory in Plato's philosophy?

6. Explain a major philosophical idea associated with the three major realist philosophers: Locke, Comenius, and James. Then evaluate these three philosophical ideas.

7. Explain a major philosophical idea associated with the three major naturalist philosophers: Hobbes, Rousseau, and Spencer. Then evaluate these three philosophical ideas.

8. What were the major contributions of John Dewey to the pragmatist philosophical tradition? Do you agree with these educational ideas?

9. Describe the existentialist attitudes toward individualism and group activity.

10. Name and describe the two types of existentialism and some major existentialist philosophers associated with each type.

Annotated Bibliography

1. Dewey, J. (1933). *How we think*. Boston: D. C. Heath.

   John Dewey's work on the scientific process and steps in critical thinking is very useful today in teaching students correct thought processes.

2. James, W. (1898). *Talks to teachers*. New York: Holt.

   William James talks to teachers and students on educational psychology and offers very practical advice for teaching and learning.

3. Kant, I. (1949). *Critique of practical reason and other writings in moral philosophy*. Translated and edited with an introduction by L. W. Beck. Chicago: University of Chicago Press.

   This is a classic work on the idealist emphasis on thought processes instead of the physical world as reality. Kant saw reality as a world of ideas and placed his emphasis on reasoning as the primary method of acquiring knowledge.

4. Neill, A. S. (1984). *Summerhill: A radical approach to child rearing*. New York: Pocket Books (a division of Simon and Schuster).

   This book describes the existentialist school established in England by A. S. Neill, in which students were allowed to make many of their own choices and to experience both success and failure for themselves.

5. Pestalozzi, J. H. (1894). *How Gertrude teaches her children* (L. E. Holland, Trans.) Syracuse, NY: George Allen and Unwin. (Original work published in 1801.)

   This book is a treatise on how mothers teach their own children.

6. Rousseau, J. J. (1911). *Émile* (B. Foxley, Trans.). London: J. M. Dent. (Original work published in 1762.)

This book is a classic treatise on the proper education of a young or gentleman boy by private tutoring, before he is exposed to the evil influences of the world.

7.   Spencer, H. (1861). *Education: Intellectual, moral and physical.* New York: Appleton.

This work emphasizes many principles of education, such as readiness, which are still useful in teaching today. Spencer's main interest is in science, particularly natural selection (evolution).

Educational Philosophies

OBJECTIVES

After reading Chapter 9, the student will be able to:

- Conceptualize the relationship between the pure philosophies and the educational philosophies

- Compare and contrast the differences between the conservative and liberal philosophies

- Identify the contributions of major educational philosophers in each of the educational philosophies

- Trace present-day movements in education to one or more of the educational philosophies

- Decide which educational philosophy incorporates her or his philosophy of learning

Introduction

How are the educational philosophies of perennialism, essentialism, progressivism, and reconstructionism related to the pure philosophies already discussed?

> Educational philosophizing concerns itself with many of the same questions as "pure" philosophy. Even where the questions are not the same they are often no more than variants. For example, while the "pure" philosopher may ask, "How does a person come to know something?" the educational philosopher may go one step further and ask, "What are the specific classroom conditions under which a person is most likely to learn?" (Rosen, 1968, p. 6)

LIBERAL VS. CONSERVATIVE PHILOSOPHIES

Dupuis (1966) categorized educational philosophies as either "liberal" or "conservative" based on the answers to four philosophical and five educational questions. He sees the conservative ideas as controlling educational practices until Jean-Jacques Rousseau and his followers revolted against these conservative views. Even these more liberal views of Rousseau were not as effective in changing educational practices because of a lack of unity between these liberal philosophical principles and the educational practices of the time. This unity of education and philosophy was accomplished by John Dewey. There was a conservative "counterrevolution" to Dewey's liberal ideas, however, and Dupuis sees the problem today as one of finding a solution to this "either–or" dilemma between liberal and conservative ideas in education. Dupuis (1966) also stated that the split personality in the philosophy of American education is partly responsible for the problems in education in the United States. Of the four educational philosophies that are examined in this chapter, perennialism and essentialism are classified as conservative, and progressivism and reconstructionism are denoted as liberal educational philosophies. Now we examine each of these educational philosophies in greater detail to see why they are so classified.

Perennialism

Perennialism, like essentialism, places its emphasis on the past. For the perennialists, truth is logical, permanent, and unchanging (Rosen, 1968):

TRUTH AS UNCHANGING

> Perennialism is a modified form of realism which is an outgrowth of the thought of St. Thomas Aquinas. Many of its tenets are, however, still deeply rooted in the Aristotelian tradition of realism. But this Aristotelian world view has had added to it the concept of God as usually defined by the Roman Catholic Church. (p. 47)

Perennialism places emphasis on everlasting values and is composed of two branches. The ecclesiastical (religious) perennialists are exemplified by Saint Thomas Aquinas (1225–1274); the lay perennialists include Mortimer Adler (1902) and Robert Maynard Hutchins (1899–1977). The lay branch of perennialism places its emphasis on reason as the major way of knowing

RELIGIOUS VS. LAY PERENNIALISTS

truth, whereas the religious branch relies on revelation. The lay group's main goal is development of the intellect, and the religious branch's goal is moral and religious development. The perennialists emphasize detailed study of the classics, and would base their curriculum on the great books. As Rosen (1968) stated, perennialists believe in faculty psychology in which "the faculty of reason is trained through the formal discipline of those subjects with the most logical organization" (p. 58). For them, the study of subjects such as Latin would exercise and train the mind in preparation for future scholastic activity. Their criteria for studying a subject would be this "mental discipline" rather than the immediate usefulness or interest of the subject to the student. The perennialist teacher would have highly developed skills of reasoning and would rely on the lecture method of passing along the truth from the past.

COUNTER-REVOLUTION TO PROGRESSIVISM

Perennialism was a counterrevolution to progressivism, but many of its themes originated earlier. For perennialists, permanence, not change, is real. The perennialists urge the study of the great masters, such as Plato and Aristotle, and of our timeless cultural heritage. Students, they say, should not follow current fads but should adjust themselves to eternal truth. The perennialists believe that people seek to answer the same questions about the meaning of life today as they did in the time of Plato and Aristotle: What does it mean to be a good and virtuous person (a question as appropriate in the time of the Watergate scandal as in the time of Plato)? Does power corrupt, and who should rule a country? Perennialists believe that the current problems of humankind, such as greed, ethical decisions, and the proper use of power, are the same as those in ancient Greece or Rome.

Educational Ideas of Perennialists

HUMAN NATURE IS UNCHANGING

What are the educational ideas of the perennialists? They believe, as has been stated previously, that human nature has not changed since the beginning of time. Because a person faces the same problems and dilemmas now as then, only a classical education can prepare every student to address these issues. Perennialists emphasize the use of reason, maintaining that students must learn to control their basic urges through reason. The job of education for the perennialists is not to adjust people to society or current

EDUCATION AS A PREPARATION FOR LIFE

trends in the world, but to adjust them to eternal truth. In opposition to the progressives, perennialists claim that schooling is merely a preparation for life and can never become a real-life situation. They would teach the 3Rs, the liberal arts, and the cultural heritage of literature and history of the United States and the world, not subjects that are fads. The curriculum

GREAT BOOKS AND CLASSICS

of the perennialists would include the **Great Books,** the classics that describe humankind's attempts to answer age-old questions. Hutchins (1936) summarized this view of education: "Education implies teaching. Teaching implies knowledge. Knowledge is truth. The truth is everywhere the same. Hence education should be everywhere the same" (p. 66). Kneller (1971) further summed up perennialist views:

Robert Maynard Hutchins, as president and chancellor of the University of Chicago, expounded the perennialist ideas of knowledge as eternal and as the chief goal of education.

(Photo courtesy of the Library of Congress and the University of Chicago.)

In short, say the perennialists, the minds of most young Americans have never really been exercised in intellectual matters, largely because teachers themselves are indifferent and give up too quickly. It is much easier to teach students at their own pace and in accordance with what they want to learn. Yet, in allowing the child's superficial inclinations to determine what he learns, we may actually hinder him from developing his real talents. Self-realization demands self-discipline, and self-discipline is attained only through external discipline (pp. 45–46)

CRITICISMS
OF PERENNI-
ALISTS

What are the major criticisms of the perennialist viewpoints with respect to education? First, the perennialists are assailed for their focus on the past. Critics accuse them of not empathizing with the current interests of learners, with the present problems of society, and with preparation of students for the future. According to Rosen (1968), "The perennialists, despite their many claims to the contrary, are advocates of a **regressive social philosophy.** They would have us solve our twentieth century problems by turning back the clock to a system of beliefs prevalent in the thirteenth century" (pp. 55–56). Another criticism of perennialism is that it is unfair to force all students into a system of education fit only for a few elite students. Even Plato in *The Republic* advocated this type of classical education only for the elite ruling class. Kneller (1971) summarized this criticism of perennialism as follows:

> Perennialists may be accused of fostering an "aristocracy of intellect" and unreasonably restricting their teaching to the classical tradition of the Great Books. They fail to appreciate that, although many children lack the particular intellectual gifts perennialism emphasizes, they nevertheless become good citizens and productive workers. To subject them to the same sort of rigorous academic training as that given to students of university caliber is to ignore this difference and perhaps to injure their personal growth. (p. 46)

Essentialism

EMPHASIS
UPON THE
PRESENT

Essentialism and perennialism are similar in some respects. Both look to the past for guidance; however, the essentialists place their faith in the 3Rs instead of the Great Books emphasized by the perennialists. The essentialists place more emphasis on the present than the perennialists. Essentialists thus aim to use basic skills to help students adjust to the real world of the present society as it is.

> How does essentialism differ from perennialism? First, it advocates a less totally "intellectual" education, for it is concerned not so much with certain supposedly eternal truths as with adjustment of the individual to the physical and social environment. Second, it is more willing to absorb the positive contributions that progressivism has made to educational methods. Finally, where perennialism reveres the great creative achievements of the past as timeless expressions of man's universal insights, essentialism uses them as sources of knowledge for dealing with problems of the present. (Kneller, 1971, pp. 60–61)

Essentialists place much more emphasis on the present than the perennialists, who have the greatest faith in the past. Perennialism and essentialism both share an emphasis on basic skills; however, whereas the main emphasis of perennialism is on the Great Books approach, the chief ideas of essentialism revolve around basic skills. Essentialism shares with idealism and realism that view that truth is immutable, permanent, and unchanging, but it differs from idealism in its view of what is real.

BASIC SKILLS
OR 3Rs

MENTAL DIS-
CIPLINE

BRICKMAN,
BESTOR, AND
SMITH

Essentialists maintain that there are certain essentials that all people should know if they are to be educated, and these are usually defined as the basic skills of reading, writing, and arithmetic. Thus, as will be discussed later, the essentialists are the forerunners of the current "**back-to-basics**" movement in American education. The essentialists focus on the effort and hard work involved in learning, in opposition to the "learning-can-be fun" attitude of the progressives. They see the teacher as a mediator between the student and the basic skills, and they promote intellectual standards. They see subject matter as the heart of education and accept the traditional methods of "mental discipline." They accentuate self-discipline as the best discipline and promote social values rather than individual experience in education. Essentialism, unlike perennialism, is opposed not to progressivism as a whole but only to certain aspects of it. Essentialists see "learning by doing" as *a* method but not *the* method of learning. According to the essentialists, learning by doing should support the total learning of the student, but they caution against overgeneralizing from a few specific experiences.

The most prominent essentialist philosophers were William Brickman (b. 1913), editor of *School and Society* magazine, and Arthur Bestor (b. 1908) and Mortimer Smith (1906–1981), both active in the Council for Basic Education. Essentialists such as Bestor blame education professors for the problems in education and would reduce or eliminate the professional education courses taken by teacher candidates. The essentialists devote their main efforts to reexamining curricular issues, to weeding out the nonessential elements in the schools, and to promoting and reinforcing the authority of the teacher in the classroom.

Educational Ideas of Essentialists

DISCIPLINE
AND SELF-
DISCIPLINE

What are the educational ideas associated with the essentialist position? Essentialists believe in discipline and self-discipline. Thus, "doing your own thing" is not a sufficient reason for including specific content in the educational process. They propose teacher-initiated learning and emphasize transmission of accumulated knowledge of the human race as our cultural heritage. Essentialists avoid fads, or what is "relevant" or popular at the moment, in favor of long-range goals and values. They emphasize basic skills at the elementary level and only essential subjects at the high school level (driver's education, sex education, and many electives would be omitted from their curriculum). Essentialists promote the internal, logical organization of subject matter, rather than an organization that would make the subject easier for the student to learn. Also, they value effort and state that little is accomplished without it, as stated by Gutek (1981):

> Learning valuable skills and knowledge requires the expenditure of time and effort. Many of the permanent and persistent interests of adult life have resulted from efforts that initially may not have been interesting or appealing to the learner. While the child's interest should not be ignored, all learning should

Essentialists see the learning of basic skills as the goal of education.

(Photo used by permission of the Indianapolis Public Schools.)

not be based on the child's limited range of experiences. The essentialist position argues that there are many things to learn that, while they may not be of immediate interest to the learner, can become both valuable and permanently interesting at a later time in a person's life. (pp. 17–18)

In many ways the essentialists' theories of education are in direct opposition to the life adjustment education movement. Life adjustment advocates believe that schools should help each individual adjust himself or herself to the broader social forces in America by using current social problems as the major focus of learning and by assuming that essential learning will occur as a by-product of the study of these problems. For example, the life adjustment advocate would encourage study of the deterioration of the ozone layer of the atmosphere, assuming that the student would acquire or refine skills in reading, speaking, writing, science, and math as he or she is motivated to read, write, and compute in studying this topic in ecology. Life adjustment education in the early 1950s was a response to the social and economic strains of World War II. To cope with these stresses following the war, the life adjustment advocates desired to expand the issues contained in the school curriculum to include the problems faced by society as well as the economic, vocational, and personal needs of youth. Gutek (1981) assessed the essentialist opposition to this life adjustment movement in the following manner:

> The essentialist attack on incidental learning was similar to the criticism that current basic education advocates have leveled against new curricular innovations, especially those of the 1960s such as the "new mathematics," the "new social studies," and the various new approaches to science education. . . . Contemporary critics of the curricular innovations of the 1960s have charged that the "discovery method" or "inquiry method" is inefficient and causes students to "reinvent the wheel" rather than master the funded knowledge of the past in an orderly way. Contemporary critics argue that the process and method of learning has been overemphasized to the detriment of content. (p. 16)

Concerning the critics of the 1960s, Gutek (1981) continued:

> While the innovators of the 1960s promised that they would teach children how to think, the critics of the 1970s and 1980s [essentialists] have argued that, in order to think, students must have something to think about. . . . They argue that the curriculum should have a content that is logically or chronologically structured. (p. 16)

A short review of the events affecting education in the 1950s, the 1960s, and the 1970s will demonstrate the influence of the essentialists and the back-to-basics movement. In 1957, the launching of *Sputnik* by the Soviet Union gave great impetus to the critics of education and to the essentialist position in favor of the back-to-basics movement in American schools. Thus, in the late 1950s the essentialist position became prominent in the United States, possibly because of *Sputnik* and possibly because of the decline of the progressive movement. Whether or not the essentialist critics of the late 1950s caused the National Defense Education Act, the emphasis of academic subject matter in teacher education programs, and the increased funding for mathematics, science, and foreign languages, the essentialists were certainly in favor of these programs. The alphabetical curriculum

ALPHABETI-
CAL CURRIC-
ULUM RE-
FORMS

GREAT SOCI-
ETY SOCIAL
PROGRAMS

RESURGENCE
OF BACK-TO-
BASICS

NEW GRASS
ROOTS ES-
SENTIALISTS
MOVEMENT

ESSENTIAL-
ISTS' CRITI-
CISMS OF ED-
UCATION

reforms of the early 1960s, such as BSCS biology, SMSG mathematics, CHEM study in chemistry, were not strictly essentialist in nature because they proposed that students learn a subject in the same way that a scholar in that academic discipline would learn it. The inquiry approach used in these projects is not part of the essentialist doctrine, and the organizational changes in American schools in the early 1960s, such as team teaching, modular scheduling, open concept schools, and individualized instruction, were not favored by the essentialists. The essentialists fared even worse in the last half of the 1960s with the advent of the Great Society social programs and the continuing Vietnam War. Instead of essentialist programs, schools were involved in compensatory education, Project Head Start, job training, and bilingual education. Activism in social problems became the rule rather than the exception.

In the mid-1970s, the back-to-basics movement had a resurgence in the United States; however, this movement differed from the preceding essentialist periods of the 1950s and the 1960s. The "new" movement began as a grass roots movement, founded by lay citizens, not by educators. It had a broader base of support from lay people and parents than the previous essentialist movements. Gutek (1981) assessed the movement in these words:

> [U]nlike other movements in educational history, the drive for basic education [in the 1970s] differed initially in that it involved few leaders of a national political or educational stature; nor were the basic education advocates enrolled in a single organization. While the back-to-basics proponents varied widely in their strategies, a common philosophical strand ran through their arguments. (p. 7)

This new essentialist movement in the 1970s was supported by a grass roots desire for accountability, minimum competency tests, and competency-based education. Professional educators were not part of the original movement and were usually relegated to responding defensively, but they were eventually forced to become involved in identifying and testing minimum competencies. The public outcry forced several state legislatures to mandate minimum competency tests for both students and teachers. In the 1980s, professional educators debated what is "basic" in education, and lay citizens were still demanding basic functional literacy and mathematical skills from students graduating from high schools (Gutek, 1981).

Many criticisms of education were made by the proponents of the back-to-basics movement in the 1970s and 1980s. These essentialists deplored social promotion, promoting a child with failing grades to keep him with his age group, as well as innovations and experiments such as electives and minicourses. The lack of emphasis on basic skills and ethical values was assailed by the essentialists. They oppose permissiveness in both the behavioral and the academic standards of the schools. The back-to-basics advocates also sounded the alarm of accountability and believed that schools were too bureaucratic and expensive. They abhorred the lack of emphasis on competition as a form of student motivation. In addition, the essentialists criticized poorly trained teachers, the schools of education, and the special jargon used by professional educators (Gutek, 1981).

CRITICISMS OF THE ESSENTIALIST MOVEMENT

Many criticisms have been leveled at the essentialists and the back-to-basics movement. As already mentioned, determining what is basic is difficult. Are art, music, and physical education basic? What about subjects such as health and social studies? This question is easily answered at the elementary school level, where reading and math are obviously basic, but becomes a quagmire at the high school level with the diversity of courses available there. Back-to-basics proponents and essentialists often fail to agree among themselves on what is basic. Most people could agree to support the back-to-basics movement if they could define what is meant by *basic*. As Gutek (1981) insisted,

> Both the friends and foes of basic education need to address the following persistent philosophical questions that have emerged in the last half century: What is a sound education? What is a school? What is the primary purpose of a school? What is the nature of the curriculum?
>
> The advocates of basic education need to ponder and answer these questions in the most coherent and comprehensive way possible so that their position is no longer based on scattered sources and conflicting opinions. Antagonists need to examine these questions in light of the historical perspective of the recurring themes of basic education. The issues raised are not fleeting ones that will go away. As they have appeared in our educational past, so they will occur in our educational future.

As has been described, the ideas of the essentialists are prominent in American education today as evidenced by the influential back-to-basics movement (see Table 9–1).

Progressivism

The third educational philosophy examined here is **progressivism**, related to the pragmatism or instrumentalism of John Dewey.

COOPERATION NOT COMPETITION

What are the main ideas of progressivism as an educational philosophy? The progressives place great faith in cooperation and social learning, rather than competition. Part of this social learning would be an emphasis on the project method or the problem-solving approach in education. The progressives thus believe that learning should be an active process and that students should do much more than receive information passively. Learning, they believe, can and should be related to the interests of the child. The teacher's role should be that of an adviser, not a "dictator" or "director" of learning.

EMPHASIS ON PROCESS

Progressives place more emphasis on the process (the means or the methods) of learning than on the end product (knowledge). The greatest reality for progressives, as for the reconstructionists, is change, and the progressives emphasize that the elementary student is a child, not a little adult (a

TABLE 9–1 ▮▮▮▮▮▮▮▮▮▮▮▮▮▮▮▮▮▮▮▮▮▮▮▮▮▮▮▮▮
Philosophy of Education

TRADITIONALIST	PROGRESSIVE
Subject-Centered	Pupil-Centered
Trailing edge of change	Cutting edge
Common core is essential	Curriculum comes from life
Emphasis on the 3Rs, spelling/achieving, and intellectual discipline	Emphasis on learning to think critically
Secondary schools should be departmentalized according to subject: a. Texts are important. b. Audiovisual is important. c. Academic scholarship (honor roll)	Teacher organizes, selects, directs experiments so that participation in activities will maximize the student's understanding and knowledge
Juvenile delinquency is due to the neglect of the school's role	If students are involved, they will become more responsible
Transmit values to the next generation	Moral aims should be based on civic and social experimentation, vocational and practical usefulness, and individual development. (Do not ignore both the social and the psychological education.)
Authority-centered or teacher-based classrooms are the best setting	Democracy is the best setting
Active student is involved in organizing his or her notes	Active school and active student

concept that Rousseau believed). They insist that education is life, not a preparation for life and learning. Students do not need to store up knowledge before they can think and solve problems. In fact, knowledge is derived from the problem-solving process. Thus, if we want students to learn about democracy, schools should be democratic institutions. For Dewey, democracy in government and education in America were closely related.

Progressive educators would not fill the head of a student with facts as one would fill a pitcher with water; they would teach students how to learn so that they can continue to learn later on their own. For progressives, CONTINUAL learning is the "continual reconstruction of experience." Their emphasis is RECON- on experience, not on the eternal truth cited by the idealists. Progressives STRUCTION think of education for the whole child and believe that education is more OF EXPERI- than subject matter alone. *Experience* and *experiment* are two key words ENCE for the progressives, as noted by Kneller (1971): "It is not the absorption of previous knowledge that counts but its constant reconstruction in the light of new discoveries. Thus, problem solving must be seen not as the search for merely functional knowledge, but as a 'perpetual grappling' with subject matter" (p. 50).

John Dewey's ideas were crucial in the progressive movement. Although

JOHN DEW-
EY'S IDEAS

Dewey preferred to call his philosophy **instrumentalism** or pragmatism, and although he believed that his progressive followers distorted many of his ideas and carried them to extremes, he is still known as the leader of the progressive education movement in the United States. It is best to examine the actual writings of Dewey to ascertain his educational beliefs because both his followers and his critics tended to distort his views. Dewey eventually denounced and disassociated himself from the progressive education movement. Thus, Dewey was first an advocate and then later a critic of progressive education.

OPPOSITION
TO DUALISMS

Dewey's educational philosophy was holistic and opposed to dualisms such as that between theory and practice, between mind and body, between thoughts and actions, and between means and ends. Dewey especially deplored the separation of the school from life outside the school. He argued against the prevalent view that knowledge should be learned and stored up so that it can be used in subsequent thoughts and actions. Dewey firmly believed that learning in schools is life, not a preparation for life. Learning is living and can best occur in actual living and in solving real problems. "Real" purposes in these actual problems can best be used to integrate learning and living. Scheffler (1966) stated this point in the following way:

> This means that the whole environment of meanings surrounding the lesson is important as potentially contributing to learning. It means, for example, that the moral atmosphere of the classroom, the encouragement of curiosity and questioning, the relations among students and with the teacher are to be considered, not as irrelevant to the curriculum but as the very basis of moral and intellectual learning which goes on in the school whether we deliberately plan it or not. It means, finally, that every item of subject matter to be taught must be provided with context in the learner's perceptions. These perceptions and, indeed, the learner's whole system of motivations must be taken with the utmost seriousness by the teacher. (p. 102)

Thus, Dewey opposed any division between humanistic and vocational education, between theoretical and applied sciences, and between thought and action.

LEARNING IS
AN ACTIVE
PROCESS

Dewey placed great emphasis on actions and experience. For him, learning was always an active process; the brain was not a passive receiver of knowledge but an active participant in or originator of meanings through problem solving. Dewey believed that experience is crucial to learning but that not all experience is educational. Hook (1966) summarized Dewey's meaning of the term *experience*:

> The term "experience" has many different meanings, but the sense which Dewey gives it makes it relevant to the human learning process. All education is occasioned by experience, but for Dewey not all experiences are genuinely educational. He regards only those experiences to which the individual reacts with informed awareness of the problem and challenge of his environment as truly educational. (p. 132)

Students must experiment and experience life to learn, according to
the progressives.

(Photo used by permission of the Indianapolis Public Schools.)

MY PEDA-   *My Pedagogic Creed,* a booklet written by Dewey (1897), contained many
GOGIC CREED of the educational beliefs on which he later elaborated. In it, he defined his
five basic principles of education. First, the individual must participate in
the social consciousness of the race; thus, Dewey emphasized social problems and experiences that he believed helped to shape the person from birth
to death. Second, the school is a part of this social process. Education, thus,
is the process of living, not preparation for life. Third, the social life of the
child is the real subject matter of education. Fourth, methods should be
given form by the child's own nature. Fifth, education is the principal means
of social progress and reform. On this final point, Dewey and the progressives would receive support from the reconstructionists as will be seen in
the next section.

The Decline of Progressive Education
What were the major criticisms of progressive education that eventually
led to its decline? Because the progressives were blamed for the problems
of education after the Soviets launched *Sputnik* in 1957, the progressive
movement, which had already been weakened by internal divisions and
external criticisms, declined dramatically in the late 1950s. The authors of
this text believe that schools are often used as scapegoats for society's

problems and difficulties. After *Sputnik*, Americans believed that the United States lagged behind the Soviet Union in the space race, and they immediately blamed the schools and especially the child-centered methods of the progressives. Cremin (1961) cut to the heart of this decline in the following analysis of the demise of the progressive movement:

> The surprising thing about the progressive response to the assault of the fifties is not that the movement collapsed, but that it collapsed so readily. . . . But, even so, one is shocked by the rapidity of the decline. Why this abrupt and rather dismal end [in the late 1950s] of a movement that had for more than a half-century commanded the loyalty of influential segments of the American public? (p. 347)

REASONS FOR THE DECLINE OF PROGRESSIVISM

What were the specific reasons for this decline of progressive education? The distortion of progressive principles by both its disciples and its critics was a major factor. Within the ranks of the progressives there developed factions of people who never seemed to be able to agree among themselves. Negativism was another factor. Progressives more often appeared to be certain of what they were against than of what they supported. Another possible factor was the excessive demands that progressive methods made on the teachers' time. Group work, individual projects, and learning by doing required more advanced preparation on the part of the teacher than the older methods of lecture and mental discipline. Progressivism also became a victim of its own success in changing American ideas about schooling and teaching methods. Some critics argue that progressives failed to keep pace with continuing changes in the mass media and social welfare, and most critics agree that the conservative shift in political and social thought after World War II provided, along with *Sputnik*, the final blow for progressivism. Finally, unlike the current basic education movement, the progressive movement was composed mostly of professional educators and failed to involve the lay public in its causes (Cremin, 1961).

FREEDOM VS. SELF-DISCIPLINE

Kneller (1971) cited additional reasons for the demise of the progressives. The progressives were criticized for allowing students to learn what they wanted to know rather than what they needed to learn. Many critics of the progressives said that the school is an artificial learning situation that can never be a real-life environment. Opponents of progressivism also doubted that self-discipline could best be developed through freedom, and these critics cited the need to use external discipline to foster self-discipline. The adversaries of the progressives also pointed out that the group decisions advocated by the progressives were not necessarily better than those made by individuals. This cooperation, the critics asserted, could result from extremes in conformity and from the tyranny of the group. The progressives, their adversaries insisted, had no monopoly on democratic principles, as the progressive movement tended to imply. Finally, Kneller (1971) cited the self-activity movement of the progressives as lacking specific goals and as being too vague to result in meaningful student activities.

DECLINE OF
PROGRESSIV-
ISM IN THE
1950s

The progressive movement had its beginnings after the Civil War and had gained a wide following among intellectuals by 1900. It grew and gained favor between 1900 and World War I as it was embraced by professional educators. The movement became fragmented in the 1920s and 1930s, and finally disappeared in the late 1950s. However, the progressives made a significant impact on education in America today, especially because of the opposition movements it spawned: essentialism and back-to-basics. Progressives believed in using education for social betterment, as did the reconstructionists, who are now examined.

Reconstructionism

CRISIS MEN-
TALITY

The last educational philosophy to be discussed here is **reconstructionism**. The main goal of reconstructionists is to change society by using education as an instrument of social reform. Thus, the behavioral sciences and cultural forces are extremely important to the reconstructionists. They believe that Americans live in an age of crisis, and there is an acute sense of urgency in their exhortations. According to Rosen (1968), "It [reconstructionism] is, in effect, an ideal of a utopian society. Philosophy is a tool; and as such, the reconstructionists say, should be used for more than just explaining experience. It must help build a better society" (p. 90). Major American leaders in reconstructionism have been George Counts (1889–1974), who wrote *Dare the Schools Build a New Social Order?* (1932); Harold Rugg (1886–1960), author of *Culture and Education in America* (1931); and Theodore Brameld (1904), whose major work was *Toward a Reconstructed Philosophy of Education* (1956).

DIFFERENCES
FROM OTHER
PHILOSOPHIES

How does reconstructionism differ from other educational philosophies and the pure philosophies? Progressives and pragmatists generally supported social change but not in the same way as the reconstructionists. The progressives wanted social change but they refused to support specific reforms in society. Rosen (1968) summarized this difference: "Reconstructionism as a philosophy of education differs from pragmatism in degree and emphasis rather than in kind. While sharing a great deal with pragmatism, it has a much more emphatic social policy" (pp. 89–90). Thus, whereas perennialism places exlcusive emphasis on the past and essentialism and progressivism place more emphasis on adjusting to the present, reconstructionism looks to the future.

SOCIAL EM-
PHASIS

The major tenets of reconstructionism can be seen in the major theses of reconstructionism as developed by Brameld (1965). There is an urgency in the cry of the reconstructionists to use education to build a new social order to prevent global self-destruction through atomic weapons. Like the progressives, the reconstructionists believe in democracy, and their new society must be controlled by the people. The logical end of national democracy, they say, is international democracy. The reconstructionists have an even greater social emphasis than the progressives. Society, the reconstructionists insist, makes people what they are. Thus, Brameld believed that group work should play an important part in schools. The reconstructionist teacher would not remain impartial but would feel obliged to persuade students, democratically, of the urgency of reconstructionism. The reconstructionists believe that the behavioral sciences are crucially important, and that both the goals and the methods of education must be modified to meet the challenging demands of the future. Thus, reconstructionists would constantly remind us that we are educating students for the future, not solely for the present.

STRENGTHS
AND WEAK-
NESSES

It is difficult to be neutral toward the reconstructionists because they are so passionate in the expression of their beliefs. Some of their strengths and weaknesses are recounted here. On the positive side, the reconstructionists do what many other philosophies fail to do when they place their major emphasis on an education for the future. Today, reconstructionists would emphasize the necessity of a world government, the need for nuclear arms control, the importance of the postindustrial society outlined by Toffler (1970), and the widespread effect that computers will have on our world. On the negative side, critics cite the pluralism evident in the United States and wonder how an entire society can support a single set of goals. Whose goals will be taught, they ask? Should teachers be biased toward specific futures for their students? Are reconstructionists engaging in indoctrination, and is this compatible with a democratic society? Are the conclusions of the behavioral sciences a strong enough base on which to build a new social order? The authors of this text doubt that Americans could agree on one vision of the future to be implemented by the reconstructionists, but we see much value in their orientation toward the future and its problems.

Conclusions on Philosophy

The philosophical conclusions of this chapter are presented in three areas: the liberal versus conservative debate in educational philosophy, the advisability of an eclectic philosophy of education, and the difference that could be made by a consistent philosophy in U.S. schools.

"EITHER–
OR" DEBATE

American schools have always been afflicted with an "either–or" debate in the philosophy of education. Educators and lay citizens disagree with each other and among themselves about whether the child or the subject matter is more important. Should school buildings be built in an open-concept design or in an arrangement of individual classrooms? Should minicourses be offered to take advantage of students' current interests at the high school level, or should students be channeled into basic skill courses? Should outside-of-school activities be part of the regular school curriculum or an extracurricular appendage to the school program? All of these questions revolve around the liberal versus conservative debate in education, and these two basic viewpoints are now examined in greater detail (see Table 9–2).

TABLE 9–2
Curriculum Organization

TRADITIONALIST	PROGRESSIVE
1. Great books program: science and math as intellectual disciplines	1. Projects such as "Why do people leave your hometown?"
2. History is good for its own sake	2. Simulate putting people on the moon
3. Spelling bees	3. Life on the Mississippi
4. Science fair	4. Helping the Public Health Service analyze streams
5. Clothing and foods	5. Making the poor aware of services available to them
6. Physical education	6. Mock zoning-board hearings
7. Sports	7. Helping minorities to get established in your school district
8. Science club	8. Designing and doing new games and teaching them to the underprivileged
9. Career day	
10. Testing (SAT, CEEB, and PSAT)	

The Conservative View

BELL'S VIEW OF EDUCATION

The conservative view of the perennialists and the essentialists is exemplified by the conservative and essentialist views of Terrel Bell, who was Secretary of Education in the Reagan administration. Bell has stated that education is the acquisition of knowledge, and he has promoted the idea of a knowledge-centered school. He opposes democracy in schools, the life adjustment curriculum, teacher–pupil planning, and the idea that learning must be enjoyable. He believes that hard work, adversity, and life's problems shape the character of students. Bell eloquently opposes the child-centered school and curricula based on the current needs and interests of students. Schools should, in his view, develop in students a lifelong thirst for intellectual knowledge, rather than accentuate their physical appetites.

> Too much time is wasted in our schools in teacher–pupil planning and committee work, and not enough is spent in vigorously seeking mastery of basic knowledge that will lead to intellectual competence and wisdom. The age in which we live is too perilous and the amount of knowledge that today's citizens must gain is too vast for us to continue to focus our attention and efforts on social adjustment processes, committee work, and setting of goals by pupils. (Bell, 1962, p. 21)

Bell does believe that the student should be active in the process of learning and also that learning should be directed toward the purpose of attaining knowledge. Bell (1962) opposes the incidental learning advocated by the progressives:

> Learning should not be activity as a process, with knowledge as an incidental by-product as the result of an activity sponsored for the sake of the activity in the name of adjustment, social interaction, and "experience getting" for its own sake. (p. 18)

He believes that this is like mistaking an effect for a cause:

> Educators who emphasize such processes as life adjustment or personality development are emphasizing results and outcomes of knowledge. This is like trying to teach a duck how to swim before it is hatched out of the egg. The duck will ultimately swim if it comes to the task or the process prepared to do so. In like manner, the child will ultimately adjust to life or develop a desired personality if he acquires knowledge. (pp. 17–18)

In much the same way, Bell (1962) made an eloquent argument for the value of the work ethic:

> There has always been more joy in work than in play. Play need only be regarded as an interval, like sleep, wherein we recoup our mental faculties and energies for more knowledge acquisition. Let our schools therefore rededicate themselves to the purpose for which they have always existed down through the ages. Knowledge-centered schools will help man to reach his ultimate destiny—which is to conquer and dominate his environment, and to place the forces of nature at the command of his will. (p. 21)

Thus, instead of adjusting people to the forces in the world, Bell would advocate gaining control of the environment through knowledge of it. Bell, it seems, is in direct opposition to the progressives in the continuing debate concerning the purposes of the schools.

The Progressive View

The progressive viewpoint is represented here by William Lauderdale and is taken from his examination (1981) of three successful progressive schools. Two of the progressive schools examined by Lauderdale are the Laboratory School established by John Dewey in Chicago and the City and Country School founded by Caroline Pratt, another progressive, in New York City. The third progressive school, which is not examined here, was the Holtville School in Alabama. It was a famous progressive school of the 1930s and 1940s that emphasized vocational and life adjustment education. The Holtville School was an innovative school thriving in a conservative and economically deprived rural area of Alabama. These three schools serve to delineate the three major factions within the progressive education movement: the experimental view (the Laboratory School of John Dewey); the child-centered emphasis (Caroline Pratt at the City and Country School in New York City); and the life adjustment faction (the Holtville School in Alabama). Now, two of these progressive schools are examined as examples of the progressive movement in education.

Dewey established the laboratory school in Chicago in 1896 to test his

THREE EXAM-
PLES OF PRO-
GRESSIVE
SCHOOLS

DEWEY'S
LABORATORY
SCHOOL

educational and psychological principles, and he himself ran the school until 1904. Dewey emphasized a relaxed atmosphere in which children could learn cooperatively. He used field trips and believed that all learning is social in nature. Chicago, he felt, provided a wide variety of museums, factories, and businesses that should be used in educating children.

> Children's interests that arose naturally from games played, stories told, or field trips taken, served as starting points for learning. However, activities that grew out of such interests were planned and shaped by the children and the teachers with an end-in-view of acquiring skills and knowledge that would provide them with greater control over their environment (Lauderdale, 1981, p. 16)

EMPHASIS ON CONSE-QUENCES AND EXPERIENCES
Problem solving was at the heart of Dewey's educational enterprise. He also placed great emphasis on consequences and experiences. He believed that thought and action are intertwined and that a thought is true only if the consequences of its actions are positive, resulting in solutions to current problems. All learning, Dewey maintained, is the result of a child's experiences. Education, for him, was the constant reconstruction of experience in the light of new experiences. Dewey insisted that individual freedom of learning could facilitate the goals of society in the long run. Lauderdale (1981) summed up Dewey's views about the needs of individuals and the requirements of the society in which they live:

> Dewey found wanting that popular notion that individual freedom and independence must be curtailed in order to establish an orderly society. For him, the issue was not one of negotiating the rights of the individual with the needs of society but one of creating social arrangements in a society through which the individual can develop as an intelligent, free human being. (p. 17)

PRATT'S CITY AND COUN-TRY SCHOOL
Caroline Pratt's City and Country School in New York City was child centered. Lauderdale saw her major methods as dramatic play, "do withs," social interaction, frequent field trips, and an emphasis on jobs. For her, the dramatic play involved Dewey's idea of the re-creation of experience and Froebel's rule that play is the work of the child. The "do withs" were blocks used in play. These blocks were not to be formed in concrete realistic objects but were to be rough. Children were to use their imagination to make them serve as the toys of play. (The authors of this text have seen children leave fancy new toys purchased by parents to play with abandoned chips of wood or old cardboard packing crates.) The social interaction and the field trips are reminders of Dewey's ideas, and the emphasis on jobs can be traced back to Johann Heinrich Pestalozzi and others. Rousseau's influence can also be seen in Caroline Pratt's ideas, as these words of Lauderdale (1981) demonstrate:

> Children's fundamental medium for the re-creation of experience was play; and for Caroline Pratt [like Rousseau], play was a most serious subject. It was through play that children began to make sense of their world, to draw rela-

tionships among ideas, and to make cause-and-effect connections within events they experienced. (p. 33)

According to Lauderdale (1981), Caroline Pratt had an experience that helped form her child-centered, progressive philosophy of education:

AN EXAMPLE
OF PRATT'S
PHILOSOPHY

The remarkable experience occurred during a visit to the home of a friend who had a six-year-old son. There she found him at play, totally absorbed in a make-believe railroad system. Spread over the room were some toys, some blocks, and any number of household items, a few scrounged from the waste basket. The boy was re-creating a world that made sense in his terms. He was an active participant in that world, building the system, controlling the movement of the trains, and supplying the variety of sounds associated with a railroad. . . . The excitement of this boy's learning stood in sharp contrast to the dulled interest in learning she had observed among so many of her settlement house children. For her, the experience sparked an enthusiasm to find a way whereby all young people might share in the re-creation or dramatization of events, i.e., dramatic play. (pp. 30–31)

SIMILARITIES
OF PROGRES-
SIVE
SCHOOLS

What were the similarities of these two progressive schools used as examples here? First, a vocational emphasis is to be found in all three progressive programs. Dewey's Laboratory School used occupations as insight into society's cultural heritage and to show how people have solved problems historically. Caroline Pratt's City and Country School found the heart of its curriculum in "jobs," and the Holtville School used work for community improvement as its central theme. Lauderdale (1981) summarized the similarities among these three progressive schools:

Although their practices varied greatly, they stood as one in their commitment to progressive principles. Their students were free to participate in decisions that affected them, to plan many of their own learning activities, and to move about freely in the performance of their work. Programs were highly individualized, and relations between teachers and students were informal and based on mutual trust. A cooperative rather than a competitive atmosphere prevailed. . . . Student evaluations were multi-dimensional and used solely as diagnostic tools rather than as instruments for rating performance. Student interests were honored and felt needs accommodated, not as ends in themselves but as springboards for learning. (pp. 58–59)

REDEFINING
THE PUR-
POSES OF ED-
UCATION

Lauderdale (1981) wrote that none of these three schools was influenced by the "cult-of-the-child" extremists, who disliked anything that restricted the freedom of the child and who gave progressive education as a whole a bad name (p. 28). The progressive educators' legacy, according to Lauderdale, was that they "set a precedent for classroom innovation by redefining the purposes of education, diversifying the curriculum, changing the roles of teachers and students, and altering the very atmosphere of the school" (p. 59). The effects of the progressive education movement can be seen today in various alternative school programs, learning contracts, group work, individualized projects for learning, student councils in many high schools, and many other forms of student participation in their own learning.

An Eclectic Philosophy

DEVELOPING
ONE'S OWN
VIEW

Experts in philosophy differ on the advisability of having an **eclectic philosophy of education.** To be "eclectic" means to take parts of various philosophies and weld them into one's own personal philosophy of education. For instance, a person could take the concept of the student as actively involved in learning from the idealists but prefer the realist view of the scientific method as the main method of gathering knowledge. One could also incorporate the pragmatic principle that values are relative and constantly changing into this eclectic philosophy. Critics of the eclectic method of developing a philosophy of education would insist that this technique does not lead to a consistent philosophy, and that one's view of reality may clash with his or her perspective on knowledge or values. In practical terms, the authors of this text believe that the philosophies of most people are, in fact, eclectic. One may believe in the scientific method of the realists but may vehemently oppose the realist view of the passive nature of the student. The most important thing is to develop one's own philosophical principles as a basis for his or her own teaching. Whether a teacher recognizes it or not, every action in the classroom is based on philosophical principles. It is crucial that teachers formulate these principles in their own minds and begin to recognize the principles on which their teaching behavior is based. If this approach means being eclectic, the authors of this text support an eclectic educational philosophy.

Can Philosophy Make a Difference?

INFLUENC-
ING ETERN-
ITY

The liberal versus conservative debate has made clear the crucial importance of a philosophy of education in practical day-to-day educational decisions. Philosophy of education can make not only *a* difference in success but *the* difference in success in teaching. It has been said many times that it is better to light one candle than to curse the darkness, and the authors of this textbook believe in this principle. Instead of decrying problems such as lack of discipline, racial differences, lack of student motivation, or lack of sufficient funds for education, a teacher should use his or her philosophy and the resources at hand to make a difference in the world. A teacher can influence eternity and may never know where his or her influence stops. One teacher can make a difference in the life of a student, and a consistent educational philosophy can make a difference in the teaching of an individual teacher.

Summary

In this chapter the educational philosophies of perennialism, essentialism, progressivism, and reconstructionism were examined. Perennialism places its emphasis on the past and portrays truth as logical, permanent, and unchanging. The religious perennialists, such as St. Thomas Aquinas, rely on revelation as the primary way of knowing, whereas the lay perennialists, such as Mortimer Adler and Robert Maynard Hutchins, place their emphasis on reason as the path to truth. The mainstays of perennialist education thought are the literary classics and the mental discipline theory of learning. Like the perennialists, the essentialists look to the past for guidance; but, unlike the perennialists, the essentialists place their faith in learning basic skills instead of reading the Great Books. In this chapter the effect of the essentialists on the current back-to-basics movement was traced, and the opposition of the essentialists to the life adjustment movement was spotlighted. Progressive ideas on education include an emphasis on process rather than product, education as life rather than as preparation for life, and the teacher's role as advisor rather than dictator. The growth of the progressive movement in the early 1900s was highlighted, and the reasons for its decline were also examined. Reconstructionism focuses on change; and its proponents, such as George Counts and Theodore Brameld, see education as an instrument to change society for the better. Finally, the liberal versus conservative debate in educational philosophy is portrayed by contrasting the ideas of leading conservative Terrel Bell with those of Caroline Pratt, founder of the child-centered City and Country School in New York City.

Glossary Terms

Questions

1. From your own experience, take a position on whether human beings are basically good or bad. Then explain which educational philosophy would be closest to your position. Why?

2. Compare and contrast the liberal and conservative philosophies of education. With which argument do you agree and why?

3. One author said that the conservative educational philosophies were predominant until Rousseau published his educational views. In what ways did Rousseau's views change educational ideas and practices?

4. List and discuss five or more pragmatic elements that were evident in the schools you observed this semester. With which of these pragmatic ideas do you agree or disagree? Are you a pragmatist?

5. Assume that you are a reconstructionist. How would you change society through education? Include your ideas on what the ideal society would be and how schools could help build such a society.

6. What kinds of support would essentialists give to the back-to-basics movement? What concerns would the progressives have about this movement?

7. How would the essentialists, the progressives, the reconstructionists, and the existentialists deal with the controversy over values education in schools?

8. Are schools either entirely traditional or entirely progressive?

9. What is the difference between progressive education and permissive education?

10. Who needs to be the most creative—the progressive teacher or the traditional teacher?

11. Is an open-concept school a progressive school? Why or why not?

12. What are the best and worst aspects of the activity method of teaching advocated by the progressives?

13. What method of teaching, progressive or traditional, is the most difficult and challenging?

14. Why is progressive education so pragmatic?

15. Are all subjects or interest areas best taught by the traditional or the progressive approach?

16. If you were going to be a doctor, a lawyer, a teacher, an engineer, or a homemaker, would you best be prepared through the traditional or the progressive approach?

17. When is subject matter more important than being taught to think?

18. Often, during a job interview, you are asked to state your educational philosophy. If asked such a question, what would be your response?

Activities for Unit IV

1. Interview a principal, a counselor, or a classroom teacher, and summarize briefly his or her educational philosophy.

2. On a continuum of educational philosophy, with essentialism at the left end and progressivism at the right end, place a check mark on the continuum to represent your position on educational philosophy. Defend your position on this continuum by writing a two-page explanation. Include philosophical evidence supporting your position.

3. Compare your personal philosophy on discipline, evaluation, and human relations with that of the philosophy of a public school teacher whom you have observed this semester.

4. Compare the philosophy of the school that you attended to the philosophy of the school in which you observed during this semester. Which

educational philosophy and/or pure philosophy would best describe each of these schools?

5. Visit an alternative school or a school with an alternative education program, and compare the principal features of this program with the progressive principles described in this chapter. How would you evaluate this alternative education program in terms of student motivation, the depth and breadth of student learning in basic skills, students' involvement in their own learning, and teacher–student interaction?

6. Construct a model city based on your projected ideas of the twenty-first century. Based on your knowledge of his philosophy, what would be Dewey's opinion of this activity?

7. Read Phi Delta Kappa Fastback No. 166, *Progressive Education: Lessons from Three Schools* (1981). In which one of the three programs described in this fastback would you feel most comfortable teaching and why? Do the same circumstances that led to the creation of these three programs still exist today? If so, what are they?

8. Write three questions that could be posed to local boards of education whose members are predominantly liberal, conservative, or existentialist in their views. Then divide the class into three groups, with one third of the class playing the role of board members and the other two thirds asking these prepared questions of the board members. After the liberal board has answered questions posed by the other groups, give the conservative and existentialist board members a chance to answer similar questions.

Annotated Bibliography

1. Adler, M. J. (1982). *The Paideia proposal*. New York: Macmillan.

   Adler advocates classical and identical education for all students, without electives or vocational education, during the elementary and secondary grades, and emphasizes Socratic discussion groups in the schools.

2. Dewey, J. (1897). *My Pedagogic Creed*. New York: Kellogg.

   This pamphlet is a concise summary of John Dewey's views on the practical education of students through life experiences. It is an excellent example of the educational ideas of the pragmatists.

3. Gutek, G. L. (1981). *Basic education: A historical perspective*. Bloomington, IN: Phi Delta Kappa Educational Foundation.

   This valuable work is a historical account of the "back-to-basics" movement in the United States.

4. Kneller, G. F. (1971). *Introduction to the philosophy of education*. New York: Wiley.

   This textbook is a classic introduction to the principles of philosophy of education and can serve as a primer in this area of study.

5. Lauderdale, W. B. (1981). *Progressive education: Lessons from three schools*, Fastback No. 166. Bloomington, IN: Phi Delta Kappa Educational Foundation.

This Phi Delta Kappa fastback surveys the principles of progressive education by examining three successful examples of progressive schools in the United States.

(Photo by Axler.)

V

The School Curriculum

Teachers and the Curriculum

How Should One Define the Curriculum?

It is very difficult to define something that includes so many facets of learning as does a school's curriculum. All curriculum specialists have written some definition to describe the curriculum as they see it. Three of these definitions are presented here:

THREE DEFI-
NITIONS

1. J. Lloyd Trump (1968) wrote that the curriculum is a vital, moving complex interaction of people and things in a freewheeling setting. it includes questions to debate, forces to rationalize, goals to illuminate, programs to activate, and outcomes to evaluate (p. 12).

2. Doll (1978) noted that the curriculum of a school is the formal and informal content and process by which learners gain knowledge and understanding and develop skills, attitudes, appreciations, and values under the auspices of their school (p. 6).

3. Hass (1983) stated that the curriculum is all of the experiences that individual learners have in a program of education. The purpose is to achieve broad goals and related specific objectives, planned in terms of a framework of theory and research or past and present professional practice (p. 4).

Each of these three authors expressed himself differently, even though all were talking about the same thing. Trump wanted the curriculum to be very active and dynamic as it exists in the schools. Doll's definition seems tame compared with Trump's and it seems to cover all imporant bases. The definition by Hass places a lot of emphasis on research and professional practice. Whichever definition you choose to follow depends on your own personal conception of what the curriculum ought to be.

TRUMP'S
DEFINITION

J. Lloyd Trump was a curriculum innovator in the 1960s who wanted high schools to change to **flexible schedules** with thirty-, twenty-, and fifteen-minute modules meeting twelve, sixteen, or twenty-four periods in a day. The benefit of flexible scheduling was to schedule more time for some classes than for other classes. For example, on some days, students need more time in biology laboratory than in lecture and discussion. Trump's flexible plan was developed when many reformers were trying to make the curriculum more relevant for the learner, and some schools found his ideas helpful. A few high schools are still operating under flexible scheduling plans.

DOLL'S DEFI-
NITION

The Doll (1978) definition is broad in coverage so as to include both the formal and the informal parts of the curriculum. The formal curriculum can be planned and observed as well as evaluated and improved. The informal curriculum, sometimes known as the hidden curriculum, is not planned and is seldom evaluated. The hidden curriculum is really the students' own curriculum as they cope with the school's bureaucratic organization and arrangements and with their social relationships inside the school. It is important for teachers to be aware of as many parts of the hidden curriculum as possible.

HASS'S DEFI-
NITION

Hass would like to see the curriculum reflect the latest research from four bases. The first base concerns *social forces*, both present and future. The teachers on the faculty of a school should know the community and the problems and concerns that exist there so that they can be in touch with their students. The second base is *human development*. Teachers need to be aware of the body of knowledge known as human growth and development so that as they teach their lessons, they can take into consideration an individual's nature and needs. Havighurst's "developmental tasks" (1948), Erikson's stages of "growth toward a mature personality" (1968), and Piaget's four stages of growth in intelligence through "**assimilation**" and "**accommodation**" (1952) help us to understand human growth and development better. The third base is the *nature of learning*. Knowing how learning occurs in students helps teachers to plan the curriculum. Your teaching practices might be based on stimulus–response conditioning, on the field theories, on Freudian theory, or on social learning, depending on your preference. The fourth base is the *nature of knowledge and cognition*. How you view the nature of knowledge depends on whether you view it as organized bodies of facts and concepts, as a fluid product of people's experience, or as a combination of the two.

Now that you have seen how three experts view the curriculum, perhaps you are ready to define it yourself. Your own definition will no doubt take into consideration many of the concepts presented by the experts, but in the end, it will be your own personal conception of what the curriculum ought to be.

What Are Some Historical Perspectives on the Curriculum?

SIGNIFICANT
WRITINGS

So that we may shed some light on the history of curriculum development, we mention here only those happenings that still have some effect on the present and that will very likely continue to have an effect in the future. In 1981, in honor of the seventy-fifth anniversary of Phi Delta Kappa, Harold Shane wrote an article for the *Phi Delta Kappan* entitled "Significant Writings That Have Influenced the Curriculum: 1906–81." To obtain data for his article, Shane wrote to 135 curriculum specialists, and 85 of them responded to an annotated list (1981) of 100 publications appearing most consistently in footnotes and in bibliographies. Shane had the specialists indicate whether they believed that a given book, article, or report had had a *major*, a *considerable*, or a *negligible* influence on curriculum theory and practice over the years 1906–1981. To achieve the distinction of having the most influence on the school curriculum, a given publication had to be rated as having had a "major" or a "considerable" influence by at least 85% of the respondents. The top ten publications are listed in order below (including ties), with some comments about their contents and their contributions.

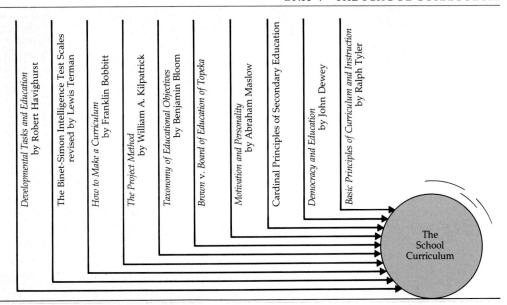

Keeping the curriculum ball rolling.

FIRST: **BASIC PRINCIPLES OF CURRICULUM AND INSTRUCTION**
BY RALPH W. TYLER (1949)

TYLER'S
PRINCIPLES

This little book by Tyler has gone through over thirty reprints. Tyler is one of the most noted American educators as well as a noted lecturer and writer. In his book, he began by asking four simple questions:

1. What educational purposes should the school seek to attain?
2. What educational experiences can be provided that are likely to attain these purposes?
3. How can these educational experiences be effectively organized?
4. How can we determine whether these purposes are being attained? (p. 1)

The logic in those four questions sets the tone for the entire book. The book is very specific. For example, Tyler wrote that if the schoolchildren in your district suffer from either a dietary deficiency or a physical condition, then your objectives in health education should reflect these concerns.

SECOND: **DEMOCRACY AND EDUCATION** *BY JOHN DEWEY (1916)*

DEWEY'S
IDEAS

John Dewey and his impact on education have been mentioned previously. In the discussion in *Democracy and Education,* Dewey wrote that he would like to have workers see more than one side of their work. "Workers," he said, "need to see the technical, intellectual, and social relationships involved in what they do" (Dewey, 1916, p. 85). In the 1980s, we heard how companies were trying to make their workers more aware of the purpose of their labor beyond just the manufacture of a product. In his theory of teaching and learning, as in the example of workers' needs, Dewey focused on the whole person.

Dewey felt that studying history as a subject resulted in too much memorization of dates and dry facts. He wanted to see the curriculum related to social concerns in our society, such as problems with insanity, poverty, public sanitation, city planning, and conservation. He wanted to see schools incorporate social studies into their curriculum. Dewey's term *social studies* included history, economics, and politics, as well as sociology. He envisioned students' discovering real problems in their communities and DEVELOPING attempting to solve these problems scientifically by collecting data, forming A SOCIAL hypotheses, and testing these hypotheses. By actually being involved in CONSCIOUS- solving real problems and by developing a social consciousness, students NESS would learn in a pragmatic way what living in a democracy is all about.

THIRD AND FOURTH (TIE): CARDINAL PRINCIPLES OF SECONDARY EDUCATION (1918)

These seven principles are covered in more detail later in this chapter. These principles were the result of the report of the National Education Association (NEA) Commission on the Reorganization of Secondary Education. The commission was most concerned that too many electives were

John Dewey emphasized work and also its relationship to society as a whole.

[Photo used by permission of the Indianapolis Public Schools.]

available to students: "Students were likely to specialize excessively or scatter their efforts over a large number of subjects having little relation to one another" (Butts, 1955, p. 576). To overcome the problem of overspecialization, the commission recommended greater correlation and fusion of subject matter around the seven principles. The core curriculum emerged as that portion of the curriculum to be taken by all students, occupying a large percentage of their school time. This general education movement is still present today and is likely to continue in the near future. The so-called SEVEN CAR-DINAL PRIN-CIPLES seven cardinal principles of secondary education are health, command of the fundamental processes, worthy home membership, a vocation, civic education, worthy use of leisure time, and ethical character. (See pages 296– 298 in this chapter for more details on the cardinal principles.)

THIRD AND FOURTH (TIE): **MOTIVATION AND PERSONALITY** *BY ABRAHAM MASLOW (1954)*

MASLOW'S HIERARCHY OF BASIC NEEDS
Maslow wrote about the hierarchy of the basic needs and how these affect motivation and personality. The physiological needs are the most prepotent of all needs. Thus, a person who is lacking food, safety, love, and esteem would hunger for food more strongly than anything else.

Maslow wrote that the higher the need, the more specifically human it is; therefore, the **self-actualization** need is shared with no other species. This uniquely human trait motivates us to become what we have the ability to become. An artist must paint, a poet must write, a teacher must teach, if they are to be ultimately at peace with themselves. Some other aspects of self-actualized people are that they

> seem to have a uniformly good appetite for food; they seem to sleep well; they seem to enjoy their sexual lives without unnecessary inhibition and so on for all the relatively physiological impulses. They are able to accept themselves not only on these low levels, but at all levels as well; e.g., love, safety, belongingness, honor, self-respect. All of these are accepted without question as worthwhile, simply because these people are inclined to accept the work of nature rather than to argue with her for not having constructed things to a different pattern. This shows itself in a relative lack of the disgusts and aversions seen in average people and especially in neurotics, e.g., food annoyances, disgust with body products, body odors, and body functions. (Maslow, 1954, p. 207)

This book gives curriculum planners and/or teachers some new insights into motivation and personality development. The book also reinforces the importance of the development of self and the ways in which schools, through proper use of the curriculum, can help in the self-actualizing process.

FIFTH AND SIXTH (TIE): **BROWN V. BOARD OF EDUCATION** *OF TOPEKA (1954)*

What can one say about the *Brown* case that has not already been said in other chapters? Even though it occurred in 1954, its major impact is still being felt as we try to right a lot of past wrongs. Racial equality through

THE *BROWN* DECISION

equal opportunity in education, in the economic arena and in the social realm, is not a fact for all Americans, but the situation is much better today as a result of the *Brown* decision.

FIFTH AND SIXTH (TIE): TAXONOMY OF EDUCATIONAL OBJECTIVES: COGNITIVE DOMAIN BY BLOOM ET AL. (1956)

BLOOM'S TAXONOMY

Most teachers are familiar with Bloom's **taxonomy** and the different levels of the cognitive domain that it identifies. One of the criticisms of the curriculum today is that teachers spend too much time asking students to recall or remember information. Facts are important to remember, but children can be challenged more by application and analysis. An illustrative test item in the application category demonstrates what is meant by applying knowledge as opposed to simply memorizing facts:

> John prepared an aquarium as follows: He carefully cleaned a ten-gallon glass tank with salt solution and put in a few inches of fine washed sand. He rooted several stalks of weed (*Elodea*) taken from a pool and then filled the aquarium with tap water. After waiting a week he stocked the aquarium with ten one-inch goldfish and three snails. The aquarium was then left in a corner of the room. After a month the water had not become foul and the plants and animals were in good condition. Without moving the aquarium he sealed a glass top on it.
>
> What prediction, if any, can be made concerning the condition of the aquarium after a period of several months? If you believe a definite prediction can be made, make it and then give your reasons. If you are unable to make a prediction for *any* reason, indicate why you are unable to make a prediction (give your reasons). (Bloom et al., 1956, p. 131)

Perhaps one of the reasons that teaching may not be focused on the higher levels of the cognitive domain is that in traditional schools there may be too much pressure to prepare children for tests that are written on the lower levels of the cognitive domain. Bloom's taxonomy has a lot to teach us, but our schools and curricula must become more flexible and less conservative to implement higher-order objectives.

SEVENTH: THE PROJECT METHOD BY WILLIAM H. KILPATRICK (1918)

KILPATRICK'S PROJECT METHOD

This essay brought a little-known professor into international fame. Kilpatrick's paper was a basic attack on traditional education, and it showed how much he agreed with John Dewey. Kilpatrick elaborated on his ideas much further in *Foundations of Method* (1925).

The later book was an extension of the original essay and made very clear Kilpatrick's disdain for the separation of knowledge and skills into separate subjects such as arithmetic and geography. He felt that these separate subjects, when applied to real life, made little sense. Kilpatrick said that education should be designed to be as "lifelike" as possible.

SELF-AC-TUALIZA-TION

Kilpatrick then became one of the major spokespersons for progressive education. His emphasis was teaching the child rather than the subject. It could also be said that he was helping the child to become self-actualized and was placing the child in the best position to be a continuous learner through problem solving. The example of the boy planting corn illustrates what Kilpatrick meant by teaching the child rather than the subject:

> "Don't you think that the teacher should often supply the plan," asks one of the participants in Kilpatrick's dialogue. "Take a boy planting corn, for example; think of the waste of the land and fertilizer and effort. Science has worked out better plans than a boy can make." Kilpatrick answers, "I think it depends on what you seek. If you wish corn, give the boy a plan. But if you wish boy rather than corn, that is, if you wish to educate the boy to think and plan for himself, then let him make his own plan." Although Kilpatrick steadfastly refused to countenance any dichotomy between "teaching subjects" and "teaching children," time and again in *Foundations of Method* he ends up choosing "boy" over "corn," with the result that his method, willy-nilly, inevitably favors the child-centered approach. (Cremin, 1961, pp. 217–218)

TEACHING
SUBJECTS
AND TEACH-
ING CHIL-
DREN

Kilpatrick's argument was that the teacher needs to be patient and to allow the learner to make a few mistakes. Kilpatrick and Dewey both caused curriculum planners to think more in terms of the learner.

EIGHTH: HOW TO MAKE A CURRICULUM
BY FRANKLIN BOBBITT (1924)

BOBBITT'S
HANDBOOK

This publication is a basic handbook for revising a school curriculum. An entire plan is clearly outlined for those involved in curriculum building. Bobbitt wrote of "education's fundamental responsibility to prepare the child for the fifty years of adulthood, and not for the twenty years of childhood and youth" (p. 8).

Bobbitt listed the major objectives of education under nine headings. Under the heading of Social Intercommunication he listed such objectives as the ability to pronounce words properly and the ability to use language that is grammatically correct. Under the heading of General Mental Efficiency, he listed traditional subjects like plant and animal life, as well as the study of human creations and inventions. The book provides a number of interesting ideas even for the current practitioner.

Relative to objectives, Bobbitt advocated "that nothing should be done by the schools that can be sufficiently well accomplished through the normal process of living." This comment is interesting in light of what has happened to the curriculum in the past few years. Schools perceive a need to incorporate more into the curriculum, such as sex education, peer counseling, drug education, and other courses thought unnecessary a few years ago. It is certain that Bobbitt himself would admit that what was normal living in one generation would change with time.

NINTH: THE BINET–SIMON INTELLIGENCE TEST SCALES/REVISED
BY TERMAN AND CHILDS (1912)

These tests were the beginning of the American testing movement. The first wide use of group intelligence testing occurred during World War I in

THE BEGIN-
NING OF THE
TESTING
MOVEMENT

1917, when the Army Alpha test was used to screen soldiers. The intelligence testing movement gathered more momentum during World War II. In education today, millions of standardized tests are used to measure achievement, intelligence, and aptitudes for various endeavors. The proper use and the misuse of tests constitute another side of the testing movement. Most educators who are involved in a screening process look at other measures of a child's ability besides his or her IQ, but test scores are still considered very important.

TENTH: DEVELOPMENTAL TASKS AND EDUCATION
BY ROBERT HAVIGHURST (1948)

HAVIG-
HURST'S DE-
VELOPMEN-
TAL TASKS

Havighurst described a developmental task as

> that task which arises at or about a certain period in the life of the individual, successful achievement of which leads to his happiness and to his success with later tasks, while failure leads to unhappiness in the individual, disapproval by the society, and difficulty with later tasks. (p. 2)

The developmental tasks outlined by Havighurst extend throughout one's lifetime. These tasks are useful to educators who are attempting to state the goals and purposes of education, and they also relate to the correct timing of our educational efforts. Havighurst introduced the concept of the

TEACHABLE
MOMENT

teachable moment as the best time for a task to be learned. His book has no doubt affected curriculum planning for the past thirty years and will continue to do so in the future.

The above list of publications and happenings concludes the top ten that have influenced the curriculum in the past seventy-five years. Three other significant publications appearing after 1960, but not included in the top ten, are now described.

GLASSER'S
*SCHOOLS
WITHOUT
FAILURE*

In *Schools Without Failure* (1969), Glasser wrote that schools are set up for failure and that successful students are those who respond in ways prescribed by the teacher. His book presents suggestions for making involvement, relevance, and thinking realities in our schools. Glasser wrote, "I believe that if a child, no matter what his or her background, can succeed in school, he or she has an excellent chance for success in life" (p. 5). His book indeed gives the reader many concrete ideas for improving schools.

TOFFLER'S
*FUTURE
SHOCK*

Alvin Toffler wrote *Future Shock* (1970) to help Americans cope with change. He described some startling evidence, such as the fact that it took the human race millions of years to attain a speed of 100 miles per hour and only another fifty-eight years to reach 400 miles per hour in the air and 18,000 miles per hour in space (p. 26). The problem with change is that it can be too massive and too rapid. All of our foundations in religion, nation, community, family, and the professions are shaking. Toffler suggested that we establish a future-facing education system, new social services, and new ways to regulate technology and that we develop a strategy for capturing control of change. He ended his book on a positive note: "By making imaginative use of change to channel change, we cannot only spare ourselves the trauma of future shock, we can reach out and humanize distant tomorrows" (p. 430).

JENCK'S *INE-QUALITY*

The last publication to be mentioned here that has had an impact on curriculum is *Inequality* (1972) by Christopher Jencks. Jencks concluded that the schools themselves make only a small difference in the cognitive and noncognitive inequality among adults. The real differences, Jencks concluded, stem from the following factors: (1) the economic origins from which a person comes; (2) the differences between rich and poor children, which are partly a matter of academic aptitude and partly a matter of money; and (3) cultural attitudes, values, and tastes for schooling, which play an even larger role than aptitude and money (p. 141). This book had a notable impact at the time of its publication.

As we enter the mid-1990s, many people are more concerned with educational achievement and test scores than they are with making the curriculum more relevant to the learner. This does not seem to be the decade for the more progressive forms of education; rather, it appears to be the decade of getting the most quality out of our traditional curriculum. Wider use of computer technology is sure to make the latter part of the 1990s exciting for those who are able to take advantage of this new phenomenon.

What Should the Aims of the Curriculum Be?

LISTING OF THE *SEVEN CARDINAL PRINCIPLES*

What should the aims of education be? This question is one of the most difficult questions for an educator to answer, and the most knowledgeable people differ on the best answer to the question. In 1918, the Commission on Reorganization of Secondary Education published a report known as the *Seven Cardinal Principles* of education. As we look over this list, we see that it is a rather complete list of goals. Some comments and questions about each of these principles may help us to realize what these aims currently mean.

Concerning health
- *Comment:* We are taught in some health classes about the parts of the human body, the enzymes in our digestive system, the food groups, and other facts.
- *Question:* Do we teach our children enough about preventive health measures, and is health given a high enough priority in the curriculum?

Concerning command of the fundamental processes
- *Comment:* Being able to do arithmetic and to communicate by reading, writing, spelling, and speaking is considered important in American democratic society.

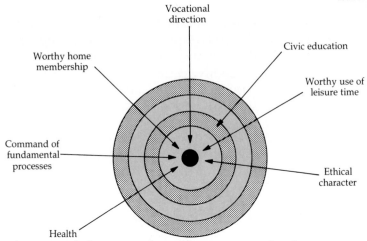

The aims of the curriculum (the Seven Cardinal
Principles—1918).

- *Question:* Why are some students allowed to graduate from our high
  schools without a command of these fundamental processes?

Concerning worthy home membership
- *Comment:* Worthy home membership no doubt includes basics such
  as food preparation, house cleaning, sewing, and raising a family.
- *Question:* Why are high school courses in these areas generally taken
  only by students on a non–college-preparatory curriculum?

Concerning vocational direction
- *Comment:* Americans value freedom of choice, but the best career
  counseling in our schools occurs at the high school level and relates
  primarily to college training.
- *Question:* Experts feel that the best career guidance plan starts at
  kindergarten and continues through high school, so why are many
  students graduating from high school with unclear goals or without
  any goals at all?

Concerning civic education
- *Comment:* Most social studies teachers discuss our nation's history,
  our democratic form of government, and the manner in which the
  people of the United States are represented in state legislatures and
  the Congress.
- *Question:* Why are many voters apathetic and uninformed about the
  voting process?

Concerning worthy use of leisure time

- *Comment:* Physical education classes stress various sports and recreational activities, and the athletic programs in our schools stress athletics for the most competitive and physically able of our students.
- *Question:* Does teaching children about the worthy use of leisure time involve more than engaging in sports? How many students are taught habits in the selective viewing of television and movies?

Concerning ethical character

- *Comment:* Ethical character can be taught and reinforced in the classroom by the teacher.
- *Question:* What good ethical behaviors did you learn from the teachers you most admired?

THREE MA-
JOR PUR-
POSES

Inlow (1966, p. 10) wrote that education has three major purposes: the **transmissive**, the **adaptive**, and the **developmental**. The transmissive purpose is passing on to each new generation the tried, if not necessarily the true. The adaptive purpose is fulfilled when we help students to acquire the skills, the knowledge, and the emotional adjustment needed to relate successfully to themselves and their world. We help students to meet their developmental purposes by guiding them to optimum growth at each maturational level.

So far, the aims of education have been discussed as they relate to absorbing information through the traditional school curricula. Other philosophers and thinkers see the aims of education in a more practical way. The influence of John Dewey, from the turn of the century onward, directed many modern-day thinkers toward the practical side of the curricula.

ALFRED
NORTH
WHITEHEAD

Alfred North Whitehead (1929) wanted to produce students who possessed both culture and expert knowledge in some special direction. Whitehead worried about teaching children inert knowledge; therefore, he stressed that *life* in all of its manifestations should be the curriculum. According to Whitehead, "The only use of a knowledge of the past is to equip us for the present" (p. 3). To illustrate what he meant, Whitehead suggested making a map of a small area using simple instruments like a surveyor's chain and compass:

> To have constructed the map of a small district, to have considered its roads, its contours, its geology, its climate, its relation to other districts, the effects on the status of its inhabitants, will teach more history and geography than any knowledge. (p. 17)

A. S. NEILL

A. S. Neill, founder of the world-famous Summerhill School, saw the aim of education as creating free citizens. He believed in having children at his school learn self-government. The students at Summerhill were free to participate or not to become involved. Neill prided himself on being voted down at general meetings; he really practiced freedom of will—the opposite of authority-centered schools:

> Neill believed in the inherent goodness of children, knowing full well that a hate-filled world would soon intrude and in many cases destroy their desire to live life as openly as possible. He was committed to participation and emotional equality; he wanted children to be as free as possible. (Snitzer, 1983, p. 56)

ALVIN TOF-
FLER

The aims of education are a little different in the view of Alvin Toffler, the author of *Future Shock* (1970): "Nothing should be included in a required curriculum unless it can be strongly justified in terms of the future" (p. 363). Like some other curriculum reformers, Toffler proposed a curriculum built around themes such as childhood, adolescence, marriage, career, retirement, contemporary social problems, and many other possible alternatives. He argued that the present, obsolete curriculum imposes standardization on the elementary and secondary schools, thus giving the pupils little choice.

These are some of the aims of the curriculum. Most of them are generally stated, but they point in a definite direction. Some aims are rather matter-of-fact and others carry with them the connotation of action and excitement. These broad purposes for education give some direction for the more specific objectives that are written for local school districts.

What Should Be Included in the Curriculum?

VARIOUS
ROLES AND
POINTS OF
VIEW

What should be included in the curriculum may be the most difficult question to answer because it depends so much on one's basic orientation as a curriculum advocate. Parents want what is best for their children; school board members must keep in mind the budget and what is best for all of the children; state school officers must keep in mind state guidelines; members of Congress are restrained by the U.S. Constitution and at the same time must be on guard to protect our national security as well as the equality of educational opportunity; and teachers should be aware of the implications of the textbooks they choose, the ability levels and individuality of the children they teach, and the new resources available to them.

BALANCE IN
THE CURRIC-
ULUM

Although most parents want what is best for their children, a good number really do not care and are willing to leave educational decisions to others. Parents with children who are talented in music, art, speech, drama, athletics, or writing may support certain programs, often not keeping curricular balance in mind. Sometimes, groups of parents boost the band or an athletic team so strongly that the program gets more attention and more money than the main academic offerings in the school. Other parents fight for programs for the gifted, for Montessori method, for special education, or for numerous other special interests.

PARENT IN-
FLUENCE

Parents also influence the curriculum by serving on textbook selection committees, and some are active lobbyists at the state level for groups such as the Parent Teachers Association and other state organizations. Still others support groups that want to censor certain books and learning materials, and some wish to restore school prayer.

THE ROLE OF
SCHOOL
BOARD MEM-
BERS

School boards represent the community as a whole, as well as the parents. Most school boards listen to the needs of the school corporation through their appointed superintendent. Most superintendents enlist the help of curriculum directors, principals, and teachers before they propose curricular changes to the board. Some school boards go outside their role as policy settlers and partially assume the role of administrator like the superintendent. When curriculum matters are decided unilaterally by the board and imposed by them on the school system, the best interests of the children may not be served. School board members can and do call attention to certain curricular needs, but these matters are best assigned to the superintendent for study and action.

DUTIES OF
STATE
SCHOOL OF-
FICIALS

State school officials represent an entire state, whose needs may be very diverse. In most states, there are industrial, urban, and rural interests to satisfy. Industrial areas are very concerned about vocational education; urban centers want money for equal educational opportunity; and rural communities want continued funding of vocational agriculture and home economics. State school boards can influence the curriculum in a number of ways, for example, through state certification requirements, which regulate how teacher-training institutions prepare their teachers. By requiring teachers to be exposed to multicultural education, educational psychology, and a set number of credit hours in a certain academic discipline, the state influences the quality of the teachers it produces; thus, indirectly, state standards influence the curriculum in those schools for which state-licensed teachers carry out the curriculum. Some states also regulate the purchase of textbooks, which may represent a type of bias in the curriculum. With regard to money, some school districts can afford a broader and

To some, fine art is an essential part of the curriculum.

(Photo used by permission of the Metropolitan School District of Washington Township.)

richer curriculum than others; however, the states do provide the poorer districts with more funding to help equalize the financial expenditures allocated by the state for each district.

INFLUENCE
OF THE U.S.
CONGRESS

Members of the U.S. Congress also influence the content of the curriculum of our nation's schools. Through categorical grants to school districts, the federal government sets the tone for the curriculum. During the *Sputnik* era, the nation worried about lagging behind the Russians in math and science, and so made plenty of funds available in these areas. One of the authors was a science teacher at this time, and his department received thousands of dollars' worth of new science equipment with the help of the federal government. Government-funded curriculum-improvement projects resulted in new textbooks in math and science. As mentioned in Chapter 6 the Smith–Hughes Act was passed in 1917 to aid vocational education, and the comprehensive Elementary and Secondary Education Act in 1965 to aid poor school districts and to help equalize educational opportunities. The federal government generally influences the curriculum in areas where state and local governments have failed to act. Ideally, its actions are motivated by what is best for our national interest.

What should be included in the curriculum is then a multifaceted question and can be answered only by reference to all of those groups that make these important decisions. Students are sometimes at the end of the list, but can provide valuable feedback about their own needs.

What Is the Hidden Curriculum?

DEFINITION

One area of the curriculum that is probably as important as, or sometimes even more important than, the actual content offered for study is the so-called hidden curriculum. It is the informal part of the curriculum that you know is there, but is difficult to see and study. Ballantine (1983) described the hidden curriculum as the part of the curriculum that refers to the 3Rs —rules, regulations, and routines—to which schools must adapt (p. 178). In this brief overview, we present some of these items that play an important role in influencing one's perception of the formal curriculum.

The Self-Concept Held by the Student

IMPORTANCE
OF SELF-CON-
CEPT

Children who have a good **self-concept** about their academic ability perform better academically. Research done by Brookover and Erickson (1975) found that changes in self-concepts about ability were followed by changes in academic achievement. Thus, it is important for teachers to encourage students to believe in themselves. Once students believe they can be high achievers, they have made the first step.

PARENTAL
INFLUENCE
ON SELF-
CONCEPT

One of the experiments by Brookover and Erickson (1975) showed that you can raise student achievement levels by working with the parents. Parents were given a set of rules and procedures and taught how to implement them as they worked with their children. Parents were told to do the following for an entire school year as they worked with their children (Brookover and Erickson, 1975):

- Don't reward any negative statements their children might make about their academic ability.
- Don't say things like "I was not a reader either."
- Tell children often and regularly, as subtly as possible, that they are academically able and ought to do better in school.
- Any positive statements their children made about their ability or achievement was to be rewarded with commendatory remarks, tokens, or prizes.
- Parents should expect small gains to occur, and these should be accompanied by increasingly higher demands on the student.
- Negative behavior or low achievement was to be overtly ignored (pp. 296–297)

As a result of this experiment, parents witnessed increased levels of performance on the part of their children and sensed that they were responsible for their children's new accomplishments.

The School Value Climate

In regard to the value climate in the schools, Ballantine (1983) considered the effects of **school social structure** and social climate on student achievement:

MEASURING
THE SCHOOL
CLIMATE

Student achievement was measured by reading and writing competencies, academic self-concept, and self-reliance. The *school social structure* was measured by teacher satisfaction with the school structure, parental involvement, differentiation in student programs, principals' reports of time devoted to instruction, and student mobility in school. The *school climate* was measured by student perceptions, teacher perceptions, and principal perceptions. The authors found that more than 85 percent of the variance in student attainment was explained by the combination of the above variables. In a summary of findings which compared improving and declining schools, Brookover and colleagues found the following: The staff of improving schools place more emphasis on accomplishing basic reading and mathematics objectives; they believe *all* students can master basic objectives and they hold high expectations; they assume responsibility for learning and accept being held accountable. Principals in improving schools are instructional leaders and disciplinarians. Brookover, in short, argues that schools *do* make a difference. (Ballantine, p. 183, emphasis added)

THE IMPOR-
TANCE OF
HIGH EXPEC-
TATIONS

The Brookover and Erickson study verifies the fact that a positive feeling on the part of the school staff toward learning and achievement does make a difference. What we are talking about is not a part of the regular formal curriculum, but those subtle things that we think about only when our attention is called to them. We have all known teachers and principals who were not responsible, who held low expectations for students, and who

This championship chess team resulted from a teacher's high expectations and students' determination.

(Photo used by permission of the Indianapolis Public Schools.)

were poor leaders, so we agree with Brookover and Erickson that schools do indeed make a difference.

The Climate in the Classroom

The classroom climate can be compared with life in the "real world." Differences in people are evident in childhood as well as when they reach their adult years, but sex bias, racial prejudice, economic bias, learning bias, and many more of these human problems are less changeable in adulthood. Thus, teachers have contact with persons in their childhood years when they are more willing to change their behavior.

TEACHER SUPPORT AND IN- VOLVEMENT

In a teacher's room, "where teacher support and involvement is at a high level, students will be more motivated toward self-improvement, academic success, and enjoyment in learning" (Ballantine, 1983, p. 188). Teachers tend to give more support to and to get more involved with children in the early grades than they do in the later school years. According to a study by Benham, Gilsen, and Oakes (1980),

> By the senior high school level, the frequency of teacher praise, encouragement, connection with guidance, and positive interaction with students had dropped by nearly 50 percent from the number of observed occurrences at the early elementary level. (p. 539)

HUMANIZING SCHOOLS

This discussion points to the need to humanize the high schools and to let the students know the teacher cares about them. The tendency to teach subjects and not students is present at the high school level, but this can all be overcome. If the students in your classes do not perceive you as a caring person, despite how much you know your subject, their academic achievement is bound to be affected.

VERBAL AND NONVERBAL INTERAC- TIONS

The climate in the classroom is partially determined by the verbal and the nonverbal interactions in the room. A significant study by Flanders (Amidon and Flanders, 1971) showed that student performance and learning are greatest when teacher influence is indirect. Flanders found that teacher talk, which is a direct influence, takes up 80% of class time. A teacher is more effective when he or she indirectly influences the class by acknowl- edging their feelings, praising and encouraging them, accepting and using their ideas, and asking them questions. A teacher is less effective when he or she directly influences the class by lecturing them, giving directions, criticizing, and justifying authority. Teacher talk is not bad, but it should be used with more discretion. The Flanders scale also points out other things that teachers should be aware of pertaining to classroom interactions, such as the importance of student talk, silence, and confusion. Teachers either in service or in training can practice Flanders' **Interaction Analysis** (see Table 10–1).

AFFECTIVE EMPHASIS

Open, flexible, and democratic classrooms stress the affective or emo- tional growth of students (Ballantine, 1983, p. 191). In such a classroom, there is less chance that a child will be isolated and neglected by either the

TABLE 10–1 ▓▓▓▓▓▓▓▓▓▓▓▓▓▓▓▓▓▓▓▓▓▓▓▓▓▓▓▓▓▓▓
Summary of Flanders' Categories for Interaction Analysis[a]

TEACHER TALK	Indirect Influence	1. *Accepts feeling:* Accepts and clarifies the feeling tone of the students in a nonthreatening manner. Feelings may be positive or negative. Predicting and recalling feelings are included.
		2. *Praises or encourages:* Praises or encourages student action or behavior. Jokes that release tension, not at the expense of another individual, nodding head, or saying "uh huh?" or "go on" are included.
		3. *Accepts or uses ideas of student:* Clarifying, building, or developing ideas or suggestions by a student. As teacher brings more of his own ideas into play, shift to category five.
		4. *Asks questions:* Asking a question about content or procedure with the intent that a student answer.
	Direct Influence	5. *Lectures:* Giving facts or opinions about content or procedure; expressing his own idea; asking rhetorical questions.
		6. *Gives directions:* Directions, commands, or orders with which a student is expected to comply.
		7. *Criticizes or justifies authority:* Statements intended to change student behavior from nonacceptable to acceptable pattern; bawling someone out; stating why the teacher is doing what he is doing; extreme self-reference.
STUDENT TALK		8. *Student talk-response:* Talk by students in response to teacher. Teacher initiates the contact or solicits student statement.
		9. *Student talk-initiation:* Talk by students, which they initiate. If "calling on" student is only to indicate who may talk next, observer must decide whether student wanted to talk. If he did, use this category.
		10. *Silence or confusion:* Pauses, short periods of silence, and periods of confusion in which communication cannot be understood by the observer.

[a]No scale is implied by these numbers. Each number is classificatory; it designates a particular kind of communication event. To write these numbers down during observation is to enumerate—not to judge a position on a scale.

SOURCE: Amidon, E. J., & Flanders, N. A. (1971). *The role of the teacher in the classroom.* Minneapolis, MN: Paul S. Amidon and Associates, Inc., p. 14.

group or the teacher. When classes are run by an authority-centered teacher, the students tend to become passive because they know that they will be listening most of the time, and they are less likely to answer questions or make decisions.

These are just a few parts of the hidden curriculum, but we have mentioned many facets of the hidden curriculum in other sections of the text. Still other parts of the hidden curriculum will be discussed in more detail in your methods classes. Some other areas that pertain to the hidden curriculum are seating arrangements for classes, the physical condition of the classrooms, the peer group influence, the whole area of power dynamics, and the teacher's personality and background.

What Are Some Organizational and Structural Decisions That Influence the Curriculum?

We can assume that somewhere, every significant aspect of curricular content has been presented to students in schools. Some schools may have a fine curriculum and excellent teachers, but such factors as classroom management, teaching methods, and the way in which the curriculum is organized and structured may be limiting factors. In this section, we concentrate on the organization and the structure of the curriculum.

Elementary School Concerns

Organizational patterns for the elementary school may include self-contained classes, grade-level teams, cross-grade teams, and nongraded classes. Some schools may have a combination of these patterns, with the lower elementary levels nongraded and the upper elementary levels graded classes. In some grades, the teachers may work on the team concept while others work in the self-contained classroom. Children can be moved **vertically** from grade to grade or from level to level and ***horizontally*** within a grade or level. Whatever is done as far as these organizational patterns are concerned, the important thing is for the schools to be flexible. According to Wiles and Bondi (1984), "A sound approach is to organize and group according to the needs of students, abilities of teachers, and availability of facilities and resources. No single pattern fits all situations" (p. 285).

NO SINGLE PATTERN

Elementary schools have done much with the grouping of students for particular purposes. The reason for grouping is to better meet the individualized needs of the children, and flexibility is the key to effective grouping. Some students may have reached a higher level of skill performance in math, yet may be lower in reading. Wiles and Bondi (1984) listed seven possible groups in which to involve students to best meet their needs:

SEVEN POSSIBLE GROUPINGS

1. *A class as a whole* can function as a group. Teachers sometimes have guilt feelings about whole class activities, but there are occasions when the teacher can address the whole class as a single group. New topic or unit introductions, unit summaries, and activities such as reports, dramatizations, and choral reading may be effectively conducted with the total class.
2. *Reading level groups* formed according to reading achievement levels are commonly found in classrooms. These groups are not static and must accommodate shifts of pupils from group to group as changes in individual achievement occur.

3. *Reading need groups* are formed to assist students in mastering a particular reading skill such as pronouncing a phonic element or finding the main idea in a paragraph.

4. *Interest groups* help students apply reading skills to other language arts and other content areas. Storytelling, recreational reading, writing stories and poems, and dramatization are activities that can be carried out in interest groupings.

5. *Practice or tutorial groups* are often used to allow students to practice oral reading skills, play skill games, and organize peer teaching situations.

6. *Research groups* allow for committee work, group projects, and other research activities. Learning centers in the classroom and research areas in the media center are often developed for research groups.

7. *Individualization* allows a student to work as an individual in selecting books and references for learning projects. Developmental programs provide for individual progress through a series of lessons. (pp. 270–271, emphasis added)

When we talk of groups at any level, we generally refer to them as either homogeneous or heterogeneous. Homogeneous groups are those that have some commonality among their members, such as the same reading level, the same math comprehension level, or the same physical performance level. Heterogeneous groups are those that contain many different levels of ability. In most schools, children perform in both kinds of groups in a single day; therefore, they can maximize their ability or talents in a special reading group or other special group and yet interact both socially and intellectually part of the day with all students.

Middle School Concerns

About eighty years ago, only about 40% of the children from elementary school went on to high school under the old eight-year/four-year plan. As HISTORICAL a result, educators conceived of the junior high school, or the six-year/ ORIGINS three-year/three-year plan. The first of these institutions was set up in Berkeley, California, in 1910, and like others to follow, its aims were to move students into high school work sooner and to focus on the unique needs of twelve- and thirteen-year-old students. In the eyes of many, what actually happened was that in the years to follow, junior high schools became mini–high schools with similar departments and extracurricular activities. Thus, they did not meet the unique developmental needs of the children being served (Steeves and English, 1978).

More recently, we have seen this intermediate age group housed in a school known more commonly as a ***middle school*** under either a Grade 5–8, Grade 6–8, or Grade 7–8 plan of organization. The most predominant organizational plan encompasses Grades 6–8 for the middle school (Steeves and English, 1978):

OPTIMUM   Debates over the optimum school district organizational plan, whether 8–4,
PLAN?   6–3–3, or 4–4–4 or some other variation are largely unproductive. The choice
           of such plans is largely arbitrary and grounded in the dictates of local pragma-

tism. Research on such patterns has failed to demonstrate clearly that any one is superior to any other. (p. 29)

High School Concerns

DEPARTMEN-
TALIZATION

Flexibility is not very descriptive of the modern high school. Most high schools are departmentalized and are much more subject centered than they are student centered. To make high schools more exciting places for students to attend, most efforts have been directed toward athletics and other extracurricular areas of concentration. Some efforts in recent times toward revitalization have been in the area of alternatives, including magnet schools and vocational schools.

RIGID ORGA-
NIZATION

The high school curriculum tends to be rigid because of societal demands that students achieve higher scores on college entrance examinations. Other reasons for rigidity in high schools, according to Wiles and Bondi (1984), are that for years most secondary schools have operated under the assumption that

1. The appropriate amount of time for learning a subject is the same uniform period of time, 50 to 60 minutes in length, six or seven periods a day, for 36 weeks out of the year.

2. A classroom group size of 30–35 students is the most appropriate for a wide variety of learning experiences.

3. All learners are capable of mastering the same subject matter in the same length of time. For example, we give everyone the same test on Chapter Five on Friday. We pass everyone from level one of Algebra to level two when June comes.

4. We assume that once a group is formed, the same group composition is equally appropriate for a wide variety of learning activities.

5. We assume that the same classroom is equally appropriate for a wide variety of learning activities. Conference rooms are not provided for teacher–student conferences. Large group facilities are not provided for mass dissemination of materials. Small group rooms are unavailable for discussion activities.

6. We assume that all students require the same kind of supervision.

7. We assume that the same teacher is qualified to teach all aspects of his or her subject for one year.

Operating on those assumptions, we have locked students into an educational egg-crate with thirty students to a cubicle from 8 A.M. to 3 P.M. five days a week. In short, schools operating under those assumptions have existed more for the convenience of teaching than for the facilitation of learning. (p. 334)

FLEXIBLE
SCHEDULING

How can the high school curriculum be made more flexible and more student centered, and thus more **humanistic**? J. Lloyd Trump (1968) and others have suggested flexible scheduling that provides a time and place for small groups, large groups, and individualized instruction. Trump outlined a schedule with fifteen-, twenty-, or thirty-minute modules instead of the conventional forty-five- or fifty-five-minute modules (p. 12). The reduced time per module would give twelve, sixteen, or twenty-four periods per day instead of the usual six- or seven-period day, but these schedules can become just as rigid if time is not used to do those things that a flexible schedule is designed to provide. William Bailey (1975) has provided us with some goals that could be reached with a flexible schedule:

OTHER IN-
NOVATIONS

1. Variable class size.
2. Variable time allotments for classes and/or block time periods.
3. Maximum use of facilities, particularly resource centers, labs, and instructional materials centers.
4. Selected students may elect seven courses or more.
5. Multiple teaching assignments, i.e., team or cooperative teaching.
6. A weekly schedule is preferable to a routinized daily schedule that, for example, maintains the same class each afternoon during poor times for concentration.
7. Facilitate independent study and individual study courses.
8. Provide students with opportunities for individualized, continuous progress learning.
9. Maximize planning time for teacher and teaching teams — should be around 25 percent.
10. Enable band and chorus to be included in a regular school day.
11. Increase the degree to which students are responsible for their own education.
12. Provide for order in daily attendance.
13. Provide for orderly but rapid changes adaptable to pep rallies, assemblies, dismissals, and other interruptions.
14. Provide for proper sequencing of the various types of instruction, i.e., lab following demonstration, small groups following lectures, etc.
15. General flexibility.
16. In addition to the intent to accommodate the above, the schedule should make it possible to carry forward present curriculum practices that have proven successful and are crucial to progress. (pp. 154–155)

Flexible scheduling is being used today in a number of high schools. Many schools have incorporated changes, such as those suggested by Wiles and Bondi, that enable the school to function more smoothly. Another problem in today's schools that inhibits innovations like flexible scheduling

ABILITY TO
USE INDE-
PENDENT
STUDY TIME

is the students' lack of maturity and apparent inability to use their independent study time efficiently. School leaders should not allow disruptive students to curtail innovations that can and will stimulate other students to greater achievements. No doubt some students may need less free time or independent study time to function properly.

The Nongraded Curricular Organization

The graded school concept is well entrenched in our society. The first graded school was installed at Boston in the Quincy School in 1848; the idea had been imported from Germany by Horace Mann. Most of our curriculum material is organized around the graded system of schooling, and there is a great deal of resistance to changing this organizational pattern. The graded system of schooling has worked for all of these years, it is said, so why change?

CHRONO-
LOGICAL AGE
VS. READI-
NESS

There is an innate error in the established graded system of schools: there is no exact correlation between the chronological age of a child and his or her readiness for a certain grade. Inlow (1966) wrote that "grading with age as a unilateral criterion assumes falsely that children of similar ages not only have similar interests and abilities, but have had similar cultural experiences as well" (p. 308). The fact is that children who enter the first grade vary in readiness, as measured by the mental age (MA) of the child, by as much as four years. Some experts feel that by the time children reach fourth grade, the span for readiness for that grade can be measured by the number for that grade. Are we trying to fit children into the wrong places, just as a carpenter might be trying to drive a square peg into a round hole?

ALTERNATIVE
TO GRADED
SCHOOLS

An obvious alternative to graded schools is **nongraded schools**. Whether these schools are located at the elementary school, middle school, or high school level, their goal is to allow more flexibility and movement within the curriculum. Ideally, these nongraded schools are there to provide continuous academic challenge and growth no matter what the age of the student. In a nongraded school, the conventional grade designations are eliminated, and three or four blocks are inserted in their place. At the elementary level, where most of the experimentation with nongraded schools has occurred, Grades 1, 2, and 3 are placed in a primary nongraded unit, and Grades 4, 5, and 6 are placed in an intermediate nongraded unit. Some educators envision nongraded education as being divided into five blocks from first grade through college.

IDENTIFYING
STUDENT
NEEDS

The nongraded school must provide a system for identifying student needs, delivering those needs in a suitable curricular package, evaluating the degree to which those needs are being met, and allowing for the continuous progress of each student. In theory, at least, each student should start and end at a different point. Most nongraded schools use multiple criteria to choose who is to be placed in a given block. Some schools use achievement as a single criterion, but other criteria may include reading level, age, or social homogeneity, and some schools deliberately impose heterogeneity, including a mixture of ages and social and emotional development.

ADVANTAGES
OF NON-
GRADED
SCHOOLS

Inlow (1966) listed the advantages of a nongraded school as follows:

1. Permits pupils to progress at their own individual rates.
2. Decisions on retardation of pupils are automatically delayed for three years.

3. Teachers have more flexibility in the selection of subject matter, in establishing its sequence, and assigning time allocations.

4. Pupil achievement, not time spent in school, constitutes the basis for evaluation.

5. Greater progress in reading is made under the nongraded than under the graded plan in the primary block. (pp. 316–317)

Inlow also listed the shortcomings of a nongraded school:

SHORTCOM-
INGS OF
NONGRADED
SCHOOLS

1. The biggest problem seems to be choosing the right vertical sequence for pupils to follow, and in what way will they follow it, as they progress through a two-, three-, or four-year nongraded curriculum.

2. After eliminating conventional grade labels, they may proceed to add others that may be no better.

3. The process of grouping children for instructional purposes is still uncertain.

4. Some incorrectly call their situation nongraded when more than one grade is represented in a typing or a Spanish class. Common ingredients of a nongraded school would be a time block longer than a year, vertical scheduling, sequential pupil progression through a given body of content, and teacher flexibility. (pp. 318–319)

A good resource on the nongraded high school is B. Frank Brown's *The Nongraded High School* (1963).

The Team Teaching Concept

Organizing the development and the delivery of the curriculum around team teaching can be very beneficial to both the teachers and the students involved. **Team teaching** can be used anywhere, but it may work best at the middle school level. When children enter the middle school, it seems like a big, impersonal organization compared to the more comfortable elementary school. According to Deibert and Walsh (1981),

SUPPORTIVE
ENVIRON-
MENT

The development of the teacher team provides the school with the type of program whereby students receive the necessary individual attention and support while gaining the benefits of a large, well-staffed, well-equipped, and diversified school. (p. 169)

MASLOW

In Maslow's (1954) **hierarchy of needs**, one progresses through five levels as he or she moves through life (see the figure on page 312). The key is that each level is built on the level below, and each level must be satisfied before the next-higher level can be attained.

Every person has the potential to be fully self-actualized or to have a complete awareness of her or his uniqueness as a person. A self-actualized person is inwardly directed in that her or his direction comes from the self. Many middle school students have not realized Maslow's level of safety when they first arrive, but through the familylike team concept, these students can be given a good sense of security in which to operate. When

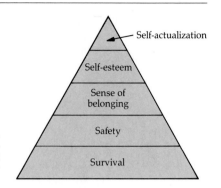

Maslow's hierarchy of needs.

(SOURCE: Data for diagram based on Maslow, A. H. [1970]. A theory of human motivation. In *Motivation and Personality,* 2nd ed. New York: Harper and Row. Copyright © 1970 by Abraham H. Maslow.)

children feel this comfortable environment, they can proceed to the next need.

> The beauty of the team concept in a school is that it breaks down the size of the institution, increases both student and teacher acceptance in the performance of tasks, and increases a sense of belonging so that eventual self-esteem and self-actualization have a better chance of being realized. (Deibert and Walsh, 1981, p. 170)

ADMINISTRA-
TIVE SUP-
PORT

Team teaching does not work in every school. The school must have an administration that fosters an **open organizational climate** as well as a staff that is enthusiastic and positive about what is going on. Leadership from the top by the principal is a key factor. Teachers from Ironwood School in Phoenix have worked successfully for ten years in teams. Among other things at Ironwood, according to Harmon (1983), "Team decisions always take account of young adolescents' need for stability, tempered by opportunities to make choices" (p. 367). This statement tends to lend support to Maslow and others, who view need satisfaction as of prime importance; thus, team teaching can be a mechanism facilitating the success of student growth.

Other advantages of team teaching were stated by Inlow (1966):

ADVANTAGES
OF TEAM
TEACHING

1. *Grouping flexibility*—For example, in a team of four teachers responsible for 120 students, one teacher could do large group instruction for 90 students, while the other three could do small group instruction with 10 students each. Multiple variations are possible making the team teaching arrangement very flexible.

2. *Better use of teacher strengths*—For instance, if one elementary school teacher is more knowledgeable than his team colleagues in a single academic area, he can extend this asset, via various grouping plans, throughout the entire group.

3. *In-service education is a by-product*—As a result of the close associations most teachers have within a group, they will experience in-service growth.

4. *Provides more time for professional duties*—Often teaching teams have noncertified personnel assigned to them, who perform such tasks as paper

grading, playground duty, or clerical duties; thus freeing the certified teacher to do the more strictly professional functions like lesson preparations. (pp. 297–299)

Inlow also stated some disadvantages of team teaching (1966):

DISADVAN-
TAGES OF
TEAM
TEACHING

1. *Sustained cooperation is difficult to achieve*—To state it bluntly, certain teachers are not mature enough to work cooperatively and productively with their colleagues in a team teaching situation. The following factors relate to this issue involving the human equation: First, it places them in a close familylike relationship wherein their paths cross hundreds of times in the course of a year. Second, the team asks that team members resolve their curriculum differences so that there will be a workable consensus. Third, team members must make collaborative decisions for unexpected occurrences. Fourth, performing under the watchful eye of colleagues is a disturbing experience for many.
2. *The curriculum problem of what should be taught*—This problem relates to what should be taught, in what way, and to what size group. It is a hard issue to resolve, but it must be resolved in order that the team may maximize effectiveness. (pp. 300–301)

Team teaching, then, can enhance the curriculum if it is organized and used with the best interests of the students and the teachers in mind. Although it has some problems, it appears that its advantages far exceed its disadvantages.

The preceding pages have presented some of the factors involved in the organization of the curriculum. There are many more, but these considerations will help the prospective teacher to realize that once curricular content is decided, the organization of that content for delivery is also vital.

GRADED VS.
NON-
GRADED?

The graded school has some inherent weaknesses, as does the nongraded school. Under the right conditions, schooling can be enhanced by the use of middle schools, nongraded blocks of time, flexible scheduling, and team teaching. The key seems to be flexibility, and the more flexible teachers are, the more they will meet the individualized needs of their students.

What Psychological Factors of Children Affect the Curriculum?

When curriculum planners get together, they inevitably want to plan a curriculum that is based on child psychology. They know that if the curriculum is psychologically based, the child will see the greatest relevance in what is being offered. Several researchers have given us a reasonably good idea of child psychology as it applies to certain age levels.

PIAGET'S
PERIODS OF
INTELLEC-
TUAL DEVEL-
OPMENT

Intellectual Development

Jean Piaget (1896–1980) gave us significant insight into the intellectual development of the human being. He described four periods of intellectual development: sensorimotor (birth to 1½–2 years), preoperational (1½–2 to

6–7 years), concrete-operational (6–7 to 11–12 years), and formal-operational (11–12 through adulthood) (Piaget and Inhelder, 1969).

SENSORIMOTOR PERIOD

Characteristic of the **sensorimotor period** is that children solve problems by using their sensory system and their motor or muscular system rather than the symbolic processes that characterize the other three major periods. Newborn infants are capable of reflexive behavior such as the rooting reflex and the sucking reflex. Both of these reflexes have survival value, as the baby locates its mother's breast through rooting and obtains its mother's milk through sucking. During this early learning period, by using their senses, humans learn a lot about the world around them. The information that infants must learn, such as the differences between hot and cold and hard and soft, is enormous, and they use only their reflexes and sense organs to begin this process.

PREOPERATIONAL PERIOD

The most characteristic feature of the **preoperational period** is the development of symbolic functioning. The symbolic functioning process occurs when the child makes one thing represent a different thing that is not present. After having seen an object, children get some mental picture of the object and are then able to imitate what they observed. Also, children use symbolic play, where they treat an object as if it were something else; for example, a doll becomes a friend or a finger becomes a gun. Also during this period, children use language to describe activities of the past and to understand some reference to the future.

CONCRETE-OPERATIONAL PERIOD

In contrast to the previous period, children who are in the **concrete-operational stage** can solve a variety of tasks. The conservation tasks that Piaget asked students to perform are interesting and demonstrate a child's progression to this period. To conserve, for example, children must recognize that differences in the size of a vessel storing liquid do not indicate changes in the volume of liquid and that the length of an object stays the same even though its position has shifted (Ault, 1983, p. 58).

FORMAL-OPERATIONAL PERIOD

An adolescent in the **formal-operational period** can construct contrary-to-fact hypotheses and reason about their new ideas. Formal-operational thinking involves three activities: (1) generating multiple hypotheses; (2) systematically checking all possible solutions; and (3) operating on operations. In generating multiple hypotheses, children at this period of development would not conclude that a man lying face-down on the sidewalk was drunk. They would instead consider other options, for example, that he may have had a heart attack, that he may be playing a joke, or that he may even have

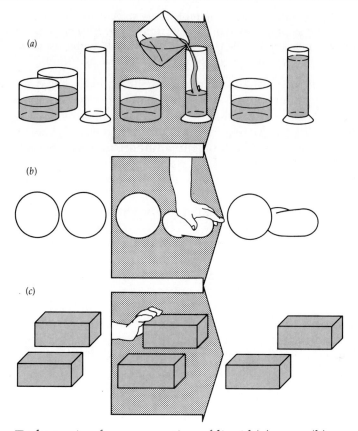

Tasks testing for conservation of liquid (a), mass (b), and length (c).

(SOURCE: From *Children's cognitive development*, 2nd ed., by Ruth L. Ault. Copyright © 1977, 1983 by Oxford University Press, Inc. Reprinted by permission.)

been hit over the head by a robber. The more possible solutions to a problem there are, the greater the need for systematic solution testing. To demonstrate systematic solution testing, a chemistry problem can be used:

> Children are shown five colorless, odorless liquids in test tubes and are asked to discover what combination of the five will produce a yellow mixture. Concrete Operational children attempt to solve this problem through trial and error. They merely start to combine the liquids. But without an overall plan of action, one which is systematic, they soon become hopelessly lost—not remembering which combinations they have already tried and which remain to be tried. Formal Operational children proceed in a more systematic fashion, often first mixing the test tubes two at a time in a logical order (first and second, first and third, first and fourth, first and fifth, second and third, and so on). Then they try combinations of three at a time, four at a time, and all five. Moreover, if Concrete Operational children stumble upon a combination which works,

they will be satisfied that the problem is solved without considering that one of the liquids may be inert and hence unnecessary. Formal Operational children will continue testing even after one solution is found, isolating the relevant factors and discarding the irrelevant. (Ault, 1983, pp. 70–71)

Finally, in operating on operations, the children begin to generate rules that are abstract enough to cover many specific instances. Roland and McGuire (1968) wrote that "The formally operational child approaches what is to Piaget the highest level of intelligence: the ability to represent, in advance of the actual problem, a full set of possibilities" (p. 50).

Therefore, Piaget gave us basic facts about the learning of the child that are useful in making intelligent curricular decisions. The ages given for the different developmental periods are meant as rough approximations only. The child is ready for the next period when he or she has accomplished the tasks of the previous period.

OPTIMAL
AGE FOR
LEARNING

Ausubel (1983) wrote about **readiness** as that time when an intellectual skill is at a particular stage of development. He wrote that most educators agree that there is an optimal age for learning, and that if learning experiences are delayed beyond this optimal period, valuable learning opportunities may be lost. **Maturation** and previous learning each contribute to one's being ready for the next level of learning, but it is very difficult to measure readiness because of its unpredictability and its lack of specificity (p. 158).

Moral Development

INDOCTRINATION

Indoctrination is a method of inculcating a set of beliefs in others without involving the critical thinking process to examine all possibilities. Historically, this was the method used in early colonial schools, especially those of the Puritans, who tried to frighten their young people from the grasp of Satan. This trend continues even in some modern-day classrooms. Gerald Paske (1985/1986) sums up the dangers of indoctrination:

> The victims of indoctrination are committed to "what," but they do not understand the "why." Thus, even when traditional conduct is no longer appropriate, the victims of indoctrination remain emotionally committed to it. They have no basis of understanding on which to rationally modify their behavior. (p. 11)

The danger for teachers lies in not teaching students to think and evaluate on their own. Teachers can easily pass on their own prejudices and misconceptions unless they place proper emphasis upon critical thinking in their classrooms. The authors of this text believe that some indoctrination is unavoidable in the early childhood years (for example, a child needs to be told never to cross a busy street before looking right and left), but that as students grow and mature, they need to learn to think critically about the values they hold. The values clarification process discussed in the next section can be an integral part of this process.

VALUES CLARIFICATION

Values are changing in our society for many reasons: Some U.S. citizens are making a big effort to understand the diverse ethnic groups that live within our pluralistic nation. Also, the dominance of the church and the family is not as strong as before World War II; thus, values that were once stressed at church and in the home are being lost. A one-school-district study in Minnesota, including interviews with 300 veteran teachers and administrators about changes in children over the past ten to twenty years, produced this comment (Hedin and Conrad, 1980):

> This passivity and dependence described by elementary teachers becomes ingrained by adolescence and, according to high school teachers, tends to harden into a generalized pattern of self-centeredness and lack of social concern. (p. 703)

The change of values indicated in the Minnesota study appears to corroborate the opinion held by some that ours is a materialistic society that is based on instant gratification and that places too much emphasis on what makes one "happy" in the short run. An example of the "me society" might be the increasing difficulty of finding people who want to dedicate their professional lives to teaching—a service occupation.

As teachers, we cannot suddenly overturn the "me society" model and insert a societal concern model, but we can help students look at the values they choose with much greater consideration. Harmin (1977) suggested a method of helping students to think more clearly about the value choices they make in life by including choosing, prizing, and acting in their deliberations:

Choosing

There are three elements in choosing: (1) making one's own judgments, (2) searching out alternatives in the choice situation, and (3) considering the consequences that will likely flow from each alternative. A word about each:

1. *Free choice.* Looking at this first part from its opposite side, I would say that a student would not be well prepared for value growth if he sought ways to avoid choices, perhaps by withdrawing from issues or timidly following the lead of others. I believe it is better for students to learn to weight evidence and to make choices independently.

2. *Alternatives.* Students should hunt for alternatives when faced with a choice situation. If a student approached issues as if they were simply either/or propositions or as if all the options were already known, he would not be well prepared to deal with values issues. The best way to find a good idea is to examine lots of ideas.

3. *Consequences.* Students should not conclude a survey of options with an impulsive or random choice. They should know how to think ahead, ma-

nipulate abstractions, make predictions about what will happen if one option or another were selected. It is on the basis of anticipated consequences, not on the basis of chance or impulse, that I prefer students make their value choices.

Prizing

It is not enough that one's rationality be engaged in value situations. One's feelings, intuitions, and deepest senses must also be engaged if values are to be completely appreciated or fully internalized. Thus the deliberation process I recommend has an element called prizing, which asks two kinds of questions: (1) How do the options in value choice feel to you? Or which choices are you most likely to prize and cherish? (2) Which options would make you feel most proud to stand up and announce as being your choice? Or which options would you feel most comfortable in being publicly associated with? A word about prizing and affirming.

1. *Prizing.* Students would not be well served in their value growth if they did not know how to get in touch with their emotional or intuitive preferences or to include those preferences in their deliberations. This is not to suggest that one should always choose what one feels like choosing. But it is to suggest that one is better served by knowing how one feels and what one's conscience may be saying than by not knowing.

2. *Affirming.* There are important advantages to students being able to share with others their personal evaluations, especially the extent to which an option feels right to them. In one sense, an opportunity to share one's values with others tests the strength of those values. When we feel proud to tell those whom we respect about a choice we made, it is a signal to ourselves that we feel positive about that choice. When we feel ashamed to tell about it, if we would rather that even our best friends knew nothing about it, it suggests that we do not feel positive about the choice. Thus, one way to get positive feedback from our subconscious selves is to ask ourselves to what extent we would be proud of others knowing about that choice. In another sense, the more we learn about how to share our values proudly and straightforwardly, the more informed our society's collective choices can be. The more we are able to take advantage of each other's insights and wisdom, the less likelihood of a demagogue leading us astray. Students who learn when and how to stand up and be counted for the things they believe in learn something important about making democracy work. They learn to maximize collective support when support is available for their position and, when it is not, they learn how to take advantage of others' thoughts in making their own decisions.

Acting

Values issues are not abstract issues. They influence what we do with our limited time and energy. To divorce value deliberations from human behavior is to divorce values from the real world. So value deliberations should include the issue of "So what?" What does a deliberation mean in terms of behavior?

Looking at this from a negative perspective, I would say that students who have not learned how to take value deliberations beyond choosing and prizing, who do not ask themselves what, if anything, it all has to do with how they spend their days, have not learned complete valuing skills. I want students to be able to look at their behaviors, both their occasional acts and the general patterns of their actions, and to compare those behaviors with what their minds tell them are intelligent choices and what their hearts tell them are choices of which they can be proud. Our minds, our feelings, and our actions must be integrated if we are to live comfortable, value-directed lives.

Briefly, then, students are helped to deliberate on values issues when they are helped to develop skills for: (1) choosing freely, (2) searching for alternatives, (3) weighing predicted consequences. (pp. 25–27)

If children can be taught to practice using the Harmin model, they will not only be taught the values clarification process; more important still, they will be taught to act on their choices. The actions the students take will teach them about the consequences of their choices. Students using the Harmin model will develop skills in problem solving and will be more actively involved in the learning process. The choice teens make to use or not to use drugs, to drink alcoholic beverages, to smoke cigarettes, or to engage in premarital sex can be tested by the Harmin process. Much more information is available on values teaching in *Values and Teaching* (1966) by Raths, Harmin, and Simon.

Literature is filled with examples of how citizens have had to make moral and ethical choices in life. Students need to be exposed to literature describing delicate ethical decisions. The literature of the Holocaust has produced some very significant stories to help students clarify their own values. James Farnham (1983) wrote about the use of the Holocaust literature in helping students to clarify ethical and moral values. Farnham likes the story in *The Sunflower*, written by Simon Wiesenthal: A Jewish prisoner who is assigned to

work in a nearby hospital is taken by a nurse one day to the bedside of a young S.S. dying of wounds. The German had a pious Catholic upbringing and is now torn with genuine remorse for the atrocities he has participated in. The Jew listens quietly, giving him the solace of confessing his sins; but, when finally he must decide to forgive the German or not on behalf of all Jewish victims, he walks wordlessly from the room. Has he done the morally right thing or not? The Jew himself is not certain. This is the hard, ambiguous ethical core of *The Sunflower*. The value of the book is enlarged by a symposium which follows the tale itself in which thirty-two eminent people offer short opinions on the Jew's silence, providing students with an example of how good will and reasoned thought can be brought to bear on vital and ambiguous ethical issues. (p. 67)

The discussion that could follow such a reading would be valuable in bringing out the ethical implications of the Holocaust. According to Farnham (1983), "Teaching students the historical and sociological facts of the Holocaust is of little value unless the ethical implications of the facts are raised" (p. 67). Teachers often teach meaningless facts without confronting the real moral and ethical issues in our society, and these opportunities are often there in our textbook literature.

Although the literature may be one source of values for class discussion, our daily experiences are also filled with examples. One of the authors remembers stories about cheating on tests, violations of fish and game laws, highway litter problems, and many more that have served as illustrations for the purpose of clarifying values. One cheating story involved one of the authors when he was in the third grade, on a day when he had failed to remember his spelling words for a test. He put together a small list of spelling words and slipped them in his desk under an empty inkwell, where they would be fully visible to him, but not to the teacher. After the test started, the teacher caught him immediately and sent him to the back of the room. Later, another cheater, who was known as the worst-behaved boy in the school, was caught by the teacher and sent to stand in the back of the room also. The original culprit stood there mortified by all of the embarrassment, but he was determined that it would never happen to him again. This is an example of learning in the "school of hard knocks."

Values emerge from our daily experiences everywhere, and as they emerge in your teaching experience, don't back away from discussing them in class. We cannot moralize as teachers, but we can involve students in ethical and moral value thinking. There is a great difference between telling children not to smoke because it is evil and explaining what cigarette tars will do to their lungs and letting them decide for themselves.

Another example of an exercise in values clarification is that of the Sanchez family and the dilemma they faced concerning a possible strike (Banks, 1987):

The Sanchez Family and the Grape Strike

Mr. and Mrs. Sanchez and their seven children came from Mexico to live in California four years ago. Mr. Sanchez had been told by relatives who had been to the United States that he could make a lot of money very quickly if he came to California. When Mr. Sanchez arrived in California, he found that it was very hard to make a living working in the fields. Since the Sanchez family has been living in California, it has had to move many times in order to follow the crops and find work. The family has traveled as far as Texas and Michigan to work in the fields.

The work in the fields is very hard. Everyone in the family, except little Carlos, works in the fields so that the family can make enough money to get by with. Even Mrs. Sanchez, who used to stay at home and take care of the home when they lived in Mexico, now must work in the fields. The pay for the work is very low. Mr. and Mrs. Sanchez find that they get further and further into debt each year.

The Sanchez family is now living in the San Joaquin Valley in California. The family went to live there to work in the grape fields. For a while everything there was okay. Recently, a lot of things have been happening in the valley that Mr. and Mrs. Sanchez do not fully understand. Most of the field workers have said that they will not work next week because the Mexican American Union, led by Juan Gonzales, who is very popular with the workers, has called a strike. The union is demanding that the owners of the grape fields pay the workers more money and give them better worker benefits. The workers who belong to the union are threatening to attack any worker who tries to go to work while the strike is on.

Mr. Sanchez is not a member of the union. He wants very much to go to work next week. He has a lot of bills to pay and needs money for food and clothing. The family simply cannot get by with the small amount of money that the union has promised to give Mr. Sanchez if he joins it and refuses to work next week. Mr. Sanchez also realizes that if the grapes are not picked within the next two weeks, they will rot. He has heard that these strikes sometimes last for months. His boss told him that if he wants to go to work next Monday morning—the day the strike is to begin—he will protect him from the unionized workers. Mrs. Sanchez thinks that Mr. Sanchez should support the strike so that he can make higher wages in the future.

Questions

1. Do you think that Mr. Sanchez and his family will go to work in the fields next Monday? Why or why not?
2. If Mr. Sanchez does go to work, what do you think will happen to him and his family?
3. If Mr. Sanchez does not go to work in the grape fields next Monday, what do you think he might do to earn money?
4. What do you think Mr. Sanchez should do? Why?
5. What would you do if you were (a) Mr. Sanchez, (b) Mrs. Sanchez, or (c) the children? Why?
6. Tell whether you agree or disagree with this statement and why: The head of a family should never let his or her spouse and children do without food and clothing need. (p. 272)

Students can read about the Sanchez dilemma, answer the questions at the end, and engage in a very sensitive values-based discussion. Many Americans have never had to think about the values discussed in these questions, but such discussions help all of us to be more sensitive to each other, no matter what our cultural and ethnic origins might be.

COGNITIVE-DEVELOPMENTAL APPROACH

KOHLBERG'S MORAL STAGES

Lawrence Kohlberg (1973) wrote about moral education's being based on cognitive development, "cognitive" because active thinking occurs on moral issues and decisions, and "development" because it moves through certain **moral stages**. Using Jean Piaget's levels of intellectual development as a base, Kohlberg redefined and validated these previous studies. As Table 10–2 indicates, the child moves from being absolutely obedient to being an authority at the preconventional level; to being loyal to the family, the group, or the nation at the conventional level; and eventually to defining her or his moral values in terms separate from the established groups' moral values at the postconventional level.

TABLE 10–2 ▰▰▰▰▰▰▰▰▰▰▰▰▰▰
Definition of Moral Stages

I. Preconventional Level

At this level, the child is responsive to cultural rules and labels of good and bad, right or wrong, but interprets these labels either in terms of the physical or the hedonistic consequences of action (punishment, reward, exchange of favors) or in terms of the physical power of those who enunciate the rules and labels. The level is divided into the following two stages.

Stage 1: The punishment-and-obedience orientation.   The physical consequences of action determine its goodness or badness, regardless of the human meaning or value of these consequences. Avoidance of punishment and unquestioning deference to power are valued in their own right, not in terms of respect for an underlying moral order supported by punishment and authority (the latter being Stage 4).

Stage 2: The instrumental-relativist orientation.   Right action consists of that which instrumentally satisfies one's own needs and occasionally the needs of others. Human relations are viewed in terms like those of the marketplace. Elements of fairness, of reciprocity, and of equal sharing are present, but they are always interpreted in a physical, pragmatic way. Reciprocity is a matter of "you scratch my back and I'll scratch yours," not of loyalty, gratitude, or justice.

II. Conventional Level

At this level, maintaining the expectations of the individual's family, group, or nation is perceived as valuable in its own right, regardless of immediate and obvious consequences. The attitude is not only one of *conformity* to personal expectations and social order, but of loyalty to it, of actively *maintaining*, supporting, and justifying the order, and of identifying with the persons or group involved in it. At this level, there are the following stages.

Stage 3: The interpersonal concordance or "good boy–nice girl" orientation.   Good behavior is that which pleases or helps others and is approved by them. There is much conformity to stereotypical images of what is majority or "natural" behavior. Behavior is frequently judged by intention—"he means well" becomes important for the first time. One earns approval by being "nice."

Stage 4: The "law and order" orientation.   There is orientation toward authority, fixed rules, and the maintenance of the social order. Right behavior consists of doing one's duty, showing respect for authority, and maintaining the given social order for its own sake.

III. Postconventional, Autonomous, or Principled Level

At this level, there is a clear effort to define moral values and principles that have validity and application apart from the authority of the groups or persons holding these principles and apart from the individual's own identification with these groups. This level also has two stages.

Stage 5: The social-contract, legalistic orientation, generally with utilitarian overtones. Right action tends to be defined in terms of general individual rights and standards which have been critically examined and agreed upon by the whole society. There is a clear awareness of the relativism of personal values and opinions and a corresponding emphasis upon procedural rules for reaching consensus. Aside from what is constitutionally and democratically agreed upon, the right is a matter of personal "values" and "opinion." The result is an emphasis upon the "legal point of view," but with an emphasis upon the possibility of changing law in terms of rational considerations of social utility (rather than freezing it in terms of Stage 4 "law and order"). Outside the legal realm, free agreement and contract is the binding element of obligation. This is the "official" morality of the American government and constitution.

Stage 6: The universal-ethical-principle orientation.   Right is defined by the decision of conscience in accord with self-chosen *ethical principles* appealing to logical comprehensiveness, universality, and consistency. These principles are abstract and ethical (the Golden Rule, the categorical imperative); they are not concrete moral rules like the Ten Commandments. At heart, these are universal principles of *justice*, of the *reciprocity* and *equality* of human *rights*, and of respect for the dignity of human beings as *individual persons*.

SOURCE: Kohlberg, L. (1973). The claim to moral adequacy of a highest stage of moral judgment. *Journal of Philosophy, 70,* 631–632.

The moral stages of Kohlberg are important considerations when it comes to curriculum development. Schools can help children move from one moral stage to a higher moral stage by engaging them in moral discussions. The important conditions for these discussions appear to be

1. Exposure to the next higher stage of reasoning
2. Exposure to situations posing problems and contradictions for the child's current moral structure, leading to dissatisfaction with his current level
3. An atmosphere of interchange and dialogue combining the first two conditions, in which conflicting moral views are compared in an open manner (Hass, 1983, p. 173)

Therefore, moral development can be accomplished through indoctrination, values clarification, and Kohlberg's cognitive-developmental approach. The teacher must decide which technique or combination of techniques is appropriate for his or her students' age and maturity level as well as for the content being taught.

Psychological Development

WATSON'S PRINCIPLES OF CHILD DEVELOPMENT

Goodwin Watson (1961) wrote psychological propositions about what we really know today concerning children and learning. He wrote that if educators use his fifty propositions, they will be on solid psychological ground (p. 2). The authors have used these fifty propositions on many occasions and have found them to be sound educationally. Two of Watson's (1961) propositions that have curricular implications follow:

Children (and adults even more) tend to select groups, reading matter, TV shows, and other influences which agree with their own opinions; they break off contact with contradictory views.

   Parents want children taught what they themselves value and believe. One of the basic educational problems is to preserve minds from being closed in—surrounded by like-minded associates, like-minded commentators, and like-minded publications. (p. 9, emphasis added)

What is learned is most likely to be available for use if it is learned in a situation much like that in which it is to be used and immediately preceding the time when it is needed. Learning in childhood, then forgetting, and then relearning when need arises is not an efficient procedure.

It was once thought that childhood was the golden age for learning. We now know that adults of forty can learn better than youths of fourteen and much better than seven-year-olds. The best time to learn is when the learning can be useful. Motivation is then strongest and forgetting less of a problem. Much that is now taught children might be more effective if taught to responsible adults. (p. 10, emphasis added)

Knowledge of these propositions may help curriculum planners to avoid training children with closed minds or teaching curriculum material that will be soon forgotten. The last proposition seems to be saying that we need to use a curriculum that leans toward teaching children self-direction in terms of how to learn rather than to give them continuous layers of subject matter.

As we plan the curriculum, we need to keep in mind the amount of attention the individual child receives in the classroom. The famous anthropologist Ashley Montagu (1983) wrote "that the most important of all basic psychological needs is the need for love" (p. 122). Montagu felt that we treat children unequally in our classrooms. Simply because children are at the same chronological age is no sign that they are at the same developmental level as well. Montagu (1983) summed up the problem very well: "The equal treatment of unequals is the most unequal way of dealing with human beings ever devised" (p. 122). The fact is that the amount of love given through special attention is diminished every time we add an additional child to a classroom.

NEED FOR
LOVE

EQUAL
TREATMENT
OF UN-
EQUALS?

Many scientists have written about the developmental needs of children. Two others besides Piaget and Kohlberg are Robert J. Havighurst and Erik H. Erikson, who are also human development theorists. All four men

hold that the development stages they describe have a fixed order, and that each person passes through these stages in this order. Successful achievement of each stage is necessary if the individual is to proceed with vigor and confidence to the next stage. There is a "teachable moment" or time of special sensitivity for each task or stage. (Hass, 1983, p. 118)

The curriculum, then, needs to be planned and organized with these developmental stages in mind. Although readiness for learning is difficult to determine, every effort needs to be made to individualize the learning process more closely.

How Do Parents Influence Their Child's Perception of the Curriculum?

Parents have great indirect influence on their child's perception of the curriculum. Many times, teachers strive to create an interest in a subject during the day only to have children exposed to negative influences by their parents toward that same subject, or toward school in general, at home that evening. Most experienced teachers often wonder why parents and teachers cannot work together to maximize learning for children. The fact is that some parents and teachers do work together and the child is the beneficiary.

PARENTS' DI-
RECT AND
INDIRECT IN-
FLUENCE

There are several areas where parents directly or subtly influence their child's perception of the curriculum. The socioeconomic circumstances of the parents and children are no doubt one of the largest factors influencing attitudes toward schooling. (See Chapter 4.) We all know of children who were brought up in poor neighborhoods, responded well to schooling, and made great successes of their lives. At the same time, we know of wealthy people who were not supportive of education and neglected their child's educational development. In both cases, these circumstances tend to be exceptions rather than common practice. Aside from the socioeconomic considerations, here are some areas in which we think parents have a big influence on their child's perception of the curriculum.

PARENTAL
EXPECTA-
TIONS

The Expectations That Parents Have

Parents who want their children to be successful work with them and help them to establish goals for themselves. A good model of parent involvement in the area of goal setting is the way in which some parents work with their children and sacrifice with them so that they can qualify for the Olympics. Many if not most of the Olympic athletes give much of the credit for their success to their parents. And most of the children who are successful in school have parents who support them and have reasonable expectations. Children are very disappointed when their parents do not hold very high expectations for them.

As a teacher, you can possibly work with your students' parents and help them to dream along with their children to set some higher goals. Some parents have not been exposed to enough of the world, through either their educational or their life experiences, to know what is really possible. As a teacher, you can open the eyes of both students and parents to a whole new world of possibilities.

Some parents have unrealistic expectations for their child. Often, these parents have been very successful and do not understand why their child is having trouble in school. If the child has a learning disability, teachers need to explain to the parents what the child's disability is and how, with a proper curricular program, he or she can become a school achiever. Some children may be emotionally or psychologically disturbed and may need special attention.

The Friends and Relatives of Parents

IMPACT OF
SIGNIFICANT
OTHERS

Friends and relatives of parents also have an influence on the parents and a direct and an indirect influence on the children. One of the authors received his value for a higher education from close family friends. Because his parents had not gone to college, they did not see the value of a college

Parental attitudes strongly influence a child's school experience.

(Photo used by permission of the Indianapolis Public Schools.)

education, as did these close family friends. Often, such relatives or friends are as great an influence on a child as the parents.

As teachers, we need to be aware of these facts and attempt to tie them into our class discussions. Using examples in our classes of how relatives and friends have helped us understand life better is a method of reinforcing values that can enhance children's perception of the curriculum. Just as parents have friends who are positive influences, some may be negative as well. If, as teachers, we become aware of such influences on children, we can attempt to focus the children away from these influences and toward more positive thinking.

The Degree of Television Monitoring That Parents Do

As we all know, children tend to watch television for long periods, sometimes for as much time as they are in school. Parents who value their children's education will regulate the amount of TV they watch. Television, like all media, has both good and bad offerings. Parents who care only that their child is quiet and not bothering them are often delighted when their child is preoccupied with TV, no matter what the quality of the program.

TELEVISION
MONITORING

Teachers can help by making parents aware of the problems that can occur when they allow their children to watch unmonitored TV. When grades are low, the teacher should question parents about their child's TV-watching habits. Many educational shows can be assigned to students so that they have a definite purpose in watching TV. Programs that are assigned as part of a class can be discussed the next day. Television has the potential to enhance a child's education if both parents and teachers can give proper direction to children.

Broadening a Child's Horizons

A child's perspective can be widened in several ways, and not all of them are expensive. In the area of reading and books, a child need not have all of these resources in the home, as public libraries, college libraries, and private sources such as relatives and friends may be easily accessible. Parents who take their children to public libraries and encourage their reading and research activities do much toward promoting their children's education. Of course, a home where there is a library or in which the parents do a lot of reading and sharing is a true bonus.

COMMUNITY RESOURCES

Another way to get children to think is to take them on trips. In large metropolitan areas, there are generally museums, zoos, government buildings, and factories, all of which invite a family visit. Many schools organize field trips to these places, but family excursions to reinforce previous visits represent excellent use of family time and money. Some children are privileged to travel extensively all over the world before they enter college, but many never venture out of their own neighborhood or village. Family trips to different locations of interest provide children with a wonderful opportunity to broaden their horizons.

READING AND TRAVEL

These two areas, reading and travel, are the raw materials from which children can build their dreams for the future. As a teacher, you can encourage both of these activities. In your talks with parents, recommend both books and trips to them. In your classes, have students present book reports and travel reports to the whole class. The world of experience can be tied to the academic world and vice versa through the involvement of your students' parents.

These, then, are a few ways in which parents can and do influence their child's perception of the curriculum. Negative-thinking parents can become positive influences if they are involved as partners with the teacher in the education of their child. Even parents with a positive attitude toward ed-

Community resources can broaden and enrich the school curriculum.

(Photo used by permission of the Indianapolis Children's Museum.)

ucation and toward the curriculum need some assistance to maximize what they can do for their child.

What Should Beginning Teachers Know About Learning Disabilities?

Most of the curriculum talk deals with children who can function in a "normal" classroom. Some children, no matter how much we would like them to function normally, are not capable for several reasons. Teachers are in a position to identify these special children and to give them the type of instruction that will help them learn.

Some History on the Problem of Learning Disabilities

SAMUEL OR-
TON

In 1937, Samuel Torrey Orton brought attention to the subject of the disorder of language development in children. Orton noted in his research that there is a certain location in the brain that affects reading ability, and it is the same site that, when damaged, causes adults to lose all aspects of reading skill (Geschwind, 1982, p. 15). Through the careful work of Dr. Orton, the details of what is a dyslexic child unfolded. There is an entrenched ignorance among some educators who label these children lazy or **hyperactive** or as kids who just will not try, when the root cause is a brain alteration in most cases.

DYSLEXIA

There are learning disabilities other than **dyslexia**, though it is the most common disorder; therefore, attention must be paid to other areas as well. Research continues, and more is certain to be learned on this topic in the near future. Two sources of further information on learning disabilities are the Association for Children with Learning Disabilities, 4156 Library Road, Pittsburgh, Pennsylvania 15234, and the Orton Dyslexia Society, 724 York Road, Baltimore, Maryland 21204.

Definition of a Learning Disability

ATTENTION
DEFICIT DIS-
ORDER

Under federal and state legislation, the child with a learning disability is referred to as having an **attention deficit disorder** (ADD). ADD children have one or more learning disabilities, many are hyperactive and/or distractible, and many develop emotional, social, and family problems. These ADD children are not mentally retarded, as they have either average or above-average intelligence. It is important to remember that in these children, if they are emotionally disturbed, the disturbance is caused by the academic difficulty they are having and not by some other family problem.

OTHER
LEARNING
DISORDERS

Many labels have been used to describe the difficulties of ADD children:

- *Dyslexia:* Reading difficulties
- *Dysgraphia:* Writing problems
- *Dyscalculia:* Math difficulty

- *Specific learning disabilities* or *perceptually impaired* or *neurologically impaired:* Perceptual, integrative, sequencing, memory, motor, or language disabilities

The Kinds of People Who Have Learning Disabilities

FAMOUS PEO-
PLE AS
LEARNING
DISABLED

All kinds of people from all economic and social levels have learning disabilities. Some people have been able to overcome their problems and lead very productive lives. Thomas Edison, Woodrow Wilson, Albert Einstein, and Nelson Rockefeller are examples of exceptionally successful individuals who overcame a learning disability.

RESULTING
FRUSTRA-
TION AND
FAILURE

More often, these children lead lives of frustration and failure. Because of their inability to read, write, and calculate properly, these children tend to be underemployed or unemployed as adults. Surveys of juvenile delinquents have shown that more than half these young people may be learning disabled. Our society depends so much on the ability to read and write that when an eighteen-year-old cannot fill out a job application, he or she is in deep trouble; thus, they may see few options open to them other than crime (Bever, 1980, p. 56). Although some people with a learning disability have become tremendously successful, there are far more who lead less fulfilling lives.

How to Diagnose Learning Disability

Because learning disabilities are of many types, and each learning-disabled child is unique, it is difficult to spot this type of individual; however, if a child has a cluster of the following symptoms and they do not disappear as he or she gets older, you may suspect a learning disability:

DIAGNOSIS

- Short attention span (restless, easily distracted)
- Reverses letters and numbers (sees "b" for "d," "6" for "9")
- Reads poorly, if at all (below age and grade level)
- Often confused about directions and time (right–left, up–down, yesterday–tomorrow)
- Personal disorganization (can't follow simple schedules)
- Impulsive and inappropriate behavior (poor judgment in social situation, talks and acts before thinking)
- Poor coordination (clumsy, has trouble using pencil, scissors, crayons)
- Inconsistent performance (can't remember today what was learned yesterday)
- Fails written tests but scores high on oral exams (or vice versa)
- Speech problems (immature speech development, has trouble expressing ideas) (Bever, 1980, p. 56)

TEAM AP-
PROACH

Once the child is recognized as possibly a learning-disabled person, school corporations, under new federal regulations, should provide a diagnostic team. The team approach ideally involves a learning-disabilities teacher, who gives a full battery of tests to determine if the child has learning disabilities and, if so, the types of disabilities; a psychologist, who assesses the child's level of intellectual functioning; a social worker or nurse, who meets with the family to learn more about the child's development, his or her behavior when not in school, and the family status; a speech therapist, who evaluates the child for speech, language, or hearing difficulties; and a physician, who does a complete physical examination. It is very important that the diagnosis be multidisciplinary, as most learning-disabled children have more than one problem area.

How to Treat a Learning-Disabled Child

MULTISEN-
SORY AP-
PROACH

After diagnosis, these children need to be placed in a classroom with teachers trained in learning disabilities. The style of teaching in most regular classrooms involves the use of one or two senses, but these children need a multisensory approach. For example, when a learning-disabled child is told something by the teacher, that child should be shown the same thing on the chalkboard and through the use of manipulative materials. In this way, the child is reached by auditory, visual, tactile, and kinesthetic means. Specifically, when outlining a paragraph, the student may have on her or his desk some small strips of paper on which to write the key thoughts and the supporting details of an idea. The outline is further enhanced by a strand of yarn laid across the paper to symbolize the concept of a common theme.

Percentage of Our Population with a Learning Disability

EXTENT OF
THE PROB-
LEM

Estimates vary about how many children are actually learning-disabled, but the federal government estimates that up to 3% of the total population have severe learning disabilities. One major, federally funded research project found that 16% of all schoolchildren have learning disabilities requiring special teaching methods. Until we can more accurately identify these children, it will be very difficult to arrive at the correct total number of individual cases.

How Does One Evaluate the Curriculum?

The curriculum needs to be evaluated, and changes or adjustments need to be made on a regular basis. Just as any rational person evaluates her or his own behavior, a school needs to evaluate its own curriculum. The curriculum is composed of many facets, some of which are difficult to measure, but schools must make the best effort possible to determine what successes and what failures their programs are having with their students.

Evaluation from Objectives

Probably the most used and most logical type of curriculum evaluation is one that is based on educational objectives written for the curriculum before instruction actually begins. According to Ralph Tyler, in *Basic Principles of Curriculum and Instruction* (1949), "The process of evaluation is essentially the process of determining to what extent the educational objectives are actually being realized by the program of curriculum and instruction" (p. 106). Tyler wrote that two important aspects of evaluation need to be examined. First, if we are looking for changes in behavior of individuals after they have been exposed to the curriculum, then we are looking not only for changes that occur immediately after a particular block of instruction but for long-term effects as well. Tyler also stated how important it is to know a student's status at the beginning of instruction so that changes resulting from instruction can be noted at the conclusion. To assess the degree of permanence of learning, the student needs to be evaluated at some time in the future. Some schools evaluate their students yearly as they move through school, and often use follow-up studies to check on their graduates.

PRETEST TO
MEASURE
CHANGES IN
BEHAVIOR

Use of this objectives-based curriculum model puts emphasis on the proper statement of the objectives at the outset. The evaluation of the curriculum tells one how well the objectives have met the original plan and suggests modifications. One of the problems with this evaluative approach is that the test influences the objectives rather than the other way around. The pressure that college entrance examinations place on students to do well has caused and is causing adjustments in the objectives being taught. The real problem is that these new objectives, shaped by the testing services, often do not match the real needs of the students.

IMPORTANCE
OF OBJEC-
TIVES

Evaluation Without Prespecified Objectives

A more progressive way of looking at the learning process involves getting the learner, with the assistance of the teacher, to come up with his or her own objectives. If teachers use a format like this for teaching, with no prespecified objectives, the evaluation must be handled differently from that used for teaching from prespecified objectives. Some school subjects lend themselves better to this type of evaluative format.

DANGER
ZONE

Teaching students about such controversial issues as peace and war, sex education, and race relations involves discussions of differing values and judgments. Teachers teaching these areas in the curriculum would be defeating their own purpose if they used prespecified objectives and expected specific outcomes. The expressive arts and the humanities lend themselves to the kinds of objectives that develop as the course moves along. The best evaluation of this type of curriculum seems to be an ongoing monitoring of the class or the project, with a constant review of the aims so that changes can be recommended to better the curriculum. Certainly, devising specific test questions to get at certain cognitive learning would not satisfy the needs of such a curriculum. Interviews with students, evaluation of specific projects completed, and other less formal methods of evaluation would work best.

Evaluation of a Curriculum Experiment

There are many evaluative designs that schools can use, but the true experimental design should be used whenever possible. The **experimental design** is generally used to measure the results of a curriculum innovation, and it is relatively free from error. Doll (1978) described how the experimental design works:

> The pupils involved in the experiment and the pupils in a control group are randomized—or randomly divided—and the teachers are selected for their similarities according to established criteria. Randomization is meant to decrease error, but it is notably difficult to achieve. After randomization, the "experimental pupils" are given the special curriculum treatment prescribed in the terms of the project while the control group receives no special treatment, continuing with the customary subject matter content and educational practices. Then, evaluation of specific learning outcomes and other outcomes is conducted for both experimental and control groups by using the same evaluation strategies and instruments for both groups. Whenever the true experimental method can be utilized, it should be selected because of its relative freedom from error and because of the confidence evaluators usually place in it. (pp. 452–453)

The experimental technique would be a good test of innovations such as new curricula in math, science, social studies, and other specific areas. The control groups would be those classes not involved in the experiment.

Standards of Achievement

When certain tests are used to evaluate individuals, the logical question is: Against what standards are they being measured? ***Norm-referenced testing*** is testing that measures a student against standards of achievement arrived at by tests that have established national, state, or local norms. When schools want to compare their students' achievements with the achievements of students in other schools in the nation, the state, or locally they use norm-referenced tests. Scores then are assigned to students on a *relative standard*, meaning that the scores are relative to the national, state, or local norms that have been established.

Another standard is the *absolute standard*, an example of which is the criterion specified by the learning objectives: "***Criterion-referenced testing*** is the measure of how well each student attains the required level of comprehension and competence specified for each objective pursued" (Kemp, 1977, p. 93). It is important to keep in mind that with criterion-referenced testing the degree of achievement is independent of the performance of other students. Students who are measured in this way, against an absolute standard, must reach a satisfactory level of performance before they can go on to the next level of learning. The terms *criterion-referenced instruction* and *competency-based instruction* are used interchangeably. In this form of evaluation, the teachers and the schools must identify those competencies that are most desired, as well as the specific criteria for achieving them.

MASTERY LEARNING

Mastery learning is another term used in connection with criterion-referenced instruction. When students meet criteria set for accomplishing objectives, they are said to have accomplished mastery learning. There is a concern that mastery learning places too much emphasis on minimum accomplishment. One method of getting around the "minimum" problem is to assign a grade of C or B to the minimum accomplishment and leave the A grade for those who achieve more than the minimum. An example follows:

> *Objective:* After taking biology and studying an ecology unit, the student will be able to answer correctly 8 out of 11 of the following items.

The questions are taken from Bloom's taxonomy at the application level:

> After the number on the answer sheet corresponding to that preceding each of the following paired items, blacken space
>
> **A**—if increase in the first of the things referred to is usually accompanied by increase in the second
> **B**—if increase in the first of the things referred to is usually accompanied by decrease in the second
> **C**—if increase in the first of the things referred to has no appreciable effect on the second

> 1. Number of lemmings in an Arctic habitat
>   Number of caribou in the same habitat
> 2. Number of lichens in an Arctic habitat
>   Number of caribou in the same habitat
> 3. Amount of carbonates dissolved in the water of a river
>   Number of clams in the river
> 4. Temperature of the environment of a mammal
>   Body temperature of the mammal
> 5. Compactness of the soil of a given area
>   Amount of water absorption by the soil after a heavy rain
> 6. Frequency of fire in a given coniferous forest
>   Number of aspen trees in the forest
> 7. Crop yield per acre of farmland cultivated in Illinois
>   Amount of soil nutrients per acre of farmland
> 8. The altitude of the environment of an animal
>   Extent to which the circulating red blood cells of the animal undergo mitosis
> 9. Extent of tree planting activity on forest land in the United States
>   Degree of water absorption by the soil per unit of area of the same land
> 10. Amount of vegetation per square yard of soil
>   Amount of available nitrate salts in the same area of soil
> 11. Amount of humus accumulated in sand during dune succession
>   Abundance of animal life in the area (p. 134)

A student who answers 8 of the items would receive a grade of C; 9 items, a B; and 10 or 11 items, an A. This is an example of mastery learning.

RELATIVE VS. ABSOLUTE STANDARDS   Standards of achievement are based on **relative standards** and **absolute standards**. When schools or teachers use either type of standard, the results will give them feedback about how successful their program or teaching has been. Analysis of the test results will lead them to either change their curriculum or be satisfied with what they have now.

DIFFICULTIES IN EVALUATION   Evaluation of the curriculum is a difficult process because it must take into consideration all aspects of the curriculum. Testing objectives for which the criteria are spelled out works very well for math or science, but for art and the humanities, another type of evaluation is needed. If you are evaluating objectives, they should be written with certain students in mind, not to comply with an outside test. The fact is that outside tests, such as the Scholastic Aptitude Test, often dictate the curriculum. The purpose of an evaluation of the curriculum is to check out changes in the behavior of students that result from instruction. This is the reason that objectives are sometimes referred to as **behavioral objectives**.

Summary

The curriculum is difficult to define and even experts do not agree on any one definition. Historically, many significant contributions have been made to curriculum development that are still used today. Some goals of curriculum development have been presented for review.

In considering what should be included in the curriculum, many groups have input—parents, school boards, state school officials, members of the U.S. Congress—but often fail to consider the special needs of one group: the students. Psychological factors that should be considered are the students' cognitive and moral development and their need for love and attention. Organizing the curriculum into elementary schools, middle or junior high schools, and high schools allows each school to meet the age needs of its students. The concepts of nongraded classes and team teaching give greater emphasis to the special needs of each child. Positive parental attitudes regarding the school curriculum have a very favorable influence on the child's perception of the curriculum. The learning-disabled deserve special attention in curriculum planning, and recent studies are discovering better ways to meet the needs of this group.

Teachers should be aware of the hidden curriculum in their classrooms. Each student's self-concept, the social structure of the school, the values of the staff toward education, and teacher–student interactions are parts of the hidden curriculum. The curriculum must become more global in outlook, and must continue to include ethnic studies. Goodlad's extensive study offers several concerns that schools' curriculum plans should address. All aspects of the curriculum must be considered in its evaluation.

Glossary Terms

Flexible Schedules, 288
Assimilation, 289
Accommodation, 289
Self-actualization, 292
Taxonomy, 293
Teachable Moment, 295
Transmissive Purpose, 298
Adaptive Purpose, 298
Developmental Purpose, 298
Self-concept, 301
School Social Structure, 302
Interaction Analysis, 304
Vertical Movement, 306
Horizontal Movement, 306
Middle School, 307
Humanistic, 308
Nongraded Schools, 310
Team Teaching, 311
Hierarchy of Needs, 311
Open Organizational Climate, 312
Sensorimotor Period, 314

Preoperational Period, 314
Concrete-Operational Period, 314
Formal-Operational Period, 314
Readiness, 316
Maturation, 316
Moral Stages, 321
Hyperactive, 328
Dyslexia, 328
Attention Deficit Disorder, 328
Dysgraphia, 328
Dyscalculia, 328
Specific Learning Disabilities, 329
Perceptually Impaired, 329
Neurologically Impaired, 329
Experimental Design, 332
Norm-Referenced Testing, 332
Criterion-Referenced Testing, 332
Relative Standards, 334
Absolute Standards, 334
Behavioral Objectives, 334

Questions

1. After reading the three definitions of curriculum, write your own composite definition.

2. How did the three significant publications appearing after 1960 differ from the top ten that came before 1960? What notable events may have caused this difference?

3. In the 1980s, should there be ten, fifteen, or twenty cardinal principles instead of the original seven? If so, what would your nominations be?

4. In what direction did John Dewey influence the curriculum? Give an example.

5. Why have we not changed our curriculum to conform to the ideas and teachings of A. S. Neill and Alvin Toffler?

6. What other groups and people influence the curriculum? Is all of this influence on the curriculum best for the educational growth of our children?

7. What are some of the psychological factors that affect how we build a curriculum?

8. Do you agree with Ashley Montagu that "The equal treatment of unequals is the most unequal way of dealing with human beings ever devised"? Why?

9. Why is the term *flexibility* not very descriptive of modern-day high schools?

10. What is the difference between dyslexia and dysgraphia?

11. What kinds of people have learning disabilities?

12. Describe the hidden curriculum. How can you as a teacher maximize learning by being aware of the hidden curriculum?

13. Distinguish the differences between evaluation from objectives and evaluation without prespecified objectives.

14. What is mastery learning? How does one overcome the "minimum accomplishment" problem?

15. Why is a teacher said to play God when he or she evaluates an absolute standard?

Annotated Bibliography

1. Bloom, B. S., Englehart, M. D., Furst, E. J., Hill, W. H., & Krathwohl, D. R. (1956). *Taxonomy of educational objectives: Cognitive domain*. New York: Longman.

    In this system of classification of thought processes, rote memory is on the lower end and synthesis is on the upper end of the scale used to categorize educational objectives such as the cognitive domain of learning.

2. Bobbitt, F. (1924). *How to make a curriculum*. New York: Houghton Mifflin.

    This classic explanation of the curriculum development process is a basic handbook for revising the school curriculum.

3. Dewey, J. (1916). *Democracy and education*. New York: Free Press.

    In his early publication on the relationship between democracy as a political system and our methods of education, Dewey points out that schools must be run as democratically as possible so that students learn the democratic processes they will need to participate in our democratic form of government.

4. Havighurst, R. J. (1948). *Developmental tanks and education*. New York: Longmans Green.

    This work describes the primary tasks that must be accomplished at each stage of an individual's development, for example, successful relationships with members of the opposite sex during late adolescence.

5. Kilpatrick, W. H. (1925). *Foundations of method*. New York: Macmillan.

    This text explains a progressive teaching method in which students learn by doing—by working on an assigned real-life problem or project.

6. Maslow, A. H. (1954). *Motivation and personality*. New York: Harper and Row.

    In this work, Maslow describes the hierarchy of needs (from physical needs at the bottom of the scale to self-actualization at the top) that all individuals experience during their lives. These needs provide the motivation for action, and one cannot advance to a higher-level need until the previous needs are satisfied.

7. Piaget, J. (1936/1952). *The origins of intelligence in children*. New York: International University Press.

Piaget proposes six stages in the development of an individual's thought processes from sensorimotor to preoperational to concrete-operational to formal-operational.

8. Tyler, R. W. (1949). *Basic principles of curriculum and instruction.* Chicago: University of Chicago Press.

Through this classic text on curriculum theory, Ralph Tyler, the "father" of the modern curriculum movement, has influenced many modern authors in this field. It was one of the earliest texts to list and explain the major steps in the curriculum development process.

- List the findings, recommendations, and criticisms of *A Nation at Risk*

- Compare and contrast the first and second waves of reform in the 1980s and 1990s

- Assess the changes in our schools as a result of *A Nation at Risk*

- Compare and contrast the following reform proposals: John Goodlad's *A Place Called School*, Mortimer Adler's *The Paideia Proposal*, Ernest Boyer's *High School: A Report on Secondary Education in America*, and the National Science Board's *Educating Americans for the 21st Century*

- Compare and contrast the reform proposals made by the state governors, William Bennett, and Ted Sizer

- Define the effective schools movement and summarize the criteria, criticisms, and implications of this movement

- Understand the uses, problems, and issues of computers and technology in schools today

CHAPTER *11*

Waves of Reform, Effective Schools, and Technology in Education

Introduction

PERIOD OF
FERMENT

The 1980s was a period of ferment and reform in American public education. Not since the wave of educational reforms that followed *Sputnik* in the late 1950s and early 1960s has there been so much pressure for change in education in the United States.

Although some forces for the reform of education appeared in the very early 1980s, the main catalyst for reform was ***A Nation at Risk:*** *The Imperatives for Educational Reform*, a report of the National Commission for Excellence in Education issued in 1983. This commission was appointed by Terrel Bell to study the causes of and solutions to problems in education that have led our country to be less productive and less competitive in international trade. Although this commission included only one public school classroom teacher on its roster of members, the report of these higher

EDUCATION
A KEY ISSUE

education, scientific, and business leaders had an enormous effect on education in the United States. Education became a key issue in national, state, and local political campaigns, Tennessee and North Carolina radically modified their educational systems with career ladder programs, and many states upgraded requirements for graduation and incorporated other educational reforms. The middle to late 1980s was an exciting time for educators because education had seldom been the center of such widespread political ferment in the United States.

REFORMS
AND TRENDS

In this chapter these reforms and trends are examined and analyzed. This analysis includes the first wave of reforms beginning in 1983, the second wave of reforms in the late 1980s, the effective schools movement, and technology in education.

The First Wave of Reforms

Introduction

WAVES AND
REFORMS

In the first section, the findings and recommendations of *A Nation at Risk* are examined and compared with those of other first-wave reform proposals by Ernest Boyer, John Goodlad, Mortimer Adler, and the National Science Board.

A Nation at Risk

FINDINGS OF A NATION AT RISK

*A NATION AT
RISK*

A Nation at Risk began with this assessment of education in the United States:

> If an unfriendly foreign power had attempted to impose on America the mediocre educational performance that exists today, we might well have viewed it as an act of war. As it stands, we have allowed this to happen to ourselves. We have even squandered the gains in student achievement made in the wake of the *Sputnik* challenge. Moreover, we have dismantled the essential support

systems which helped make those gains possible. We have, in effect, been committing an act of unthinking, unilateral education disarmament. (National Commission on Excellence in Education, 1983, p. 5)

INDICATORS
OF RISK

The commission cited many indicators that American public education was "at risk." Studies of student achievement show that American students are low achievers compared with other industrialized nations. Furthermore, 23 million Americans, including 13% of all seventeen-year-olds, are **functionally illiterate.** High school students score lower, on average, on standardized achievement tests than during the *Sputnik* era. Also, the scores on the **Scholastic Aptitude Test (SAT)** declined steadily from 1963 to 1980. In addition, many high school students lack the higher-order thinking skills essential in the modern world.

FINDINGS
CONTENT

What was wrong with American public schools that allowed them to fall so low? The findings of the commission's report were divided into four areas: content, expectations, time, and teaching. With respect to content, the conclusion was that our schools have too many electives, the schools allow students too much choice in electives as opposed to required courses, and too few students elect to take the more difficult courses in math, science, and foreign language (National Commission on Excellence in Education, 1983, pp. 18–19). With respect to content the commission concludes:

> Secondary school curricula have been homogenized, diluted, and diffused to the point that they no longer have a central purpose. In effect, we have a cafeteria-style curriculum in which the appetizers and desserts can easily be mistaken for the main courses. (National Commission on Excellence in Education, 1983, p. 18).

LOWERED EX-
PECTATIONS

In regard to the second area, expectations, the commission found evidence of a lowering of academic expectations and standards. The amount of homework assigned was declining; **minimum competency** was becoming the maximum in many schools; and fewer difficult courses were required of all students, especially in science and math. In addition, high school graduation requirements were low and included too many electives, and college entrance requirements were low at some schools that are required to admit any high school graduate. Furthermore, textbooks were watered down; and the percentage of school revenue spent on textbooks and other educational materials had decreased.

TIME

TEACHING

The findings regarding time and teaching were especially critical of education in the United States. Comparison of our students with those in foreign countries revealed that American students spend fewer hours per day and fewer days per year in school and that much of this time is wasted on nonacademic activities or classroom discipline. The commission also criticized the lack of time spent on mastering study skills necessary for future learning. The findings concerning teaching included the following: too few academically able students are attracted to teaching, teacher preparation programs empahsize methods over subject-area content, teachers'

One fear of *A Nation at Risk* was that children might lose their desire for learning.

(Photo used by permission of the Indiana State Teachers Association.)

salaries are too low compared with other professions, and severe teacher shortages exist in the areas of math and science.

RECOMMENDATIONS OF A NATION AT RISK

RECOMMEN-
DATIONS

From these findings the *A Nation at Risk* commission made specific recommendations in the same four areas: content, expectations, time, and teaching. For content, the commission recommended strengthening high school graduation requirements by mandating four years of English and three years each of mathematics, science, and social studies as well as one

CONTENT—
NEW BASICS

semester of computer science; these were to be called the **"five new basics."** In addition, for students going on to college the commission recommended two years of a foreign language. Concerning standards and expectations,

HIGHER
STANDARDS

the commission suggested improving textbooks (and providing funds for development of textbooks in thin-market areas, such as gifted and talented programs); administering standardized achievement tests frequently, especially at points of transition from one level of schooling to another; raising college admission requirements; and preventing grade inflation by ensuring that grades given are indicators of academic achievement.

MORE TIME
ON TASK

In the area of time, the report emphasized a longer seven-hour school day, a longer 200- to 220-day school year, and more effective use of time during the school day through better classroom management and discipline procedures, better student attendance, and reduction of the administrative paperwork burden on teachers. Lastly, the commission recommended rais-

TEACHING
CAREER LAD-
DERS

ing teachers' salaries, developing career ladder programs for teachers, adopting an eleven-month contract for teachers to encourage curriculum revision and professional development, raising the academic standards for teacher candidates, and using monetary incentives in the form of grants and loans to relieve the current shortages of science and mathematics teachers. A final category of recommendations encouraged leadership and fiscal support for upgrading the nation's public schools.

CRITICISM OF A NATION AT RISK

A Nation at Risk encountered several criticisms after its release in 1983. Both vocational education and elementary education had been omitted from

CRITICISMS
OF *A NATION
AT RISK*

the report. The commission seemed to be indicating that most, if not all, students should pursue an academic program and attend college after graduation from high school. A curriculum report of the National Association of Secondary School Principals (NASSP), on the other hand, suggests integration of academic and vocational skills. This NASSP report concludes,

> The reality in today's postindustrial information service society is that everyone needs to be prepared for employment and have at least minimal competency in the basic skills. Yet our educational system, in large part, continues to function as if students can be educated through mutually exclusive tracks. ("Making Common Cause," 1980, p. 1)

ACADEMIC
VS. VOCA-
TIONAL

Thus, the "either/or" idea of an academic versus a vocation education implied in *A Nation at Risk* seems to be outdated in the modern world. *A Nation at Risk* also seems to concentrate on the high school level, omitting emphasis on the essential basic skills developed at the elementary and junior high/middle school levels. Furthermore, the recommendations appear to emphasize **"quick-fix" solutions** that can be easily mandated or legislated, such as increased graduation requirements, longer school days, and a longer school year, rather than restructure of the schools and the way teachers work with each other. Other critics have cited the emphasis on cognitive skills rather than on affective or attitudinal dimensions in the *At Risk* report.

TOP DOWN
VS. BOTTOM
UP

Also, *At Risk* was issued from on high rather than from a "grass roots" effort at educational reform; it was prepared primarily by leaders in science, business, and universities, not by public school teachers. In fact, only one practicing public school teacher was a member of the commission. Experts caution that true educational reform can only occur as teacher's attitudes are modified and that this attitudinal change is unlikely unless teachers are involved from the outset in the reform movement. Despite these criticisms, *At Risk* continues to have an effect on our schools. Other selected reform reports are examined and compared with *At Risk* in the next section.

John Goodlad's A Place Called School

Goodlad's (1984) study of schooling in the United States was motivated by the lack of good, scientifically collected data on schools. Schooling in the United States is such a broad topic and our country is so diverse that securing a representative random sample for study is almost impossible. DIVERSE Instead, Goodlad and his associates obtained a sample containing maximum SAMPLES diversity and representativeness. They eventually selected thirteen communities in seven sections of the country. Thirty-eight schools were studied, each differing from the others in several significant characteristics, such as location, size, student population characteristics, and family income. Twenty trained data collectors were sent into each community, where they remained for a month and eventually collected data from 8,624 parents, 1,350 teachers, and 17,163 students. According to Goodlad, "No single study has made detailed observations of over 1,000 classrooms" (p. 18). Many of the questions asked were directed specifically toward the curriculum.

LACK OF IN-   The first concern of the study is related to the lack of intellectual devel-
TELLECTUAL opment in the schools. Goodlad defined intellectual development as the
DEVELOP- ability to think rationally; the ability to use, evaluate, and accumulate
MENT knowledge; and the desire for further learning. The data showed little evidence that the instruction given in schools goes much beyond mere acquisition of information or memorization of facts. Rarely did these researchers find students who were trying to understand implications or explore possible applications of the information presented. Basically, they saw students who were preoccupied with the knowledge level of Bloom's taxonomy.

Goodlad speculated that the reason children are learning at a lower cognitive level is that the precedent or model for most of the curriculum emerges from the dominant English-language arts and mathematics curric-
MATH SCI- ula. Our society sets a high value on mastery of English and mathematics,
ENCE MODEL so how these areas are taught tends to influence how the rest of the curriculum is taught. Social studies and the sciences are more often taught through lectures on dry, inert facts rather than through problem solving and visits to natural settings or state legislatures.

As a young man, one of the authors lived on a farm and experienced many natural learning opportunities to which most school-aged children growing up in the 1990s are not exposed. A few of these farm experiences included caring for and selling chickens and eggs; planting, caring for, and harvesting crops; caring for animals; maintaining machinery; and solving
MORE ACTIV- practical problems. These experiences were very useful and stimulating to
ITIES NEEDED a young person, so much so that he preferred being on the farm to being in the classroom. It appears that with modern technology such as computers,

video equipment, transportation, laboratory equipment, and outside resources, today's teachers could plan more activities and problem-solving experiences under the auspices of the school.

The second concern relates to schools' not helping the individual toward personal development. At the lower elementary level, teachers appear to teach with the idea that the topics they introduce will aid personal development, but subject matter rather than the person seems to dominate as the child reaches the upper elementary grades. Also, as students move to the higher grades, teachers tend to concentrate their goals on the tests they give instead of the personal development of the student. The "how" and "why" aspects of subject matter should be dealt with to help children with their personal development. As Kilpatrick recommended, we want to develop the "boy" and not the "corn" (Cremin, 1961, p. 218). Projects that cause children to think and to become actively involved with both mind and body would aid personal development. For example, children who devise and carry out their own plan for involving senior citizens in their education do a lot toward developing their own character. Children who observe the misuse of paper in their own classrooms and decide, with the help of their teacher, to save paper and encourage other classrooms to do the same learn a valuable lesson in conservation and in acting on their own beliefs.

A third concern pertains to the best use of leisure time. Most schools provide for student participation in baseball, basketball, soccer, football, and volleyball, but when they graduate, students find themselves ill prepared for individual sports, like golf, tennis, skiing, badminton, and racketball. The Goodlad study revealed that schools have not changed much over the years in that they neglect the physical skills needed to play individual sports. Is it possible that many schools' athletic programs influence, to a large degree, what is taught in physical education classes? No doubt, the encouragement and development of leisure-time activities are neglected.

A fourth concern is that schools neglect social development. Teamwork is fostered in physical education classes, but more often, the activities stress competition. Goodlad favors deliberate cultivation of the values and skills of constructive social interaction and group accomplishment.

A fifth concern is the lack of development of such **existential qualities** as hope, courage, and love of humankind. These qualities are generally fostered through literature in myths, fairy tales, novels, drama, and poetry. The study showed that the early years of schooling appear to be shockingly devoid of fairy tales. Fairy tales have the ability to symbolize, through the use of dragons and heros, the challenges, problems, and opportunities that life presents. In the lower tracks of English courses, children did not seem to be studying poverty, disease, violence, and prejudice in some of the good literature. Most English classes were repetitively preoccupied with the mechanics of usage.

A sixth concern is that the public is blaming the schools for not teaching

PERSONAL
DEVELOP-
MENT

USE OF LEI-
SURE TIME

SOCIAL DE-
VELOPMENT

EXISTENTIAL
QUALITIES

Goodlad says that students need to develop their individual skills through sports such as swimming.

(Photo by Bill Locker.)

exactly the things they seem to be preoccupied with teaching. The major criticism in the 1980s was that schools are not teaching the fundamentals, but according to Goodlad's study, fundamentals are emphasized, to the neglect of other areas of the curriculum. Could it be that neglect of the lively parts of the curriculum at the higher level of the cognitive domain is making schools, and schooling in general, dull and uninteresting, leading to disinterest in all parts of the curriculum? We all know that the fundamentals are important (these are generally known as the 3Rs), but maybe the most neglected fundamentals are literature, social studies, and science.

EMPHASIS ON FUNDAMENTALS

The complete study by John Goodlad and his associates is found in ***A Place Called School*** (1984), which contains some valuable current information on the state of schooling and education in the United States.

Mortimer Adler's Paideia Proposal

PAIDEIA PROPOSAL

In 1982, one year before *At Risk* was issued, Dr. Mortimer Adler published ***The Paideia Proposal*** in which he outlined an identical curriculum for every child, regardless of ability, from Grades 1 through 12. All vocational education and electives would be eliminated under his plan. Adler believes that despite their many individual differences, children are the same as far as their human nature is concerned. Therefore, schools should offer a **one-track system of education.** He sees the division of students into different tracks, such as college-bound and non–college-bound, or into liberal education versus vocational education as an elitist view of education. Instead, he prefers equal opportunity for all students, regardless of their intellectual ability. Adler makes an analogy between students of varying ability and

ONE-TRACK SYSTEM

The fundamentals of math are being practiced by these mathletes.

(Photo used by permission of the Metropolitan School District of Washington Township.)

sponges of different size; the students absorb different quantities of the same-quality education, just as the sponges soak up different amounts of the same liquid. Adler maintains that in present-day schools, the various-sized sponges, (or students of varying ability) absorb different types of liquid (education of varying quality) — the large sponges (brighter students) absorb cream; the medium-sized sponges (average students), regular milk; and the small sponges (slow students), skim milk or even dirty water (watered-down curricula). Adler believes that as a democracy, it is essential that we treat all students equally, and his two main objectives or goals include earning a good living and leading a good human life, both of which are promoted by a rigorous liberal arts and general education, not by vocational education. All students would take a one-semester introduction to careers in Grade 12; all other vocational education would come after high school. All electives and course choices would be eliminated under *The Paideia Proposal*, but all students would be required to take auxiliary subjects, such as physical education, care of the body, and manual arts (typing, cooking, sewing, wood- and metalworking, automobile driving, and repair of electrical household equipment).

The Paideia Proposal implies many criticisms of both current education and teacher-preparation programs. He believes that teachers are **facilitators of learning** and that students must do their own learning. Adler's plan involves the acquisition of fundamental knowledge through lectures and

VARIOUS-
SIZED
SPONGES

NO ELEC-
TIVES

TEACHERS AS
FACILITATORS

assignments, the development of intellectual skills through coaching by the teacher and practice by students, and the refinement of questioning and discussion skills through Socratic seminars. Thus, personal involvement of students in their own learning is a primary tenet of the Adler plan of education. The current preparation of teachers is also criticized by Adler who believes that teachers have not received quality education themselves and that working conditions, salaries, and other compensation are inferior compared with other professions. Adler believes that the main business of schools is teaching and learning, not keeping the peace, balancing budgets, enforcing laws, or promoting justice. Adler concludes that education and democracy mutually reinforce each other:

EDUCATION
ESSENTIAL
TO DEMOC-
RACY

> The two—**universal suffrage** and universal schooling—are inextricably bound together. The one without the other is perilous delusion. Suffrage without schooling produces mobocracy, not democracy—not rule of law, not constitutional government by the people as well as for them. . . . We are all sufferers from our continued failure to fulfill the educational obligations of a democracy. We are all victims of a school system that has only gone halfway along the road to realize the promises of democracy. (Adler, 1982, pp. 3–4, emphasis added)

Ernest Boyer's High School: A Report on Secondary Education in America

HIGH
SCHOOL RE-
PORT

TWELVE
PRIORITIES

In the same year that *A Nation at Risk* was published, the Carnegie Foundation for the Advancement of Teaching issued **High School: A Report on Secondary Education in America,** written by Ernest Boyer (1983). This report recommended twelve priorities in its agenda for action. The first was an emphasis on vision and clear goals for American public schools. The second was emphasis on the centrality of language and English proficiency in the curriculum. In the third recommendation Boyer spelled out the core curriculum for the first two years of high school in detail. This core curriculum would be required of all students and would include literature, U.S. history, Western civilization, non-Western civilization, science, mathematics, technology, two years of a foreign language, the arts, civics, health, and the world of work. This core curriculum is innovative because it requires that all students take a foreign language and world history (Western and non-Western) which are not required in all school districts now. The fourth suggestion involves the transition from work to learning: the last two years of high school are envisioned as a transition school in which the student can elect to take advanced classes in an academic subject and/or to explore career options. The fifth recommendation was a bold requirement for a new service requirement called the **"new Carnegie Unit."** This new unit would involve students in volunteer work in the community or at school.

FROM
SCHOOL TO
WORK

NEW CARNE-
GIE UNIT

"FIFTH-
YEAR" PRO-
GRAMS

In the sixth recommendation, Boyer outlined the Carnegie panel's program of teacher education, which emphasizes a **"fifth-year" teacher education program,** improved continuing education, a career ladder for teaching professionals, and competency tests for teachers. The seventh recommendation focuses on instruction and suggests a variety of reforms in teaching

Boyer recommends a new Carnegie Unit that would involve students in volunteer work in the community or the school.

(Photo used by permission of the Indianapolis Public Schools.)

TEACHING
AND TEXT-
BOOKS
COMPUTERS
AS TOOLS

styles and textbooks. Eighth is the establishment of ten technology resource centers in the country to demonstrate the latest in computer technology and to arrange seminars for teachers on up-to-date use of the computer as a teaching tool. Boyer and his panel of experts believe that the computer can be used as a tool to extend the teacher's reach, not to replace the teacher. Ninth, the report emphasized the need to be flexible to fit purpose;

PATTERNS
TO FIT PUR-
POSES

examples include flexible scheduling, schools-within-schools, and special arrangements for gifted and talented students as well as remedial programs for slower students. (Note that *The Paideia Proposal* suggested one track for all students.) The ninth recommendation also proposed establishment of a network of residential academies in science and mathematics across the country for gifted students in these academic areas.

ADMINISTRA-
TORS, TRAN-
SITIONS, AD-
VISORY
COUNCILS

In its last three recommendations, this report on the American high school suggests a program for preparing principals that includes administration internships (similar to student teachers); strengthening of the transitions between elementary, junior high/middle schools, and high schools; and establishment of parent–teacher–student advisory councils as well as a network of community/citizen coalitions for education to aggressively support public schools (Boyer, 1983, pp. 301–319).

DIFFERENCES
IN KIND AND
DEGREE

Boyer makes several other cogent general observations of American schools. He is concerned that high schools differ not simply in degree but in the kind of education they provide. He foresees that high schools in our nation will serve more and more minority students—students whom the

American high school has served least well in the past. He is troubled by the emphasis on "the system" instead of individual schools and the quality of the relationship between teachers and students (Boyer, 1983, pp. xii–xiii).

EVALUATION OF BOYER'S IDEAS

The authors of this textbook applaud Boyer's emphasis on technology, global education, and service to school and community as components of the high school program. Boyer cites the decline in SAT scores, but he balances this news by citing other tests that show that "in 1980 seventeen-year-olds were doing about as well in their total reading ability as they were ten years earlier" (Boyer, 1983, p. 26). He says that although the American public "wants it all," the high school should concentrate on four major goals: (1) communication and critical thinking; (2) knowledge about themselves, their human heritage, and their interdependent world; (3) preparation for work and further education; and (4) social and civic obligations (Boyer, 1983, pp. 66–67). Boyer criticizes schools offering a preponderance of practical courses to the majority of students while limiting enrollment in academic courses such as foreign languages, advanced science courses, and higher-level mathematics courses to a few students. He further states that "many school people seem more concerned about how long students stay in school than they are about what students should know when they depart" (Boyer, 1983, p. 83). This position is similar to the cafeteria of electives or smorgasbord criticism in *A Nation at Risk*. The authors of this textbook concur with Boyer's emphasis on basic English literacy skills and also his interdisciplinary emphasis in the core curriculum. In the opinion of the authors of this textbook, the splintering of knowledge caused by the lack of an interdisciplinary approach in today's schools is one of the major defects in our schools, preventing practical application of these principles and conceptual learning in many high school courses. We also support Boyer's criticisms of present vocational programs as either irrelevant or inadequate because they train students for the glamour occupations, such as computer programming, instead of the service-oriented jobs that are likely to proliferate in the future. The authors also support the criticisms of textbooks (Boyer, 1983, p. 142) and Boyer's suggestion for a five-year teacher preparation program grounded in the liberal arts and sciences (pp. 176–177).

National Science Board's Educating Americans for the 21st Century

Discussion of the National Science Board's report on science and mathematics education in the United States, ***Educating Americans for the 21st Century,*** can be divided into three sections: causes, remedies, and recommendations. The National Science Board cites the following causes of deficiencies in precollege science and technology education in the United States: (1) too little classroom time is spent on these subjects, (2) there are not enough good curricular materials to demonstrate practical applications of science and to motivate students, and (3) there has been a decline in the

CAUSES OF DEFICIENCIES

The National Science Board suggests requiring science and technology studies for all students daily.

(Photo used by permission of the Indiana Department of Education.)

number of qualified science teachers (National Science Board, 1982, p. 25). In regard to remedies, the report suggests that all students from kindergarten through Grade 11 should be required to study science and technology daily, that new curricular materials be developed, and that new initiatives be implemented in teacher-training programs in the United States (National Science Board, 1982, p. 25). The National Science Board states that although the emphasis in the reform movement after *Sputnik* was on understanding science concepts, the reform movement in the 1960s and 1970s stressed concrete experiences and practical applications (National Science Board, 1982, p. 28). The Science Board cautions that in the short run, a greater emphasis on science courses may exacerbate the shortage of science teachers.

> The critical shortage of teachers for mathematics and science in the schools will in the long run be alleviated by a curriculum which motivates and prepares students for science and technology-oriented careers. But in the short run, any intensification of mathematics and science education will make the shortage worse, while different emphases in curriculum content will widen the gap in teacher preparedness. (National Science Board, 1982, p. 28)

The National Science Board recommends **magnet schools** for students talented in science and mathematics as a possible solution to these problems. The group stresses that they are not a panacea, however; but they

MAGNET
SCHOOLS—A
PANACEA?

recommend that the federal government play a significant role in designing and implementing such magnet schools. They suggest using the land grant model to set up these experimental schools with close ties to universities and industry (National Science Board, 1982, pp. 220–222). *Educating Americans for the 21st Century* concludes:

> The class of the year 2001 was born this year, and as we look to the twenty-first century, we are struck by a remarkable spectacle: unless we initiate major changes today, we will perpetuate an education system designed for the covered wagon in the space age. Magnet schools offer a strategy of low-cost, high-visibility, incremental change that can transform American education. (National Science Board, 1982, p. 223)

COMPARED
TO *AT RISK*

It should be mentioned that both *A Nation at Risk* and Boyer's *High School* also note the shortage of mathematics and science teachers and suggest remedies, for example, loans to students who are preparing to teach and who are talented in mathematics and science.

CONCLU-
SIONS ON
FIRST WAVE

In summary, five first-wave reform proposals have been examined. *A Nation at Risk* issued findings and recommendations in five major areas: content, standards, time, teaching, and fiscal support. *The Paideia Proposal* of Mortimer Adler suggested a one-track academic and liberal education that omitted all electives and almost all vocational education and emphasized student–teacher interaction in academic coaching and Socratic seminars. Ernest Boyer's *High School* suggested requiring student service to the community or school, implementing five-year teacher education programs grounded in the liberal arts and sciences, placing a new emphasis on computer technology as a tool in the classroom, and improving vocational education as well as academic education. Although Adler abhors electives and vocational education in the K–12 curriculum, Boyer supports both if they are used correctly. In *A Place Called School* John Goodlad based his conclusions on research grounded in classroom observations of elementary schools. He emphasized academic knowledge, personal development, leisure time, social development, and existential qualities such as love of humankind. Finally, the National Science Board's report, *Educating Americans for the 21st Century*, focused on improvements in science and mathematics education, emphasizing magnet schools as a solution to these problems.

The Second Wave of Reforms

PREVIEW OF
REFORMS

The initial wave of reforms, including *A Nation at Risk, The Paideia Proposal, A Place Called School, High School,* and *Educating Americans for the 21st Century,* was followed by a second wave of reforms in reaction to the first wave. The first wave emphasized organizational and legislative reforms such as time-on-task, time spent in school, teacher qualifications, and so on. The second wave spotlighted the teaching act itself, with emphasis on collaboration among teachers and other reforms in working relationships. Opinions representing this second wave of reforms are now presented and include the differences between the first and second waves, the causes of the second wave, second-wave reforms in secondary schools, tensions resulting from the second wave, reasons for failure of the reforms, proposed reforms, and William Bennett's assessment on whether the nation is *still* at risk.

Differences Between the First and Second Waves of Reform

What are the differences between the first and second waves of educational reforms of the 1980s?

COMPARISON OF FIRST AND SECOND WAVES

The first wave set out to raise standards, lengthen schools days and years, and generally to raise the rigor of American public education. It has brought to everyone's attention that all is not well with our schools and that preserving public education will take major investments of time, money, and effort. Unfortunately, it is based on a narrow conception of education. (Michaels, 1988, p. 3)

FIRST WAVE

QUICK-FIX SOLUTIONS

The first wave concentrated on looking backward and on the quick-fix solutions of increased learning time, increased graduation requirements, and more frequent assessment of educational results. In contrast, the second wave of reforms in the late 1980s emphasized individual schools and working relationships among teachers and students. The new-wave reforms included an emphasis on high-order thinking skills; students' ability to understand what they learn, instead of to memorize by rote; an improved school environment of personalization and trust; flexible use of time; increased decision making at the local school level; and encouragement of a **collegial, participatory school environment** among students and staff (Michaels, 1988, p. 3). However, Ken Michaels, writing in *Educational Leadership*, cautions that educators may ruin the effect of this second wave because it is possible to "do" the items on this list and still not deviate from the status quo:

ENDS VS. MEANS

In the past, for example, schools added ten minutes to the homeroom and proclaimed they had a flexible schedule; teachers took turns lecturing to large groups of students and called it team teaching; a one-week unit on basic set operations inserted into an algebra course made it "modern math." Tinkering with the external trappings of schooling will not result in the kinds of changes we need. The entries on my abbreviated list are not the *ends* of reform; they are the *means* we must use to create different models of schooling. (p. 3)

SECOND WAVE

STRUCTURING THE ENVIRONMENT

This second wave of reforms is based on relationships, philosophical beliefs, values, and human nature in general. The new schools should develop an environment to educate as well as train, by emphasizing high-order thinking, skills for critically viewing the mass media, and a sense of ownership of students in their own learning. The emphasis here is not so much on "teaching" as on structuring an environment for student learning. The local school's teachers must have autonomy and flexibility to make more decisions about the learning of their students. The professional isolation of teachers must be decreased by building cooperation and colleague-

COOPERA-
TION AND
COLLEAGUE-
SHIP

ship among them. Furthermore, greater recognition and rewards must be provided for both teachers and students. The teaching profession must be made attractive to bright college students, and some form of **mentoring** or **career ladders** should be developed so that master teachers can assist those just entering the profession. Michaels suggests that educators need "to take their eyes off the rearview mirror of first-wave reform and look carefully at the 21st century" (Michaels, 1988, p. 3). Educators now have an opportunity as never before to restructure the teaching profession, the school environment, and student learning. The time for "tinkering" with American public schools is past.

RESTRUC-
TURING THE
PROFESSION

> [S]ignificant educational improvement of schooling, not mere tinkering, requires that we focus on entire schools, not just teachers or principals or curricula or organization or school community relations but all of these and more." (Goodlad, 1984, preface)

Causes of the Second Wave

COMMON
THREADS

What caused this second wave of educational reform in the 1980s? The major causes seem to be teacher shortages, changing family patterns, and pressure from business groups. The doors to other professional careers have opened up to women, who traditionally constitute the majority of teachers, and the brightest women often enter other fields instead of teaching. Another factor is the subservient working conditions of teachers, who often have little to say about key curricular and teaching decisions in their schools.

> Teaching has historically been a female occupation, but the women who were always there are not there any more. The last two decades have seen more and more younger women move into what were traditionally male occupations, with fewer entering education. Better working conditions, higher status positions, greater recognition, higher salaries, greater autonomy, and more control over working conditions have attracted women to other fields of endeavor. (Lieberman, 1988, p. 5)

POSSIBLE
SHORTAGES

In recent years the teaching force has been aging because fewer staff members have been added in most school districts. Also, fewer students have been graduating as certified teachers and entering teaching. Thus, when teachers who were hired thirty or more years ago retire in the late 1980s and early 1990s, there will be a shortage of qualified replacements.

APATHY AND
ATTITUDES

Two other causes of this reform movement can be identified. One of the causes of this shortage and of the second wave of reforms has been the changing family structure, which has resulted in apathy toward schools and a lack of respect toward teachers. The social and economic changes in the 1980s have been reflected in the many negative attitudes toward schools. These changes range from the lack of adequate financing for education to drug abuse; also, a large percentage of the population currently do not have children of school age. The second cause of the second wave of reforms stems from the reports of business groups calling for changes in education to make the United States more competitive in world markets. Thus, the reforms arise in a crisis situation and the schools are the scapegoat for the failures of society in general.

> What we see, then, is the coming together of important and disparate social forces with a common interest in reforming the nation's schools: governors making education the number one priority in their states; universities calling for massive reform of teacher preparation in their own institutions; business concerned with reform because of the need for better educated workers; and teacher associations recognizing that they must play a significant role in restructuring and professionalizing teaching if they are to influence the direction of change. This is an unprecedented, if uncoordinated, coalition of forces calling for structural reforms. (Lieberman, 1988, p. 5)

Tension and Collaboration Resulting from the Second Wave

TENSIONS

Both tension and collaboration have resulted from the second wave of reform sweeping American public education in the late 1980s. Any attempt to reform changes the way things have always been done in schools. Thus, career ladder plans and collaborative arrangements among teachers seem to be in opposition to the belief that all teachers are equal from their first day in the classroom and that teachers work independently in their separate classrooms. Lieberman (1988) calls this the **"egalitarian ethic"** and warns that teachers may oppose working collectively to solve problems as suggested by the second wave of reforms (p. 7). Another source of tension is the parent–child relationship that has often existed between principals and teachers. Principals and other administrators must learn to treat teachers as adult professionals who make the key instructional decisions in schools instead of as children to be told what to do. A third source of tension stems from the previous adversarial relationships between teachers and administrators, which has been fostered by collective bargaining and work stoppages in recent years.

> Somehow, a new dialogue must take place; and a new set of organizational arrangements must be created so that all members of the school community can be involved in building a collaborative culture. (Lieberman, 1988, p. 7)

COLLABORA-
TION

The collaboration resulting from this second wave of reforms could reshape and change teaching dramatically, encouraging quality young people to enter the teaching profession and experienced teachers to remain in teaching. Veteran teachers could share their expertise with interns and beginning teachers, who would benefit from being exposed to the modeling of experienced teachers. All teachers would be decision makers, collaboratively solving problems in a collegial model relationship. These instructional problems would be solved by professionals "on site" at the local school level, not at the district, state, or national level. This restructuring of schools may involve mentor teachers, local teacher centers, and teacher leaders who would be powerful models of professionalism (Lieberman, 1988,

What Would "Help a Lot" to Improve Education?

A Metropolitan Life survey of the American teacher probed both teachers and parents about what they thought would "help a lot" to improve education. A total of 2,011 parents and 1,002 teachers responded to the survey.

▇ percentage of parents supporting this concept.

☐ percentage of teachers supporting this concept.

Original data for this photo essay came from the Metropolitan Life Survey of the American Teacher 1987: *Strengthening Links Between Home and School.*

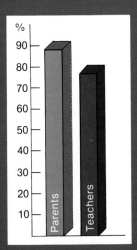

Having the school notify parents immediately about problems involving their children emerged as the number one item that would help improve education and the home/school connection.

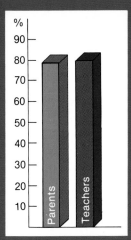

Having parents limit television watching until all homework is finished ranked high on the list.

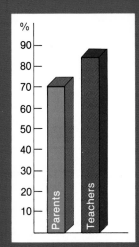

Having parents spend more time with their children in support of school and teachers was indicated as another important factor in helping improve the quality of education.

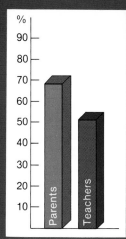

Establishing a homework hot-
line for students to call for
homework advice was seen as
a viable way to assist students
in achieving success in school.

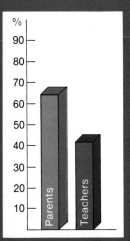

Distributing a newsletter to
parents to inform them about
what is happening in school
was also noted as a method for
improving communication.

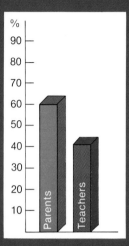

Offering in-service training for teachers on how to involve parents more effectively in the educational process was also seen as an important concept to support.

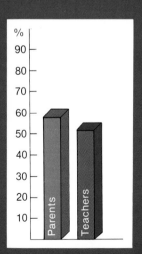

Getting teachers and parents to meet and talk about school policies ranked high in survey results.

EMPOWER-
MENT OF
TEACHERS

pp. 5–6). Teachers must be **empowered** to work together in doing a professional job.

> [W]e may indeed have a real opportunity to change the teaching profession . . . to provide greater recognition and status for teachers who have suffered too long from mythological and oversimplified definitions of their work; . . . [to] reshape teaching as an occupation to encourage young people to become teachers and more experienced teachers to share their expertise. (Lieberman, 1988, p. 7)

Reasons for Failure of Reforms

REASONS FOR
FAILURES

Arthur Combs (1988) has examined the reasons for the failure of past reform efforts and the new assumptions of these second-wave reforms. He says that the earlier reforms failed because they concentrated on changing "things" rather than people, because they were based on only partially correct assumptions, and because the reforms were dictated from above and passed down to teachers for implementation. Instead, Combs advises us to concentrate on changing people's beliefs; to emphasize processes, not preconceived outcomes; to first determine our priorities; and to start with the local problems of teachers. He suggests identifying and eliminating the barriers to reforms, whether from inertia, philosophies, or lack of resources (Combs, 1988, pp. 39–40).

> To change people's beliefs requires creating conditions for change rather than imposing reforms. It calls for open systems of thinking rather than the closed systems most reforms are accustomed to. (Combs, 1988, p. 40)

Three Models of Reform Proposals

PREVIEW

The second wave of reform generally emphasizes on-site change at the local school building level; but proposals for larger reforms have been made by the state governors, by William Bennett, and by Ted Sizer.

STATE GOVERNORS' PROPOSALS

FIVE STEPS

Honestschlager and Cohen (1988) suggest five steps that the nation's governors should take during the second wave of reforms. First, states should expect to assume greater responsibility for educational goals and standards. Second, states must develop more appropriate and realistic sanctions for school districts who perform poorly. Third, states must stimulate local inventiveness. Fourth, states should reduce regulations that interfere with local autonomy. Fifth, states must perfect their assessment systems to accurately reflect the state's educational goals and to measure higher-level educational outcomes in the second wave.

WILLIAM BENNETT'S PROPOSAL

William Bennett, the former U.S. Secretary of Education, outlined a model curriculum for kindergarten through eighth grade before leaving office in

A MODEL
CURRICULUM

1988. Bennett, like Mortimer Adler, advocates early exposure of children to good literature and a curriculum rich in content starting in the early grades. He emphasizes instruction in basic skills in the early grades and provides guidelines for K–8 instruction in English, social studies, science, mathematics, foreign language, fine arts, and physical education/health. Criticizing the bland basal readers in use today, Bennett calls for a reading program built around the classics. He proposes a social studies curriculum introducing customs, holidays, and mapmaking in the early grades to be followed by U.S. history in Grades 4 and 5 and world history in Grades 6 and 7. Eighth graders would study world geography and government. Experimentation, problem solving, and hands-on experience would be stressed in mathematics under this plan; and creativity would be the emphasis of fine arts classes. Students would begin foreign-language instruction in the fourth grade; a health/physical fitness program, including drug abuse, would begin in kindergarten. Greater emphasis on homework as well as on increasing time-on-task was also part of Bennett's proposal, which was praised

These children are involved in hands-on experience in mathematics, as recommended by William Bennett.

(Photo used by permission of the Pentathalon Institute.)

by representatives of the National Education Association and of the Association for Supervision and Curriculum Development (ASCD) (Gold, 1988, pp. 38–40).

TED SIZER'S PROPOSAL

ALIENATION

INCENTIVES
FOR STU-
DENTS

Ted Sizer, in an interview with Ron Brandt of ASCD (1988), suggested that schools are mirrors of society and that our American society does not really value adolescents, which results in **alienation,** drug abuse, and other problems. Sizer, who is involved with the Coalition for Essential Schools, believes that people in politics and education are beginning to realize that business-as-usual and complacency will no longer suffice in our information-age, globally competitive society. Sizer believes that educators must provide incentives for students to engage their minds deeply and must reorganize the way time is used in classrooms to facilitate this engagement. Intellectual development must be the main purpose of schools, he says; and he supports the **Socratic discussion groups** suggested by Mortimer Adler. Sizer states that we must group and regroup students frequently (Brandt, 1988, p. 31). He believes that all parts of the educational delivery system must be changed.

ACTIVE
LEARNING

> For example, if you want to rearrange your program to make kids more active, to let them derive answers rather than simply memorize them, that obviously affects not only the speed with which you move over the subject matter, but also the blocks of time necessary for the kids to engage in it. The teachers and principals will tell you this can't be done piecemeal. That means that planning must be comprehensive, indeed. (Brandt, 1988, p. 36)

Are Schools Still at Risk?

FOLLOW-UP
REPORT

PROGRESS

Are the U.S. public schools still at risk? In 1988 William Bennett issued a five-year follow-up report on *A Nation at Risk* and concluded that although the nation's schools are still at risk, much progress has been made toward improvement. In Bennett's words, "We're seeing progress. We're doing better. But we're not where we should be. . . . We are still at risk" (Beck, 1988, p. 54).

What progress has been made in improving U.S. schools? Every state has adopted some of the proposed reforms since *A Nation at Risk* was published in 1983. Forty states have raised high school graduation requirements, and in nineteen states students must pass a test before receiving their high school diplomas. With respect to teacher education and certification, forty-six states have mandated competency tests for beginning teachers, and twenty-three states have initiated alternative teacher certification. Average teacher salaries have been increased nationally at twice the rate of inflation to $28,031. The decline in SAT scores has been halted and slightly reversed; the combined verbal and mathematical scores have risen sixteen points since 1980 to begin recovering the ninety-point decline from 1963 to 1980. These trends are depicted in Figure 11–1, which illustrates the SAT scores

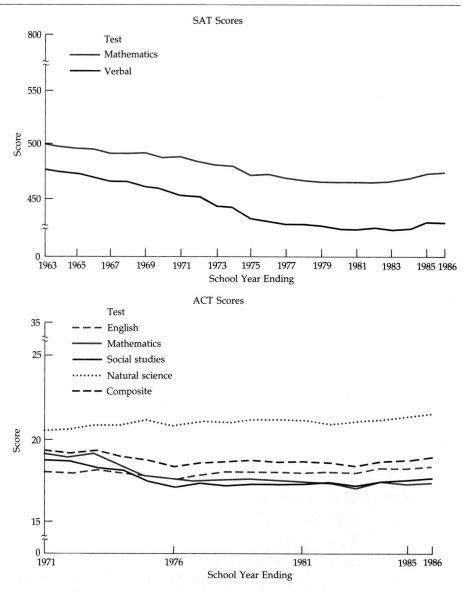

Figure 11–1 Trends in college entrance examination scores. Total SAT scores declined steadily from 1963 to 1980, for an overall decline of ninety points, but have increased by sixteen points since 1980. The increase of nine points from 1984 to 1985 was the largest annual increase in recent years and represented a recovery to 1975 levels. There was no further increase in 1986, however. The composite ACT score declined somewhat from the early 1970s to the mid-1970s. The composite score of 18.8 in 1986 was the highest since 1974.

(SOURCE: The College Board [SAT scores] and the American College Testing Program [ACT scores].)

from 1963 to 1986. This trend is especially significant as more students are taking the test then ever before (Beck, 1988, p. 54).

PROBLEMS IN EDUCATIONAL REFORMS

CONTINUING
PROBLEMS

Several problems still remain in assessment of our schools. Experts cannot even agree on elementary statistics because of the differences in the nation's 15,747 school districts. The National Education Association (NEA) cites lack of funding as a cause of many educational problems, whereas Bennett and many other education critics think we are already spending a sufficient amount of money on education in the United States (Beck, 1988, p. 55). Bennett advocates more state reporting of test scores, district by district, to link financing with results in a move toward **accountability.** Fourteen states now do this, and the number is expected to increase in the next few years. Bennett also advocates a new autonomy for teachers but favors linking it with accountability wherever possible. The largest criticism of the first wave of educational reforms in the period 1983 to 1988 is that these reforms have not significantly improved the education of black and Hispanic students in the inner-city areas of large U.S. cities. Two additional criticisms concern the 30% dropout rate nationwide and the lower science and mathematics achievement scores of U.S. students compared with students in many developed countries (Beck, 1988, p. 55). *Newsweek* summarized other criticisms of the reform movement as follows:

> Bennett says one signal achievement of the reform movement has been "discovering what works": recruiting and rewarding good teachers, strengthening the content of instruction, and instituting accountability. But there is still little consensus outside his office on how to achieve those goals. Teachers' unions still resist many forms of merit pay, alternative certification, and competency testing. Some educators think the current wave of test mania is hampering curriculum reforms by encouraging teachers to "teach the test." Others say it is the only way to quantify progress and some even call for a national student-achievement test, with results reported state by state. A few experts fear that tougher graduation requirements have actually encouraged marginal students to leave school. (Beck, 1988, p. 55)

RALPH TYLER'S EVALUATION OF EDUCATIONAL REFORM MOVEMENTS

OUTSIDE ORI-
GINS

In a 1987 article in the *Phi Delta Kappan*, Ralph Tyler, the father of the curriculum movement in U.S. schools, reflected on current and past reforms as well as difficulties with these reform movements. Tyler said that most reform movements originate outside of the profession of education and are not based on dependable information. In fact, he hinted that schools have been used as a scapegoat for the United States' failure to compete with the Russians in space science in the 1950s and with the Japanese in manufacturing in the 1980s. The commissions making these reform reports assume that all schools have the problems listed when only some schools may be afflicted. These reformers often fail to plan pilot studies to test the soundness of their proposals and to provide training for all teachers to use new curriculum materials. Worse, he says, these reformers establish contradictory goals for schools, for example, advocating equity for minorities and at the same time imposing additional graduation requirements in the 1980s.

Furthermore, Tyler states that reform proposals fail because they lack focus, because they are not accompanied by implementation plans, and because the resources necessary for their implementation are not provided (Tyler, 1987, p. 279). Tyler has "found that it takes six or seven years to get a reform really working as intended. Most implementation plans greatly underestimate the amount of time required" (1987, p. 280). In addition, he notes that reforms require changes in people, especially in their attitudes, as well as in aspects of the teaching-learning system. Tyler concludes that reforms can be successful in U.S. schools but that these reform movements cannot be left in the control of forces who have little understanding of schools and teaching (Tyler, 1987, p. 280).

Conclusions on Reforms in Education

What conclusions can be drawn from this discussion of educational reforms? Groups outside of education should be prevented from using the

schools as a **scapegoat** for society's problems in other areas, such as business or military competition. The first wave of reforms concentrated on simplistic solutions to U.S. educational problems, such as increasing the amount of time spent in school, the teacher education requirements, the high school graduation requirements, and the testing of student progress. The second wave concentrates on restructuring the way teachers work with

students and emphasizes career ladders, the empowerment of teachers to make major decisions in curriculum and instruction, and collaboration among teachers, ending the traditional isolation of teachers in eggcrate classrooms. The second wave of reforms also emphasizes process, rather than product, and changing the attitudes of teachers toward their roles in schools. The authors of this text see this period as most exciting for teachers and students of education. Never before have we had such a sustained interest in educational reform at the local, state, and national levels, and never have we had such an opportunity to make such significant differences in the education of our children and in the teaching profession itself.

Effective Schools

Introduction

This section of the chapter deals with the **effective schools movement,** which in many ways parallels the reform movements of the 1980s. First, an overview of the research on effective schools is presented; then reactions to and criticisms of these ideas are examined.

Definitions of Effective Schools

The factors linked by research to effective schools have been defined in many different ways. Lawrence Stedman (1987) identified the five major

KEY FACTORS
factors in the effective schools formula as (1) strong leadership of the school principal, (2) high expectations of students by the teachers, (3) concentration of emphasis on basic skills, (4) an orderly school environment, and (5) frequent and systematic evaluation of students (Stedman, 1987, pp. 215–223). Murphy and Hallinger (1985) list a similar, but not identical, set of essentials for effective schools. They find a clear sense of purpose to be associated with effective schools. Other authors call this sense of purpose a "vision" of what the school should be, but the idea is the same. Schools cannot achieve a goal unless they first define it. Murphy and Hallinger point out that early studies on effective schools failed to link these overall goals to specific levels of student achievement on standardized tests, but later studies did link school goals and student achievement. The school factor identified by Murphy and Hallinger related to a set of core standards within a rich curriculum. These core standards are called "basic skills" by some researchers; Murphy and Hallinger do not believe that these core standards should limit the scope of course offerings to only basic skills. The third factor they identified was high expectations of student achievement, which include regular assignment and grading of homework. A commitment to educate each student as fully as possible was the fourth factor. Fifth was providing a special reason for each child to go to school through student involvement in meaningful activities. The last three standards were a safe, orderly learning environment; a sense of community or cohesiveness; and a problem-solving attitude (Murphy and Hallinger, 1985, pp. 18–22). Other factors associated with effective schools are high self-concept of students and parental involvement in a rich program of school activities, both academic and cocurricular.

ASSUMP-
TIONS
Several assumptions can be identified from this overview of effective schools research. First, it is assumed that schools will be more effective if they have a vision of the future and clearly identified goals. Second, the principal's leadership seems to be the key factor in these schools. *All* students are assumed to be capable of learning, and basic skills are learned and evaluated regularly. An orderly school environment makes this learning possible; and students, as well as parents and teachers, have meaningful involvement in planning and participating in the school program.

Criticisms of Research on Effective Schools

CRITICISMS
Some criticisms have surfaced concerning research on effective schools. Stedman (1987) has criticized the back-to-basics emphasis in this research as limiting the school curriculum. He believes that research has not provided evidence that the five factors listed earlier in this section are characteristic of effective schools. Stedman further believes that standardized test scores in mathematics and reading are too narrow a base on which to judge total school achievement. He asserts that emphasis on a narrow range of basic skills in effective schools research widens the gap between inner-city schools, which emphasize basic skills, and suburban schools, which, he says, emphasize creative problem solving. Stedman (1987) identifies nine

broad categories of interrelated factors that he believes are related to effective schools: ethnic and racial pluralism, parent participation, shared governance with teachers and parents, academically rich programs, skilled use and training of teachers, personal attention to students, student responsibility for school affairs, an accepting and supportive environment, and teaching aimed at prevention of problems (pp. 215–224).

DEFENSE OF
EFFECTIVE
SCHOOLS

Wilbur Brookover (1987), who with Lawrence Lezotte was the originator of the research on effective schools, defends the research that he has supervised against these criticisms. He asserts that Stedman has distorted the original research on effective schools in several ways. First, Stedman has narrowed the emphasis on "student achievement" in this original research to "basic skills." Brookover says that emphasis on basic skills does not limit achievement in other areas of the curriculum. Brookover also believes that the primary purpose of frequent assessment of students is evaluation of the curriculum, not the students or teachers as Stedman suggests. Furthermore, Brookover criticizes Stedman's assumption that only minority students are supposed to make significant gains in test scores under effective schools programs. *All* students should be able to make these gains, he says. Brookover also criticizes Stedman's nine factors, especially the parent participation factor:

> In our study of a random sample of Michigan elementary schools, we found that a measure of parent interaction in the school was significantly *negatively* associated with mean student achievement in higher socioeconomic student populations. On the other hand, parent interaction was slightly *positively* associated with higher student achievement in a sample of predominantly black schools. (Brookover, 1987, p. 226)

LABELING
AND DISTOR-
TION?

Brookover states that while the effective schools research does have several limitations, these can best be addressed by additional stringent research methodologies, not by labeling the effective schools movement as a back-to-basics approach and by distorting its findings, as Stedman seems to have done (Murphy and Hallinger, 1985, pp. 226–227).

Computers and Technology

Introduction

Closely related to our vision of educational reforms and the future is the discussion of the place of technology. Many experts on the use of computers in education predict that the computer of tomorrow will be analogous to the pencil of today; some even prognosticate that children will learn with computers at home instead of at school. However, the consensus seems to be that computers will be a tool of teachers and students, not a replacement for the teacher. Unlike the use of educational technology in the past, such as educational television and teaching machines, the computer is not a fad; it is having a tremendous impact on society in general, as well as on

A TOOL, NOT
A PANACEA

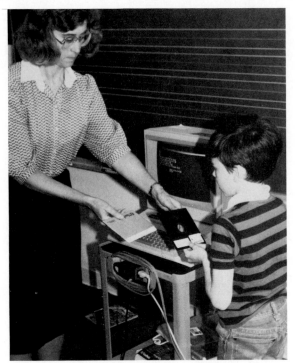

Using the computer as a tool for effective learning.

(Photo used by permission of the Indiana Department of Education.)

education. Because of this pervasive influence of computers on society and because we are entering the information age in which access to and use of information are key to success, it seems logical to predict that computers will also be a key element in educating children and young people in the future. Whether the influence of computers is revolutionary or evolutionary is yet to be seen.

PERVASIVE
INFLUENCE

Computers have affected every aspect of society. At supermarket check-out counters computers read prices, and department store computer cash registers record an inventory of products. Banks are so dependent on computers that they cannot quote account balances when their computers are down. Industrial robots controlled by computers are assuming many industrial functions and changing industrial employment patterns. Bills and letters to customers are printed by computers in many businesses, and even small businesses use computer accounting programs to keep their records. Microchips are found everywhere, in children's toys, in calculator watches, in hearing aids, and in implanted medical devices. Military defense systems are computer controlled, and soldiers of the future will need a high level of technological training to operate these systems. In medicine and health, laser technology and biochemical engineering have become commonplace. In addition computers control prosthetic devices for paraplegics and large-

NEW TERMS

print monitors for the visually impaired. The literature is replete with such new terms as *"infoglut"* (information overload), *telecommuters* (people who work at home via computers), and *flexiplaces* (flexibility in work sites). The authors of this text do not believe that teachers should fear this technology **(technophobia)**, but that they should be able to use it as a tool in teaching (Shane, 1983, p. 126).

Uses and Issues of Computers and Technology in Education

PROGRESSION OF USES

The use of computer technology in education began with record keeping and has now spread to almost every area of the public school curriculum. Computers were first used to keep school academic records and print report cards, but now the computer is found in the classroom from kindergarten through Grade 12 in the public schools. Elementary pupils use personal computers to learn writing skills, and word processing instruction begins in upper elementary school or middle school grades. Social studies students can utilize computer simulations, and high school chemistry students can perform dangerous experiments safely on the computer. Advanced accounting classes are often taught using the computer, and computer word processors are rapidly replacing typewriters in typing classes. Some music theory classes are using special computer programs to compose music, and industrial arts classes can study the use of computers in the design of automobiles and other products. Art and design classes can also make use of computers extensively. Thus, a metamorphosis has occurred in the school curriculum, with computer technology leading the way.

ACTUAL USE?

Despite these possibilities, to what extent is the computer actually used in schools today? As part of the National Assessment of Educational Progress (NAEP) in 1986, the first nationwide assessment of students' computer-related knowledge, skills, attitudes, and experience was undertaken. This study found that although students' attitudes toward computers were overwhelmingly positive, a majority of students had not used computers in any single subject area. For instance, 53% of students in the third grade, 39.4% of those in the seventh grade, and only 29% of those in the eleventh grade had used computers in mathematics classes. The respective percentages for English/reading were 25%, 23.9%, and 16.9%; for science, 12.8%, 11.6%, and 15.4%; and for social studies, 11.7%, 10.2%, and 4.6%. The percentages for art and music were about 0.7% at Grade 7 and 4% at Grade 11, although much higher use was reported in Grade 3 at the elementary level in these subjects. About one third of all students had never used computers in class. In conclusion,

> the NAEP data show that computers are not widely used to learn traditional subjects, such as mathematics, science, and English. (La Pointe and Martinez, 1988, p. 60)

EQUITY AND ACCESS

Furthermore, the NAEP survey found that equity and access are significant factors in the acquisition of computer skills. At all three grade levels in the study, boys demonstrated more computer competence than girls and

A persistent question concerning computers is whether equal access is granted to minority students.

(Photo used by permission of the Metropolitan School District of Washington Township.)

had greater access to computers at home. Black and Hispanic minority students scored lower on computer competency than white students, and the schools they attended were less likely than other schools to use microcomputers. It seems as if home access to computers is a crucial factor in computer competence, and students do not have equal access to computers at home (La Pointe and Martinez, 1988, pp. 59–61).

A TAXON-OMY OF USES

What are the classifications of computer use in today's schools and how are these related to Bloom's taxonomy? Drill and practice, tutorials, simulations, application courseware, programming, and educational games seem to be the most common uses in current school programs. Drill and practice, which are used for remediation and reinforcement, involve only the lower levels of Bloom's taxonomy, knowledge and comprehension. Tutorials, which are utilized to teach new concepts or skills, also emphasize the lower levels of knowledge and comprehension. Simulations emphasize the top four levels of Bloom's **taxonomy,** which are application, analysis, synthesis, and evaluation. Simulations allow students to make decisions concerning situations that simulate real-life experience. Application software, such as word processing, electronic spreadsheets, and art or music packages, also emphasize Bloom's top four levels, whereas educational strategy games can encompass the top three levels of analysis, synthesis, and evaluation (Stronge, 1987, pp. 18–19).

"WHO" BE-
COMES A
PRIORITY?

Which students should use computers in schools, especially when computers and class time are limited? All students should have experience with computers periodically during their school careers. Gifted students can be taught higher-level thinking skills by computers, but all students need these same skills, not only the gifted. In fact, there are many reasons low achievers should use computers. First, low achievers find computers an attractive means of learning subject matter because of the great interest in computer technology. Second, computers can simulate situations that would be impossible for students to control in real life. Teachers should not assume that low achievers lack an ability for or an interest in higher-order thinking or problem solving through computer activities (Patterson, 1987, p. 38).

Other Problems and Issues Concerning the Use of Computers in Schools

GAMES VS.
EDUCATION?

ETHICS AND
COPYING?

KEYBOARD-
ING?

TEACHERS AS
PROGRAM-
MERS?

What other problems and issues are associated with the use of computers in schools? The greatest single use of computers by students of all ages is in playing games at home and sometimes at school. Although some of these games are educational, many students become addicted to games at the expense of other educational opportunities. Another problem has been the quality of educational software available for students, although this has improved in recent years. A further difficulty involves the ethics of copying programs; school systems can minimize this problem by joining consortiums, such as the Minnesota Educational Computer Consortium, or by purchasing a **"site license,"** which gives the school district the right to make for its own use as many copies of a computer program as it deems necessary. Students must be taught, however, that copying programs, and especially selling them to others, is illegal. As computer use begins in elementary school, or earlier, a problem arises as to when keyboarding should be taught. Presently, of course, typing or keyboarding is rarely taught before the ninth grade, by which time students may have developed many bad typing habits that they may have to unlearn. Two other problems involve teachers and the computer. Should all teachers be taught to program the computer? The consensus seems to be that all teachers do not need this knowledge. The salient analogy here would be that a driver does not need to be able to build or repair a car to use or drive it. All teachers need to know how to select and use software, but they are not necessarily required to program the computer or to produce software. Another issue involves the inservice training of teachers in the use of computers. Many school districts have such programs and offer salary or credit incentives to entice teachers to take them.

A COMPUTER
CURRICULUM

What should be taught at each grade level in regard to computers? In the early days many high schools had **computer literacy** programs because many students came to high school with little knowledge or experience in this area. Currently, however, **computer literacy** programs are most often found in elementary grades, and specific skills are taught at each grade level. Junior high or middle schools now further these skills with **word processing, spreadsheets,** and other application programs, whereas programming, usually in more than one computer language, is an elective at the high school level. In other words, basic computer knowledge is taught early in the curriculum, with some required computer work in the middle schools or junior high schools and higher-level programming courses as high school electives.

Examples of Innovative Computer Use in Schools

PAPERT'S
PROGRAM

Two examples of innovative computer use are now examined. The first program was designed by Seymour Papert, creator of the Logo computer language and professor of mathematics and education at the Massachusetts Institute of Technology. This program, called "Project Headlight," is used at the Hennigan Elementary School in Boston. It is described as "a computer intensive Logo-based project that emphasizes a high computer to student ratio" (Parker, 1986, p. 10). Project Headlight emphasizes how children relate to what they are learning, not just the knowledge itself. One way this is done is to allow pupils to take apart and put together two "sacrificial" computers on the first day of the project. The program integrates the use of computers with homemade instruments for a music course. In Papert's words, "I think it's important that computer high tech and low tech be in the same activity, in the same room, at the same time. This is the theme of this project; it's also a theme of how we look at the future" (Parker, 1986, p. 11).

COMPUTER-
BASED WRIT-
ING PROJECT

Alan M. Lesgold describes a computer-based writing project at the University of Pittsburgh's Falk School where IBM PC Jr.'s are used to teach writing skills through word processing. Lesgold states that "Computer literate students will be able to distinguish between the routine tasks from which computers can release them and more sophisticated capabilities—framing and solving problems, communicating visually and verbally—that are least likely to be automated" (Lesgold, 1986, p. 7). This program aims to improve writing skills by making word processing easily accessible to students, thus giving them additional practice in composing their thoughts. Lesgold believes that computer programs can be developed that point out the line in which the spelling or syntactical error is found but force the student to discover and correct the error for himself or herself. He says that computer programs are already available for teaching the skills involved in outlining thoughts, and believes that student exercises to develop ideas for essays could also be computer based. Even though teaching writing skills requires much teacher time in paper grading, Lesgold believes that computers can ease the workload of teachers considerably (Lesgold, 1986, p. 9).

CONCLU-
SIONS
     In conclusion, educational technology in computers reached a turning point in the 1985–1986 school year and has "moved from a curiosity to a useful tool that will help schools provide better curriculum and instruction" (Valdez, 1986, p. 4). The present applications of computer technology are geared more toward the creative aspects of teaching instead of drill and practice as in previous years. Higher-order thinking skills, not content-specific instruction, seems to be the wave of our technological future.

Summary

In this chapter the two waves of educational reform in the 1980s, the recent effective schools movement, and the increasing importance of technology in education were examined. With respect to the first wave of reform in the early 1980s, the findings, recommendations, and criticisms of *A Nation at Risk* were summarized. Four other proposals in this early wave of reforms were also analyzed: John Goodlad's *A Place Called School*, Mortimer Adler's *The Paideia Proposal*, Ernest Boyer's *High School: A Report on Secondary Education in America*, and the National Science Board's *Educating Americans for the 21st Century*. The second wave of reforms was then summarized and compared with the first wave. In addition, three proposed models for educational reform were included as examples of the second wave. Definitions, criticisms, and implications of the effective schools movement and the uses, issues, and problems concerning computers and technology in education were explored. Current examples of innovative computer programs in public elementary and secondary schools were given.

Glossary Terms

A Nation at Risk, 339
Functionally Illiterate, 340
Scholastic Aptitude Test (SAT), 340
Minimum Competency, 340
Five New Basics, 341
Quick-Fix Solutions, 342
Existential Qualities, 344
A Place Called School, 345
The Paideia Proposal, 345
One-Track System of Education, 345
Facilitators of Learning, 346
Universal Suffrage, 347
High School: A Report on Secondary Education in America, 347
New Carnegie Unit, 347
Fifth-Year Teacher Education Program, 347

Educating Americans for the 21st Century, 349
Magnet Schools, 350
Collegial, Participatory School Environment, 352
Mentoring, 353
Career Ladders, 353
Egalitarian Ethic, 354
Empowerment, 355
Alienation, 357
Socratic Discussion Groups, 357
Accountability, 359
Scapegoat, 360
Effective Schools Movement, 360
Infoglut, 364
Flexiplaces, 364
Technophobia, 364

Questions

1. How has education in elementary and secondary schools changed since the publication of *A Nation at Risk* in 1983? What are the advantages and disadvantages of these reforms?

2. What valid ideas for reform do you see in the proposals of John Goodlad, Mortimer Adler, and Ernest Boyer? With which one of these authors do you most agree? Why?

3. What innovative approaches can you imagine to alleviate the shortage of science and math teachers in our elementary and secondary schools? What is your reaction to the proposals of the National Science Board?

4. Compare and contrast the first and second waves of educational reform in the 1980s and 1990s. What are the criticisms of each?

5. Compare and contrast the reform proposals of William Bennett, Ted Sizer, and the state governors.

6. Define "empowerment" of teachers and evaluate its effectiveness in educational reform.

7. Do you believe that U.S. schools are still "at risk"? Why or why not?

8. What specific characteristics have been shown to be associated with effective schools?

9. Evaluate an elementary or secondary school with which you are familiar according to the criteria for effective schools.

10. Summarize the criticisms of the research on effective schools. What do you think are the pros and cons of this movement?

11. Identify the major issues presented by computers and technology in education. What are the pros and cons of each issue?

12. What do you see as the proper uses of computers in education? How do you plan to use computers in your own teaching?

13. Evaluate the innovative school programs using the computer that are presented in this chapter. What are the advantages and disadvantages of each?

Activities for Unit V

1. Choose one of the top ten writings that have influenced the curriculum, research it in detail, and draw your own conclusions about its lasting value and contribution. Report your findings to the class.

2. The authors have raised some questions relating to the practice of the original Seven Cardinal Principles of education. Answer each of these questions and propose a curricular answer to each question.

3. Try Alfred North Whitehead's idea of surveying a small district and comparing it with another district. Involve the whole class in this project.

4. After observing a lesson being taught in school, analyze whether it was psychologically sound in terms of the findings of the works of Piaget, Kohlberg, or Watson.

5. Plan a minilesson in your content area, keeping in mind the developmental stage of most of the children in the class. Before presenting the lesson to the children, have three or more of your peers assess its developmental level.

6. Research the pros and cons of homogeneous and heterogeneous grouping of students. Report your findings to the class.

7. Describe how the modern-day high school can be made more flexible to best accomplish the needs of serious students. This could be a group or class project. Flexible scheduling, nongrading, and team teaching may be a good place to start.

8. Read an article that relates to how parents influence the curriculum in our schools. Summarize the article and share your findings with the class.

9. Plan a lesson for a class in which you will encounter exploratory experiences, involving the positive use of TV. Assign a program for the students to watch, and plan follow-up activities for them to do the next day. TV documentaries would be good for this purpose.

10. With the permission of the principal, the teacher, and the child, do a case study of a learning-disabled child. After doing the study, make some recommendations as to the best curriculum and technique to use with this child.

11. Speculate on why teachers are more effective if they use indirect influence rather than direct influence in their teaching style, according to Flanders.

12. Take the content area you are being trained to teach and make some global objectives for your future classes. Examples for science:
   a. Make a list of the major scientific discoveries around the world and the people who made them.
   b. Examine why fewer scientific discoveries are made in undeveloped countries. What are some of the reasons behind this lack of scientific development? What would improve the situation?

13. Examine a test that has norm references. Determine how the test manufacturer arrived at the norms used in the test.

14. Make a chart comparing the reform proposals of the 1980s and 1990s.

15. Interview a principal and a teacher on their assessments of recent educational reforms.

16. After reviewing the reform proposals of the 1980s and early 1990s,

make a list of "unfinished business"—changes that still need to be made in our schools.

17. Identify recent educational reforms that have failed or succeeded and the reasons for their failure or success.

18. Design a specific proposal to improve an elementary or secondary school with which you are familiar to make it more effective.

19. Visit the computer labs of two or three local elementary or secondary schools. Assess the progress of these schools in the use of computers and technology.

20. Invite an expert on computers and technology to speak on current trends in this area.

Annotated Bibliography

1. Bennett, W. J. (1988). *American education: Making it work*. Washington, DC: U.S. Government Printing Office.

   This assessment by the U.S. Secretary of Education describes how far we have come in education and what we still need to do to improve our schools.

2. Boyer, E. L. (1983). *High school: A report on secondary education in America*. New York: Harper and Row.

   In this report written for the Carnegie Foundation for the Advancement of Teaching, Boyer surveyed the current state of American secondary education, including descriptions of a troubled institution; an exploration of its mission and its goals; an example of a school that works; and connections between high schools and public colleges and corporations.

3. Brookover, W. B., & Lezotte, L. W. (1979). *Changes in school characteristics coincident with changes in student achievement*. East Lansing: Institute of Research on Teaching at Michigan State University.

   This report led to the effective schools movement, which became very influential in the 1980s and continues in the 1990s.

4. Good, T. L., & Brophy, J. E. (1984). *Looking in classrooms*, 3rd ed. New York: Harper and Row.

   Brophy and Good state that teachers are often not aware of much of their behavior in the classroom and this lack of awareness often results in inappropriate and self-defeating behavior. They describe a variety of techniques that can be used to increase a teacher's awareness of behavior in the classroom. Thus, the focus of this volume is on classroom observation.

5. Goodlad, I. I. (1984). *A place called school*. New York: McGraw-Hill.

   In his study, John Goodlad surveyed thirteen communities in seven sections of the country. The thirty-eight schools studied differed in location, size, student population characteristics, and family income. Twenty trained data collectors were sent into each community where they remained for a month and eventually collected data from 8,624 parents, 1,350 teachers, and 17,163 students. No other study has contained such detailed observations of more than 1,000 classrooms.

6. Honestschlager, D., & Cohen, M. (1988). The governors restructure schools. *Educational Leadership, 45,* 42–43.

This article surveys the efforts of governors to reform education in their states.

7. National Commission on Excellence in Education. (1983). *A nation at risk: The imperatives for education reform.* Washington, DC: U.S. Government Printing Office.

This report outlines deficiencies in education in the United States, as well as findings and recommendations with respect to content, standards and expectations, use of time and leadership, and fiscal support.

8. Shane, H. G. (1983). The silicon age. II. Living and learning in an information epoch. ***Phi Delta Kappan,*** *65,* 126–129.

In this article, the noted futurist Harold Shane explores what living and learning in the new information age will be like for today's students.

[Photo used by permission of the Library of Congress.]

VI

Legal Elements of Education

Teachers' Legal Rights and Responsibilities

OBJECTIVES

After reading Chapter 12, the student will be able to:

- Identify and delineate the functions of the various courts in the federal court system

- Understand the state court structure, duties of state courts, and state procedures

- Articulate the legal powers of the federal government in regard to education

- Understand teachers' contractual and employment rights

- Explain teachers' rights to organize and bargain collectively and to engage in political activity

- Comprehend teachers' roles in handling and dealing with the rights and responsibilities of pupils

- Appreciate the rights and responsibilities of teachers in disciplining students

- Define the tort liability of teachers and describe situations in which teachers could be legally negligent

Introduction

Teachers, like all other citizens, have legal rights. Along with those rights, however, come certain responsibilities. Because the teaching profession is charged by society with the important task of developing the intellectual capabilities of its citizens, including its future leaders, the responsibilities are especially crucial.

This chapter presents teachers' rights and responsibilities in four basic areas: (1) certification, (2) contracts, (3) control of students, and (4) tort liability. In addition, certain miscellaneous areas deemed important for teacher candidates are introduced.

First, however, a brief overview of the American court system is necessary, to provide the background for teachers' rights and responsibilities.

The American Court System

Because the common law is derived from court decisions, and because the written law is subject to interpretation by the courts, it will help the student becoming acquainted with the law for the first time to understand the basic structure of the court system of the United States.

There are actually two separate court systems, the federal and the state. The federal courts operate in every state and territory, side by side with the courts of each individual state. But the authority of the two court systems differs. Federal courts handle only those cases that involve a federal question, that is, cases that involve the U.S. Constitution, federal statutes and administrative rules, or disputes between the states.

The Federal Court Structure

In its general form, the federal court system is simple to describe and understand. It is a three-tiered system. On the bottom tier is the U.S. district court. It is a court of "original jurisdiction" (first hearing), or simply a trial court.

In the middle of the federal court system sit the U.S. courts of appeal. When a case has been tried in the court of original jurisdiction, the loser has a right to appeal the case to a higher court. Remember that these courts are solely courts of review, or of appeals; they have no original jurisdiction.

At the very top of the federal court system stands the U.S. Supreme Court. It has both original and appellate jurisdiction, although it rarely exercises the former. The court uses its discretion to decide which of the approximately 5,000 cases a year it will hear, and only those that have broad and general interest to the nation's welfare are considered.

Because there is no higher court in the nation, the decisions of the Supreme Court are final; however, there are three ways by which the decisions, or their effects, can be changed. First, the court may reverse itself. Second, the Constitution can be amended. Third, decisions of the Supreme Court can be changed by an act of Congress.

Of the three kinds of federal court, only the Supreme court was established by constitutional mandate. Except for the power to change the number of justices, to approve the U.S. President's appointments, to impeach, and to set salaries, Congress has no direct power over the Supreme Court. It is up to Congress to provide for the rest of the federal court system. It did this beginning with the Judiciary Act of 1789 followed by the Judicial Code in 1911, which established our current three-tiered system.

The State Court Systems

The state court systems resemble the federal system in that they, too, are three-tiered; that is, there are trial courts, courts of appeal, and one court of ultimate review, usually called a supreme court, in each state. In addition to the three tiers, nearly every state has a number of inferior or minor courts that take care of small civil claims and petty criminal cases. Remember that each state has complete control over its own court system and that no two states have exactly the same system.

In the remainder of this chapter teachers' rights and responsibilities are discussed in the areas of certification, contracts, control of students, and tort liability.

Teacher Certification

For entrance into a profession, a license or certificate is usually required. One of the major reasons for certification is to ensure the public a certain standard of performance by the members. To qualify for certification and for admission to the profession, an individual must meet the required qualifications, and these are usually of such a nature as to prepare one to

LICENSING
perform adequately. One of the reasons that certificates are required of public school teachers in all states was stated clearly by the Indiana Supreme Court as far back as 1866: "It was intended by the requirement of a certificate . . . to guard against the squandering of a sacred public fund, upon persons assuming to teach without being capable of performing a teacher's duties" (*Harrison School Township v. Conrad*, 26 IND 337 1866).

The teaching certificate is not a property right; that is, it is not the result of a contract between the state and the teacher. No absolute rights, such as guaranteed employment or tenure rights, are conferred by the certificate

NO ABSO-
LUTE RIGHTS
on the holder. Rather, the teaching certificate is a personal privilege granted by the state to an individual and may not be transferred, sold, or bartered to another person. Because the state has the power to issue certificates, it also has the power to revoke them. One who holds a license to teach does so at the pleasure of the issuing agency.

States vary in the causes for which a teaching certificate can be revoked. In some states, the causes are listed by statute; in other states, the statutes

CAUSES FOR
REVOCATION
say nothing. Where the statutes do list the causes, only those listed can be used to revoke a certificate; any reasons not specifically enumerated in the statute do not constitute legal grounds for revocation. Many states legislate

To be certified, every prospective teacher must fulfill the licensing requirements of the state in which she or he wishes to teach.

[Photo by Axler.]

as grounds for revocation of a teacher's certificate such things as incompetency, intentional neglect of duty, or immorality.

It is customary for state legislatures to delegate the setting of requirements for teaching certificates to the state board of education. The state
department of public instruction is usually assigned the administrative task
of issuing the certificates. When questions arise, particularly over whether
a certificate should be issued to a particular applicant, the state board of
education settles the matter.

Increasingly, state boards of education are turning to the colleges that
prepare teachers for recommendations to accompany the applications of
graduates for teaching certificates. The objective is to involve the teacher-
training institutions, as much as possible, in the certification process.

One of the more irritating hurdles that a teacher must face when moving
from state to state is getting properly certified. No two states have exactly
the same requirements, and all states require their own certificates. There
are three ways in which a person properly prepared to teach in one state
may secure the certificate of another state:

SECURING
CERTIFICATES
FROM OTHER
STATES

First, he or she can meet all the requirements as listed. This is done
usually when a person builds his or her college program around those

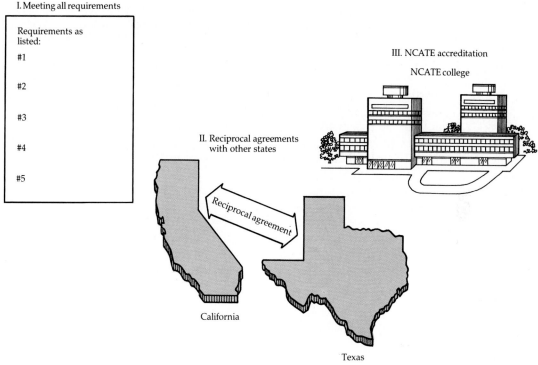

Three considerations for teaching approval in other states.

specific requirements. In other words, the student knew the requirements and then aimed to meet them from the beginning.

Second, he or she can secure a certificate through **reciprocity.** This means that the state in which he or she wants a certificate has an agreement with the state in which he or she currently holds one to reciprocate in granting certificates to each other's licensed teachers. These are usually bilateral agreements (involving only two states); however, one state may have reciprocity agreements with as many states as it desires.

Third, he or she can graduate from a college accredited by the National Council for the Accreditation of Teacher Education (NCATE). At one time, over half the states granted teaching certificates if any one of those accredited institutions would certify that a graduate had met the requirements for certification in the state in which the accredited institution was located and would also recommend the graduate for the specified certificate. This seems to be a promising method for arriving at some kind of nationwide standardization of certification requirements.

Another promising method is to have a coalition of states agree to common certification requirements. In May 1984, over two thirds of the fifty states had joined the Interstate Certification Project, through which initial certification among member states is greatly simplified.

Teachers' Contracts

Nearly two million teachers are under contract in the public elementary and secondary schools each year, and each one of them represents a teacher's contract. A recent study of court cases in which teachers were litigants revealed that nearly half of them related to teachers' contracts and tenure rights. Clearly, then, the subject of teacher contracts merits serious consideration by the person preparing to teach.

To adequately understand the legal aspects of teacher contracts, it is helpful to know some essential facts about contracts in general. All contracts under the common law possess certain elements on which their validity depends. A valid contract, including a contract for teaching services, has five basic elements, the absence of any one of which is enough to render the contract null and of no effect:

ELEMENTS OF
A VALID
CONTRACT

1. The contract must be between competent parties.
2. The contract must be based on mutual assent.
3. The contract must contain a valid consideration.
4. The contract must contain rights and liabilities sufficiently definite to be enforceable.
5. The contract must be of such a nature as not to be prohibited by statute or common law.

The major concepts contained in each element follow.

COMPETENCY OF THE PARTIES

ELIGIBILITY

To be competent to contract for a teaching position, a teacher must have both eligibility and capacity to contract. By *eligibility* is meant the possession of certain qualifications prescribed by statute, usually for certain classes of professional people such as teachers, lawyers, and doctors. Possession of a valid teaching certificate makes a teacher eligible to contract.

CAPACITY

Capacity, with respect to the teacher, refers to such requirements as age, citizenship, marital status, and similar factors that are usually required by the state legislature. For example, a minor cannot legally enter into a contract and so would not have the capacity to do so. With respect to school boards, statutory authority to contract is, with few exceptions, vested in each of them, and this gives them the legal capacity.

MUTUAL ASSENT

OFFER AND
ACCEPTANCE

The negotiations leading to a contract can be categorized into *offer* and *acceptance*. For these to happen, there must exist a concurrence of assent on the part of both the offeror and the offeree about the conditions of the contract. There must be neither doubt nor difference between the parties.

VALID CONSIDERATION

SALARY AND
BENEFITS

In the legal sense, consideration consists of the act, or the promise, of surrendering some legal right at the request of another party. It is the price that one party pays for the act or promise of another. In a teaching contract, the consideration promised by the school district is the salary and other monetary benefits; the teacher promises her or his services. Unless the contracting parties reach agreement about the consideration, there will be no contract.

DEFINITE RIGHTS AND LIABILITIES

SPECIFIC
ENOUGH TO
BE ENFORCE-
ABLE

It is a well-settled principle of law that a contract lacks validity when the rights and liabilities of the contracting parties are not sufficiently definite as to be enforceable. A promise to pay a teacher "good wages" is not definite enough; a specific amount of money must be offered. Other things that should be definitely stated in a teacher's contract are (1) the beginning and ending dates of employment; (2) the nature of the services to be performed by the teacher; and (3) all other things required by statute.

NOT PROHIBITED BY LAW

LEGAL

It is logical to expect that a contract entered into in violation of a law would be invalid. Among the more common statutes barring or limiting the making of a valid contract are those concerning contracts made on Sunday, made in restraint of trade, based on gambling or usurious interest rates, or made orally when the statutes require them to be in writing.

OTHER CON-
TRACTUAL
FACTORS

In addition to the elements just discussed, other factors concerning contracts are worthy of consideration. State statutes, existing as well as future ones, are considered a part of all public school contracts. When a state passes a statute requiring public school teachers to belong to and to contribute to the teachers' retirement system, that statute pertains to all teachers, even those already under contract.

IMPLIED
POWERS

State boards of education and state departments of public instruction possess explicit or implied powers to prescribe rules and regulations for the government of the public schools. Whenever these state agencies make such rules, and if the rules are reasonable and within the agency's power to make, they can be enforced even if they affect the terms of a teacher's contract.

RULES OF LO-
CAL SCHOOL
BOARDS

Likewise, rules and regulations of local school boards, when not arbitrary, unreasonable, capricious, or unjust, become, by implication, an integral part of each teacher's contract. This principle pertains to rules passed *after* a contract becomes effective, as well as to those in effect when the contract is signed. Furthermore, the board must make some reasonable attempt to communicate new rules to all employees, such as a general announcement or notification by letter, before compliance can be expected.

Contracts may be terminated by mutual consent at any time; however, termination of a contract by only one of the contracting parties without the consent of the other is called **breach of contract**. A teacher holding a

TERMINA-
TION OF
CONTRACTS

valid contract with a school district may not simply abandon it by notifying the board. State statutes usually provide a procedure for resignation, which the teacher must follow to be legally discharged from the obligations of the contract. In some states, the law allows that a probationary teacher under contract may resign on twenty-one days' written notice. Other states do not make it quite so easy for teachers to get out of a contract. "Contract jumping" after a certain date in the summer, usually August 1 or 15, is the target of legislation in a number of states.

SAFEGUARDS

Whereas school boards are given certain safeguards against the abandonment of contracts by teachers, as just described, teachers are protected to an even greater extent against such actions on the part of school boards. Whereas state laws usually give teachers the right to resign during the term of a contract, school boards can resort to no such procedure. To release a teacher under contract against her or his will, the board must charge her or him with failure to perform the duties required. The most common charges in such cases are immorality, insubordination, neglect of duty, and incompetence. Evidence must then be supplied by the board to substantiate its charges.

RENEWAL OF
CONTRACTS

Teachers not on **tenure** do not need to be rehired by the school board on the expiration of a contract, and the board usually need not give the reason for not rehiring a teacher. However, a number of states have what is called a *continuing-contract law*, which protects teachers from dismissal during a period of several months just before a new school year begins. The continuing contract law requires a school board to notify all nontenured teachers by a prescribed date in the spring, usually around May 1, if they are *not* to be rehired for the following school year. The law gives teachers not so notified the right to claim a contract at their proper place on the salary schedule for the coming year.

Teachers on tenure are commonly referred to as being on *indefinite contract*. This simply means that once a teacher gains tenure, his or her contract is automatically renewed from year to year without any requirement for official action by either the school board or the teacher, who, of course, continues in his or her proper place on the salary schedule. The only way a tenured teacher can be legally dismissed is by the procedure prescribed by the tenure statute in that state. Tenure and some of its implications, including dismissal, are discussed later.

Other Rights of Teachers

Teachers have both rights and responsibilities, just like anyone else; however, they must be viewed from the standpoint of the teacher, and from such a standpoint, a number of unique aspects are discernible. A discussion of teachers' rights will be followed by a look at their responsibilities.

At one time, teachers in this country were little better off than factory and mine workers were before the unions became strong enough to effect changes for the better. They were, in many instances, told what to teach, where to live, and what they could or could not do. In addition, they worked for very low salaries and few, if any, fringe benefits. To sum it all up, teachers at one time had very few rights.

As progress in other areas was noticed, teachers began to seek and to win concessions, until a sizable body of "teachers' rights" had been built. In the 1950s, teachers began to organize effectively, much as labor had been doing for several decades, and through collective bargaining, they have gained new rights and solidified their positions with respect to old ones. Some of the more important rights now legally held by teachers are discussed in the following paragraphs.

Salaries

It is a well-established principle of law that school boards have the power to fix teachers' salaries as long as no statute is violated and the boards do not act in an arbitrary and capricious manner.

MINIMUM
SALARIES

In some states, the legislature determines the minimum salary that can be paid to any public school teacher by passing a minimum salary law. Such laws generally base minimum salaries on only two factors: training and experience. In those states, public school districts cannot pay a teacher less than the amount stipulated in the state schedule. Most school districts, however, adopt **salary schedules** that are higher than the minimums required by state schedules. When this occurs, such districts establish new minimums, and no teachers may be paid a salary lower than that called for by their local salary schedule for a person with their training and experience, except on rare occasions.

The most common reason for placing an individual teacher below his or her normal place on the salary schedule, which is approved by the courts in several states, is the failure of the teacher to improve himself or herself professionally. When the board requires the teachers of the district to complete additional college credits or to participate in certain in-service programs, or allows approved travel to substitute for either of the first two requirements as a prerequisite to remaining in the proper place on the salary schedule, failure to do so results in a lower salary than is called for by the schedule. The Supreme Court of Missouri included membership in local, county, state, and national education associations as a factor in professional improvement, when it ruled that a teacher who refused to join them had no right to remain on the salary schedule.

There is little, if any, legal precedent to prevent a school board from increasing the salaries of teachers above their rightful place on the schedule. Should a board want to recognize outstanding performance in such a way, it can.

The salary schedule is not a contract between the teacher and the board. It is in the nature of a declaration of policy by the board and may be revised at any time. Of course, once teachers' contracts based on a certain salary schedule are signed, changing the schedule has no effect on those contracts. Once the contract period ends, however, a new salary schedule can go into effect.

Whenever factors other than training and experience are used as bases for determining classifications in a salary schedule, great care must be taken. Of course, courts may vary in their viewpoints, but in general, it is a good rule not to use factors that distinguish between teachers as married or unmarried, as black or white, as male or female, and as having dependents or having no dependents.

EXTRA PAY
FOR EXTRA
WORK

A school board may require teachers to perform duties other than those required in the classroom and extending beyond regular school hours without paying them additional salary. On the other hand, a board may choose to give teachers "extra pay for extra work." Should it choose not to, the board must be careful to see that such assignments (1) are equitably distributed among all the teachers; (2) are related to teaching duties (janitorial service, police service, and school bus driving are said by a New York court not to be so related); and (3) are related to a teacher's qualifications (the science club, for example, should not be assigned to an English teacher with no science background).

MISSED
SCHOOL
DAYS

Teachers are entitled to their salaries when schools are closed for reasons beyond their control. In some states, the courts have ruled that teachers do not even have to report for duty on such days though ordered to do so. It is generally conceded that days of school missed for such reasons may be made up at times as on Saturdays and during Christmas or Easter vacation. However, it is probable that additional salary would be required if lost days were made up after the expiration date on the teachers' contracts, which is usually in late May or in June.

Retirement

RETIREMENT
VS. PENSION

All of the states have teacher retirement plans. There is a legal distinction between a **retirement** plan and a **pension**. In the latter, the teacher is not required to contribute a part of her or his salary to the plan; in the former, the teacher and usually the school district or the state both contribute. The state has no obligation to pay a pension, but it may do so if the people desire. On the other hand, a retirement plan is contractual in nature, and the state assumes an obligation to the teachers enrolled in it.

VESTED
RIGHTS

Such obligations are not absolute, however. There is no question but that the state has the obligation to pay the teachers an amount equal to their contributions, because the teachers' rights become *vested*, at least to that amount, when they are required to contribute to the plan. If the statute requires interest to be paid, that, too, becomes part of the state's contractual obligation.

The contribution of the state is not as clear-cut. When the state's share of retirement benefits is paid to a member only after she or he retires based on a formula that does not go into effect until then, a contractual relationship does not arise until retirement. This means that once a member retires and her or his benefits are computed, the state may not lower them; however, the benefit schedule may be lowered before the teacher retires.

Some states pay their share to the account of each member of the plan every year during active service, so that when a member retires, the state's share is already fully paid. In those cases, both the member's share plus interest and the state's share plus interest become a contractual obligation of the state. It should be kept in mind, however, that the member must qualify for retirement benefits under the laws of the state before he or she can claim the state's share. His or her own contributions, usually plus interest, revert to him or her whenever he or she leaves the state or leaves teaching for a stated minimum length of time.

ANSWERS TO
QUESTIONS

When questions about retirement arise, the teacher can turn to the retirement fund officials, to the state education association, or to the state department of public instruction for help. Providing adequately for our elderly people has become an important social responsibility; therefore, teachers should know as much as possible about their retirement rights.

Leaves of Absence

In earlier times, when a teacher was absent from his or her job for any reason, he or she often was not paid for the days missed. However, as the school year lengthened, as professional organizations became more active, and as work pressures increased, the practice of allowing teachers leaves of absence with pay became a regularly accepted practice.

At first, school boards, through local rules and regulations, took the initiative in this matter. But one by one, state legislatures have faced the issue by passing laws that guarantee teachers limited leaves of absence for specified reasons with full pay. Leaves of absence for certain other reasons can also be obtained, but without pay.

The most common type of leave with full pay is sick leave. Nearly all of the states have enacted legislation mandating sick leave in some form for regular teachers. The average number of days of sick leave per year in those states is about ten. Most of them also allow unused sick leave to accumulate, the number of such days usually being left to the local school boards. As many as 180 days have been allowed to accumulate in some districts.

SICK LEAVE

In addition to allowing sick leave days to accumulate, some local districts have encouraged teachers to claim them judiciously by allowing them to be used as the basis for a form of severance pay. In other words, when a teacher retires, he or she is paid for all unused sick leave at the rate of pay of his or her last year of teaching.

SICK LEAVE
AS A FORM
OF SEVER-
ANCE PAY

It is not necessary for there to be a statute in a state for teachers to be given sick leave. Local school boards may grant sick leave as long as there is no statute forbidding the practice. In many of the states with sick leave statutes, local boards have the authority to exceed the number of days required by the statute, and many local school districts do just that. The practice of allowing sick leave accumulated in one school district to be

ACCUMULA-
TION OF SICK
LEAVE

transferred to and used in another district in the same state is now fairly common. So far, no unused sick leave is transferrable from one state to another.

Leave for a death in the immediate family is also common. In some states, a statute requires all school boards to grant this type of leave. Where there is no statute, boards have the legal right to grant it if they wish. The usual number of days granted for this leave is from three to five, and any unused days are generally not cumulative. The "immediate family" is usually limited to spouse, children, parents, and grandparents.

DEATH IN
THE IMMEDI-
ATE FAMILY

Personal leave has been getting more attention since 1965. This allows teachers two or three days a year to take care of personal matters or to perform civic duties. It is usually in addition to sick leave and the leave for a death in the immediate family, and as for those two kinds of leave, it provides for full pay for the number of days allowed by the law.

PERSONAL
LEAVE

Sabbatical leave has so far not been commonly granted to public elementary and secondary school teachers. It is thought of mostly in connection with colleges and universities. However, there are sabbatical leave programs in some of the wealthier and/or more progressive school districts now, and the practice is certain to be expanded. A sabbatical is a leave granted to a teacher after serving a certain number of years in the district, usually six or seven. The teacher is paid while on sabbatical, but the amount varies greatly among districts. The common practice in colleges and universities is to provide the teachers with full pay for one semester and with half pay for two semesters. A few public school districts follow this practice, but most of them grant smaller amounts.

SABBATICAL
LEAVE

The reasons for which sabbatical leaves may be given are usually strictly controlled. Professional improvement is the objective of most of them. Thus, further study and travel closely related to one's teaching field are the most common reasons approved by boards for sabbaticals.

Maternity leaves may be with or without pay, depending on the circumstances. Until 1974, nearly all maternity leaves were without pay and were strictly regulated by local school boards with respect to when a pregnant teacher had to begin the leave and when she could return to teaching. *Cleveland Board of Education v. La Fleur* (414 U.S. 632), a 1974 U.S. Supreme Court decision, changed all that. At issue was a board rule requiring every pregnant teacher to take an unpaid leave of absence five months before the birth of her child and specifying a return after the child had reached three months of age.

MATERNITY
LEAVE

The Court decided that the blanket five-month leave before birth, as well as the three-month return date, was arbitrary and did not consider the individual needs and capabilities of each affected teacher. It reasoned that the ability to teach effectively is an individual matter to be decided by each teacher in conjunction with her physician and the school administration.

Furthermore, in most states, pregnancy is now considered a physical condition that qualifies the teacher for sick leave. When advised by her physician to take a pregnancy leave, the teacher may apply accumulated

PREGNANCY
AS SICK
LEAVE

sick leave to be paid for those days. Of course, once all sick leave is used, the leave reverts to being an unpaid one.

The leaves previously discussed are nearly always given with full or partial pay. Other leaves provided by many school boards are not accompanied by salary. The advantage of a leave without pay accrues mainly to the tenured teacher. By being granted a leave, a tenured teacher does not have to give up his or her tenure rights. The main advantage of a nonsalaried leave to a nontenured teacher is the implication by the board that he or she will be rehired when the leave expires, although there is no legal guarantee.

LEAVE WITH-
OUT PAY

Another common reason for leave without pay is professional improvement. Although a small number of schools allow sabbatical leaves to be used for this purpose, most such leaves are nonsalaried. Service in the armed forces is still another reason. Some states make it mandatory for school boards to give a leave of absence to regular teachers going into service whether they are on tenure or not, thus guaranteeing them a job in the same district when they return.

Tenure

Teacher tenure is a much misunderstood phenomenon. Many people think of it as guaranteeing a teacher his or her job. The legal purpose of tenure, however, is to provide an orderly means for the dismissal of teachers. At one time, it was not uncommon for school boards to dismiss teachers for little or no reason. That is no longer a customary procedure because board practices today are a great deal sounder and more ethical than they were earlier in our history. The advent of negotiations between teacher groups and school boards has now created a new factor to be considered with respect to tenure, that is, the freedom with which a teacher can negotiate with his or her employer. Without tenure laws to protect him or her, the teacher would find it difficult to negotiate effectively.

ORDERLY
MEANS OF
DISMISSAL

To achieve tenure status, a teacher must nearly always serve a probationary period in a school district, generally three years, although state requirements vary from two to five years. During the probationary period, the teacher serves under an annual contract, which means that the board can refuse to renew it at the end of any school year.

PROBATION-
ARY PERIOD

Tenure refers to one's status within a particular school district. Thus, probationary time served in one district is not transferred to another. When a teacher moves from one district to another, she or he must serve the required probationary period in the new district to achieve tenure there, even though she or he may have been on tenure in the previous district. Usually, the probationary period requirement must be met by serving those years consecutively. For example, if a state requires a three-year probationary period and a teacher serves two consecutive years, then takes a leave of absence, he or she may have to begin the probationary period over again. Service as a substitute teacher, a special teacher, a part-time teacher, or a supply teacher ordinarily does not count toward tenure status.

APPLICABLE
TO ONLY A
SINGLE DIS-
TRICT

About four fifths of the states have tenure laws of some kind. Although they differ in detail, they all provide for two things: (1) continuing employment of the teacher who has acquired tenure status as long as the service rendered remains satisfactory and (2) a specific procedure to be followed if there is just cause for dismissal.

PROCEDURE
FOR DIS-
MISSAL

The procedure for dismissing a tenured teacher is set by statute. Although the specific details may vary by state, the four steps that follow summarize fairly well the procedure commonly followed:

1. A notice from the school board that dismissal is contemplated
2. A statement of the charges
3. The right to a hearing before the school board with counsel
4. The right to appeal—to a higher educational authority in the state and/or to the courts

REASONS FOR
DISMISSAL

The reasons for which a tenured teacher may be dismissed must be defined by statute. The courts have consistently refused to uphold dismissals for reasons not contained in the tenure law. There is a considerable variety of reasons among the states, but among the more common ones are incompetency, immorality, insubordination, neglect of duty, and reduction of staff because of a drop in enrollment. Some states allow some leeway to local boards by including as a reason for dismissal in the tenure law the phrase "and for other just and good cause." This is not a mandate for school boards to dismiss tenured teachers for any reason whatsoever, because the courts have required the reasons under that clause to be related to the performance of a person as a teacher.

FOLLOWING
THE EXACT
PROCEDURE

Both the school board and the tenured teacher being dismissed must follow the procedure exactly as outlined by the tenure statute. Failure to do so nearly always results in the loss of one's rights under that law. For example, if the statute requires a teacher to ask for a hearing with the board within five days of receiving a statement of charges, failure of the teacher to do so means that he or she forfeits the right to a hearing.

TENURED VS.
NONTENURED

In contrast to the **nontenured teacher**, who works under an annual contract, the tenured teacher need not be reappointed annually. He or she is entitled to a succession of contracts for an indefinite period as long as his or her behavior does not expose him or her to dismissal for one of the reasons listed in the tenure statute. Thus, it is commonly said that a tenured teacher is on "indefinite contract." A school board need not send new contracts to its tenured teachers each year unless it wishes to change some of the conditions in the contract. As far as salary is concerned, tenured teachers receive what the salary schedule calls for whether or not they get a contract each year.

Academic Freedom

Academic freedom is a term that implies both freedom for the teacher and the responsibility necessary to maintain it. The courts have insisted that academic freedom is not an unlimited right of a teacher to speak, think, and believe as she or he wishes in the classroom. Rather, the teacher has the responsibility to consider such things as the standards of the community, the laws of the state and nation, the age and capacity of her or his students, and the fact that her or his rights as a teacher are not the same as the rights of an ordinary citizen. Because a teacher believes in Christianity, for example, is not a good reason that she or he should be allowed to teach about it as the only true religion. How free should a teacher be to teach about sex? Academic freedom does not give the teacher the license to teach students that sexual intercourse between single students under eighteen is proper, because this violates certain statutes. Academic freedom does not mean academic license. It is the freedom to do good and not to teach evil. Academic freedom cannot authorize a teacher to teach that murder or treason is good.

ACADEMIC FREEDOM, NOT ACADEMIC LICENSE

There is no clear definition of academic freedom available. In general, the term refers to the freedom that teachers should have to discuss all aspects of a subject with their students without imposing their own viewpoints. A teacher should have the freedom to state his or her own viewpoint as one among others but should not have the right to propagandize it as the only view. When teachers believe that they are restricted by their superiors, or by the community, in their freedom to teach, they should go to the courts.

NO CLEAR DEFINITION

Right to Organize and Bargain Collectively

There is no doubt today that teachers have the right to organize and to join employee organizations. There was some doubt of this until the 1960s, but now most states have enacted statutes specifically permitting it.

The right to negotiate, or bargain, with school boards is not quite as clear-cut as the right to organize. The key concept in negotiations is that school boards have the right to bargain with teachers if they wish to, but unless a state statute compels them, they are not required to bargain. It can be done, without statutory compulsion, only at the board's discretion.

COLLECTIVE BARGAINING

One by one, the states are passing negotiation or **collective bargaining** laws. These laws require school boards to negotiate with teacher organizations, and they also spell out the procedures for negotiation, as well as for settling an impasse between board and teachers. Exclusive negotiation rights have caused some problems, especially in those states without negotiations statutes. In general, though, the teacher organization with the greatest membership is given the right to bargain for all the teachers in a school district. Minority organizations and individuals, however, must be given the right to be heard. The statutes usually define the procedure for determining which organization will have exclusive bargaining rights.

NO LEGAL RIGHT TO STRIKE

At the present time, public school teachers in most states, as government employees, do not have the legal right to strike. The fact that teachers have gone on strike, and probably will in the future, does not make striking legal. The major penalty for striking is dismissal, and teachers realize that a school board will not dismiss all who have gone on strike because replacements cannot be found. Today, however, there is considerable evidence indicating that public opinion is growing in support of legalizing teacher strikes. At least eight states now permit limited right-to-work stoppages, but only after certain mandatory conditions have been met.

Probably the greatest problem faced by both sides in negotiations is the **impasse**, which is that point where disagreement prevails and neither side will give in or compromise. Three methods are usually available. The first of these, mediation, occurs when both sides agree to employ a third party for the purpose of helping them reach an agreement. The mediator makes suggestions, persuades, cajoles, or praises in an attempt to get the negotiating parties to agree; however, nothing in this procedure is binding on either side.

MEDIATION

Fact finding occurs when a third party (often from outside the district) is employed to conduct a study of the situation and to present a factual report, which is usually publicized. It is then hoped that public opinion will cause one or both sides to change positions and an agreement to be reached. Again, nothing is binding on either party.

FACT FIND-
ING

Arbitration occurs when two disputing parties engage a third party (if arbitration is compulsory, the arbiter may be appointed) to hear both sides, to study the situation, and then to make a decision. Only a few states permit binding arbitration at this time (which means that the decision of the arbiter is binding on both parties), and those states vary in how it can be used. Arbitration is not popular with either public employees or public employers and is being met with great resistance in most states. One good reason is that such a procedure takes the decision-making authority from the school board, which it has long held by statute.

ARBITRATION

Political Activity

FEW LIMITA-
TIONS

The kind of political activity in which a teacher engages makes a difference. A teacher may engage in the normal political activities of any citizen outside the classroom. Limitations are placed on him or her only when there is some detrimental relation to his or her job as a teacher. For example, if the time required for political activities prohibits the teacher from adequately performing his or her duties, the board may require the teacher to curtail his or her political duties or risk dismissal.

NO RIGHT
TO PROPA-
GANDIZE

Teachers have no right to impose their political views on their captive audience, the students. Academic freedom gives teachers the right to discuss politics, political parties and platforms, and candidates, but not the right to propagandize in the classroom.

The right of public school teachers to hold political office varies among the states: some allow it, others do not. Indiana allows its public school teachers to hold political office but requires them to take a leave of absence while holding public office (during the legislative session if elected to the legislature), and if campaigning for office requires a great deal of time, the local school board has the power to place them on leave for the campaign as well.

Loyalty Oaths

In the early 1960s, nearly three fourths of the states had a constitutional, statutory, or administrative requirement for a loyalty oath by teachers as a prerequisite to teaching. Many teachers oppose such a requirement, mainly because they believe that it discriminates against them as a particular class of people. "Why aren't other groups or classes of people required to take a loyalty oath for employment?" they ask. State courts have consistently upheld loyalty oath laws; however, the U.S. Supreme Court has ruled some GUILT BY AS- loyalty oath laws unconstitutional when it found them to be too vague for SOCIATION fair interpretation or to be based on the principle of "guilt by association," indicting members of certain organizations such as the Communist Party. This does not necessarily indicate that all loyalty oath laws are headed for extinction, but that some may be invalid if challenged.

Discrimination in Employment

No one has an inherent right to be employed as a teacher in the public schools. The highest of qualifications does not change this principle. On the other hand, a person may *not* be refused a position solely on the basis of race, creed, color, sex, age, handicap, or national origin. The courts have repeatedly said, in decisions since World War II, that distinctions in employment or nonemployment of persons on these bases alone are in violation of the Due Process and Equal Protection clauses of the Fourteenth Amendment.

To curb discriminatory practices, states have enacted "fair employment

Sample loyalty oath.

(SOURCE: Adapted by permission from the Indiana Department of Education.)

IMPORTANT: State law requires the loyalty affidavit to be signed and notarized on each application and requires the applicant to keep one copy.

LOYALTY AFFIDAVIT

I solemnly swear (or affirm) that I will support the Constitution of the United States of America, the Constitution of the State, and the laws of the United States and the state, and will, by precept and example, promote respect for the flag and the institutions of the United States and of the state, reverence for law and order, and undivided allegiance to the government of the United States of America.

Signed _____
(Applicant)

Subscribed and sworn to before me, a Notary Public, this _____ day of _____ 19 ___

My commission expires _____. Notary Public _____

NOT VALID WITHOUT STAMP OR SEAL OF NOTARY PUBLIC

CURBING
DISCRIMINA-
TORY PRAC-
TICES

practices" and **"antidiscrimination" laws**. The purpose of fair employment practices is to provide opportunities for members of minority groups to secure adequate employment and to create public attitudes that reject discriminatory practices. These laws actually extend beyond discrimination as it is commonly understood and forbid certain expressions of prejudice.

The federal government added its weight and enlarged the scope of the applicability of racial antidiscrimination in employment when it passed the Civil Rights Act of 1964. Title VII of that act contains the criteria pertinent to employment.

USE OF TESTS

Since 1964, the U.S. Supreme Court has clarified Title VII through a number of decisions. The use of tests has been one of the most contentious issues related to discrimination in employment, especially when a test results in the disqualification of a disproportionate number of minority applicants. In general, a test may be used as a means of determining job qualification when there is a positive relationship between the test results and job performance, and when there is no provable attempt on the part of the employer to discriminate.

FOURTEENTH
AMENDMENT

Principles of law similar to those involved in hiring are applicable when promotions and staff reductions take place. Either Title VII or the Equal Protection Clause of the Fourteenth Amendment is the basis for legal action when discrimination is suspected.

REVERSE DIS-
CRIMINA-
TION

At times, members of a majority group feel the sting of discrimination when attempts to remedy minority discrimination are overemphasized. This is called *reverse discrimination*, and it has been addressed by the courts on several occasions. The U.S. Supreme Court has held unconditionally that the terms of Title VII "are not limited to discrimination against members of any particular race" (*McDonald v. Santa Fe Trail Transportation Co.*, 427 U.S. 273, 1976). Quota systems, which prescribe definite percentages or numbers of one race or minority group, without regard to other factors, have been declared illegal by the Court.

SEX DISCRIM-
INATION

Sex discrimination has also been the focus of federal legislation and resulting court cases. Until the 1970s, unequal treatment in employment based on sex was legally sanctioned; however, as racial minorities gained in their battle for equal rights, women began to realize that action was also needed to better their position. The legal bases for nearly all sex discrimination cases have been the Equal Pay Act, Title VII of the Civil Rights Act of 1964, and Title IX of the Education Amendments of 1972.

The areas of greatest emphasis, in which significant gains for women have been made, are those concerning pregnancy-related policies, differential treatment of men and women in retirement programs, and sex bias in hiring, promotion, and pay.

In addition to discrimination by race and sex, considerable attention has been paid in recent years to discrimination based on age and on handicap. For additional information about those subjects, see the reference section near the end of this book.

Duty-Free Lunch Periods

Teachers have long maintained that they should have the privilege of eating lunch during the school day entirely free from any kind of responsibility. Most schools make no such provisions for their teachers. Some states have enacted statutes giving teachers such a right. The amount of duty-free lunchtime averages about thirty minutes in those states, and the statute usually prescribes the hours during which the free time must be used. The validity of these statutes has so far not been successfully challenged in the courts.

Right to Hold Other Employment or Positions

MAKE
TEACHERS
UNFIT?

Public school teachers do have the right to hold employment outside the school system while under contract. It is only when such outside employment substantially interferes with the effective performance of their teaching duties, or when the outside work is of such a nature as to make teachers unfit for their positions (such as bookie or gambler or, in one case, a waitress in a "dive"), that boards have the right to dismiss them or require them to give up the outside job.

Lunchroom duty continues to be a responsibility of teachers.

(Photo by Axler.)

Fringe Benefits

Without express statutory permission, it is generally assumed that school boards may spend public funds for any purpose that is reasonably necessary to promote the interests of the schools. With the fierce competition for employees of the 1950s and 1960s, most school authorities adopted the philosophy that it was necessary to provide not only competitive salaries but fringe benefits as well. These have remained a vital part of teacher compensation ever since. The most common fringe benefits are prepaid hospital and medical plans, life insurance, retirement plans, leaves with pay, severance pay, and workers' compensation.

WORKERS'
COMPENSA-
TION

Although **workers' compensation** is in effect in most states by statute and has been upheld by the courts, many teachers are unaware of either its benefits or its requirements. The benefits usually consist of payment of a weekly allowance during the period in which a teacher cannot work. To qualify for workers' compensation benefits, a teacher must be accidentally injured "out of" and "in the course of" his or her employment in the school. "Out of" one's employment refers to the relationship of the activity from which the injury arose to one's duties as a teacher. The question to answer here is: Did your job require you to do the act that caused the injury? "In the course of" refers to whether or not you were actually in the act of performing the job required of you when the injury occurred. It is interesting to note that such incidents as heart attacks and coming down with the measles have been judged by the courts to be compensable "injuries" under workers' compensation laws.

Control of Students

Whenever people have rights, they also have responsibilities, and people who have responsibilities often incur liabilities that grow out of neglecting or forgetting them. The greatest legal responsibility that a teacher has is for the health, safety, and well-being of the students placed in her or his care. From the standpoint of the law, teachers must know what they can or cannot do with respect to their students. When they do things they shouldn't do or don't do the things they should do, teachers may incur a personal liability, usually in the form of money damages.

There are also certain things that the teacher or the school can do to control students. A school could not operate unless certain rules were established and enforced with respect to the admission, attendance, assignment, graduation, and behavior of its students. The teachers have the responsibility to carry out such rules and regulations.

With young people in school at least half of the year, many of them even more, the responsibility for and thus the control of them must be lodged with the school and its personnel, at least for the time they are in school or are engaged in school-sponsored activities. The courts have come to define this relationship of the teacher standing in place of the parent as *in loco parentis*.

It should not be assumed that ***in loco parentis*** gives the teacher exactly the same powers over the pupils as the parents have. The teacher's authority is less broad than that of the parent because the teacher's control is limited

IN LOCO PAR-
ENTIS

to situations within his or her jurisdiction as a teacher. The parent, for example, controls the manner and mode of religious training and the type of medical and dental treatment that the child receives. The teacher can control none of those things because they lie outside the scope of his or her authority as a teacher. Note, however, that limiting the *in loco parentis* relationship to the scope of a teacher's authority does not confine that authority merely to the school premises and to school hours. Whenever the orderly operation of the school is endangered, a teacher has the right to control the actions or words of a student, whether or not on the school premises or during school hours.

As long as the teacher exercises control of pupils in a *reasonable* manner, he or she will not be denied such control. In addition, a teacher's control

LIMITED BY
SCHOOL
RULES

is sometimes limited by school board rules and by statutes. Thus, if not restricted by rule or law and if his or her demands are not unreasonable, the teacher has the common law right to direct how and when each pupil shall attend to his or her appropriate duties and the manner in which the pupil shall conduct himself or herself.

There are certain things pupils must do, and there are certain other things they cannot do. It is usually up to the teacher to see that those things are either done or not done, as the case may be. When the rules governing the

RIGHT TO
PRESCRIBE
PENALTIES

"do's" or "don'ts" are violated, the teacher then has the right to prescribe penalties. When penalizing students, the teacher should make certain that the rule broken was a reasonable one and that the penalty is also reasonable. The paragraphs that follow discuss some of these requirements and the penalties that often go with them.

Pupil Dress and Appearance

There is no disagreement with the fact that schools have the right to regulate the dress and appearance of their students. The question that the

DEGREE OF
REGULATION

courts are called on to answer is the *degree* of regulation that the schools can exercise. Objectors to excessive regulation contend that the student is being deprived of the First Amendment right of free expression (a form of freedom of speech).

What the court looks for in cases dealing with the regulation of pupil dress and appearance in school is evidence that the orderly operation of the school is being eroded by the dress or appearance in question. For a regu-

ORDERLY OP-
ERATION OF
A SCHOOL

latory rule of this kind to be reasonable, there must be a logical relationship between it and the efficient operation of the school. Teachers and administrators should be careful to compile specific evidence to this effect before making or enforcing a rule regulating pupil dress and appearance.

A case dealing with pupil dress of a slightly different nature, but a fairly common occurrence nevertheless, involved a high school girl who was suspended from school for refusal to wear a prescribed uniform in her gym class. It was contended that wearing the uniform subjected the girl to an immodest display that was in violation of her religious beliefs. A compromise was reached when the court held that the girl could be required to attend the class, but that she could not be required to wear the prescribed outfit nor to engage in exercises that would be immodest in ordinary apparel.

PRESCRIBED
UNIFORMS

In another case where the school required that a certain garb be worn by students, the court looked for a relationship between the requirement and the reason for wearing the garb. A high school senior refused to wear a cap and gown at commencement, whereupon the school board refused to give her a diploma. The court said that it could see no relation between wearing a cap and gown and the educational objectives of the school. The student could be barred from the commencement exercises, but not from receiving her diploma.

DRESS RE-
LATED TO
REQUIRE-
MENTS

Pupil Driving

Most high schools today have huge parking lots, and most of the space is used by students who drive to school. This circumstance, of course, brings up the question of what control school authorities may exercise over student drivers. The answer is not as simple as the question, however, because the issue involved is the power of the school to regulate the use by students of public roads and streets. Those who object to the regulation of student driving by the school contend that this is a matter for the civil authorities and is not within the implied powers of school boards.

POWER TO
REGULATE

A school board may designate where students must park, and it may also prohibit student driving during school hours without permission, as long as the prohibition's primary purpose is the safety of the students and/or the orderly operation of the school. Where there is evidence to show that students driving their cars on the public streets around the school endanger the safety of other students, the school may take any reasonable steps to control the practice. A common rule approved by schools is to require students to park their cars in designated areas when they arrive at school and to prohibit them from driving without written permission until they leave for home. A common penalty for rulebreakers is to deprive them of driving rights for a period. Of course, if the student's home location requires transportation, the school must provide it during this period.

REGULATING
PARKING

Some schools require student drivers to deposit their car keys in the office when they arrive at school. The reasoning is that the cars cannot be driven until the keys are given back to the drivers, and the principal can thus tightly control student driving during school hours. There are two weaknesses in this plan. The first one is that the students may have duplicate keys. The second weakness is of a legal nature. Under the law of bailments, the principal could become the bailee for all the cars for which keys are turned in. Any damage done to the cars during the time the keys are held could be charged to the principal. No case of record has been heard

CONTROL OF
CAR KEYS

on that subject, but some legal experts express the opinion that it could happen.

Pupil Marriages

Many schools have reported problems as a result of student marriages. Whether the problems result from the marriages or from the reaction of the school officials to the marriages is sometimes difficult to determine. At any rate, school boards have gone to great lengths to discourage students from getting married or to penalize married students by suspending, expelling, or barring them from participation in extracurricular activities.

As far as the legality of the school board efforts is concerned, much is left to be desired. The board may certainly discourage marriage by persuasion or logic, but there are no legal measures that it may effectively use to prevent student marriages.

SUSPENSION AND EXPULSION OF MARRIED STUDENTS

As recently as the 1960s, many school boards adopted rules expelling students who got married on the grounds that (1) expulsion would serve as an example and thus deter pupils planning marriage from going through with it, and (2) the unmarried students associating with married ones in the schools would somehow become less moral. The courts have upheld neither point of view. In fact, a Mississippi court ruled:

> Marriage is a domestic relation highly favored by the law. When the relation is entered into with correct motives, the effect upon the husband and wife is refining and elevating, rather than demoralizing. Pupils associating in school with a child occupying such a relation, it seems, would be benefited instead of harmed. (*McLeon v. State ex rd. Colmer,* 154 Miss. 468, 1929)

Admission Requirements

Although it may be correct to say that a child has the right to attend a public school, that right is not absolute. If it were, school authorities would have a difficult time with certain children. The courts have generally said that attendance at a public school is a privilege that is granted a child, but under such terms and conditions as the lawmaking power, within constitutional limits, may see fit to impose.

PRIVILEGE NOT A RIGHT

Thus, a school board may, under certain conditions, deny admission to a child. One of these conditions is age. A school board may determine the age for admission to the first grade or kindergarten. It may even set a cutoff date, meaning that children reaching the age of five or six after a specified date will not be admitted to kindergarten or the first grade until the following year. The usual cutoff date is the first of September, October, November, or December. Some states have statutes specifying admission cutoff dates. Local boards must conform to those, of course.

CONDITIONS OF DENIAL

Another condition for admission that may be imposed by a school board is the requirement to take a physical examination or to be vaccinated. The requirement for vaccination sometimes leads to conflict with religious beliefs. Certain religions forbid their members to receive vaccinations, blood transfusions, and other medical treatment of that sort. The reasoning

VACCINATIONS?

Although education is a right, school authorities may set admission requirements such as age and proper immunization, which must be satisfied at the time of registration.

(Photo by Axler.)

of the courts in ruling on that conflict was well stated by the Supreme Court of Kentucky in 1948:

> Religious freedom embraces two conceptions, freedom to believe and freedom to act. The first is absolute but, in the nature of things, the second cannot be . . . the constitutional guarantee of religious freedom does not permit the practice of religious rights dangerous or detrimental to the lives, safety or health of the participants or to the public. (*Mosier v. Barren County Board of Health*, 215 S.W. 2d 967, 1948)

Children may not only be refused admission to a public school for failure to be vaccinated but may also be expelled if they are already in attendance. State statutes that address the subject prescribe the legal procedure within their boundaries.

Attendance Requirements

PENALTIES
AGAINST
PARENTS

All of the states have **compulsory attendance laws.** The constitutionality of such laws has frequently been challenged, but the courts have consistently upheld them. The courts have reasoned that an enlightened citizenry is essential for our form of government, as well as for our survival; thus, parents should be required to relinquish custody of their children to the school during certain specified years in order that minimum educational standards may be attained. Penalties are assessed against the parents if their children do not attend school while within the age of compulsory attendance, unless there is a legal reason for being absent.

Children may be placed in whatever grade or at whatever level the school officials decide on, provided there are reasonable grounds for such placement. When a child transfers from another school, for example, the public school officials may place him or her in the same grade or any other grade that a reasonable assessment of his or her abilities may indicate. Courts will not overrule a decision of this kind, which is based on professional competence, unless there is clear evidence of whim or capriciousness on the part of the board.

RIGHT TO ASSIGN STUDENTS

The school board also has a right to assign a student to any attendance unit (building) within the district. Ordinarily, pupils attend the school nearest their residence, but if a school is crowded, the board may assign pupils to another school not as conveniently located. A pupil has no legal right to attend a particular school within a district merely because he or she lives in it, or because his or her parents want the child to attend a particular school.

INTEGRATION AS A REASON

Since the *Brown v. Board of Education of Topeka* case in 1954 invalidated school segregation, pupil assignment has become a major factor in the **integration** process. Some school boards have used the discretion usually given them with respect to pupil assignment for the purpose of creating or maintaining segregation. From the many court decisions on this subject, one thing is clear: pupil assignment may not be made with racial **segregation** as the objective. As a matter of fact, the converse is true. Court decisions in the 1970s required pupil assignments to be made with *desegregation* as the objective. Thus, the busing of children within a school district—and even between school districts—has, on occasion, been mandated by the courts.

Obviously, all children within the compulsory attendance age limits cannot benefit from school. The various state legislatures and the courts have recognized this fact, so there are statutes and court decisions alike that set forth the circumstances under which such children are legally excused.

EXCUSED ABSENCE

The most common reason for an excused absence from school is illness. No statute or court will require a child to attend school when attendance would endanger his or her health or well-being. School officials may take reasonable steps to check on students, such as requiring a signed statement from the doctor for a prolonged illness or for a student who is absent for that reason quite frequently.

Other common reasons for nonattendance are mental or physical incompetence, living a great distance from school or having to travel a dangerous route without transportation, serving as a page in the legislature, a death in the immediate family, exposure to a contagious disease, and suspension or expulsion. At one time, the courts approved the substitution of "equiv-

MIXED OPIN-
IONS CON-
CERNING
HOME IN-
STRUCTION

alent home instruction" for attendance at a recognized school, but decisions in the 1950s and 1960s reversed this attitude. On that subject, the courts recognized that a highly qualified teacher may be secured to provide home instruction, but that even the best teacher could not provide the child with experiences in group activity and social outlook comparable to those provided in the public school. Court decisions in the 1970s and 1980s have been mixed, with some state courts approving home instruction, and others not.

THE QUES-
TION OF RES-
IDENCE

The question of residence as related to the payment of tuition for attending a particular school is sometimes puzzling. Public schools are free from tuition in all states, most of them by constitutional mandate. This mandate has been intepreted to mean that tuition is free only in the school district in which the student is a resident. Generally, the residence of a student is with his or her parents or legal guardian. Whenever a student lives with someone other than his or her parents or guardian, the criterion for determining whether he or she is a resident for school purposes is the primary reason for his or her living there. If it is to provide him or her with a better home, he or she is considered a resident; if it is to take advantage of the schools, he or she has to pay tuition as a nonresident. Orphans and children on welfare are usually considered residents of the homes to which they are assigned.

Suspension and Expulsion

REASONS

If attending a public school were an absolute right of an American child, **suspension** and **expulsion** would be impossible. Many teachers and administrators are thankful that such is not the case. Any students whose presence is clearly inimical to the best interests of the school, regardless of age, may be excluded. Of course, the school board must have sufficient evidence to support such charges if challenged by the student and his or her parents.

SUSPENSION
VS. EXPUL-
SION

Suspension is temporary exclusion from school, usually for several days; expulsion is more permanent, but usually only for the remainder of the term or school year. Because expulsion is a far more serious penalty, many states require the school board to make this decision, whereas suspension is often left to the discretion of the superintendent or the principal.

DEPRIVED OF
AN EDUCA-
TION?

Neither of these two penalties for misconduct is looked on with favor by the courts or by the teaching profession. Some incorrigible pupils violate regulations for the very purpose of being removed from school. When a pupil is denied school attendance, he or she is being deprived of an education, the one thing that he or she needs the most. There are some students, however, whose presence is extremely detrimental to the good of the school. When all else has failed, suspension or expulsion could be the only remedy.

DUE PROCESS

Some states enacted "student due process statutes" in the 1970s. The common elements in those laws require schools to draw up a set of reasonable rules and penalties, and they prescribe the **"due process"** steps that must be taken before a student can be suspended or expelled.

In-school detention is one form of discipline.

(Photo by Axler.)

Academic Penalties for Behavioral Violations

LOWERING GRADES?

A common practice in the schools is to penalize a student for misconduct by lowering her or his grades. Although there is very little legal precedent in this area, it is generally agreed that an obvious resort to such practice would not be upheld in a court of law. First, it is poor practice because it is illogical; neither is it based on any acceptable educational theory. Second, the consequences to the student may be so detrimental as to cause the penalty to be out of all proportion to the offense.

GRADES AND OTHER PEN-ALTIES?

For example, a bright student could be just mischievous enough to irritate some of her teachers to the point where they lowered her grades sufficiently to prevent her from securing a valuable college scholarship. Or an average student who was apt to get caught while violating school rules could be kept from graduating. This is a difficult practice to defend, especially when the misconduct is quite obviously removed from the realm of academic grades. One principal lowered the grades of a boy who would not conform to the rules on student driving. Another boy had his grades lowered because he was caught drinking alcoholic beverages at a school dance.

CHEATING AND PLAGIA-RISM

Where there is some reasonable relationship of the misconduct to academic grades, the practice would probably win approval. Cheating on an exam and **plagiarism** are examples. It could be logically argued that the grades would have been lower if the cheating or plagiarism had not occurred.

Paying for Damages

RESTITUTION

At this time, only a few states have statutes requiring parents to assume financial responsibility for acts of their children. In the majority of states, then, it would be useless to bring suit against a child to collect for any damage he or she may have caused to school property, unless the child holds assets in his or her own right. As a result, some schools have resorted to suspending or expelling students who have damaged school property until payment has been made by either the student or his or her parents. The courts have distinguished between damage caused by mischievous or careless acts and that caused willfully or maliciously. Unless a statute does make the parents liable, the school cannot require a student to pay for damage caused by negligence or carelessness, nor can the student be punished for it. If the damage is inflicted willfully or maliciously, however, recovery or punishment, or both, may well be upheld in court.

Corporal Punishment

Once the most common methods of controlling student misbehavior, **corporal punishment** has been declining in use for the past several decades; however, it is still used often enough so that all teachers ought to be acquainted with its legal aspects. The educational merits and demerits of corporal punishment are not discussed here.

RIGHT TO
USE

Teachers have the right to use corporal punishment as long as a statute or a local school board rule does not forbid it. Only New Jersey, Massachusetts, and the District of Columbia have such a statute at this time. It is safe to say, however, that most teachers in the United States have the right to administer corporal punishment, although in many school districts that do not forbid it, strict procedures are set up to regulate it.

ASSAULT
AND BAT-
TERY

A teacher who administers corporal punishment may be charged either with assault and battery or with breaking a local school board rule. **Battery** is any intentional touching of a person, his or her eyeglasses, or his or her clothing without his or her consent or without being privileged. **Assault** is causing fear or apprehension of a battery. Assault can be committed without battery, but battery generally includes assault. If an assault alone causes an injury, charges may be brought. For example, an upraised arm may cause a pupil to duck and hit his or her eye on a sharp corner or other object and thus inflict serious damage.

An assault and battery charge is upheld by a court only if the teacher inflicted immoderate punishment or caused some permanent injury and did so with malice or with wicked motives. Seldom will a criminal charge of assault and battery be brought against a teacher; most parents prefer a civil charge, in part, because damages can then be sought.

The best advice for teachers to follow might be summed up in the following points:

1. Be sure there is no statute prohibiting corporal punishment.
2. Check the local school board regulations closely, first, to find out if

corporal punishment is prohibited, and second, if it is not, to learn the proper procedures if it is prescribed.

3. Never strike a child when angry or with malice.

SOME GUIDE-
LINES FOR
CORPORAL
PUNISHMENT

4. Inflict only moderate punishment. Do not take the chance of leaving the child with a permanent injury.

5. The punishment should be suited to the age, sex, size, and physical strength of the child.

6. The punishment should be in proportion to the offense.

7. Be sure the rule being enforced with corporal punishment is a reasonable one.

8. The child punished should be under the jurisdiction of the person doing the punishing. If not, the punisher is not *in loco parentis* and is thus not privileged (see the definition of *battery* given earlier).

Detention

Another common method of enforcing school rules and regulations is keeping the student after school. If the detention is for a reasonable time and was assigned for a good and related cause, there seems to be little objection RISK OF LIA- to it from a legal standpoint. However, where detention involves a student BILITY who depends on a school bus to get home, there may be some risk of liability should the student walk, hitchhike, or ride home without someone other than his or her parents and be injured while doing so. It would be much safer to mete out some other punishment to such students.

Student Search and Seizure

The use of drugs by school-aged students became widespread in the 1970s. To combat such use in the schools, the practice of searching for illegal drugs (or tobacco or alcohol) on the persons or in the lockers or automobiles FOURTH of students became fairly common. Students found with drugs in their AMENDMENT possession turned to the **Fourth Amendment** of the U.S. Constitution, which protects individuals against arbitrary searches by requiring state agents to obtain a warrant based on probable cause before conducting a search. The public school, it was said, was an agent of the state.

Until 1985, the courts ruled on student search and seizure cases using one of three approaches: (1) the Fourth Amendment does not apply because school officials function as private citizens; (2) the Fourth Amendment does THREE AP- apply, but the doctrine of *in loco parentis* lowers the standard in determin- PROACHES ing the reasonableness of a search; or (3) the Fourth Amendment applies, and probable cause is required before conducting a search. It was difficult for schools to know exactly where they stood as long as the courts in different state and federal jurisdictions differed in their interpretation of the situation.

Early in 1985, the U.S. Supreme Court handed down a decision that should stabilize the law and allow school officials to draw up rules that will withstand legal protests. In a case originating in New Jersey, the Court,

On the grounds of "reasonable suspicion," school officials may search students' lockers for illegal or regulated substances.

(Photo by Axler.)

by a 6–3 majority, declared that public schools fell under the second approach enunciated in the preceding paragraph (*New Jersey, Petitioner v. T.L.O.*, U.S. Sup. Ct., 1985). Although the Fourth Amendment does apply, public schools will not be held to the same standard of **"probable cause"** to which the police are held. School officials may search students or their

PROBABLE
CAUSE VS.
REASONABLE
SUSPICION

purses, lockers, or automobiles parked on school property on the basis of **"reasonable suspicion."** A search of a student by a public school official is reasonable under the Fourth Amendment if there are reasonable grounds for suspecting that the search will reveal evidence of a student's violation of either the law or the rules of the school. The method of search must then be reasonably related to the objectives of the search and may not be excessively intrusive in light of the age and sex of the student and the nature of the infraction.

In the New Jersey case, a teacher's report that the student had been seen smoking in the lavatory in violation of school rules provided enough reasonable suspicion to justify the school officials' decision to open her purse to look for cigarettes. The detection of cigarette rolling papers in the purse gave rise to reasonable suspicion that she was carrying marijuana and justified further search of the purse for contraband.

Tort Liability of Teachers

SAFETY AND
WELL-BEING

When someone has a responsibility, as teachers do, for the safety and well-being of the students assigned to them, there is a good chance that a slipup will occur and that the responsibility will not be properly fulfilled. Should this happen, the teacher could incur a legal liability that would require the payment of money for any damage that may be done to the person or property of another.

LEGAL
AGENTS

Every person is legally responsible for his or her own acts or the acts of his or her **legal agents.** A person who negligently drives his automobile through a plate glass window, for example, commits a **tort** against the person who owns the window, and the courts will permit the owner to recover damages. Thus, a tort occurs when one person acts wrongfully and such an act causes real injury or damage to the person or property of another. Wrongful acts pertaining to contracts, however, are not torts.

SPOKEN
WORD

A tort may also arise from the spoken word. One who causes injury to the reputation of another by use of the written or spoken word may be held accountable and may be made to pay damages to the injured party.

WRONGFUL
ACTIONS

Wrongful actions that lead to a tort are called *negligence*. In other words, when a person acts negligently and causes injury to another, that is a tort. Negligence is defined as failing to do what a reasonably prudent person would have done in similar circumstances, or doing what a reasonably prudent person would not have done in similar circumstances.

REASONABLE
PRUDENT
PERSON

It is difficult to define a reasonably prudent person. He or she is an ideal but is always of the same class of persons as the one with whom he or she is being compared. When one is trying to determine whether a teacher acted as a reasonably prudent person, for example, he or she would be measured against a reasonably prudent teacher, not an engineer or laborer. The courts try to figure out what a hypothetically reasonable and prudent teacher would have done in a similar situation, and if the accused teacher did not act in that way, he or she would be held liable for a tort.

Negligence is composed of four elements, all of which must be proved by a plaintiff to win a claim:

NEGLIGENCE

1. *Duty*—The defendant owed the plaintiff a duty of reasonable care.
2. *Breach of that duty*—The defendant failed to perform the duty in the manner of a reasonably prudent person.
3. *Causation*—The defendant's actions actually caused the injury and were proximate to it.
4. *Damage or injury*—The plaintiff must have suffered a *real* loss, not merely imaginary and usually not just financial.

REASONABLE
STANDARDS

If we analyze these elements from the standpoint of a teacher, it is clear that teachers have the duty to exercise reasonable care for the safety and well-being of students in their charge. As for the second element, the duty a teacher owes her or his pupils is breached when she or he fails to perform it in the manner of a reasonably prudent teacher. It is important to recognize that the standards of care vary with the ability of the students and with the type and the place of the activity in which they are engaged. For example, younger children need greater care than older ones, mentally retarded children need greater care than those with normal intelligence, and the laboratory or the physical education area requires greater care than the ordinary classroom.

ELEMENT OF
CAUSATION

The element of causation requires the plaintiff to prove (1) that the event causing the injury would not have occurred *but for* the defendant's conduct, and that (2) there was an unbroken connection between the wrongful act and the injury, the sequence being such as to make it just to hold the defendant responsible. Should any other actions or factors intervene between the acts of the defendant and the injury, the responsibility for the injury may shift.

"REAL" LOSS
OR DAMAGE

For there to be liability for tort, the plaintiff must, in most cases, have suffered a real loss or damage. A *real loss* is defined as a crippling or permanent injury to the physical person or damage to tangible property. Financial loss alone is too difficult to assess, the courts say, although in some types of libel and slander, an exception to this general rule is made.

CONTRIBU-
TORY NEGLI-
GENCE

COMPARA-
TIVE NEGLI-
GENCE

The teacher charged with a tort has several defenses. One is to show the absence of any one of the four elements of negligence. Another defense, ***contributory negligence***, constitutes behavior on the part of the plaintiff contributing to the injury or damage he or she has suffered, such behavior not conforming to the standard required for his or her own protection. This standard varies according to the age, intelligence, sex, physical characteristics, and training of each person. Contributory negligence is much more likely to be a factor with an older, intelligent child than with a young, retarded child. If both parties contribute to the injury, neither can recover, except in a few states where the damages are prorated according to the amount each party's acts contributed to the loss. This is called ***comparative negligence***.

A third defense to which a defendant in a tort liability case may resort is called ***assumption of risk***. Players and spectators alike assume the *normal* risks involved in an athletic contest, although the risks of an unsafe field or unsafe apparatus or equipment can be grounds for liability. Thus, a high school boy voluntarily out for football is legally regarded as assuming the normal risks of injury connected with that sport and will not stand to collect damages for any injuries unless someone's negligent action, above and beyond the usual circumstances, caused them. As in contributory negligence, the age, intelligence, sex, physical characteristics, and training of each person are important factors in determining the assumption of risk.

ASSUMPTION OF RISK

Supervision is the area in which most cases of tort liability originate. Teachers are responsible for the supervision of all students specifically assigned to them, as well as of other students temporarily passing in and out of their jurisdiction. For example, playground duty may involve not a specific list of students, but all the students who come and go. Hallway duty is similar.

REASONABLE SUPERVISION OF STUDENTS

A teacher is not expected to be everywhere at once, nor is he or she expected to foresee all possible consequences. As long as the teacher is in the area he or she is assigned to supervise and remains alert to what is going on, the teacher is supervising in a reasonable manner. An example of inadequate supervision would be the teacher who let his pupils out on the playground for recess but remained in his room while they played. He could see most of them from his classroom window. One of the pupils was injured because of some horseplay, but he was powerless to stop the activity before the accident occurred. Had he been on the playground, he would have been in a much better position to prevent the horseplay.

Sometimes, a supervisory assignment is unreasonable; for example, the principal may assign too many students or too large an area to one teacher. In that case, if an injury occurs because of inadequate supervision, and if the teacher makes a reasonable effort to supervise, the principal could be held liable.

UNREASONABLE ASSIGNMENTS

Field trips often present added supervisory problems. For one thing, the standard of care that a teacher must exercise is usually higher because the conditions encountered on a field trip present more dangers than the classroom. Another problem is the permission slip sent home with the students for the parents to sign. This slip usually contains a statement to the effect that the parents will not hold the school or the teacher liable in case of an injury to their child. Many teachers rely on that signed statement as a release from all liability. There is no legal basis for the exception because parents cannot sign away their children's rights. Nevertheless, the use of permission slips is highly recommended because they show evidence of planning on the part of the teacher, they provide the parents with information about the child, and they just may help to deter a parent whose child was injured on the trip from bringing suit.

FIELD TRIPS

USE OF SCHOOL PROVIDED TRANSPORTATION

A teacher should use school-provided transportation whenever available, not only for field trips but for any other activity that requires students to

Field trips present special responsibilities for teachers.

(Photo used by permission of the Indianapolis Public Schools.)

PRINCIPAL–
AGENT RELA-
TIONSHIP

be transported. Unless the teacher has automobile insurance specifically covering the hauling of passengers, there will probably not be sufficient liability coverage in case of an injury to a student rider.

Sending pupils on errands may result in liability for the teacher. **A "principal–agent" relationship** is set up when a pupil runs an errand for the benefit of a teacher. Under this relationship, the **"principal"** assumes all responsibility for the acts of the **"agent"** as well as for the agent's safety. Thus, if a student is injured or damages someone's property while on an errand, the liability that may accrue would revert to the teacher who sent the student.

TREATMENT
OF INJURIES

First aid and the treatment of injuries may present some problems to teachers. The courts hold that teachers are reasonably intelligent people and therefore expect them to react intelligently in an emergency. Thus, teachers are expected to render one of the common types of first aid when the situation requires it. But emergency first aid is all a teacher should administer. When an emergency no longer exists, treatment begins, and teachers have no license to practice medicine. If the condition of a student given medical treatment by a teacher worsens as a result of the treatment, liability could result. On the other hand, if an obvious emergency presents itself and a teacher does not give first aid, if a common kind is required, the teacher could also be liable if the student's condition worsens.

LIBEL VS.
SLANDER

The one area of tort liability for which an injury to the physical person or actual damage to property is not a required element is defamation of character. A simple definition of defamation is making statements that lower or "defame" the character of another person. Written defamation is called ***libel;*** spoken defamation is called ***slander.***

PRIVILEGE IS
A PROTEC-
TION

Teachers often say uncomplimentary things about some of their students. These could be defamatory and could lead to a slander suit, depending on how and to whom they were said. When a teacher makes statements, verbally or in writing, about a student to a person with a bona fide interest in that student, the statements are privileged. Privilege is a protection given to those who are required to make statements about others in the course of their daily activities, some of which may be defamatory in nature. The law of privilege recognizes that it is essential that true information be given whenever necessary to protect one's own interests, those of third parties, and certain interests of the public.

ABSOLUTE
AND QUALI-
FIED

There are two kinds of privilege: absolute and qualified (or conditional). Absolute privilege covers occasions of such great importance to the public that they entitle the utterer to speak out fearlessly, knowing that she or he is immune from suit. It is usually reserved for judges in connection with judicial proceedings, lawmakers during legislative sessions, and certain executives or government employees in the discharge of their duties.

Teachers come under qualified privilege that grants immunity from liability as long as the speaker does not abuse the privilege. Abuse occurs when the speaker does not honestly believe what he or she says or has no reasonable grounds for believing it. Telling the truth is usually, but not always, a good defense against defamation. If the truth is spoken but the intent is to willfully and maliciously impugn the character of another, the speaker may be judged liable.

The important points for teachers to remember are (1) not to say anything defamatory about anyone else unless it becomes necessary; and (2) when it is necessary, to say or write it only to those who have a bona fide interest in the person. When a guidance counselor, the principal, or an adviser requests information about a student, a teacher is privileged to transmit anything she or he believes to be true, no matter how defamatory it may sound.

Immunity from Liability

Although teachers are always liable for their negligent actions as individuals, the school districts for which they work may be immune from tort liability. Most of the states are still under what is called the ***immunity doctrine,*** which means that the government cannot be held liable for the negligent acts of its employees, agents, and officials. A public school district is a governmental agency and is thus immune in those states. It follows, then, that where the school district cannot be successfully sued, injured parties will sue the individual whose negligence caused the injury. That is why teachers are often the defendants in tort liability cases.

IMMUNITY DOCTRINE

There are several states, however, where statutes now permit suits in tort to be brought directly against the school district. In several others, the courts have removed the immunity doctrine (which is based on common law) with respect to governmental agencies, and in those states, school districts may now be sued for tort. Finally, several states have so-called **save-harmless statutes,** which do not allow the school district to be sued but do allow it to pay the damages and court costs for its employees' negligence, provided the incident occurred while the employees were performing duties connected with their jobs in the district.

SAVE-HARM-LESS STAT-UTES

In the states described in the preceding paragraphs, the public school teachers are protected from serious financial loss by the school district itself. In all other states, the teachers must have insurance to protect them. School districts usually carry personal liability insurance on their employees. If the judgment against a teacher is for more than the amount covered by the insurance, the teacher is liable for the difference. In some states, the teachers' organizations carry liability policies on each member, although these policies may not give enough protection.

PERSONAL LI-ABILITY IN-SURANCE

Summary

The bases of the written law are the federal and state constitutions; the statutes passed by federal, state, and local legislative bodies; and the rules and regulations adopted by regulatory and administrative agencies. The common law derives mainly from court decisions as they interpret the written laws and settle disputes over matters not covered by written law.

Knowledge of the structure of the American court system is necessary if one is to clearly understand school law. There are two court systems in the United States: the federal system and the state system. The federal court system includes the federal district courts, the circuit courts of appeal, and the U.S. Supreme Court. The state courts consist of local courts, appellate courts, and (in most states) supreme courts.

Teachers have certain rights, but each right is accompanied by related responsibilities. Therefore, along with the various legal rights of teachers, the professional responsibilities that accompany them should be learned.

Teachers must have certificates, issued by the states, to teach in public schools. Differing requirements by the states cause problems for teachers who move across state lines, but several steps are being taken by the states to reach a solution.

All states have specific statutes pertaining to teachers' contracts, which must include the five basic elements of a valid contract: (1) competent parties, (2) mutual assent, (3) valid consideration, (4) sufficient definition, and (5) legal subject matter.

Besides certification and contracts, there are other legal rights of teachers to be considered. Among these are salaries and fringe benefits; retirement plans; leaves of absence (with or without pay); tenure; academic freedom; the right to organize and bargain collectively; the right to engage in political activity and to be free from discrimination based on race, sex, age, or handicap; duty-free lunch periods; and the right to hold other employment.

The control of students is an important element of teaching. Lack of control nearly always leads to a poor learning environment for the students, and it could also lead to the reprimand or dismissal of the teacher. For these reasons, the states require the schools to control the behavior, the appearance, and the activities of students in a reasonable manner. Schools are encouraged to create reasonable rules with accompanying penalties and to enforce them with appropriate procedures that follow due process principles. As a result, students may be legally suspended or expelled, corporally punished, detained, and searched.

All teachers are legally responsible for the safety, health, and well-being of the students under their supervision. If they breach that responsibility by doing something that a normally prudent teacher would not do or by not doing something that a normally prudent teacher would have done in similar circumstances, they are negligent. If that negligence is the actual and proximate cause of a real injury to students under their supervision, the teachers can be held liable by a court of law and may be required to pay damages. This is called *tort liability.*

The courts, however, recognize that teachers cannot be all places at one time or see all things that go on. Consequently, the courts have emphasized the point that as long as teachers take reasonable precautions to prevent injuries, they will not be held liable.

Glossary Terms

Reciprocity, 381	Continuing-Contract Law, 384
Breach of Contract, 383	Indefinite Contract, 384
Tenure, 384	Salary Schedule, 385

Questions

1. What is the relationship between federal and state courts in regard to school law decisions? Give some examples of cases that would be more likely to be settled at the state or federal level.

2. Explain the five basic elements of a valid teaching contract.

3. Define *tenure*. Can a tenured teacher who transfers from one school district to another claim tenure in the new district?

4. How much freedom does a teacher have to state his or her own viewpoint on controversial issues within the classroom?

5. Explain the terms *quotas* and *discrimination*. How have these affected educational practices?

6. What is *in loco parentis?* What are the rights and restrictions that *in loco parentis* gives teachers?

7. How have the courts ruled in regard to compulsory attendance laws? How do you personally feel about these laws?

8. Differentiate between the terms *suspension* and *expulsion.* Give some examples of each.

9. What is wrong with using grades as penalties? What are some alternatives?

10. In terms of tort liability, define *negligence* and give the four elements that must be present for negligence to be proved.

Activities for Unit VI

1. Visit a state or federal court and report to the class what you have observed.

2. Invite a local lawyer who handles school law cases to discuss past cases.

3. Invite a professor of school law to come to your class and discuss major principles of school law.

4. Interview a superintendent or a school board member in regard to the amount of litigation that occurs yearly in the school district. Try to ascertain the magnitude of yearly legal costs in a school district.

5. Clip newspaper articles concerning school litigation to be placed on the classroom bulletin board.

6. Ask a principal what due process procedures are employed in his or her school district. What has been the effect of due process procedures on school discipline and special education decisions?

7. Research the *Brown v. Board of Education of Topeka* case (1954) and demonstrate its relationship to the Fourteenth Amendment.

8. Interview a school superintendent in regard to the procedure that he or she uses in the process of termination of a tenured and a nontenured teacher.

9. Review articles in the *Phi Delta Kappan* on compulsory school attendance, and summarize the pros and cons of the issue.

10. Research the topic of desegregation by investigating a case in your state.

11. Research and evaluate a Saturday school or an in-school suspension program in a school district within your area.

12. Research in a law library any case on tort liability. What significance does this case have for education?

Annotated Bibliography

1. Cohen, J. H. (1989). Legal challenges to testing for teachers certification: History, impact and future trends. *Journal of Law and Education, 18,* 229–265.

   This is the best single article on teachers' certification. The article lays out all cases one would need to know in researching this area. The information covers the National Commission on Excellence in Education and *A Nation at Risk,* and sets out the law in terms of case law related to those issues.

2. Feld, D. E. Right to discipline pupil for conduct away from school grounds or not immediately connected with school activities. 53 ALR3d 1124 (all new law updated yearly).

   The right of schools to discipline a pupil for misconduct away from school grounds or not connected with school activities is discussed.

3. Hursh, R. D. Teachers' civil liability for administering corporal punishment to pupil. 43 ALR2d 469 (all new law updated yearly).

    The liability to which teachers are subject in regard to administrating corporal punishment is described.

4. *Miller v. Griesel* (1974) Ind. 308 N.E. 2d 701.

    This case is, perhaps, the most significant teacher liability case in the entire United States. Much research can be completed by merely following normal legal research procedures to update this case.

5. Selbee, M. L. (1988). The essentials of employee discharges. *Indiana School Boards Association Journal, 28,* 25–29

    This very good article on teacher contracts and discharges is keyed to Indiana law, and includes charts and teacher classifications.

6. Schopler, E. H. Right of a student to hearing on charges before suspension or expulsion from educational institution. 58 ALR2d 903 (all new law updated yearly).

    The right of students to a hearing prior to suspension or expulsion from school is described.

[Photo courtesy of the Library of Congress.]

VII

Control and Governance of Education

OBJECTIVES

After reading Chapter 13, the student will be able to:

- Understand the evolution of and the current issues in state and local governance.

- Perceive the roles of state and local governments in the governance and control of education

- Recognize the role of the various state agencies and state public officials in the governance of education

- Be cognizant of the powers, limitations, duties, and methods of selection of local school boards

- Become aware of the powers, duties, and responsibilities of a local school superintendent

Local and State Governance and Control of Education

Introduction

DEFINITIONS
OF GOVER-
NANCE AND
CONTROL

Students of education and prospective teachers want to understand the
"system" in which they will be working, just as new executives want to
understand the corporate structure of the industries in which they work.
To accomplish this, it is necessary to study the control and governance of
education. First, one must differentiate between governance and control.
The authors of this text feel that although the definitions of these terms
have much in common, **governance** should be used for the formal system
of government management of the education function of society, whereas
control of education includes any person or group having an organized
influence on education in the United States. Thus, *control* is a broader term
and includes informal influences on education from special-interest groups
such as parents' organizations and taxpayers' groups. Such groups do not
have legal responsibilities for the running of schools and are not hired by
those who do have statutory authority, but they can have a major impact
on how the schools function.

Questions

RELATION-
SHIPS
AMONG THE
THREE LEV-
ELS OF GOV-
ERNMENT

Numerous questions are raised and examined in this chapter. What should
be the relationship of local, state, and federal governments in governing
education? What should be the role of lay citizens and professional educators in making decisions about schools? Should the primary objectives of
schools be intellectual, social, personal, vocational, or a combination of
these? What is the governance system for education at the state level? What
are some problems that states have in controlling education, and what are
some possible solutions? What are the roles of the state legislatures, the
state boards of education, the state departments of education, the chief
state school officers, and the state courts in governing education? At the
local level, what are the duties and responsibilities of local school boards
and local school superintendents in the governance of education? What
problems are caused by the variation in the wealth of local districts, and
what are some possible remedies for this situation? What are the roles of
the U.S. Constitution, the U.S. Congress, the U.S. Department of Education,
the U.S. Secretary of Education, and the federal courts in the governance
of education? Who should control the public schools, and what should be
the role of special-interest groups? What alternatives to public schools are
available to students in the United States, and how are private schools
governed?

Evolution of Governance

Before we examine the details of the system of governance of schools in
the United States, it is necessary to provide a short history of the evolution
of the governance and control of education in the United States.

Although statutes such as the Massachusetts laws of 1642 and 1647 providing for free public schools had already been passed, the American schools were primarily private or church related in the late 1600s and in the 1700s. The control of these early schools was concentrated in church groups or individuals. Thomas Jefferson proposed a system of free public elementary schools for Virginia, but his original proposal was defeated. The

PROMINENT LAWS AND LEADERS

public school movement in the United States was founded on the later work of Horace Mann in Massachusetts and of Henry Barnard in Connecticut. Most of the early public schools were small one-room primary schools established by local communities, encouraged by state laws that permitted, but did not require, schools to be set up at public expense wherever a small cluster of families desired to establish them. This pattern of small, local school districts was to remain the most common configuration in the United States in the 1800s and during most of the 1900s. The county unit became the predominant pattern of organization in the South, and the town school was the most common in New England. States began to require rather than merely permit local communities to establish schools supported by local taxes.

Who would govern or control these schools? Early school laws passed by the colonies contained language that would give local civil officials, instead of special school boards, the power to control schools. The early state legislatures passed regulations for schools, and the local town officials

CIVIL CONTROL VS. SPECIAL BOARDS

provided day-to-day supervision of the local school. There was no state bureaucracy in these early days, no state board of education, nor any chief state school officer. According to Campbell, Cunningham, Nystrand, and Usdan (1980), "There were no separate boards of education for the first 200 years of our history" (p. 64). Schools were very simple and small during this period; and the states believed that they were to protect and encourage schools, not to establish and support them. Thus, for 200 years, the schools were governed by the same governmental bodies as governed the towns as a whole. In the 1820s, however, the Massachusetts legislature established school boards, called **town school committees,** as separate governmental bodies to run the schools, providing local governance for schools separate from the local government of cities and towns. Special governance for schools became a reality at the state level also. According to Campbell et al., "special government for education was soon to emerge, first in the form of a chief state school officer, often called a state superintendent of public instruction, and later a state board of education" (p. 64). By 1870, thirty-six of the states had created such a position; by 1900, all states admitted to the Union, forty-four in number, had chief state school officers; all states since admitted to the Union also have such officials. Thus, a special system of governance for education has been established at both the local and the state levels in the United States.

Even though lay control and inspection of local schools were established early in American history, a necessity later arose for professional administrators to run the day-to-day operation of the public schools under policy guidelines established by lay school boards. In the local schools, these persons were called **head teachers** or *principal teachers*, and they usually also taught classes. With the growth of cities and the increased size of school districts because of the combination of smaller districts, the supervision of schools became too time consuming for lay school board members

EARLY SU-
PERVISION
AND ADMIN-
ISTRATION

who held other full-time employment; thus, the post of superintendent of schools was created in each local district. At first, the duties of both the principal and the superintendent were mostly clerical, consisting of keeping records such as enrollment and attendance figures, but soon, persons in these positions took on more substantial duties in the supervision of local schools and local school districts.

How could this evolution of governance and control of American public schools be summarized? First, the American schools are not a national system; instead, they grew from the local, grass roots level. Second, in the United States, control of policymaking for public schools has traditionally been placed in the hands of laypeople, not professional administrators. However, the daily operaton of schools and the administration of policy decisions reside in professional educational administrators, such as princi-

EMPHASIS ON
LAY CON-
TROL

pals or superintendents. Meanwhile, a change from a majority of private and/or church-related schools to public and secular schools had taken place. In most places in the United States, private schools became alternatives to public schools, which enrolled the vast majority of students in the country.

> The basis for state control over education was pretty well established as early as 1820 by constitutional and statutory provisions of the states which made up the union . . . 13 of the 23 states had constitutional provisions for education, seventeen had statutory provisions, and only two states—Rhode Island and Tennessee—had neither constitutional nor statutory provisions for education. (Campbell et al., 1980, p. 64)

However, the governance of schools has continued to become more complicated as the American society has grown more complex:

SECULARIZA-
TION AND
EGALITARI-
ANISM

> Our early schools, largely under the control of the local communities, seemed to serve a rural, homogeneous society rather well. . . . The schools of today are not only the product of forces noted above (such as secularization and egalitarianism); they also exist in a complex, largely urban, and pluralistic society. Morever, world-wide ideologies and practices affect today's schools beyond the wildest dreams of the citizens of this nation during the last century. Under these circumstances the questions of organization and control of American schools have new meanings and require fresh analyses. (Campbell, 1980, pp. 10–11)

Although much can be learned from studying the historical background of governance and control in American schools, the modern world may require some changes in the traditional governance of schools. Citizens must learn to preserve the best and most sacred of these traditions while also fostering some modifications to adapt to changing circumstances.

State Governance of Education

Introduction

EDUCATION IS A STATE FUNCTION

In the United States, education is primarily a function of fifty state governments. Education is controlled, legally, by state government. Teachers are state employees, school board members are state officials, and the taxes used to support schools are state and local taxes. However, the states have chosen to delegate the day-to-day operation of the schools to local school boards and the local school districts under broad state guidelines. Historically, education has been viewed as one of the powers left up to the states or "reserved to the states and to the people," as put forth in the **Reserved Powers** Clause of the Tenth Amendment of the U.S. Constitution:

> Although the Constitution of the United States contains no direct reference to education, most state constitutions have specific provisions which make education a legal responsibility of the state. Moreover, the statutes of most states stipulate in considerable detail how schools are to be governed. Much of this control is delegated to district boards of education and to other bodies, all of which become a part of the state system of education. In a sense, then, we have 50 systems of education in America, but in many respects these various systems are similar. (Campbell et al., 1980, p. 61)

The state has the power to establish, and to abolish, local school districts, which are legally quasi corporations created by the state. The states can also force the consolidation or the reorganization of local schools, as they have done in many states in the past three decades for purposes such as efficiency and monetary savings. Today, there are fewer school districts nationwide than there were twenty or thirty years ago because of this reorganization process. Although many residents in small rural communities have opposed this reorganization, by which they would lose a local high school in their community, the process of reorganization has continued because it has been mandated by state legislatures and state boards of education, which have the authority in these matters.

State Powers

The states can either grant local districts broad power or, conversely, limit the powers of these local districts severely. What are the primary powers that the states exercise in their control of local schools?

1. *Control of information*—The states require reports from local school districts and conduct studies of local school practices.

2. *Technical services*—The states provide technical services in areas such as curriculum and programs for both the mentally and physically handicapped and the gifted.

3. *Regulation of standards*—The states regulate standards for such things as attendance, textbooks, and fiscal records.

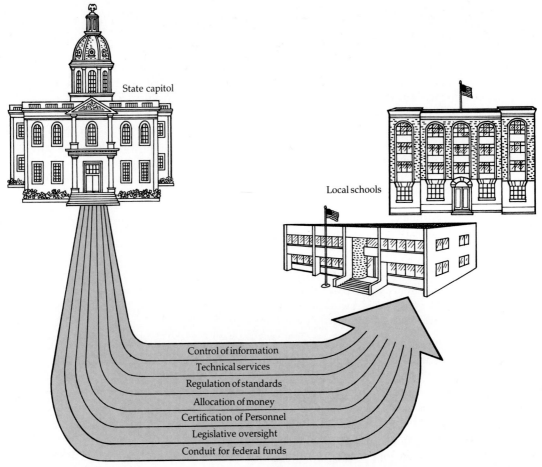

State capitol

Local schools

Control of information

Technical services

Regulation of standards

Allocation of money

Certification of Personnel

Legislative oversight

Conduit for federal funds

Primary powers of the state.

4. *Allocation of money*—The states appropriate and allocate money for the operation of local schools, but local schools supplement these appropriations with money raised locally.

5. *Certification of personnel*—The states now determine the nature of preservice and in-service preparation programs for teachers, but the states are currently being challenged by universities and teachers' organizations for the control of these activities.

6. *Legislative oversight*—The states, through state departments of education, oversee and help implement legislative mandates.

7. *State legal review*—State courts settle differences in the interpretation of state laws regarding schools.

STATE CON-
TROLS

8. *Conduit for federal funds*—The states receive funds from the federal

government and enforce federal regulations established for federal school programs.

Some of these state controls are exercised by the state department of education, and others are controlled directly by the governor, the state attorney general, the state auditor, the state legislature, or other state agencies concerned with building codes or health standards. The inability of many local school districts to adequately finance their schools in recent years has led to an increase in direct state involvement in education. Herman (1977) summarized the state education powers:

> Individual states differ in the specifics of their control over local decision makers. Practically all of them, however, administer a wide variety of federal programs, many of them have labor relations (collective bargaining) legislation, a few have formal accountability models and all have a great proliferation of bureaucrats that write and interpret a mountain of rules and regulations to be obeyed by local school districts. (p. 154)

In the next sections of this textbook, the educational functions of the state constitutions, the state legislatures, the state boards of education, the state departments of education, and the state superintendent of schools are examined in greater detail.

State Constitutions

EDUCATION EXPLICIT IN STATE CONSTITUTION

The states have the constitutional and statutory powers to control and regulate the schools within their borders. Each state has a constitution created by a constitutional convention. The convention delegates are elected; and thus, the state constitutions and their educational mandates ultimately reflect the will of the people of the state. The federal government has only specific **powers** given (or "delegated") to it by the U.S. Constitution. However, state governments have all powers except those that are prohibited to them by the U.S. Constitution or by their respective state constitutions. State constitutions deal with education explicitly, whereas the U.S. Constitution does not mention education, dealing with it only by implication. Krohne (1982) explicated further the language used in state constitutions:

> Historically, however, all state constitutions address the general concept that the legislature is responsible for providing a free public education system. A few state constitutions make this responsibility discretionary (or optional) such as Mississippi. . . . Most, however, are written using such words as "shall," "will," or "must" instead of "may" as a clear directive of acceptance to providing educational opportunities to its citizenry. (pp. 22–23)

A MIDWESTERN EXAMPLE

Let us use the state of Indiana as an example of the constitutional provisions in the states in general. In 1816, the Indiana State Constitution provided, "as soon as circumstances will permit," for the establishment of a tuition-free educational system from elementary school through the university level, but financial circumstances never permitted the state legislature to fully carry out this generous charge. The Indiana legislature did enact permissive legislation to permit property owners at the local level to levy a tax for school construction, but through the 1840s, education was basically a function of local government with little state involvement. Krohne (1982) summarized the origin of the Indiana State Superintendent and the Indiana State Board of Education:

> Following the new Indiana State Constitution in 1852, which made no provisions for a state board of education but did provide for a state superintendent, a law was passed which among other things established a state board of education in Indiana. The first state board was created by section 147 of the School Law of 1852, and was made up of the state superintendent, the auditor, the treasurer, the secretary of state, and the governor. In 1855, the attorney general was added as a sixth member. The first recorded meeting was June 7–10, 1853, which appears to mark the beginning of the Indiana State Board of Education. (p. 32)

State Legislatures

The state legislatures have **plenary** or "full" **powers** to control education within their states, but this full power is limited both by pressures to provide funds for other state services and by various checks and balances in the U.S. federal system of government. The important concept to remember is that the state legislature is the "big school board" in each state and that its actions supersede those of any local school boards in the state, which are created by, and can be abolished by, the state legislature. The state superintendent and the state board of education can propose and recommend education legislation, but only the state legislature can pass laws concerning education.

PLENARY OR FULL POWERS

The **checks-and-balances** limitations on the power of a state legislature in regard to education are the first type of control on the education powers of the state legislature. First, the state legislature cannot act against the contents of the federal or state constitutions regarding education. All legislation passed in the United States, including laws passed by state legislatures, is subject to the prohibitions and limitations of the U.S. Constitution. The parts of the U.S. Constitution that are most often cited by the courts in ruling on education are the First Amendment, the Fifth Amendment, the Fourteenth Amendment, and Article 1, Section 10, on obligations of contracts. (See Chapter 14 for further details on the federal role in education.) Second, the courts have ruled that state legislatures cannot be unreasonable in their use of power and that they cannot delegate their full power over education to other agencies.

CHECKS AND BALANCES

Competition for funding with other state services also limits each state's ability to use the authority that it possesses in the area of education. One problem faced by state legislatures is special-interest legislation aimed narrowly at one issue, such as "creationism" versus evolution in the teaching of science. A second problem for state legislatures in the area of education is the public demand for **accountability** in education. As a result, state

COMPETITION FOR FUNDING AND ACCOUNTABILITY

State legislatures are the major source of control over education.

(Photo courtesy of the Indiana State Department of Education.)

legislatures are enacting more and more specific legislation on rules concerning schools, including competency testing for both teachers and students, property tax controls, and collective bargaining.

Collective bargaining, for example, is one of the main issues in the struggle between school boards and teacher associations, with each side trying to gain power through legislative action. Collective bargaining laws are continually being modified where they already exist, and are sought in states where they have not yet been established. On one side of the issue are those, including many state legislators, who feel that too much power has been taken from local school boards and that it is time to restore local control. On the other side are teachers' associations, who seek legislation to strengthen the position of their members in the collective bargaining process (Pipho, 1980, p. 38).

State legislatures find themselves caught between many competing and antagonistic forces, with their full powers over education limited in many

STATE COL-
LECTIVE BAR-
GAINING
LAWS

COMPETING
FORCES

legal, constitutional, and practical ways. In recent years, the educational problems faced by state legislatures have also been exacerbated by such general societal problems as inflation, energy costs, and the decline of the school-aged population. As you can readily see, the "big school board" of the state legislature has more problems and limitations than ever before in its history.

State Boards of Education

CARRY OUT STATE POL-ICY MAN-DATES

Although the state legislatures have full powers over education and enact legislation to set general education policy for the state, they have established **state boards of education** to carry out these state policy mandates. Most of these state boards of education have similar powers but vary extensively in their size, their methods of selection, their terms of office, and their relationship to the superintendent of public instruction. At first, the state boards of education were composed of state officials elected to govern the state as a whole and not elected for the specific education function. These *ex officio* members included the governor, the secretary of state, the attorney general, and the auditor, but eventually board members came to be chosen for their specific educational purpose, either by appointment by the governor or by election by the citizens of each state. According to Campbell et al. (1980), "In 1972 board members in 31 states were appointed by the governor; in thirteen states were elected by the people; and in five states they acquired office in other ways" (p. 66). Thus, most state boards of education today are made up largely of lay citizens rather than professional educators. In recent years, there has been a trend toward having the members of the state board of education elected by the citizens of the state.

State Departments of Education

ADMINISTER STATE POL-ICY

Most states have established state departments of education to administer the general policies of the state boards of education and have given them a variety of functions. One of the duties of the **state department of education** is to regulate and enforce minimum educational standards. Another function is to operate schools for the blind and the deaf. Still another duty is to help the schools improve their operations. State departments of education provide assistance to local school districts in planning, research, and evaluation. The state departments of education perform a leadership role in improving schools in their respective states.

CONDUITS FOR FEDERAL FUNDS

The divisions of a typical state department of education include administration, finance, teacher certification and licensing, instructional services, curriculum, vocational and adult education, vocational rehabilitation, and junior colleges. The most salient feature of state departments of education is that they act as a conduit for channeling federal funds to the local school districts. In many states, one half to two thirds of the personnel of the state department of public instruction are supported through federal money paid to the states to administer federal programs in education. In addition, the state department of education administers the state's financial contribu-

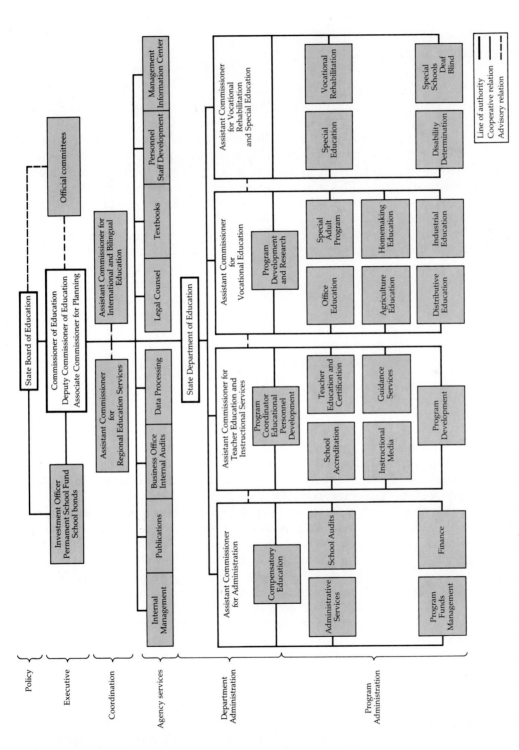

Lines of authority in the Texas Education Agency

(SOURCE: Pearson, J. B., and Fuller, E. (Eds.). (1969). *Education in the States: Historical development and outlook.* National Education Association of the United States, Washington, D.C., p. 1221.)

tions to education, making budget control a powerful function of the state education agencies.

State Superintendents of Education

TOP STATE SCHOOL OF-FICIAL

The **state superintendent of education** is the top state school official in all states. He or she usually heads the state department of education and either is the chief executive officer of the state board of education or is selected independently of that group by election or appointment. In nineteen states, the state superintendent of education is elected by popular vote, and in twenty-six states, he or she is appointed by the state board of education. In five states, the state superintendent is appointed by the governor. The state superintendents who are elected by popular vote or appointed by the governors are legally state officers. Those who are appointed by state school boards are considered employees, not officers, of their states. If we relate

METHODS OF SELECTION

the method of selection of the state superintendent to that of the state board of education, fifteen states have a state superintendent and a state board of education appointed by the governor, eleven states have an elected state board of education that appoints the state superintendent, and thirteen states have an elected state superintendent but an appointed state board of education. In five states, both are appointed, and in six states both are elected. Only Wisconsin has no state board of education (Krohne, 1982, p. 28).

State Courts

The state courts also have an indirect influence on educational policy in a state because they interpret the education provisions in the state's constitution, establish common law by making decisions on educational questions brought before them, and decide whether state statutes are "constitutional" in terms of being in harmony with the state constitution.

INTERPRET STATE CON-STITUTION AND LAWS

Although the state's power over education is subject to these controls, the state courts in general have been reluctant to interfere with the state's operation of the schools as long as the state acts in a reasonable and prudent manner. State school-finance plans are particularly being challenged in the state courts, and many of these courts have ruled that the unequal educational opportunities caused by inequities in school finance within a state are a violation of state constitutional provisions. These recent court decisions have encouraged school-finance-reform legislation in many states. (See Chapter 15 for more details on this reform movement.) Thus, the state courts have had a significant influence on state educational concerns.

Conclusions on State Governance

Most authorities in education are predicting an increased state role in education for a variety of reasons. First, education is legally a state function, not a local function. Even though the states have historically delegated the daily operation of the schools to the local school districts, numerous factors

INCREASED STATE ROLE

are currently forcing the states to become more active in education. One reason has been that local revenue sources have been inadequate. This factor, combined with inflation and local property tax freezes, has forced the states to assume a greater role in school finance. Another reason for increased state influence is the recent demand for accountability in education, which has resulted in specific legislation on accountability in about half the states. Increasing teacher power also leads to more state jurisdiction, as seen in the establishment by twenty-three states of state-level professional practices boards composed mostly of teachers.

LIMITED FEDERAL ROLE IN EDUCATION

A second major reason for the growth in state leadership in education has been the trend in recent years for the president to limit the federal role in education. Although both Presidents Nixon and Carter stressed the need to cut back federal involvement in education in favor of an increased state role, President Reagan wanted to dismantle the federal education establishment and to eliminate the recently formed cabinet-level Department of Education. Although President Reagan did not carry out these proposals, he has given impetus to state leadership in education. Merit pay and career ladder plans in Tennessee and North Carolina show that the states are currently taking the lead in educational reform, encouraged by the president and the U.S. Department of Education. The states have increased power and authority because all federal aid is administered by the states, which act as proxies for the federal government. An additional reason for the growth in state power and influence in education is the increased number of mandates from the state legislature and the demand for more accountability in education. State education agencies are the logical choice to establish and implement legislative mandates for competency tests for both teachers and students.

What are some predictions for the role of the states in education? The role of the states in planning, evaluation, and research will increase as a result of these legislative mandates. Increasingly able personnel will be attracted to the state departments of education because of larger salaries supported primarily by federal funds. It is also predicted that state legislatures will often become "traffic cops" mediating among various state interest groups, and that special state problems of the 1990s will center on lids on taxes, inflation, and accomplishing more with fewer resources.

FUTURE TRENDS IN STATE GOVERNANCE

Additional future trends in state governance of education are foreseen by Herman (1977, pp. 143–144). He believes that there is a trend toward spending identical amounts for the education of each student in the state regardless of the taxable wealth available at the local district level. Herman foresees a continuation of categorical aid (aid for special purposes such as special education) to stimulate innovation at the local level. The trend, in his opinion, is for the states to take away decision-making powers from the local school district level. Some state categorical aid programs will be only partially funded, and some will not be worth the local effort needed to initiate and sustain them.

What are the major problems involved in the state governance of educa-

MAJOR PROB-
LEMS

tion? First, the states often mandate educational programs, such as those for special education students, but at the same time fail to provide adequate financial resources to carry out these plans, leaving the local school districts to find the necessary funds. The states often do not provide adequate financing of education in inflationary times or do not decide on fiscal allocations of funds far enough in advance to give local officials sufficient planning time to meet deadlines. Paperwork for state education agencies requires an excessive amount of local school officials' time and energy.

SCOPE OF DE-
CISIONS

Educational decisions made at the state level include the scope and extent of the instructional programs, including standards, compulsory attendance, minimum length of school year, selection of textbooks, and required courses of study; certification of personnel, including approval of the programs of teacher-training institutions and the certification of school personnel; facilities standards; and financial support, which encompasses a ceiling on local school district taxes, stipulations for how the school budget is to be prepared and what budget categories should be used, and approval of the local school district budget. The execution of educational governance at the state level is performed by the governor, the chief state school officer, the state board of education, and the state department of education, with a few functions handled by other state agencies. Remember that, subject to some limitations, the state legislatures have plenary or full powers over public education in their respective states because education is a power reserved to the states and the people by the U.S. Constitution and because the states must delegate any powers exercised by school districts at the local level.

Local Governance of Education

Introduction

DAY-TO-DAY
OPERATION
AT THE LO-
CAL LEVEL

Although the states have the legal authority to provide public education in the United States, they have delegated the day-to-day operation of public schools to local school districts in each state. These local school districts are, thus, the basic administrative unit for school organization in the United States. The states' policy of delegating authority to local school boards and the courts' practice of permitting local school boards any reasonable and prudent use of this authority have made the local school district the most important unit in American education, according to many educational experts. Campbell et al. (1980) summarized the powers delegated to the local school districts:

> In brief, the duties of school board members include the right to establish schools, to build school houses, to employ a superintendent, to establish necessary rulers to manage and govern the schools, and to raise and expend money. The courts have consistently held that such delegations by the state legislature to district boards of education are appropriate. (p. 75)

CREATED BY
THE STATE

The **local school district** is a unit of government, created by the state, with quasi-corporate powers. It is given the power to administer a public school or a public school system and is controlled by a local board of education. It has the power to tax, the power to make contracts, and the right to employ a superintendent if it chooses. Thus, these local school districts are creations or extensions of the state, which can create, destroy, or modify them, an important point to remember in studying the reorganization of local districts. The state can make these local school districts autonomous and independent, or dependent and subservient to the state control agencies.

VARIATION
IN LOCAL
UNITS

Some 16,000 school districts exist in the United States, making them the most numerous units of local government. They vary tremendously in size (from huge metropolitan districts like Los Angeles and Chicago to small districts with a handful of schools), wealth, power, and effectiveness of operation. "Their diversity illustrates the tenaciousness with which Americans hold to these remnants of localism and grass-roots expression of the public will" (Campbell et al., 1980, pp. 90–91).

INTERMEDI-
ATE OR
COUNTY
UNITS

Many states have established an intermediate or county unit between the local and state levels in the governance of education. Historically, the more centralized county unit of organization for education began in the South, where people were spread farther apart than in New England, where the town or township was the local unit of governance. This intermediate or county unit is another example of the state's proclivity to delegate the supervision of schools closer to the actual operation of the schools. This county unit, consisting of the county superintendent of schools and a county board of education, makes certain that local schools operate according to state legislative mandates and state board of education rules. These intermediate units are more common in states having numerous small rural districts and schools, which need this additional kind of supervision:

> While the function of the intermediate unit is not always clear, the county superintendent or county board is usually charged with preparing information and making reports to the state department of education, assisting in the reorganization of school districts, registering teachers' certificates, assisting in the supervision of rural schools, assisting with in-service education of teachers, and providing some special services in weak districts. (Campbell et al., 1980, p. 76)

Thus, these county governance units, which are found in about one half of the states, are set up to provide services that small school districts cannot provide for themselves.

Local School Boards

Local school boards, as well as local school districts, are creations of the state legislature, which also has the power to abolish or modify them if it wishes. Membership on local school boards consists of lay citizens, not

Local school boards implement state school policies as well as make local policies.

(Photo used by permission of the Indianapolis Public Schools.)

LAY CITIZENS professional educators. This lay control of local school boards is the salient feature of education in the United States. These local school boards are the policymakers in education, whereas the administrators and the teachers only carry out and implement those policies passed by the local board of education. Thus, two important principles to be remembered about the American governance of education are that school policy is formulated by lay school boards and then is administered by local school officials. An individual school board member has no official decision-making authority unless he or she is attending an official school board meeting. Local school board members should not interfere as individuals in the daily operation of the schools, just as the school administration should refrain from making school policy decisions without approval of the local school board. Local school board members are legally "agents" of the state, whereas local school administrators are "employees" of the local school district and the local school board. School boards generally have from three to seven members; and members serve terms of three, four, or six years. Other than some reimbursement for expenses, school board members seldom receive a salary (Campbell et al., 1980).

POWERS OF LOCAL SCHOOL BOARDS
The powers of the local school board come from the state legislature in the form of statutes interpreted by the state courts. These powers are granted by statute, fairly and necessarily implied from those powers expressly EXTENSIVE granted, and essential to accomplishing the goals set for the local schools POWERS by the state. The board, as has been said, must act as a whole and cannot

delegate powers that are mandated for the boards alone to perform, such as employing teachers. The superintendent recommends candidates for teaching positions, but only the board in a duly constituted board meeting can put them under contract. In addition, the local school board has no choice but to carry out state education mandates, such as special education programs or pupil competency testing. Local boards of education have the power to establish schools, to hire administrators and teachers, to tax and to borrow money, to draw up attendance boundaries, to determine curricula, and to pass school budgets.

LIMITATIONS ON LOCAL SCHOOL BOARDS

Many formal and informal controls and limitations exist on this wide power exercised by local school boards. The formal legal controls originate with the state legislature and the state board of education. The procedures for selecting school board members (see Methods of Selection) and the behavior of board members after they are selected are prescribed by state statutes. These state laws govern the size of the board, the length of term of the members, the method of filling vacancies, the time and location of regular board meetings, the procedures for special board meetings, and the duties of school board members. Although local school boards may have the right to raise money through local taxes, often a ceiling is set by law on the tax rate that can be levied. In addition, state laws often specify specific procedures that must be followed by local boards of edcuation in the expenditure of money. For example, new building, renovation, or major equipment purchases might by law need approval by local district referendum (Campbell et al., 1980).

FORMAL CONTROLS

An informal limitation on local school boards relates to public pressure. School boards have external and internal responsibilities. The internal duties are concerned with management responsibilities, but the external duties involve the relationship of the schools to the public that the school board serves. Especially in large, diverse school districts, many pressure groups compete for the attention of the school board. Because being a school board member is not a full-time job and pays a minimum salary, board members often feel persecuted when the public threatens, harasses, and criticizes them during public board meetings (many times concerning emotional issues over which they have little control, such as federal desegregation mandates). Campbell et al. (1980, pp. 191–192) believe that public schools often become the political arena for attempts to reconcile social controversies. As a result, school boards often become **scapegoats** for public frustration on issues such as busing, prayer in schools, reduction in teaching staff, school reorganization, and school closings.

INFORMAL CONTROLS

METHODS OF SELECTION

ELECTION VS. APPOINTMENT

How are school board members selected for American schools? The two primary methods are by appointment and by public vote. The greatest number of school boards have elected members; only 14% of school board

SHOULD LOCAL SCHOOL BOARDS EXIST?	
Pros	Cons
1. Boards provide lay involvement in and control of education.	1. Boards have responsibility without funding power.
2. They promote grass-roots support.	2. They lack autonomy of action.
3. Decisions are made closest to level of implementation.	3. They lack expertise.
	4. They lack a broad vision of education.
4. Special local knowledge is brought to decisions.	5. Districts vary greatly in wealth.

HOW SHOULD MEMBERS BE SELECTED?			
Appointment		Election	
Pros	Cons	Pros	Cons
1. High-quality people are appointed. 2. Members have interests of whole community as motivation.	1. Members chosen because of "political connections."	1. It's democratic. 2. Grass-roots political support.	1. Single-issue interest. 2. Campaigning is divisive and expensive and deters many qualified candidates. 3. Members are elected because of "negative politics," i.e., being against something.

Controversy over local school boards.

members are appointed to their posts. In many communities with appointed school boards, the board members are appointed by the mayor, the city council, the county council, the county commissioners, or a combination of these. Appointive boards often have limitations on the number of members from one political party.

ADVANTAGES OF AP-POINTED BOARDS

The advantages of appointive boards are that high-quality, capable community leaders who would not volunteer to run for election to the school board are often selected, and that appointed board members usually have broad community interests at heart, not just specific, single interests, which often motivate individuals to seek election to a school board. A disadvantage of appointive boards is the possible political influence involved in the appointment of members by officials who are actively engaged in political parties, such as mayors and council members.

NONPAR-TISAN ELEC-TIONS AND NOMINATION PROCEDURES

Of the school boards composed of elected members, most are selected through nonpartisan elections, either at large in the school district or by subdistricts within the school district itself. In school districts with elected boards, the nomination procedure becomes very important. Many of these districts have umbrella grass roots citizens' groups or planning committees that slate candidates for school board election, others use caucuses of all eligible voters in the district or petitions to select candidates.

The advantages of elected local school boards include a democratic selection process and grass roots political support. The disadvantages include the political campaigning necessary in an election, the single-issue politics and negative motivation "against something" that motivate many of these candidates, and the loss of many qualified candidates who are not motivated to seek political office by running in an election.

ADVANTAGES OF ELECTED BOARDS

WHO SERVES AND WHAT MOTIVATES MEMBERS

We now come to the questions of who serves on school boards, what the personal characteristics of school board members are, and what motivates these members to serve on school boards. About half the elected school board members have special-interest motivation for seeking election, and the other half profess broad community-oriented objectives (Campbell et al., 1980, pp. 196–197). This leaves no doubt that pressure on single issues such as busing, school finance, and the closing of specific schools does motivate many individuals to seek elected school board positions. Men continue to constitute the majority of school board members, but the percentage of minorities on school boards is increasing. Women are usually elected, not appointed, and constitute a minority of school board members. The trend in school board membership is toward including both younger and older persons as members, toward higher income levels of board members, and toward higher levels of education. Many experts predict that in the future, more minorities and women will serve as school board members. The most common categories of the professions of school board members are managers and owners of businesses, professionals, farmers, and homemakers. For a few individuals, such as former President Jimmy Carter of Georgia, school board membership may lead to a political career, but for most members, service on the school board is their highest political or public service office.

SINGLE ISSUE CANDIDATES

PROS AND CONS OF LOCAL SCHOOL BOARDS

There are advantages to having local school boards: citizens are involved in the educational process, there is grass roots support for education, decisions are made close to the level of implementation, and local board members know the special circumstances of the school. One of the biggest problems with local school boards today is that they have retained responsibility for local programs but have lost control of the power to finance these programs fully because of property tax freezes and increased state aid to education. A smaller percentage of school funds is raised at the local level controlled by the school board, and yet many new mandates flow from the state to the local school each year. The local school boards seem to be caught in the middle of these pressures, as we will see in Chapter 15. Many factors seem to be encroaching on the relative autonomy that school

LESS AUTON-OMY

districts enjoyed in the past, and many expect the school districts to have even less autonomy in the future. Lay school boards are chastised for lacking the expertise needed in today's society in areas such as collective bargaining and school finance. Another criticism of local school districts is their variation in wealth, especially assessed valuation, and, thus, in educational opportunity. Critics assert that a state or national system of education would be more efficient and would eliminate the disparity between the have's and the have-not's in present local school districts. In spite of these criticisms, local school districts and school board members seem to be permanent fixtures in American education.

Local School Superintendents

The local superintendent of schools is appointed to the position by the local school board and can be dismissed by this same group, although this is an elected office in some Southern states. (It is interesting that school administrators do not have a guarantee of tenure or automatic contract renewal after a specified number of years as a trial period. Superintendents CARRIES OUT and other school administrators may have earned tenure as teachers but POLICIES OF cannot attain it for administrative positions.) The local superintendent of THE BOARD schools is the chief executive of the board of education and carries out the policies approved by this board. Many local superintendents serve small school districts and have little or no central office staff to help them carry out their duties. In populous urban areas, superintendents may have a large central office staff with differentiated duties in areas such as finance, curriculum, planning, special services, elementary education, and secondary education. Thus, the duties of a superintendent of schools can vary from the supervision of a few teachers in a small school district to the supervision of hundreds of central office staff members and thousands of teachers.

BOARD FOR-
MULATES
POLICY AND
THE SUPER-
INTENDENT
IMPLEMENTS

The most important delineation of the powers and duties of the superintendent, compared with those of the local school board, is that the board formulates policy for the local school district, and the superintendent implements or carries out this board policy. When a school board member interferes in the daily operation of a school or a school district, he or she has overstepped the bounds of the sole duty of the board to make policy. The powers of a local school superintendent are given to her or him by the local board of education and include recommending teachers and administrators to be employed by the board, proposing a budget for the local school district, recommending changes in both physical facilities and curriculum, and recommending purchases of materials to be made by the district. Thus, the local superintendent has both business management and curriculum and supervision functions.

SUPERINTEN-
DENT AS ME-
DIATOR

Many modern school superintendents are essentially mediators among various **special-interest** and pressure **groups.** It is hoped that the superintendent will be a leader in directing the future course of the school district and the community through her or his duty to educate both the board and the local citizens on issues of concern to schools. In practice, this is not

The local school superintendent serves as the chief spokesperson for the local district in the community.

(Photo used by permission of the Metropolitan School District of Lawrence Township.)

always the case, although the superintendent does wield enormous power through appointments, administration of the budget, and visibility in the community. However, it is believed by many experts on education that local school boards and superintendents have had their power eroded by encroachments from state and federal government, as will be seen in Chapter 14. Even the power of teachers' organizations and the limitations on property taxes supported by local citizens' groups have greatly decreased the actual clout of local school superintendents in many school systems.

CHARACTER-
ISTICS OF SU-
PERINTEN-
DENTS

What are the characteristics of persons who serve as local school superintendents, and what are the possibilities of superintendency as a career? The vast majority of local superintendents are males, but some females are entering the field. Finance is usually rated as the top issue by superintendents, but teacher militancy, race relations, and changing societal values are also important to superintendents (Campbell et al., 1980, pp. 224–225). The superintendency is not a very stable career for many: the median term of a superintendent in one position is four years, and the median length of a person's entire career in the superintendency is seven years. Apparently, the pluralism and pressures in American society have made this a difficult position for one person to hold for an extended period.

What conclusions can be drawn and what predictions can be made about superintendency in the future? Because of the consolidation and reorganization of local districts, the number of superintendents may decline slightly in future years. However, better selection procedures and improved preparation programs with less emphasis on academic course work and greater emphasis on internships and field experience may improve the quality of local superintendents. A doctorate is increasingly required for superintendents in large school districts. Some education experts, such as Kirst and Garms (1980), see centralization and loss of local power as the key factors in the role of the superintendent in the future. During recent decades, superintendents and school boards have seen their areas of discretionary power eroded from both the top and the bottom. From the top, state and federal governments as well as the courts increased their roles in education, thus diminishing local control. Also, private interest groups such as the Ford Foundation, the Council for Basic Education, the Education Commission of the States, and the Council for Exceptional Children raised their concerns and used their influence to shape educational policy. And from the bottom, superintendents and school boards found their powers tied to local collective bargaining contracts. There seems to be no reason to believe that this trend will be reversed in the future.

THE EROSION
OF THEIR
POWER

Conclusions on Local Governance

Some general conclusions and future predictions can be drawn from this discussion of local governance and control. First, although local school boards and superintendents will continue to have the legal authority to run day-to-day educational programs, several factors would seem to portend limits on this authority. Many of the problems surface at the local level, but many key decisions (especially financial decisions) are made at the state level, leaving the local board of education with the problems but without the means to deal with them. The growth of power of both teachers' organizations and special-interest groups of lay citizens also limits the effective power of the local school board. Another factor in the loss of power of local school boards has been the increase in state and federal regulations, such as rules for special education and the handicapped.

LIMITS ON
AUTHORITY

Herman (1977) summarized the variety of state and federal regulations and other pressures on school boards:

> Arbitrators tell you how to interpret master contracts with employees; individual pupil's rights provide hearings on any student disciplinary actions; MIOSHA [state occupational safety agency] inspectors levy fines and temporarily close down equipment and school plants; inspectors investigate to determine whether or not the local district is meeting affirmative action quotas; unemployment compensation is paid, with the approval of the reviewing agency, for a bus driver who quit the job —payment was made during the summer when other bus drivers were not collecting salaries; the types and quantity of food to be served students is [sic] determined by federal and state agents if the district wishes to receive reimbursement; a plan for the busing of local students to achieve desegregation is agreed to by the courts and federal agencies; the district needs [to] establish an educational program for a month old child whose doctor has certified him as being handicapped; the local teachers' union or association

threatens to strike if the provisions suggested by the state and national teachers' associations are not included in the master contract negotiated with the local board of education; and ad infinitum. (pp. 146–147)

Thus, it seems certain that school boards will be asked to do more with fewer financial resources and increased state and federal regulations, in addition to augmented pressure from teachers' organizations and lay groups. School board members will find themselves mediating the pressures from these groups and others, too, in future years.

Summary

The most important concept for students to understand from this chapter about educational governance is that education is a state function. States, however, generally delegate the actual operation of schools to the local school district, while maintaining their powers of oversight and ultimate authority. The governance of education has evolved from early colonial laws that gave local civil authorities the permission to establish schools if they so desired to a hierarchy of special governance for education, with a state board of education and a chief state school officer in each state. The governance issues of funding, lack of uniformity, and present economic realities have also been spotlighted in this chapter. The origin of state "reserved powers" in the U.S. Constitution was examined, as was the authority of the state legislatures, the state boards of education, and the state superintendents of education; Indiana was used as an example of governance in a typical state. On the local level, the powers and limitations of local school boards were surveyed, including the method of selection and the possible motivation of local school board members. Finally, the duties of local school superintendents, as well as problems and solutions at the local governance level, were outlined. It was found that many local school boards and superintendents feel that their authority has been eroded in recent years by court intervention, militant teachers' organizations, and state control of school finances through Proposition 13–like property tax freezes.

Glossary Terms

Governance, 422
Town School Committees, 423
Head Teacher, 424
Reserved Powers, 425
Delegated Powers, 427
Plenary Powers, 428
Checks and Balances, 428
Accountability, 428

State Board of Education, 430
State Department of Education, 430
State Superintendent of Education, 432
Local School District, 435
Local School Board, 435
Scapegoat, 437
Special-Interest Groups, 440

Questions

1. Make a list of special-interest groups that influence your state legislature. Which ones have the most influence in your state?

2. What is the title of the person in charge of the department of education in your state? What are his or her major responsibilities?

3. Why is there a trend toward fewer school districts? What are the advantages and disadvantages of consolidation?

4. Why do school districts resist reorganization into larger units?

5. How does a person become a member of a school board in your state?
   a. From what socioeconomic level do most school board members come?
   b. What are the legal requirements for school board members?
   c. What are the two primary methods of selecting school board members?
   d. What personally motivates persons to run for the school board in your community?
   e. How has single-issue politics affected school board elections in your state?

6. Distinguish between the role of the superintendent and the role of the school board in relation to administration and policy formation. In what ways can these lines become blurred, and what problems can this blurring cause?

7. What are the general duties, as defined by law, of your state school board?

8. What are some of the ways in which the public can be involved in the selection of school board candidates?

9. What are the advantages and the disadvantages of having a lay school board?

10. List the major powers and duties of your local school board.

11. Are school board members compensated for their duties in your state? If so, how much are they paid? Do you think the compensation is adequate? Why or why not?

Annotated Bibliography

1. *Becoming a better board member.* (1982). Washington, DC: National School Boards Association.

   This publication is a practical guide for school board members. Prospective teachers can use it to gain insight into how a school board actually works.

2. Campbell, R. F., Cunningham, L. L., Nystrand, R. O., & Usdan, M. D. (1989). *The organization and control of American schools*, 6th ed. Columbus, OH: Charles E. Merrill.

   This latest edition of a classic text on school finance includes a discussion of local, state, and federal finance, as well as the roles of the courts, boards of education, superintendents, principals, teachers, and special-interest groups in school finance decisions.

3. Garms, W. I., Guthrie, J. W., & Pierce, L. C. (1978). *School finance: The economics and politics of public education.* Englewood Cliffs, NJ: Prentice-Hall.

    This classic text on the structure and financing of public schools includes an overview of local and state governance.

4. *The school board and the instructional program.* (1981). NSBA Research Report, 1981–1982. Washington, DC: National School Boards Association.

    This research report reviews the literature on the role of school boards and the results of a national survey on the operation of local school boards.

Federal Governance and Control of Education

Introduction

FEDERAL IN-
FLUENCE

The third level of governance in American education comprises federal controls and influence on United States schools. Historically, Americans have felt that the day-to-day operation of their schools, including curriculum, qualifications of teachers, selection of textbooks, and regulation of school buildings, should be controlled at the local level; however, the federal government has had a profound influence on American schools through federal money appropriated for education, regional resource centers that support federal education programs, categorical grants that support national interests in vocational education, and federal court decisions concerning desegregation and sex discrimination.

DELEGATED
VS. RESERVED
POWERS

What are the three types of powers granted to governmental units in the United States, and how do these powers affect the federal role in education in the United States? In the U.S. Constitution, **delegated powers** are the powers expressly granted to the national government and the U.S. Congress. In other words, the federal government has only those specific powers listed in the Constitution. In contrast, all other **powers** are **reserved** to the states and to the people by the Tenth Amendment to the Constitution. Some powers, such as the authority to raise money through taxation, are granted to both the federal and the state governments. In addition, certain powers, such as the power to conduct foreign affairs, are forbidden to the states by the federal Constitution. Education is not mentioned in the U.S. Constitution, is not delegated to the national government, and therefore is reserved to the states. The federal courts have ruled that the federal government has "implied" powers, which are the powers necesary to carry out the authority specifically delegated to the federal government. It is in these "implied" powers that the federal government's authority is found. If education is necessary for the national defense or the general welfare (delegated functions of the federal government), the national government has the authority to pass and implement certain education legislation. Usually, this legislation is in areas where the states have failed to act, such as vocational education. Remember, however, that the federal government has limited and implied powers in education, whereas the state powers are plenary, or full, in this area.

HISTORY OF
FEDERAL IN-
VOLVEMENT

Historically, the federal government has been involved in public education since the land ordinances of 1785 and 1787, but the total amount of federal assistance for education was small until the Russians launched *Sputnik* in 1957. Federal aid increased after *Sputnik*, the high point being the Elementary and Secondary Education Act (ESEA) of 1965. In the 1970s and 1980s, the federal influence on education declined, but the federal government continues to be involved in public education. In fact, the federal programs related to education are so diverse, so numerous, and so dispersed among various federal agencies that it is difficult, if not impossible, to determine how much money the federal government does spend on educational activities. Students of education in the United States must realize that although education is not mentioned in the U.S. Constitution, the federal influence on education has been present and extensive from the earliest days of our nation.

The U.S. Constitution and Education

ENUMER-
ATED POW-
ERS AND IM-
PLIED
POWERS

The U.S. Constitution contains no direct mention of education for two reasons. First, when the Constitution was adopted, the federal government had only limited (or enumerated) powers, or those that were implied from the enumerated powers. Second, the states did not yet have public school systems because most schools in the late 1700s were parochial and private. The framers of the Constitution conceived of the national government as limited and circumscribed. The Tenth Amendment, included as part of the Bill of Rights in order to gain ratification and approval for the Constitution, states that "The powers not delegated to the United States by the Constitution, nor prohibited by it to the states, are reserved to the states respectively, or to the people." Thus, as education was not mentioned as a federal power, it was reserved to the states. In fact, the Ninth Amendment in the Bill of Rights makes it clear that the framers of the Constitution wanted the broadest powers in the hands of the states and the people when it insisted that "The enumeration in the Constitution, of certain rights, shall not be construed to deny or disparage others retained by the people." The powers of the people and the individual were so broad that they had all powers not expressly listed in the Constitution itself.

GENERAL
WELFARE
CLAUSE

One of the provisions of the Constitution that affects education indirectly is found in Article I, establishing the powers of Congress or the legislative branch of the federal government. Article I, Section 8, is commonly called the **General Welfare Clause** because it provides for the powers of Congress in regard to the common defense, the general welfare, and the levying and collection of taxes. It states, in part, "The Congress shall have Power to levy and collect Taxes, Duties, Imports and Excises, to pay the Debts and provide for the common Defense and general Welfare of the United States." This means that the federal government has the right to levy and collect taxes to support public education because the federal courts have decreed that Congress cannot provide for the general welfare and for the national defense without being able to make certain that proper educational opportunities exist for U.S. citizens. Thus, the federal courts, and particularly the U.S. Supreme Court, have "implied" powers in the realm of education from this elastic General Welfare Clause. The last paragraph in Article I is called the **Elastic Clause** and gives Congress the necessary and proper authority to carry out these earlier powers: "To make all Laws which shall be necessary and proper for carrying into Execution the foregoing Powers." Johns and Morphet (1975) asserted, "The General Welfare Clause has been used extensively during the past forty years to justify the expansion of old federal activities, and the addition of new activities of the federal government" (p. 364). Thus, Article I, Section 8, the General Welfare Clause of the Constitution, has been used by the U.S. Supreme Court to allow expansion of the federal role in education.

Three amendments to the Constitution, the First, Fifth, and Fourteenth, have figured prominently in court cases related to the public schools. The **First Amendment** states, "Congress shall make no law respecting an establishment of religion, or prohibiting the free exercise thereof; or the right of the people peaceably to assemble, and to petition the Government for a redress of grievances." This amendment has been used by the U.S. Supreme Court in school-related cases in decisions involving the separation of church and state, freedom of the press, freedom of speech, and freedom to assemble. The **Fifth Amendment** states in part that no person shall be deprived of life, liberty, or property without due process of law and that private property should not be taken for public use without proper compensation to the owners. This Due Process clause has been used by the federal courts in cases involving students' rights and teachers' rights, especially in discipline and punishment cases. The **Fourteenth Amendment,** which was passed after the Civil War, guarantees the rights and privileges of U.S. citizens to residents of all the states in these words:

THREE AMENDMENTS

DUE PROCESS OR EQUAL PROTECTION CLAUSE

> No State shall make or enforce any law which shall abridge the privileges or immunities of citizens of the United States; nor shall any State deprive any person of life, liberty, or property, without due process of law; nor deny to any person within its jurisdiction the equal protection of the laws.

This clause, commonly called the *Equal Protection Clause*, extends the federal due process to the state level. (See Unit VI for more information on these topics.)

The U.S. Congress and Education

INTERPRETATION OF IMPLIED POWERS

Congress has been granted wide powers in education by the U.S. Supreme Court's interpretation of **implied powers,** the General Welfare Clause, and the Elastic Clause in the U.S. Constitution. The first federal legislation concerning education was passed by Congress under the Articles of Confederation and consisted of land grants in federal territories for the purpose of establishing and supporting public elementary schools. These were included in legislation establishing methods of surveying and dividing up the western lands. Later in the 1860s, federal lands were given for the establishment of land grant colleges in each state by the Morrill Act. In 1917, Congress passed the Smith–Hughes Act, establishing the federal role in stimulating vocational education through categorical grants for specific purposes, with requirements for matching state funds. Congress was providing stimulation for needed changes in public education from a total college preparatory emphasis to an additional concern for vocational education caused partly by World War I.

The legislation passed by Congress for relief during the Great Depression of the 1930s and World War II in the 1940s accelerated this trend toward

A chief school official testifies at a U.S. Congressional hearing.

(Photo used by permission of the Indianapolis Public Schools.)

more federal involvement in education. Again, Congress, spurred on by national emergencies and defense requirements, stepped in to correct omissions at the state level in educational programs. Two of the relief measures passed by Congress were the Civilian Conservation Corps (CCC), which provided jobs related to conservation of natural resources for young people who were unemployed during the Great Depression, and the National Youth Administration (NYA), which provided funds for students to attend school during the Depression. In 1941, Congress passed the Lanham Act for national defense reasons. This law aided local governments, which were overwhelmed by a large influx of students into areas where war industries or military installations for World War II were located.

The 1950s and 1960s saw a greatly increased involvement of Congress in education. The major legislation passed by Congress during this twenty-year period included extensions of the original G.I. Bill of Rights benefits for veterans; the National Science Foundation, which was established in 1950 to promote education in the sciences; the National Defense Education Act (NDEA) of 1958; the Vocational Education Act passed in 1963; and the Elementary and Secondary Education Act of 1965, which supported the education of children of low-income families. It seemed as if Americans believed that every social, political, and economic problem in the United States could be solved by education legislation passed by Congress. Inevitably, these high expectations were followed by a period of doubt that federal education programs could accomplish these herculean tasks. As Campbell, Cunningham, Nystrand, and Usdan (1980) state, "The boom in federal influence began to slow down about 1970. The seventies were a time of reappraisal, retrenchment, and redirection in federal involvement in education" (p. 35). Campbell et al. also believe that the research studies in the 1970s and 1980s have cast doubt on the ability of educational programs to make a difference in solving society's problems and deficiencies.

PUBLIC LAW
94-142

Despite this general retrenchment of education in the 1970s, at least one major piece of legislation affecting education was passed during this period. In 1975, Congress passed Public Law 94-142 concerning the education of handicapped children. As a result of Public Law 94-142 and state regulations governing handicapped students, local school districts were required to prepare individual educational plans (IEPs) for every handicapped student, to provide a "least restrictive" education environment, with mainstreaming where appropriate, and to provide medical support services such as occupational therapy and physical therapy for such students. The cost of implementing these requirements is a tremendous burden to local school districts because the federal government pays only a fraction of these expenses.

IMPACT OF
PUBLIC LAW
94-142

What has been the impact of Public Law 94-142 on local school districts, other than its cost? The positive impact of Public Law 94-142 on local school districts has been fourfold. It has increased cooperation between parents, schools, and other agencies serving the needs of handicapped children. It has increased the knowledge of all concerned about the education of these special children. New priorities have been established for the use of resources and funds, and special education has also come to be considered as a legitimate part of the total school program (Atkin, Allen, and Wachter, 1980, pp. 120–121). Perhaps the greatest effect of Public Law 94-142 has been the influence it has exerted on the regular school programs. The regular school students have been brought into closer contact with these special students through mainstreaming and have been exposed to their similarities and differences. It is hoped that these regular students will learn that they are more similar to than different from students in special education classes. Because of the IEPs required by special education legislation, the public is beginning to demand that individualized educational plans be drawn up for regular students as well. Special education programs have served as models for implementing competency testing and for developing remedial programs for regular school students. Greater cooperation has resulted between teachers in the regular school program and special education teachers, because of mainstreaming and the work of resource teachers who serve as bridges between the two programs. The authors of this text have also observed that special education students behave differently and often more positively when mainstreamed with regular school students than when attending special education classes. "Every decision regarding handicapped children will somehow affect the total program for all students" (Atkin et al., 1980, p. 120). Thus, the terms *mainstreaming, least restrictive environment,* and *due process* for special education students have become common terms in the language of education since 1975.

CONTINUED
RETRENCH-
MENT IN THE
1980s

The 1980s seemed to continue the retrenchment in federal legislation on education. With enrollments down and money tight, the federal government attempted to return the burden for education back to the states.

However, there is no doubt that Congress has had an impact on education throughout American history, especially since the 1950s through categorical grants for specific purposes perceived as both urgently needed for national priorities (such as for defense or for economic development) and consistently neglected at the local and state levels.

The U.S. Department of Education and the U.S. Secretary of Education

Throughout U.S. history, programs of education have been administered by numerous Cabinet-level departments and other agencies of the federal government. For example, the schools for military dependents located abroad are administered by the U.S. Department of Defense, and schools on Indian reservations in the United States are run by the Bureau of Indian Affairs in the U.S. Department of the Interior. So many federal agencies have been involved in administering federal educational activities that even an overview of federal activities in education is difficult, but the most visible national education agency has been the U.S. Office of Education in the Department of Health, Education, and Welfare.

DIFFUSION OF PROGRAMS

The National Education Association (NEA) had been lobbying for many years for the creation of a Cabinet-level department of education, to be

President George Bush speaks before the President's Education Summit with Governors, September 1989.

(Photo used by permission of Carol T. Powers, The White House.)

CABINET-
LEVEL DE-
PARTMENT

separated from the Department of Health, Education, and Welfare and to replace the Office of Education. NEA representatives argued that establishment of such a high-level education department headed by a Cabinet-level secretary of education would enhance the prestige of both American public school teachers and American education in general. Although many opponents view this idea as an example of special-interest legislation for the sole advancement of teachers, the bill that established this Cabinet-level department was passed in Congress during President Jimmy Carter's administration. In spite of extensive lobbying by the NEA, it passed by only four votes in the House of Representatives, certainly not the mandate for the new department that the NEA had sought. During his campaign for the presidency, Ronald Reagan, who succeeded Carter as president, called for abolition of the **Department of Education** as a Cabinet-level position, but he eventually appointed Terrel Bell to succeed Shirley Hufstedler as the second U.S. Secretary of Education. Bell, a conservative from the West, operated under and shared President Reagan's philosophy of a limited federal role in education. He attempted to motivate educational improvements by the various states, and the programs that he supported encompassed merit pay and master teacher or career ladder plans in several states, including Tennessee and North Carolina. Bell was succeeded in 1985 by William J. Bennett, who continued the conservative thrust of this office, and by Lauro Cavazos under Presidents Ronald Reagan and George Bush.

IMPLICA-
TIONS OF
THE CHANGE

What are the implications of the establishment of the Department of Education to replace the former Office of Education in the Department of Health, Education, and Welfare? First, this department is only an administrative agency, carrying out the will of Congress. It cannot make education laws, only the policies to carry them out. Second, the new department had mostly a public relations advantage; it took over the functions of the old Office of Education and some education functions that had been conducted by other cabinet-level departments. It made education more visible and gave the Secretary of Education more access to the president. Savage (1980) believes that the new Department of Education is just an administrator, not a policymaker, in education and concluded:

> In all but foreign policy, Congress calls the shots. In education, Congress creates a new program, says how much money it will get, says exactly how it will be distributed, who will get it, and what they can and cannot spend it for. The Office of Education or the Department of Education simply sends out the checks. (p. 117)

MORE INFLU-
ENCE?

Although the Department of Education may have more influence than Savage believes, it is true that almost all of the federal programs in education are for specific purposes, such as vocational education, and that this categorical aid is established by Congress, not the Department of Education. Congress also has a proclivity to pass laws expanding existing educational programs and creating new programs rather than cutting back or eliminating existing programs. Therefore, Congress, rather than the U.S. Depart-

Former Education Secretary Terrel H. Bell was a motivator of state reforms in education.

(Photo used by permission of the Indiana State Teachers Association.)

ment of Education, seems to wield the real power over education in the United States.

Quattlebaum's report (1951) concerning the U.S. Office of Education and the administration of federal education activities (which seem to be appropriate to describe the U.S. Department of Education as well) led Campbell et al. (1980) to conclude:

> One, these activities were extensive and widespread. Two, the money appropriated for such activities was appreciable. Three, the United States Office of Education had meager influence and even less control over this vast program. Four, there was apparently little, if any, coordination of the programs of the several federal agencies. (p. 30)

SPLINTERED
PROGRAMS

Thus, the federal education programs are splintered among numerous federal agencies, and the Department of Education has little control over them. Students of education should remember that the federal government administers its aid to public schools not directly, but always through state education agencies, and that the Cabinet rank of education was threatened by the conservative views of President Reagan and others.

The Federal Courts' Influence on Education

POWER OF
JUDICIAL RE-
VIEW

The federal courts rule on cases involving the interpretation of laws passed by Congress, and the U.S. Supreme Court has the power of **"judicial review"** and can decide which powers are "implied" as "necessary and proper" for both the states and the federal government. The power of judicial review was established by John Marshall, the first Chief Justice of the U.S. Supreme Court. Under this power, the Court can rule on the constitutionality of laws passed by the Congress and, if necessary, declare them unconstitutional (or null and void). Constitutional issues such as public aid to private schools, the separation of church and state, due process in students' and teachers' rights, and integration of schools have been addressed by the federal courts over the years.

Campbell et al. (1980) synthesized the variety of educational issues on which the state and federal courts have ruled:

VARIETY OF
ISSUES

> Let us summarize these legal milestones as they pertain to the public schools. In response to social, economic, and political development in this country, there was first the establishment of public schools by constitutional and statutory provisions. As time went on, attendance of pupils in school and payment of taxes for school purposes were required. In the latter half of the nineteenth century the public school program was extended to include the secondary level. Convictions about the importance of public schools, however, were not sufficient to eliminate the nonpublic school. While the doctrine of separation of church and state still pertains, it does not rule out the use of some public money for the benefit of pupils (not the schools themselves) in nonpublic schools, nor does it prohibit a limited amount of cooperation between school and religious bodies. Finally, the obligation of the public school to serve all

children without regard to race or color has been given rigorous interpretation by our highest court. (p. 15)

(See Chapter 13 for more detailed information on these court decisions.)

EDUCATION AS A SCAPE-GOAT

Because educational and social issues seem to be intertwined, education has often been the battleground—and sometimes the scapegoat—for society's social issues. Schools are shaped by society to accomplish its purposes, whether they be education of the handicapped or integration of the races. In fact, federal court decisions have often mandated actions that were unpopular in some sections of the United States, such as racial integration of the public schools. The federal courts have ruled on the confidentiality of student records based on the Family Educational Rights and Privacy Act of 1974 and on the equal treatment of female employees and students under Title IX of the Educational Amendments of 1972. However, the implementation of these federal court rulings depends on the respect that the majority of Americans have for their laws, as seen by the thirty-plus years of struggle to fully implement the desegregation ruling in the 1954 *Brown* decision of the U.S. Supreme Court. Education and the federal courts are likely to continue to be in the center of social conflict and often to be blamed by society for its unsolved problems.

Who Should Control the Public Schools?

QUESTIONS ABOUT CONTROL

The debate continues in the 1990s concerning who should control the public schools. Should the control be at the local, state, or national level of government? How much control should school administrators have in education? Should the state governors, state school boards, or state superintendents of public instruction be in complete charge of education in their states? What should be the role of parents and local community leaders in educational policy? What is the role of local school board members in the education process? Should teachers' organizations and unions be able to dictate conditions of employment and other policies to local school boards? What role should university professors and teacher-training institutions play in the education process? Should public school students, the consumers of education, have a role in educational policy decisions?

EMPOWER-MENT AT THE LOCAL LEVEL?

Concerning the role of school administrators in school decisions, many superintendents see an erosion of authority and power at the local district level, with more local responsibility than ever but with less power to solve educational problems locally. Principals see the need for power to run their schools at the local building level and cite numerous studies showing the principal to be the key to teacher morale and educational excellence at the local level. According to Robert Schain, the principal of Wingate High School in Brooklyn, New York, "We don't need structural changes in the ways schools are governed so much as we need a new attitude on the part of both professionals and the public" ("How Should Schools Be Ruled?" 1980, p. 104). He believes that education must become a top priority if the current problems in governance of education are to be surmounted. He feels that the public is simply not committed to excellence in education. Although many speak of the need for good public schools, budgets are cut, so that resources are not available for needed programs. Salaries and status accorded educators are also low, keeping capable people from entering or remaining in the field, and the media feature negative stories about the schools, belying the claim that first-rate schools are a top priority for Americans.

John Prasch, a superintendent, cited the social climate that opposes both shared values and consensus. He accused us of being suspicious of our own institutions, leading citizens to cut off the resources needed for public schools. He castigated our inadequate decision-making processes and con-

IMPORTANCE OF SOCIAL CLIMATE

cluded, "The best evidence of our inability to reach decisions efficiently is how frequently we turn to the courts" ("How Should Schools Be Ruled?" 1980, p. 105). He criticized legislatures for their procrastination in making important education decisions—making many just before they adjourn—instead of using an orderly decision-making process. It is easy for these examples to see that school administrators at all levels are increasingly frustrated by their role in the governance of education.

What is the feeling of government officials at the local, state, and federal levels concerning their roles in the governance of education? A governor

ACCOUNTA-BILITY

cited problems such as increasing demands for accountability in education, the era of scarcity and limits, the decline in the school-aged population, economic recessions decreasing funds for all state services, and taxpayer revolts against further education spending. A member of the Virginia State Board of Education foresaw a greater state role in education, citing the increasing financial problems of local school districts and the taxpayer concerns about the increasing federal bureaucracy ("How Should Schools Be Ruled?" 1980, p. 106). Anne Campbell, Commissioner of Education in Nebraska, also emphasized the "strings" attached to federal aid to education:

> Except for issues involving a clear national interest, educational policy is a state responsibility—and most states delegate a great deal of authority to local districts. But prescriptive federal legislation and regulations are increasingly limiting the latitude within which states and local districts can work. In areas such as vocational education, education of the handicapped, and bilingual education, there is far too much specificity in federal directions. ("How Should Schools Be Ruled?" 1980, p. 103)

Campbell said that most local citizens may agree with the federal goals but resent the increased financial burdens placed on local taxpayers to carry them out.

Carl Perkins, a member of the U.S. House of Representatives from Kentucky, admitted that the role of the federal government in education has expanded recently but counteracted the myth that the federal government's share of education funding has increased. He cited statistics to show that

The State Board of Education is at the heart of controversy over who should control education.

[Photo used by permission of the Indiana Department of Education.]

FEDERAL
SPENDING AT
A CONSTANT
LEVEL

because of inflation and increasing education costs, the federal government's share of funding for schools has remained at an almost constant 8%. He admitted that the public perceives a greater control of education by the federal government through its regulations, but claimed that Congress has attempted to reduce the burdensome paperwork connected with federal education programs. He emphasized that federal education aid has always been, and will continue to be, categorical in nature for very specific programs and purposes related to the national interests, not a general or block grant aid to education ("How Should Schools Be Ruled?" 1980, p. 109). Thus, from the viewpoint of Congress, the perception of increased federal control of educational governance is exaggerated and incorrect.

How do local community leaders, teachers' organizations, and professors in university teacher-preparation programs view the governance–control issues and their roles? Many local community leaders believe that improvement of education should begin at the local school with shared decision-

VARIOUS
VIEWS OF
CONTROL

making involving parents, students, and other citizens, who they feel have been left out of the decision-making process. Carl Marlburger, a parent advocate, believes that if students and parents are not included in the governance of education through shared decision-making, the existence of public schools will be threatened in future years. He sees teachers' organizations as gaining more power in the present governance structure ("How Should Schools Be Ruled?" 1980, p. 108).

Yet, one teachers' organization official sees the erosion of local decision-making power as the current trend. Norman Goldman, Director of Instruction for the New Jersey Education Association, cited the implementation of statewide competency testing programs for students as "governance by testing" and believes that this emphasis on testing will lead to less local

EROSION OF
LOCAL
POWER

control of education in the future ("How Should Schools Be Ruled?" 1980, p. 103). Albert Shanker, President of the American Federation of Teachers, agreed that local power over education is decreasing, but he worried that this power is being fragmented instead of concentrated in one source, where it can be used effectively to promote education. He believes that future educational leaders will need to be more informed about both finance and politics because financial and political considerations seem to be controlling education to a greater degree now than in the past ("How Should Schools Be Ruled?" 1980, p. 105).

Schools of education in American universities have been blamed by the public, the state legislatures, and other public officials for the perceived "failures" of the present educational system. Although university professors of education have been used as scapegoats by the public during educational WHO'S TO crises, they, too, see the same erosion of local power mentioned by other BLAME? reference groups. Michael Kirst, Professor of Education at Stanford University and President of the California State Board of Education, put the problem in these words:

> Over the last two decades public education in the United States has been legalized, centralized, and bureaucratized at an increasing rate. The discretionary zone of local superintendents and boards has been squeezed progressively into a smaller and smaller area, especially during the last decade.
>
> It is simplistic, however, to call this change "centralization"; there is no central control point but rather a fragmented oligopoly. Local school boards are subject to pressures from higher authorities—federal and state legislatures, agencies, and courts; and from outside interests like Educational Testing Service and the Council for Exceptional Children. Moreover, the shift of influence to higher levels has not resulted in a commensurate loss of pressure from local sources. ("How Should Schools Be Ruled?" 1980, pp. 103–104)

What conclusions can be drawn from this discussion of who should control education? The era of extreme local control seems to be at an end, INCREASED but most experts do not wish to put the control of schools at the federal PRESSURES level of government. A trend can be discerned toward increased direct BUT LESS involvement of the states in education, particularly in the financing of POWER schools and in the reform of education. Most experts see the local school board as having increased pressures but less real power than in previous years. Most advocate shared decision making in education but caution against the fragmentation of the political clout of education groups. Alvin Toffler, the author of *Future Shock* and *The Third Wave*, summarized the problems and possible solutions:

> Some problems cannot be solved on a local level. Others cannot be solved on a national level. Some require action at many levels simultaneously. Moreover, the appropriate place to solve a problem doesn't stay put. It changes over time.
>
> To cure today's decision logjam resulting from institutional overload, we need to divide up the decisions and reallocate them—sharing them more widely and switching the site of decision-making as the problems themselves require. . . .
>
> The issue is not "either/or" in character. It is not decentralization in some absolute sense. The issue is rational reallocation of decision-making in a system that has overstressed centralization to the point at which new information flows are swamping the central decision makers. ("How Should Schools Be Ruled?" 1980, pp. 102–103)

Thus, although Toffler was discussing the problems of government in general, his solutions seem relevant to educational governance as well.

The Influence of Special-Interest Groups on Educational Governance

In addition to the formal legal controls of local school boards, state legislatures, the U.S. Congress, and the courts, numerous informal controls on education are exercised by various **special-interest groups.**

Types of Special-Interest Groups

What types of groups attempt to influence education by lobbying in state legislatures or in the U.S. Congress on educational issues? The first and most important of the special-interest groups are the local, state, and national organizations of teachers, administrators, and school board members. Some of the teachers' organizations consider themselves professional organizations, and others are known as unions. (See Chapter 17 on education organizations for more detailed information.)

EDUCA-
TIONAL OR-
GANIZA-
TIONS

Taxpayer groups concerned about the cost of education constitute a second type of special-interest group lobbying on education legislation. In this category are included business groups, such as the state chamber of commerce or the National Association of Manufacturers; farm organizations, such as the Farm Bureau; and taxpayers' associations, such as those that supported Proposition 13 in California. In many agricultural states, the Farm Bureau opposes additional educational expenditures, whereas labor organizations, such as the AFL–CIO, have generally supported educational spending, which usually benefits their members' children.

TAXPAYER
GROUPS

A third category of special-interest groups includes school-related groups, such as the special education organizations, groups promoting education for the gifted, and the National Congress of Parents and Teachers.

SCHOOL-RE-
LATED
GROUPS

A fourth type of special-interest group includes ethnic minorities, such as blacks and Hispanics, who desire a better education for members of their group.

A final type of special-interest group includes right-wing religious organizations, such as the Moral Majority, which were influential in educational debates in the 1980s. These organizations seem to be afraid that the schools are undermining the moral character of U.S. youth by not allowing prayer in public schools and by failing to emphasize values in public schools. It seems clear that a multitude of groups are attempting to influence education legislation for their own specific purposes.

RELIGIOUS
ORGANIZA-
TIONS

Effect of Special-Interest Groups

What influence do these special-interest groups have on education? One of the problems in passing education legislation is that the various education groups do not speak with one voice. Many state legislators often complain

This famous cartoon, which originally appeared in *Harper's Weekly* in 1871, illustrates the delicate balance between church and state.

(Photo used courtesy of the Library of Congress.)

PROBLEMS RELATED TO SPECIAL-INTEREST GROUPS

that lobbyists related to education cannot agree on what is best for education. For example, teachers' groups often do not agree with superintendents' groups or organizations of school board members on issues such as school finance or collective-bargaining legislation. State legislators are often confused by these conflicting demands of education's special-interest groups, and as a result, education legislation suffers. Another problem influencing the effectiveness of education groups is related to the increasing militancy of teachers. Because of teachers' attitudes and collective-bargaining legislation, teachers' organizations have excluded principals and other administrators who formerly were members of these groups. This same teacher militancy has led to an estrangement between teachers and lay citizens in many communities, making confrontation, instead of conciliation and collaboration, the *modus operandi*. As has been explained, the growth of special-interest groups has been one of the reasons for the decline in power at the local school district level of education.

Whereas most authorities see teachers' organizations as very influential

IMPACT OF
SPECIAL-IN-
TEREST
GROUPS ON
DECISION
MAKING

in education legislation, Donmoyer (1980) found in his research that the impact of professional educators on decision making is lessening even as they participate more fully in the political process. Earlier findings seemed to indicate that educational interest groups played a significant role in legislative policymaking. But Donmoyer concentrated on curriculum legislation rather than on funding legislation, as had been done earlier, and found that professional educators' groups played only a minor supporting role in the legislative process. Thus, it seems that organizations of professional educators have been relegated to responding to initiatives of others in areas such as competency testing and professional standards, although they have more influence on school finance legislation in many states.

FUTURE
TRENDS

What does this influence of special-interest groups in education mean for the future? It would seem that the control of education will be more divided and splintered in the years ahead, so that it will be necessary for special-interest groups to form coalitions to implement common objectives in state and national legislatures. Kirst and Garms (1980) suggested that more money and effort on the part of teachers' organizations should be used at the state level rather than at the national level if these organizations want to increase their effectiveness in lobbying for educational legislation. The trend toward a multiplicity of special-interest groups also means that administrators must be trained to mediate conflict between these groups and that no one voice will speak for education in future years.

Governance and Control of Private or Parochial Schools

STATE REGU-
LATION OF
PRIVATE
SCHOOLS

How are private and parochial schools governed, and how does this process differ from the governance of public schools? Attendance at private or parochial schools does satisfy the states' compulsory attendance laws, but the states do have the right to make private or parochial schools meet certain standards, such as public health, safety, building requirements, and zoning laws. It is generally agreed that the states also have the authority to regulate and to inspect private schools to determine if they meet standards for curriculum and teacher training. State requirements for citizenship training, particularly teaching about the electoral process, must be met by private and parochial schools as well as public schools. However, the states differ widely in the strictness of their regulation of and their enforcement of regulations in private or parochial schools. The percentage of the total student population in attendance at nonpublic schools varies significantly from state to state and from region to region in the United States. States such as Rhode Island, Connecticut, Pennsylvania, Massachusetts, New York, and New Jersey have higher enrollment of pupils in private schools, whereas southern states, such as North Carolina, West Virginia, and Georgia, and western states, such as Wyoming, Utah, and Oklahoma, have small nonpublic enrollments. Historically, the enrollments in nonpublic schools, which are not supported by public taxes, showed a steady increase until the 1970s. Because of financial pressures, many private and parochial schools have closed since the mid-1970s, and there has been a 10% decline in the number of pupils enrolled in nonpublic schools during this period.

Church-Related Private Schools

TWO TYPES OF NON- PUBLIC SCHOOLS

Nonpublic schools can be divided into two types: church related and non–church-related. The vast majority of these schools have a religious affiliation, and only 15% of the total is made up of non–church-related schools. Over half the church-related schools are Roman Catholic, followed by Lutheran and Seventh Day Adventist. Even the religious schools vary in their governance and control: some are controlled by groups of parents, whereas others are under direct church control. For example, some Roman Catholic schools are under the direct control of the parish, and others are run by religious orders or private Roman Catholic groups.

ROMAN CATHOLIC SCHOOLS

The diocese is the equivalent to the local public school district in the governance of Roman Catholic schools. The bishop oversees Roman Catholic schools in the diocese, and the priest has jurisdiction over the schools in his parish. Because of the burden created by these schools on church officials, a superintendent of schools and a board of education have been created in each diocese. The Roman Catholics have expanded the percentage of lay members on these diocesan school boards to over 40%. In corresponding fashion, most parishes in the Roman Catholic church also have parish boards of education. Parish Roman Catholic schools are financed by parish contributions and by tuition paid by the parents of the students. However, only about one half of Roman Catholic students of elementary school age attend Roman Catholic schools, and about one third of Roman Catholic high school–aged students attend Catholic high schools. Increased financial costs resulting from inflation and the decline of membership in the religious teaching orders have forced the closing of many Roman Catholic schools in the last decade.

REDUCED PUBLIC FI- NANCIAL BURDEN

The Roman Catholic schools remove a great financial burden from the public schools by educating millions of American youth. Three fourths of students enrolled in nonpublic schools are in Roman Catholic schools. If all Catholic schools were closed, the increase in the cost of educating the students in the public schools would be catastrophic. It should also be noted that private and parochial school parents also pay taxes to support public schools as well as pay tuition to nonpublic schools. Thus, the effect of nonpublic schools on public education is potentially tremendous. In addition, Roman Catholic schools and other nonpublic schools provide an alternative to public schools and have often stimulated innovation in education and sparked changes in the public schools.

Non–Church-Related Private Schools

The second type of nonpublic school is not related to churches or religious groups. These nonchurch or nonsectarian schools constitute only 10% to

PRIVATE SEC-
TARIAN
SCHOOLS

15% of the total enrollment in nonpublic schools in the United States. They range from small store-front schools to prestigious college preparatory schools. These schools have many problems in common with church-related schools. Many face uncertain enrollments, unstable finances, and the pressure of inflation. Some of these prep schools also have the image of snobbishness to overcome, whether they deserve this reputation or not. According to Campbell et al. (1980), "In general the quality of independent school education is sufficiently high that states need not be concerned unduly about supervising them" (p. 9). However, the states have the same authority to supervise nonsectarian or non–church-related schools as they have over church-related schools.

Campbell et al. (1980) summarized the importance of these nonpublic schools as follows:

> [T]o understand the schools of America one must look at the public and the non-public schools. The presence of the nonpublic school affects in many ways the organizaton and control of public schools. Also, events in some public school systems have given impetus to nonpublic alternatives. (p. 9)

Conclusions About Governance and Control

What general conclusions can be drawn in the area of governance and control of education in the United States? The conditions in public education changed drastically in the late 1970s and in the 1980s compared with the 1950s and 1960s:

LOSS OF LO-
CAL FREE-
DOM

> The decade of the 1970s was marked by paradox. Many school districts accustomed to rapid and sustained growth since World War II faced decline for the first time. Increasing enrollments, new facilities, and program extensions gave way to retrenchment, reductions in (work) force, and program cutbacks. The pronounced nature of these changes coupled with school finance uncertainties and the impact of the courts on the schools placed new stresses on the governance and management of education. The future of local school districts appears to be caught up in the question of whether or not our political system, functioning through the mechanisms of local districts, states and federal centers of responsibility can carry its burdens. (Campbell et al., 1980, p. 113)

Critics of the increase in federal rules and regulations pertaining to education in the last two decades see a loss of local freedom in the governance and control of U.S. schools. Not all educators agree with this view. Some feel that centralization of the process of financial support for schools is possible without centralization of administration and operational control (Johns and Morphet, 1975).

CENTRALIZA-
TION VS. DE-
CENTRALIZA-
TION

Education students must decide for themselves whether centralization or decentralization is better for the future of governance in education. Those who favor decentralization believe that it encourages local citizens' interest and participation in the governance of schools, whereas those who support more centralization in school governance stress the improvement in school financing that is possible under a more centralized governance. Some of the control and finance questions that education students need to examine were listed by Herman (1977):

1. How much of the financial resources of the federal, state, and local units of government should be placed into the education of the children and youth of this country?

2. Should the unit of government mandating that specific educational and social programs be conducted at the local school district level be required to provide the funding for the mandated programs?

3. Should every child be provided with an equal educational opportunity regardless of the degree of wealth that exists within the locality of his parents' residence? . . .

4. If collective bargaining is permitted by public employees, should the state take over this function in order to balance the resources brought to the task by a local Board of Education and by a unified national, state, and local teachers' union or association?

5. What agency or group is to have final decision-making authority about the multitudes of programs and functions carried on at the local school district level? Also, how much responsibility and control is to be given to the local level and its agents, the state level and its agents and the federal level and its agents? (p. 162)

Summary

In our examination of the U.S. Constitution, it was found that education is not mentioned directly in this document but that education is a power reserved to the states and to the people by the Tenth Amendment. The federal involvement in education, however, has been justified by the "implied" powers of Article I, Section 8 (the General Welfare Clause), and by three amendments to the Constitution, the First, the Fifth, and the Fourteenth. The role of the U.S. Congress in passing educational legislation was surveyed, with highlights on key federal legislation from the Morrill Act in the 1860s through Public Law 94-142 and the federal retrenchment in educational funding in recent years.

The evolution of the Office of Education into the Cabinet-level U.S. Department of Education, including the implications of this change for the prestige of education in general, was traced. The federal courts were also found to have exerted great influence on education in the United States, sometimes making education the scapegoat for severe national problems.

Finally, several specific issues concerning governance and control in general were addressed. First, future trends in the governance of education were discussed, as was the issue of who should control the public schools. Then, the influence of special-interest groups at all levels of government, as well as the governance of private and parochial schools in the United States, was scrutinized.

In Chapter 15, we examine in greater detail school finance, a topic closely related to the questions of control and governance.

Glossary Terms

Questions

1. What is the significance of each of the following parts of the U.S. Constitution?
    a. First Amendment
    b. Tenth Amendment
    c. Fourteenth Amendment
    d. General Welfare Clause (Article I, Section 8)
2. What was the significance of the establishment of the U.S. Department of Education? What benefits have accrued to education as a result of this event?
3. In what ways has federal assistance improved the state departments of education?
4. What is the relationship between the state departments of education and federal aid to education?
5. Give five examples of how the federal government is involved in education. Is it important for the federal government to be involved in each of these areas? Why or why not?
6. Of the three levels of control of education in the United States (local, state, and federal), which one has the primary responsibility for control of education, and what are the functions of the other two levels in education?

Activities for Unit VII

1. Plan an individual visit to your state legislature. Interview a lobbyist, and talk with a conservative and a liberal state legislator. Summarize your findings.
2. Interview a member of the state board of education in your state. Find out about his or her duties and about the amount of influence he or she has on education in the state.

3. Ask your U.S. Representative what have been the differences in the function of the current U.S. Department of Education compared with the old Office of Education. Has this change been an improvement?

4. Contact a state legislator and inquire about the function of the state department of education. In what ways has this department been effective? In what ways does it need to be improved?

5. Interview a person from another country. Compare the local control of education used in the United States with the national control of education found in France, Japan, or another country.

Annotated Bibliography

1. Atkin, R., Allen, L. I., & Wachter, H. H. (1988). P. L. 94–142 and local district governance. *Educational Leadership, 38,* 120–121.

    The impact of Public Law 94–142 on the governance of local school districts and their special education programs is explained.

2. How should schools be ruled? (1980). *Educational Leadership, 38,* 102–105.

    Various experts in all areas of education discuss how they feel schools should be governed. These experts include superintendents, principals, school executives, and union leaders.

3. Johns, R. L., & Morphet, E. L. (1975). *The economics and financing of education: A systems approach,* 3rd ed. Englewood Cliffs, NJ: Prentice-Hall.

    This book is a classic text on the basic principles of school finance in the United States.

4. Savage, D. G. (1980). Education of a new department. *Educational Leadership, 38,* 117–118.

    The development and implementation of the Cabinet-level Department of Education is traced. The thesis of this article is that the Department of Education does not originate policy and has little chance of streamlining administration of federal programs.

[Photo used by permission of the Metropolitan School District of Washington Township.]

VIII

Financing Education

OBJECTIVES

After reading Chapter 15, the student will be able to:

- Delineate the primary state and local taxes used to support education

- Understand the role of the "foundation program" in state financing of education

- Explain possible reforms and solutions to state and local problems in financing schools

- Differentiate between a progressive and a regressive tax

- Perceive the advantages and disadvantages of the property tax as a primary source of educational funding

Local and State Financing of Education

Introduction

REASONS FOR
STUDYING FI-
NANCE

Why should students of education study educational finance? The "bottom line" in any endeavor or organization is usually money: "What can we accomplish with the resources at our disposal?" Because resources are scarce and limited by nature, the question becomes one of priorities: "What is most important for us to do, given these limited financial resources?" The 1970s and early 1980s have been an era of limits, and as a result, questions of educational finance have taken center stage. Whereas the schools received much financial support in the 1950s and 1960s, the public mood turned toward taxpayer revolts and refusal to support bond issues for education in many states in the 1970s and the early 1980s. Coupled with this public mood in these two decades were inflation, the energy crunch, and a decline in the school-aged population. In addition, financial pressures on local, state, and national governments forced education to compete fiercely with other needs, such as defense spending and police officers' pensions for tax dollars. Economic recessions in the late 1970s and the early 1980s exacerbated this problem, making educational finance one of the top two issues, along with discipline, in most polls of teachers and administrators in the 1980s. Another reason for the study of educational finance by students of education and by all citizens is that education is one of the biggest business enterprises, in terms of dollars spent, in the entire nation. In many states, the expenditures for education make it the biggest "business" in the state, and many times, education, from kindergarten through the university, consumes more than half the state's budget. A third reason to study school finance is that the salaries of teachers and administrators are closely related to financial conditions in the local school system. Because concern about adequate salaries is uppermost in the minds of many teachers and prospective teachers, the financing of education is an important topic. Attracting high-quality people into teaching may depend on educational finance and higher salaries for teachers.

FINANCE
QUESTIONS

Many important educational questions are discussed in Unit VIII. How well do states fund education? What are the primary state taxes used to raise money for education? What problems exist in using these taxes, and can the states move toward full state funding for education in the future? What local taxes are earmarked for education, and what are the strengths and deficiencies of these taxes? What are some possible solutions to inequities in the local property tax? What percentage of school revenues comes from local, state, and federal sources? What is the history of federal aid, and has it increased or decreased in recent years? What is the difference between "categorical aid" and "block grants," and what effect does each have on education? What are the major specific federal programs in education, and what is the purpose of each? What problems do critics see in federal aid, and are there any possible solutions to these difficulties? What are the current trends in federal aid, and how will they influence education? What is the budgeting process, including the major divisions of funds in educational accounting and in the planning, programing, budgeting system, a system for linking financial resources to educational outcomes? How may vouchers, tax credits, performance contracting, and accountability contribute to solutions to educational finance problems? What conclusions can be drawn regarding educational finance, and what future trends can be discerned?

VARIABLES IN PUBLIC SUPPORT FOR EDUCATION   What personal characteristics influence a citizen's viewpoint on educational finance, and what variables affect a local community's spending for education? Campbell, Cunningham, Nystrand, and Usdan (1980) found that the two most important personal factors that influence a citizen's financial support of education are occupation and the number of years of schooling the person has had. To a lesser degree, they found that age, race, and religion can help to predict a person's financial support of education, but that income, sex, and type of community were variables not closely associated with support of education by citizens. The three variables that influence the expenditures of a local community for education include the wealth of the local district, variations in government access and control, and differentials in the educational aspirations of the district. Thus, the assessed valuation of the school district and the educational aspirations that parents have for their children affect the financial resources available for education in that community.

In the following sections of this unit, state, local, and federal financial support of education is examined.

State Support

Introduction

The percentage of total public school **revenues** coming from state sources has been increasing in recent years. According to the National Center for Education Statistics (NECS) (1988b), in the 1969–1970 school year, 52% of

TABLE 15–1

Summary of the Sources of Public School Revenues from School Years 1959–1960 through 1986–1987

SCHOOL YEAR ENDING	PERCENT OF REVENUE FROM		
	Local	State	Federal
1960	56	39	4
1970	52	40	8
1980	43	47	10
1987	44	50	6

SOURCE: National Center for Education Statistics (1988). *The condition of elementary and secondary schools*, Vol. I, p. 34.

public elementary and secondary school revenues nationwide came from local sources, and only 40% came from state sources. In 1979–1980, however, 47% came from the states and only 43% could be traced to local sources. Thus, it can be seen that the local share of revenue for public elementary and secondary education, formerly over 50%, is declining and STATE SHARE that the state share is increasing, reaching the 50% level. (See Table 15–1.) INCREASING (Note that during this ten-year period between 1969–1970 and 1979–1980 the federal share remained more stable, rising from 8% in 1969–1970 to a high of 10% in 1979–1980 but reverting back to the 6% level in 1986–1987.) This same source (NCES, 1988b) shows that the percentage of the **gross national product (GNP)** spent on public and private education at the elementary, secondary, and university levels increased from 4.8% in 1959 to a high of 7.5% in 1970, and then declined to 6.8% in 1986. Clearly, until the last few years, the nation was spending a greater percentage of its resources on education at all levels, and the states have assumed a greater role in financing public elementary and secondary education (Figure 15–1).

One of the major problems with state support of education is the enor-

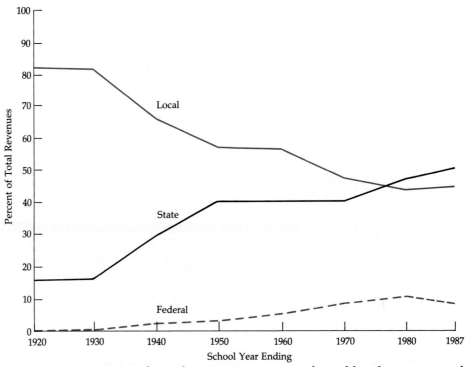

Figure 15–1   National trends in revenue sources for public elementary and secondary education: Selected school years ending 1920–1987.

(SOURCE: National Center for Education Statistics (1988). *The condition of education, elementary and secondary education,* Vol. I, p. 35.)

TABLE 15–2 ▅▅▅▅▅▅▅▅▅▅▅▅▅▅▅▅▅▅▅▅▅▅▅▅

Total Expenditures of Educational Institutions Related to the Gross National Product (GNP), by Level of Institution: 1959–1960 to 1986–1987

SCHOOL YEAR	GNP (in billions)	TOTAL EXPENDITURES FOR ALL EDUCATIONAL INSTITUTIONS (in millions)	
		Amount	Percent of GNP
1	2	3	4
1959–1960	$495.8	$23,860	4.8
1961–1962	533.8	28,503	5.3
1963–1964	606.9	34,440	5.7
1965–1966	705.1	43,682	6.2
1967–1968	816.4	55,652	6.8
1969–1970	963.9	68,459	7.1
1970–1971	1,015.5	75,741	7.5
1971–1972	1,102.7	80,672	7.3
1972–1973	1,212.8	86,875	7.2
1973–1974	1,359.3	95,396	7.0
1974–1975	1,472.8	108,664	7.4
1975–1976	1,598.4	118,706	7.4
1976–1977	1,782.8	126,417	7.1
1977–1978	1,990.5	137,042	6.9
1978–1979	2,249.7	148,308	6.6
1979–1980	2,508.2	165,627	6.6
1980–1981	2,732.0	182,849	6.7
1981–1982	3,052.6	197,801	6.5
1982–1983	3,166.0	212,081	6.7
1983–1984	3,405.7	228,597	6.7
1984–1985	3,772.2	247,657	6.6
1985–1986[a]	4,010.3	269,485	6.7
1986–1987[b]	4,235.0	289,500	6.8

[a] Preliminary.
[b] Estimated.

Note. Total expenditures for public elementary and secondary schools include current expenditures, interest on school debt, and capital outlay. Data for private elementary and secondary schools are estimated. Total expenditures for colleges and universities include current-fund expenditures and additions to plant value. Excludes expenditures of noncollegiate postsecondary institutions. Some data have been revised from previously published figures. Because of rounding, details may not add to totals.

SOURCE: National Center for Education Statistics (1988). *Digest of education statistics,* p. 29. This table was prepared in November 1987.

TABLE 15–3 ▮▮▮▮▮▮▮▮▮▮▮
Current Expenditure per Pupil in Average Daily Attendance in Public Elementary and Secondary School, by State: School Years Ending 1970 and 1986

STATE	EXPENDITURE PER PUPIL (1985–1986 dollars)		PERCENT[a] INCREASE	STATE	EXPENDITURE PER PUPIL (1985–1986 dollars)		PERCENT INCREASE
	1970	1986			1970	1986	
United States	$2,351	$3,752	59.6	Missouri	$2,041	$3,189	56.2
Alabama	1,567	2,565	63.6	Montana	2,253	4,091	81.6
Alaska	3,234	8,253	155.2	Nebraska	2,122	3,634	71.3
Arizona	2,075	3,093	49.1	Nevada	2,217	3,440	55.2
Arkansas	1,635	2,658	62.5	New Hampshire	2,083	3,542	70.0
California[a]	2,498	3,543	41.8	New Jersey	2,928	5,395	84.3
Colorado	2,126	3,975	87.0	New Mexico	2,037	3,195	56.9
Connecticut	2,741	4,743	73.1	New York	3,823	6,011	57.3
Delaware	2,593	4,610	77.8	North Carolina	1,764	2,982	69.0
District of Columbia	2,934	5,337	81.9	North Dakota	1,987	3,481	75.2
Florida	2,110	3,529	67.3	Ohio	2,103	3,527	67.7
Georgia	1,694	2,966	75.1	Oklahoma	1,742	3,146	80.7
Hawaii	2,422	3,807	57.2	Oregon	2,664	4,141	55.4
Idaho	1,738	2,484	42.9	Pennsylvania	2,540	4,416	73.8
Illinois	2,620	3,781	44.3	Rhode Island	2,568	4,667	81.8
Indiana	2,097	3,275	56.2	South Carolina	1,765	3,058	73.3
Iowa	2,432	3,619	48.8	South Dakota	1,988	3,051	53.5
Kansas	2,221	3,829	72.4	Tennessee	1,631	2,612	60.2
Kentucky	1,571	2,486	58.3	Texas	1,798	3,298	83.4
Louisiana	1,867	3,187	70.7	Utah	1,804	2,390	32.5
Maine	1,995	3,472	74.0	Vermont	2,326	4,031	73.3
Maryland	2,646	4,450	68.2	Virginia	2,039	3,520	72.6
Massachusetts	2,475	4,562	84.3	Washington	2,637	3,881	47.2
Michigan	2,604	4,176	60.3	West Virginia	1,930	3,528	82.8
Minnesota	2,603	3,941	51.4	Wisconsin	2,543	4,168	63.9
Mississippi	1,443	2,362	63.7	Wyoming	2,466	5,114	107.4

[a] Estimated by the Center for Education Statistics.
Note. 1985–1986 dollars are based on the Consumer Price Index, prepared by the Bureau of Labor Statistics, U.S. Department of Labor. These data do not reflect differences in inflation rates from state to state.

SOURCE: National Center for Education Statistics (1988). *The condition of education: Elementary and secondary education,* Vol. 1, p. 93.

VARIATION
IN FINAN-
CIAL ABILITY
OF STATES

mous variation in the financial ability of the states to support public elementary and secondary education. In 1986, the **personal income per capita** varied from less than $9,716 in Mississippi to $18,627 in New Jersey and $19,599 in Connecticut. Similar variations exist in expenditure per pupil in average daily attendance (ADA) in public elementary and secondary schools in the individual states. Whereas the national average is $3,752 per pupil, Mississippi spends $2,362 per pupil and Alaska spends $8,253 per pupil. The three states in addition to Alaska that spend more than $5,000 per pupil in ADA are New Jersey, New York, and Wyoming, as well as the District of Columbia (NCES, 1988b). (See Table 15–3.) From these figures, it can be easily determined that wealthy states can spend more than twice as much per pupil in ADA in public elementary schools than can the poorest states.

DEFINITION OF TERMS   Several terms in school finance should be defined before the topic of school funding is examined in more detail. These terms are **foundation programs, average daily attendance (ADA), average daily membership (ADM),** and **assessed valuation.** Garms, Guthrie, and Pierce (1978) defined the *foundation* or *flat grant program* as "a certain amount of 'basic' education that should be provided on an equal basis to all. Any amount beyond that provided by the flat grant or foundation guarantee is a local luxury, not to be aided by the state" (pp. 79–80).

EXAMPLES OF FOUNDATION FUNDING   Nationwide state support for school funding averages about 50% of total school revenues, and most is distributed under a foundation funding plan (Benson, 1975). To understand foundation funding, let us examine three hypothetical school districts within a single state, each having 1,000 students (see Figure 15–2). The purpose of foundation funding is to provide an adequate education to every child in a state. To this end, the state government estimates an annual cost per pupil for basic education. Generally, this is a single value, but sometimes states set higher amounts for secondary than for elementary pupils (Benson, 1975). This figure per pupil times the

Figure 15–2   Foundation funding.

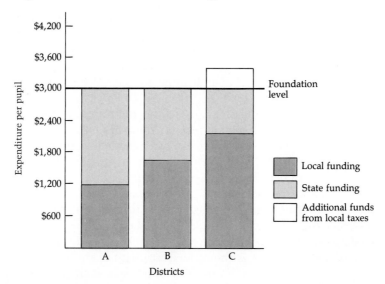

number of students in a district determines the total foundation program cost per district. For the purpose of this example, the state sets a figure of $3,000 per pupil, which results in a foundation program cost of $3 million for each of our three districts ($3,000 × 1,000 pupils = $3 million).

FAIR LOCAL CONTRIBUTION

State governments do not ordinarily provide the entire amount of the foundation cost but require local districts to make what Benson (1975) called a **"fair local contribution."** The fair local contribution is generally raised by the state's requiring local districts to levy a property tax at a rate determined by the state, say, 5%. Looking at District A of our example, suppose the assessed value of property in the district is $24 million, or $24,000 per pupil. A **property tax levy** for schools of 5% would therefore raise $1,200,000, or $1,200 per pupil. The state would then provide the balance of the foundation funding, or $1,800,000 for the district, $1,800 per pupil in District A. The state is providing 60% of this district's foundation budget for education, a higher percentage than the national average because of the lower-than-average property values of the district. District B, on the other hand, has property whose assessed value is $34 million, or $34,000 per pupil. With a 5% property tax levy this district can raise $1,700,000 ($1,700 of the needed $3,000 per pupil), with the state contributing $1,300,000, or 43% of the budget. District B falls nearer the national average. District C may be a district with a larger commercial base, for its assessed property value is $44 million. It raises $2.2 million with the 5% property tax, thereby costing the state only $800,000, or 27% of the total foundation budget.

THREE EXAMPLES

ADDITIONAL FUNDS OR FREEZE?

If a local school district desires to spend more money per student than the state's foundation program provides, it can attempt to raise the additional money through a higher local property tax rate—unless the local district is under a state property tax freeze or Proposition 13–like state legislation. Should District C residents decide that they wish to improve their schools beyond the programs provided by the state's foundation amount, they could raise their property tax rate to say, 6%. By so doing they could now raise $2,640,000 locally, $2,200,000 of which would fall under the foundation program. The state would still provide $800,000 and the district would have an additional $440,000, or $440 per pupil, to expand their programs.

ADA AND ADM

Average daily attendance is based on the number of students actually in attendance at a school, not just on the rollbooks. It is calculated from a tally of the number of students in attendance and those legally excused for the school year; then this total is divided by the number of days in the school year. In contrast, the average daily membership is based on the total number of students enrolled in school each day, whether or not they are actually in attendance. In other words, the ADM is tied to enrollment, not to attendance. In school systems with large numbers of absent or missing students, this difference between the ADA and the ADM is significant.

Assessed valuation is the official estimate of the value of property for the purpose of taxation and is usually much less than the market value of the

ASSESSED
VALUATION

property, many times only one third of the market value. The tax rate is then set as so many cents per hundred dollars of assessed valuation, not of the market value. For example, a house with a market value of $100,000 may be assessed for tax purposes at $33,000 (assessed valuation). If the tax rate for schools is set at 10 cents per hundred dollars of assessed valuation, this hypothetical homeowner would pay $33 in taxes per year to support the schools. The actual rates and amounts would be much higher, and it should be remembered that the financing of other units of local government besides schools would also be included in the final tax rate.

DIVISIONS
INTO FUNDS

What are the various divisions or "funds" into which the local school district budget is divided? These funds can be thought of as separate accounts, and it should be remembered that money from one fund (account) cannot be transferred to another without special state approval. Thus, money from the cumulative building fund cannot ordinarily be used to pay teachers' salaries, which are an operating expense. In Indiana, for example, state law provides for four funds: a general fund for current operating expenses, such as utility costs and teachers' salaries; a debt service fund to pay interest on district borrowing; a cumulative building fund for capital expenditures such as those for buildings and equipment; and a transportation fund to pay for the costs of transporting students, except for the purchase of school buses. All of these "funds" have separate tax levies in Indiana, and money from one fund may not be transferred to another fund without special state approval. Almost every state limits the borrowing capacity of schools for capital outlay purposes, such as school buildings, equipment, and buses. This limit is usually expressed as a percentage of assessed valuation, and beyond this limit, bonds may not be authorized even by a vote of the residents of the district. Many states require a referendum of the voters in the local school district to approve bond issues, but Indiana has no such provision.

TRENDS IN
STATE FI-
NANCE

How much responsibility should the states have to finance public elementary and secondary education? The trend is clearly toward the states' funding an increasing percentage of education costs, but state legislators must weigh the money required for public education with the demands of other public services, such as prisons, mental health facilities, welfare, and highways. This question also involves issues such as the scope of state responsibilities, local control, property tax relief, and equalization. Because almost all public school revenue comes directly or indirectly from taxes, the next sections of this chapter examine the two major state taxes: the state sales tax and the state individual and corporate income taxes.

State Sales Tax

ADVANTAGES
AND DISAD-
VANTAGES

In 1987, forty-five of the states had a statewide sales tax to raise revenue. What are the advantages and disadvantages of the tax and what trends can be discerned in its use? First, the state **sales tax** is a relatively painless way to collect tax revenue because the majority of this money is paid in small amounts as purchases are made. Second, the burden is placed on citizens

Divisions of local school district budgets: transportation, debt servicing, capital expenses, and operating expenses.

(Photos by Axler.)

who spend money, not on those who save it. One disadvantage is that the impact of the sales tax falls more heavily on citizens who are poor and are forced to spend most of their money on the necessities. It should be noted, however, that many states exempt necessities such as food and medicine from the sales tax to alleviate this problem. Another disadvantage is that because revenues from the sales tax are based on the purchase of goods, the amount of money collected can decrease rapidly during a recession or depression, when fewer purchases are made. The sales tax is relatively elastic, however, and it brings in an abundance of revenue in more prosperous times.

SALES TAX
TRENDS

What are the trends in state tax use, rates, coverage, and exemptions? (See Table 15–4.) The sales tax is a significant source of state revenues, but it has remained fairly constant over the last six years. Again, all but five states (Alaska, Delaware, Montana, New Hampshire, and Oregon) levy such a tax, and those states that do have sales taxes do not have a tendency to raise them. Motor fuels, tobacco, and alcohol tax revenues have also shown an increase recently (Kane, 1988). In the early 1980s, 3% or 4% was a common rate for state sales taxes (Due, 1982), but inflation and the lack of federal aid has made states more dependent on this income, and rates slowly increased toward the end of the decade.

A MAJOR
SOURCE OF
STATE REVE-
NUE

State Income Taxes

The greatest increase has been in the state income tax revenues, which reached a high of 39.2% in 1987. After the sales tax, individual and corporate **income taxes** combined are used by more states than any other major

TABLE 15–4

Percent Distribution of State Tax Collections by Major Tax Category

YEAR	SALES AND GROSS RECEIPTS TAXES	INCOME TAXES	LICENSE TAXES	OTHER
1957	58.1	17.6	15.1	9.2
1967	58.2	22.4	11.4	8.0
1977	51.8	34.3	7.1	6.8
1982	48.5	36.7	6.2	8.6
1983	48.9	36.7	6.2	8.2
1984	48.7	37.8	6.1	7.4
1985	48.8	37.8	6.4	7.0
1986	49.2	37.6	6.5	6.7
1987	48.5	39.2	6.5	5.8

SOURCE: Kane, V. (1988). *The book of the states* (1988–1989 edition). The Council of State Governments, Lexington, KY, Vol. 27, p. 265.

The state sales tax is one of the chief sources of state revenue, but its pros and cons as a fair tax are a matter of debate.

(Photo by Axler.)

source of revenue. Together with the sales tax these two sources combined for a total of 88% of state revenue. (See Table 15–4.) In the six states that do not collect individual income taxes, the burden falls on other sources. Forty-six states have some form of corporate taxes, although these are generally kept low by the competition between states to attract businesses and industries to their areas (Kane, 1988, pp. 376–378).

ADVANTAGES AND DISADVANTAGES

What are the advantages and disadvantages of the individual personal income tax? First, it is based on the "ability to pay" principle, and citizens with larger income pay a larger total tax bill. It should be noted, however, that some state individual income taxes are not **progressive**; that is, the wealthier citizens do not pay a higher rate than the poorer citizens. The same rate applies to all citizens (unlike the federal income tax, which is progressive), although the total amount of money paid by the higher-income citizens may be higher. Second, the revenue from this tax may increase or decrease according to economic conditions in the state, in contrast to the local property tax, which can be levied on property whether people are working or spending money or not.

Inequality between districts is one of the major problems in school funding. Property-rich districts can provide many extras, such as this performing arts center,
while property-poor districts struggle for necessities.

(Photo by Axler.)

State Finance Problems and Possible Solutions

What are the major problems of the states in school finance, and what
solutions are proposed to alleviate these difficulties? First, the history of
these school finance problems and reforms is reviewed.

During the 1950s and 1960s, enrollments in the U.S. public schools grew
rapidly, and increased funds were spent to build new buildings and to hire
new teachers. However, in the late 1970s, public school enrollments peaked,
and the period of rapid growth in education came to an end, caused by the
DECLINE IN   decline in enrollments coupled with the increased opposton of taxpayers
ENROLL-   to school revenue increases. When funds became tight, the inequalities in
MENTS AND   the financing of education became more prominent.
INCREASED
OPPOSITION   As major funding for schools comes from property taxes, property-poor
districts often need tax rates two or three times those of property-rich
districts to raise the same amount of capital per pupil for education. (For
example, in Figure 15–2, District A would need a property tax rate of 9%
to raise the same amount of money for schools as District C, with a 5%
levy.) The courts have ruled in California, Minnesota, Texas, New Jersey,
Wyoming, Kansas, Connecticut, and Idaho that education or equal protection clauses in the state constitutions were violated by existing methods
INEQUALITY   of funding schools. Yet, the job of finding solutions to the problem fell to
BETWEEN   state legislators, as the courts offered no remedies. The legislators found
DISTRICTS   themselves facing the need to control or cut back spending on education

and at the same time to guarantee that the quality of each child's education was not unduly dependent on the wealth of his or her local school district (Garms et al., 1978, pp. 339–340).

RETRENCH-
MENT AND
REFORM

Thus, the forces demanding retrenchment in educational spending and those forcing reform in educational finances hit state legislators simultaneously in the early 1970s. This process culminated the *Serrano* decision of the U.S. Supreme Court in 1971, which declared that public school finance laws that made the quality of a student's education dependent on the wealth of a local school district were unconstitutional:

> Equalizing educational resources would not have been so difficult had additional state dollars been available to increase spending in poor districts nor would budget tightening have been so difficult if everyone's budget were squeezed by the same amount. Combining reform and retrenchment was politically explosive, however. These became the underlying themes of what has come to be known as the school finance movement. (Garms et al., 1978, p. 340)

EDUCATORS
NOT IN CON-
TROL

One of the problems for educators was that they were not in control of this **school finance reform** movement. Legislators and governors, not educators, made the decisions on school reform in the 1970s. Add to this the role of the state and federal courts, and it can be easily seen that educators were not in control of the school finance reforms during this period. In addition, the old educational coalition of teachers and administrators was splintering, partly because of differences on how tight money should be spent and how limited resources should be allocated. Teacher militancy, collective bargaining, and accountability issues resulted from the breakup of this education coalition.

The major state educational finance program before the 1970s was the foundation or flat grant per pupil, which was explained earlier in this chapter. What were the criticisms leveled by reformers at this program?

REFORMERS'
CRITICISMS

First, poorer school districts that had much less than wealthier districts in assessed valuation of property had to use higher school tax rates to raise the money needed for an adequate education program. Often, even after suffering higher tax rates on their property, these poorer districts were not able to offer adequate educational programs to their students.

POORER DIS-
TRICTS,
HIGHER
RATES

A second criticism of the foundation **school finance plans** was that a flat grant per pupil failed to take into consideration that education costs more per pupil in urban areas than in rural areas of the United States. Whereas large cities receive the state support per pupil, their costs, including teachers' salaries, are significantly higher than in most rural areas. One reason for this situation is that high local taxes for other government services prevent large cities from raising local taxes for schools.

URBAN VS.
RURAL

A third criticism of the old school finance plans was that many poor districts had an inordinate number of special education students, who were more costly to educate than the average public school student. The foundation or flat grant program of the states provided the same number of dollars to a school district for each student, regardless of the cost of educating that student. The states, in addition, often passed laws requiring more special classes and special services for these special students, without appropriating the state money to fund these requirements, forcing local school districts to take money from other parts of the school budget to meet these needs.

In summarizing the criticisms of the state foundation programs, Benson (1975) hypothesized the conditions under which such a foundation program would work:

WOULD
WORK IF . . .

Under certain circumstances, the foundation program could (would) work quite well. First, there should be no major differences in prices that school districts pay for teachers' services, instructional materials, school houses, maintenance, etc., as one moved from one part of the state to the other. Second, districts would need to be large enough to include more or less equal proportions of children who are costly to educate, or some action would be required to see that even small districts had no more than their proper share of costly children—children requiring say, bilingual teachers. Third, the local taxable resources per student would need to be more or less uniform among the districts of the state. (pp. 80–81)

THREE EXAM-
PLES

Regarding Benson's third point, you will remember the examples from Figure 15–2, in which the wealthiest district, District C, was able to raise $2,000 per pupil of the foundation amount of $3,000 from the 5% local property tax. Yet, some school districts have much greater property value than District C. Consider a fourth district, District D, which is heavily industrial, having an assessed valuation per student of $120,000. With the basic property tax rate of 5%, District D raises $6,000 per pupil for education with no more sacrifice than the other districts must make to get the minimal state funding level of $3,000 per pupil.

REVOLTS
AND FREEZES

Another problem leading to school finance reforms in the 1970s was taxpayers revolts and **property tax** limitations or **freezes,** which were often part of the reforms passed by state legislatures (Pipho, 1981):

Taxpayer revolts, slashed budgets, and now federal cutbacks—many states are facing the strictest spending limits of the decade. Ever since California voters approved Proposition 13 in the summer of 1978, the mood of the country has moved steadily toward lower spending for education. To date, 17 states have adopted either constitutional or statutory limits on taxation or spending. Some states have been harder hit than others. Although comparing states is difficult, the industrial states of the North appear hardest hit by legislated spending limits combined with inflation-driven cost increases, declining enrollments, and a recession-triggered drop in tax receipts. (p. 722)

POOR FISCAL
CONDITIONS
OF THE
STATES

Thus, the poor **fiscal** condition of the states has increased the pressure for school finance reforms. Nearly all states were experiencing a deterioration in their financial condition in the early 1980s, caused by a decrease in federal aid, changes in the corporation and individual income taxes, and a severe national economic recession. Clearly, the industrial states of the North and the Northeast are most affected, as they lost population because

Economic recession and the shutdown of important industries adversely affect education.

(Photo by Bill Locker.)

of declines in the automobile and steel industries as a result of foreign competition and lack of modernization. The southern and western states, in contrast, are generally gaining in population, wealth, and industries. School finance in these latter areas is less a problem because of increased population, industrialization, and wealth in the South and the West. For example, the governor of Michigan, hard hit by the decline in the automobile industry, ordered a 25% reduction in state expenditures in 1981, including a 50% cut in property taxes, an increase in the sales tax from 4% to 5.5%, and a limit on increases in taxes to 6% a year unless citizens vote for a larger increase. In Indiana, the 5% increase in school funding in 1981 was the lowest in ten years, and educators in this state worried that the school revenue increases would fail to keep up with the inflation rate (Pipho, 1981). Because the states estimate their revenues in advance to prepare their budgets, high estimates often lead to cuts in proposed spending, whereas low estimates result in budget surpluses. As Pipho (1981) wrote, "Either way, states walk a fiscal tightrope" (p. 722).

REFORMS AND SOLUTIONS

What reforms have been proposed as solutions to these problems in state educational finances? First, the state reforms in the 1970s are examined. Then, reforms used in five states are studied. Next, the obstacles to state school finance reform and the accomplishments of these state reforms are investigated. Finally, conclusions and predictions for the future are summarized.

1970s SCHOOL FINANCE REFORMS

What were the school finance reforms of the 1970s? About half the states enacted public school finance reforms in the 1970s, most of these in the early 1970s before the enrollment declines, **recessions**, and fiscal crunch of the late 1970s and the early 1980s. These reform movements used the citizens' growing resistance to increases in local property taxes to demonstrate how state taxes could replace school revenue from the property taxes. By the mid-1970s, an economic recession had caused further concern about government spending and had made significant reforms more difficult to execute. Also, by the late 1970s, declining public school enrollments made it difficult to convince state legislators that more and more funds were necessary to educate fewer and fewer students. These reforms usually included statutory or constitutional limits on taxation or spending for education, or both. The issues in this reform movement included "accommodation between wealthy districts and poor districts, urban–rural tensions, conflicts between taking care of special needs and supporting the basic program" (Fuhrman, 1980, p. 123).

OBSTACLES TO FINANCE REFORM

What are the obstacles to public school finance reform, and what were the accomplishments of these reforms in the 1970s? One of the obstacles was the failure of the federal government to adequately support state public school finance reforms. Only the federal Title I program of compensatory education channels more funds to poor school districts than to the wealthy systems and greater aid to financially hard-pressed urban districts than to more affluent suburban districts. A small number of federal block (general) grants for education have also given states more flexibility in putting funds where they are most needed at the local level, but most federal aid is still categorical (that is, for specific purposes, such as vocational education). Callahan and Wilkins (1976) concluded, "At this point, the federal government seems to be interested in supporting state equalization efforts only if it costs very little money" (pp. 9–10).

POSITIVE AC-COMPLISH-MENTS

The positive accomplishments of these public school finance programs have been numerous. First, the local school property taxes have been reduced or at least have been prevented from increasing. Second, in some states, property taxes have been made more equitable and fair. Third, the debate in state legislatures sparked by school tax reform legislation has raised the public consciousness on issues in education. Fourth, disadvantaged students and less wealthy taxpayers have benefited from these finance reforms. Greater equity between poor and wealthy districts has resulted, but this improvement has been spotty and uneven at best.

CONCLU-SIONS

Many of the predictions for school finance in the 1980s have become reality. **User fees** to finance education are utilized more fully, especially for nonrequired courses, such as drivers' education. Increasingly, parents directly pay a greater share of their children's educational costs through tuition and fees for summer schools and special courses. The pressure to accomplish more with fewer resources was the slogan for the 1980s. Fuhrman (1980) envisioned accountability and competency testing for both teachers and students as the wave of the future, predicting that these forced state legislatures to appropriate more money for remediation for students who fail these tests (pp. 123–124). Doyle (1982) agreed and further suggested that education will be forced to consider "productivity" as a major goal for both teachers and students by emphasizing time-on-task, mastery learning, ability grouping, and giving priorities to objectives. Many states will continue to increase their share of the cost of public elementary and secondary education; a few states may adopt full state funding, with governance decisions still being made at the local level. As we move into the 1990s, many of these predictions have come true.

PREDICTIONS In the 1990s the state and local communities will be seriously challenged to meet the needs generated by increased enrollment, for example, the need for additional school personnel, especially in the elementary grades. This increase also affects the ADA per pupil gain. As more resources are used to meet the increasing needs, the gain per pupil will decrease. Teachers' salaries are on the rise, and although there is a vast difference among states, we must look at the impact of this at the state and local levels. Congress continues to reduce the budget deficit, and it is expected that the federal government's share of public school finances will continue its downward trend in the 1990s, thus exerting more pressure at the state and local levels to compensate for this loss of revenue while trying to meet the increasing financial needs of pubic elementary and secondary schools (NEA, 1988, p. 5).

Local public school finances are now examined in more detail.

Local Support

Introduction

EMPHASIS ON PROPERTY TAXES Local support for education comes primarily from the **local property tax.** This tax is among the most criticized and controversial of all the taxes used to support public schools. The property tax can be defined as a tax on real property (land and improvements such as buildings) and personal property, such as household furnishings.

> Local revenues are drawn primarily from property taxation. For the most part, property tax yields are obtained from levies on "real property": owner-occupied houses, apartment houses, hotels, factories, warehouses, stores of all kinds, and land. The property tax rate can conveniently be thought of as a percentage levy, for example, a "$4.00 per $100" property tax rate means that taxes in the current year are 4 percent of the *assessed value* of the property. Assessed value is presumed to bear a relationship to the sale value of the property in the market, and by conventional practices properties are assessed as some fraction of their presumed true or sale value. A house, for example, may be assessed at 25 percent of its market value, so a "$4.00 per $100" school tax rate is actually a tax rate equal to 1 percent of market value. Assessment ratios are supposed to be the same for different pieces of property, at least those in the same class (e.g., houses vs. factories), and those situated in a given taxing jurisdiction. (Benson, 1975, p. 79)

VARIATION IN PROPERTY TAX The property tax for the support of education is truly "local" because it varies from school district to school district in each state. Thus, a suburban school district could have a school tax rate that varies from that of a nearby urban system and from those of other suburban systems as well. The advantages of this tax are its dependability and stability. Whereas fluctuations in retail sales may cause variations in state sales tax collections, and whereas economic recessions can cause decreases in the revenue from state personal or corporate income tax, personal property always exists in each

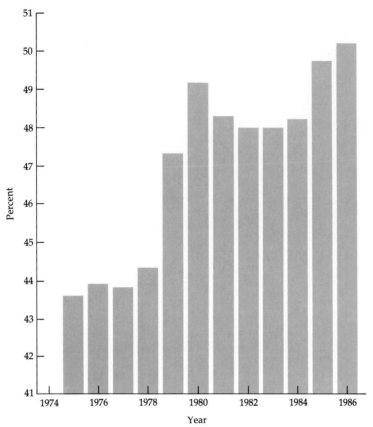

Figure 15–3   State support (of total revenues) for public schools in the United States, 1975–1986.

(SOURCE: Statistical Abstract of the United States, 1987, p. 123.)

school district and can be taxed to fund public schools. In this section, the following topics are addressed: other local taxes besides the property tax, problems and inequities in local property tax assessment, the **"regressive"** nature of the property tax, the increased choices provided for the wealthy by the property tax, the lack of flexibility in the property tax, the effect of population shifts on property tax revenue, and the failure of state aid to equalize local support of public schools. In addition, the effects of the "taxpayer revolt" on the property tax and possible solutions to property tax problems are examined.

Other Local Taxes

Before more detailed discussion of the local property tax, it is necessary to explain other local taxes briefly. There are several other sources of income on which school systems may rely when tax support is insufficient. A state excise tax, or intangibles tax, and a county-adopted local-option income

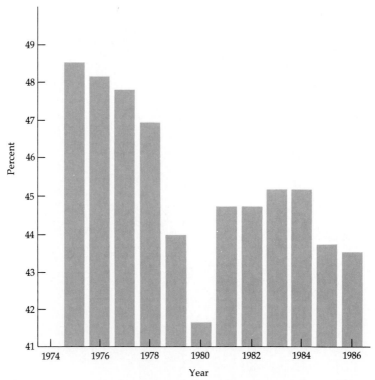

Figure 15–4   Local support (of total revenues) for public schools in the United States, 1975–1986.

(SOURCE: Statistical Abstract of the United States, 1987, p. 123.)

tax serve as examples. Nontax sources include transfer tuitions, money from the sale of school property, and gifts or contributions. Many local school systems are setting up foundations to seek contributions to support programs for which tax revenues are not sufficient.

Local Property Taxes

PROBLEMS AND INEQUITIES

Is the property tax a good tax? What are its problems and inequities? Should it be used more or less extensively to support local public schools? These issues are now examined in detail.

ASSESSMENT INEQUITIES

One problem with respect to the local property tax concerns the assessment inequities of its application. The usual practice in most states is to have the county or township assessor, usually elected, assess the property in his or her jurisdiction once every five or ten years. Several difficulties are associated with this system. First, the assessors are usually politicians who lack formal training in proper assessment procedures. Second, in the past, some of these officials have been politically corrupt, accepting bribes

Many local school systems are setting up foundations to provide for needs not met by tax revenues, for example, this special physical training equipment for special education students.

(Photo by Axler.)

to lower assessments on commercial, industrial, or private property. Third, because individual assessors assess the property in each county or taxing unit, the assessment on identical property varies from jurisdiction to jurisdiction because of a lack of common standards and procedures. A fourth problem with this system is the difficulty of keeping up with changes in property values when full assessments are usually carried out only every five or ten years. For example, in the late 1970s and the early 1980s when the nation experienced rampant inflation, the assessed valuation of property did not always reflect the increase in property values resulting from inflation.

PROPERTY TAX AS A RE-GRESSIVE TAX
    A second area of difficulty with the local property tax is that it is a regressive tax. A **regressive tax** is defined as a tax that takes a greater percentage (not amount, but percentage) from those who have the least ability to pay. In other words, the citizens who have the least wealth and resources pay a greater percentage of the property tax than people at the upper end of the scale. For example, a widow who owns her home but who has very little income must pay property taxes on the same basis as everyone else. Also, a local resident could own much property but have little cash on hand to pay the taxes on this property. A progressive tax, on the other hand, would take a greater percentage of tax revenue from those

people who have the greatest ability to pay. Wealthier people usually pay a greater "amount" in taxes, but who pays a larger "percentage" of her or his resources in taxes is the issue here. The state sales tax is also criticized by some as regressive, but this would partially depend on whether food, medicine, and other necessities were exempted from the sales tax.

INCOME TAX
AS A PRO-
GRESSIVE
TAX

The best example of a progressive tax is the federal income tax, with its many exemptions and deductions. Many state income taxes are not as progressive as the federal income tax because these state income taxes are gross taxes with few exemptions and deductions.

MORE
CHOICES FOR
WEALTHY

Other criticisms of the use of a local property tax for the support of public schools are that this tax gives the wealthy more choice of which schools their children attend, and that population shifts have made this tax inadequate for financing urban education. Although wealthy families have always had more choice in educating their children than poor families because they could afford to send their offspring to private schools, upper-income families have more choice even within the public schools. By buying houses in suburbs where schools can spend more money per pupil or in sections of large cities with superior schools, upper-income families can "purchase" a good education for their children, whereas poor families cannot usually afford to change their place of residence to escape poor schools.

REDUCED AS-
SESSED VAL-
UATION IN
CENTRAL
CITY AREAS

A second related problem is the population shift from central urban areas to suburban and rural areas in many states. The more affluent citizens flee to the suburbs along with business and industry, leaving a greatly reduced assessed valuation for the support of public schools in central urban areas. In addition, of the pupils who remain in these areas, a large percentage are minorities or have problems, for example, disabilities, that make them more expensive to educate. Urban areas also often suffer most from inflation and the high costs of teachers' salaries. Pinkney (1980) insisted that all Americans will suffer if this trend continues. Failing to take this "flight" from central urban areas and the high cost of educating inner-city students into consideration, Pinkney believes, is sabotaging the next generations of American youth, and he believes that, in the long run, this sabotage will create a problem for all Americans, not just those in inner-city areas.

LACK OF
FLEXIBILITY
AND FAILURE
TO EQUALIZE

PROBLEMS OF
INFLATION?

Additional criticisms of the use of the property tax to finance public schools are the lack of flexibility inherent in this tax and the failure of state aid to equalize local support. The criticism of lack of flexibility concerning the property taxes involves the recent controls that have been placed on these taxes in most states. Placing lids or caps on total property tax levies or rates does not allow school districts to deal with inflation or with changes in local conditions, such as an influx of new students or the loss of tax revenues from a major industry. Also, the so-called equity or equalizing features of state aid formulas have, in general, failed to make up for differences in ability to raise revenue for schools at the local level. Although Indiana has had some increases and modifications in its initial property tax freeze, the overall effect has been to increase school revenues at a rate much less than the rate of inflation in the years since 1973, while at the same time mandating schools to do more in expensive areas such as special education.

TAXPAYER REVOLT

A taxpayer revolt beginning with Proposition 13 in California in 1978 has exacerbated the problems of the local property tax. It should be remembered that in many states, citizens of local school districts must approve increases in school funding or borrowing in a referendum. In turning down increases CITIZENS' in these local taxes, citizens have been demonstrating their dissatisfaction DISSATISFAC- with the spending for government in general and for schools in particular. TION Public elementary and secondary schools were shut down for brief periods in Ohio and other states when voters failed to approve the funds needed to operate them. Statewide limits on local taxes, such as Proposition 13 in California, have often, but not always, been accompanied by increases in state funding.

What have been the causes of this revolt by American taxpayers in the years after Proposition 13 in 1978? Sharp increases in taxes have been suggested as a possible cause; however, John Due (1982) found that state and local expenditures as a percentage of the gross national product (GNP) had remained fairly constant since 1972, and that the local property tax as a percentage of the GNP increased slowly up to 1971–1972 and then declined. Thus, although taxes have risen, state and local taxes as a percentage of the GNP have not increased significantly. Inflation has also been cited by some people as a cause of the property tax revolt. John Due (1982), however, asserted, "Most of the population clearly is not adversely affected; incomes have kept up with the cost of living and values of typical assets have risen even more rapidly than inflation" (p. 278). It should be remembered, however, that older citizens on fixed incomes have been adversely affected by the rampant inflation of the late 1970s and the early 1980s.

CAUSES OF   Instead of either inflation or sharply increasing taxes, the real causes of TAXPAYER the taxpayer revolt would seem to be emotional. Because of the Watergate REVOLTS scandal and other factors, there seems to be a widespread feeling that government is inefficient and corrupt, that inflation is caused by excess government spending, and that schools are offering too many "frills." The public sees verbal Scholastic Aptitude Test (SAT) scores declining and public school enrollment decreasing at the same time that expenditures for schools are on the increase. Many voters are aghast at the pressure of unions for salary increases for government employees, including teachers, and at skyrocketing welfare costs in large urban areas of the United States. At the EMOTIONAL same time, these citizens are bombarded with distasteful government reg- ISSUES AND ulations, such as speed limits of fifty-five miles per hour, mandatory mo- ANTIGOV- torcycle helmet laws, pollution controls, and occupational health and safety ERNMENT regulations. Although the purpose of these laws is to help and protect FEELING citizens, many people see them as government meddling in their lives and taking away their freedoms. The general populace has also been reacting to minority rights legislation with a backlash against quotas and other government rules. At the same time inflation is rising and pushing citizens into higher federal income tax brackets without any increase in their real income. Many of these reasons are emotional and simplistic, but they cause citizens to lash out at their government. Where can citizens quickly and directly "get back at" the government? The easiest place is in referendums for school revenue at the local level. As John Due (1982) concluded, "much of the anti-tax sentiment has little to do with taxes per se. The votes are votes against inflation and irritating regulations and government actions, not just against taxes" (p. 281). Thus, the "taxpayer revolt" centers on emotional issues, and the schools are used as scapegoats for the general conditon of society. One of the greatest dangers of this movement is the tendency to make important educational decisions in an irrational manner and thus to harm future generations of young people in the United States.

EIGHT TRENDS FROM TAX-PAYER RE-VOLT MOVE-MENT

What conclusions can be drawn from this taxpayer revolt movement? Hartley (1981) listed eight specific trends resulting from this movement: It will result in more centralized state governance and control of education, causing a major shift from local to state financing of public education. Educators will be forced to form new coalitions to offset the taxpayers in revolt. Statewide collective bargaining for teachers' salaries and an increase in user fees for education will be legacies of this movement. In addition, Hartley believes that less variation within states in spending for education, changes in school budgeting procedures, and more pressure to justify supervisory positions in schools will result from this revolt. He even foresees a voucher plan and a possible constitutional amendment to require a balanced budget as results at the federal level. Others even predict the abolition of local school districts and local boards of education as an outcome of the taxpayers' revolt. Not all of these trends and predictions will come true, but they are warning signs for the educational community of serious problems for public schools in the years ahead.

INEVITABLE CONSE-QUENCES

The hazards of the tax revolt expenditure limitation movement for education as well as for other basic state and local government functions are obvious. How serious they will prove to be remains to be seen. The bandwagon was rolling at full tilt in 1981, with politicians leaping on at each opportunity. But the bandwagon appears to be slowing down—as the consequences of drastic tax reduction and federal budget cuts become apparent. Services that people want must be reduced, and competent personnel must be let go. California voters in 1980 rejected a proposal to cut state income taxes in half, and most of the proposals in 1980 and 1981 were defeated at the polls. (Due, 1982, p. 284)

PROPOSALS TO ALLE-VIATE PROP-ERTY TAX PROBLEMS

POSSIBLE SOLUTIONS TO LOCAL PROPERTY TAX PROBLEMS

What are some of the solutions proposed to solve or alleviate these problems with the local property tax? Common sense should lead Americans to believe that the wealthiest nation on earth must reexamine its spending priorities. Education, not automobiles, microwave ovens, and videotape recorders, should be America's first priority. Certainly, a paradox exists when in such a wealthy country, the beginning of a new school year recently found over a million children on the streets because of lack of funds for their schools. Additional money may not guarantee better education, but without more adequate funding the very survival of some public school systems is at risk.

> Those citizens who seemingly fail to care about the survival of public education in urban areas fail to realize that the real destiny of all Americans is tied together. The destiny of all school systems (urban, suburban and private) is tied together; we all must share the concerns and blame and put the rhetoric into concrete action. (Pinkney, 1980, p. 69)

FULL STATE
FUNDING?

INCREASED
FEDERAL
AID?

COST-EFFEC-
TIVE
SCHOOLS?

USE OF EX-
EMPTIONS?

TOO DE-
PENDABLE
TO BE
DROPPED?

The possible solutions include full state funding of education, as now exists in Hawaii. The U.S. Constitution clearly makes education a state responsibility by failing to mention it as a federal power and therefore delegating it, by omission, to the states. Increased federal aid is another alternative, but this is not likely because the federal percentage of public school revenue has remained fairly constant for many years, and because the purpose of federal aid has been to stimulate reform in education, not to provide general support for schools. Also, many citizens fear that increased federal aid will lead to a loss of local control of education. Others refute this argument by insisting that local control is a myth, as schools are legally a state, not a local, responsibility. They assert that local governance and control can exist even if the majority of public school revenues comes from federal or state sources. Another possible solution to the financial problems of schools is to hold teachers more accountable for the "products" they produce by testing student performance periodically. Many businesspeople prod schools to be more "cost effective," in business terms. A more practical solution to the property tax problems may be to use exemptions to eliminate the hardships caused for the poor by this tax. As Benson (1975) suggested, "the property tax is too productive of revenue to be abandoned in the short run" (p. 91). Rather, he suggested that the administration of the property tax be moved to the state level to eliminate some of the abuses in the assessment and the administration of this tax. All in all, the property tax is too dependable a source of revenue to be abandoned. Instead, it should be improved by the elimination of abuses wherever possible.

Summary

This chapter has focused on how adequately state and local governments are now financing public education, showing that states and local school districts vary widely in their expenditures per pupil for education. Several important terms in educational finance were defined, such as a *foundation program*, *flat grant*, and *average daily attendance*. Illustrative examples of a foundation program and of two primary state taxes used for education (state sales tax and state income tax) were delineated. In addition, present state school finance problems, culminating in the school finance reform programs of the 1970s and 1980s, were surveyed. The main feature of local support for education was found to be the local property tax, which varies for each school district. This tax is regressive, not progressive, and has many disadvantages; however, because the local property tax is a stable source of revenue, it is likely to continue to be used to finance schools in the future, but perhaps with homestead exemptions added to ameliorate its regressive nature. The advantages and disadvantages of the local property tax were discussed, as were the taxpayer revolts against such taxes in recent years.

Glossary Terms

Revenues, 473
Gross National Product (GNP), 474
Per Capita Personal Income, 476
Foundation Program, 477
Average Daily Attendance (ADA), 477
Average Daily Membership (ADM), 477
Assessed Valuation, 477
Fair Local Contribution, 478
Property Tax Levy, 478
Sales Tax, 479

Income Tax, 482
Progressive Tax, 482
School Finance Reforms, 484
School Finance Plan, 484
Property Tax Freezes, 485
Fiscal, 485
Recession, 486
User Fees, 487
Local Property Tax, 488
Regressive Tax, 489, 491
Progressive Tax, 491

Questions

1. What are the primary local and state taxes used to support education in your community? Explain whether each is regressive, proportionate, or progressive.
2. List several advantages and disadvantages of the use of the local property tax for the support of education.
3. What is your favorite tax for educational support? Why?
4. Explain the statement, "Education is big business."
5. What are the pros and cons of accountability for the schools?
6. In what ways have states reformed their financial support for education in recent years? Which of these reforms would you support? Why?
7. Describe the importance of the assessed valuation of a school district in its ability to adequately fund an educational program.
8. Describe how one private school in your community is financed. What limitations are placed on this school by its funding sources?
9. As an individual taxpayer, would you rather live in an industrial or a residential area? Why?

Annotated Bibliography

1. Adams, E. K. (1982). *A changing federalism: The condition of the states*, Report No. F82-1. Denver, CO: Education Finance Center, Education Programs Division of the Education Commission of the States.

    This booklet deals with the fiscal conditions of the fifty states in the 1980s as political and economic forces were altering the structure of the government and education.

2. Duke, A. L. (1984). *Decision making in an era of fiscal instability*, Fastback No. 212. Bloomington, IN: Phi Delta Kappa Educational Foundation.

    This fastback discusses the options currently available for financing public education and the consequences of each option, with emphasis on decision making and reactions to retrenchment.

3. Garms, W. I., Guthrie, J. W., & Pierce, L. C. (1978). *School finance: The economics and politics of public education*. Englewood Cliffs, NJ: Prentice-Hall.

    This classic text on the structure and financing of public schools includes the politics of school finance reform.

4. Gibson, J. T. (1981). *Financing education: An administrative approach*. Washington, DC: University Press of America.

    This book is a simplified overview of school finance designed to overcome the lack of knowledge of school finance demonstrated by most teachers.

5. Gurwitz, A. S. (1982). *The economics of public school finance*. Cambridge, MA: Ballinger Publishing Co. (a subsidiary of Harper and Row).

    The first part of this educational policy study presents in some detail the aspects of economic theory used in analyzing school finance systems. The second part casts the general problem of reforming school finance in the framework most amenable to economic analysis and presents a summary of the most relevant economic research.

Federal Support of Education

OBJECTIVES

After reading Chapter 16, the student will be able to:

- Explain the differences between categorical grants and block general grants in the federal support of education

- Explain the pros and cons of federal involvement in the financing of education

- Identifiy the significance of *Serrano v. Priest* and other federal and state court decisions on public school finance

- Comprehend the role of tuition tax credits and voucher plans as possible solutions to school finance problems

Federal Aid to Schools

GOOD NEWS
AND BAD
NEWS

Moses came down from the Mountain to address the assembled multitude. In his arms he bore two Tablets. He said, "I have some good news and some bad news. First the good news. There are only Ten Laws to be obeyed and they are inscribed on these two Tablets. The bad news is that one hundred strong men must accompany me up the Mountain to carry down the regulations." (Wise, 1981, p. 484)

FEDERAL AID
IN PERSPEC-
TIVE

RETRENCH-
MENT AND
SCARCITY

This quotation illustrates the reaction of many citizens and educators to the federal role in education, but in reality, the federal government has never provided more than 9.3% of the total expenditures for public elementary and secondary education. In 1974 the federal government provided a little over 8% of these funds, and the federal share increased to a high of approximately 9.2% in 1980. It then declined to 7.4% in 1982 and 6.4% in 1986 during the retrenchment of the Reagan administration, when the emphasis was shifted back to state and local governments (see Figures 16–1 and 16–2). Not only have the percentages of federal aid decreased, but actual dollar amounts of federal aid declined during the 1980s.

This trend sets the scene for the era of limits that has begun for both government and education. Such words as *retrenchment, scarcity,* and *priorities* seem to occur more frequently in the literature on education.

World War II was followed by a decade of economic growth and expansion

Figure 16–1   Federal support (of total revenues) for public schools in the United States, 1975–1986.

(SOURCE: Statistical Abstract of the United States, 1987, p, 123.)

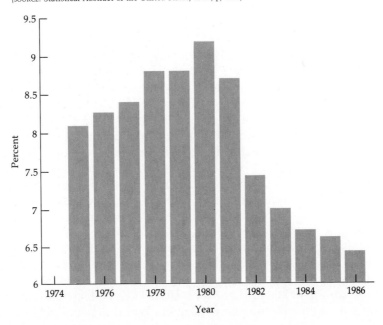

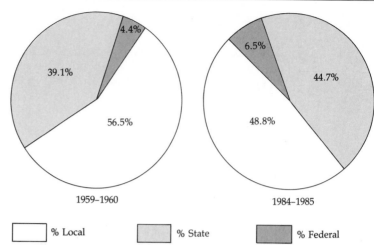

Figure 16–2   Local, state, and federal public school revenues as a percentage of total revenues for the school years 1959–1960 and 1984–1985.

(SOURCES: Digest of Education Statistics, 1985–1986, p. 80; Digest of Education Statistics, 1987, p. 35.)

PRIORITIES AND LIMITS

in America, but the New Federalism now demands that priorities be set and limits be maintained in all areas, including education. Doyle (1982) addressed school board members in the following words:

> You are on the firing line, because you are in the undesirable position of dealing with scarcity. In political and financial terms, you are now playing a zero-sum game. Each slice of pie dished up for education means that much less for some other sector. And within the education enterprise itself, each slice for one education program means that much less for another. (p. 23)

In other words, as in the 1980s, education is not going to receive automatic increases in funds in the 1990s; it must compete with other government services, such as police and fire protection, welfare, mental health, and highways, for the revenue it does receive. Various education programs will compete with each other for funds and survival. The New Federalism of President Reagan returned more of the responsibility for improving education to state and local officials, diminishing the federal role in education. According to Doyle (1982, p. 25), although the conservative federal government was the most easily identifiable cause of diminishing federal aid, it was actually a reflection of the times. Lack of economic expansion coupled with the increased demand for social programs for an aging population forced schools to compete head-to-head for the available resources. Doyle believes that school districts must reorder their priorities, spending more funds on reading and the three 3Rs, rather than on such courses as drivers' education. He sees the most obvious solution as statewide funding of public education and stated that Proposition 13–type legislation promoted such a remedy. He predicted a continued but modest federal presence in education

COMPETITION WITH OTHER GOVERNMENT SERVICES

COMPETITION FOR AVAILABLE RESOURCES

but emphasized that the real battles of educational finance will be fought at the state, not the local or federal, level.

In the late 1970s and the early 1980s, the trend in state government was to regain initiative and control over programs from the federal government. During the 1960s, increasing numbers of federal dollars were transmitted through state governments to local public school districts. The states, in turn, used the federal funds granted to them to administer the various STATES DE-PENDENT ON FEDERAL SUPPORT federal programs to augment their own contingent of consultants and supervisors. At first, these staff additions were just icing on the cake, and the basic cake itself was provided with state funds. By 1979, however, Pipho (1981, p. 125) stated that 20% to 30% of state education department budgets came from federal funds. Thus, the state education agencies have become dependent on federal support, and many state legislatures spent the late 1970s and early 1980s attempting to regain control over the 20% to 30% of state education department revenue that came from federal sources.

INCREASING STATE CON-TROL The states do seem to be seizing the initiative as education becomes an important political issue in state politics. Instead of simply serving as a conduit for federal aid, the states are increasingly seeking to control the direction of educational policy within their borders.

Besides the modest federal role in education and the new era of limits, it is necessary for the student of education to understand the nature of the FEDERAL AID AS CATEGOR-ICAL, NOT GENERAL federal aid itself. Federal aid has traditionally been "categorical," that is, for specific programs and purposes, not general aid to education. In other words, federal money cannot be spent for any current needs in public schools but must be used for specific programs to help the poor, the disadvantaged, the handicapped, the minorities, or the vocational education student. "Block grants," on the other hand, would provide more flexibility to the states and to local school districts in the use of federal money, and in 1981, thirty federal educational programs were combined into one block grant for the states, demonstrating a trend toward more federal block grants in the future, according to Kirst (1982, p. 72). However, it is important to realize that most current federal aid is designated for specific purposes. Among these purposes are improving reading effectiveness, vocational education, guidance and counseling, school social work, school health, and special education. It remains to be seen whether more federal block grants will replace the present **categorical aid** in the future.

What are the real and perceived problems connected with federal aid to education? One of the problems is related to the categorical grants already PROBLEMS OF FEDERAL AID discussed, which critics contend give no **discretionary power** to officials at the local and state levels on how federal funds are to be spent. In addition, some federal programs require **matching funds** from the state and the local levels, further reducing the money available to finance other educational programs. The biggest problem, however, is the **mandates** and **regulations** associated with federal aid to education. Often, the mandates accompanying federal aid, especially regulations regarding special education and the handicapped, cost more than the federal funds provide for these programs. Also,

MANDATES
AND REGU-
LATIONS

although federal aid would seem to be an appropriate vehicle for reducing the disparity between the states in their ability to support public schools, federal aid does not seem to be accomplishing this purpose. In fact, federal aid seems to equalize these differences among states only slightly, and although Title I of the Elementary and Secondary Education Act (ESEA) provides more aid to poorer school districts, many federal programs seem to help wealthy districts more than poor districts (Campbell, Cunningham, Nystrand, and Usdan, 1980, pp. 383–384).

POSSIBLE SO-
LUTIONS TO
PROBLEMS

What are some possible solutions to these problems associated with federal aid to education? Replacement of categorical aid with **block grants** would give local and state leaders more flexibility in meeting needs at these levels, but some argue that block grants would diminish the federal government's role as an innovator in promoting change in education at the state and local levels. Reducing the number of federal mandates and regulations is also a possible remedy, but few experts foresee this development in the future. The states, however, do seem to be seizing more initiative in controlling their educational programs, and the New Federalism of the Reagan administration encouraged state efforts to solve educational problems. It would appear that the modest percentage of school revenues coming from the federal government will not be sufficient to equalize the

Federal aid provides funds for special educational programs, but not for general programs for all children.

(Photo used by permission of the Metropolitan School District of Washington Township.)

disparities between the states in their ability to finance public schools. More will be said about this problem when solutions to school finance issues are discussed later in this chapter.

What are the future trends in regard to federal aid to education? First, the federal presence in education will continue to be modest, and the dollar amounts of this aid may actually decrease in future years. Second, general aid in the form of block grants is unlikely to replace federal categorical aid for specific purposes, such as vocational education, in spite of recent emphasis on revenue sharing and the consolidation of categorical grants into a few block grants. Third, the major purpose of federal aid to education will continue to be the stimulation of state and local officials to put more resources into programs that are in the national interest but that have been slighted at the state and local levels, such as programs for the handicapped and the disadvantaged. As Doyle (1982) concluded, "This, I say, is the reality of the '80's: a substantially diminished federal role in education no matter who occupies the White House." He believes that the era of limits is here to stay and has not simply been caused by the conservative policy of the Reagan administration. **Recessions, inflation,** tax revolts, decreases in the schoolaged population, and pressure to fund other government services are the real causes of the era of limits, and they guarantee that scarcity, retrenchment, and priorities will be significant in the future of federal aid to education.

FUTURE
TRENDS IN
FEDERAL AID

In the next section, the influence of federal and state courts on educational finance is examined.

The Courts and Educational Finance

Introduction

The federal and state courts have had a significant impact on educational finance, especially in recent years. Increasingly, educational policy is determined by the courts, from desegregation decisions to rulings on school finance, because of the greater use of **litigation** by society in general.

> Enter the courts on the issue of education finance. As is well known, the courts in a number of states have ruled that the existing system of education finance discriminates against poor people or—at the best—distributes educational resources in an irrational fashion. The general order or remedy is for state governments to play a more active role in educational resource allocations (though some of the more popular reform schemes would leave considerable discretionary powers over spending at the local level, as long as the state acts to equalize local taxing power). (Benson, 1978, p. 78)

FINANCES
CONTROL-
LING
SCHOOLS?

In fact, increasingly, the finances are controlling the schools, instead of the schools shaping their finances. Federal and state court decisions have forced state legislatures to restructure their entire system of financing schools at a time when the states must do more with less money because of state and federal pressures for increased aid to the handicapped and minorities. Thus,

Each child should receive the same attention and opportunities, regardless of the wealth of the school district.

(Photo used by permission of the Indianapolis Public Schools.)

every dollar used to equalize educational opportunity must result in a dollar-for-dollar decrease in educational spending in another area.

In the next sections the background of the school finance reform movement and the *Serrano* v. *Priest* (1971) decision—its results, its significance, and its possible negative consequences—are examined.

Background of the School Finance Reform Movement

Arthur E. Wise, John E. Coons, William Cane, and Stephan Sugarman were pioneers in the movement for public school finance reform. They suggested that the quality of education within any state should not depend on the wealth of the local school district. They suggested that the state collect and distribute all revenue to local public school districts and attempt to equalize the tax bases of local school districts by revising equalization formulas and by redrawing local district boundary lines.

EQUALIZA-
TION FOR-
MULAS

FATHER OF
THE FINANCE
MOVEMENT

Arthur Wise (1981) has generally been credited with being the father of this movement, which led to numerous state court decisions on school finance. Although Wise advocated full state financing of education, he believed that local operation of these districts was possible and was preferable to state operation of schools. He believed that the main problem concerned the distribution of state school funds, not how these funds were raised at the state level. Wise emphasized that the then-current inequality in the ability of local school districts to finance education within a state ought to be illegal. Wise became interested in school finance reform when he wrote a term paper for a graduate course in school law. This paper was later published in the *Administrator's Notebook* (1965) and led to a general reexamination of school financing at the state level. His ideas resulted in lawsuits on public school finance in several states.

Serrano v. Priest *and Related Cases*

The landmark state court decision on school finance reform is the *Serrano v. Priest* decision (5 Cal. 3d 584) of the California Supreme Court in 1971: "The Serrano criterion merely requires that the quality of education (usually defined as amount spent per child) shall not be a function of community wealth, but only of the wealth of the state as a whole" (Garms, Guthrie, and Pierce, 1978, p. 218). This decision seemed to eliminate local flat grant or foundation programs, which allowed local school districts to spend more per child if they wished, but it did not outlaw the state or local property tax to finance education if the funds were distributed equally among the school districts in the state. In fact, the *Serrano* decision did not specify a particular school finance program, although it did provide that district spending should not be related to the taxable wealth of that school district. It declared the school finance system in the state of California at that time unconstitutional, arguing that this system violated the guarantees of equal protection in both the state and the federal constitutions. Benson (1978) summarized the background of this decision:

QUALITY OF EDUCATION INDEPENDENT OF DISTRICT'S WEALTH?

> On August 23, 1968, a suit was filed by school children and their taxpaying parents of a number of Los Angeles school districts. The case, *Serrano v. Priest*, listed the state treasurer, the state superintendent of public instruction, and several other state and local officials as defendants. Plaintiffs claimed that there were disparities in educational provision among the districts of California; that these disparities arose primarily as a result of differences in taxable wealth per student; and that educational opportunities in low-wealth districts were substantially inferior to those available to children attending schools in high-wealth districts. (p. 339)

RODRIGUEZ V. SAN ANTONIO

Public school finance lawsuits followed in several other states. In *Rodriguez v. San Antonio Independent School District* (337 F. Supp. 280, 1971), a state court ruled that the Texas educational finance system was unconstitutional because it violated the Equal Protection Clause of the Fourteenth Amendment to the U.S. Constitution. In 1973, this case was appealed to the U.S. Supreme Court, which reversed the decision of the Texas court and thus prevented a nationwide uniform solution to the inequities in school finance. In other words, the Supreme Court ruled that equalization of school finance was not a federal problem and should be decided at the state level. After this decision, action took place in various state courts in Alaska, Connecticut, Florida, Georgia, Kansas, Maine, Missouri, New Jersey, New York, Ohio, Oregon, and West Virginia.

Results and Significance of Serrano v. Priest

What have been the results of *Serrano* and related decisions? The most important result of these state court decisions has been to put pressure on state legislatures to reform their school finance programs. These decisions

PRESSURE
FOR STATE
REFORMS

established the concept of *fiscal neutrality* in school finance. This term means that a child's education may not be determined by the wealth of a local school district. Another effect was the domino effect, which caused challenges to school finance plans to be filed in the courts of numerous other states. In addition, these cases placed in jeopardy the school finance systems in every state except Hawaii, which has statewide public school financing. Thus, state legislatures were forced to consider major revisions of their school finance programs to avoid further litigation. *Serrano* and related state court decisions have made a permanent impact on public school finance in the various states, both through what these decisions said and through what they did not say.

Possible Solutions to Problems in School Finance

OVERVIEW OF
SOLUTIONS

What possible solutions to the problems of school finance were accentuated by the *Serrano* case and other state school financing court decisions? The possible and suggested solutions include power equalizing, full state funding, tuition tax credits, vouchers, and private grants to public education. In addition, an increase in federal funds, restructuring educational priorities, mandating the same expenditure for each pupil nationwide, accountability, performance contracting, and school consolidation have been proposed as possible solutions to school finance problems in the United States. Each of these suggested remedies is examined briefly in this section, and the likelihood of use is assessed.

Two of the most prominent solutions are power equalizing and full state funding of public education. **Power equalizing** equalizes the ability to raise dollars per pupil at the same tax rates but does not mandate the rate or the resulting expenditure level. Under power equalizing a variety of levels of educational quality would be available in a school system; and a family could choose the level of quality it prefers, realizing that taxes would vary according to the level of quality chosen. **Full state funding** would result if all local public school revenues were raised through state taxes and were then distributed to the local school districts. Hawaii has had full state funding of K–12 public education for many years, and recently Florida also adopted a full state funding plan.

FULL STATE
FUNDING

Many people argue that because education is legally a state function, it should be supported entirely by state funds. It is further asserted that state taxes are more equitable than local taxes, such as the local property tax. Even statewide funding of education would not solve the financial problems in the nation, however, because states, too, vary greatly in their ability to support schools. Less wealthy states would have to greatly increase their tax rates to raise the same revenue provided by lower rates in wealthier states. Full state funding is an acceptable solution under the *Serrano* decision because the money spent per pupil would be a function of state wealth, not of the wealth of the local school district. Full state funding would not mandate that an equal number of dollars be spent on educating each child in the state but would require that state money be allocated to local districts based on the learning requirements of its children and the local costs of educating them. Under full state funding, local districts would lose only their power to tax, but not their powers to hire, fire, and promote teachers. This plan retains the advantages of local control but provides statewide financing for all districts in the state. Several states seem to be moving toward a combination of power equalizing and full state funding to finance education in their states.

Other major solutions that have been suggested include **tuition tax credits** and vouchers to finance education. Both of these plans would further the interests of private and parochial schools by allowing parents to choose which schools their children would attend. Critics of these plans assert that they would foreshadow the demise of public schools as we now know them and would increase the educational disparity between poor and wealthy students. Proponents claim that these plans would introduce free enterprise and competition to revitalize education in the United States. TUITION TAX Even if weak schools fail to go out of business, they say, the schools in CREDITS general will be stronger and more progressive. Historically, the Reagan administration favored tuition tax credits for parents who send their children to private schools, allowing these parents to deduct a portion of the tuition that they pay from the income on which they must pay federal income taxes. The Bush administration also encourages and favors parental choice. Leonard (1982) assessed the results of tuition tax credits:

> If tuition tax credits are approved by the Congress, they may change elementary and secondary education in important ways. First, the Administration estimates that such credits would cost the federal government $2.7 billion in fiscal year 1982, the cost rising to nearly $7 billion by fiscal year 1986. The government would have to recoup this loss of revenue somehow—most likely through future cuts in federal education spending. Another round of budget cuts could well wipe out some programs and leave others at subsistence level. Second, some observers believe that tuition tax credits will bring a jump in private school enrollments, compounding the problems that public schools already face because of enrollment declines. Proponents of tuition tax credits argue that such credits should not affect public school enrollments adversely; public schools will merely be forced to improve the quality of their programs in order to compete for students who will now be able to afford private schools, they say. (p. 601)

Thus, Leonard anticipated less money for public schools and a decline in public school enrollments if tuition tax credit legislation is passed by Congress.

The **voucher plan,** in contrast to tuition tax credits, was originally proposed in 1955 by Milton Friedman, an economist at the University of

The allowance of tuition tax credits or the use of vouchers would help the private and parochial schools. The question arises whether this type of funding would subsequently hurt the public schools.

(Photo used by permission of the Archdiocese of Indianapolis.)

VOUCHERS

Chicago. Under Friedman's plan, governments would guarantee each child a minimum level of education by giving parents vouchers each year redeemable for a certain sum of money toward tuition at any "approved" school. Schools participating, both public and private, would have to meet minimum government standards in their educational programs to be "approved" and to be eligible to receive payment for their vouchers. Parents would be free to choose the school best suited to their child's needs and to supplement the voucher amount with additional money if they so desire.

Because the original Friedman voucher proposal would permit parents to supplement the government voucher with additional funds of their own, it would not meet the criteria set down in the *Serrano* decision unless it were modified to eliminate this problem.

PROS AND CONS OF VOUCHERS

There are both pros and cons to such a voucher system. On the positive side, parents would have expanded choices in providing for their children's education and would not be forced to use one school or teacher about which they have no particular enthusiasm. Also, theoretically, the presence of competition for students would improve both the quality and the variety of educational programs. Teachers' salaries, proponents contend, would become more responsive to the fluctuations of the economy and, presumably, would be forced upward by the pressure of competition. On the negative side is the contention that such a plan would increase class and racial distinctions and would segregate rather than integrate the population. Additionally, it is argued that some rural areas would not have alternatives to public schools; that the values instilled by schools of various religious groups would vary, breaking down the common core of values necessary to perpetuate our society; and that it would be difficult for parents to judge

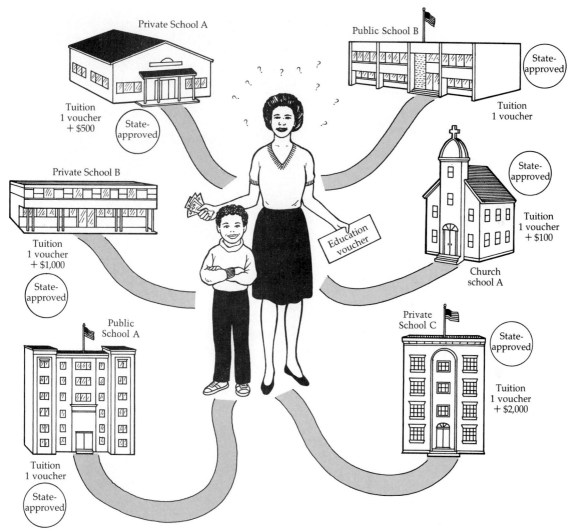

Private School A

Public School B

State-approved

Tuition
1 voucher

Tuition
1 voucher
+ $500

State-approved

State-approved

Private School B

State-approved

Tuition
1 voucher
+ $100

Tuition
1 voucher
+ $1,000

Church
school A

State-approved

Education
voucher

Public
School A

Private
School C

State-approved

Tuition
1 voucher
+ $2,000

Tuition
1 voucher

State-approved

The voucher system.

the quality of the various school alternatives. Opponents of this voucher plan assert that the greatness of the United States has resulted from its public schools and that this plan would weaken them by making them a dumping ground for only poor and disadvantaged students.

MODIFICA-
TIONS TO
VOUCHER
PLAN

To answer some of these criticisms, Friedman suggested modifications to his original proposal. Under this revised voucher plan, parents who want to send their children to nonpublic schools would receive a voucher or payment equal to the cost of educating each child in the local public school. Thus, the size of the grant or voucher would be determined mainly by per-pupil educational expenses at the local level.

The property tax is a regressive tax, hitting hardest those citizens with limited or fixed incomes.

(Photo by Axler.)

OTHER REMEDIES   What other possible remedies have been proposed for the present problems in school finance? First, some suggest contributions from foundations and corporations to replace the loss of funds, especially federal funds, for public education. Ninety-five percent of these monies, however, goes to higher education, not to public elementary and secondary schools. Thus, it

FOUNDA-
TIONS AND
CORPORA-
TIONS?

seems unlikely that private sources would replace any loss of public revenue for K–12 schools, even though some public school districts are forming private foundations to seek contributions for their schools. Private charitable foundations do not have sufficient resources to make up for the loss of public funds to education. Related to this solution would be the increased emphasis on "user fees," under which students would pay a portion of their own costs for education, especially for electives such as drivers' education classes.

MORE FED-
ERAL AID?

Other suggested solutions are numerous and varied. One is an increase in federal aid to education, but the trend seems to be toward less, rather than more, federal aid for public elementary and secondary schools, with the percentage of funds from federal aid remaining fairly constant over the long run. Another proposed solution is to use the shortage of public school funds to restructure the priorities in American education and to place more emphasis on basics such as reading and mathematics. The authors of this book believe that the restructuring of priorities must take place in the society as a whole, not just in education. They castigate American society for placing its spending priorities on entertainment and automobiles rather than on the education of its children. Yet another remedy suggested by the *Serrano* case would equalize all educational expenditures in a state by mandating that the same number of dollars be spent on each child in the state while allowing the funds to be raised by taxes at the local level. Still other solutions that have been proposed for the problems of public school finance are performance contracting, greater use of accountability, and more emphasis on the consolidation of smaller schools.

PERFOR-
MANCE CON-
TRACTING?

ACCOUNTA-
BILITY AND
CONSOLIDA-
TION?

Thus, although many solutions to school finance problems have been proposed, no one solution can be seen as the answer at this time; however, increased state funding seems to be the most likely course in most states. The prospects for educational finance in the 1990s appear bleak, especially when compared with public school funding in previous decades. It is possible, however, that some continued progress will be made in school finance reform in the next decade.

Summary

This chapter began by emphasizing the stability of the percentage of the K–12 public school revenues originating from the federal government, which has remained steady at about 6% to 8% in recent years, with little prospect of increasing in the foreseeable future. The problems associated with federal aid were examined, and possible solutions to these problems were suggested. The realities of the 1980s and 1990s seem to be diminished federal presence in education and increased state initiative through school finance reforms and career ladder programs. Significant terms in federal aid, such as *categorical grant* and *block grant*, were defined, and their influence on education was examined. This chapter also traced the background of the school finance reform movement and surveyed its future prospects, including the influence of *Serrano v. Priest* and related court cases. Possible solutions to these school finance problems suggested in this chapter were full state funding, the voucher plan, and tuition tax credits. The advantages and disadvantages of each of these solutions were discussed, along with future trends in school finance.

Glossary Terms

Categorical Aid, 501	Inflation, 503
Discretionary Power, 501	Litigation, 503
Matching Funds, 501	Fiscal Neutrality, 506
Mandates, 501	Power Equalizing, 506
Regulations, 501	Full State Funding, 506
Block Grants, 502	Tuition Tax Credits, 507
Recessions, 503	Voucher Plan, 507

Questions

1. Define categorical support for education. What are the advantages and disadvantages of this approach?

2. Summarize the views of both the advocates and the opponents of federal aid to education.

3. Which state probably would receive the greatest amount of federal aid? Why?

4. Identify five future trends for educational finance in the United States. Be certain to relate these trends to local, state, and federal support of education.

5. What are the dangers and rewards to public education of implementing a voucher plan for financing the education of youth? How do you feel personally about this issue?

Activities for Unit VIII

1. Choose two school districts in your state and demonstrate the inequality between them with respect to financial support for education.

2. Of the expenditure per pupil for education in your school district, how much is paid by the state and how much comes from local taxes? What does the federal government contribute per pupil?

3. Find two or three periodical articles in the *Education Index* dealing with the pros and cons of the proposed voucher plans for education. How do you feel personally about this issue?

4. Invent and describe your ideal plan for financing public schools. Demonstrate how it would be equitable to all groups involved.

5. Research the funding per pupil in average daily attendance (ADA) in the top five states and the bottom five states in the United States. What conclusions about school finance can you draw from these data?

6. How is the local tax rate for a school district determined in your state? What steps or controls are involved in this process?

7. If support per pupil in ADA were magically doubled in your state, how would you spend the additional funds?

Annotated Bibliography

1. Advisory Commission on Intergovernmental Relations. (1981). *Intergovernmentalizing the classroom: Federal involvement in elementary and secondary education in the federal role in the federal system: The dynamics of growth* (a series of commission reports). Washington, DC: Advisory Commission on Intergovernmental Relations.

   This commission report traces the history of federal involvement in public education and discusses contemporary issues surrounding this role.

2. McMahon, W. W., and Geske, T. G. (Eds). (1982). *Financing Education: Overcoming inefficiency and inequity.* Urbana: University of Illinois Press.

   Various authors are represented in this collection of readings on the issues of social efficiency and equity in financing schools.

3. McNett, I., et al. (1982). *Early alert: The impact of federal education cutbacks on the states.* Washington, DC: Institute of Educational Leadership.

   This is a compilation of newspaper articles on the impact and implications for education of cutbacks in federal aid in the 1980s.

4. Miller, R. A. (Ed.) (1981). *The federal role of education: New directions for the eighties.* Washington, DC: Institute for Educational Leadership.

   This paperback contains selected readings by various authors on the federal role in education including current policy dilemmas, federal–state relationships, and prescriptions for future policies.

5. Robinson, G. E., & Protheroe, N. J. A. (1987). *Cost of education: An investment in America's future.* Arlington, VA: Educational Research Service.

   This comprehensive study of the cost of education and its effects or benefits addresses the importance of considering both the effectiveness and the probable costs of educational changes and reforms.

{Photo used by permission of the Indiana State Teachers Association.}

IX

Educational Organizations

Educational Organizations

OBJECTIVES

After reading Chapter 17, the student will be able to:

- Gain a historical perspective of the role of teachers' organizations in American education

- Realize the importance of teachers' organizations in the supporting role they play in representing the teacher

- Compare the policies and goals of the American Federation of Teachers (AFT) and the National Education Association (NEA)

- Determine the role that teachers' organizations play in the collective bargaining process

- Select other organizations that will help her or him in professional development

The Purpose of Teachers' Organizations

PROVIDE A
FORUM

The primary purpose of teachers' organizations—or unions, as some people prefer to call them—is to provide a forum in which teachers can unify to prepare their case for presentation to the school board, the state legislature, and the U.S. Congress. Teachers normally present the school board with a contract proposal that is dealt with through the collective bargaining process. Teachers are often affiliated with state teachers' organizations that have certain employees registered as lobbyists during each state's legislative sessions. Legislators, many times, rely on teacher **lobbyists** for valuable information and for help in writing education bills. At the federal level, teachers are represented by lobbyists from the large parent organizations for teachers—the National Education Association (NEA) and the American Federation of Teachers (AFT).

Why Belong to a Teachers' Organization?

UNIFYING
VOICE

First, individual teachers choose to belong to teachers' organizations to support the unified voice of teachers. Teachers are cognizant of the power and influence that come from unifying into one group. Second, teachers like to belong because of member benefits such as insurance plans, travel agency and car rental agreements, book clubs, educational journals, newsletters, and legal assistance. Third, some teachers enjoy taking an active role in organizations and rising to leadership within them. A fourth reason is that membership may help a teacher to feel more involved in the educational process. On the negative side, a few teachers may join because of a feeling of coercion from colleagues. Some dedicated teachers' organization members feel that those who fail to join and pay their fair share are "freeloaders." Frequently, some teachers do not belong because the organizations support one issue with which they disagree or because of personal dislike of an officer or a member.

How Effective Are Teachers' Organizations?

POLITICAL
SUCCESSES

The effectiveness of teachers' organizations in achieving their goals depends on the issue in question and on whether one is referring to implications at the local, state, or federal level of government. There was an impressive show of power and influence during the 1980 presidential elections, when more teacher delegates attended the Democratic National Convention than any other organized group. The NEA teachers were pleased with President Carter for his leadership in changing the U.S. Office of Education to the Cabinet-level Department of Education, and they came in force to nominate him for a second term. Teachers were able to celebrate a victory for Carter at the convention but were not able to elect him in November. The AFT did not have the same interest in getting a U.S. Department of Education

Teachers' organizations increase the power of individual professional educators through collective action.

(Photo used by permission of the Indiana State Teachers Association.)

as did the NEA, but the AFT does support the department now that it has been established.

BARGAINING AND GRIEV-ANCES

The effectiveness of teachers' organizations in representing teachers at the bargaining table and in **grievance procedures** seems to be improving. An increasing number of issues, both monetary and nonmonetary, are now included in the bargaining process. Administrators, who were once in a very authoritative position, are now almost afraid to say or do anything for fear of teacher grievances or a lawsuit. Teachers' organization power in relation to collective bargaining and teachers' grievances may be a sign of effectiveness in influencing school administration and school boards, but this shift may be only temporary until the power struggle levels off. Most administrators are still in control of their buildings and their school systems, but some administrators are not aware of, nor do they have the time to exercise, all their legal rights and responsibilities. Probably, a true measure of effectiveness will come when both administrators and teachers can work harmoniously as a team for the benefit of the students.

A Brief History of Two Major Teachers' Organizations

In the early days of schooling in America, only a few individual teachers registered their complaints, as shown in two isolated examples:

EZEKIEL
CHEEVER

In 1766 Ezekiel Cheever, who had established a "Town Free School" in Charlestown, Massachusetts, found himself in unusually tight financial straits. His pittance of a salary had not been paid on schedule, schools in nearby towns had lured away some of his pupils, and his schoolhouse was falling apart. Cheever spoke up at a town council meeting and by his audacity persuaded the selectmen to promise that they would "take care the schoolhouse be speedily amended because it is much out of repair" and see to it that his yearly salary was paid (the constables, he told them, being "much behind him"). Cheever also won their promise that no other schoolmaster would "be suffered or set up in the town."

CALEB
BINGHAM

Another instance of "militancy" took place during the 1790s elsewhere in Massachusetts. Schoolmaster Caleb Bingham was a modest and, usually, a timid man. But the town fathers had not paid him or the other teachers for months. Instead, they were handed a paper certifying that the town owed them a certain sum. These certificates or "town orders" could then be sold at the bank for a considerable discount. Bingham decided he had had enough. When he received his next certificate, he advertised it for sale in the town newspaper, in effect publicizing the fiscal state of the community. This public insult led to a town meeting, to which Bingham was summoned by a constable. Called on for his apology, Bingham gave a brief account of his frustrations. "I have a family and need the money," he explained. "I have done my part of the engagement faithfully, and have no apology to make to those who have failed to do theirs. All I can do is to promise that if the town will punctually pay my salary in the future, I will never advertise their orders for sale again." Reportedly the town treasurer slapped him on the shoulder and said, "Bingham, you are a good fellow; call at my office after the meeting and I will give you the cash." Presumably, Bingham had no further trouble collecting what was due him. (Donley, 1976, p. 4)

Most of the early teachers were not like Cheever and Bingham, and they did what was expected of them with few complaints. Teachers were ex-

EMERGING
FROM PAS-
SIVITY

pected to teach and to do numerous other chores, and to keep quiet. Because teachers were of a rather passive nature, teachers' organizations were slow in emerging as a powerful force in education. Some old-time teachers would not recognize the profession today.

TEACHERS
ORGANIZE

The first teachers' association, the Society of Associated Teachers of New York City, was established in 1794. Later, county and city teachers' organizations were set up across the country, and thirty state teachers' associations were formed between 1840 and 1861. From the beginning, teachers have been torn between emphasizing society's needs for good education and emphasizing their own economic benefits. On the side of emphasizing society's needs were those who wanted to protect the welfare of our country by being very service oriented. Historically, teachers have remained service oriented, but they have become less reticent about protecting their own economic benefits.

TABLE 17–1

Leading Similarities of and Differences Between the AFT and NEA

SIMILARITIES	DIFFERENCES
1. Both are for the betterment of teacher welfare.	1. Ages: NEA—1857 AFT—1917.
2. Both participate in the collective-bargaining process by assisting bargaining teams at the local level.	2. The AFT is affiliated with the American Federation of Labor and the Congress of Industrial Organizations (AFL–CIO).
3. Both favor the strike as a last resort when agreements cannot be reached.	3. The AFT believes in voice votes, whereas the NEA believes in the secret ballot for major offices.
4. Both provide supplemental services for teachers such as insurance, car rental, and travel.	4. Size (approximate): NEA 1,920,000 AFT 450,000
5. Both are big lobbying organizations for education at the state and federal levels. Both use the efforts of political action committees (PACs).[a]	5. The AFT is most active in our largest metropolitan areas.
6. State and local affiliations are integral parts of both of the national organizations.	6. The NEA makes extensive field and research services available to teachers.
7. Both use unified dues to unite local, state, and national organizations financially.	7. The NEA provides uniserve directors to help local affiliates.[b]
8. Both strongly support public education.	8. NEA dues are higher than AFT dues.

[a] Historically, the NEA promoted education from both the teachers' and the administrators' sides, but since collective bargaining, they primarily aid the teachers.
[b] A uniserve director is a full-time NEA employee who helps with the collective bargaining process and other matters relating to teachers' welfare. Uniserve directors are well-trained professionals located in each state, and are key officials in the NEA operation.

Differences and Similarities Between the AFT and the NEA

The leading similarities and differences between the American Federation of Teachers and the National Education Association are outlined in Table 17–1. There are additional similarities and differences, but those that are listed stand out as the most important ones. Most of the items listed in Table 17–1 are described in greater detail later in the chapter.

History of the NEA

The first of the two major teachers' organizations was formed in Philadelphia in 1857 by forty-three educators. Called the National Teachers' Association, it later became known as the National Education Association and has now grown to 1.9 million members from every state in the nation.

Dual purposes were proposed for the National Teachers' Association: to elevate the character and advance the interests of the profession of teaching, and to promote the cause of popular education in the United States. Most of the early discussions centered on promoting the need for public education in America, and this is still one of the prime interests of the NEA.

Resolutions passed by the NEA give us an idea of what the organization
stood for during those early years. The following historical resolutions reveal something of the social and educational philosophy of the members of the NEA:

- 1876. Resolved, next to liberty, education has been the great cause of the marvelous prosperity of the Republic in the first century of its history, and is the sure and only hope of its future.
- 1889. Universal suffrage without universal education is a national peril. The aim of the school is not training of the mind alone, but the training of the man.
- 1894. Education is the inalienable right of every child of our Republic.
- 1915. The people of each and every nation need to sink their nationalism in a larger internationalism. . . .
- 1932. No nation can afford to entrust its children to incompetent teachers.
- 1944. Education should prepare each generation to meet the social, economic, and political problems of an ever changing world. (Wesley, 1957, pp. 369–370)

In 1892 and in 1910, firm resolutions were made in support of the public schools. The 1915 resolution in support of internationalism is not very different from the NEA's present support of multicultural education.

Not until 1925 did the classroom teacher become a full-fledged participant in NEA activity. Before this time, school administrators did all of the policymaking in the association. In two democratizing moves by the NEA in the 1920s and 1930s, classroom teachers became full members, and a National Representative Assembly of Delegates was established. Teachers could then have a voice in the National Representative Assembly. Still, there was no evidence of great militancy during this period.

Throughout the years, the NEA had accumulated over thirty departments. These departments are listed here in four categories (Wesley, 1957):

Departments of the NEA

1. *Administration*
    a. American Association of School Administrators, 1870
    b. Department of Elementary School Principals, 1921
    c. National Association of Women Deans and Counselors, 1918
    d. National Association of Secondary School Principals, 1927
    e. National Council of Administrative Women in Education, 1932

2. *Curriculum Areas*
    a. American Association for Health, Physical Education, and Recreation, 1937

    b. American Industrial Arts Association, 1939
    c. Association for Supervision and Curriculum Development, 1929
    d. Department of Home Economics, 1930
    e. Department of Vocational Education, 1875
    f. Music Educators National Conference, 1940
    g. National Art Education Association, 1933
    h. National Association of Journalism Directors, 1939
    i. National Council for the Social Studies, 1925
    j. National Council of Teachers of Mathematics, 1950
    k. National Science Teachers Association, 1895
    l. Speech Association of America, 1939
    m. United Business Education Association, 1892

3. *Instruction of Selected Groups or Classes*
    a. American Association of Colleges for Teacher Education, 1948
    b. Association for Higher Education, 1942
    c. Department of Kindergarten–Primary Education, 1884
    d. Department of Rural Education, 1907
    e. International Council for Exceptional Children, 1941
    f. National Association of Public School Adult Educators, 1955

4. *Service*
    a. American Educational Research Association, 1930
    b. Department of Audio-visual Instruction, 1923
    c. Department of Classroom Teachers, 1913
    d. National Association of Educational Secretaries, 1946
    e. National Retired Teachers Association, 1951
    f. National School Public Relations Association, 1950

DISAFFILIA-
TIONS

By 1976, because of disaffiliation of these departments, only four remained with the NEA. The underlying cause of the dissatisfaction was the **adversarial relationship** inherent in the collective bargaining process (West, 1980, p. 84). The NEA had decided to promote the cause of collective bargaining in the 1960s, and this decision led administrators who had been strong leaders of the NEA to disaffiliate with the association. The nonadministrator affiliates, however, were probably influenced by other factors as well (West, 1980, p. 85). There is now a continuing relationship with these disaffiliated organizations, and the NEA has simplified its organizational structure and clarified its public image. On pages 535–543, collective bargaining is discussed in detail, and it should become clearer to the reader why most of these disaffiliations took place.

PROMOTING
CIVIL RIGHTS

    The NEA has a long history of promoting civil rights in our country. One example was the Prince Edward County, Virginia, Free School Association, which was supported by the NEA. Prince Edward County closed its public schools rather than comply with the *Brown* decision in 1954 to integrate their schools. The NEA assisted by asking its membership to donate money to keep the Free School Association going during this tense period: "The

PROFILE OF KEITH GEIGER

Keith Geiger was elected President of the National Education Association in 1989.

[Photo used by permission of the National Education Association.]

Keith Geiger was elected president of the National Education Association in July 1989. He replaced Mary Hatwood Futrell who had been president of the organization since 1983. Geiger served as the vice-president of the NEA during the period that Futrell was president.

Throughout his 25-year career in education, Geiger has worked in numerous professional, political, and negotiating capacities at every level of the NEA. He was a member of NEA's 1976 Presidential Screening and Endorsement Committee and has been a delegate to two Democratic National Conventions. Previously he served as president of the Michigan Education Association and the Livonia (Michigan) Education Association in which city he was a high school mathematics and science teacher. Geiger was born in Pigeon, Michigan, where he attended high school; earned his B.A. at Asbury College, Wilmore, Kentucky; received his M.A. at Peabody College, Nashville, Tennessee; and has done postgraduate work at the University of Michigan.

Geiger is involved in a wide variety of community activities and other professional organizations. He is currently a member of the National Council for the Accreditation of Teacher Education (NCATE) Executive Committee; the Labor Committee of the Martin Luther King, Jr., Federal Holiday Commission; and the Commission on Presidential Scholars. In 1988, he served as a judge for *USA Today*'s All-Academic Team and the National League of Cities Innovations Awards Competition. He also was part of a delegation invited to observe the Chilean presidential election in October 1988. Geiger served as a delegate to meetings of the World Confederation of Organizations of the Teaching Profession in 1975, 1982, 1984, 1986, and 1988. He is listed in *Who's Who in Labor*.

During Geiger's campaign for president of the NEA, he presented himself as a tough but flexible leader who has aggressively challenged management at the bargaining table while knowing how to cooperate at the conference table. He has pledged to help the few states that have no collective bargaining law pass one.

The Bush Administration calls the choice plan in education a cornerstone of education reform. This plan allows parents to send their children to any public school of their choice. Geiger opposes the choice plan, but favors enough flexibility to allow magnet schools, alternative schools, and other options that offer some variety. He favors raising the level of education in all schools, in contrast to the choice plan, which may upgrade only a few schools. He believes that most of the choice plans now being tested do not provide for student transportation and that they tend to shortchange the schools not included.

Although Geiger wants to see the NEA look more like a union, he is expected to follow reforms and policies instituted by Mary Hatwood Futrell for the most part. In reference to his presidency, he said "You will not see a big about-face in this organization." Futrell is widely credited with bringing teachers into the mainstream of the education reform movement through their participation in teacher leadership training, dropout prevention, and literacy programs. Further, like Futrell, Geiger is expected to support such issues as school reform, recruitment of minority teachers, and better education for low-income children.

superintendent of the Free School Association later told the NEA staff the schools could not have opened without the NEA's prompt assistance" (West, 1980, p. 104).

SEPARATE STATE AFFILIATES

There had been both black and white affiliates of the NEA in the South, and in another case, the NEA issued four suspensions of state affiliates in 1969. The goal was to gain mergers of the two separate state affiliates in these states. By 1977, unification was completed when the two associations in Louisiana merged. John Ryor, then president of the NEA, declared, "The doctrine of separate but equal has no place in the teaching profession" (West, 1980, p. 122). The 1954 *Brown* decision of the U.S. Supreme Court regarding "separate but equal" as being inherently unequal was the power behind both of these actions by the NEA.

RESOLUTIONS PROCESS

Policy decisions are made by the NEA in the following manner. Any teacher member can submit resolutions to the Resolution Committee for a hearing. Resolutions are voted on by the committee, and before each delegate assembly, the proposed resolutions are printed for the delegates to consider before voting. At the delegate assembly, approximately 8,690 delegates have an opportunity to debate and vote on the proposed resolutions. The representative assembly meets annually, and in 1988, they passed 249 resolutions, which then became part of the policy of the association. Resolution A-2 on public education is presented here:

> The National Education Association believes that the priceless heritage of free public educational opportunities for every American must be preserved and strengthened. Members of the Association are encouraged to show their support of public education by sending their children to public schools.

PRICELESS HERITAGE

> Free public schools are the cornerstone of our social, economic, and political structure and are of utmost significance in the development of our moral, ethical, spiritual, and cultural values. Consequently, the survival of democracy requires that every state maintain a system of free public education that prepares its citizens to—

> a. Achieve **functional proficiency in English,** with emphasis on the development of those basic reading, writing, speaking, and listening skills essential for success in other disciplines and everyday life
>
> b. Compute effectively enough to ensure their ability to procure and/or dispense services and materials necessary to their health and general well-being
>
> c. Use critical thinking, creative thinking, and problem-solving skills
>
> d. Exercise attitudes of good citizenship, societal productivity, and global awareness
>
> e. Appreciate the aesthetic and moral qualities of life
>
> f. Formulate values for their lives that will lead to continual growth and self-fulfillment
>
> g. Recognize and appreciate the cultural, social, political, and religious differences found throughout the nation and the world
>
> h. Use leisure time effectively and develop sound physical health habits
>
> i. Develop skills in the practical/vocational and fine arts

The Association urges its state and local affiliates to intensify efforts to maintain and strengthen comprehensive programs of education that aspire to these goals. (*NEA handbook*, 1988–1989, pp. 203–204, emphasis added)

NEW BUSI-
NESS ITEMS

The NEA also sets policy by passing new business items during the representative assembly. Three of these new business items passed during the 1988 assembly were as follows:

Tobacco-Free Environment

SMOKE-FREE?

The NEA, through normal channels of communication, shall encourage and assist state and local affiliates to create a tobacco-free environment in the public schools.

Role of Parents/Primary Guardians in Educational Process

PARENTAL
RESPONSIBIL-
ITY

The NEA should communicate with its state and local affiliates and with local school governing bodies that it is the responsibility of parents/primary guardians to become involved in the educational process of each child—in homework, achievement, and behavior. The NEA should encourage more interaction among parents/primary guardians and the educational process in the classroom because the parents/primary guardians are fundamentally the driving force behind each student's success. This should be accomplished prior to the end of the 1988–89 school year.

Youth Gangs and Violence

NEGATIVE
FACTORS

The NEA will include in each of NEA's national and regional conferences a component dealing with the problem of youth gangs and individual youth violence in the schools. (*NEA handbook*, 1988–1989, pp. 281–290)

POLICY AND
ADMINISTRA-
TION

The policies of the NEA are administered by the 140-member board of directors and the 9-member executive committee. The president is a member of the executive committee, and he or she directs the administration of policy. Priorities among the multitude of resolutions and new business items are sorted out by the board of directors and the executive committee. The president also consults with the executive director, whose main function is to implement the policies of the NEA. The schematic outline (Figure 17–1) depicts the NEA working structure and lists the important committees of the association.

The executive secretary of the NEA presides over a staff of 550 at the NEA headquarters in Washington, DC, and six regional offices. It is the responsibility of the executive secretary to take the policy developed by the representative assembly and turn it into action. The highest elected officer in the NEA is the president, who presides over the **representative assembly** and the executive board. These two positions have separate functions, and it is important that the incumbents understand each other's role.

History of the AFT

TEACHERS'
UNION

Unlike the NEA, which has preferred the term *teachers' association,* the American Federation of Teachers, from the beginning, used the term **union** to describe itself. The first teacher's union was formed in 1897 in Chicago

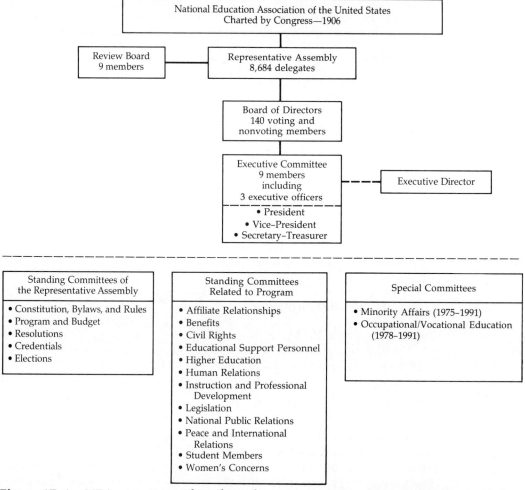

Figure 17–1   NEA structure. This chart does not include ad hoc committees of the Board of Directors and Executive Committee.

(SOURCE: *NEA handbook* (1988–1989). Washington, DC: National Education Association, p. 10.)

and became known as the Chicago Teachers Federation (CTF). Even in those early days, low salaries and job security were the highest priorities to be dealt with by the young union.

EARLY UNION AD-VOCATES

In 1902, Jane Addams, the social settlement reformer in Chicago, encouraged the teachers to affiliate with the American Federation of Labor. John Dewey, the famous educational philosopher, actively urged all instructors to join in common cause with the laborer. Dewey once said that he cherished his union card second only to his teaching certificate. In fact, he held AFT card number 1 (Braun, 1972, p. 48). As most teachers came from lower-middle-class origins and thought that unions were a lower-class activity, they needed to be convinced that the affiliation with labor was acceptable. After the affiliation with labor took place in 1902, Margaret Haley, editor of the *CTF Bulletin*, explained the affiliation as follows:

> Not only has the time arrived when public school teachers must take a position on the serious economic and political questions pressing for solution. . . . but the public school as an institution must be either democratic or autocratic. A democratic form of government cannot be maintained with autocratic principles controlling the schools either in their administration or methods of teaching. The labor interests lie in popular, democratic government, and in the maintenance of democracy. It is the largest organized force of democracy. The only people you can depend upon to act permanently with you are those whose interests are identical with yours. We expect by affiliation with labor to arouse the workers and the whole people, through the workers, to the dangers confronting the public schools from the same interests and tendencies that are undermining the foundations of our democratic republic. It is necessary to make labor a constructive force in society, or it will be a destructive force. If the educational question could be understood by the labor men, and the labor question by the educators, both soon would see they are working to the same end, and should work together. (Braun, 1972, p. 48)

No wonder Jane Addams was interested in the CTF: the organization supported many reform movements such as women's suffrage, municipal ownership of public utilities, and direct primaries. The CTF was the force behind the successful passage of the Illinois Child Labor Law in 1903, and it supported the proposal to have an elected schoolboard in Chicago. The spread of democracy throughout our republic, particularly concerning education, was a dominant theme of the teachers' union. During the 1930s, prominent advocates of progressive education were active in the union, and George Counts became the president of the AFT. The progressives, according to the John Dewey model, wanted to see the schools become the agent for a democratic society (Eaton, 1975, p. 74).

REASONS FOR UNION POPULARITY   One of the reasons that the CTF became so popular with the teachers in Chicago was the failure of the NEA to relate to the classroom teacher during this period. Most of the leadership of the NEA was then composed of college presidents and school district superintendents, who relegated the classroom teacher to the role of listener. In the early 1900s, the CTF was composed entirely of grade school or elementary teachers, mostly female, who wanted a voice in the American education movement.

AFT FOUNDED   The American Federation of Teachers was established in Chicago in 1916. The AFT was formed from four local unions, including the CTF. Among the goals that the union supported were free schools, free textbooks, and compulsory education. In these early days, members of the AFT perceived themselves as simply a more radical group working within the structure of the NEA (Eaton, 1975, p. 18). It was not until 1921 that the AFT considered itself a competitor rather than a part of the NEA.

AFT PLAT-
FORM

During the period 1916–1929, the AFT adopted a **social platform** that remained consistent through the 1960s. The major points for which the AFT fought were the following:

1. Greater pay and better working conditions for all teachers
2. Equal pay for teachers regardless of race, creed, or sex
3. Tenure provisions for teachers
4. The granting of sabbatical leaves for teachers
5. Equalizing the pay and benefits between elementary and secondary teachers
6. The political freedom of teachers to belong to organized parties, participate in political activities, and espouse political candidates outside of their teaching duties
7. The inclusion of teachers on boards of education
8. Academic freedom for teachers to discuss national and international issues in the classroom setting
9. Protection of women teachers from unfair hiring practices, dismissals due to marriage, and the failure of boards of education to provide maternal leaves
10. Recognition of the special education plight of the black American and his teacher. Promotion of equal pay and school facilities and recognition of the need to publicize the inequities of Negro education
11. Gaining a role for the teacher in the process of school administration especially in matters pertaining to the profession or in the instruction of children.
12. The inclusion of laboring-class peoples on boards of education
13. Condemnation of plans that would separate vocational programs of education from regular school settings
14. Resistance to those groups who sought to use the schools to indoctrinate children, such as the National Association of Manufacturers, U.S. Chamber of Commerce, American Legion, and others
15. Opposition to secondary school ROTC and military training courses
16. Support for the workers' education movement
17. Federal aid to education
18. The establishment of a cabinet-level Department of Education (Eaton, 1975, pp. 168–69)

GROWTH OF
AFT

By 1947 the AFT had grown to eighty-six chartered locals, which included groups in twenty-four of the twenty-five U.S. cities of more than 100,000 population (Donley, 1976, p. 4). In 1961, after a rough campaign, the United Federation of Teachers (UFT), an AFT affiliate, won from their rival, the Teachers' Bargaining Organization (TBO), an NEA **affiliate,** the right to represent all New York City teachers at the bargaining table. "The union (UFT) victory in New York City was probably the biggest single success in the history of teacher organizing in the United States" (Donley, 1976, p. 49). The AFT victory in New York increased AFT membership and motivated teachers in the larger cities to new and greater efforts. At the time of

PROFILE OF ALBERT SHANKER

Albert Shanker, long-time president of the American Federation of Teachers.
(Photo used by permission of the American Federation of Teachers.)

Albert Shanker was born in New York City in 1928, the son of Polish immigrants. Both of his parents were active in trade unionism and in the Roosevelt New Deal. As a child he marched in parades to honor Franklin D. Roosevelt. Always an excellent student, Shanker earned a bachelor's degree from the University of Illinois.

As a youngster, he lived in the Ravenswood area of Queens, a Jew in a primarily Irish area. It was here, as an eight-year-old boy, that Shanker experienced an incident of ethnic discrimination that nearly took his life. He was hung by a rope from a tree by a gang of boys who accused him of killing Jesus, but he was saved by a woman who ran to his aid. Later, at the University of Illinois at Urbana, he found that the only living quarters offered to Jewish students were located six miles from campus. No doubt such incidents caused Albert Shanker to become committed to the civil rights movement. Thus, his New York union contributed large sums of money to Martin Luther King's voter registration drive in Alabama.

After some teaching experience in Harlem and Queens, Shanker slowly, but surely, rose in union leadershp to become president of the American Federation of Teachers and vice-president of the American Federation of Labor (AFL–CIO). In 1984, he was elected to a sixth two-year term as president of the AFT. Donley (1976) wrote, "Albert Shanker's rise to leadership in the AFT began when the New York City teachers chose his local union as their representative in 1961. Later he directed a merger of the AFT and NEA teachers in New York State. He then emerged as one of the most powerful teacher leaders in the nation" (p. 124). He strongly supports the public school system and is opposed to tax credits, school voucher proposals, and state and local tax-cut movements.

In July 1989, Shanker spoke to union members about how to reform our nation's schools. During his speech he compared our top students who are measured on the National Assessment to those in Europe and Canada who take a similar exam. The results show that our student population achieves at the top level, at the rate of 3% to 6% compared with 16% to 30% in these other countries. The top level on the National Assessment refers to students who can either read editorials in newspapers, write a good letter, and/or solve a two-step verbal problem. His conclusion, after looking at these data, is that the U.S. educational system has no choice but to reform and change the way we are now educating our children. He would like to see the schools freed from the bureaucracy under which they now function so that they can do things differently to raise the achievement levels of their students. Responsibility for the budget and the allocation of monies would be placed in the hands of the schools so that the professional teachers and administrators could make decisions without the constraints of the school board and the heavily layered bureaucracies that exist in most large city school systems.

Shanker proposes that we give teachers real incentives, financial

and otherwise, to make the needed changes. Every five years, assessments would be made of those schools participating in the incentive
plan; and schools demonstrating the highest achievements would be
financially rewarded. The money for the rewards would come from
the federal government. The lowest award would be $15,000 per in-
dividual teacher; the highest awards would range from $150,000 to
$200,000 per individual teacher, depending on the number of schools
enrolled in the incentive program.

As we move into the 1990s it will be interesting to watch the
progress of the Shanker proposal. Shanker feels that some form of this
proposal has a real chance because of the current crisis in education
and the fact that George Bush wants to be our "education president."

the New York victory, AFT membership was 60,715 teachers, whereas NEA
membership was 1,300,000 teachers. The NEA then started concentrating
on better service to teachers in the larger urban areas, which had been long
neglected by them.

SUCCESS IN
LARGE CITIES

The AFT had an illustrious beginning, John Dewey being one of its chief
advocates. Its greatest successes have been in the largest cities of our
country, where there is an established union tradition. Its commitment to
civil rights and the laborer is well established. Where the AFT moves in
the next ten years will depend largely on Albert Shanker, its president and
one of the most influential leaders in the entire labor movement.

Merger Talks

DREAM FOR
A MERGER

David Sheldon won the presidency of the AFT in 1968 with a pledge to
open **merger** negotiations with the NEA. By that time, the AFT had won
bargaining rights in nearly every major city, including New York, Boston,
Philadelphia, Detroit, Chicago, Cleveland, and Gary. The AFT had only
200,000 members, but it represented nearly a half million teachers at the
bargaining table. Sheldon was able to convince antimerger forces within
his own organization that the strength of the AFT in the larger cities was
enough to keep it from being swallowed up by the larger NEA forces. A
merger of the Flint, Michigan, union with a much larger NEA affiliate in
1968 was cause for hope that at long last there might be a merger of the
two national organizations. Both David Sheldon and Albert Shanker had
dreamed of and planned for the day when there could be a national merger
of the two unions. The goal, after merger, would be nationwide teacher
strikes to elicit massive federal aid to education.

ROADBLOCKS
TO MERGER

There were too many roadblocks to merger in the late 1960s, some that
Sheldon did not foresee. Many rank-and-file members of the AFT were
former NEA members, and they knew full well that some NEA representatives had made deals with school boards to help eliminate the union.

There were black teachers in the South who knew that the NEA had backed off on desegregation measures. Probably, most importantly, as far as the AFT was concerned, there was too much dissension within their own staff. Sheldon's leadership ability was being questioned, and as a result, he gave up the merger issue.

In 1969, NEA President Elizabeth D. Koontz made informal inquiries directed to David Sheldon about merger talks, but by 1970, the NEA had officially banned merger talks. Still, there were unofficial merger talks at the NEA conventions. One of the largest roadblocks to merger, as far as the NEA was concerned, was the AFT's affiliation with the AFL–CIO (Eaton, 1975, p. 197). Sheldon had been willing to consider merger talks without the AFL–CIO affiliation, but Shanker insisted on AFL–CIO membership. Albert Shanker was himself a block to merger talks because of his strong AFL–CIO stand. (See Figure 17–2.)

AFL–CIO AF-
FILIATION?

Whatever the historical interactions between the NEA and the AFT regarding a possible merger, the current positions of both organizations are as follows:

A Single National Organization of Educators

The 1976 Representative Assembly reaffirms the Association's policy concerning a single national organization of educators as follows:

The Representative Assembly reaffirms the NEA's desire to unite all educators in a single national organization. The Representative Assembly further recognizes that a merger with the AFT, the AAUP, and other appropriate organizations could contribute to that end. The NEA believes, however, that if a merger is to produce true "unity," the resulting organization must embody the following basic concepts: (a) no affiliation with the AFL–CIO and no obligation to the institutional positions and objectives of the AFL–CIO; (b) guaranteed minority group participation in the governance and operation of the new or-

UNITY?

Figure 17–2   Merger issues.

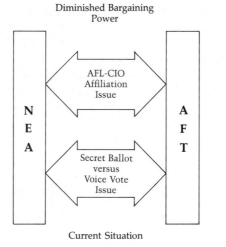

ganization; (c) the use of the secret ballot to elect the officers and change the governing documents of the new organization.

The Representative Assembly authorizes the NEA president to enter into discussions regarding the possible establishment of a single national organization embodying the foregoing concepts if and when the president, in conjunction with the Executive Committee, believes that such discussions will be productive. (*NEA handbook*, 1988–1989, pp. 297–298)

The AFT Official Policy on Merger

MERGER?

The official AFT policy on merger, established in 1972, includes the following provisions:

Before any AFT local or state federation may engage in unity talks with another organization, it shall receive approval of two-thirds vote of the AFT executive council. Before any agreement between an AFT local or state federation and another organization shall become final it must be approved by two-thirds vote of the AFT executive council and by a majority vote in a membership referendum of the AFT local or state federation involved. (Dashiell, 1982, pp. 5–6)

SECRET BAL-LOT?

Although the AFL–CIO issue is a big problem blocking merger, the **secret ballot** is another difficult issue to settle. The NEA simply believes that its delegate assembly would be undemocratic without the secret ballot. In 1982, the AFT reaffirmed a commitment to voice vote, although some members of the AFT are trying to change this rule. If the two organizations ever do merge, the voice of teachers will be more powerful than ever before.

The Collective Bargaining Process

EARLY HU-MILIATION

The authors once heard a story of a township trustee whose wife enjoyed insulting teachers on payday by having them line up behind the family sedan. The wife of the trustee would then use the trunk lid as a desk and proceed to distribute the salaries. The humiliated teachers wanted to keep their jobs, so they lined up and did not overtly complain. Now, most teachers negotiate for their salaries through the collective bargaining process, and they receive their money in a dignified manner.

At the present time, there is no federal law governing the **collective bargaining process.** In the absence of such a law, approximately thirty states have written laws that deal with the question in a comprehensive way. Of the remaining states, some are now considering passage of a collective bargaining law, but some states even prohibit the process by law. In most cases, teachers are at least allowed to discuss working conditions with school boards.

Elections

In states where there are laws governing negotiations, an election is generally held to enable one organization to gain sole bargaining rights for all the teachers in a school system. Teachers are represented at the bargaining table by either the NEA or AFT local affiliates or by other teachers' repre-

EITHER–OR REPRESENTA-TION

sentation groups, so that the negotiation process can be simplified. When a teachers' organization wins an election over rival groups, it gains **exclusive bargaining rights** with the school board in that district. These elections are supervised by the Public Employee Relations Board (PERB) set up in many states to administer the public employee collective bargaining law.

EXCLUSIVE BARGAINING RIGHTS

Once a union has gained exclusive bargaining rights, it must represent fairly all persons in that bargaining unit. The bargaining unit generally contains members of rival unions and nonmembers, as well as members of the majority teacher organization in that district. Two cases, one in Michigan and one in Rhode Island, are presented here to indicate what a delicate issue fairness is to the bargaining unit.

BROAD DIS-CRETION

> The first case again involves the Detroit Federation of Teachers, which agreed to a two-year contract that raised regular teachers' salaries in both years but raised the pay of emergency substitute teachers in the second year only. An emergency substitute filed suit alleging that this disparate treatment constituted a breach of the union's duty of fair representation. A Michigan court upheld the contract. It noted that a union must have *broad discretion in considering proposals and in recommending a combination of contract provisions that in its judgment represents the best total agreement.* Accordingly, to avoid utter chaos in labor relations and to keep the interventions of the courts to a minimum, a breach of the duty of fair representation is proved only when there is "showing of bad faith, arbitrary or discriminatory action, or fraud." (*McGrail v. Detroit Federation of Teachers*, 1973, emphasis added)

The Rhode Island Supreme Court reached a somewhat different result in a very interesting and widely discussed case involving a union's duty of **fair representation** while handling teachers' grievances.

> In the summer of 1972 the Warwick, Rhode Island, school board posted a vacancy notice for the position of chairman of the high school business department. The vacancy was a *"promotional position"* that, according to the union/board contract, was to be filled on the basis of qualifications; but if the qualifications of two or more candidates were considered equal, the job would go to the person with the most seniority in the Warwick school system. After reviewing the qualifications of the four applicants for the position, the school board appointed Richard Belanger. An unsuccessful applicant, Arthur Matteson, who had more Warwick seniority than Belanger, filed a grievance with the union. The union pressed Matteson's grievance all the way to binding arbitration, where a panel of three arbitrators held that Matteson should have been selected for the position. After a year as department chairman, Belanger was demoted to classroom teacher and Matteson assumed the chairmanship.

FAIR REPRE-SENTATION

> Belanger then wrote the union, requesting that a grievance be pursued on his behalf. The union refused on the ground that to do so would be inconsistent with its earlier advocacy of Matteson's grievance and with the union/board agreement that binding arbitration would be the final step in grievance proceedings. Belanger filed suit alleging in part that the union breached its duty of fair representation when it agreed to press Matteson's grievance. A lower court agreed with Belanger and ordered him reinstated as department chairman. Matteson and the union appealed.

The Rhode Island Supreme Court found that the union failed to represent fairly all members of the bargaining unit when it agreed to pursue Matteson's grievance without ever contacting Belanger or considering his qualifications for the position. The court termed as "simplistic" the union's defense that Matteson was the only member of the bargaining unit grieving the selection of Belanger. The court stated: "It should have been apparent to the union that Matteson's grievance, although theoretically against the School Committee, was in reality against Belanger." Because Belanger was also a member of the union's bargaining unit, the union had an obligation to ascertain Belanger's qualifications before determining that the seniority clause should control the selection. The court stated that it would have been sufficient to investigate "in an informal manner. . . . so long as its procedure affords the two employees the ability to place all the relevant information before the union." Even though the court could find no evidence of bad faith on the part of the union, it held that the arbitrary refusal to consider Belanger's qualifications before championing Matteson's cause was "a clear breach of the duty of fair representation."

Despite this holding, the Rhode Island Supreme Court refused to reinstate Belanger to the chairmanship. Even though Belanger's right to fair representation was breached by the union's advocacy of Matteson's grievance, the qualificatons of both men were fully and fairly considered by the arbitration panel. The school board "forcefully" argued Belanger's suitability for the job, yet the arbitrators ruled for Matteson. This led the court to conclude that even if the union had considered Belanger's qualifications, it still would have elected to press Matteson's grievance and the identical result would have ensued. Accordingly, Belanger could not demonstrate that he was actually harmed by the union's breach of the duty of fair representation.

Taken together, the Michigan and Rhode Island cases confirm that a *duty of fair representation attaches to both bargaining and grievance proceedings*. The duty compels neither neutrality by the union in disputes between its members nor equality of results. What is required, however, is a broad consideration of the interests of all members of the bargaining unit. Although states will differ in their application of the duty of fair representation, the principles articulated by the Michigan and Rhode Island courts are likely to be important considerations in any such case. (*Belanger v. Matteson*, pp. 15–17)

DETERMINA-
TION BY
ELECTIONS

In order that the exclusive bargaining agent not abuse its privileges, most states have built-in safeguards to protect the other groups. When sufficient dissatisfaction builds up against the exclusive bargaining representative, an election can be called to reestablish which agent will be the exclusive bargaining representative. Also, in most states, before the contract is made law, members of the entire group, including rival unions and nonunion members, are given an opportunity to ratify the contract. Flygare (1977) summarized this important point:

> Even though the exclusive bargaining representative may have the privilege of sitting at the bargaining table without interference from rival teachers' organizations, it still must perform in accordance with the wishes of its whole constituency. If not, it may suffer the embarrassment of having the agreements it hammered out with the school board rejected by the teachers or, worse yet, it may lose its status as exclusive bargaining representative at the next election. (p. 20)

The Scope

The **scope of bargaining** that teachers enter into with school boards varies greatly from state to state and from school district to school district (Figure 17–3). Some of the topics commonly included are salaries, insurance, sabbaticals, student discipline, the curriculum, tenure, and emergency leave. Some items that cannot be bargained for are those that violate constitutional principles; those that are already clearly determined by state law, such as tenure provisions; those that are subject to accrued contractual rights, such as sick leave; and, in some states, those topics that are considered the exclusive prerogative of management. The scope of what teachers bargain for is very important because, without much breadth allowed, the law is shallow, and bargaining many become a waste of time for all concerned (Flygare, 1977, p. 25).

ITEMS TO BE NEGOTIATED

The Process Itself

The bargaining process is generally started by the selection of a bargaining team from the faculty and the recruitment of someone to represent the board of education. The spokespeople for the teachers are frequently bargaining specialists from the teachers' organization or officers of the teachers' organization, whereas the school board is more often represented by a professional negotiator, who is often an attorney. Bargaining works best when one person speaks for each side. The teachers begin by presenting their contract proposals to the board. The board members consider the teachers' **proposals** and then come forward with **counterproposals.** This first round of proposals on both sides usually comprises lavish demands from the teachers and sparse offers from the board. Negotiations continue from counterproposal to counterproposal until either a contract is agreed on or an **impasse** has been reached.

PROPOSALS AND COUNTERPROPOSALS

Most states with collective bargaining laws have set down orderly ways of resolving impasses between the two parties. **Mediation** is the first step

MEDIATION

Figure 17–3   The scope of bargaining.

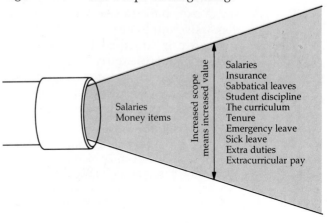

Collective bargaining between school districts and teachers' organizations is often complex and lengthy.

(Photo used by permission of the Indiana State Teachers Association.)

taken, and it involves having the state Public Employees Relations Board select a labor mediator. The mediator remains impartial and tries to narrow down the issues, to improve communication, and to make specific recommendations that are not binding on either party. A mediator's recommendations are usually not made public. Mediators are often able to prevent a work stoppage by improving communication between the groups. Because mediators have little power, relying primarily on personal dynamics, some say that mediation is a waste of time, but it appears to be a necessary part of an orderly process.

Fact finding is the next step in the process of impasse resolution. Many

FACT FIND-
ING

of the same techniques are used by the fact finder as were used by the mediator, but his or her recommendations are made public. Making certain facts a part of the public record puts a great deal of pressure on both the teachers and the school board to come forward with reasonable proposals. One disadvantage of fact finding is that there is a widespread belief among teachers' unions that if they hold out until fact finding, they will gain more in the ultimate settlement. Whatever disadvantages there may be, fact finding is another method of getting both parties to come to a voluntary solution of their differences.

ARBITRATION

Finally, **arbitration** is used to settle disputes that go beyond fact finding. It is commonly known as *binding arbitration* because both parties agree to let the arbitrator decide what is fair for both sides. Many arbitrators try to divide the settlement down the middle so as not to be unfair, but neither side generally likes the results. The results of arbitration settlements have caused boards to formulate their final offer very carefully, as that is what is used to make the "split-the-difference" award.

FINAL-OFFER
ARBITRATION

Because of the problems with arbitration settlements, a new system called **final-offer arbitration** has been devised. In this case, both parties are asked to make their final offer, and the arbitrator chooses one or the other of the proposals. This system causes both sides to carefully consider their final offer and provides some incentive for voluntary settlement. Table 17–2 summarizes the bargaining process.

Strikes

STRIKES?

Both the NEA and the AFT were opposed to **strikes** at one time, but both organizations now approve of strikes. AFT affiliates were the first to call for strikes. The 1963 strike threat in New York City by the UFT caused the following reactions from William B. Carr, the executive secretary of the NEA:

INCREASED
MILITANCY

> The tactics used in New York City before the opening of schools do not represent values that can be taught to American public school children—disturbing extremes were reached when some of their leaders openly called on all teachers to defy both the statutes and court injunction. (Donley, 1976, pp. 52–53)

Charles Cogen, President of the UFT, responded:

> Teachers are setting a good example. Civic courage and idealism should be practiced by those who teach it. I am confident that our strikes have enhanced the respect which students have for their teachers. (Donley, 1976, p. 52)

ILLEGAL
STRIKES?

Carr was referring to the Condon–Wadlin Law in New York, which provided penalties for striking civil employees. Public school teachers have felt for years that it is unfair that they are prevented from striking, whereas teachers in private schools can legally engage in strike activity. Teachers are often linked with police and firefighters as civil employees, but they believe that they should not be associated in this manner because their occupation

TABLE 17–2 ▰▰▰▰▰▰▰▰▰▰▰▰▰▰▰▰▰▰▰▰▰▰▰▰▰
Major Steps in the Process of Collective Bargaining

Depending on the state, the following are the usual steps:

MAJOR STEPS

First: Selection of the bargaining teams for both sides (school board and teachers).

Second: Presentation of the teachers' contract proposal to the board of education.

Third: Presentation of the board's counterproposal.

(At this point there may be several proposals and counterproposals before both sides decide that they are at an impasse.)

Fourth: Either an *agreement* or an *impasse* is reached. If an *impasse* is reached, the following occurs:

Fifth: *Mediation* leading to an *agreement* or an *impasse*. If an *impasse* is reached, the following occurs:

Sixth: *Fact finding.* In most states this is the final step, and the two groups must continue bargaining until they reach an *agreement.*

In a few states, however, the following occur:

Seventh: *Arbitration.* This means that the dispute between the board of education and the teachers will be determined by a mutually-agreed-to arbitrator. Often an agreed-to settlement by an arbitrator is binding on both parties.

Eighth: In most states, *strikes* are not permitted, but in a few cases, the teachers can strike if they have followed all of the collective bargaining steps and no agreement has been reached. Several states list penalties for striking.

---

does not involve the health and safety of the public as is the case of the other two groups.

DOMINANCE
BY ADMINIS-
TRATORS

When Carr spoke for the NEA in the 1960s, the NEA was a different kind of organization, dominated by administrators. By 1980, more than ten years after Carr's departure from the association, attitudes toward strikes and teacher militancy had changed so that they were very much in line with the thinking of the AFT. The NEA strike policy as of 1984 is as follows:

F-8 Strikes

NEA STRIKE
POLICY

The National Education Association denounces the practice of keeping schools open during a strike. It believes that when a picket line is established by the authorized bargaining unit, crossing it is strikebreaking. This unprofessional act jeopardizes the welfare of school employees and the educational process.

The Association also believes that the chances of reaching voluntary agreement in good faith are reduced when one party to the negotiation process possesses the power to use the courts unilaterally against the other party.

The Association recommends several procedures to be used in resolution of impasse—such as mediation, fact finding, binding arbitration, political action, and strike—if conditions make it impossible to provide quality education. In event of a strike by school employees, extracurricular and cocurricular activities must cease. Appropriate teacher training institutions should be notified that a strike is being conducted and urged not to cooperate in emergency licensing or placement practices that constitute strikebreaking.

The Association condemns the use of ex parte injunction, jailing, setting excessive bail, fines, firing of members, decertification of an organization as the bargaining agent, loss of association rights, and revocation or suspension of tenure, licensure, and retirement benefits in school work stoppages. The Association also condemns denial of credits to students who have honored a work stoppage. The Association urges state and federal governments to enact, where they do not exist, statutes guaranteeing school employees due process of law when a work stoppage occurs, including the right to present their case to the state or courts, before back-to-work orders are issued.

SUPPORT FOR
STRIKERS

The Association urges its affiliates to establish practices and procedures to supply financial and emotional support as well as external and internal publicity for any unit local engaged in a strike. (*NEA handbook*, 1988–1989, p. 242)

Not only has the NEA approved of strikes, but it has become very specific about how its striking rights are to be guarded. Both the AFT and the NEA now believe that the strike is the ultimate way to resolve an impasse during the collective bargaining process.

PERMIT
STRIKES?

There are a few states that permit strikes by teachers. Until better collective bargaining laws are passed by the states that do legally allow teachers to withhold their services, teachers will remain frustrated by the system.

Strikes, when they occur, affect teachers, parents, children, and communities.

(Photo used by permission of the Indiana State Teachers Association.)

The system of collective bargaining is an orderly process for resolving contract disputes between the teachers' organizations and the school boards. Before the collective bargaining laws, teachers had to work with their administrators and school boards to produce a contract, and often, the decision was an arbitrary one made by the board. The teachers had no legal right to argue for their point of view. Some say that now that teachers, as far as collective bargaining is concerned, are on an equal basis with administrators, an adversarial rather than a congenial relationship has resulted. Adversarial relationships between administrators and teachers, many say, are the reason that we have an erosion of public support of education. Others point out that if the public is upset by adversarial conflicts between teachers and administrators, it is because the public does not understand the collective bargaining process and that it is up to the teachers, the administrators, the school boards, and the media to tell the true story. One fact is that adversarial relationships of the collective bargaining types are not allowed in totalitarian countries. Flygare (1977) expressed the hope of many when he wrote:

> After all has been said about statutes, court rulings, and the like, the hope remains that teachers and school boards can settle their differences of opinion with civility and with eyes focused on the quality of education. (p. 49)

Agency Shop

DUES FOR ALL?

One of the most controversial items concerning teachers and union membership is the so-called **agency shop provision.** Unions or teachers' organizations believe that the exclusive representative organization ought to be paid dues by all members of a teaching staff whether they belong to that union or not. Unions assert that bargaining costs a lot of money and takes a lot of time, and that all members of a teaching staff receive equal benefits whether they are members of the bargaining unit, are members of a rival union, or are not members of any union. Union members sometimes refer to these nonpaying members of a teaching staff as freeriders or freeloaders. The nonpayers consider themselves independent thinkers who want to preserve their freedom of choice.

PRO AND CON

There are obviously strong arguments to support both sides of this controversial issue: the union needs financial support for the work that it has been elected to do, and nonmembers want freedom of choice. Some say that a possible compromise would be to have all members of a teaching staff pay a reasonable fee, but not one that is equal to the full union membership dues that regular members must pay. This solution would eliminate the objection that some nonmembers have to being required to support the broader causes of the AFT and the NEA when their views differ. The difficulty here is figuring out what a fair assessment would be in relation to the real cost of collective bargaining. To protect those who are already members of the school corporation from being forced to belong, it could be decided that the "agency fee" would be assessed only from all new teachers entering the school system, who will have the opportunity to accept or reject the "agency fee" provision at the time of hiring.

MINORITY
UNIONS PAY
TWICE?

Members of competing minority unions object to having to pay full membership fees in two unions, only one of which represents their views. Some say that for competing **minority unions,** a proportionate cost of the bargaining process that is conducted by the majority union should be all that the minority union members are asked to pay. Minority unions need to support themselves financially and in other ways so that they can continue to put adequate pressure on the majority union to do the job it has been elected to do.

FORCED
UNIONISM?

The agency shop provision is not a resolved issue. A group called Concerned Educators Against Forced Unionism, a division of the National Right to Work Committee, has been formed simply to fight the agency shop provision. Whether a compromise can be worked out to settle this dispute will be interesting to observe.

The Political Action Committee (PAC)

Teachers' organizations have been supporting political candidates for years, but these efforts have increased since the 1970s. During the 1974 congressional campaign, the NEA and the AFT spent about $3.5 million to elect "friends of education." The Carter–Mondale ticket was heavily supported by the teachers in 1976 and in 1980. Their political clout has been growing because their organizations have grown in numbers and their **political action committees** have become more effective. Besides helping to elect Jimmy Carter in 1976, NEA-backed candidates in congressional races won in large numbers. Albert Shanker's AFT was also very effective in the larger cities.

POLITICAL
CLOUT

The NEA's political action committee, known as NEA-PAC, was begun in 1972. Today, it is one of about 2,500 PACs in the country, which spent a grand total of $130 million on the 1980 elections. The NEA's determination to influence national elections through political action was demonstrated in a forceful speech by the president of the NEA in 1973. In her concluding speech to the 1973 representative assembly, President Helen Wise said:

POLITICAL
GOALS

The NEA has indeed awakened and we are on our way. Our first major objective, politically and legislatively, will be to reverse the national leadership in Washington and put a friend of education in the White House and more friends of education in Congress.

We will initiate a grass roots campaign that will bring about the victories that we must have in 1976, and if that means building a war chest to get friends of education elected—then we need to keep the old lid open and continue to plunk in the money.

One thing is certain—the NEA will never again sit out a national election.

In fact, we will build NEA's political force over the next two years to the point where the Presidential candidates will seek NEA endorsement. (West, 1980, p. 194)

Wise was blowing the bugle for events to come. The assistance that NEA members gave the Democratic ticket in 1976, 1980, 1984, and 1988 was considerable. Concerning the 1976 election, Carter's campaign manager Hamilton Jordan said, "The mass support from teachers was critical to our winning this very close election. All over the nation, we turned to NEA for assistance. We asked for help and they delivered" (Elam, 1981, p. 170). President Carter then kept his promise for greater financial support for education and for the establishment of a U.S. Department of Education, which became a reality during his term.

MASS
TEACHER
SUPPORT

How successful the NEA-PAC effort has been can be measured by the number of candidates it has endorsed who have won elections.

ENDORSING
CANDIDATES

> In 1972 the NEA-PAC endorsed 32 candidates. Twenty-six were elected—80% of those endorsed.
> In 1974, 229 candidates for the House were elected of 282 endorsed, and 21 Senatorial candidates were elected from 28 endorsed—another 80% record. . . .
> The 1978 elections produced a 77% success ratio, with 197 out of 247 endorsed candidates winning election to the House and 13 out of 24 winning their Senate races. . . .
> One of the gratifying developments of the more aggressive political action policy, according to NEA leaders, is that more and more candidates are consulting with them prior to the election on the association's legislative goals and priorities. (West, 1980, p. 200)

POLITICAL
SUCCESSES

In the 1980 elections, NEA-backed candidates won in 209 of the 278 House races, a drop to a 75% level from 77% success ratio in 1978 (Elam, 1981, p. 171). Part of the reason for the 1980 drop was that PACs from the Far Right, such as the National Concerned Citizen's PAC, exerted a huge effort in defeating liberal candidates in 1978. Historically, for example, the National Concerned Citizen's PAC spent more on anti–Birch Bayh and anti–George McGovern campaigns than the NEA-PAC was able to raise for 309 of its endorsed candidates combined (Elam, 1981, pp. 171–172). Birch Bayh and George McGovern were two of the best friends that education had in the U.S. Senate.

AMA-PAC
VS.
NEA-PAC

Elam (1981) compared the PAC effort made by the American Medical Association (AMA) with that of the NEA-PAC in the 1980 elections. In 1980, the average U.S. physician earned $68,000 annually from private practice, compared with the average teacher, who earned $17,264. The AMA had 230,000 members (out of a potential 394,000) at the time, and the NEA, 1,680,566 members (out of a potential 3,000,000). The AMA member contributed $250 for national dues, and the NEA member paid $48 nationally for dues. Of the AMA members, 35% contributed $12.75 annually to their PAC, whereas about 20% of the NEA members made PAC contributions, averaging less than $1 per contributor. In the 1980 national elections, the AMA-PAC contributed $1,405,000, compared with only $337,000 spent by the NEA-PAC. Of the AMA-endorsed candidates, 81% won in 1980, compared with less than 75% of the NEA-endorsed candidates (p. 172). It would appear that if teachers want to improve their potential for helping to elect national candidates, their effort in both amount and number of contributors to the NEA-PAC must improve. The NEA has an average of 6,000 members in every congressional district; their potential for political contracts is enormous. According to Chapman (1980), "Most teachers are bright, articulate, and reasonably well-informed, making them naturals for political activism" (p. 10).

GIANT STEP?
Some feel that if teachers can ever unify in the belief that friends of education elected to local, state, and national offices do make a difference, teaching and the field of education will have taken a giant step. Teachers will need to shed completely the age-old belief that politics is a dirty business in which teachers ought not involve themselves. Many teacher leaders say that teachers need to take the time and provide the dollars to elect public officials who will speak up for the true merits of maintaining the kind of public schools that have made our country great.

Special Professional Organizations

This chapter on educational organizations would not be complete without mention of a few special **professional organizations** associated with selected fields of preparation. Becoming acquainted with professional journals printed by these organizations in your major and/or minor fields will cause you to ask probing questions that will lead to answers earlier rather than later in your career. Students often find exciting new ideas in these journals to use in early field experiences or later during student teaching.

PHI DELTA
KAPPA
Some organizations, like Phi Delta Kappa, deal with education in general and not with any specific discipline or branch of study. People who belong to Phi Delta Kappa are known as Kappans, and they are very proud of their professional journal known as *Phi Delta Kappan. Phi Delta Kappan* is published ten times a year, and it is sent all over the world to nearly 125,000 members. The september issue generally contains the Annual Gallup Poll of the Public's Attitudes Toward the Public Schools. The main purpose of Phi Delta Kappa is to promote quality education, particularly public education, as essential to the democratic way of life. If one needs some in-depth information on a topic, the organization publishes minibooks, called *fastbacks*, which now list nearly three hundred titles.

Another example of an educational organization that has a wide appeal is the Association for Supervision and Curriculum Development (ASCD). Classroom teachers, curriculum coordinators, supervisors, professors of education, and many other professionals involved in education are included in its membership. The primary purpose of the ASCD is the improvement of education at both the elementary and the secondary levels. *Educational*
ASCD
Leadership, the ASCD's professional journal, covers many timely educa-

tional topics. The ASCD yearbook focuses on one current topic of interest to educators, such as humaneness or lifelong learning. This is an organization to be involved in if you are interested in keeping up with or making curricular changes yourself.

For a complete listing of all educational organizations, consult a current copy of Volume 1 of *The Encyclopedia of Associations* (Akey, 1990). A few examples taken from *The Encyclopedia of Associations* are presented in the Appendix.

Summary

The main intention of this chapter has been to acquaint the beginning teacher with the two partisan teacher organizations in the United States. Whether a teacher belongs to one, both, or none of these organizations, the AFT and NEA will be a factor in that teacher's career in the public schools. The purposes of these organizations, as well as the reasons for and benefits of membership, were examined. The degree of their effectiveness depends a lot on how they function locally at the bargaining table, how they lobby in the state legislatures, and what effect they have on the U.S. President and the Congress.

The collective bargaining process was presented to give the reader a view of the way in which it is set up, its scope, and the process that it entails. Some general comments were made, but in the absence of a federal collective bargaining law, each state is somewhat different. Strikes, which are illegal in most states, are backed as a last resort by both the NEA and the AFT. The agency shop is another controversial issue for teachers to resolve; at this time, it appears to be mostly a local issue. Political action committees, or PACs, have been increasingly active, particularly on the national scene. The AFT and NEA invested much money and effort into the last four presidential elections, and there is no sign that this effort will diminish with time.

Glossary Terms

Lobbyists, 518

Grievance Procedures, 519

Resolutions, 522

Adversarial Relationship, 523

Functional Proficiency in English, 526

Representative Assembly, 527

Teachers' Association, 527

Union, 527

Social Platform, 530

Affiliate, 530

Merger, 533

Secret Ballot, 535

Collective Bargaining Process, 535

Exclusive Bargaining Rights, 536

Broad Discretion, 536

Fair Representation, 536

Scope of Bargaining, 538

Proposals, 538

Counterproposals, 538

Impasse, 538
Mediation, 538
Fact Finding, 539
Arbitration, 540
Final-Offer Arbitration, 540
Strikes, 540

Agency Shop Provision, 543
Minority Unions, 544
Political Action Committees
 (PACs), 544
Professional Organization, 546

Questions

1. In what ways are the NEA and the AFT moving closer together?
2. What are some comparisons between union leaders Albert Shanker and Keith Geiger?
3. Is a merger between the NEA and the AFT a real possibility? Discuss the pros and cons of such an outcome.
4. The collective bargaining process causes an advocacy position to be developed by both the teachers and the school administration. Discuss the pros and cons of this situation.
5. Why do teachers' organizations take such a strong stand against tuition tax credits?
6. Besides being tied together financially, what are some other benefits of local, state, and national teachers' organizations?
7. How would you feel about being a member of a militant teachers' organization?
8. The NEA and the AFT endorse mainly Democratic Liberals. Suppose you are a strong Republican. What will you do? How do you rationalize your views?
9. What will your fellow workers think if you do not join and take part in a teachers' organization? Will you accept the benefits along with those who pay the dues and work within the organization?
10. Make a list of the differences and the similarities between the NEA and the AFT. Why are the two organizations so different and yet so similar?
11. What is the present status of the U.S. Department of Education? Why did the NEA want the department so much?
12. What is the controversy surrounding the "agency shop" provision in many teachers' contracts?
13. What is a uniserve director? What are his or her duties?
14. Why is political action on the part of the teacher an accepted part of her or his function as a teacher?
15. Why do teachers sometimes strike? What risks do they take? What is your state law on teachers' strikes?

Activities for Unit IX

1. Simulate collective bargaining. A simulation game called *A Collective Bargaining Simulation in Public Education*, by Marcus H. Sandver and Harry R. Blame, can be purchased from Grid Inc., 4666 Indianola Avenue, Columbus, OH 43214.

2. Analyze the problems that caused a teachers' strike in your state. What alternatives were open to the teachers, and what solutions were finally arrived at?

3. Invite members of the AFT, the NEA, and other teachers' groups to debate the pros and cons of their points of view before your class.

4. Attend a conference or a workshop sponsored by a teachers' organization in your local area. Report to the class concerning the general value of such a workshop or conference.

5. Invite a school administrator and/or a mediator to talk to you in regard to how he or she feels about working with teachers' organizations during contract negotiations.

6. Go on a field trip to a labor union office with some prewritten questions about unions; then, draw your own comparisons of the union philosophy and the NEA philosophy.

7. Play a videotape, if one is available, of the collective bargaining process. After viewing the tape, write down any questions you have about collective bargaining, and then discuss the questions in class.

8. Invite a uniserve director to your class to discuss her or his function in the NEA structure.

9. Write for or collect the legislative proposals of the state NEA, the state AFT, and the state school boards' association. How are they similar to and different from each other?

10. Invite a state legislator to talk about pending education bills. What are some differences between the role of a legislator and the role of a union lobbyist?

11. Who are the real leaders in your state in the promotion of education? Make a list of these people and debate in class the merits of their stands on educational issues.

12. Simulate in your own class various leadership roles in teachers' organizations. By rotating roles throughout a quarter or a semester, you can experience what being a member of a union is like. Some roles are building representative, chief lobbyist, and president of the union.

13. Secure an invitation to a local teachers' organization meeting. Summarize the deliberations at the meeting and be prepared to discuss the meeting with the class.

14. Ask your state legislative representative if you can act as a page for him or her during the legislative assembly.

15. Find out if there are any local alternatives to either the state NEA or AFT affiliates. Report on these to the class.

Annotated Bibliography

1. Donley, M. O. (1977). *The future of teacher power in America*, Fastback No. 98. Bloomington, IN: Phi Delta Kappa Educational Foundation.
The history of teacher's organizations is traced from their beginning to the late 1970s. The author wrote his Ph.D. thesis on the history of U.S. teachers' organizations and is an authority on this area.

2. Flygare, T. J. (1977). *Collective bargaining in the public schools*, Fastback No. 99. Bloomington, IN: Phi Delta Kappa Educational Foundation.
Although this fastback was written in 1977, most of the concepts about the bargaining process remain the same in the 1990s. For one who desires to know more about the process of collective bargaining, the author supplies much information.

3. *NEA handbook, 1988–1989.* Washington, DC: National Education Association.
Published annually, the *NEA Handbook* provides basic information on the Association, including goals and objectives, the program, administrative figures, and names, addresses, and telephone numbers of key elected leaders and staff.

4. Wesley, E. B. (1957). *NEA: The First Hundred Years.* New York: Harper and Brothers.
The history of the NEA until its centennial year, 1957, is reviewed. Some of the events in American education in which the association played a prominent part are described.

5. *The Encyclopedia of Associations.* Detroit: Gale Research Co., Book Tower.
More than 30,000 national and international organizations are listed by name, address, and phone number; executive director; date of founding; number of members; publications; conventions; and a description of the organization's goals.

Appendix

Dates of Key Educational Events in America

1607	Jamestown colony was founded.
1620	Plymouth colony was founded.
1635	Boston Latin Grammar School was opened.
1636	Harvard was founded.
1642	Massachusetts passed a law requiring compulsory education (not necessary in schools).
1647	Old Deluder Satan Act of Massachusetts called for schools in every town with more than fifty households.
1648	First property tax for support of schools was passed in Dedham, Massachusetts.
1690	*New England Primer* was first published in Boston; it was used until 1802.
1693	William and Mary College was founded.
1701	Society for the Propagation of the Gospel in Foreign Parts was founded to educate slaves and Indians.
1746	Princeton University was founded.
1751	Benjamin Franklin's Philadelphia Academy was established (private secondary education).
1776	Phi Beta Kappa was founded at William and Mary College.
1779	Thomas Jefferson wrote the Bill for More General Diffusion of Knowledge, a plan for free public education for residents of Virginia (not including slaves).
1780	Sunday school movement began in England.
1785	The Land Ordinance set aside one section of each township to support education in western areas of the country.
1787	The Northwest Ordinance set aside one section for schools and two townships for a university.
1789	U.S. Constitution was adopted.
1794	The first teacher association was established—Society of Associated Teachers of New York City.
1797	Monitorial school was started in England by Andrew Bell.
1880–1850	Academy movement dominated secondary education.
1805	The New York Free Society was formed by DeWitt Clinton.
1818	Monitorial school was begun in the United States.
1819	The *Dartmouth College* case established the rights of private schools.
1820s	Infant school societies begun in England were formed in major U.S. cities.
1821	First American high school was established in Boston (English Classical School).
1821	Troy Female Seminary was opened by Emma Willard to provide secondary education to women.

1825	University of Virginia was founded.
1827	Massachusetts required establishment of high schools in cities.
1828	Hartford Seminary was opened by Catherine Beecher to educate girls.
1831	Frenchman Victor Cousin issued a report on Prussian education—*The Cousin Report.*
1834	Pennsylvania passes the Free School Act, doing away with pauper schools.
1836	First McGuffey Reader was printed.
1837	An American report was issued on Prussian education—*The Stowe Report.*
1837	Mount Holyoke College for women was established by Mary Lyon.
1837	Horace Mann was appointed secretary of the State Board of Education in Massachusetts.
1840	First child labor law was enacted in Rhode Island.
1840s–1850s	Horace Mann, "father of public education," reformed the public education system of Massachusetts.
1852	Massachusetts passed the first law requiring compulsory school attendance.
1853	New York Free School Society turned over its "schools for the poor" to the city of New York as public schools.
1855	First kindergarten in the United States was opened by Mrs. Carl Schurz, conducted in German.
1856	First coeducational high school was opened.
1857	National Education Association was formed.
1860	First English-speaking kindergarten was opened in Boston by Elizabeth Peabody.
1862	Morrill Land Grant Act endowed land grant colleges in each state.
1867	Henry Barnard, public school reformer for Connecticut, became first U.S. Commissioner of Education.
1868	Hampton Institute was founded by Samuel Chapman Armstrong to educate blacks.
1874	The *Kalamazoo* case established the public high school as a legitimate part of the public school system.
1875	Progressive education movement in the United States was begun by Francis Wayland Parker.
1880	Tuskegee Institute was founded by Booker T. Washington for education of blacks.
1892	The Committee of Ten of the National Education Association proposed the first organized secondary school curriculum.
1896	In *Plessy v. Ferguson,* the U.S. Supreme Court upheld the right of railroads to segregate passengers by race—"separate but equal" doctrine.
1896	University of Chicago laboratory school was begun by John Dewey.

1897	First teachers' union was formed—Chicago Teachers Federation.
1909	First junior high schools were established in Columbus, Ohio, and Berkeley, California.
1914	Smith–Lever Cooperative Agriculture Extension Act provided for national aid in distribution of information about agriculture and home economics.
1916	American Federation of Teachers was formed.
1917	Smith–Hughes Act provided vocational education in schools below the college level.
1919	Progressive Education Association was formed in Washington, DC.
1944	GI Bill of Rights provided free education for World War II veterans.
1946	National School Lunch Act was passed.
1948	In the *McCollum* case, the U.S. Supreme Court ruled religious instruction in the public schools to be unconstitutional.
1952	GI Bill of Rights was extended to veterans of Korea.
1954	In *Brown v. Board of Education of Topeka,* the U.S. Supreme Court ruled that segregated schools are unequal and must be abandoned.
1958	National Defense Education Act provided scholarships for college and graduate students.
1962	U.S. Supreme Court ruled prayer and Bible reading in the public schools to be unconstitutional.
1964	Economic Opportunity Act (EOA) set up the Job Corps and Head Start programs.
1964	Civil Rights Act of 1964 gave the U.S. Justice Department power to enforce desegregation of schools.
1965	The Elementary and Secondary Education Act (ESEA) provided federal aid to elementary and secondary education programs, especially to those aimed at the poor and minorities.
1966	GI Bill of Rights was extended to veterans of Vietnam War.
1972	Title IX of the Education Amendments made discrimination on the basis of sex illegal.
1974	Family Educational Rights and Privacy Act established the confidentiality of student records.
1975	Education for All Handicapped Children Act provided for "mainstreaming" of handicapped children.
1978	In the *Bakke* case, the U.S. Supreme Court ruled against reverse discrimination.
1982	U.S. Supreme Court ruled that the state of Texas must provide public education for children of illegal aliens.
1983	The National Commission on Excellence in Education (created in 1981) issued *A Nation at Risk,* a report on the quality of education in the United States.
1985	The Carnegie Forum on Education and the Economy was founded.

1987   National Board for Professional Teaching Standards was established.

Special Professional Organizations

The organizations are arranged by areas of special interest. The two principal general teachers' organizations, the American Federation of Teachers and the National Education Association, are listed at the end.

Art

NATIONAL ART EDUCATION ASSOCIATION (Arts)(NAEA)
1916 Association Drive   Phone: (703) 860–8000
Reston, VA 22091   Thomas A. Hatfield, Exec. Dir.
Founded: 1947. **Members:** 11,500. **Staff:** 11. **Regional Groups:** 4. Teachers of art at elementary, secondary, and college levels; colleges, libraries, museums, and other educational institutions. Studies problems of teaching art; encourages research and experimentation. Serves as clearinghouse for information on art education programs, materials, and methods of instruction. **Publication:** *Art Education*, bimonthly. Educational journal reporting on current issues, problems, and approaches in visual art education, including curriculum, teaching strategies, and innovative and exemplary programs. **Price:** Included in membership dues: $50/year for nonmembers.

Bilingual Education

NATIONAL ASSOCIATION FOR BILINGUAL EDUCATION (NABE)
1201 16th Street, NW, Rm. 408   Phone: (202)822–7870
Washington, DC 20036   Joseph W. Beard, Admin.
Founded: 1975. **Members:** 3,000. **State Groups:** 32. Educators, administrators, paraprofessionals, community and lay people, and students. Purposes are to recognize, promote, and publicize bilingual education. Seeks to increase public understanding of the importance of language and culture. Utilizes and develops student proficiency and ensures equal opportunities in bilingual education for language-minority students. Works to preserve and expand the nation's linguistic resources. **Publications:** (1) *Journal*, 3/year (2) *Newsletter*, 8/year.

Curriculum

ASSOCIATION FOR SUPERVISION AND CURRICULUM DEVELOPMENT (ASCD)
225 North Washington Street   Phone: (703) 549–9110
Alexandria, VA 22314   Gordon Cawelti, Exec. Dir.
Founded: 1921. **Members:** 35,000. **Staff:** 30. **Affiliated Units:** 52. Professional

organization supervisors, curriculum coordinators, directors of curriculum, consultants, professors of education, classroom teachers, principals, superintendents, parents, and others interested in school improvement at any level of education: elementary, secondary, college, or adult. **Publications:** (1) *Educational Leadership*, 8/year. (2) *Yearbook*. Also publishes *Update* and booklets.

Early Childhood

NATIONAL ASSOCIATION FOR THE EDUCATION OF YOUNG CHILDREN (Childhood Education)(NAEYC)
1834 Connecticut Avenue, NW — Phone: (202) 232–8777
Washington, DC 20009 — Dr. Marilyn M. Smith, Exec. Dir.
Founded: 1926. **Members:** 62,000. **Staff:** 35. **Budget:** $2,000,000. **Local Groups:** 350. Teachers and directors of preschool and primary schools, kindergartens, child-care centers, cooperatives, church schools, play groups, and groups having similar programs for young children; early childhood education and child development professors, trainers, and researchers. Open to all individuals interested in serving and acting on behalf of the needs and rights of young children, with primary focus on the provision of educational services and resources. **Publications:** (1) *Early Childhood Research Quarterly.* (2) *Young Children*, bimonthly; journal covering developments in the practice, research, and theory of early childhood education; includes work reviews, calendar of events, record reviews, research reports, and Washington update.

Elementary Education

ASSOCIATION FOR CHILDHOOD EDUCATION INTERNATIONAL (ACEI)
11141 Georgia Avenue — Phone: (202) 363–6963
Wheaton, MD 20902 — James S. Packer, Exec. Dir.
Founded: 1892. **Members:** 11,000. **Staff:** 11. **State Groups:** 36 **Local Groups:** 350. Teachers, parents, and other adults interested in promoting good educational practices for children from infancy through early adolescence. **Publications:** *Childhood Education*, 5/year. Also publishes bulletins, *Bibliography of Books for Children*, and portfolio on nursery school and kindergarten.

English

NATIONAL COUNCIL OF TEACHERS OF ENGLISH (NCTE)
1111 Kenyon Road — Phone: (217) 328–3870
Urbana, IL 61801 — John C. Maxwell, Exec. Dir.
Founded: 1911. **Members:** 102,000. **Staff:** 80. **State Groups:** 50. **Local**

Groups: 89. Teachers of English at all school levels: elementary, secondary, and college. **Publications:** (1) *English Journal*, 9/year. (2) *Language Arts*, 9/year. (3) *College English*, 8/year. (4) *Council-Grams*, 5/year. (5) *College Composition and Communication*, quarterly. (6) *English Education*, quarterly. (7) *Research in the Teaching of English*, quarterly. (8) *Director*, annual. Also publishes books and pamphlets and issues cassettes and "literary maps."

French

AMERICAN ASSOCIATION OF TEACHERS OF FRENCH (AATF)
57 East Armory   Phone: (217) 333–2842
Champaign, IL 61820   Fred M. Jenkins, Exec. Sec.
Founded: 1927. **Members:** 30,000. **Local Groups:** 76. Teachers of French in public and private elementary and secondary schools, colleges, and universities. **Publications:** (1) *French Review*, bimonthly (directory included in May issue). (2) *National Bulletin*. (3) *Directory*, annual.

German

AMERICAN ASSOCIATION OF TEACHERS OF GERMAN (AATG)
523 Building, Suite 201   Phone: (609) 663–5264
Route 38   Robert A. Govier, Exec. Dir.
Cherry Hill, NJ 08034
Founded: 1926. **Members:** 6,500. **Staff:** 6. **Local Groups:** 60. Professional and educational society of teachers of German at all levels. **Publications:** (1) *German Quarterly*. (2) *Newsletter*, quarterly. (3) *Unterrichtspraxis*, semiannually.

Gifted Children

NATIONAL ASSOCIATION FOR GIFTED CHILDREN (NAGC)
675 Lovell Road, Suite 140   Phone: (612) 784–3475
Pines, MN 55014   Joyce Juntune, Exec. Dir.
Founded: 1954. **Members:** 7000. **Staff:** 7. **Budget:** $600,000. **State Groups:** 22. Librarians, teachers, university personnel, administrators, and parents. To advance interest in programs for the gifted. Seeks to further education of the gifted and to enhance their potential creativity. **Publications:** (1) *Gifted Child Quarterly*. (2) *National Association for Gifted Children—Communique*, quarterly. Also publishes newsletter on the educational and familial needs of gifted children. Reports on federal legislative actions that affect gifted children and describes new educational materials for the gifted. Includes news of association activities.

Home Economics

HOME ECONOMICS EDUCATION ASSOCIATION (HEEA)
1201 16th Street, NW   Phone: (202) 822–7844
Washington, DC 20036   Catherine A. Leisher, Exec. Dir.
Founded: 1927. **Members:** 3,700. **Budget:** $54,000. Teachers and supervisors of home economics education. Seeks to promote effective programs of home economics education, to supplement existing services available to home economics educators, and to cooperate with other associations in related fields. **Affiliated With:** National Education Association. **Publications:** *Home Economics Educator*, quarterly newsletter. **Price:** Included in membership dues; $15/year. **Circulation:** 3,000. Also publishes booklets, reports, monographs, and other materials.

Honorary Organization: Phi Delta Kappa

PHI DELTA KAPPA
Eighth Street and Union Avenue   Phone: (812) 339–1156
Bloomington, IN 47401   Dr. Lowell C. Rose, Exec. Sec.
Founded: 1906. **Members:** 116,000. **Chapters:** 550. Professional, honorary, and recognition fraternity, education. **Publications:** (1) *Phi Delta Kappan*, monthly. (2) *CEDR Quarterly.* (3) *News, Notes, and Quotes*, quarterly. Also publishes *PAR (Practical Applications of Research)* and monographs.

Industrial Arts/Vocational Education

NATIONAL ASSOCIATION FOR TRADE AND INDUSTRIAL EDUCA-
TION (NATIE)
P.O. Box 1665   Phone: (703) 777–1740
Leesburg, VA 22075   Dr. Ethel M. Smith, Acting Exec. Dir.
Founded: 1974. **Members:** 1,400. **State Groups:** 24. Educators in trade and industrial education. Works for the promotion, development, and improvement of trade and industrial education. Provides leadership in developing support for greater identity in federal legislation. **Publications:** *NATIE News Notes*, quarterly association and industry newsletter; includes book reviews, calendar of events, research updates, and statistics. **Price:** Included in membership dues.

Library

AMERICAN LIBRARY ASSOCIATION (ALA)
50 East Huron Street   Phone: (312) 944–6780
Chicago, IL 60611   Robert Wedgeworth, Exec. Dir.
Founded: 1876. **Members:** 37,000. **Staff:** 220. **Regional Groups:** 56. Librar-

ians, libraries, trustees, friends of libraries, and others interested in the responsibilities of libraries in the educational, social, and cultural needs of society. **Publications:** (1) *Booklist*, semimonthly (except August). (2) *American Libraries*, monthly (except July/August). (3) *Choice*, 11/year. Also publishes books and pamphlets.

Mathematics

NATIONAL COUNCIL OF TEACHERS OF MATHEMATICS (NCTM)
1906 Association Drive   Phone: (703) 620–9840
Reston, VA 22091   Dr. James D. Gates, Exec. Dir.
Founded: 1920. **Members:** 70,000. **Staff:** 45. **State and Local Groups:** 190. Teachers of mathematics in grades K–12, two-year colleges, and teacher education personnel on college campuses. **Publications:** (1) *Arithmetic Teacher*, 9/year. (2) *Mathematics Teacher*, 9/year. (3) *Journal for Research in Mathematics*, 5/year. (4) *News Bulletin*, 5/year. (5) *Yearbook*. Also publishes booklets, pamphlets, reprints, and teaching aids.

Music

MUSIC TEACHERS NATIONAL ASSOCIATON (MTNA)
617 Vine Street   Phone: (513) 421–1420
Suite 1432   Robert J. Elias, Exec. Dir.
Cincinnati, OH 45202
Founded: 1876. **Members:** 23,500. **Staff:** 9. **State Groups:** 51. Professional society of music teachers in studios, conservatories, music schools, public and private schools, colleges, universities, and undergraduate and graduate music students. **Publications:** (1) *American Music Teacher Magazine*, 6/year. (2) *Directory of Nationally Certified Teachers*, annually. Also publishes national courses of study and books.

Physical Education

AMERICAN ALLIANCE FOR HEALTH, PHYSICAL EDUCATION, RECREATION AND DANCE (AAHPERD)
1900 Association Drive   Phone: (703) 476–3400
Reston, VA 22091   Robert K. Windsor, Exec. V. Pres.
Founded: 1885. **Members:** 42,000. **Staff:** 54. **State Groups:** 54. **Regional Groups:** 6. Students and educators in physical education, dance, health, athletics, safety education, recreation, and outdoor education. **Publications:** (1) *Journal of Physical Education and Recreation*, 9/year. (2) *Update*, 9/year. (3) *Health Education*, 6/year. (4) *Research Quarterly*. (5) *News Kit on Programs for the Aging* (feature of *Update*), semiannually. (6) *Leisure Today*,

2/year. Also publishes manuals and handbooks through their Sports Library for Girls and Women.

Reading

INTERNATIONAL READING ASSOCIATION (IRA)

P.O. Box 8139   Phone: (302) 731–1600
800 Barksdale Rd.   Ralph C. Staiger, Exec. Dir.
Newark, DE 19711

Founded: 1956. **Members:** 61,000. **Staff:** 80. **Local Groups:** 1,100. Individuals engaged in the teaching or supervising of reading at any school level. **Publications:** (1) *Journal of Reading,* 8/year. (2) *Reading Teacher,* 8/year. (3) *Reading Today,* 8/year. (4) *Lectura y Vida,* quarterly. (5) *Reading Research,* quarterly. Also publishes books and monographs (10–20/year).

Science

NATIONAL ASSOCIATION OF BIOLOGY TEACHERS (NABT)

11250 Roger Bacon Drive   Phone: (703) 471–1134
Reston, VA 22090   Dr. Wayne A. Moyer, Exec. Dir.

Founded: 1938. **Members:** 6,000. **Staff:** 7. Professional society of biology teachers and others interested in teaching of biology at secondary and college levels. **Publications:** (1) *American Biology Teacher,* 9/year. (2) *News & Views,* bimonthly.

NATIONAL SCIENCE TEACHERS ASSOCIATION (NSTA)

1742 Connecticut Avenue, NW   Phone: (202) 328–5800
Washington, DC 20009   Bill G. Aldredge, Exec. Dir.

Founded: 1895. **Members:** 63,000. **Staff:** 5. Teachers "seeking to foster excellence in the whole of science teaching." **Publications:** (1) *The Science Teacher,* 9/year. (2) *Science and Children,* 8/year. (3) *Energy and Education Newsletter,* bimonthly. (4) *Journal of College Science Teaching,* 6/year. (5) *Bulletin,* 3/year. Also publishes curriculum development and professional materials, teaching aids, career booklets, and audiovisual aids.

Social Studies

NATIONAL COUNCIL FOR THE SOCIAL STUDIES (NCSS)

3615 Wisconsin Avenue, NW   Phone: (202) 966–7840
Washington, DC 20016   Elizabeth Scott, Acting Dir.

Founded: 1921. **Members:** 25,000. **Staff:** 8. **State Groups:** 9. **Local Groups:** 109. Teachers of social studies, including civics, geography, history, and political science. **Publications:** (1) *Social Education,* 7/year. (2) *Newsletter,* 5/year. (3) *Bulletins,* 3/year.

Spanish

AMERICAN ASSOCIATION OF TEACHERS OF SPANISH AND POR-
TUGUESE (AATSP)
P.O. Box 6349   Phone: (601) 325–2041
Mississippi State, MS 39762   Richard B. Klein, Exec. Dir.
Founded: 1917. **Members:** 12,000. **Local Groups:** 74. Teachers of Spanish
and Portuguese languages and literature and others interested in Hispanic
culture. **Publications:** (1) *Hispania*, quarterly. (2) *Director*, annually.

Special Education

FOUNDATION FOR EXCEPTIONAL CHILDREN (Special Education)(FEC)
1920 Association Drive   Phone: (703) 620–3660
Reston, VA 22091   Robert L. Silber, Exec. Dir.
Founded: 1971. **Members:** 1,000. **Staff:** 4. Institutions, agencies, educators,
parents, and persons concerned with the education of gifted or handicapped
children. Established to further the educational, vocational, social, and
personal needs of the handicapped child or youth and the neglected educational needs of the gifted. **Publications:** *Foundation for Exceptional Children—Focus*, 3/year. Also publishes newsletter providing information on
the foundation's programs, committees, financial support, and board of
directors; carries profiles of scholarship recipients and of active members;
features award winners and grant recipients.

General Teachers' Organizations

AMERICAN FEDERATION OF TEACHERS (AFT)
11 Dupont Circle, NW   Phone: (202) 797–4400
Washington, DC 20036   Albert Shanker, Pres.
Founded: 1916. **Members:** 580,000. **Locals:** 2,100. **Affiliated With:** AFL–
CIO. Promotes collective bargaining for teachers and other educational
employees. **Publications:** (1) *American Teacher*, monthly (September–May).
(2) *American Educator*, quarterly.

NATIONAL EDUCATION ASSOCIATON (Teachers)(NEA)
1201 16th Street, NW   Phone: (202) 833–4000
Washington, DC 20036   Don Cameron, Exec. Dir.
Founded: 1857. **Members:** 1,600,800. **Staff:** 600. **State Groups:** 53. **Local
Groups:** 10,000. Professional organization and union of elementary and
secondary school teachers, college and university professors, administrators, principals, counselors, and others concerned with education. **Publications:** (1) *Reporter*, 8/year. (2) *Today's Education*, quarterly. (3) *Handbook*,
annually.

Source. Akey, D. S. (Ed.). (1990). *Encyclopedia of associations*. Detroit: Gale Research Co., Book Tower.

CODE OF ETHICS
of the Education Profession

ADOPTED BY THE 1975 NEA REPRESENTATIVE ASSEMBLY

Preamble

The educator, believing in the worth and dignity of each human being, recognizes the supreme importance of the pursuit of truth, devotion to excellence, and the nurture of democratic principles. Essential to these goals is the protection of freedom to learn and to teach and the guarantee of equal educational opportunity for all. The educator accepts the responsibility to adhere to the highest ethical standards.

The educator recognizes the magnitude of the responsibility inherent in the teaching process. The desire for the respect and confidence of one's colleagues, of students, of parents, and of the members of the community provides the incentive to attain and maintain the highest possible degree of ethical conduct. The Code of Ethics of the Education Profession indicates the aspiration of all educators and provides standards by which to judge conduct.

The remedies specified by the NEA and/or its affiliates for the violation of any provision of this Code shall be exclusive and no such provision shall be enforceable in any form other than one specifically designated by the NEA or its affiliates.

Principle I—Commitment to the Student

The educator strives to help each student realize his or her potential as a worthy and effective member of society. The educator therefore works to stimulate the spirit of inquiry, the acquisition of knowledge and understanding, and the thoughtful formulation of worthy goals.

In fulfillment of the obligation to the student, the educator—

1. Shall not unreasonably restrain the student from independent action in the pursuit of learning.
2. Shall not unreasonably deny the student access to varying points of view.
3. Shall not deliberately suppress or distort subject matter relevant to the student's progress.
4. Shall make reasonable effort to protect the student from conditions harmful to learning or to health and safety.
5. Shall not intentionally expose the student to embarrassment or disparagement.
6. Shall not on the basis of race, color, creed, sex, national origin, marital status, political or religious beliefs, family, social or cultural background, or sexual orientation, unfairly:
   a. Exclude any student from participation in any program;
   b. Deny benefits to any student;
   c. Grant any advantage to any student.
7. Shall not use professional relationships with students for private advantage.
8. Shall not disclose information about students obtained in the course of professional service, unless disclosure serves a compelling professional purpose or is required by law.

Principle II—Commitment to the Profession

The education profession is vested by the public with a trust and responsibility requiring the highest ideals of professional service.

In the belief that the quality of the services of the education profession directly influences the nation and its citizens, the educator shall exert every effort to raise professional standards, to promote a climate that encourages the exercise of professional judgment, to achieve conditions which attract persons worthy of the trust to careers in education, and to assist in preventing the practice of the profession by unqualified persons.

In fulfillment of the obligation to the profession, the educator—

1. Shall not in an application for a professional position deliberately make a false statement or fail to disclose a material fact related to competency and qualifications.
2. Shall not misrepresent his/her professional qualifications.
3. Shall not assist entry into the profession of a person known to be unqualified in respect to character, education, or other relevant attribute.
4. Shall not knowingly make a false statement concerning the qualifications of a candidate for a professional position.
5. Shall not assist a noneducator in the unauthorized practice of teaching.
6. Shall not disclose information about colleagues obtained in the course of professional service unless disclosure serves a compelling professional purpose or is required by law.
7. Shall not knowingly make false or malicious statements about a colleague.
8. Shall not accept any gratuity, gift, or favor that might impair or appear to influence professional decisions or actions.

Source. Reprinted by permission of the National Education Association, Washington, D.C.

American Federation of Teachers

BILL OF RIGHTS

THE TEACHER IS ENTITLED TO A LIFE OF DIGNITY EQUAL TO THE HIGH STANDARD OF SERVICE THAT IS JUSTLY DEMANDED OF THAT PROFESSION. THEREFORE, WE HOLD THESE TRUTHS TO BE SELF-EVIDENT:

I

TEACHERS have the right to think freely and to express themselves openly and without fear. This includes the right to hold views contrary to the majority.

II

THEY SHALL be entitled to the free exercise of their religion. No restraint shall be put upon them in the manner, time or place of their worship.

III

THEY SHALL have the right to take part in social, civil, and political affairs. They shall have the right, outside the classroom, to participate in political campaigns and to hold office. They may assemble peaceably and may petition any government agency, including their employers, for a redress of grievances. They shall have the same freedom in all things as other citizens.

IV

THE RIGHT of teachers to live in places of their own choosing, to be free of restraints in their mode of living and the use of their leisure time shall not be abridged.

V

TEACHING is a profession, the right to practice which is not subject to the surrender of other human rights. No one shall be deprived of professional status, or the right to practice it, or the practice thereof in any particular position, without due process of law.

VI

THE RIGHT of teachers to be secure in their jobs, free from political influence or public clamor, shall be established by law. The right to teach after qualification in the manner prescribed by law, is a property right, based upon the inalienable rights to life, liberty, and the pursuit of happiness.

VII

IN ALL cases affecting the teacher's employment or professional status a full hearing by an impartial tribunal shall be afforded with the right to full judicial review. No teacher shall be deprived of employment or professional status but for specific causes established by law having a clear relation to the competence or qualification to teach, proved by the weight of the evidence. In all such cases the teacher shall enjoy the right to a speedy and public trial, to be informed of the nature and cause of the accusation; to be confronted with the accusing witnesses, to subpoena witnesses and papers, and to the assistance of counsel. No teacher shall be called upon to answer any charge affecting his employment or professional status but upon probable cause, supported by oath or affirmation.

VIII

IT SHALL be the duty of the employer to provide culturally adequate salaries, security in illness and adequate retirement income. The teacher has the right to such a salary as will: a) Afford a family standard of living comparable to that enjoyed by other professional people in the community; b) To make possible freely chosen professional study; c) Afford the opportunity for leisure and recreation common to our heritage.

IX

TEACHERS shall not be required under penalty of reduction of salary to pursue studies beyond those required to obtain professional status. After serving a reasonable probationary period a teacher shall be entitled to permanent tenure terminable only for just cause. They shall be free as in other professions in the use of their own time. They shall not be required to perform extracurricular work against their will or without added compensation.

X

TO EQUIP people for modern life requires the most advanced educational methods. Therefore, the teacher is entitled to good classrooms, adequate teaching materials, teachable class size and administrative protection and assistance in maintaining discipline.

XI

THESE rights are based upon the proposition that the culture of a people can rise only as its teachers improve. A teaching force accorded the highest possible professional dignity is the surest guarantee that blessings of liberty will be preserved. Therefore, the possession of these rights impose the challenge to be worthy of their enjoyment.

XII

SINCE teachers must be free in order to teach freedom, the right to be members of organizations of their own choosing, without coercion or intimidation must be guaranteed. In all matters pertaining to their salaries, fringe benefits, working conditions and other terms and conditions of employment, they shall be entitled to bargain collectively through representatives of their own choosing with their officially designated employers, such negotiations to culminate in a written legal contract.

Source. Reprinted by permission of the American Federation of Teachers, Washington, D.C.

References

ADAMS, E. K. (1982). The fiscal condition of the states. *Phi Delta Kappan, 63,* 598-600.

ADLER, M. J. (1982). *The Paideia proposal.* New York: Macmillan.

Advisory Commission on Intergovernmental Relations. (1977). *Significant features of fiscal federalism, 1976–77.* Washington, DC: U.S. Government Printing Office.

AKEY, D. S. (ED.) (1990). *Encyclopedia of associations,* 24th ed., Vol. 1. Detroit, MI: Gale Research Company, Book Tower.

AMIDON, E. J., & FLANDERS, N. A. (1971). *The role of the teacher in the classroom.* Minneapolis, MN: Paul S. Amidon and Associates.

ANDERSON, L. F. (1931). *Pestalozzi.* New York: McGraw-Hill.

ANRIG, G. (1986). Teacher education and teacher testing: The rush to mandate. *Phi Delta Kappan, 67,* 447–451.

ARCHAMBAULT, R. D. (ED.) (1966). *Dewey on education: Appraisals.* New York: Random House.

ATKIN, R., ALLEN, C. I., & WACHTER, H. H. (1980). PL 94-142 and local district governance. *Educational Leadership, 38,* 120–121.

AULT, R. L. (1983). *Children's cognitive development.* New York: Oxford University Press.

AUSUBEL, D. P. (1983). Viewpoints from related disciplines: Human growth and development. In G. Hass (Ed.), *Curriculum planning: A new approach,* pp. 155–163. Boston: Allyn and Bacon.

BACON, F. (1901). *Novum organum.* New York: Collier and Son. (Originally published in 1620.)

BAILEY, W. J. (1975). *Managing self-renewal in secondary education.* Englewood Cliffs, NJ: Educational Technology Publications.

BALLANTINE, J. H. (1983). *The sociology of education.* Englewoods Cliffs, NJ: Prentice-Hall.

BALLINGER, C., KIRSCHENBAUM, N., & POIMBEAUF, R. (1987). *The year round school: Where learning never stops.* Bloomington, IN: Phi Delta Kappa Educational Foundation.

BANERJEE, S. (Feb.–Mar. 1983). Use and misuse of the media. *World Health,* pp. 18–20.

BANKS, J. (1977). *Multiethnic education: Practices and promises.* New York: Longman.

BANKS, J. A., (1987) *Teaching strategies for ethnic studies,* 4th ed. Newton, MA: Allyn and Bacon.

BASH, J. H. (1973). *Effective teaching in the desegregated school,* Fastback No. 32. Bloomington, IN: Phi Delta Kappa Educational Foundation.

BECK, M. (1988). A nation still at risk. *Newsweek, 45,* 54–55.

BELL, C. A., CASTO, G., & DANIELS, D. S. (1983). Ameliorating the impact of teenage pregnancy on parent and child. *Child Welfare, 62,* 167–173.

BELL, T. H. (1962). *A philosophy of education for the space age.* New York: Exposition Press.

BENHAM, B. J., GILSEN, P., & OAKES, J. (1980). A study of schooling: Students' experiences in schools. *Phi Delta Kappan, 61,* 337–340.

BENNETT, C. (1979). Interracial acceptance in desegregated schools. *Phi Delta Kappan, 60* (5), 683.

BENSON, C. S. (1975). *Educational finance in the coming decade.* Bloomington, IN: Phi Delta Kappa Educational Foundation.

BENSON, C. S. (1978). *The economics of public education,* 3rd ed. Boston: Houghton Mifflin.

BEVER, S. (1980). *Building a child's self-image.* St. Paul: Minnesota Association for Children and Adults with Learning Disabilities.

BLACK, H. C. (1979). *Black's Law Dictionary,* 5th ed. St. Paul, MN: West Publishing.

BLAU, J., & BLAU, P. (1983). The cost of inequality: Metropolitan structure and violent crime. *American Sociological Review, 47,* 114–129.

BLOOM, B. S., ENGLEHART, M. D., FURST, E. J., HILL, W. H., & KRATHWOHL, D. R. (1956). *Taxonomy of educational objectives: cognitive domain.* New York: Longman.

BOBBITT, F. (1924). *How to make a curriculum.* New York: Houghton Mifflin.

BORDEAUX, D. B. (1982). How to get kids to do what's expected of them in the classroom. *Clearing House, 55,* 273–278.

BOURKE, W., & FURNISS, R. (1987) After school discussion helps problem students. *Phi Delta Kappan, 69,* 241–242.

BOYD, W. (1963). *The educational theory of Jean Jacques Rousseau.* New York: Russell and Russell.

BOYER, E. L. (1983). *High school: A report on secondary education in America.* New York: Harper and Row.

BOYER, E. L. (1988). *Report card on school reform.* New York: Carnegie Foundation for the Advancement of Teaching.

BRAMELD, T. (1956). *Toward a reconstructed philosophy of education.* New York: Dryden Press.

BRAMELD, T. (1965). *Education for the emerging age.* New York: Harper and Row.

BRANDT, R. (1985). On teaching and supervising: A conversation with Madeline Hunter. *Educational Leadership, 42,* 61–66.

BRANDT, R. (1988). On changing secondary schools: A conversation with Ted Sizer. *Educational Leadership, 45,* 30–36.

BRAUN, R. J. (1972). *Teachers and power*. New York: Simon and Schuster.

BRICKMAN, W. (1966). *John Dewey: Master educator*. New York: Atherton Press.

BRODINSKY, B. (1976). Twelve major events that shaped America's schools. *Phi Delta Kappan, 58,* 68–77.

BROOKOVER, W. B. (1987). Distortion and overgeneralization are no substitutes for sound research. *Phi Delta Kappan, 69,* 225–227.

BROOKOVER, W. B., & ERIKSON, E. L. (1975). *Sociology of education*. Homewood, IL: Dorsey Press.

BROWN, B. F. (1963). *The nongraded high school*. Englewood Cliffs, NJ: Prentice-Hall.

BROWN, B. F. (1980). A study of the school needs of children from one-parent families. *Phi Delta Kappan, 61,* 537.

BULLOCK, C. S., III, & ROGERS, H. R., JR. (1975). *Racial equality in America.* Pacific Palisades, CA: Goodyear Publishing.

BUTLER, J. D. (1968). *Four philosophies and their practice in education and religion.* New York: Harper and Row.

BUTTS, R. F. (1955). *A cultural history of Western education.* New York: McGraw-Hill.

BUTTS, R. F. (1978). *Public education in the United States.* New York: Holt, Rinehart and Winston.

BYRD, D., SHROCK, S., & CUMMINGS, O. (1986). Arthur Andersen & Co., society cooperative implications from a big-eight accounting firm. *Mirrors of Excellence, Association of Teacher Educators,* pp. 10–15.

CALLAHAN, J. J. & WILKINS, W. H. (1976). State school finance reform in the 1970s. In J. J. Callahan & W. H. Wilkins (Eds.), *School finance reform: A legislator's handbook,* pp. 1–11. Washington, DC: National Conference of State Legislatures.

CALLAHAN, J. J., & WILKINS, W. H. (Eds.) (1976). *School finance reform: A legislator's handbook.* Washington, DC: National Conference of State Legislatures.

CAMPBELL, R. F., CUNNINGHAM, L. L., NYSTRAND, R. O., & USDAN, M. D. (1980). *The organization and control of American schools,* 4th ed. Columbus, OH: Charles E. Merrill.

CARLSSON-PAIGE, N., & LEVIN, D. (1989). Advocating regulation of children's television. *Education Week,* Feb. 15, p. 32.

CARNEGIE FORUM. (May 1986). *A nation prepared: Teachers for the 21st century.* Report of the Task Force on Teaching as a Profession of the Carnegie Forum on Education and the Economy. Princeton, NJ: Carnegie Foundation.

The Carnegie Foundation for the Advancement of Teaching. (1988). *Report card on school reform: The teachers speak.* Princeton, NJ: Carnegie Foundation.

CARROLL, S. (1982). The search for equity in school finance. In W. W. McMahon & T. G. Geske (Eds.), *Financing education: Overcoming inefficiency and inequity,* pp. 237–266. Urbana: University of Illinois Press.

CHAPMAN, S. (1980). NEA seizes power: The teachers' coup. *The New Republic, 183*(15), 9–11.

Child abuse and neglect (1975). U.S. Department of Health, Education and Welfare, Publication No. (OHD) 75-30073, Vol. 1. Washington, DC: Superintendent of Documents, U.S. Government Printing Office.

Child abuse prevention and treatment act, (P.L. 93-247), 1974.

COMBS, A. W. (1988). New assumptions for educational reform. *Educational Leadership, 45,* 38–40.

COMMAGER, H. S. (1976). *The people and their schools,* Fastback No. 79. Bloomington, IN: Phi Delta Kappa Educational Foundation.

CONDRY, J. (1987) T.V. As educator. *Action in Teacher Education, 9* (2), 15–26.

COONS, J. E., & SUGARMAN, S. D. (1978). *Education by choice.* Berkeley: University of California Press.

COORSCH, R. (1982). The low down on alcoholism. *Consumer's Research Magazine, 65* (Oct.), 4.

CORTÉS, C. E. (1983). Multiethnic and global education: Partners for the eighties? *Phi Delta Kappan, 64,* 568–571.

COUNTS, G. (1932). *Dare the school build a new social order?* New York: John Day.

CREMIN, L. A. (1961). *The transformation of the school.* New York: Random House.

CREMIN, L. (1970). *American education: The colonial experience, 1607–1783.* New York: Harper.

CRUICKSHANK, D. R., & BROADBENT, F. W. (1968). *The simulation and analysis of problems of beginning teachers.* Brockport: New York State University.

CUBBERLEY, E. P. (1934). *Public education in the United States.* New York: Houghton Mifflin.

DASH, L. (1989). *When children want children: The urban crisis of teenage childbearing.* New York: William Morrow.

DASHIELL, R. (1982). *Report on the 66th annual convention of the American Federation of Teachers.* Washington, DC: National Education Association.

DAVIS, M. (1988). Prejudice is more than black and white. *Educational Leadership, 45,* 28

DEDRICK, C. V., HAWKES, R. R., & SMITH, J. K. (1981). Teacher stress: A descriptive study of the concerns. *National Association of Secondary School Principals Bulletin, 65,* 31–35.

DEFOE, J., & BREED, W. (1988). Youth and alcohol in television stories, with suggestions to the industry for alternative portrayals. *Adolescence, 23* (91), 533–549.

DEIBERT, J. P., & WALSH, K. J. (1981). Maslow and team organization. *Clearing House, 55,* 169–170.

DEROCHE, E. F., & KUJAWA, E. (1982). A survey of teacher supply and demand in the West. *Phi Delta Kappan, 63,* 566–567.

DEWEY, J. (1897). *My pedagogic creed.* New York: Kellogg.

DEWEY, J. (1916). *Democracy and education.* New York: Free Press (Macmillan).

DEWEY, J. (1933). *How we think.* Boston: D. C. Heath.

DEWEY, J. (1964). The way out of educational confusion. In R. D. Archambault (Ed.), *John Dewey on education,* pp. 422–426. New York: Random House. (Original pamphlet published by Harvard University Press in 1931.)

DIXON, M. (1978). *Women in class struggle.* San Francisco: Synthesis Publications.

DOGOLOFF, L. (1988). Drug prevention programs—Strong policies, strong actions. *Curriculum Report of the National Association of Secondary School Principals, 17,* 1–6.

DOLL, R. C. (1978). *Curriculum improvement.* Boston: Allyn and Bacon.

DONLEY, M. O. (1976). *Power to the teacher.* Bloomington: Indiana University Press.

DONMOYER, R. (1980). Educators and the legislative process. *Educational Leadership, 38,* 128–129.

DOYLE, D. P. (1982). Your meager slice of New Federalism could contain delicious options for schools. *The American School Board Journal, 169,* 23–25.

DUE, J. (1982). Shifting sources of financing education and the taxpayer revolt. In W. W. McMahon & T. G. Geske (Eds.), *Financing education: Overcoming inefficiency and inequity,* pp. 267–286. Urbana: University of Illinois Press.

DUPUIS, A. M. (1966). *Philosophy of education in historical perspective.* Chicago: Rand McNally.

DURKHEIM, E. (1897). *Suicide.* New York: Macmillan

EATON, W. E. (1975). *The American Federation of Teachers, 1916–1961: A history of the movement.* Carbondale and Edwardsville: Southern Illinois Press; London and Amsterdam: Feffer and Simons.

EBY, F. (1952). *The development of modern education.* New York: Prentice-Hall.

Economic report of the President. (1989). Washington DC: Superintendent of Documents, U.S. Government Printing Office.

EDELMAN, M. W. (1983). 1982 elections—Their implications for families and children in 1983. *Young Child, 38,* 25.

Educational Research Service, Inc. (1985a). *Fringe Benefits for Teachers in public schools, 1984–85.* Princeton, NJ.

Educational Research Service, Inc. (1985b). *Scheduled salaries for professional personnel in public schools, 1984–85: Part 1. National Survey and Wages in Public Schools.* Princeton, NJ.

ELAM, S. M. (1981). The National Education Association: Political powerhouse or paper tiger? *Phi Delta Kappan, 63,* 169–174.

ERICKSON, E. (1968). *Identity: Youth and crisis.* New York: Norton.

FANTINI, M.D. (1982). Toward a national public policy for urban education. *Phi Delta Kappan, 63,* 545.

FARMER, J. (1975). Toward equal educational opportunity. In *American Education,* pp. 16–20. Washington, DC: U.S. Department of Health, Education, and Welfare, Office of Education.

FARNHAM, J. F. (1983). Ethical ambiguity and the teaching of the Holocaust. *English Journal, 72,* 67.

First-year teacher support/induction program in California. (Nov. 1988). Encinitas Union School District, presentation at a national conference of the National Council of the States Inservice Education.

Florida Department of Education. (1985). Section 231-17 Rule 6A-5075, Florida Statutes, p. 306.

FLYGARE, T. J. (1977). *Collective bargaining in the public schools,* Fastback No. 99. Bloomington, IN: Phi Delta Kappa Educational Foundation.

FOXLEY, C. H. (1979). *Nonsexist counseling: Helping women and men re-define their roles.* Dubuque, IA: Kendall/Hunt.

FRASER, B. G. (1977). *The educator and child abuse.* Chicago: National Committee for Prevention of Child Abuse.

FRIEDMAN, M. S. (1953). *Martin Buber, the life of dialogue.* Chicago: University of Chicago Press.

FRIEDMAN, M. (1955). The role of government in education. In R. A. Solo (Ed.), *Economics and the public interest,* pp. 127–128. New Brunswick, NJ: Rutgers University Press.

FRIEDMANN, R. (1987). Changing how society views children. *Children Today,* July–Aug. pp. 10–14.

FRYMIER, J. (1988). *Graphs of America: Facts about crucial issues facing the United States today,* U.S. Census Data. Bloomington, IN: Phi Delta Kappa Educational Foundation.

FUHRMAN, S. (1980). School finance reform in the 1980's. *Educational Leadership, 38,* 122–124.

FUNK, F., SHARPE, D., & USHER, M. (1986). The Disney approach to people management and training. *Mirrors of Excellence, Association of Teacher Educators,* pp. 29–35.

FUTRELL, M. (1988). Teachers feel they have too little to say. *The Indianapolis Star,* Sept. 11, p. A–10.

GARFINKEL, B., et al. (1988). *Responding to adolescent suicide.* pp. 1–29. Bloomington, IN: Phi Delta Kappan Task Force on Adolescent Suicide, Phi Delta Kappan Educational Foundation.

GARMS, W. I., GUTHRIE, J. W., & PIERCE, L. C. (1978). *School finance: The economics and politics of public education.* Englewood Cliffs, NJ: Prentice-Hall.

GEORGE, P., & MOONEY, P. (1986). The Miami Boys Club Delinquency Prevention Program. *Educational Leadership,* pp. 76–78.

GESCHWIND, N. (1982). Why Orton was right. *Annals of Dyslexia, 32,* 13–30.

GIBSON, J. T. (1981). *Financing education: An administrative approach.* Washington, DC: University Press of America.

GIL, D. G. (1969). What schools can do about child abuse. *American Education, 5,* 3.

GLASSER, W. (1969). *Schools without failure.* New York: Harper and Row.

Global perspective for teacher education. (1983). Washington, DC: American Association of Colleges for Teacher Preparation.

GOLD, D. L. (1988). Bennett presents model plan for K–8 curriculum. *Education Week, 8,* 1 and 38–40.

GOOD, H. S., & TERRER, J. D. (1973). *A history of American education.* New York: Macmillan.

GOODHUE, T. (1988). Meeting concerns about sex abuse in schools. *Education Week,* pp. 56 and 48.

GOODLAD, J. I. (1984). *A place called school.* New York: McGraw-Hill.

GORMAN, S. F. (1982). Crackdown on drunk driving. *Senior Scholastic, 115,* 8.

GOUGH, P. (1976). *Sexism: New issue in American education,* Fastback No. 81. Bloomington, IN: Phi Delta Kappa Educational Foundation.

GRADY, J. B. (1980). Peer counseling in the middle school: A model program. *Phi Delta Kappan, 61,* 710.

GRANT, M. A. (1983). How to desegregate and like it. *Phi Delta Kappan, 63,* 539.

GREULING, J. W., & DEBLASSIE, R. R. (1980). Adolescent suicide. *Adolescence, 15* (Fall), 589–601.

GRUBER, F. C. (1973). *Historical and contemporary philosophies of education.* New York: Thomas Y. Crowell.

GUTEK, G. L. (1981). *Basic education: A historical perspective.* Bloomington, IN: Phi Delta Kappa Educational Foundation.

HALPERIN, S., et al. (1988). *The forgotten half: Non–college-bound Students in America.* William T. Grant Foundation Commission on Work, Family and Citizenship. *Phi Delta Kappan, 69,* 409–414.

HAMBERG, B. V. (1980). Peer counseling can identify and help troubled youngsters. *Phi Delta Kappan, 61,* 562.

HAMLIN, K., & HERING, K (1988). Help for the first-year teacher: Mentor, buddy, or both? *National Association of Secondary School Principals Bulletin,* Sept. pp. 125–127.

HARMIN, M. (1977). *What I've learned about values education,* Fastback No. 91. Bloomington, IN: Phi Delta Kappa Educational Foundation.

HARMON, S. B. (1983). Teaming: A concept that works. *Phi Delta Kappan, 64,* 366–367.

HARRIS, J., HEID, C., INGERSOLL, G., & PUGH, R. (1985). *Brown to Buckley: A study of desegregation, integration, and student attitudes in seven Marion County, Indiana School Districts.* Indianapolis/Bloomington, IN: Indiana University, Center for Urban and Multicultural Education Office of School Programs.

HARTLEY, H. J. (1981). 1980's education scenario: From tax revolt to governance reform. *Music Educators Journal, 67,* 35–39.

HASS, G. (1983). *Curriculum planning.* Boston: Allyn and Bacon.

HAVIGHURST, R. J. (1948). *Developmental tasks and education.* New York: Longmans Green.

HAWLEY, R. (1987). Schoolchildren and drugs: The fancy that has not passed. *Phi Delta Kappan, 68,* K1–K8.

HAWLEY, W. D. (1983). Achieving quality integrated education—With or without federal help. *Phi Delta Kappan, 64,* 355–356.

HEDIN, D., & CONRAD, D. (1980). Changes in children and youth over two decades: The perceptions of teachers. *Phi Delta Kappan, 61,* 703.

HERMAN, J. J. (1977). *Administrator's practical guide to school finance.* West Nyack, NJ: Parker.

HICKS, J. D. (1957). *The federal union,* 3rd ed. Cambridge, MA: Riverside Press.

HITZ, R., & ROPER, S. (1986). The teacher's first year: Implications for teacher educators. *Action in Teacher Education, 8* (3), 65–71.

HOLMES GROUP, INC. (1986). *Tomorrow's teachers: A report of the Holmes group,* pp. 1–86. East Lansing, MI: Holmes Group.

HONESTSCHLAGER, D., & COHEN, M. (1988). The governors restructive schools. *Educational Leadership, 45,* 42–43.

HOOK, S. (1966). John Dewey: His philosophy of education. In R. D. Archambault (Ed.), *Dewey on education: Appraisals,* pp. 127–159. New York: Random House.

How should schools be ruled? (1980). *Educational Leadership, 38,* 102–105.

HUDELSON, S. (1987). The role of native language literacy in the education of language for minority children. *Language Arts, 64* (8), 827–841.

HUNTER, M. (1985). What's wrong with Madeline Hunter? *Educational Leadership, 42,* 57–60.

HUTCHINS, R. M. (1936). *The higher learning in America.* New Haven, CT: Yale University Press.

Indiana Department of Public Instruction, Division of School Finance. (1981). *Digest of public school finance in Indiana: 1981–83 Biennium.* Indianapolis: Indiana Department of Public Instruction.

INLOW, G. (1966). *The emergent in curriculum.* New York: Wiley.

JACQUES, M. J. (1982). The Metropolitan Youth Education Center: A Colorado solution to the problem of high school dropouts. *Phi Delta Kappan, 64,* 136–137.

JAMES, W. (1890). *The principles of psychology.* New York: Holt.

JAMES, W. (1898). *Talks to teachers.* New York: Holt.

JENCKS, C. (1972). *Inequality.* New York: Basic Books.

JOHNS, R. L., & MORPHET, E. L. (1975). *The economics and financing of education: A systems approach,* 3rd ed. Englewood Cliffs, NJ: Prentice-Hall.

JOHNSON, C. (1963). *Old-time schools and school books.* New York: Dover.

JOHNSON, J., & BENEGAR, J. (1981). *Global issues in the curriculum grades 5–8.* Boulder, CO: Social Science Education Consortium, Inc., IRIC Clearing House for Social Studies/Social Science Education, Global Perspective in Education.

KAMMANN, R. (1972). The case for making each school in your district different and letting parents choose the one that's best for their child. *American School Board Journal, 159,* 37–38.

KANE, V. (1988). State tax collections in 1987. In *Book of the States* (1988–1989 edition), Vol. 27. Lexington, KY: Council of State Governments.

KATZ, M. S. (1976). *A history of compulsory education laws.* Bloomington, IN: Phi Delta Kappa Educational Foundation.

KEESHAN, B. (1983). Families and television. *Young Child, 38,* 55.

KEMP, J. E. (1977). *Instructional design.* Belmont, CA: Fearon–Pitman.

KEPPEL, F., & MESSERLI, J. (1975). Horace Mann's client. *American Education, 11,* 18–21.

KERMAN, S. (1979). Teacher expectations and student achievement. *Phi Delta Kappan, 60,* 716–718.

KERMAN, S., & MARTIN, M. (1980). *Teacher expectations and student achievement.* Bloomington, IN: Phi Delta Kappa Educational Foundation.

KILPATRICK, W. H. (1918). *The project method.* New York: Teachers' College, Columbia University.

KILPATRICK, W. H. (1925). *Foundations of method.* New York: Macmillan.

KIRST, M. W. (1982). Why there's a financial squeeze on schools and what to do about it. *Learning, 10,* 70–72.

KIRST, M. W., & GARMS W. I. (1980). Public school finance in 1980's. *Education Digest, 46,* 5–8.

KNELLER, G. F. (1971). *Introduction to the philosophy of education.* New York: Wiley.

KOHLBERG, L. (1973). The claim to moral adequacy of a highest stage of moral judgment. *Journal of Philosophy, 70,* 630–646.

KRAUSHAAR, O. F. (1976). *Private schools: From the Puritans to the present.* Bloomington, IN: Phi Delta Kappa Educational Foundation.

KROHNE, P. W. (1982). *An analysis of the state board of education in Indiana—Its composition, organization, and operation, and areas of jurisdiction.* Unpublished doctoral dissertation, Indiana University, Bloomington.

LANDSMAN, L. (1988). 10 resolutions for teachers. *Phi Delta Kappan, 69,* 373–374.

LANIER, J., AND FEATHERSTONE, J. (1988). A new commitment to teacher education. *Educational Leadership, 46,* 18–22.

LAPOINTE, A. E., & MARTINEZ, M. E. (1988). Aims, equity, and access in computer education. *Phi Delta Kappan, 70,* 59–61.

LASLEY, T. J. (1980). Preservice teacher beliefs about teaching. *Journal of Teacher Education, 31,* 38–41.

LAUDERDALE, W. B. (1981). *Progressive education: Lessons from three schools.* Bloomington, IN: Phi Delta Kappa Educational Foundation.

LEE, S., BRYANT, S., NOONAN, N., & PLIONIS, E. (1987). Keeping youth in school: A public–private collaboration. *Children Today,* July-Aug., pp. 15–20.

LEONARD, M. (1982). Reaganomics and K–12 education: Some responses from the private sector. *Phi Delta Kappan, 63,* 600–602.

LESGOLD, A. M. (1986). Preparing children for a computer-rich world. *Educational Leadership, 43,* 7–11.

LIEBERMAN, A. (1988). Expanding the leadership team. *Educational Leadership. 45,* 4–9.

LINDSEY, P., & LINDSEY, O. (1974). *Breaking the bonds of racism.* Homewood, IL: ETC Publications.

MAEROFF, G. (1988). Withered hopes, stillborn dreams: The dismal panorama of urban schools. *Phi Delta Kappan, 69,* 633–638.

MAGNUSON, E. (1983). Child abuse: The ultimate betrayal. *Time, 122* (Sept. 5), 20–22.

Making common cause: Integrating academic and vocational studies. (1980). *Curriculum Report, 18,* 1–8.

MASLOW, A. H. (1954). *Motivation and personality.* New York: Harper and Row.

MASON, K. (1979). Responsibility for what's on the tube. *Business Week,* No. 2598 (Aug. 13).

MATTHEWS, D. B. (1989). *Stress management training: A component in teacher education.* Paper presented at the Annual Conference of the Association of Teacher Educators, St. Louis, MO, Feb. 18–22, 1989.

MCINTIRE, R. G., HUGHES, L. W., & SAY, M. W. (1982). Houston's successful desegregation plan. *Phi Delta Kappan, 63,* 538.

MCKENRY, P. C., TISHLER, C. L. & CHRISTMAN, K. L. (1980). Adolescent suicide and the classroom teacher. *Education Digest, 46,* 43–45.

MCKIBBIN, M. (1988). Alternative teacher certification programs. *Educational Leadership, 46,* 32–35.

MCMAHON, W. W., & GESKE, T. G. (EDS.) (1982). *Financing education: Overcoming inefficiency and inequity.* Urbana: University of Illinois Press.

MEYER, A. E. (1967). *An educational history of the American people,* 2nd ed. New York: McGraw-Hill.

MEYER, A. E. (1975). *Grandmasters of educational thought.* New York: McGraw-Hill.

MICHAELS, K. (1988). Caution: Second wave reform taking place. *Educational Leadership, 45,* 3.

MIEL, A., & KIESTER, E., JR. (1967). *The shortchanged children of suburbia.* New York: American Jewish Committee.

MITCHELL, D., & PETERS, M. (1988). A stronger profession through appropriate teacher incentives. *Educational Leadership, 46,* 74–78.

MONROE, P. (1940). *Founding of the American public school system.* New York: Macmillan.

MONTAGU, A. (1983). My idea of education. In G. Hass (Ed.), *Curriculum planning: A new approach,* pp. 121–123. Boston: Allyn and Bacon.

MOORE, M. (1982). How I killed someone. *Washington Post,* Mar. 13, p. 10.

MOOREFIELD, S. (1972). One woman's fight. *American Education, 10,* 30–31.

MURPHY, E. M. (1983). *The environment to come: A global summary.* Washington, DC: Population Reference Bureau.

MURPHY, J., & HALLINGER, P. (1985). Effective high schools—What are the common characteristics? *NASSP Bulletin, 69,* 18–22.

MYERS, P. E. (1981). The principal and the beginning teacher. *National Association of Secondary School Principals Bulletin, 65* (444), 70–75.

National Center for Education Statistics. (1982). *Digest of education statistics 1982.* Washington, DC: U.S. Department of Education.

National Center for Education Statistics. (1988a). *Digest of education statistics.* Washington, DC: U.S. Department of Education, Office of Educational Research and Improvement.

National Center for Education Statistics. (1988b). *The condition of education: Elementary and secondary education,* Vol. 1. Washington, DC: U.S. Department of Education.

National Center for Education Statistics and Bureau of Labor Statistics. (1980–1981). *Occupational outlook handbook: Teaching occupations.* Washington, DC: U.S. Government Printing Office.

National Commission on Excellence in Education. (1983). *A nation at risk: The imperatives for education reform.* Washington, DC: U.S. Government Printing Office.

National Education Association. (1970). *Estimates of school statistics, 1970–71.* Washington, DC.

National Education Association. (1979). *Estimates of school statistics, 1979–80.* Washington, DC.

National Education Association. (1983). *Rankings of the states, 1982,* National Education Association Research Memo. Washington, DC.

National Education Association. (1988). *Estimates of school statistics, 1987–88* as provided by the State Department of Education, p. 5.

National Science Board Commission on Precollege Education in Mathematics, Science and Technology. (1982). *Educating Americans for the 21st Century,* pp. 25–26, 96–99, 220–223.

NEA handbook, 1988–1989. Washington, DC: National Education Association.

NIETO, C. (1986). The California challenge: Preparing teachers for a growing Hispanic population. *Action in Teacher Education,* Spring, pp. 1–8.

NORTON, A., (1987). Families and children in the year 2000. *Children Today,* July–Aug., pp. 6–9.

NUNN, G. D., & PARISH, T. S. (1982). Personal and familial adjustments as a function of family type. *Phi Delta Kappan, 64,* 141.

ODDEN, A., & AUGENBLICK, J. (1981). State policy makers view school finance in the 1980's. *Education Digest, 46,* 13–15.

ORLOSKY, D. E. (Ed.) (1988). *Society, schools, and teacher preparation,* a Report to the Commission on the Future Education of Teachers (Teacher Education Monograph No. 9). Washington, DC: ERIC Clearinghouse on Teacher Education.

O'REILLY, J. (1983). New insight into alcoholism. *Time, 121,* (Apr. 25) p. 25.

ORLICH, D. (1989). Education reforms: Mistakes, misconceptions, miscues. *Phi Delta Kappan, 70,* 512–517.

ORNSTEIN, A. C. (1980). Teacher salaries, past, present, future. *Phi Delta Kappan, 61,* 677–679.

OVANDO, C. J. (1983). Bilingual/bicultural education: Its legacy and its future. *Phi Delta Kappan, 64,* 564–568.

OVERTON, B. (1979). *The abused or neglected child: How can we help?* Speech given to various professional gatherings, Fort Benjamin Harrison Help Center, Indianapolis, IN.

OZMON, H., & CRAVER, S. (1972). *Busing: A moral issue,* Fastback No. 7. Bloomington, IN: Phi Delta Kappa Educational Foundation.

PARKER, J. L. (1986). Papert points the way. *Electronic Education, 6,* 10–12.

PASKE, G. H. (1985–1986). The failure of indoctrination: A response to Wynne. *Phi Delta Kappan, 43,* 11–12.

PATTERSON, J. H. (1987). Computers and low achievers: Looking beyond drill and practice. *Electronic Education, 6,* 38.

PEARSON, J. B., & FULLER, E. (Eds.) (1969). *Education in the states: Historical development and outlook.* Washington, DC: National Education Association.

PESTALOZZI, J. H. (1894). *How Gertrude teaches her children* (L. E. Holland, Trans.). Syracuse, NY: George Allen and Unwin. (Original work published in 1801.)

PFEFFER, C. R. (1981). Suicidal behavior of children. *Exceptional Children, 48,* 170–172.

PIAGET, J. (1952). Jean Piaget. In C. A. Murchison (Ed.), *A history of psychology in autobiography,* Vol. 4. Worcester, MA: Clark University Press.

PIAGET, J. (1957). *John Amos Comenius.* Paris: United Nations Educational, Scientific, and Cultural Organization.

PIAGET, J., & INHELDER, B. (1969). *The psychology of the child.* New York: Basic Books.

PINKNEY, H. B. (1980). American dilemma: Financing public education. *National Association of Secondary School Principals Bulletin, 64* (439), 68–73.

PIPHO, C. (1980). State legislatures and the schools. *Educational Leadership, 38,* 125–127.

PIPHO, C. (1981). Rich states, poor states. *Phi Delta Kappan, 62,* 722–723.

PLATO. (1929). *The Republic* (A. D. Lindsay, Trans.). London: J. M. Dent (Original work written circa 350 B.C.)

PRESTON, D. J. (1980). *Young Frederick Douglass, the Maryland years.* Baltimore: Johns Hopkins University Press.

Progressive education: Lessons from three schools, Fastback No. 166. (1981). Bloomington, IN: Phi Delta Kappa Educational Foundation.

PURSELL, W. M. (1976). *A Conservative School: The A+ School in Cupertino,* Fastback No. 67. Bloomington, IN: Phi Delta Kappa Educational Foundation.

QUATTLEBAUM, C. A. (1951). *Federal educational activities and educational issues before Congress,* 3 vols. Washington, DC: U.S. Government Printing Office.

The Random House college dictionary, rev. ed. (1980). New York: Random House.

RATHS, L., HARMIN, M., & SIMON, S. (1966). *Values and teaching.* Columbus, OH: Charles E. Merrill.

RAYWID, M. A. (1981). The first decade of public school alternatives. *Phi Delta Kappan, 62,* 551–554.

REED, D. (1986). Wanted: More black education students. *Action in Teacher Education,* Spring, pp. 31–36.

RHODES, F. (May 1988). *One-third of a nation. A Report of the Commission on Minority Participation in Education and American Life,* pp. 1–33.

ROBERTSON, N. L., & ROBERTSON, B. T. (1977). *Education in South Africa,* Fastback No. 90. Bloomington, IN: Phi Delta Kappa Educational Foundation.

ROLAND, T., & MCGUIRE, C. (1968). The development of intelligent behavior: Jean Piaget. *Psychology in the Schools, 5,* 47–52.

ROSEN, F. B. (1968). *Philosophic systems and education.* Columbus, OH: Charles E. Merrill.

ROSSI, A. S. (1971). Equality between the sexes: An immodest proposal. In M. H. Garskof (Ed.), *Roles women play: Readings toward women's liberation.* Belmont, CA: Brooks/Cole.

ROUSSEAU, J-J. (1911). *Émile* (B. Foxley, Trans.). London: J. M. Dent. (Original work published in 1762.)

ROUSSEAU, J-J. (1913). *The social contract* (G. D. H. Cole, Trans.). London: J. M. Dent. (Original work published in 1762.)

RUGG, H. O. (1931). *Culture and education in America.* New York: Harcourt Brace.

SANCHEZ, N. (1987). Bilingual education: A barrier to achievement. *Bilingual Education,* Dec., pp. 42–43.

SAVAGE, D. G. (1980). Education of a new department. *Educational Leadership, 38,* 117–118.

SCHEFFLER, I. (1966). Educational liberalism and Dewey's philosophy. In R. D. Archambault (Ed.), *Dewey on eduction: Appraisals,* pp. 96–110. New York: Random House.

SCHLECHTY, P., & INGWERSON, D.   (1987). A proposed incentive system for Jefferson County teachers. *Phi Delta Kappan*, Apr. 585–590.

SCHLEMMER, P.   (1981). The zoo of school. Evolution of an alternative. *Phi Delta Kappan, 62*, 558–560.

The school's role in community life.   (1982). *Contemporary Education, 53*(3), 123–125. (Reprinted from *School and Community*, Oct. 1964.)

SEDINGER, C.   (1988). *The first step in professional growth and development: The beginning teacher program in Broward County, Ft. Lauderdale, Florida, p. 3.* Broward County Schools: Florida.

SEIBEL, M., & MURRAY, J.   (1988). Early prevention of adolescent suicide. *Educational Leadership, 45*, 48–51.

SELDEN, H. L.   (1975). Kalamazoo and high school too. *American Education, 11*, 22–24.

SELDEN, J.   (1975). Learning by the numbers. *American Education, 11*, 25–27.

SELIGSON, M.   (1986). Child care for the school-aged child. *Phi Delta Kappan, 67*, 637–640.

Senate & House of Representatives.   (1989). *Congressional resolution designating the month of March as "Women's History Month."* Santa Rosa, CA: National Women's History Project.

SHANE, H.   (1981). Significant writings that have influenced the curriculum: 1906–81. *Phi Delta Kappan, 62*, 311–314.

SHANE, H. G.   (1983). The silicon age. II. Living and learning in an information epoch. *Phi Delta Kappan, 65*, 126–129.

SMITH, A. D., & REID, W. J.   (1982). Family role revolution. *Journal of Educational Social Work, 18*, 51–57.

SMITH, E. J.   (1981). Adolescent suicide: A growing problem for the school and family. *Urban Education, 16*, 279–296.

SNITZER, H.   (1983). A. S. Neill remembered. *Educational Leadership, 41*, 56.

SPENCER, H.   (1861). *Education: Intellectual, moral, and physical.* New York: Appleton.

SPENCER, S.   (1979). Childhood's end. *Harper's magazine, 259*, 16–19.

STEDMAN, L. C.   (1987). It's time we changed the effective schools formula. *Phi Delta Kappan*, Nov., pp. 215–223.

STEEVES, F. L., & ENGLISH, F. W.   (1978). *Secondary curriculum for a changing world.* Columbus, OH: Charles E. Merrill.

STRONG, G.   (1983). It's time to get tough on alcohol and drug abuse in schools. *American School Board Journal, 170*, 23–24.

STRONGE, J.   (1987). Think of this. *Electronic Education, 6*, 18–19.

Subcommittee on Juvenile Justice of the Committee on the Constitution, U.S. Senate.   (1981). *Oversight hearing to fashion programs to remove the juvenile from a crime cycle*, Oct. 22, 1981, Serial No. j-97-70.

SUMMERS, A.   (1979). Angels in purgatory: Los Angeles awaits two decisions on mandatory busing for desegregation. *Phi Delta Kappan, 60*, 718–723.

The Supreme Court, the limits that create liberty and the liberty that creates limits.   (1964). *Time* (Oct. 9), pp. 48–58.

TARCHER, J.   (1982) *Return to excellence in education and quality in our classrooms Marva Collins' way.* New York: St. Martin's Press.

The Carnegie Foundation for the Advancement of Teaching. (1988). *Report card on school reform: The teachers speak.* Princeton, NJ: Carnegie Foundation.

The teacher and the drug scene, Fastback No. 26. (1973). Bloomington, IN: Phi Delta Kappa Educational Foundation.

TEETER, R. (1983). *The opening up of American education.* Lanham, MD: University Press of America.

TERMAN, L. M., & CHILDS, H. G. (1912). A tentative revision and extension of the Binet–Simon measuring scale of intelligence. *Journal of Educational Psychology, 3,* 61–74, 133–143, 198–208, 277–289.

TOFFLER, A. (1970). *Future shock.* New York: Random House.

TOFFLER, A. (1980). *The third wave.* New York: Morrow.

TRUMP, J. L. (1968). *Secondary school curriculum improvement.* Boston: Allyn and Bacon.

TYACK, D. B. (1974). *The one best system.* Cambridge, MA: Harvard University Press.

TYLER, R. W. (1949). *Basic principles of curriculum and instruction.* Chicago: University of Chicago Press.

TYLER, R. W. (1981). The U.S. vs. the world: A comparison of educational performance. *Phi Delta Kappan, 62,* 207–310.

TYLER, R. W. (1987). Education reforms. *Phi Delta Kappan, 69,* 227–280.

Uniform Crime Reports for the United States. (1987). Federal Bureau of Investigation, U.S. Department of Justice, Washington, DC.

U.S. Bureau of the Census. (1971). *Residential finance survey, 1970.* Washington, DC: U.S. Government Printing Office.

U.S. Bureau of the Census. (1980). *State government tax collections in 1980.* Washington, DC: U.S. Government Printing Office.

U.S. Department of Commerce, Bureau of the Census. (1984). *Statistical abstract of the United States.* Washington, DC: U.S. Government Printing Office.

U.S. Department of Commerce, Bureau of the Census. (1985). *Statistical abstract of the United States.* Washington, DC: U.S. Government Printing Office.

U.S. Department of Health and Human Services. (1987). *National trends in drug use among American high school students and young adults, 1975–1986.* Rockville, MD: National Institute on Drug Abuse.

U.S. Department of Health and Human Services, Public Health Service, Alcohol, Drug Abuse, and Mental Health Administration. (1982). *Television and behavior: Ten years of scientific progress and implications for the eighties,* Summary Report, Vol. 1. Washington, DC: Superintendent of Documents, U.S. Government Printing Office.

U.S. Department of Labor (1985). Major Job and Training Program. *Congressional Digest,* Apr., pp. 102 and 103.

U.S. Public Health Service. (1972). *Television and growing up: The impact of televised violence.* Washington, DC: U.S. Government Printing Office.

VALDEZ, G. (1986). Realizing the potential of educational technology. *Educational Leadership, 43,* 4–6.

VALVERDE, L. A. (1978). *Bilingual education for Latinos.* Washington, DC: Association for Supervision and Curriculum Development

Violence in schools: Causes and remedies, Fastback No. 46. (1974). Bloomington, IN: Phi Delta Kappa Educational Foundation.

Vision of reform: Implications for the education profession. (Fall 1986). The Report of the ATE Blue Ribbon Task Force, John Sikula, Chair. Reston, VA: Association of Teacher Educators.

WATSON, G. (1961). *What psychology can we trust?* New York: Teacher College Press.

WATTS, D. (1986). Alternative routes to teacher certification: A dangerous trend. *Action in teacher education*, Summer, pp. 25–29.

WESLEY, E. B. (1957). *NEA: The first hundred years*. New York: Harper and Brothers.

WEST, A. M. (1980). *The National Education Association: The power base for education*. New York: Free Press (Macmillan).

WHITEHEAD, A. N. (1929). *The aims of education*. New York: Macmillan.

WILES, J., & BONDI, J. C. (1984). *Curriculum development: A guide to practice*. Columbus, OH: Charles E. Merrill.

WILLIAMS, J. (1988). *Eyes on the prize*. Penguin Books.

WILLIE, C. V. (1984). *Old and new ideas about school desegregation*. Cambridge, MA: Harvard University Graduate School of Education.

WISE, A. E. (1965). Is denial of equal educational opportunity constitutional? *Administrator's Notebook, 13,* 1–4.

WISE, A. E. (1981). School finance reform: A personal statement. *The Educational Forum, 45,* 485–492.

YANKELOVICH, D, & KAAGAN, L. (1979). Two views on Proposition 13: One year later—What it is and what it isn't. *Social Policy, 10,* 19–23.

Glossary

Absolute Standard A standard of measurement in which arbitrary points are established for obtaining each letter grade. For example, if 70% is the lowest passing grade, all students who receive 70% or higher pass, but all students who receive less than 70% fail.

Academic Freedom The freedom or authority that teachers should have to discuss all aspects of a subject with their students without imposing their own viewpoints on students. It involves both freedom and responsibility (to consider laws, community standards, and age or capacity of the students).

Academy The second type of secondary school established in the colonies; founded in 1751 by Benjamin Franklin. The curriculum of these schools was more practical and less classical.

Accommodation An individual's reaction to the external environment or the outside world as described by Jean Piaget.

Accountability (1) Requirement that one give an explanation of the results of one's works; that is, a teacher must answer for the learning or lack of learning of his or her students. (2) Defining the responsibility for students' optimal learning per money expended for education.

Adaptive Purpose Purpose of education that is fulfilled when teachers help students to acquire the skills and knowledge and make the emotional adjustment needed to relate successfully to themselves and their world.

Additives Sections or units on minorities that are added to the mainstream curriculum, rather than integrated with the contributions of all races and ethnic minorities into the mainstream curriculum.

Adversarial Relationship Relationship characterized by disagreement between two parties, who promote their own views as to how issues should be resolved.

Affiliate Subgroup or branch of a state or national organization, for example, a state teachers' organization may be a branch of the National Education Association.

Agency Shop Provision Labor term used to describe a union that all employees must join and pay dues to.

Alienation Mental change preventing the person affected from leading a normal existence.

Alternative Certification   State-approved plan that legally enables a person to teach whether or not the person has gone through the normal channels of teacher training and has been state certified.

Alternative School Movement   Group of nontraditional schools with a curriculum that is considered more relevant to student needs and an approach that attempts to humanize the educational process.

Anti-discrimination Laws   Laws passed by the states and Congress to provide opportunities for members of minority groups to secure adequate employment, and to create public attitudes that reject discriminatory practices.

Arbitration   Procedure of the collective bargaining process in which both parties appoint a third party to hear both sides of the issues, study the situation, and make a decision that is binding on both parties.

Asian-Americans   Americans related to people from countries of the Far East.

Assault   Causing fear or apprehension of battery, which is intentional touching without permission or privilege.

Assessed Valuation   Official estimate of the value of property for the purpose of taxation.

Assimilation   Internalizing of a concept as described by Jean Piaget.

Assumption of Risk   Defense against tort liability in which players and spectators alike assume the normal risks involved in an athletic contest. The age, intelligence, sex, physical characteristics, and training of each person are important factors in determining the assumption of risk.

Attention Deficit Disorder (ADD)   Disorder characterized by inability or less ability to learn. A person with a learning disability is said to have attention deficit disorder.

Average Daily Attendance (ADA)   Daily attendance based on number of students present, not just enrolled, in a school.

Average Daily Membership (ADM)   Daily attendance based on students enrolled in the school district on a given day.

Axiology   Branch of philosophy concerned with ethics (what is right) and aesthetics (what is beautiful).

Back-to-Basics   A movement emphasizing the 3Rs and the essentials of education that began in the the 1950s and was reborn in the 1980s.

Battery   Intentional touching of a person, his or her eyeglasses, or his or her clothing without consent or privilege.

Behavioral Objectives   Objectives or goals written from the student's point of view and evaluated in terms of observed changes in the student's behavior. Behavioral objectives usually include the action or behavior to be specified, the conditions and restrictions under which the behavior will be accomplished, and the criteria of acceptable performance.

Biculturalism   Existence of two cultures in one nation.

Bilingualism   Ability to speak two languages, usually the native language and the language of the adopted country.

Blacks   Persons of Afro-American descent.

Block Grants   Federal funds appropriated in broad areas to give local and state leaders in education more flexibility in meeting the needs of the levels.

Breach of Contract   Termination of a contract by one of the contracting parties without the consent of the other party.

Broad Discretion   Leeway in the scope of decision making, allowing for wide interpretation of the powers to make proposals.

Building Drug-Free Schools   Comprehensive drug education program (grades K–12) that is designed to eliminate drugs in schools by implementing policies system-wide.

Career Ladder   Program that provides for the professional advancement of teachers from student teaching or internships through beginning teacher placement to master teacher status, with pay and responsibility increasing with each step on this ladder.

Carnegie Forum   Group appointed by the Carnegie Foundation with a ten-year agenda to explore the link between economic growth and education of the people who will make that growth possible, including teachers.

Categorical Aid   Federal funds appropriated for specific programs, such a special education, not general aid to education.

Checks and Balances   Power of one branch of government to exercise certain control over other branches of government, for example, the veto that the president of the United States has over laws passed by the U.S. Congress.

Clinical Theory of Instruction   Framework for teaching, developed by Madeline Hunter, based upon the premise that the teacher is a decision maker.

Coherence Theory of Truth   Hegel's belief that an individual fact or idea has no value until it fits into a system with other facts and ideas.

Collective Bargaining   Process in which school boards negotiate with organizations representing teachers in a step-by-step manner clearly spelled out by state law, on issues specifically mentioned in the law.

Collegial Participatory School Environment   School setting in which all teachers are empowered to make crucial decisions about student learning and in which teachers and administrators work together equally to prevent problems, solve problems, and plan for student learning.

Comparative Negligence   Proration of damages according to the amount that each party's acts contributed to the damage, loss, or injury.

Composite Indicators of Changes in Average Salaries and Wages Paid by Public School Systems (CIC)   Index of all the variations in salaries and wages paid by the public schools and how they change.

Compulsory Attendance Laws   State laws requiring students to attend school for a specific number of years to attain at least the minimum education necessary to be an enlightened citizen.

Computer Literacy   Ability to use the computer on a beginning level with simple computer commands and programs.

Concrete-Operational Stage   Piaget's development stage at which a child solves a variety of tasks. For example, a child must recognize that differences in the size of vessels storing liquid do not indicate changes in the volume of liquid.

Consumer Price Index (CPI)   Index measuring the change in the cost of typical wage-earner purchases of goods and services expressed as a percentage of the cost of goods and services in some specified base period.

Continuing-Contract Law   Law that gives teachers not notified by May 1 of their dismissal the right to claim a contract at their proper place on the salary schedule for the next school year.

Contributory Negligence   Behavior on the part of the plaintiff contributing to the injury or damage that he or she has suffered, such as behavior not conforming to the standard required for her or his own protection.

Cooperating Teacher   Classroom teacher paid and assigned by the university to guide, direct, or facilitate the training of a preservice teacher at a school building location.

Copybooks   Books made by students in which they copied lessons and practiced penmanship.

Corporal Punishment   Physical discipline, as when an adult (teacher, parent, and others) strikes a child or student with his or her hand, a paddle, or another instrument to punish the child for misbehavior.

Counterproposals   Set of propositions that one party in a labor dispute makes in response to earlier propositions by the other party.

Counter-Reformation   Reform movement in the Roman Catholic Church that followed the Protestant Reformation. The Jesuits are an example of this movement.

Criterion-Referenced Testing   Tests that measure how well a student attains the required level of comprehension and competence specified for each objective pursued.

Culturally Pluralistic Society   Existence of a variety of cultural and ethnic groups in one society, as in the United States.

Cultural Pluralism   The opportunity of all ethnic and social groups to develop their own cultural experiences within a single society.

Dame School   Early colonial school, with origins in England, that was run by ladies (hence the name) who made extra money by taking children into their homes and teaching them the basic fundamentals.

Delegated Powers   Specific powers granted to the federal government in the U.S. Constitution.

Department of Education   A cabinet level department of the Executive Branch of the Federal Government established in 1979 to replace the former Office of Education in the Department of Health, Education and Welfare.

Developmental Purpose   Purpose of education that is fulfilled when students are guided to optimum growth at each maturational level.

Discretionary Power   Power of local and state education officials to determine how federal funds are spent.

Due Process   Legal steps that must be taken if a student is to be suspended or expelled, such as written notice, a hearing, and counsel of a lawyer.

Dyscalculia   Impairment of the ability to do mathematical problems because of brain injury or disease.

Dysfunctional Family   Family that does not operate within the norms of society because of an impairment, for example, alcoholism, divorce.

Dysgraphia   Inability to write properly.

Dyslexia   Inability to read understandingly.

Eclectic Philosophy of Education Personal philosophy of education developed by combining parts of various philosophies.

Educating Americans for the 21st Century Report issued in 1982 on the condition of science and mathematics education in the United States. The problems were surveyed and solutions offered.

Effective Schools Movement Movement in education initiated by Wilbur Brookover and others to study the characteristics of schools that produce the best learners as certified by standardized achievement tests. This movement emphasized vision of purpose, high standards and expectations, and the belief that all students are capable of learning if given the proper instruction.

Egalitarian Ethic Theory that all teachers are equal, no matter what their experience, ability, or education, and that all teachers should make classroom decisions on their own without input from other educators.

Egalitarian Marriage Model of an ideal family unit in which the husband and wife share all roles in the household equally.

Elastic Clause Common name for Article I, Section 8, of the U.S. Constitution. (See *General Welfare Clause* in this glossary.) Through interpretation by the federal courts, many powers have been implied from this General Welfare or Elastic Clause.

Elitists Any group that maintains itself by holding a certain power over others, as opposed to a group that maintains itself by its own merit. For example, kings and queens in the past maintained an elite caste (nobles) around them.

Empowerment Granting teachers the power to make crucial decisions on teaching and learning at the local school or classroom level, instead of simply implementing decisions made by the administrative hierarchy.

Enlightenment A European intellectual movement in the seventeenth and eighteenth centuries that instigated revolutionary developments in art, philosophy, and politics through the use of reason, the power by which man understands the universe and improves his own condition.

Epistemology Branch of philosophy concerned with truth and knowledge.

Essentialism Educational philosophy that stresses the 3Rs and a return to the basics. The focus is on the present and on using basic skills to help students adjust to the real world.

Ethnic Diversity Existence in one population of members of a variety of ethnic groups.

Ethnic Enclave Group of people of the same ethnicity or national origin who remain distinct rather than blend or "melt" in with others.

Ethnic Encapsulation Tendency to participate primarily in one's own ethnic community and, often, the tendency to believe that one's ethnic group is superior to other ethnic groups.

Ethnic Groups Groups characterized by identical national origin, religion, race, and/or other cultural characteristics, for example, blacks, Hispanics, and Native Americans.

Ethnocentric Characterized by or based on the attitude that one's own group is superior to other groups.

Exclusive Bargaining Rights Legal approval of one bargaining group or union as representing all of the employees in a bargaining unit, usually the school district; obtained by an election supervised by a Public Employee Relations Board.

Existential Qualities   Qualities such as hope, courage, and love of humankind, which are generally fostered through myths, fairy tales, novels, drama, and poetry.

Existentialism   Philosophy that maintains that existence (being) precedes essence (meaning). It stresses personal choice and making the most of the situation in which one finds oneself.

Experimental Design   Research design used to measure the value of curriculum innovations that is relatively free from error. The experimental design uses a randomized sample, a control group, and an experimental group.

Expulsion   Exclusion from school for the remainder of the term or school year.

Facilitators of Learning   Teachers or other individuals who set conditions under which students can do most, if not all, of their own learning.

Fact Finding   Process in which a neutral party examines the issues, makes recommendations, and publicizes the recommendations. This process is not binding on either party, but mobilizes public awareness and support for the fact finder's recommendations.

Fair Local Contribution   Amount generated by a state-mandated local property tax.

Fair Representation   Responsibility of a union, once it has gained exclusive bargaining rights, to represent all dues-paying persons equitably, whether or not they are members of the union.

Feminist   A person who supports political, social, and economic equality of the sexes.

Feudal System   Medieval political institution having roots in the Roman period. The king was the chief overlord, and all nobles owed allegiance to him. As long as the nobles were loyal to the king, they received the king's protection.

Fifth Amendment   Fifth Amendment to the U.S. Constitution, which states that no person shall be deprived of life, liberty, and property without due process of law and that private property should not be taken for public use without proper compensaton to the owners. Commonly referred to as the Due Process Clause, it has been used by the federal courts in cases involving students' rights and teachers' rights, especially in cases of discipline and punishment.

Fifth-Year Teacher Education Program   Curriculum program for training teachers in which the teacher candidate completes a regular bachelor's degree in liberal arts and/or sciences in the first four years and then completes a fifth year of study in education, both theory and practice, before being granted a preliminary license to teach in public elementary and secondary schools.

Final-Offer Arbitration   Process in which both parties in a labor dispute make their final offer and agree to allow an arbitrator to choose one of the two final proposals as the final contract agreement.

First Amendment   First Amendment of the U.S. Constitution which provides for separation of church and state, freedom of the press, freedom of speech, and freedom of assembly.

Fiscal   Referring to the financial affairs of schools.

Fiscal Neutrality   Legal concept that a child's education may not be determined by the wealth of a local school district.

Five New Basics   Basic subjects required of all students in public high schools as recommended by the *A Nation at Risk* report: Four years of English, three years each of mathematics, science, and social studies, and one semester of computer science.

Flexible Schedules Arrangement by which students attend classes of different length on the same day or various days during the week.

Flexiplaces Flexibility with respect to work sites. A computer terminal in the home can be a flexiplace.

Formal-Operational Period Piaget's developmental stage at which the child (adolescent) is able to construct contrary-to-fact hypotheses and reason about their ideas.

Foundation Program Guarantee of specific amount of money for each child in every state district in the state for basic education.

Fourteenth Amendment Fourteenth Amendment to the U.S. Constitution, commonly called the Equal Protection Clause, which guarantees the rights and privileges of U.S. citizens to residents of all the states. It was passed after the Civil War and extends the federal due process to the state level.

Fourth Amendment Fourth Amendment to the U.S. Constitution, which protects individuals against arbitrary searches by requiring state agents first to obtain a warrant based on probable cause.

Fringe Benefits Benefits above and beyond the wages paid to an employee, for example, sick leave, health insurance, and personal leave.

Full State Funding Type of funding in which all local public school revenues are raised at the state level and no local property tax funds or other local taxes are needed for public schools.

Functional Proficiency in English Ability to demonstrate those basic reading, writing, speaking, and listening skills essential to success in other disciplines and everyday life.

Functionally Illiterate Unable to read and understand or write at a level necessary to function in the society.

General Educational Development Text (GED) This equivalency test is an alternative way for dropouts to earn a high school diploma.

General Welfare Clause Article I, Section 8, of the U.S. Constitution providing for the powers of Congress in regard to the common defense, the general welfare, and the levying and collection of taxes. The courts have ruled that education is part of the General Welfare Clause and that Congress can enact legislation concerning education under the mandate in this clause.

Governance Formal system of government management of the education function of society.

Grammar School Secondary school in which boys between the ages of twelve and sixteen were taught Greek grammar and literature. Grammar schools in the colonies were secondary in nature, designed to be preparatory schools for colleges, and emphasized the classics.

Grammaticus The teacher who taught in the Roman grammar school.

Great Books Timeless classics of literature on which the perennialists based their educational philosophy.

Grievance Procedure Process of working through a formal complaint registered by a person or persons regarding a work situation.

Gross National Product (GNP) Total value of goods and services produced by the residents of a nation during a specific period.

Group Facilitator   Person who directs a group, gives feedback to its members, and helps the members give constructive feedback to one another.

Head Start   Comprehensive program that provides health, educational, and social services with the aim of moving preschool children and their families toward self-efficiency.

Head Teacher   Early school principal who served as a teacher and an administrator simultaneously.

Here's Looking at You   Drug education curriculum for Grades K–12 emphasizing risk factors and engaging students in a variety of learning activities.

Hierarchy of Needs   A structure of five levels of human needs developed by Abraham Maslow through which each person must pass, with each level built on the level below and in which one level must be satisfied before the next level can be attained.

High School: A Report on Secondary Education in America   Report written by Ernest Boyer and published by the Carnegie Foundation for the Advancement of Teaching in 1983 that recommends twelve priorities in its agenda to reform American public secondary education.

Hispanics   Descendents of the people of Spain, Portugal, or Latin America.

Holmes Group   Group of large research-based universities intent on eliminating undergraduate teacher education and establishing the master's degree as a prerequisite to the initial teaching certificate.

Horizontal Movement   Flexible pattern whereby students can be moved within a grade or level.

Hornbook   Colonial schoolbook more closely resembling a paddle than a book with pages. It generally contained the alphabet, the benediction, and the Lord's Prayer. Instead of being covered with cellophane paper it was covered with a translucent sheet made from a cow's horn.

Humanist   The Renaissance humanist was a scholar who believed that human nature was perfectible only if it was allowed to develop through an understanding of the ancient classics. Modern humanists believe that humans, rather than God, are the source of reality.

Humanistic   Characterized by a focus on the human interest of the students.

Hyperactive   Excessively active.

Idealism   Traditional philosophy that identifies reality as spirit, mind, soul, or ideas.

Immunity Doctrine   Legal doctrine that states the government cannot be held liable for the negligent acts of its employees, agents, and officials.

Impasse   Deadlock in negotiations indicating the failure to reach a contract agreement between two parties, such as a school district and teachers as represented by a teachers' organization.

Implied Powers   Powers not specifically written into the U.S. Constitution but inferred or implied from general clauses, such as the General Welfare Clause, by the U.S. Supreme Court.

In loco parentis   Legal term stating that teachers have authority over pupils similar to but not as broad as that exercised by their parents as long as teachers act in a "reasonable" manner (as defined by the courts).

Incentives Motivating factors, financial and otherwise, that inspire professional growth in a teacher.

Income Tax Revenues collected from an individual or corporation on the basis of income.

Infant School A school for three-, four-, and five-year-old children from poor families who worked in factories, which taught religion and the 3 Rs, but concentrated on play, singing, dancing, and nursery care.

Indefinite Contract Type of contract, for teachers with tenure, that is automatically renewed yearly without any official actions by either the teacher or the school board; the teacher continues at her or his proper place on the salary schedule.

Inflation Period of rising prices, when fewer goods and services can be purchased for a set amount of money.

Infoglut Information overload caused by the electronic media and the expansion of knowledge occurring in the modern world.

Instrumentalism John Dewey's pragmatic philosophy emphasizing the process (instrument) of learning rather than the end product. Instrumentalism stresses "how" to learn more than "what" is learned.

Integration Incorporation as equals into the same school of members of different races, by busing, magnet schools, or other means.

Interaction Analysis Refers to a scale developed by Ned Flanders that points to things teachers should be aware of with respect to classroom interactions.

Internment Camps Prison-like camps used to separate many Japanese-Americans from the mainstream American population during World War II.

Internship Program Program in place in a number of states by which a first-year teacher gains field experience (paid or unpaid) and is thus helped to adapt to the teaching environment. Normally, a mentor teacher is assigned to each intern during this period.

Jacksonian Democracy That form of democracy exhibited in Andrew Jackson's presidency in which the base of voting citizens was widened to include all males. This process caused more interest in the public schools.

Job Corps Federal program in which residential centers for disadvantaged young men and women provide basic education, vocational training, counseling, and health care to help prepare them for jobs and responsible citizenship.

Job Training Partnership Act (JTPA) Law passed by the Congress in 1982 providing for a system of block grants to states to support local training and employment programs for the economically disadvantaged.

Judicial Review Power assumed by the U.S. Supreme Court to decide whether a law is constitutional or unconstitutional. It is often used by this court to decide which powers can be implied as "necessary and proper" for both the states and the federal government.

Latchkey Children Children who must let themselves out and in before and after school because no adult is available to supervise them at those times.

Learned Bias Prejudgment based on the learning process and experiences in the external world, not on innate qualities.

Legal Agent Person acting under the direction or authority of another person; the latter person is legally responsible for the actions of the former.

Libel   Written statements that lower or "defame" the character of another person.

Linguistic Minority   A group whose language is not used daily by the majority of society.

Litigation   Use of courts and the legal system to settle disputes.

Lobbyist   Person representing a special-interest group who is engaged in urging the passage of legislation particular to that group's cause.

Local School Boards   Group of appointed or elected lay citizens who establish local school district policies within state guidelines, who hire the local school superintendent, and who approve budgets as well as employees' contracts.

Local School District   State-created unit of government with quasi-corporate powers, such as the powers to administer school, to tax, and to employ teachers. The state can destroy or modify these local school districts at any time.

Local Property Tax   Tax on real property (land and buildings) as well as personal property (furnishings) that varies from local district to local district.

Logic   Branch of philosophy concerned with how one thinks and reasons; includes inductive and deductive reasoning.

Ludus   Roman elementary or primary school where reading, writing, and arithmetic were taught.

Lyceum   Early form of organized adult education founded by Josiah Holbrook in 1826 in Millbury, Massachusetts, which became popular in the midwestern and northeastern United States.

MADD (Mothers Against Drunk Driving)   Organization of mothers, many of whom have lost children as a result of alcohol abuse, who have banded together to combat this problem.

Magnet Schools   Public elementary or secondary schools that specialize in one area (for example, science or math) of study and attract students from throughout a school district without a specific attendance area within the district.

Mandates   Rules for spending funds appropriated at the local, state, or national level.

Mass Media   Forms of communication (television, film, radio, newspaper, magazines) designed to reach the majority of the people.

Matching Funds   Tax funds that the federal government requires to be raised at the local or state level before federal funds can be allocated and used at the local and state levels.

Maternity Leave   Time off from teaching with or without pay for pregnancy and child care; the former position is available to the teacher upon her return to work after a specified period.

Maturation   Internal ripening process through which the student becomes physically ready to accomplish a specific task.

Mediation   Process in which a neutral person is asked to help the two parties in a labor dispute reach an agreement by narrowing the issues, improving communications, and making specific recommendations that are not binding on either party.

Megaethnic Group   Any large cultural group that has assimilated many smaller ethnic and minority groups to become the dominant culture.

Melting Pot Concept   Social and cultural assimilation of immigrants into a society.

Mental Discipline Ability to think logically. Subjects like math are considered better suited for developing mental discipline than music and art.

Mentor Teacher Master teacher who performs all the tasks expected of a cooperating teacher, but in most cases is assigned to a first-year teacher and for a longer duration. The emphasis is on being a good model for the intern.

Mentoring Planned program in which an experienced teacher advises and assists new teachers during the first one or two years of teaching. Mentoring usually also involves the participation of the principal, the visitation of the neophyte teachers' classes, and a decision on licensing and future employment.

Merger Combination of two groups with similar goals into one large group.

Metaphysics Branch of philosophy concerned with the fundamental nature of reality.

Middle School School that houses Grades 5–8, 6–8, or 7 and 8.

Minimum Competency Lowest level of achievement necessary to obtain a passing grade on school work. Every student should achieve at this level before proceeding to the next level.

Minority Union Unions that have lost out in the election for representation at the bargaining table, but may remain as a minority union in the same school district.

Mirrors of Excellence Book published by the Association of Teacher Educators that gives examples from business and industry that can be used as models to improve teacher education.

Monitorial School School in which a paid master teacher instructed several monitors who in turn taught the masses. In some monitorial schools, one paid master was responsible for 500 or more students.

Moral Stages Stages, such as those defined by Lawrence Kohlberg and others, of moral and ethical decision-making, based upon the cognitive stages of Piaget.

Morality System of moral values used to guide everyday life.

Multiethnic Education Education characterized by a curriculum that acquaints students with, and promotes acceptance and understanding of, the many diverse ethnic groups within a society.

Multiethnic Model Method of teaching in which every historical and social event is viewed from the perspective of different cultural and ethnic groups. A multiethnic model supports the idea that there exist stages of ethnicity that one can attain, as in the model proposed by James Banks.

A Nation at Risk Report issued in 1983 by the National Commission on Excellence in Education that surveys the present state of public education and makes specific recommendations for reforming education.

National Board for Professional Teaching Standards Proposed (not existing) group that would grant certificates to those teachers that attain a high level of competence at the national level.

National Council for Accreditation of Teacher Education (NCATE) National nongovernmental accrediting agency whose purpose is to promote high-quality teacher education by ensuring that institutions meet its standards.

National Institute of Mental Health (NIMH) Agency in the Department of Health and Human Services in the Executive Branch of the federal government that provides a national focus for federal efforts to deal with mental health problems.

Native Americans   American Indians.

Naturalism   Oldest of the major traditional philosophies embodying the belief that reality is the physical world as it appears to one's senses.

Negligence   Failure to exercise the care that a prudent person usually exercises, leading to a tort.

New Carnegie Unit   New unit of credit toward high school graduation proposed by Ernest Boyer in *High School: A Report on Secondary Education in America* that would involve students in volunteer work in the school or community for high school credit.

New England Primer   Tiny, yet important book used in early New England schools. It was filled with Biblical verses that warned youngsters about going to Hell.

Noncertified Teacher   Person who may have some training to be a teacher, but is not fully certified by state standards to serve as a teacher.

Nongraded School   School in which grade designations are eliminated, and three or four broad groupings are inserted in their place.

Nonreferenced Testing   Tests that measure a student's achievement against standards of achievement of other students that have been arrived at by tests with established national, state, or local norms.

Nontenured Teacher   Teacher who is on an annual contract and has not been granted tenure either because he or she has not worked in the district for seven years or for other reasons.

Object-Teaching Lessons   Lessons described by Pestalozzi that relate to real objects in the child's environment.

Old Field Schools   Abandoned cabins located in old, worn-out tobacco fields (hence the name) in the South in which poor whites received a meager and/or crude education.

One-Track System of Education   Plan that provides all students, regardless of their intellectual ability, equal opportunity to receive elementary and secondary education by requiring all students to take the same basic courses, thereby eliminating separate "tracks" for college-bound and non–college-bound students.

Open Organizational Climate   The type of administrative structure in a school that breaks down normal barriers between teachers and the administration, providing a climate where ideas and concepts can be freely exchanged and formulated.

Paideia Proposal   Plan proposed by Mortimer Adler in which every child, regardless of ability, would be taught the same curriculum from Grades 1 through 12. The focus would be on group discussion and classical literature; electives and vocational education would be eliminated.

Paternal Deprivation   Lack of nurturing of children by their father because of his obligations outside the home or his absence from the home.

Paternalistic   Acting like a father figure toward those over which one has authority; for example, William Penn acted paternalistic toward blacks and Indians.

Pauper School   School established for the purpose of providing free or inexpensive education for poor children.

Pedagogical Journals   Periodical publications emphasizing teaching methods in education.

Peer Acceptance   Acceptance by those of equal status.

Pension Plan State plan in which the school district, but not the teacher, is required to contribute a specific sum to a fund that will be paid to the teacher upon retirement.

Per Capita Income Average income per person in a population group (for example, a state).

Perennialism Educational philosophy maintaining that truth is logical, permanent, and unchanging. It places much credence in the classics or Great Books approach to learning, with an emphasis on the past instead of the present or future.

Personal Leave Two or three days per year granted to teachers to take care of personal business and/or civic duties.

Philosophy Belief system a person develops concerning existence, reality in the world, truth, and knowledge.

A Place Called School A 1984 study supervised by John Goodlad based on detailed observations of more than 1,000 classrooms and on a sample composed of schools containing maximum diversity and representativeness.

Plagiarism Use of someone else's written work without giving credit to the source.

Plenary Powers Full powers given to a governmental unit; for example, the states have plenary power to control education.

Political Action Committees (PACs) Groups organized to collect funds to help political candidates or influence legislation.

Pragmatism Traditional philosophy, originating in the United States, focusing on the belief that the meaning of an idea is determined by its consequences. It was developed in opposition to idealism and stresses practicality and "what works." Also called *instrumentalism* or *experimentalism.*

Preoperational Period Piaget's developmental stage characterized by symbolic functioning. At this stage, for example, a child can make one object represent another object that is not present.

Preservice Teacher Student still involved in teacher training; one who has not yet entered the classroom as a fully trained and certified teacher.

Principal–Agent Relationship Situation in which a pupil (agent) runs an errand for the benefit of a teacher (principal party). The principal party assumes all responsibility for the acts of the agent as well as for the agent's safety.

Probable Cause Stringent standard to which police officers are held as a basis for search and seizure.

Professional Organization Group of persons specially trained and certified in a particular field, such as teaching, medicine, and law.

Progressive Education Twentieth-century innovation that is the opposite of traditional education. The learner is fully involved in the process of problem solving and the thinking process.

Progressive Tax Tax that takes a greater percentage of revenues from those people who have the greatest ability to pay.

Progressivism Educational philosophy stressing the experience of the learner and learning as an active process. Cooperation, social learning, and the process of learning rather than the end product are emphasized.

Project Charlie Program that focuses on raising young people's (K–6) self-esteem as a way to prevent them from using drugs.

Project SMART   Program for seventh graders addressing alcohol use and utilizing resistance training (saying "no").

Property Tax Freeze   Limitation on property taxes set by a legislature.

Property Tax Levy   Tax based on a percentage of the value of land and improvements (for example, buildings) raised at the local level and often used to help finance public education.

Proposals   Set of propositions offered by one side in a labor dispute as a beginning for discussion in the negotiation process.

The Quest Program   Program that emphasizes drug-free youth, not just drug education, by involving students in a community service project to build self-confidence.

Quick-Fix Solutions   Legislated or administered remedies for the problems in public education, such as more hours in the school day, more school days per year, and more testing of students, rather than changes in the way teachers work with students and with other teachers.

Readiness   State of being physically and mentally prepared to accomplish the developmental tasks appropriate to one's age and level of maturity.

Realism   Traditional philosophy claiming that the physical world, as it appears to one's senses, is the real world and that the universe is governed by an orderly system of natural laws. It is similar to naturalism but has a more fully developed epistemology (theory of knowledge).

Reasonable Suspicion   Suspicion, based on reason, that a search will reveal evidence of a student's violation of either the law or school rules. It is the standard now required of school officials by the courts for search and seizure.

Recession   Reduction in economic activity.

Reciprocity   Mutual exchange of privileges, as when a teacher licensed in one state is granted a corresponding license in another state because of an agreement between the two states.

Reconstructionism   Educational philosophy embodying the use of education as a tool or instrument with which to change society for the better. This philosophy places its emphasis on the prevention of world crises through constructive social change.

Regressive Social Philosophy   Philosophy emphasizing the past and the belief that current problems can be solved by turning back the clock to previous centuries. It was a term used to criticize the perennialists.

Regressive Tax   Tax that takes a greater percentage from those who have the least ability to pay.

Regulations   Rules or methods required for operation, for example, the rules accompanying federal aid to education.

Relative Standard   Standard of measurement by which a student's score is compared with the scores of other students on a national curve with 10% A's, 20% B's, 40% C's, 20% D's, and 10% F's.

Representative Assembly   Group of individuals assembled for the purpose of passing resolutions pertaining to the entire organization, as in the National Education Association.

Reserved Powers   Powers not specifically given to the federal government by the U.S. Constitution and thus left to the states.

Resistance Training Method of training used in drug education in which students practice saying "no" to pressures to drink.

Resolutions Decisions passed by a democratically controlled body expressing their position on a variety of issues pertaining to the existence of that organization.

Retirement Plan State plan in which the teacher and the school district both contribute to a fund that will be paid to the teacher over a period when she or he terminates his or her service to a state after a specified required number of years of teaching.

Revenues Income that a state or national government collects and receives into the treasury for public use.

Reverse Discrimination Situation in which members of a minority group are favored over those of a majority group on the basis of race, sex, age, or handicap.

Role Model Person who sets a positive example for others and is respected for the choices he or she makes.

Sabbatical Leave Time away from regular duties (usually one semester or one year), with or without pay, that is granted to a teacher for further education or educational travel. The position is held open for the teacher.

SADD (Students Against Drunk Driving) Organization of teens who try to combat alcohol abuse.

Safety Net Used to describe the process of providing disadvantaged youth a chance to be "saved" from a life dependent on government assistance; government programs that enable those persons who are not able to provide for themselves with the minimum level of support and necessities for an independent life, including vocational training and job skills if appropriate.

Salary Schedule Chart of teachers' basic salaries based on education and years of experience.

Sales Tax Revenue based on the purchase of goods.

Save-Harmless Statutes State laws that do not allow school districts to be used but do allow them to pay damages and court costs for employees' negligence, provided that the incidents occurred while employees were performing duties connected with their jobs in the district.

Scapegoat Person or group that is blamed for the actions of another person or group. For example, schools have been blamed for the failure to put the first man in space.

Scholastic Aptitude Test (SAT) Test published by the Educational Testing Service of Princeton, New Jersey, that evaluates the ability of high school students to do college-level work.

School Finance Plan Distribution and spending plan of a school district based on income provided by state and local resources.

School Finance Reforms Movement in the 1970s emphasizing the equalizing of educational opportunities for every student while cutting back on spending.

School Social Climate Composite of teachers' satisfaction with school structure, parental involvement, differentiation in student programs, principals' reports of time devoted to instruction, and student mobility in school.

Scientific Spirit Questioning of the causes and effects of the phenomena in the universe.

Scope of Bargaining   Topics that may legally be discussed in the bargaining process such as salaries, fringe benefits, and working conditions.

Secret Ballot   Vote, such as a paper ballot as opposed to a voice vote, conducted in such a way that no one can identify for whom anybody else voted.

Secular Education   Education that stresses life here on earth rather than any religious belief.

Segregation   Separation of different races or ethnic groups with respect to educational opportunities, housing, transportation, and other facilities.

Self-Actualization   Full realization of one's potential.

Self-Concept   Mental image of oneself; also, belief in oneself.

Sensorimotor Period   Developmental stage at which children solve problems by using their sensory system and their motor or muscular system rather than the symbolic processes that characterize Piaget's other three major periods.

Sex Role Stereotype   Mental image some people have of the roles of men and women, often founded on inaccurate perceptions.

Site License   Permission to use certain computer programs and disk materials in a specific school district for a yearly fee, the district having the right to make as many copies of a computer program as it deems necessary for use *only* in that district.

Slander   Utterance of charges or misrepresentations that damage the reputation of another.

Social Platform   Propositions pertaining to issues of mostly a societal nature, for example, protection of women teachers from unfair hiring practices.

Socratic Discussion Groups   Teaching method in which probing questions are used to elicit responses and discussion from students.

Socratic Method   Method developed by Socrates that teaches people to think logically through a dialectical technique of questioning.

Special-Interest Groups   Groups that attempt to influence education by lobbying in state legislatures and the U.S. Congress on educational issues. Special-interest groups include organizations of teachers, parents, and administrators; taxpayer groups; organizations promoting the education of the gifted, special education students, or ethnic minorities; and religious groups with an interest in education.

Specific Learning Disabilities or Perceptually Impaired or Neurologically Impaired   Perceptual, integrative, sequencing, memory, motor, or language disabilities.

Spreadsheet   Labor-saving system of charting information through the use of a computer with the capability of recording, storing, and retrieving information.

Standard Preparation   Those programs, normally supervised by NCATE and state agencies, for the certification of teachers, including subject matter courses, methods courses, field experiences, and student teaching or internship programs.

State Board of Education   State educational governing board set up by state law or by the state constitution to formulate general educational policies for the state, including minimum educational standards.

State Department of Education   State educational agency established by state law or by the state constitution to administer, regulate, and enforce minimal educational standards set up by the state legislature and the state board of education.

State Superintendent of Education   Top state school official who usually heads the state department of education. He or she is either the chief executive officer of the state board of education or is selected independently of that group by election or appointment.

Stress   Internal disturbance that causes one to be less than fully productive in the course of a day; bodily or mental tension resulting from factors that tend to alter an existing state of balance.

Strikes   Work stoppage in which employees refuse to perform their usual tasks until an agreement is reached with their employer.

Sunday School Movement   Movement that started in England in 1780 and then spread to the United States for the purpose of educating poor factory working children on their day off, before child labor laws were enacted.

Supply and Demand   Overall need for teachers relative to the number of teachers available. Supply refers to the number of credentialed teachers who are ready to teach at a given time. Demand refers mainly to the number of teacher vacancies at any given time for certain types of credentialed teachers.

Suspension   Temporary exclusion from school for a specific short period (usually three to five days).

Taxonomy   System of classification of educational objectives into three domains—cognitive, affective, and psychomotor—developed by Benjamin Bloom.

Teachable Moment   The best time for a task to be learned, as used by Havighurst.

Teachers' Association   Name used by members of the NEA before the era of collective bargaining. At that time, the NEA wanted to avoid use of the term *union*.

Team Teaching   Team teaching is a method whereby two or more teachers work together to teach a large class for a longer block of time, and work together on the curriculum during a common planning time. It is characterized by taking advantage of teacher strength.

Technophobia   Fear of technology, for example, fear of using bank teller machines or computers.

Tenth Amendment   Tenth Amendment to the U.S. Constitution which delegates the power to establish public schools to the states. This amendment probably owes its passage to the fact that the Founding Fathers feared a strong federal government.

Tenure   Status granted after a certain period to a teacher protecting him or her from summary dismissal. Tenure is usually granted after seven years of employment in one school district and cannot be transferred to any other school district.

TESA (Teacher Expectations and Student Achievement)   Professional improvement model that sensitizes the preservice teacher to the unique needs of the children or young adults in a classroom.

Title IX   Legal act that led to a government program intended to end discrimination by not allowing anyone to be excluded from participation on the basis of sex.

Toleration   Toleration of a religious nature, as exemplified by the Quakers, is openness to other religious groups seeking refuge in the United States.

Tort   Legal term for a wrongful act by one person causing real injury or damage to the person or property of another.

Town School Committee   Early school board separate from the local city/town governments in colonial Massachusetts.

Transmissive Purpose   Purpose of education that relates to passing on to each generation the tried, if not necessarily the true.

Tuition Tax Credits   Deduction of a portion of the tuition that parents who send their children to private schools pay, from the income on which they must pay federal income taxes.

Typology   Classification based upon types, such as the Banks typology.

Union   Organization of workers employed in a similar industry to press for better wages and working conditions.

Universal Suffrage   Legal condition under which all persons over a certain age can exercise the right to vote in local, state, and national elections, regardless of race, sex, religion, national origin, or wealth.

Urban Schools   Schools located within city limits and usually inhabited by an economically poorer and disadvantaged student population than suburban schools.

User Fee   Fee paid directly by parents for special nonrequired (elective) courses and summer school to help finance education.

Value Clarification   Process by which an individual identifies his or her beliefs and values by discussing them in group situations with other individuals who have different values. No "right" or "wrong" answers should be expected.

Vertical Movement   Flexible pattern in which students can be moved from grade to grade or from level to level.

Voucher Plan   Proposal by Milton Friedman that the government guarantee each child a minimum level of education by giving parents certificates or vouchers each year that would be redeemable for a certain sum of money toward any "approved" school, public or private.

Whole Child Initiative (WCI)   An idea that brings parents, teachers, and other community members together to provide a vision of excellence and positive experiences for the benefit of youth.

Word Processing   Labor-saving system of recording, storing, and retrieving typewritten data through the use of a computer.

Workers' Compensation   State insurance program to cover injuries to a worker sustained "out of" or "in the course of" his or her employment.

Index

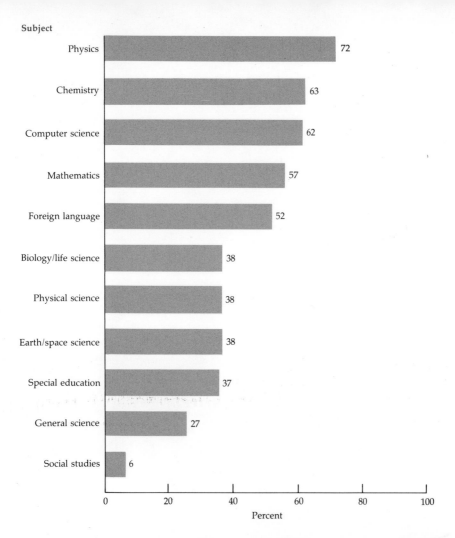

Subject	
Physics	72
Chemistry	63
Computer science	62
Mathematics	57
Foreign language	52
Biology/life science	38
Physical science	38
Earth/space science	38
Special education	37
General science	27
Social studies	6

Percent: 0 20 40 60 80 100

Above: Percentage of high school principals who reported difficulty in hiring

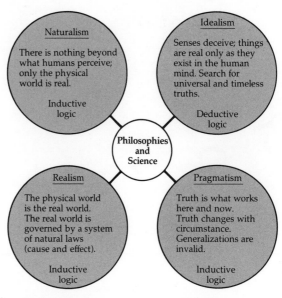

Naturalism
There is nothing beyond what humans perceive; only the physical world is real.

Inductive logic

Idealism
Senses deceive; things are real only as they exist in the human mind. Search for universal and timeless truths.

Deductive logic

Philosophies and Science

Realism
The physical world is the real world. The real world is governed by a system of natural laws (cause and effect).

Inductive logic

Pragmatism
Truth is what works here and now. Truth changes with circumstance. Generalizations are invalid.

Inductive logic

Right: Relationships among the traditional philosophies and science